Birnbaum's 97
Mexico

W9-BBW-924

A BIRNBAUM TRAVEL GUIDE

Alexandra Mayes Birnbaum
EDITORIAL CONSULTANT

Lois Spritzer
Editorial Director

Laura L. Brengelman
Managing Editor

Mary Callahan
Beth Schlau
Senior Editors

Patricia Canole
Gene Gold
Susan McClung
Associate Editors

Marcy S. Pritchard
Map Coordinator

Susan Cutter Snyder
Editorial Assistant

HarperPerennial
A *Division* of HarperCollins*Publishers*

For Stephen, who merely made all this possible.

FIRST EDITION

ISSN 0749-2561 (Birnbaum Travel Guides)
ISSN 0883-1209 (Mexico)
ISBN 0-06-278255-X (pbk.)
96 97 98 99 ❖/RRD 5 4 3 2 1

Cover design © Drenttel Doyle Partners
Cover photograph © David Hiser

BIRNBAUM TRAVEL GUIDES

Bahamas, and Turks & Caicos
Bermuda
Canada
Cancun, Cozumel & Isla Mujeres
Caribbean
Country Inns and Back Roads
Disneyland
Hawaii
Mexico
Miami & Ft. Lauderdale
United States
Walt Disney World
Walt Disney World for Kids, By Kids
Walt Disney World Without Kids

Contributing Editors

Patricia Alisau
Trudy Balch
Frederick H. Brengelman
Paul Hagerman
Richard Harris
Letti Klein
Wendy Luft
Thérèse Margolis
Erica Meltzer
Anne Millman
Shari Dawn Rettig
Pancho Shiell
Carol Zaiser

Maps

B. Andrew Mudryk

Contents

Getting Ready to Go

Practical information for planning your trip.

The Cities

Thorough, qualitative guides to each of the 28 cities most often visited by vacationers. Each section offers a comprehensive report on the city's most compelling attractions and amenities—highlighting our top choices in every category.

Diversions

*A selective guide to a variety of unexpected pleasures,
pinpointing the best places to pursue them.*

Unexpected Pleasures and Treasures

Directions

*Mexico's 10 major driving routes, covering the main
north-south and east-west highways that lead from
border crossings and major cities to the country's
farthest jungles and beaches.*

Glossary

Foreword

Mexico remains the most popular foreign destination for US travelers, despite the fact that recent years have been especially confusing for folks heading south of the border. The rollercoaster ride that continues to characterize Mexico's political, personal, financial, and industrial relationships with other North American countries—and the rest of the world, for that matter—has been mirrored by severe swings in currency relationships, and there has never been a time when an up-to-date guide to Mexico was a more useful travel tool.

That's why we've tried to create a guide to Mexico that's specifically organized, written, and edited for today's demanding traveler headed to this increasingly complex country. This is a traveler for whom qualitative information is infinitely more desirable than mere quantities of unappraised data. We realize that it's impossible for any single writer to visit thousands of restaurants (and nearly as many hotels) in any given year and provide accurate appraisals of each. And even if it were physically possible for one human being to survive such an itinerary, it would of necessity have to be done at a dead sprint, and the perceptions derived therefrom would probably be less valid than those of any other intelligent individual visiting the same establishments. It is, therefore, both impractical and undesirable (especially in a large, annually revised and updated guidebook *series* such as we offer) to have only one person provide all the data on the entire world. Instead, we have chosen what we like to describe as the "thee and me" approach to restaurant and hotel evaluation and, to a somewhat more limited degree, to the sites and sights we have included in our text. What this really reflects is personal sampling tempered by intelligent counsel from informed local sources.

This guidebook is directed to the "visitor," and such elements as restaurants have been specifically picked to provide the visitor with a representative, enlightening, and above all pleasant experience. Since so many extraneous considerations can affect the reception and service accorded a regular restaurant patron, our choices can in no way be construed as an exhaustive guide to resident dining. We think we've listed all the best places, in various price ranges, but they were chosen with a visitor's enjoyment in mind.

Other evidence of how we've tried to tailor our text to reflect modern travel habits is apparent in the section we call diversions. Where once it was common for travelers to spend a Mexican visit seeing only the obvious sights, today's traveler is more likely to want to pursue a special interest or to venture off the beaten track. In response to this trend, we have collected a series of special experiences, so that it is no longer necessary to wade through a pound or two of superfluous prose just to find unexpected pleasures and treasures.

Finally, I also should point out that every good travel guide is a living enterprise; that is, no part of this text is carved in stone. In our annual revisions, we refine, expand, and further hone all our material to serve your travel needs better. To this end, no contribution is of greater value to us than your personal reaction to what we have written, as well as information reflecting your own experiences while using the book. Please write to us at 10 E. 53rd St., New York, NY 10022.

We sincerely hope to hear from you.

Alexandra Mayes Birnbaum

ALEXANDRA MAYES BIRNBAUM, editorial consultant to the *Birnbaum Travel Guides*, worked with her late husband, Stephen Birnbaum, as co-editor of the series. She has been a world traveler since childhood and is known for her travel reports on radio on what's hot and what's not.

Mexico

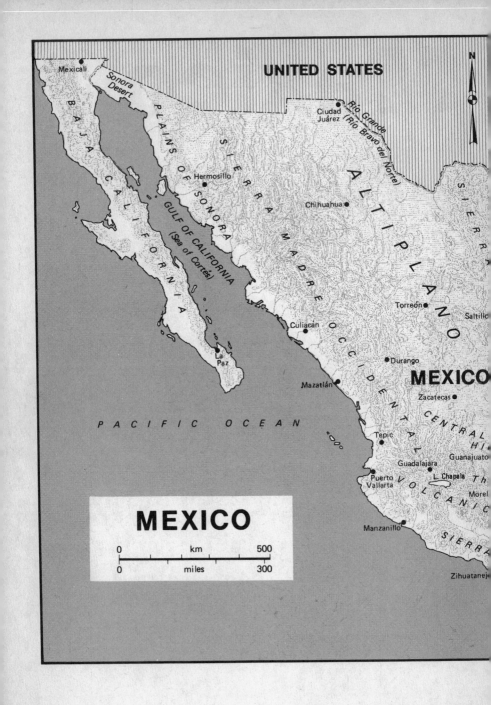

MEXICO

UNITED STATES

Mexicali

Sonora Desert

BAJA CALIFORNIA

PLAINS OF SONORA

SIERRA MADRE OCCIDENTAL

Ciudad Juárez

Río Grande (Río Bravo del Norte)

Hermosillo

GULF OF CALIFORNIA (Sea of Cortés)

Chihuahua

ALTIPLANO

SIERRA

Torreón

Saltillo

La Paz

Culiacan

Durango

MEXICO

Mazatlán

Zacatecas

PACIFIC OCEAN

Tepic

CENTRAL

HI

Guadalajara

L. Chapala

Guanajuato

Th

Puerto Vallarta

VOLCANIC

Morel

Manzanillo

SIERRA

Zihuataneje

| 0 | km | 500 |
| 0 | miles | 300 |

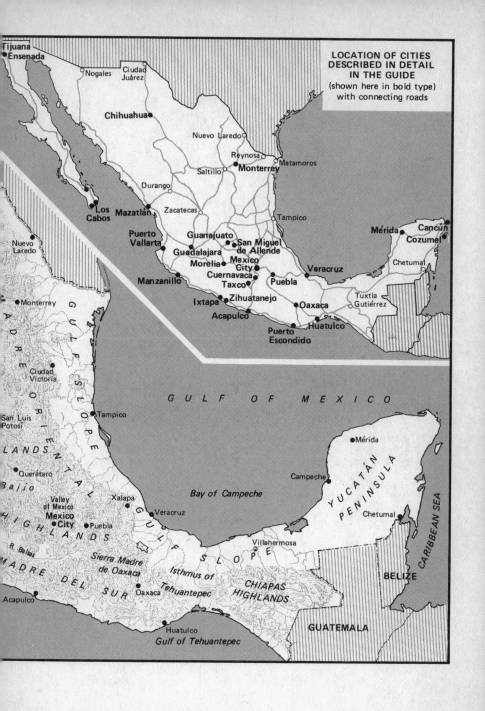

LOCATION OF CITIES
DESCRIBED IN DETAIL
IN THE GUIDE
(shown here in bold type)
with connecting roads

How to Use This Guide

A great deal of care has gone into the organization of this guidebook, and we believe it represents a breakthrough in the presentation of travel material.

Our text is divided into five basic sections, in order to best present information on every possible aspect of a Mexican vacation. Our aim is to highlight what's where and to tell you as much as we can about what you need to know—how, when, where, how much, and what's best—to make the most intelligent choices possible.

Here is a brief summary of what you can expect to find in each section. We believe that you will find both your travel planning and en route enjoyment enhanced by having this book at your side.

GETTING READY TO GO

A mini-encyclopedia of practical travel facts with all the precise data necessary to create a successful trip to Mexico. Here you will find how to get where you're going, plus selected resources—including useful publications, and companies and organizations specializing in discount and special-interest travel—providing a wealth of information and assistance useful both before and during your trip.

THE CITIES

Our individual reports on the Mexican cities most visited by tourists and business travelers offer short-stay guides, including an essay introducing the city as a contemporary place to visit; an *At-a-Glance* section that's a site-by-site survey of the most important, interesting, and unique sights to see and things to do; *Sources and Resources,* a concise listing of pertinent tourism information, such as the address of the local tourist office, which sightseeing tours to take, where to find the brightest nightspot or hail a taxi, which are the shops that have the finest merchandise and/or the most irresistible bargains, and where the best golf, tennis, fishing, and swimming are to be found; and *Best in Town,* which lists our cost-and-quality choices of the best places to eat and sleep on a variety of budgets.

DIVERSIONS

This section is designed to help travelers find the best places in which to engage in a variety of exceptional experiences, without having to wade through endless pages of unrelated text. In every case, our particular suggestions are intended to guide you to that special place where the quality of experience is likely to be highest.

DIRECTIONS

Here are 10 driving itineraries, from Baja's hidden beaches to the jungle ruins of the Maya. DIRECTIONS is the only section of this book that is organized geographically, to cover the major north-south and east-west routes that lead from border crossings and major cities to the farthest reaches of the country.

GLOSSARY

This section provides helpful information that you may need on your trip. In Mexico, measurements may be expressed in either US or metric units, and temperatures measured in Celsius or Fahrenheit. The weights and measures table provides approximate equivalents, as well as formulas for conversion. In addition, there is *Useful Words and Phrases,* a brief introduction to the Spanish language that will help you to make a hotel or dinner reservation, order a meal, mail a letter, and even buy toothpaste in Mexico. Though most resorts in major cities have English-speaking staff, at smaller establishments (particularly in rural areas), a little knowledge of Spanish will go a long way.

To use this book to full advantage, take a few minutes to read the table of contents and random entries in each section to get a firsthand feel for how it all fits together. You will find that the sections of this book are building blocks designed to help you put together the best possible trip. Use them selectively as a tool, a source of ideas, a reference work for accurate facts, and a guidebook to the best buys, the most exciting sights, the most pleasant accommodations, and the tastiest foods—*the best travel experience* that you can possibly have.

Getting Ready to Go

Getting Ready to Go

When to Go

The Mexican climate ranges from the subtropical heat, humidity, and abundant rainfall of the Gulf and Caribbean Coasts to the semiarid Baja Peninsula and the temperate highlands of the central plateau. Nearly perfect winter weather has made coastal areas such as Cancún and Cozumel in the Caribbean and Acapulco on the Pacific Coast popular winter vacation destinations. On the other hand, the relatively high elevation of much of the country's interior tempers the summer heat, making inland areas such as Cuernavaca and Oaxaca attractive to summer visitors. Travel during the off-seasons (winter inland and summer on the coast) and shoulder seasons (the months immediately before and after the peak months) also can offer relatively fair weather and smaller crowds, and often is less expensive.

If you have a touch-tone phone, you can call *The Weather Channel Connection* (phone: 900-WEATHER) for current worldwide weather forecasts. This service, available from *The Weather Channel* (2600 Cumberland Pkwy., Atlanta, GA 30339), costs 95¢ per minute; the charge will appear on your phone bill.

Traveling by Plane

SCHEDULED FLIGHTS

Airlines offering flights between the US and Mexico include *Aero California* (from Los Angeles, California only), *Aerolitoral, Aeromar* (from San Antonio, Texas only), *Aeroméxico, Aero Poniente, Alaska Airlines, America West, American, American Eagle, American Trans Air, Continental, Delta, Iberia, LACSA, Mexicana, Midway* (to Cancún only), *Northwest, TACA, Taesa, TWA, United,* and *USAir*. Airlines serving domestic routes within Mexico include *Aero California, Aero Caribe, Aerolitoral, Aero López, Aeromar, Aeroméxico, Aeromorelos, Aero Poniente, Aviacsa, Mexicana,* and *Taesa*.

FARES The great variety of airfares can be reduced to the following basic categories: first class, business class, coach (also called economy or tourist class), excursion or discount, and standby, as well as various promotional fares. For information on applicable fares and restrictions, contact the airlines listed above or ask your travel agent. Most airfares are offered for a limited time and sell out quickly. Once you've found the lowest fare for which you can qualify, purchase your ticket as soon as possible.

RESERVATIONS Reconfirmation is strongly recommended for all international flights. It is essential that you call to confirm your round-trip reservations— *especially the return leg*—as well as any flights within Mexico.

SEATING You usually can reserve a specific seat when purchasing your ticket; otherwise, seats are assigned on a first-come, first-served basis at check-in. Seating charts may be available from airlines and are included in the *Desktop Flight Guide* (Official Airline Guides, PO Box 51703, Boulder, CO 80321; phone: 800-323-3537 for orders; 708-574-6000 for information; fax: 708-574-6565).

SMOKING US law prohibits smoking on flights scheduled for six hours or less within the US and its territories on both US and foreign carriers. These restrictions do not apply to most nonstop flights between the US and international destinations, although a number of US carriers have independently banned smoking on some of their flights. For example, at press time, *American Trans Air, Continental, Delta, Midway, Northwest* and *USAir* did not permit smoking on flights between the US and Mexico. A free wallet-size guide that describes the rights of nonsmokers under current regulations is available from *ASH* (*Action on Smoking and Health;* DOT Card, 2013 H St. NW, Washington, DC 20006; phone: 202-659-4310).

SPECIAL MEALS When making your reservation, you can request one of the airline's alternate menu choices for no additional charge. Though not always required, it's a good idea to reconfirm your request the day before departure.

BAGGAGE On major international airlines, passengers usually are allowed to carry on board one or two bags that will fit under a seat or in an overhead compartment and to check two bags in the cargo hold. Specific regulations regarding dimensions and weight restrictions vary among airlines, but a checked bag usually cannot exceed 62 inches in combined dimensions (length, width, and depth) or weigh more than 70 pounds. There may be charges for additional, oversize, or overweight luggage, and for special equipment or sporting gear. Note that baggage allowances may be more limited on domestic routes within Mexico. When you check your bags, make sure that the tags the airline attaches are correctly coded for your destination.

IMPORTANT NOTE

During busy holiday seasons, some airlines may not accept any luggage exceeding the standard allowances—even for an additional fee. If you think you might need to bring extra luggage at such times, contact the airline before your trip.

CHARTER FLIGHTS

By booking a block of seats on a specially arranged flight, charter operators frequently can offer travelers bargain airfares. If you do fly on a charter, however, read the contract's fine print carefully. Federal regulations permit charter operators to cancel a flight or assess surcharges of as much as 10% of the airfare up to 10 days before departure. You usually must book in advance, and once booked, you may not be able to change your flight—a good reason to buy trip cancellation insurance (see *Insurance,* below). Also, make your check out to the company's escrow account, which provides some protection for your investment in the event that the charter operator fails. Additional information on charter flights is provided in the publication *Jax Fax* (397 Post Rd., Darien, CT 06820; phone: 800-952-9329 for subscriptions; 203-655-8746 for information; fax: 203-655-6257).

DISCOUNTS ON SCHEDULED FLIGHTS

COURIER TRAVEL In return for arranging to carry documents or to accompany some kind of freight, a traveler pays only a portion of the total airfare (and sometimes a small registration fee). One agency that matches would-be couriers with courier companies is *Now Voyager* (74 Varick St., Suite 307, New York, NY 10013; phone: 212-431-1616; fax: 212-219-1753).

Courier Companies

Discount Travel International (169 W. 81st St., New York, NY 10024; phone: 212-362-3636; fax: 212-362-3236).

Halbart Express (147-05 176th St., Jamaica, NY 11434; phone: 718-656-8279; fax: 718-244-0559).

Midnite Express (925 W. Hyde Park Blvd., Inglewood, CA 90302; phone: 310-672-1100; fax: 310-330-2358).

Publications

Air Courier Bargains: How to Travel World-Wide for Next to Nothing, by Kelly Monaghan (The Intrepid Traveler, PO Box 438, New York, NY 10034; phone: 800-356-9315 for orders; 212-569-1081 for information; fax: 212-942-6687).

Travel Unlimited (PO Box 1058, Allston, MA 02134-1058; no phone).

CONSOLIDATORS AND BUCKET SHOPS These companies buy blocks of tickets from airlines and sell them at a discount to travel agents or directly to consumers. Since many bucket shops operate on a thin margin, be sure to check a company's record with the *Better Business Bureau*—before parting with any money.

Cheap Tickets (6151 W. Century Blvd., Los Angeles, CA 90045; phone: 800-377-1000; fax: 800-454-2555).

Council Charter (205 E. 42nd St., New York, NY 10017; phone: 800-800-8222 or 212-661-0311; fax: 212-972-0194).

Discount Travel International (address above).

Fare Deals Travel (9350 E. Arapahoe Rd., Suite 330, Englewood, CO 80112; phone: 800-878-2929 or 303-792-2929; fax: 303-792-2954).

Southwest Travel Systems (1001 N. Central Ave., Suite 575, Phoenix, AZ 85004; phone: 800-STS-TRAVEL or 602-255-0234; fax: 602-255-0220).

STT Worldwide Travel (9880 SW Beaverton Hillsdale Hwy., Beaverton, OR 97005; phone: 800-348-0886 or 503-641-8866; fax: 503-641-2171).

Unitravel (1177 N. Warson Rd., St. Louis, MO 63132; phone: 800-325-2222 or 314-569-0900; fax: 314-569-2503).

LAST-MINUTE TRAVEL SERVICES These are clubs or agencies that provide members or clients with information on imminent trips and other bargain travel opportunities. Some of the clubs charge an annual fee; others offer free membership. Note that despite the names of some of the services listed below, you don't have to wait until literally the last minute to make travel plans.

Discount Travel International (address above).

FLY ASAP (PO Box 9808, Scottsdale, AZ 85252-3808; phone: 800-FLY-ASAP or 602-224-9504; fax: 602-224-9533).

Last Minute Travel (1249 Boylston St., Boston, MA 02215; phone: 800-LAST-MIN or 617-267-9800; fax: 617-424-1943).

Moment's Notice (7301 New Utrecht Ave., Brooklyn, NY 11204-5137; phone: 718-234-6295; fax: 718-234-6450).

Spur of the Moment Cruises (411 N. Harbor Blvd., Suite 302, San Pedro, CA 90731; phone: 800-4-CRUISE or 310-521-1070 in California; 800-343-1991 elsewhere in the US; 24-hour hotline: 310-521-1060; fax: 310-521-1061).

Traveler's Advantage (3033 S. Parker Rd., Suite 900, Aurora, CO 80014; phone: 800-548-1116 for information; 800-835-8747 for member services; fax: 303-368-3985).

Vacations to Go (1502 Augusta Dr., Suite 415, Houston, TX 77057; phone: 713-974-2121 in Texas; 800-338-4962 elsewhere in the US; fax: 713-974-0445).

Worldwide Discount Travel Club (1674 Meridian Ave., Miami Beach, FL 33139; phone: 305-534-2082).

GENERIC AIR TRAVEL These organizations offer a service similar to airline standby, except that they sell seats on not one but several scheduled and charter airlines. One pioneer of generic flights is *Airhitch* (2472 Broadway, Suite 200, New York, NY 10025; phone: 212-864-2000 in New York City; 800-326-2009 elsewhere in the US; fax: 212-864-5489).

BARTERED TRAVEL SOURCES Barter—the exchange of commodities or services in lieu of cash payment—is a common practice among travel suppliers. Companies that have obtained travel services through barter may sell these services at substantial discounts to travel clubs, who pass along the savings to members. One organization offering bartered travel opportunities is *Travel World Leisure Club* (225 W. 34th St., Suite 909, New York, NY 10122; phone: 800-444-TWLC or 212-239-4855; fax: 212-564-5158).

CONSUMER PROTECTION

Passengers whose complaints have not been satisfactorily addressed by the airline can contact the *US Department of Transportation* (*DOT;* Consumer Affairs Division, 400 Seventh St. SW, Room 10405, Washington, DC 20590; phone: 202-366-2220). Also see *Fly Rights* (*Consumer Information Center,* Department 133B, Pueblo, CO 81009; phone: 719-948-3334; fax: 719-948-9724). If you have safety-related questions or concerns, write to the *Federal Aviation Administration* (*FAA;* 800 Independence Ave. SW, Washington, DC 20591) or call or fax the *FAA Consumer Hotline* (phone: 800-322-7873; fax: 202-267-5087). If you have a complaint against a local travel service in Mexico, contact the Mexican tourist authorities or Mexico's consumer protection agency, the *Procuradoria Federal del Consumidor* (208 Calle José Vasconcelos, Sixth Floor, Colonia Condensa, México, DF 06140, México; phone: 52-5-211-1723; fax: 52-5-211-2052 or 52-5-211-9475; and 127 Av. Revolución, Colonia Escandón, México, DF 11800, México; phone: 9-1-800-90313, toll-free, in Mexico, or 52-5-272-5056; fax: 52-5-272-7511).

Traveling by Ship

Your cruise fare usually includes all meals, recreational activities, and entertainment. Shore excursions are available at extra cost, and can be booked in advance or once you're on board. An important factor in the price of a cruise is the location (and sometimes the size) of your cabin. Charts issued by the *Cruise Lines International Association* (*CLIA;* 500 Fifth Ave., Suite 1407, New York, NY 10110; phone: 212-921-0066; fax: 212-921-0549) provide information on ship layouts and facilities, and are available at some *CLIA*-affiliated travel agencies.

The *US Public Health Service* (*PHS*) inspects all passenger vessels calling at US ports. For the most recent summary or a particular inspection report, write to the *National Center for Environmental Health* (Attention: Chief, Vessel Sanitation Program, 1015 N. America Way, Room 107, Miami, FL 33132; phone: 305-536-4307; fax: 305-536-4528). Most cruise ships have a doctor on board, plus medical facilities.

For further information on cruises and cruise lines, consult *Ocean and Cruise News* (PO Box 92, Stamford, CT 06904; phone/fax: 203-329-2787). And for a free list of travel agencies specializing in cruises, contact the *National Association of Cruise Only Agencies* (*NACOA;* 3191 Coral Way, Suite 630, Miami, FL 33145; phone: 305-446-7732; fax: 305-446-9732).

International Cruise Lines

Carnival Cruise Lines (3655 NW 87th Ave., Miami, FL 33178-2428; phone: 800-327-9501 or 305-599-2600; fax: 305-471-4740).

Celebrity Cruises and Fantasy Cruises (5200 Blue Lagoon Dr., Miami, FL 33126; phone: 800-437-3111 or 305-262-6677; fax: 800-437-9111 or 305-267-3505).

Clipper Cruises (7711 Bonhomme Ave., St. Louis, MO 63105-1956; phone: 800-325-0010 or 314-727-2929; fax: 314-727-6576).

Commodore Cruise Line (4000 Hollywood Blvd., S. Tower, Suite 385, Hollywood, FL 33021; phone: 800-237-5361; fax: 800-654-9031).

Costa Cruises (80 SW Eighth St., Miami, FL 33130; phone: 800-462-6782; fax: 305-375-0676).

Crystal Cruises (2121 Ave. of the Stars, Los Angeles, CA 90067; phone: 800-446-6620 or 310-785-9300; fax: 310-785-0011).

Cunard (555 Fifth Ave., New York, NY 10017; phone: 800-5-CUNARD, 800-221-4770, or 212-880-7300; fax: 718-786-2353).

Dolphin Cruise Line (901 South America Way, Miami, FL 33132-2073; phone: 800-222-1003 or 305-358-2111; fax: 305-358-4807).

Holland America Line/West Tours (300 Elliot Ave. W., Seattle, WA 98119; phone: 800-426-0327 or 206-281-3535; fax: 800-628-4855 or 206-281-7110).

INTRAV (7711 Bonhomme Ave., St. Louis, MO 63105-1961; phone: 800-456-8100 or 314-727-0500; fax: 314-727-9354).

Majesty Cruise Line (same address as *Dolphin Cruise Line,* above; phone: 800-532-7788 or 305-536-0000; fax: 305-358-4807).

Norwegian Cruise Line (95 Merrick Way, Coral Gables, FL 33134; phone: 800-327-7030 or 305-445-0866; fax: 305-448-6406).

OdessAmerica Cruise Company (170 Old Country Rd., Mineola, NY 11501; phone: 800-221-3254 or 516-747-8880; fax: 516-747-8367).

P&O Cruises (2815 Second Ave, Suite 400, Seattle, WA 98121; phone: 800-340-7674 for reservations; 800-774-6237 for information; fax: 206-728-3982).

Princess Cruises (10100 Santa Monica Blvd., Los Angeles, CA 90067; phone: 800-421-0522 or 310-553-1770; fax: 310-284-2844).

Radisson Seven Seas Cruises (11340 Blondo St., Omaha, NE 68164; phone: 800-285-1835, 800-333-3333, or 402-498-5072; fax: 402-498-5055).

Royal Caribbean Cruise Lines (1050 Caribbean Way, Miami, FL 33132; phone: 800-327-6700 or 305-539-6000; fax: 800-722-5329).

Seabourn Cruise Line (55 Francisco St., Suite 710, San Francisco, CA 94133; phone: 800-929-9595 or 415-391-7444; fax: 415-391-8518).

Special Expeditions (720 Fifth Ave., New York, NY 10019; phone: 800-762-0003 or 212-765-7740; fax: 212-265-3770).

Sun Line Cruises (1 Rockefeller Plaza, Suite 315, New York, NY 10020; phone: 800-872-6400 or 212-397-6400; fax: 212-765-9685).

Traveling by Train

If you are interested in traveling to Mexico by train, note that there is no direct service from the US. *Amtrak* (phone: 800-USA-RAIL) serves El Paso (Texas), San Diego (California), and Yuma (Arizona). From El Paso, you can take a bus across the border to Ciudad Juárez; from San Diego and Yuma, there are buses to Mexicali. Trains depart from Ciudad Juárez and Mexicali for Mexico City.

Mexico has some 13,000 miles of rail lines. Most routes begin or end in Mexico City, although there also are regional lines, such as those along developed sections of the Pacific Coast. Note, however, that passenger service no longer is provided on some lines (such as from Veracruz to Cancún), and that modern-day bandits make some routes unsafe.

Although train travel in Mexico costs less than in the US, schedules can be erratic, the range of accommodations may be limited, and English-speaking personnel are not always available. Two classes of tickets are sold— *Primera Especial* (first class) and *Segunda Clase* (second class); reservations are required for first class seats. In some cases, dining and bar cars may be available, and you may be able to reserve overnight accommodations. It is best to travel light—Mexican trains do not have baggage cars, so you will have to carry your own luggage onto the train and keep it with you.

A word of warning: There are no official porters at Mexican train stations, although you will encounter numerous individuals offering to carry your bags. Be advised—releasing your belongings to their custody is at your own risk.

Tickets for Mexican trains can be purchased in the US from *Mexico Adventures* (6400 Airport Rd., Suite D, El Paso, TX 79925; phone: 800-322-4888 or 915-775-9955; fax: 915-775-9958) and *Mexico by Train* (PO Box 2782, Laredo, TX 78044; phone: 800-321-1699 or 210-725-3659; fax: 210-571-3659).

Companies offering rail tours in Mexico include *Mexico Adventures* (address above), *South Orient Express* (16800 Greenspoint Park Dr., Suite 245N, Houston, TX 77060; phone: 800-659-7602 or 713-872-0190; fax: 713-872-7123), *Mexico by Train* (address above), and *Sanborn Tours* (PO Drawer 519, McAllen, TX 78502; phone: 800-395-8482 or 210-682-9872; fax: 210-682-0016).

FURTHER INFORMATION

Timetables and publications with information on *Amtrak* fares, routes, and stations are available at train stations, and also can be obtained be calling *Amtrak*'s central information number (phone: 800-USA-RAIL) or writing to *Amtrak Corporate Headquarters* (60 Massachusetts Ave. NE, Washington, DC 20002-4225).

For information on Mexican rail service, contact the main office of Mexican National Railways (*Ferrocarriles Nacionales de México;* Estación Central de Buenavista, Departamento de Tráfico de Pasajeros, Av. Insurgentes Nte. and Av. Mosqueta, México, DF 06358, México; phone: 52-5-547-8655; fax: 52-5-547-8972). Information also is available at branch offices located throughout the country.

Traveling by Bus

Should you wish to travel to Mexico by bus, note that direct bus service is available only to the US border or just over the border into Mexico. In the US, *Greyhound* (phone: 800-231-2222) provides service to Brownsville, McAllen, Laredo, and El Paso (Texas), as well as Calexico, San Diego, and San Ysidro (California); in Mexico, *Greyhound* buses stop at Matamoros, Nueva Laredo, and Tijuana. From these points, you can transfer to Mexican buses to continue the journey south. Once in Mexico, you can purchase tickets for the US leg of the return trip from *Greyhound de México* (707 Calle Amores, México, DF 03310, México; phone: 52-5-669-0986 or 52-5-669-1287).

Bus tickets in Mexico are even less expensive than train fares, and the country is well served by local and express (long-distance) buses. Both first and second class tickets are sold; only first class tickets can be reserved. Where possible, always opt for first class buses, which are more likely to be air conditioned and may have toilets on board. Tickets usually are purchased on a cash-only basis at the bus station on the day of travel. If you do not have reservations and you are traveling during peak travel periods or on holidays, be sure to purchase your tickets as early as possible on the day of departure.

On most local bus routes, reservations are not necessary and the ticket is purchased on the bus. Note that buses are the main form of public transportation in rural areas and often are very crowded, and that purchasing a ticket does not guarantee you a seat.

Mexico City is the hub for most Mexican bus routes, and travelers can purchase tickets from there to destinations throughout the country. Among the major bus companies operating out of Mexico City are *Autobuses de Oriente, Enlaces Terrestres Nacionales, Transportes Chihuahuenses, Transportes del Norte, Omnibus de México,* and *Autotransportes Tres Estrellas de Oro.* These companies are based in one of the four super-terminals in the city, according to the region of the country they serve:

Main Bus Terminals

Terminal Central del Norte (Northern Terminal; 4907 Av. de los 100 Metros; phone: 52-5-587-1552).

Terminal Central del Sur (Southern Terminal; 1320 Taxqueña; phone: 52-5-689-9745 or 52-5-689-9718).

Terminal Central del Poniente (Western Terminal; 122 Av. Sur; phone: 52-5-271-0038).

Terminal Central de Oriente (Eastern Terminal; 200 Calzada Ignacio Zaragoza; phone: 52-5-542-7098).

Traveling by Car

Driving is the most flexible way to tour Mexico. When planning your driving route, however, be *very* conservative in estimating driving time. In some areas, *driving or stopping by the roadside after dark can be very dangerous.*

DRIVING IN MEXICO

As in the US, driving in Mexico is on the right side of the road and passing is on the left. Pictorial direction signs are standardized under the International Roadsign System and their meanings are indicated by their shapes—triangular signs indicate danger, circular signs give instructions, and rectangular signs provide information. Note that toll roads in Mexico are privately run and can be quite expensive. For example, at press time, the one-way toll for traveling the full length of the toll road between Mexico City and Acapulco—covering a distance of 415 kilometers (approximately 257 miles)—was 255 pesos ($34).

In Mexico, distances are measured in kilometers (km) rather than miles (1 mile equals approximately 1.6 kilometers; 1 kilometer equals approximately .62 mile) and speed limits are in kilometers per hour (abbreviated km/h in Mexico). Speed limits usually are 100 to 120 km/h (62 to 74 mph) on highways, 80 km/h (50 mph) on main roads, and 40 to 50 km/h (25 to 31 mph) in towns and near schools. Seat belts are required by law for front seat passengers.

CROSSING THE BORDER

Mexican regulations regarding driving a car across the border from the US are both complicated and stringent—and change frequently. Although the information below was correct at press time, be sure to contact the Mexican tourist authorities regarding any changes *before* you set out on your trip.

To enter Mexico by car, you will need the following: Proof of citizenship, your driver's license, and the car's registration or title, as well as a Mexican tourist card (see *Entry Requirements and Customs Regulations,* below), a car permit, a Temporary Import Permit, and a Vehicle Promise Return Form. You also may be asked to show proof of US automobile insurance (also see "Automobile Insurance," below). In addition, although not *required,* using a major credit card to pay the car permit application fee will simplify the process and substantially reduce costs (see below).

You can obtain the car and Temporary Import permits and the Vehicle Promise Return form from *Mexican Customs* officials at the border. As there often are long delays at border crossings, however, you might want to consider the services offered by *Sanborn's Mexico Insurance Service* (main office: 2009 S. 10th St., McAllen, TX 78503; phone: 210-686-0711 or 210-682-1354; fax: 210-686-0732) and the *American Automobile Association* (*AAA;* main office: 1000 AAA Dr., Heathrow, FL 32746-5063; phone: 407-444-7000; fax: 407-444-7380). Any *Sanborn's* office and some *AAA* branch offices near the border can provide and fill out the forms for you and make the necessary copies. There are express check-in lines at the border for those who arrive with the forms already completed. *Sanborn's* charges a $25 fee for this service ($10 if you also purchase Mexican car insurance through them). The *AAA* service is free to members and available to non-members for a fee (often around $25, although the fee varies between branches).

After the forms have been processed by *Mexican Customs* officials, you will be allowed to cross the border temporarily to bring these documents to a nearby branch of the *Banco del Ejército*. There you must pay a fee of $12 *by credit card* (cash is not accepted).

If you do not have a credit card, you will be required to provide the bank with a bond equal to between 2% and 5% of the value of your car. This bond can be purchased from representatives of a bonding company located in a *Banco del Ejército* branch. You can obtain a refund when leaving Mexico—minus a hefty $125 processing fee—but note that cash refunds are available only at the particular *Banco del Ejército* branch where the bond was issued. Refund requests can be processed at other branches, but your refund will be sent to you by check after you return to the US.

Once you have paid the credit card fee or obtained the bond, you will be given proof of payment to bring back to *Mexican Customs* officials at the border. You then will be issued a car permit.

Banco del Ejército branches are located in the following Mexican border towns: Agua Prieta, Ciudad Acuña, Ciudad Juárez, Ciudad Miguel Alemán, Colombia, Matamoros, Mexicali, Naco, Nogales, Nuevo Laredo, Ojinaga, Palomas, Piedras Negras, Reynosa, San Luis Río Colorado, Sonoyta, Tecate, and Tijuana.

In addition to the requirements discussed above, the following regulations apply if you do not own the car you are driving into Mexico:

- If the owner of the car will not be accompanying you on your trip, and he or she is a member of your immediate family (father, mother, brother, sister, son, daughter, or spouse), you must have a notarized letter from that family member releasing the car to you. If the owner of the car is not a family member, he or she must *personally* obtain the car permit at the border and provide customs officials with the notarized release letter.
- If the car was rented or leased in the US, you must have a credit card and the rental contract in your own name, as well as a notarized letter from the company authorizing you to drive the vehicle across the border. Note, however, that at press time, few of the major US car rental companies allowed cars rented in the US to be driven into Mexico.
- If you are driving a company car, you must have a credit card, your employee ID, and a notarized letter from the company certifying that you have permission to drive the car in Mexico.

AUTOMOBILE INSURANCE

Note that US insurance policies are not recognized in Mexico and you will have to purchase separate Mexican insurance (including personal liability coverage). Some US insurance agents can have a policy written for you through a Mexican insurance company. You also can purchase this coverage through any office of *Sanborn's Mexico Insurance Service* (see "Crossing the Border," above) or from other companies located in US border towns. When renting a car to pick up in Mexico, the car rental company usually will obtain the necessary insurance for you.

For information on companies that sell Mexican insurance, as well as additional information on car entry regulations, call the *Mexican Ministry of Tourism*'s toll-free information line (phone: 800-482-9832). Information also is available from the *Mexican Government Tourism Office for Surface Transportation* (2707 N. Loop W., Suite 440, Houston, TX 77008; phone: 713-880-8772; fax: 713-880-0286).

MAPS

Among the best maps are those available from *Guía Roji* (31 José Moran, Colonia San Miguel Chapultepec, México, DF 11850, México; phone: 52-5-515-0384 or 52-5-515-7963; fax: 52-5-277-2307) and Mexico's *Instituto Nacional de Estadística, Geografía e Informática* (*INEGI;* Asesor de Centro Ventas, Av. Héroes de Nacozari, Nivel Acceso, Fraccionamiento Jardín del Parque, Aguascalientes 20270, México; phone: 52-49-182232; fax: 52-49-180739). Additional resources include the *Rand McNally Cosmopolitan Map of Mexico* and the *Rand McNally Road Atlas: US, Canada and Mexico* (Rand McNally, 150 E. 52nd St., New York, NY 10022; phone: 212-758-7488). A good source for maps of all kinds is *Map Link* (25 E. Mason St., Suite 201, Santa Barbara, CA 93101; phone: 805-965-4402; fax: 800-MAP-SPOT or 805-962-0884).

AUTOMOBILE CLUBS AND BREAKDOWNS

To protect yourself in case of breakdowns while driving in Mexico, and for travel information and other benefits, consider joining a reputable automobile club. The largest of these is the *American Automobile Association* (*AAA;* main office: 1000 AAA Dr., Heathrow, FL 32746-5080; phone: 407-444-7000; general fax: 407-444-7380; travel department fax: 407-444-4584). Before joining this or any other automobile club, however, check whether it has reciprocity with Mexican clubs such as the *Asociación Mexicana Automovilística* (*AMA;* 7 Calle Orizaba, Colonia Roma, México, DF 06700, México; phone: 52-5-208-8329; fax: 52-5-207-4448) and the *Automóvil Club de México* (59 José María Iglesias, Colonia Tabacalera, México, DF 06030, México; phone: 52-5-705-0258; fax: 52-5-546-0665).

In addition, the *Mexican Ministry of Tourism*'s emergency road service fleet, known as the *Angeles Verdes* ("Green Angels"), patrols major Mexican highways from 8 AM to 8 PM. Except for parts and fuel, their assistance is free. The nationwide number in Mexico for the Green Angels is 5-250-8221. Note, however, that there may not be anyone at this number who speaks English. For English-language assistance 24 hours a day, call the *Mexican Ministry of Tourism* (phone: 250-0123 or 250-0151 in Mexico City; 91-800-90392, toll-free, elsewhere in Mexico).

GASOLINE

In Mexico, gasoline is produced and distributed by *Petróleos Mexicanos (PEMEX),* the government-owned oil company, and is sold in liters (approximately 3.8 liters = 1 US gallon). Leaded *(Nova),* unleaded *(Magna sin),* and diesel (also called *diesel* in Mexico) fuels are available.

RENTING A CAR

You can rent a car through a travel agent or international rental firm before leaving home, or from a local company once in Mexico. Reserve in advance.

Most car rental companies require a credit card, although some will accept a substantial cash deposit. The minimum age to rent a car is set by the company; some also may impose special conditions on drivers above a certain age. Electing to pay for collision or loss damage waiver (CDW or LDW) protection will add to the cost of renting a car, but releases you from full financial liability for the vehicle. (Also see "Automobile Insurance," above.) Possible additional costs include drop-off charges and one-way service fees.

Whether you arrange the rental in advance or upon arrival in Mexico, you will need your US driver's license, proof of US citizenship, and a copy of the rental contract. (Note that this contract must be kept with you at all times while you are in Mexico—do not leave it in the car.)

Below is a list of international car rental companies with offices in Mexico. For the names and phone numbers of international and local companies in particular Mexican cities, see *Sources and Resources* in THE CITIES.

Avis Rent A Car (phone: 800-331-1084).

Budget Rent A Car (phone: 800-472-3325).

Dollar Rent A Car (phone: 800-800-4000).

Hertz Rent A Car (phone: 800-654-3001).

National Car Rental (phone: 800-227-3876).

Payless Car Rental (phone: 800-PAYLESS).

Sears Rent A Car (phone: 800-527-0770).

Thrifty Car Rental (phone: 800-367-2277).

Package Tours

A package tour is a collection of travel services that can be purchased in a single transaction. Its principal advantages are convenience and economy—

you don't have to make individual arrangements for each service, and the cost usually is lower than that of the same services purchased separately. Tour programs generally can be divided into two categories: escorted or locally hosted (with a set itinerary) and independent (usually more flexible).

When considering a package tour, read the brochure *carefully* to determine exactly what is included and any conditions that may apply, and check the company's record with the *Better Business Bureau*. The *United States Tour Operators Association* (*USTOA*; 211 E. 51st St., Suite 12B, New York, NY 10022; phone: 212-750-7371; fax: 212-421-1285) also can be helpful in determining a package tour operator's reliability. As with charter flights, to safeguard your funds, always make your check out to the company's escrow account.

Many tour operators offer packages focused on special interests such as the arts, nature study, or sports. *All Adventure Vacations* (5589 Arapahoe, Suite 208, Boulder, CO 80303; phone: 800-537-4025 or 303-440-7924; fax: 303-440-4160) represents such specialized packagers. Many also are listed in the *Specialty Travel Index* (305 San Anselmo Ave., Suite 313, San Anselmo, CA 94960; phone: 415-459-4900 in California; 800-442-4922 elsewhere in the US; fax: 415-459-4974).

Below is a list of companies offering package tours to Mexico. Note that companies described as wholesalers accept bookings only through travel agents.

Package Tour Operators

Adventure Center (1311 63rd St., Suite 200, Emeryville, CA 94608; phone: 510-654-1879 in northern California; 800-227-8747 elsewhere in the US; fax: 510-654-4200).

AIB Tours (2500 NW 79th Ave., Suite 211, Miami, FL 33122; phone: 305-715-0056 in Florida; 800-242-8687 elsewhere in the US; fax: 305-715-0055). Wholesaler.

Alaska Airlines Vacations (PO Box 68900, Seattle, WA 98168-0900; phone: 800-468-2248; fax: 206-433-3374).

American Airlines FlyAAway Vacations (offices throughout the US; phone: 800-321-2121).

American Museum of Natural History Discovery Tours (Central Park W. at 79th St., New York, NY 10024; phone: 800-462-8687 or 212-769-5700; 212-769-5755).

American Wilderness Experience (PO Box 1486, Boulder, CO 80306; phone: 800-444-0099 or 303-444-2622; fax: 303-444-3999).

Anglers Travel (3100 Mill St., Suite 206, Reno, NV 89502; phone: 800-624-8429 or 702-324-0580; fax: 702-324-0583).

Angling Travel and Tours (c/o *John Eustice & Associates, Ltd.*, 1445 SW 84th Ave., Portland, OR 97225; phone: 800-288-0886 or 503-297-2468; fax: 503-297-3048).

Apple Vacations East (7 Campus Blvd., Newtown Sq., PA 19073; phone: 800-727-3400 or 610-359-6500; fax: 610-359-6524). Wholesaler.

Backroads (1516 Fifth St., Berkeley, CA 94710; phone: 800-462-2848 or 510-527-1555; fax: 510-527-1444).

Baja Expeditions (2625 Garnet Ave., San Diego, CA 92109; phone: 800-843-6967 or 619-581-3311; fax: 619-581-6542).

Barron Adventures (16501 Pacific Coast Hwy., Suite 100, Sunset Beach, CA 90742; phone: 310-592-2050; fax: 310-592-2069).

Butterfield & Robinson (70 Bond St., Suite 300, Toronto, Ontario M5B 1X3, Canada; phone: 800-678-1147 or 416-864-1354; fax: 416-864-0541).

Caiman Expeditions (3449 E. River Rd., Tucson, AZ 85718; phone: 520-299-1047; fax: 520-299-8920).

California Academy of Sciences (Attention: Travel Division; Golden Gate Park, San Francisco, CA 94118; phone: 415-750-7222; fax: 415-750-7346).

Ceiba Adventures (PO Box 2274, Flagstaff, AZ 86003; phone: 520-527-0171; fax: 520-527-8127).

Certified Vacations (110 E. Broward Blvd., Ft. Lauderdale, FL 33302; phone: 800-233-7260 or 305-522-1440; fax: 305-357-4687).

Collette Tours (162 Middle St., Pawtucket, RI 02860; phone: 800-752-2655 in New England; 800-832-4656 elsewhere in the US; fax: 401-727-4745).

Continental Vacations (offices throughout the US; phone: 800-634-5555).

Coral Way Tours (9745 Sunset Dr., Suite 104, Miami, FL 33173; phone: 800-882-4665 or 305-279-3252; fax: 305-279-3167).

Delta's Dream Vacations (PO Box 1525, Ft. Lauderdale, FL 33302; phone: 800-872-7786).

Dvorak's Kayak and Rafting Expeditions (17921 US Hwy. 285, Nathrop, CO 81236; phone: 800-824-3795 or 719-539-6851; fax: 719-539-3378).

Earthwatch (680 Mt. Auburn St., PO Box 403BG, Watertown, MA 02272; phone: 800-776-0188 or 617-926-8200; fax: 617-926-8532).

Ecosummer Expeditions (main office: 1516 Duranleau St., Vancouver, British Columbia V6H 3S4, Canada; phone: 800-465-8884 or 604-669-7741; fax: 604-669-3244; US mailing address: 936 Peace Portal Dr., PO Box 8014-240, Blaine, WA 98231).

Far Flung Adventures (PO Box 377, Terlingua, TX 79852; phone: 800-359-4138 or 915-371-2489; fax: 915-371-2325).

Far Horizons (PO Box 91900, Albuquerque, NM 87199-1900; phone: 800-552-4575 or 505-343-9400; fax: 505-343-8076).

Fishing International (PO Box 2132, Santa Rosa, CA 95405; phone: 800-950-4242 or 707-539-3366; fax: 707-539-1320).

Forum Travel International (91 Gregory La., Suite 21, Pleasant Hill, CA 94523; phone: 510-671-2900; fax: 510-671-2993 or 510-946-1500).

Frontiers International (100 Logan Rd., Wexford, PA 15090-0959; phone: 412-935-1577 in Pennsylvania; 800-245-1950 elsewhere in the US; fax: 412-935-5388).

Funjet Vacations (PO Box 1460, Milwaukee, WI 53201-1460; phone: 800-558-3050 for reservations; 800-558-3060 for customer service). Wholesaler.

Gadabout Tours (700 E. Tahquitz Canyon Way, Palm Springs, CA 92262; phone: 800-952-5068 or 619-325-5556; fax: 619-325-5127).

Globetrotters (139 Main St., Cambridge, MA 02142; phone: 800-333-1234 or 617-621-9911; fax: 617-577-8380).

Globus and Cosmos (5301 S. Federal Circle, Littleton, CO 80123-2980; phone: 800-851-0728 for information; 800-221-0090 for reservations; or 303-797-2800; fax: 303-798-5441). Wholesaler.

GWV International (300 First Ave., Needham, MA 02194; phone: 800-225-5498 or 617-449-5460; fax: 617-449-3473). Wholesaler.

Himalayan Travel (112 Prospect St., Stamford, CT 06901; phone: 800-225-2380 or 203-359-3711; fax: 203-359-3669).

International Expeditions (1 Environs Park, Helena, AL 35080; phone: 800-633-4734 or 205-428-1700; fax: 205-428-1714).

Journeys (4011 Jackson Rd., Ann Arbor, MI 48103; phone: 800-255-8735 or 313-665-4407; fax: 313-665-2945).

Kerrville Tours (PO Box 79, Shreveport, LA 71161-0079; phone: 800-442-8705 or 318-227-2882; fax: 318-227-2486).

LATOUR (15-22 215th St., Bayside, NY 11360; phone: 800-825-0825 or 718-229-6500; fax: 718-229-6978).

Liberty Travel (for the nearest location, contact the central office: 69 Spring St., Ramsey, NJ 07446; phone: 201-934-3500; fax: 201-934-3888).

Maupintour (PO Box 807, Lawrence, KS 66044; phone: 800-255-4266 or 913-843-1211; fax: 913-843-8351). Wholesaler.

Maya Route Tours (PO Box 1948, Murray Hill Station, New York, NY 10156; phone: 212-683-2136; fax: 212-575-7730).

Mayflower (1225 Warren Ave., PO Box 490, Downers Grove, IL 60515; phone: 800-323-7604 or 708-960-3430; fax: 708-960-3575).

Mountain Travel-Sobek (6420 Fairmount Ave., El Cerrito, CA 94530; phone: 510-527-8100 in California; 800-227-2384 elsewhere in the US; fax: 510-525-7710).

MTA International (1717 N. Highland Ave., Suite 1100, Los Angeles, CA 90028; phone: 800-876-4682 or 213-462-6444; fax: 213-461-7559). Wholesaler.

Nantahala Outdoor Center Adventure Travel (13077 Hwy. 19 W., Bryson City, NC 28713-9114; phone: 800-232-7238 for reservations; 704-488-2175 for information; fax: 704-488-2498).

National Outdoor Leadership School (288 Main St., Lander, WY 82520; phone: 307-332-6973; fax: 307-332-1220).

Natural Habitat Adventures (2945 Center Green Court South, Boulder, CO 80301; phone: 800-543-8917 or 303-449-3711; fax: 303-449-3712).

Nature Expeditions International (PO Box 11496, Eugene, OR 97440; phone: 800-869-0639 or 503-484-6529; fax: 503-484-6531).

New England Vacation Tours (PO Box 560, West Dover, VT 05356; phone: 800-742-7669 or 802-464-2076; fax: 802-464-2629). Wholesaler.

Northwest World Vacations (c/o *MLT*, 5130 Hwy. 101, Minnetonka, MN 55345; phone: 800-328-0025 or 612-989-5000; fax: 612-474-0725). Wholesaler.

Oceanic Society Expeditions (Ft. Mason Center, Building E, San Francisco, CA 94123; phone: 800-326-7491 or 415-441-1106; fax: 415-474-3395).

Outland Adventures (PO Box 16343, Seattle, WA 98116; phone/fax: 206-932-7012).

Pacific Rim Paddling Company (621 Discovery St., PO Box 1840, Victoria, British Columbia V8W 2Y3, Canada; phone: 604-384-6103; fax: 604-361-2686).

PanAngling Travel Service (180 N. Michigan Ave., Room 303, Chicago, IL 60601; phone: 800-533-4353 or 312-263-0328; fax: 312-263-5246).

Pleasant Holidays (2404 Townsgate Rd., Westlake Village, CA 91361; phone: 800-242-9244 or 818-991-3390; fax: 805-495-4972).

Quasar Tours (1523 W. Hillsborough Ave., Tampa, FL 33603; phone: 800-444-1770 or 813-237-4990; fax: 813-238-4175). Wholesaler.

Questers Tours & Travel (581 Park Ave. S., Suite 1201, New York, NY 10016; phone: 800-468-8668 or 212-251-0444; fax: 212-251-0890).

Regina Tours (401 South St., Room 4B, Chardon, OH 44024; phone: 800-228-4654 or 216-286-9166; fax: 216-286-4231).

REI Adventures (PO Box 1938, Sumner, WA 98390-0800; phone: 800-622-2236 or 206-891-2631; fax: 206-395-4744).

Sanborn Tours (PO Drawer 519, McAllen, TX 78502; phone: 800-395-8482 or 210-682-9872; fax: 210-682-0016).

See & Sea Travel (50 Francisco St., Suite 205, San Francisco, CA 94133; phone: 415-434-3400 in California; 800-348-9778 elsewhere in the US; fax: 415-434-3409).

Sierra Club Outings (730 Polk St., San Francisco, CA 94109; phone: 415-923-5630).

Smithsonian Associates Study Tours (1100 Jefferson Dr. SW, Room 3045, Washington, DC 20560; phone: 202-357-4700; fax: 202-786-2315).

Solar Tours (1629 K St. NW, Suite 604, Washington, DC 20006; phone: 800-388-7652 or 202-861-5864; fax: 202-452-0905). Wholesaler.

Steppingstone Environmental Education Tours (PO Box 373, Narberth, PA 19072; phone: 800-874-8784 or 610-649-3891; fax: 610-649-3428).

Sun Holidays (7280 W. Palmetto Park Rd., Suite 301, Boca Raton, FL 33433; phone: 800-243-2057 or 407-367-0105; fax: 407-393-3870). Wholesaler.

Sunmakers (S. Tower, 100 W. Harrison, Suite 350, Seattle, WA 98119; phone: 800-841-4321 or 206-216-2900; fax: 800-323-2231). Wholesaler.

Tauck Tours (PO Box 5027, Westport, CT 06881; phone: 800-468-2825 or 203-226-6911; fax: 203-221-6828).

Tours and Travel Odyssey (230 E. McClellan Ave., Livingston, NJ 07039; phone: 800-527-2989 or 201-992-5459; fax: 201-994-1618).

TNT Vacations (2 Charlesgate W., Boston, MA 02215; phone: 800-262-0123 or 617-262-9200; fax: 617-638-3445). Wholesaler.

TRAVCOA (PO Box 2630, Newport Beach, CA 92658; phone: 800-992-2004 or 714-476-2800 in California; 800-992-2003 elsewhere in the US; fax: 714-476-2538). Wholesaler.

Travel New Orleans (400 Magazine St., Suite 201, New Orleans, LA 70130; phone: 800-535-8747 or 504-561-8747; fax: 504-565-3550). Wholesaler.

Travel Impressions (465 Smith St., Farmingdale, NY 11735; phone: 800-284-0044 or 516-845-8000). Wholesaler.

TravelWild International (PO Box 1637, Vashon Island, WA 98070; phone: 800-368-0077 or 206-463-5362; fax: 206-463-5484).

Trek America (PO Box 189, Rockaway, NJ 07866; phone: 800-221-0596 or 201-983-1144; fax: 201-983-8551).

Tropical Adventures Travel (111 Second Ave. N., Seattle, WA 98109; phone: 800-247-3483 or 206-441-3483; fax: 206-441-5431).

TWA Getaway Vacations (Getaway Vacation Center, 10 E. Stow Rd., Marlton, NJ 08053; phone: 800-GETAWAY; fax: 609-985-4125).

Unique World Travel (39 Beechwood Ave., Manhasset, NY 11030; phone: 516-627-2636 in New York State; 800-669-0757 elsewhere in the US; fax: 516-365-1667). Wholesaler.

United Vacations (PO Box 24580, Milwaukee, WI 53224-0580; phone: 800-328-6877; fax: 414-351-5256).

Victor Emanuel Nature Tours (PO Box 33008, Austin, TX 78764; phone: 800-328-VENT or 512-328-5221; fax: 512-328-2919).

Wide World of Golf (PO Box 5217, Carmel, CA 93921; phone: 800-214-4653 or 408-624-6667; fax: 408-625-9671).

Wilderness: Alaska/Mexico (1231 Sundance Loop, Department BB, Fairbanks, AK 99709; phone/fax: 907-479-8203).

Wildland Adventures (3516 NE 155th St., Seattle, WA 98155; phone: 800-345-4453 or 206-365-0686; fax: 206-363-6615).

Insurance

The first person with whom you should discuss travel insurance is your own insurance broker. You may discover that the insurance you already carry protects you adequately while traveling and that you need little additional coverage. If you charge travel services, the credit card company also may provide some insurance coverage (and other safeguards). Below is a list of the basic types of travel insurance and some of the companies specializing in such policies.

Types of Travel Insurance

Automobile insurance: Provides collision, theft, property damage, and personal liability protection while driving. (For information about Mexican automobile insurance requirements, see *Traveling by Car,* above.)

Baggage and personal effects insurance: Protects your bags and their contents in case of damage or theft at any point during your travels.

Default and/or bankruptcy insurance: Provides coverage in the event of default and/or bankruptcy on the part of the tour operator, airline, or other travel supplier.

Flight insurance: Covers accidental injury or death while flying.

Personal accident and sickness insurance: Covers cases of illness, injury, or death in an accident while traveling.

Trip cancellation and interruption insurance: Guarantees a refund if you must cancel a trip; may reimburse you for additional travel costs incurred in catching up with a tour or traveling home early.

Combination policies: Include any or all of the above.

Travel Insurance Providers

Access America International (PO Box 90315, Richmond, VA 23230; phone: 800-284-8300 or 804-285-3300; fax: 804-673-1491).

Carefree (c/o *Berkely Care,* Arm Coverage, 100 Garden City Plaza, Fifth Floor, PO Box 9366, Garden City, NY 11530; phone: 800-645-2424 or 516-294-0220; fax: 516-294-0268).

NEAR Services (PO Box 1339, Calumet City, IL 60409; phone: 708-868-6700 in the Chicago area; 800-654-6700 elsewhere in the US; fax: 708-868-6706).

Tele-Trip (c/o *Mutual of Omaha,* 3201 Farnam St., Omaha, NE 68131; phone: 800-228-9792 or 402-351-5754; fax: 402-351-2456).

Travel Assistance International (c/o *Worldwide Assistance Services,* 1133 15th St. NW, Suite 400, Washington, DC 20005-2710; phone: 800-821-2828 or 202-331-1609; fax: 202-331-1530).

Travel Guard International (1145 Clark St., Stevens Point, WI 54481; phone: 800-826-1300 or 715-345-0505; fax: 800-955-8785).

Travel Insured International (PO Box 280568, East Hartford, CT 06128-0568; phone: 800-243-3174 or 860-528-7663; fax: 860-528-8005).

Disabled Travelers

Make travel arrangements well in advance. Specify to all services involved the nature of your disability to determine if there are accommodations and facilities that meet your needs.

Publications

Access Travel: A Guide to the Accessibility of Airport Terminals (Consumer Information Center, Department 575A, Pueblo, CO 81009; phone: 719-948-3334; fax: 719-948-9724).

Air Transportation of Handicapped Persons (Publication #AC-120-32; *US Department of Transportation,* Distribution Unit, Utilization and Storage Section, M-45.3, 33-410 75th Ave., Landover, MD 20785; phone: 301-322-4961; fax: 301-386-5394).

The Diabetic Traveler (PO Box 8223 RW, Stamford, CT 06905; phone: 203-327-5832; fax: 203-975-1748).

Directory of Travel Agencies for the Disabled and Travel for the Disabled, both by Helen Hecker (Twin Peaks Press, PO Box 129, Vancouver, WA 98666; phone: 800-637-2256 for orders; 360-694-2462 for information; fax: 360-696-3210).

The Disabled Driver's Mobility Guide (*American Automobile Association,* Traffic Safety Department, 1000 AAA Dr., Heathrow, FL 32746-5063; phone: 407-444-7961; fax: 407-444-7956).

Handicapped Travel Newsletter (PO Drawer 269, Athens, TX 75751; phone: 941-540-7612; fax: 941-540-7238).

Handi-Travel: A Resource Book for Disabled and Elderly Travellers, by Cinnie Noble (*Easter Seals/March of Dimes National Council,* 45 Sheppard Ave. E., Suite 801, Toronto, Ontario M2N 5W9, Canada; phone/TDD: 416-250-7490; fax: 416-229-1371).

Holidays and Travel Abroad, edited by John Stanford (*Royal Association for Disability and Rehabilitation,* address below).

On the Go, Go Safely, Plan Ahead (*American Diabetes Association,* National Service Center, 1660 Duke St., Alexandria, VA 22314; phone: 800-232-3472 or 703-549-1500; fax: 703-549-6995).

Travel for the Patient with Chronic Obstructive Pulmonary Disease (c/o Dr. Harold Silver, 1601 18th St. NW, Washington, DC 20009; phone: 202-667-0134; fax: 202-667-0148).

Travel Tips for Hearing-Impaired People (*American Academy of Otolaryngology,* 1 Prince St., Alexandria, VA 22314; phone: 703-836-4444; fax: 703-683-5100).

Travel Tips for People with Arthritis (*Arthritis Foundation,* 1314 Spring St. NW, Atlanta, GA 30309; phone: 800-283-7800 or 404-872-7100; fax: 404-872-0457).

The Travelin' Talk Newsletter (*Travelin' Talk,* PO Box 3534, Clarksville, TN 37043-3534; phone: 615-552-6670; fax: 615-552-1182).

Traveling Like Everybody Else: A Practical Guide for Disabled Travelers, by Jacqueline Freedman and Susan Gersten (Modan Publishing, PO Box 1202, Bellmore, NY 11710; phone: 516-679-1380; fax: 516-679-1448).

The Wheelchair Traveler, by Douglass R. Annand (123 Ball Hill Rd., Milford, NH 03055; phone: 603-673-4539).

Organizations

ACCENT on Living (PO Box 700, Bloomington, IL 61702; phone: 800-787-8444 or 309-378-2961; fax: 309-378-4420).

Access: The Foundation for Accessibility by the Disabled (1109 Linden St., Valley Stream, NY 11580; phone/fax: 516-568-2715).

American Foundation for the Blind (11 Penn Plaza, Suite 300, New York, NY 10001; phone: 800-232-5463 or 212-502-7600; fax: 212-502-7777).

Mobility International (main office: 25 Rue de Manchester, Brussels B-1070, Belgium; phone: 32-2-410-6297; fax: 32-2-410-6874; US address: *MIUSA,* PO Box 10767, Eugene, OR 97440; phone/TDD: 503-343-1284; fax: 503-343-6812).

MossRehab Hospital Travel Information Service (telephone referrals only; phone: 215-456-9600; TDD: 215-456-9602).

National Rehabilitation Information Center (8455 Colesville Rd., Suite 935, Silver Spring, MD 20910-3319; phone: 301-588-9284; fax: 301-587-1967).

Paralyzed Veterans of America (*PVA;* PVA/Access to the Skies Program, 801 18th St. NW, Washington, DC 20006-3585; phone: 202-872-1300 in Washington, DC; 800-424-8200 elsewhere in the US; fax: 202-785-4452).

Partners of the Americas (1424 K St. NW, Suite 700, Washington, DC 20005; phone: 800-322-7844 or 202-628-3300; fax: 202-628-3306).

Royal Association for Disability and Rehabilitation (*RADAR;* 12 City Forum, 250 City Rd., London EC1V 8AF, England; phone: 44-171-250-3222; fax: 44-171-250-0212).

Society for the Advancement of Travel for the Handicapped (*SATH;* 347 Fifth Ave., Suite 610, New York, NY 10016; phone: 212-447-7284; fax: 212-725-8253).

Package Tour Operators

Accessible Journeys (35 W. Sellers Ave., Ridley Park, PA 19078; phone: 800-846-4537 or 610-521-0339; fax: 610-521-6959).

Accessible Tours/Directions Unlimited (Attention: Lois Bonanni, 720 N. Bedford Rd., Bedford Hills, NY 10507; phone: 800-533-5343 or 914-241-1700; fax: 914-241-0243).

Beehive Travel (77 W. 200 S., Suite 500, Salt Lake City, UT 84101; phone: 800-777-5727 or 801-578-9000; fax: 801-297-2828).

Classic Travel Service (275 Madison Ave., Suite 2314, New York, NY 10016-1101; phone: 212-843-2900; fax: 212-944-4493).

Dahl's Good Neighbor Travel Service (124 S. Main St., Viroqua, WI 54665; phone: 800-338-3245 or 608-637-2128; fax: 608-637-3030).

Dialysis at Sea Cruises (PO Box 218, Indian Rocks Beach, FL 34635; phone: 800-544-7604 or 813-596-4614; fax: 813-596-0203).

Flying Wheels Travel (PO Box 382, Owatonna, MN 55060; phone: 800-535-6790 or 507-451-5005; fax: 507-451-1685).

The Guided Tour (7900 Old York Rd., Suite 114B, Elkins Park, PA 19027-2339; phone: 800-783-5841 or 215-782-1370; fax: 215-635-2637).

Hinsdale Travel (201 E. Ogden Ave., Hinsdale, IL 60521; phone: 708-325-1335; fax: 708-325-1342).

MedEscort International (*Lehigh Valley International Airport*, PO Box 8766, Allentown, PA 18105-8766; phone: 800-255-7182 or 610-791-3111; fax: 610-791-9189).

Prestige World Travel (5710-X High Point Rd., Greensboro, NC 27407; phone: 800-476-7737 or 910-292-6690; fax: 910-632-9404).

Sprout (893 Amsterdam Ave., New York, NY 10025; phone: 212-222-9575; fax: 212-222-9768).

Weston Travel Agency (134 N. Cass Ave., PO Box 1050, Westmont, IL 60559; phone: 708-968-2513; fax: 708-968-2539).

Single Travelers

The travel industry is not very fair to people who vacation by themselves—they often end up paying more than those traveling in pairs. There are services catering to single travelers, however, that match travel companions, offer travel arrangements with shared accommodations, and provide information and discounts. Helpful information for those traveling alone also is provided in the newsletter *Going Solo* (Doerfer Communications, PO Box 123, Apalachicola, FL 32329; phone/fax: 904-653-8848).

Organizations and Companies

Gallivanting (515 E. 79th St., Suite 20F, New York, NY 10021; phone: 800-933-9699 or 212-988-0617; fax: 212-988-0144).

Globus and Cosmos (5301 S. Federal Circle, Littleton, CO 80123-2980; phone: 800-851-0728 for information; 800-221-0090 for reservations; or 303-797-2800; fax: 303-798-5441).

Jane's International Travel and Sophisticated Women Travelers (2603 Bath Ave., Brooklyn, NY 11214; phone: 800-613-9226 or 718-266-2045; fax: 718-266-4062).

Jens Jurgen's Travel Companion Exchange (PO Box 833, Amityville, NY 11701; phone: 800-392-1256 or 516-454-0880; fax: 516-454-0170).

Marion Smith Professional Singles (611 Prescott Pl., N. Woodmere, NY 11581; phone: 800-698-TRIP, 516-791-4852, 516-791-4865, or 212-944-2112; fax: 516-791-4879).

Partners-in-Travel (11660 Chenault St., Suite 119, Los Angeles, CA 90049; phone: 310-476-4869).

Solo Flights (612 Penfield Rd., Fairfield, CT 06430; phone: 800-266-1566 or 203-256-1235).

Travel Companions (*Atrium Financial Center*, 1515 N. Federal Hwy., Suite 300, Boca Raton, FL 33432; phone: 561-393-6448 in Florida; 800-383-7211 elsewhere in the US; fax: 561-393-6448).

> *Travel in Two's* (239 N. Broadway, Suite 3, N. Tarrytown, NY 10591; phone: 914-631-8301 in New York State; 800-692-5252 elsewhere in the US).
>
> *Umbrella Singles* (PO Box 157, Woodbourne, NY 12788; phone: 800-537-2797 or 914-434-6871; fax: 914-434-3532).

Older Travelers

Special discounts and more free time are just two factors that have given older travelers a chance to see the world at affordable prices. Many travel suppliers offer senior discounts—sometimes only to members of certain senior citizens organizations (which may offer travel benefits of their own). When considering a particular package, make sure the facilities—and the pace of the tour—match your needs and physical condition.

Publications

> *Going Abroad: 101 Tips for Mature Travelers* (Grand Circle Travel, 347 Congress St., Boston, MA 02210; phone: 800-221-2610 or 617-350-7500; fax: 617-423-0445).
>
> *The Mature Traveler* (GEM Publishing Group, PO Box 50400, Reno, NV 89513-0400; phone: 702-786-7419).
>
> *Take a Camel to Lunch and Other Adventures for Mature Travelers,* by Nancy O'Connell (Bristol Publishing Enterprises, PO Box 1737, San Leandro, CA 94577; phone: 510-895-4461 in California; 800-346-4889 elsewhere in the US; fax: 510-895-4459).
>
> *Unbelievably Good Deals & Great Adventures That You Absolutely Can't Get Unless You're Over 50,* by Joan Rattner Heilman (Contemporary Books, 180 N. Stetson Ave., Suite 1200, Chicago, IL 60601; phone: 800-621-1918 or 312-540-4500; fax: 800-998-3103 or 312-540-4687).

Organizations

> *American Association of Retired Persons* (AARP; 601 E St. NW, Washington, DC 20049; phone: 202-434-2277).
>
> *Mature Outlook* (Customer Service Center, 6001 N. Clark St., Chicago, IL 60660; phone: 800-336-6330; fax: 312-764-5036).
>
> *National Council of Senior Citizens* (1331 F St. NW, Washington, DC 20004; phone: 202-347-8800; fax: 202-624-9595).

Package Tour Operators

> *Elderhostel* (75 Federal St., Boston, MA 02110-1941; phone: 617-426-7788).
>
> *Gadabout Tours* (700 E. Tahquitz Canyon Way, Palm Springs, CA 92262; phone: 800-952-5068 or 619-325-5556; fax: 619-325-5127).
>
> *Grand Circle Travel* (347 Congress St., Boston, MA 02210; phone: 800-221-2610 or 617-350-7500; fax: 617-346-6700).

Grandtravel (6900 Wisconsin Ave., Suite 706, Chevy Chase, MD 20815; phone: 800-247-7651 or 301-986-0790; fax: 301-913-0166).

Interhostel (*University of New Hampshire,* Division of Continuing Education, 6 Garrison Ave., Durham, NH 03824; phone: 800-733-9753 or 603-862-1147; fax: 603-862-1113).

Mature Tours (10 Greenwood La., Westport, CT 06880; phone: 800-266-1566 or 203-256-1235; fax: 203-259-7113).

OmniTours (104 Wilmot Rd., Deerfield, IL 60015; phone: 800-962-0060 or 708-374-0088; fax: 708-374-9515).

Saga International Holidays (222 Berkeley St., Boston, MA 02116; phone: 800-343-0273 or 617-262-2262; fax: 617-375-5950).

Money Matters

The basic unit of Mexican currency is the **peso,** which is divided into 100 **centavos.** The peso is distributed in coin denominations of 1, 5, 10, 20, and 50 centavos, and 1, 2, 5, 10, 20, and 50 pesos, and in bills of 1, 10, 20, 50, 100, 200, and 500 pesos. At the time of this writing, the exchange rate for Mexican currency was 7.5 pesos to $1 US. Note, however, that because of the continuing volatility in the value of the peso, this could change significantly by the time of your trip.

Be forewarned: After a period of extreme devaluation of the peso, the so-called *Nuevos Pesos* ("new" pesos) were issued a few years ago by the Mexican government. Although bills initially had the words "Nuevos Pesos" printed on them, the bills now being issued no longer carry this designation, and are referred to simply as "pesos"; both versions of the new pesos are legal tender. Note, however, that the old pesos no longer have any value, and a small amount of this worthless currency still may be (illegally) in circulation. To avoid the possiblity of being cheated, it's a good idea to familiarize yourself with the new currency before your trip.

Exchange rates are listed in international newspapers such as the *International Herald Tribune.* Foreign currency information and related services are provided by banks and companies such as *Thomas Cook Foreign Exchange* (for the nearest location, call 800-621-0666 or 312-236-0042; fax: 312-807-4879); *Harold Reuter and Company* (200 Park Ave., Suite 332E, New York, NY 10166; phone: 800-258-0456 or 212-661-0826; fax: 212-557-6622); and *Ruesch International* (for the nearest location, call 800-424-2923 or 202-408-1200; fax: 202-408-1211). In Mexico, you will find the official rate of exchange posted in banks, airports, money exchange houses, hotels, and some shops. Since you will get more pesos for your US dollar at banks and money exchanges, don't change more than $10 for foreign currency at other commercial establishments. Ask how much commission you're being charged and the exchange rate, and don't buy money on the black market (it may be counterfeit). Estimate your needs carefully; if you overbuy, you lose twice—buying and selling back.

CREDIT CARDS AND TRAVELER'S CHECKS

Most major credit cards enjoy wide domestic and international acceptance; however, not every hotel, restaurant, or shop in Mexico accepts all (or in some cases any) credit cards. When making purchases with a credit card, note that the rate of exchange depends on when the charge is processed. Most credit card companies charge a 1% fee for converting foreign currency charges. It's also wise to carry traveler's checks while on the road, since they are widely accepted and replaceable if stolen or lost. You can buy traveler's checks at banks and some are available by mail or phone. Keep a separate list of all traveler's checks (noting those that you have cashed) and the names and numbers of your credit cards. Both traveler's check and credit card companies have international numbers to call for information or in the event of loss or theft.

CASH MACHINES

Automated teller machines (ATMs) are increasingly common worldwide, and most banks participate in international ATM networks such as *MasterCard/Cirrus* (phone: 800-4-CIRRUS) and *Visa/PLUS* (phone: 800-THE-PLUS). Using a card—with an assigned Personal Identification Number (PIN)—from an affiliated bank or credit card company, you can withdraw cash from any machine in the same network. The *MasterCard/Cirrus ATM Location Directory* and the *Visa/PLUS International ATM Directory 1997* provide locations of network ATMs worldwide and are available from banks and other financial institutions.

SENDING MONEY ABROAD

Should the need arise, you can have money sent to you in Mexico via the services provided by *American Express MoneyGram* (phone: 800-926-9400 for information; 800-866-8800 for money transfers) or *Western Union Financial Services* (phone: 800-325-6000 or 800-325-4176). In some cases, you also can have money wired to you via a direct bank-to-bank transfer from the US. Arrangements can be made with the participating institutions. If you are down to your last cent and have no other way to obtain cash, the nearest *US Consulate* (see *Consular Services,* below, for addresses) will let you call home to set matters in motion.

Accommodations

For specific information on hotels, resorts, and other selected accommodations, see *Checking In* in THE CITIES, sections throughout DIVERSIONS, and *Best en Route* in DIRECTIONS.

RENTAL OPTIONS

An attractive accommodations alternative for the visitor content to stay in one spot is a vacation rental. For a family or group, the per-person cost can be reasonable. To have your pick of the properties available, make inquiries at least six months in advance.

The *Worldwide Home Rental Guide* (3501 Indian School Rd. NE, Suite 303, Albuquerque, NM 87106; phone: 800-299-9886 or 505-255-4271; fax: 505-255-0814) lists rental properties and managing agencies. In addition, *Rental Directories International* (*RDI;* 2044 Rittenhouse Sq., Philadelphia, PA 19103; phone: 215-985-4001; fax: 215-985-0323) publishes a directory called *The Islands, Mexico & Hawaii,* which lists vacation properties that can be rented directly from the owners.

Rental Property Agents

At Home Abroad (405 E. 56th St., Suite 6H, New York, NY 10022-2466; phone: 212-421-9165; fax: 212-752-1591).

Condo World (4230 Orchard Lake Rd., Suite 3, Orchard Lake, MI 48323; phone: 800-521-2980 or 810-683-0202; fax: 810-683-5076).

Creative Leisure (951 Transport Way, Petaluma, CA 94954; phone: 800-4-CONDOS or 707-778-1800; fax: 707-763-7786).

Europa-Let (92 N. Main St., Ashland, OR 97520; phone: 800-462-4486 or 503-482-5806; fax: 503-482-0660).

Hideaways International (767 Islington St., Portsmouth, NH 03801; phone: 800-843-4433 or 603-430-4433; fax: 603-430-4444).

La Cure Villas (275 Spadina Rd., Toronto, Ontario M5R 2V3, Canada; phone: 800-387-2726 or 416-968-2374; fax: 416-968-9435).

Property Rentals International (1 Park W. Circle, Suite 108, Midlothian, VA 23113; phone: 800-220-3332 or 804-378-6054; fax: 804-379-2073).

Rent a Home International (7200 34th Ave. NW, Seattle, WA 98117; phone: 206-789-9377; fax: 206-789-9379).

Rent a Vacation Everywhere (*RAVE;* 135 Meigs St., Rochester, NY 14607; phone: 716-256-0760; fax: 716-256-2676).

VHR Worldwide (235 Kensington Ave., Norwood, NJ 07648; phone: 201-767-9393 in New Jersey; 800-633-3284 elsewhere in the US; fax: 201-767-5510).

Villa Leisure (PO Box 30188, Palm Beach, FL 33420; phone: 800-526-4244 or 407-624-9000; fax: 407-622-9097).

Villas and Apartments Abroad (420 Madison Ave., Suite 1003, New York, NY 10017; phone: 212-759-1025 in New York State; 800-433-3020 elsewhere in the US; fax: 212-755-8316).

Villas International (605 Market St., Suite 510, San Francisco, CA 94105; phone: 800-221-2260 or 415-281-0910; fax: 415-281-0919).

HOME EXCHANGES

For comfortable, reasonable living quarters with amenities that no hotel could possibly offer, consider trading homes with someone abroad. The following companies provide information on exchanges:

HomeLink USA (PO Box 650, Key West, FL 33041; phone: 800-638-3841; phone/fax: 305-294-1448).

Intervac US/International Home Exchange (PO Box 590504, San Francisco, CA 94159; phone: 800-756-HOME or 415-435-3497; fax: 415-435-7440).

Loan-A-Home (7 McGregor Rd., Woods Hole, MA 02543; phone: 508-548-4032).

Worldwide Home Exchange Club (main office: 50 Hans Crescent, London SW1X 0NA, England; phone: 44-171-823-9937; US office: 806 Brantford Ave., Silver Spring, MD 20904; phone: 301-680-8950).

HOME STAYS

United States Servas (11 John St., Room 407, New York, NY 10038; phone: 212-267-0252; fax: 212-267-0292) maintains a list of hosts worldwide willing to accommodate visitors free of charge. The aim of this nonprofit program is to promote international understanding and peace, and *Servas* emphasizes that member travelers should be interested mainly in their hosts, not in sightseeing, during their stays.

ACCOMMODATIONS DISCOUNTS

The following organizations offer discounts of up to 50% on accommodations throughout Mexico:

Carte Royale (1 Premier Plaza, 5605 Glenridge Dr., Suite 300, Atlanta, GA 30342; phone: 800-218-5862 or 404-250-9940; fax: 404-252-9162).

Encore Marketing International (4501 Forbes Blvd., Lanham, MD 20706; phone: 800-638-0930 or 301-459-8020; fax: 301-731-0525).

Entertainment Publications (2125 Butterfield Rd., Troy, MI 48084; phone: 800-445-4137 or 810-637-8400; fax: 810-637-2035).

Great American Traveler (Access Development Corp., PO Box 27563, Salt Lake City, UT 84127-0563; phone: 800-548-2812 or 801-262-2233; fax: 801-262-2311).

Hotel Express International (International Concepts Group, 14681 Midway Rd., Dallas, TX 75244; phone: 800-866-2015, 800-770-2015, or 214-497-9792; fax: 214-770-3575).

Impulse (6143 S. Willow Dr., Suite 410, Englewood, CO 80111; phone: 303-741-2457; fax: 303-721-6011).

International Travel Card (6001 N. Clark St., Chicago, IL 60660; phone: 800-342-0558 or 312-465-8891; fax: 312-764-8066).

Privilege Card (3391 Peachtree Rd. NE, Suite 110, Atlanta, GA 30326; phone: 800-236-9732 or 404-262-0255; fax: 404-262-0235).

Quest International (402 E. Yakima Ave., Suite 1200, Yakima, WA 98901; phone: 800-742-3543 or 509-248-7512; fax: 509-457-8399).

BE FOREWARNED

Visitors should be aware that the word *motel* may have a very different connotation in Mexico than in the US. While a Mexican *hotel* provides accommodations similar to the US version, a *motel* often serves another purpose—and rents rooms by the hour. These *auto-hoteles,* as they are also advertised, have curtained garages to insure the privacy of any "guests" who might not like their license plates seen. Many an unsuspecting tourist has pulled into a *motel* hoping to enjoy a relaxing evening, only to discover that there is no furniture (other than one very conspicuous bed), no closet, and no phone in the room.

Time Zones

With a few exceptions, most of Mexico operates on central standard time. Mountain standard time is observed in the western coastal states of Sonora, Sinaloa, and Nayarit, as well as in Baja California Sur, across the Gulf of California. Baja California Norte operates on pacific standard time and is the only Mexican state that observes daylight saving time. Thus, from the first Sunday in April to the last Sunday in October, the time in Baja California Norte (and in most of the US) becomes one hour later in relation to the rest of Mexico.

Business and Shopping Hours

Mexican businesses often are open weekdays from 9 or 10 AM to 5 or 6 PM, with a one-hour break for lunch, although some take a longer break (about two hours) in the afternoon and stay open until around 7 PM. Shops usually are open weekdays and Saturdays from around 9 or 10 AM to 8 or 9 PM, with a one- or two-hour break in the afternoon. In major cities and tourist areas, shops may stay open as late as 10PM and also may be open on Sundays. Department stores and malls often are open seven days a week from 9 or 10 AM to 8 or 9 PM, but may stay open as late as 10 or 11 PM.

Banking hours in Mexico generally are weekdays from 9 AM to 3 PM, although some banks are open from 9 AM to 1 or 1:30 PM, and may reopen from 4 to 6 PM. Banks in major cities and resort areas sometimes offer longer hours—usually from 8:30 or 9 AM to 5 or 6 PM. Money exchange houses (called *casas de cambio* or just *cambios*) often are open seven days a week from 8 or 9 AM to 2:30 PM. In larger cities and tourist areas, *cambios* may open at 7 or 8 AM and stay open from until 8 or 9 PM (or as late as midnight in major airports), sometimes without a break.

Holidays

Below is a list of the public holidays in Mexico and the dates they will be observed this year. Note that the dates of some holidays vary from year to year; others occur on the same day every year.

> *New Year's Day* (January 1)
> *Constitution Day* (February 5)
> *Flag Day* (February 24)
> *Birthday of Benito Juárez* (March 21)
> *Holy Thursday* (March 27)
> *Good Friday* (March 28)
> *Labor Day* (May 1)
> *Cinco de Mayo* (May 5)
> *Independence Day* (September 16)
> *Columbus Day* (October 12)
> *President's State of the Nation Address* (November 1)
> *All Souls' Day;* known in Mexico as the *Day of the Dead* (November 2)
> *Anniversary of the Mexican Revolution of 1910* (November 20)
> *Feast of Our Lady of Guadalupe* (December 12)
> *Christmas* (December 25)
> *Banks closed for annual balance* (December 31)

Mail

Almost every town in Mexico has a post office. Most branches are open weekdays from 9 AM to 5 PM (although main post offices in major cities and tourist areas may be open as late as 7 PM) and Saturdays from 9 AM to 1 or 2 PM. Stamps also are sold at airports and major bus and train stations, as well as at some hotels and stores. There are public mailboxes *(buzones)* on street corners and mail drops in large hotels and office buildings. Note, however, that it is much safer to mail letters and packages directly from post offices.

When sending mail between between Mexico and the US, always use airmail and allow at least 10 days for delivery. Note that the inclusion of postal codes in Mexican addresses is *essential;* delivery of your letter or parcel may depend on it. In addition, all packages mailed to or from Mexico should be registered. If your correspondence is especially important, you may want to send it via an international courier service, such as *FedEx* (phone: 800-GO-FEDEX in the US; 91-800-90011, toll-free, in Mexico) or *DHL Worldwide Express* (phone: 800-225-5345 in the US; contact a local *DHL* office in Mexico).

You can have mail sent to you care of your hotel (marked "Guest Mail, Hold for Arrival") or main post offices in Mexico (the address should include *"a/c Lista de Correos, Poste Restante, Principal Oficina,"* the Mexican equivalent of US "General Delivery"). Many *American Express* offices in Mexico also will hold mail for customers ("c/o Client Letter Service"). Information on this service is provided in the pamphlet *Worldwide Travelers' Companion,* available from any *American Express* travel office. Note that *US Embassies* and *Consulates* abroad will hold mail for US citizens *only* in emergency situations.

Telephone

In general, direct dialing is possible between Mexico and the US, although when calling from small towns or remote areas in Mexico, you still may need the assistance of an international operator. Public telephones are widely available. There also are telephone calling centers from which long-distance calls can be made. The number of digits in phone numbers varies throughout Mexico.

The procedures for making calls to, from, and within Mexico are as follows:

To call Mexico from the US: Dial 011 (the international access code) + 52 (the country code for Mexico) + the city code + the local number.

To call the US from Mexico: Dial 95 (the international access code) + 1 (the US country code) + the area code + the local number.

To make a call from one Mexican city code coverage area to another: Dial 91 + the city code + the local number. Note: the 91 prefix also must be dialed when calling a toll-free number in Mexico.

To make a call within the same Mexican city code coverage area: Dial the local number.

Although some Mexican pay phones—particularly in rural areas—still take coins, most public telephones in metropolitan and tourist areas accept only special *Ladatel* phone debit cards. (These telephones also may accept long-distance calling cards—see below.) *Ladatel* cards are sold at the offices of *Teléfonos de México* (*TELMEX;* 190 Parque Villa, Colonia Cuauhtémoc, México 06599, México; phone: 52-5-222-1212), as well as at post offices and some hotels, restaurants, stores, and newsstands.

You can use a telephone company calling card number on any phone, and some pay phones take major credit cards (*American Express, MasterCard, Visa,* and so on). Also available are combined telephone calling/bank credit cards, such as the *AT&T Universal Card* (PO Box 44167, Jacksonville, FL 32231-4167; phone: 800-423-4343). Similarly, *Sprint* (8140 Ward Pkwy., Kansas City, MO 64114; phone: 800-226-8472) offers *VisaPhone,* through which you can add phone card privileges to your existing *Visa* card.

Companies offering long-distance phone cards (without additional credit card privileges) include the following:

AT&T (295 N. Maple Ave., Basking Ridge, NJ 07920; phone: 800-CALL-ATT).

Executive Telecard International (4260 E. Evans Ave., Denver, CO 80222; phone: 800-950-3800).

LDDS/Worldcom (1 International Center, 100 NE Loop 410, Suite 400, San Antonio, TX 78216; phone: 800-275-0200).

MCI (323 Third St. SE, Cedar Rapids, IA 52401; phone: 800-444-4444; and 12790 Merit Dr., Dallas, TX 75251; phone: 800-444-3333).

Sprint (address above; phone: 800-PIN-DROP).

Note that you may not be able to use some of the cards listed above (or service may be limited) when making calls between Mexico and the US. Contact the card issuer for information before your trip.

Hotels routinely add surcharges to the cost of phone calls made from their rooms. Long-distance telephone services that may help you avoid this added expense are provided by a number of companies, including *AT&T* (International Information Service, 635 Grant St., Pittsburgh, PA 15219; phone: 800-874-4000), and *Executive Telecard International, LDDS/Worldcom, MCI,* and *Sprint* (addresses above). Note that some of these services can be accessed only with the companies' long-distance calling cards (see above). In addition, even when you use such long-distance services, some hotels still may charge a fee for line usage.

AT&T's Language Line Service (phone: 800-752-6096) provides interpretive services 24 hours a day for telephone communications in Spanish (and numerous other languages). Useful telephone directories for travelers include the *AT&T Toll-Free 800 National Shopper's Guide* and the *AT&T Toll-Free 800 National Business Guide* (phone: 800-426-8686 for orders), the *Toll-Free Travel & Vacation Information Directory* (Pilot Books, 103 Cooper St., Babylon, NY 11702; phone: 516-422-2225; fax: 516-422-2227), and *The Phone Booklet* (Scott American Corporation, PO Box 88, W. Redding, CT 06896; no phone).

Important Phone Numbers

Emergency assistance: The nationwide emergency assistance number is 06. For assistance in English, dial 91-800-90392 (toll-free), 525-250-0123, or 525-250-0151.

International operator (English-speaking): Dial 09.

Local information: Dial 04.

Nationwide information: Dial 07.

Long-distance operator (for calls within Mexico): Dial 02.

Electricity

Like the US, Mexico uses 110-volt, 60-cycle, alternating current (AC). Appliances running on standard current can be used without converters.

If traveling to more remote areas, bring along a plug adapter set for use with the few older outlets that may differ from those in the US.

Staying Healthy

For up-to-date information on current health conditions, call the Centers for Disease Control's *International Travelers' Hotline:* **404-332-4559.** The Centers for Disease Control also publishes *Health Information for International Travel, 1997,* which provides worldwide information on health risks and vaccination requirements. It can be ordered from the *Superintendent of Documents* (*US Government Printing Office,* PO Box 371954, Pittsburgh, PA 15250-7954; phone: 202-512-1800; fax: 202-512-2250).

The *US Public Health Service* recommends diphtheria, tetanus, and hepatitis B shots for anyone planning a trip to Mexico. In addition, for adults who have received only the standard childhood vaccination against polio, a second innoculation is advised. Influenza shots are advised, particularly for senior citizens. Children also should be innoculated against polio, measles, mumps, and rubella.

Especially in urban areas, Dengue fever can be carried by mosquitoes, although the risk to travelers usually is low. In rural and jungle areas, Chagas' disease and malaria also can be transmitted through insect bites. The best protection is to wear proper clothing (covering as much of the skin surface as possible); antimalarial tablets and a strong insect repellent also are advisable. Bites from snakes, spiders, and scorpions can be serious and must be treated immediately.

One health problem commonly associated with travel to Mexico is an unpleasant—but usually short-lived—intestinal disorder sometimes called "Montezuma's Revenge." The most effective way to avoid this illness (as well as much more serious conditions, such as cholera, infectious hepatitis, and typhoid fever) is *never* to drink the tap water—do not even brush your teeth with it. Stick to bottled water (if unavailable, boil the water or use water purification tablets) or other bottled or canned beverages. Stay away from fresh fruit juices and mixed alcoholic drinks (which may contain tap water) and any drinks served with ice. Similarly, do not eat salads, uncooked vegetables, or unpeeled fruit. Milk sold in stores is pasteurized and safe to drink, but beware of spoilage due to improper refrigeration. Avoid unpasteurized or uncooked dairy products and raw (or undercooked) seafood, and *never* buy food from street vendors.

When swimming in the ocean, be careful of the undertow (the water running back down the beach after a wave has washed ashore), which can knock you off your feet, and riptides (currents running against the tide), which can pull you out to sea. Sharks are found in coastal waters, but rarely come close to shore. Jellyfish—including Portuguese men-of-war—are fairly common, as are eels and sea urchins. And note that coral reefs, while beautiful, can be razor sharp.

Another common problem for travelers to Mexico is sunburn. Note that the risk of overexposure is not limited solely to coastal areas; the sun's intensity in inland areas, particularly at higher altitudes, also can be quite strong. When spending any length of time outdoors, take appropriate precautions—including the use of a sunscreen with a Sun Protection Factor (SPF) of 15 or higher.

In parts of Mexico at elevations above 5,000 feet (Mexico City, for example, is 7,800 feet above sea level), visitors unaccustomed to the thinner air may experience altitude sickness. If possible, travel to higher altitudes gradually. Otherwise, for the first few days, try to keep physical exertion and stress to a minimum and limit your consumption of alcohol, which can aggravate this condition. Those planning an extended stay in Mexico City also should note that air pollution can be a serious problem and may adversely affect individuals with pulmonary and respiratory conditions.

Major cities and tourist areas in Mexico are well supplied with doctors, hospitals, clinics, and pharmacies—some open 24 hours—which carry most of the drugs available in the US. In smaller towns and rural areas, pharmacies usually are not open around the clock; if you need a prescription filled during off-hours, contact a local hospital or clinic for information about on-call pharmacists, or go directly to a hospital emergency room.

Should you need non-emergency medical attention, ask at your hotel for the house physician or for help in reaching a doctor. Lists of English-speaking doctors and dentists also may be available from the *US Embassy* and *Consulates.* **In an emergency: Go to the emergency room of the nearest hospital, dial one of the emergency numbers provided in *Telephone*, above, or call an operator for assistance. If possible, someone who can translate into Spanish should make the call.**

When traveling abroad, be extremely cautious about injections, because reusable syringes and needles may be used and sterilization procedures sometimes are inadequate. If you have a condition that requires periodic injections, bring a supply of syringes with you or buy disposable syringes at a local pharmacy. To avoid potential problems with customs authorities when entering or leaving Mexico, bring a doctor's note stating that the syringes are required for treatment of a medical condition.

Additional Resources

Global Emergency Services (2720 Enterprise Pkwy., Suite 106, Richmond, VA 23294; phone: 804-527-1094; fax: 804-527-1941).

Health Care Abroad/Global (c/o *Wallach and Co.,* PO Box 480, Middleburg, VA 22117-0480; phone: 800-237-6615 or 540-687-3166; fax: 540-687-3172).

International Association for Medical Assistance to Travelers (*IAMAT;* 417 Center St., Lewiston, NY 14092; phone: 716-754-4883; and 40 Regal Rd., Guelph, Ontario N1K 1B5, Canada; phone: 519-836-0102; fax: 519-836-3412).

International Health Care Service (440 E. 69th St., New York, NY 10021; phone: 212-746-1601).

International SOS Assistance (8 Neshaminy Interplex, Suite 207, Trevose, PA 19053-6956; phone: 800-523-8930 or 215-244-1500; fax: 215-244-2227).

Medic Alert Foundation (2323 Colorado Ave., Turlock, CA 95382; phone: 800-ID-ALERT or 209-668-3333; fax: 209-669-2495).

Travel Care International (PO Box 846, Eagle River, WI 54521; phone: 800-5-AIR-MED or 715-479-8881; fax: 715-479-8178).

Traveler's Emergency Network (*TEN;* PO Box 238, Hyattsville, MD 20797-8108; phone: 800-ASK-4-TEN; fax: 301-559-5167).

TravMed (PO Box 5375, Timonium, MD 21094-5375; phone: 800-732-5309 or 410-453-6380; fax: 410-453-6371).

U S Assist (2 Democracy Center, Suite 800, 6903 Rockledge Dr., Bethesda, MD 20817; phone: 800-895-8472 or 301-214-8200; fax: 301-214-8205).

Consular Services

The American Citizen Services section of the *US Embassy* or *Consulate* is a vital source of assistance and advice for US travelers abroad. If you are injured or become seriously ill, the embassy or consulate can direct you to sources of medical attention and notify your relatives. If you become involved in a dispute that could lead to legal action, the embassy or consulate can provide a list of English-speaking attorneys. In cases of natural disasters or civil unrest, consular offices handle the evacuation of US citizens if necessary.

The *US State Department* operates an automated 24-hour *Citizens' Emergency Center* travel advisory hotline (phone: 202-647-5225). You also can reach a duty officer at this number from 5:15 PM to 10 PM, eastern standard time, seven days a week; at other times, call 202-647-5226. For faxed travel advisories and other consular information, call 202-647-3000 using the handset on your fax machine; instructions will be provided. Using a personal computer with a modem, you can access the consular affairs electronic bulletin board (phone: 202-647-9225).

For further information, also see the *US State Department*'s brochure *Tips for Travelers to Mexico.* It can be ordered from the Superintendent of Documents (*US Government Printing Office,* PO Box 371954, Pittsburgh, PA 15250-7954; phone: 202-512-1800; fax: 202-512-2250).

The U.S. Embassy and Consulates in Mexico

Embassy

Mexico City: 305 Paseo de la Reforma, Cuauhtémoc, México, DF 06500, México (phone: 52-5-211-0042; 24-hour emergency number: 52-5-560-3317; fax: 52-5-511-9980 or 52-5-208-3373).

Consulates

Ciudad Juárez: *Consulate General,* 924 Av. López Mateos Nte., Ciudad Juárez, Chihuahua 32000, México (phone: 52-16-113164; fax: 52-16-169056).

Guadalajara: *Consulate General,* 175 Progreso, Guadalajara, Jalisco 44100, México (phone: 52-3-825-2700 or 52-3-825-2998; fax: 52-3-826-6549).

Hermosillo: *Consulate,* 141 Monterrey, Hermosillo, Sonora 83260, México (phone: 52-621-72375; fax: 52-621-72578).

Matamoros: *Consulate,* 2002 Av. Primera, Colonia Jardín, Matamoros, Tamaulipas 87330, México (phone: 52-88-124402; fax: 52-88-122171); *Consulate,* 3330 Av. Allende, Colonia Jardín, Nuevo Laredo, Tamaulipas 88260, México (phone: 52-871-40512; fax: 52-871-147984).

Mérida: *Consulate,* 453 Paseo de Montejo, Mérida, Yucatán 97000-12, México (phone: 52-99-255409 or 52-99-255011; fax: 52-99-256219).

Monterrey: *Consulate General,* 411 Av. Constitución Pte., Monterrey, Nuevo León 64000, México (phone: 52-83-452120; fax: 52-83-3452120, ext. 461).

Tijuana: *Consulate General,* 96 Calle Tapachula, Colonia Hipodrómo, Tijuana, Baja California Norte 22420, México (phone: 52-66-817400; fax: 52-66-818016).

Entry Requirements and Customs Regulations

ENTERING MEXICO

A US citizen needs a tourist card and an official photo ID to enter Mexico. Tourist cards can be obtained in the US at *Mexican Ministry of Tourism* offices and from *Mexican Consulates,* as well as from authorized airline ticket offices and travel agencies. Tourist cards also are issued at Mexican government border offices. US citizens must provide proof of US citizenship (passport, certified copy of a birth certificate, or voter registration card) and an official photo ID—a passport fulfills both these requirements. Naturalized citizens must present their naturalization papers (originals or certified copies); affidavits of citizenship are *not* accepted.

In addition, a minor (under 18) traveling alone must have written permission from both parents or legal guardians. If a minor is traveling with one parent or guardian, a letter signed by the other (or proof of sole custody) is required. If the whereabouts of the other parent are unknown, a judge's letter may be required; and if one parent is deceased, officials may ask to see a copy of the death certificate.

When you arrive in Mexico, you must sign the tourist card in the presence of a Mexican immigration official. You also may be required to present proof of your US citizenship again, so bring the necessary documentation with you. (For information about documents needed to drive a car across the border into Mexico, see *Traveling by Car.*) A tourist card allows you to stay in Mexico for up to six months.

A visa is required for study, residency, work, or stays of more than six months. Proof of means of independent financial support is pertinent to the acceptance of any long-term–stay application. For further information, US citizens should contact the *Mexican Embassy* or the nearest *Mexican Consulate* well in advance of their trip.

You are allowed to enter Mexico with the following items duty-free: three liters of liquor, 400 cigarettes (two cartons), 50 cigars, a camera, a camcorder, and 12 rolls of film and/or videocassettes. Note that only those over 18 (the legal drinking age in Mexico) are permitted to bring liquor into the country.

Travelers arriving by air or sea also are allowed additional gift items— such as electronics, appliances, and toys—not exceeding $300 in value; those arriving by land are allowed $50 in such items. (No duty is assessed on clothes and other items for your own use that you have packed in your luggage.) To avoid paying duty unnecessarily (either when entering Mexico or returning to the US), it is advisable to register expensive items—such as computer equipment—with *US Customs* before your trip and with Mexican customs authorities when entering Mexico.

Note: In addition to the originals, it's a good idea to bring along a set of photocopies of documents you may need to present to Mexican immigration officers. Also leave extra copies at home.

DUTY-FREE SHOPS

Located in international airports, duty-free shops provide bargains on the purchase of goods imported to Mexico from other countries. But beware: Not all foreign goods are automatically less expensive. You *can* get a good deal on some items, but know what they cost elsewhere. Also note that although these goods are free of the duty that *Mexican Customs* normally would assess, they will be subject to US import duty upon your return to the US (see below).

VALUE ADDED TAX (VAT)

Called *Impuesto al Valor Agregado (IVA)* in Mexico, this sales tax (15% at press time) is built into the price of most goods and services, except such basics as food, toiletries, and some medicines. Unlike many other countries that assess value added taxes, however, there currently is no provision for foreigners to obtain a refund of the tax. For additional information, contact the *Secretaría de Hacienda y Crédito Público* (37 Paseo de la Reforma, Módulo 5, Second Floor, México, DF 06066, México; phone: 52-5-227-0297; fax: 52-5-228-3902).

RETURNING TO THE US

You must declare to the *US Customs* official at the point of entry everything you have acquired in Mexico. The standard duty-free allowance for US citizens is $400. If your trip is shorter than 48 continuous hours, or if you have been outside the US within 30 days of your current trip, the duty-free allowance is reduced to $25. Families traveling together may make a joint customs declaration.

A flat 10% duty is assessed on the next $1,000 worth of merchandise; additional items are taxed at a variety of rates (see *Tariff Schedules of the United States* in a library or any *US Customs Service* office). Some articles are duty-free only up to certain limits. The $400 allowance includes 200 cigarettes (one carton), 100 cigars, one liter of liquor, and one liter of perfume. The $25 allowance includes 50 cigarettes, 10 cigars, four ounces of liquor, and four ounces of perfume. In addition, the Generalized System of Preferences (GSP), which allows US citizens to bring certain goods into the US duty-free, applies to Mexico. Each day you are abroad, you also can ship up to $200 in gifts (excluding alcohol, perfume, and tobacco) to the US duty-free.

Antiques and paintings or drawings that are at least 100 years old also are duty-free. However, you must obtain a permit from the *Instituto Nacional de Antropología e Historia* (Departamento Juridico, 45 Córdoba, Colonia Roma, México, DF 06700, México; phone: 52-5-533-4976 or 52-5-511-0844; fax: 52-5-533-2015) to take archaeological finds or other artifacts out of Mexico.

FORBIDDEN IMPORTS

US regulations prohibit the import of some goods sold abroad, such as fresh fruits and vegetables, most meat products (except certain canned goods), and dairy products (except fully cured cheeses). Also prohibited are articles made of materials from plants or animals on the endangered species list.

FOR ADDITIONAL INFORMATION Consult one of the following publications, available from the *US Customs Service* (PO Box 7407, Washington, DC 20044; phone: 202-927-6724): *Currency Reporting; Importing a Car; International Mail Imports; Know Before You Go; Pets, Wildlife, US Customs;* and *Pocket Hints.* Also see *Travelers' Tips on Bringing Food, Plant, and Animal Products into the United States,* available from the *United States Department of Agriculture, Animal and Plant Health Inspection Service (USDA-APHIS-LPA;* 4700 River Rd., Unit 51, Riverdale, MD 20737; phone: 301-734-7280; fax: 301-734-5221). With a touch-tone phone, you can access recorded information on a variety of customs-related topics by calling the general *US Customs Service* phone number above.

For Further Information

Mexican Government Tourism Offices in the US are the best sources of travel information. Offices generally are open on weekdays, during normal business hours. There also is a 24-hour information hotline in Mexico City (phone: 800-482-9832 in the US; 250-0123 or 250-0151 in Mexico City; 91-800-90392, toll-free, elsewhere in Mexico). For information on entry requirements and customs regulations, contact the *Mexican Embassy* or a *Mexican Consulate.*

Mexican Ministry of Tourism Offices

California: 10100 Santa Monica Blvd., Suite 224, Los Angeles, CA 90067 (phone: 310-203-8191; fax: 310-203-8316).

Illinois: 70 E. Lake St., Suite 1413, Chicago, IL 60601 (phone: 312-606-9252; fax: 312-606-9012).

New York State: 405 Park Ave., Suite 1401, New York, NY 10022 (phone: 212-838-2949; fax: 212-753-2874).

Texas: 5075 Westheimer, Suite 975-W, Houston, TX 77056 (phone: 713-629-1611; fax: 713-629-1837).

Washington, DC: 1911 Pennsylvania Ave. NW, Washington, DC 20006 (phone: 202-728-1750; fax: 202-728-1758).

The Mexican Embassy and Consulates in the US

Embassy

Washington, DC: 1911 Pennsylvania Ave. NW, Washington, DC 20006 (phone: 202-728-1600; fax: 202-797-8458); *Consular Section,* 2827 16th St. NW, Washington, DC 20009 (phone: 202-736-1000; fax: 202-797-8458).

Consulates

Arizona: *Consulate,* 486 N. Grand Ave., Nogales, AZ 85621 (phone: 520-287-2521; fax: 520-287-3175); *Consulate,* 1990 W. Camelback Rd., Suite 110, Phoenix, AZ 85015 (phone: 520-242-7398/9; fax: 520-242-2957); *Consulate,* 553 S. Stone Ave., Tucson, AZ 85701 (phone: 520-882-5595; fax: 520-882-8959).

California: *Consulate,* 331 W. Second St., Calexico, CA 92231 (phone: 619-357-3863 or 619-357-4132; fax: 619-357-6284); *Consulate,* 830 Van Ness Ave., Fresno, CA 93721 (phone: 209-233-3065; fax: 209-233-6156); *Consulate General,* 2401 W. Sixth St., Los Angeles, CA 90057 (phone: 213-351-6800 or 213-351-6825; fax: 213-389-6864); *Consulate,* Transportation Center, 201 E. Fourth St., Room 209, Oxnard, CA 93030 (phone: 805-483-4684; fax: 805-385-3527); *Consulate,* 9812 Old Winery Pl., Suite 10, Sacramento, CA 95827 (phone: 916-363-3885; fax: 916-363-0625); *Consulate,* 588 W. Sixth St., San Bernardino, CA 92401 (phone: 909-888-3155; fax: 909-889-8285); *Consulate General,* 1549 India St., San Diego, CA 92101 (phone:

619-231-8414; fax: 619-231-4802); *Consulate General,* 870 Market St., Suite 528, San Francisco, CA 94102 (phone: 415-392-5554; fax: 415-392-3233); *Consulate,* 380 N. First St., Suite 102, San Jose, CA 95112 (phone: 408-294-3414/5; fax: 408-294-4506); *Consulate,* 828 N. Broadway, Santa Ana, CA 92701 (phone: 714-835-3069; fax: 714-835-3472).

Colorado: *Consulate General,* 707 Washington St., Suite A, Denver, CO 80203 (phone: 303-830-0601 or 303-830-0607; fax: 303-830-2655).

Florida: *Consulate General,* 1200 NW 78th Ave., Suite 200, Miami, FL 33126 (phone: 305-716-4977; fax: 305-593-2758); *Consulate General,* 823 Colonial Dr., Orlando, FL 32830 (phone: 407-894-0514; fax: 407-895-6140); *Consulate,* 1717 W. Cass St., Tampa, FL 33606 (phone: 813-254-5960; fax: 813-251-2032).

Georgia: *Consulate General,* 3220 Peachtree Rd. NE, Atlanta, GA 30305 (phone: 404-266-2233; fax: 404-266-2302).

Illinois: *Consulate General,* 300 N. Michigan Ave., Second Floor, Chicago, IL 60601 (phone: 312-855-1380; fax: 312-855-9257).

Louisiana: *Consulate General,* World Trade Center Building, 2 Canal St., Suite 840, New Orleans, LA 70130 (phone: 504-522-3596; fax: 504-525-2332).

Massachusetts: *Consulate,* 20 Park Plaza, Suite 506, Boston, MA 02116 (phone: 617-426-8782; fax: 617-695-1957).

Michigan: *Consulate,* 600 Renaissance Center, Suite 1510, Detroit, MI 48243 (phone: 313-567-7713; fax: 313-567-7543).

Missouri: *Consulate,* 1015 Locust St., Suite 922, St. Louis, MO 63101 (phone: 314-436-3233; fax: 314-436-2695).

New Mexico: *Consulate,* Western Bank Building, 401 Fifth St. NW, Albuquerque, NM 87102 (phone: 505-247-2139; fax: 505-842-9490).

New York State: *Honorary Consul of Mexico,* 1875 Harlem Rd., Buffalo, NY 14212 (phone: 716-895-9800; fax: 716-895-9947); *Consulate General,* 8 E. 41st St., New York, NY 10017 (phone: 212-689-0456/7/8/9; fax: 212-545-8197).

Pennsylvania: *Consulate,* Bourse Building, 111 S. Independent Mall E., Suite 1010, Philadelphia, PA 19106 (phone: 215-922-4262; fax: 215-923-7281).

Texas: *Consulate,* 200 E. Sixth St., Suite 200, Austin, TX 78701 (phone: 512-478-2866; fax: 512-478-8008); *Consulate,* 724 E. Elizabeth St., Brownsville, TX 78520 (phone: 210-542-4431; fax: 210-542-7267); *Consulate,* N. Tower, 800 N. Shoreline Blvd., Suite 410, Corpus Christi, TX 78401 (phone: 512-882-3375; fax: 512-882-9324); *Consulate General,* 8855 N. Stemmons Freeway, Dallas, TX 75247 (phone: 214-630-7341/2/3; fax: 214-630-3511); *Consulate,* 300 E. Losoya St., Del Rio, TX 78840 (phone: 210-774-5031; fax: 210-774-6497); *Consulate,* 140 Adams St., Eagle Pass, TX 78852 (phone: 210-773-9255/6; fax: 210-773-9397); *Consulate General,* 910 E. San Antonio Ave., El Paso,

TX 79101 (phone: 915-533-3644/5; fax: 915-532-7163); *Consulate General,* 3015 Richmond St., Suite 100, Houston, TX 77098 (phone: 713-524-2300; fax: 713-523-6244); *Consulate,* 1612 Farragut St., PO Box 659, Laredo, TX 78042 (phone: 210-723-6360 or 210-723-6369; fax: 210-723-1741); *Consulate,* 600 S. Broadway, McAllen, TX 78501 (phone: 210-686-0243/4; fax: 210-686-4901); *Consulate,* 511 W. Ohio St., Suite 121, Midland, TX 79701 (phone: 915-687-2334; fax: 915-687-3952); *Consulate General,* 127 Navarro St., San Antonio, TX 78205 (phone: 210-227-9145/6/7; fax: 210-227-1817).

Utah: *Consulate,* 458 E. 200 S., Salt Lake City, UT 84111 (phone: 801-521-8502/3; fax: 801-521-0534).

Virginia: *Consulate,* 5121 E. Virginia Beach Blvd., Suite E2, Norfolk, VA 23502 (phone: 804-461-4553; fax: 804-466-8595); *Consulate,* 2420 Pemberton Rd., Richmond, VA 23233 (phone: 804-747-1961; fax: 804-747-1574).

Washington State: *Consulate,* 2132 Third Ave., Seattle, WA 98121 (phone: 206-448-3526; fax: 206-448-4771).

The Cities

Acapulco
(pronounced Ah-kah-*pul*-ko)

The mere mention of Acapulco usually brings a string of extravagant images to mind. Whether or not you consider these superlatives justified, Acapulco's reputation as an international beach resort borders on legendary. Throughout the year, and especially in the winter, tourists from all over the world descend on the hotel-lined gem of a bay facing the Pacific Ocean, generating a momentum that is in itself a kind of homage to this resort's reputation.

How you personally feel about Acapulco will depend, in large part, on your reaction to the sheer number of tourists around you—more than three million people visit Acapulco every year. If you don't mind sharing the pleasures of the sun with lots of other similarly inclined folk, Acapulco's beaches can be among the most compelling destinations in the Western Hemisphere.

More than any other Mexican city, Acapulco exudes sensuality. The first thing you're bound to notice is that during the day no one ever wears more than bathing trunks or a bikini. People are constantly flaunting their bodies, even on the city's buses or in supermarkets. At night, the sounds of tropical guitar and pop music drift through the air, mingling with the gentle music of the ocean, the palm leaves rustling in the soft, languorous wind, and the murmur of hushed conversations.

The first Spaniard to discover the Bahía de Acapulco (Acapulco Bay) was Francisco Chico. Under orders from Cortés to find natural harbors from which to launch the search for a Spice Islands route, he happened upon the bay in 1521. By 1579 Acapulco had become the only official port between the Americas and Asia. Luxury items such as silk, porcelain, spices, and ivory were transported from China and Japan via the Philippines by boat to fast-growing Acapulco. The rich cargoes were carried by mule train to Mexico City, from where they were sent on to Veracruz for shipment to Spain. This profitable trade did not go unnoticed by such pirates as Sir Francis Drake, who preyed on the Spanish galleons. Acapulco's *Fuerte de San Diego* (Fort of St. James) was constructed to defend the port against pirate raids.

After Mexico's War of Independence (1810–21), trade with the Orient ceased. Acapulco became a forgotten fishing village until 1922, when a paved road from Mexico City was finally built, but even then it was another 10 years before it got its first tentative start as a resort. Acapulco really came into its own in the late 1950s, when it became known as "The Riviera of the West."

Since then, Acapulco's reputation as a resort has dipped and soared like the parasailers who take off from Playa la Condesa. The rich and famous still go to Acapulco; they just don't talk about it the way they used to. In addition, the stress of coping with such huge numbers of visitors and the concomitant growth of the resident population (to nearly 540,000, with unofficial estimates approaching 1.5 million), which has made Acapulco one of the fastest-growing cities in the world, has overtaxed the city's resources.

Early this decade, the government began investing $300 million in several projects designed to revitalize Acapulco and its environs, including the construction of a superhighway between Cuernavaca and Acapulco that cuts driving time from Mexico City to about four hours. Acapulco's main street, Costera Miguel Alemán—known simply as "la Costera"—is now a well-maintained seaside avenue, and the beaches are cleaner than they used to be. Open-air markets along the beach and on vacant lots around the city have reduced the number of pushy street vendors. White-uniformed, multilingual "tourist police" now patrol the Costera, providing visitors with information. There is still room for improvement, especially in town and up in the mountains, where most of the residents live in substandard conditions. Still, there is too much to be prized about Acapulco for it to ever lose its luster. You have only to look down on the city at dusk from the heights of a casita in the luxurious *Las Brisas* complex to appreciate its unique character. The lights flicker like diamonds on an endless necklace, the dark water offering a muted reflection of the blinking brightness.

Acapulco At-a-Glance

SEEING THE CITY

Most people get their first breathtaking view of the bay—from the summit of the hill above the southern border of the city (at the entrance to *Las Brisas* and the Acapulco Diamante development)—as they drive in from the airport. (Airport Road also is known, for good reason, as the Carretera Escénica, or Scenic Highway.) For a special treat, try dining at one of the high-rise, roof garden restaurants, or go parasailing (a dangerous activity, though fun).

SPECIAL PLACES

These days the action in Acapulco centers along the Costera Miguel Alemán, the broad avenue that runs along the bay. To the left (as you face the ocean) beyond the southwestern headland is Puerto Marqués and then the open sea, as well as the fashionable *Acapulco Princess* and *Pierre Marqués* hotels. To the right is Caleta, where many of Acapulco's first hotels still operate, although many are rather run-down now. Because the sea is Acapulco's prime attraction, look first at the beaches. All are federal property, and the hotels have no jurisdiction over them. For safety's sake, we recommend avoiding completely isolated beaches; lifeguards are on hand at hotel beaches, but they may not work the more remote spots. And be very careful if you have sensitive skin: Two hours on an Acapulco beach, even in the early morning, can roast you.

CALETA AND CALETILLA This pair of pretty, sheltered beaches—their names mean "cove" and "little cove"—along the western rim of the bay beyond the *malecón* (seaside walkway) and *Fuerte de San Diego* are known as "the morning beaches" because of the early sun they get. Ringed with older hotels and resorts, they still are popular with longtime Mexican tourists. Although they may not be as serene—or as clean—as other more popular spots, they are very often crowded (especially since they are bisected by the walk to the *Mágico Mundo Marino* aquarium; see below). They still offer good swimming, though some sections are polluted. There's also a lot of boat traffic; launches are for rent at the pier, and boats leave regularly for Isla la Roqueta. Also for rent are small sailboats, kayaks, and paddleboats.

ISLA LA ROQUETA The beach on this uninhabited island is popular with families because the waters are calm and the sands white and beautiful. Snorkeling and scuba diving are excellent on the island's northern side, and there are surfboards for rent. Fishing is good, and kayaks are available. Also here is *Aca-Zoo,* a small, state-operated zoo with a certain Robinson Crusoe charm. It's closed Tuesdays; there's an admission charge (no phone). There's ferry service from and to Caleta; buy tickets from the kiosk on the beach.

PLAYA PAPAGAYO (PARROT BEACH) This beautiful wide swath of sand in front of *Parque Papagayo* has two names—the other is "El Morro" (The Rock), for the large rock formations just offshore.

LA CONDESA Running from the *Continental Plaza Acapulco* to *El Presidente* hotels, this is the most tourist-infested stretch of sand these days. It's also where the bright beach cafés, swinging bars, and scantiest bikinis are found. One section of the beach is popular with gays. Your best bet is just to sunbathe here; the waters are rough, and there's always a strong undertow. La Condesa offers sailboats for rent; there are also rental facilities for windsurfing, parasailing, and water skiing. Up by the Costera are a number of nice luncheon spots with music for dancing.

ICACOS *La Palapa* and the *Hyatt Regency* hotels share this strand, the first true beach on the Bahía de Acapulco (Acapulco Bay) as you drive in from the airport. The sheltered waters are calm and quiet, and the beach less hectic than the more popular spots. About 20 feet from the beach is Plaza Francia, an excellent sunning spot complete with small wooden patio. The plaza was built and donated by Acapulco's sister city of Cannes, France.

PLAYA REVOLCADERO Ten miles (16 km) southeast of town, in front of and on either side of the *Acapulco Princess* and *Pierre Marqués* hotels, this beach is a favorite of the rich and pampered. The water is great for body-surfing, as it's on the open Pacific, but beware of the sometimes vicious undertow. Those who enjoy a canter on the sand may rent ponies here.

BARRA VIEJA This stretch of beach about 24 miles (38 km) southeast of Acapulco is where the Laguna de Barra Vieja meets the Pacific. A marina is being built here (though work has been halted temporarily). The water on the Pacific side is too treacherous for swimming, but small boats are available for exploring the lagoon, fringed with palm and banana trees full of tropical birds. There are also horses for rent. *Pescado a la talla* (fish sliced in strips and marinated in spicy—though not hot—adobo sauce), said to have originated here, is for sale at the small thatch-roofed restaurants along the beach.

PIE DE LA CUESTA Formerly the private turf of Acapulco regulars, this beach has come to the attention of foreign tourists as well, so it's usually crowded. Ten miles (16 km) northwest of the city proper, it's a wonderful place to order a potent *coco loco* (perhaps at *Tres Marías,* on the beach), cuddle up in a hammock, and cement friendships as the sun goes down. Continue to the *Castillo del Rey León* beach club, where visitors can enjoy a buffet and use the pool, tennis court, and hammocks for a small fee, as well as pay a free visit to the small, rustic zoo (phone: 849905/6). At the *Parador del Sol,* there's an all-inclusive club where you can lunch and relax for the day (Km 5, Barra de Coyuca; phone: 602003 or 601648; fax: 601649). Note that this section of the coast has the area's most dangerous undertows: Sun, don't swim.

OTHER SIGHTS

LA QUEBRADA Acapulco's famous *clavadistas* (cliff divers) plunge from a 150-foot cliff here into a shallow inlet. Each dive must be perfectly timed to coincide with an incoming wave, or the diver risks being bashed against the jagged rocks. *La Perla* (at *Plaza las Glorias El Mirador* hotel; see *Checking In*) remains the best spot to watch the divers, who hurl themselves off the cliff at 1, 7:30, 8:30, 9:30, and 10:30 PM daily year-round. The best time is in the evening, when the cliffs are floodlit and the last diver is armed with two oversize torches, blazing a trail against the dimming sky.

EL CENTRO (OLD TOWN) Downtown Acapulco was the heart of town before the Costera hotel strip took over, and some say it remains the city's soul. Enter from Calle Azueta at the north end of the Costera, and wander crowded, narrow streets filled with itinerant musicians, shopkeepers, and residents. For shopping that's a world away from the Costera's chic boutiques, head south a few blocks to the central market on the other side of the wide canal, where blocks and blocks of clothing, crafts, household goods, and curiosities will tempt you.

PLAZA JUAN ALVAREZ (ZÓCALO) This square in downtown Acapulco is dominated by the *Catedral de Acapulco* (Cathedral of Acapulco), an oddity built in 1930 with Byzantine towers and a mosque-like dome. Opposite, at the waterfront, stands a monument to national heroes Guerrero, Morelos, Hidalgo, and Cuauhtémoc, the last Aztec emperor.

MURAL DIEGO RIVERA A spectacular and little-known mural by one of Mexico's most famous artists surrounds a private home in the hills of Acapulco. Although the house is closed to the public, the mural (a must-see) may be viewed by taking the road that leads to the *Casablanca* hotel (at the gas station about four blocks past the *zócalo*). Bear left at the fork and continue up to the site.

FUERTE DE SAN DIEGO (ST. JAMES FORT) Acapulco's most historic sight was built in 1617 to protect the port from pirates (it was rebuilt after an 18th-century earthquake). It was here that the insurgents defeated the royalists in the early 1800s. The fort now houses an interesting museum that chronicles the history of Acapulco from pre-Hispanic times through the War of Independence from Spain. Closed Mondays. Admission charge. A few blocks left of the *zócalo,* across from the piers and customs house (phone: 839730).

MÁGICO MUNDO MARINO (MAGICAL MARINE WORLD) In this large aquatic park is a museum devoted to marine life, water slides, lovely cataracts, several restaurants, and an aquarium. Open daily. Admission charge. On a small peninsula accessible by a walkway from Caleta (phone: 831215 or 831193).

LAGUNA COYUCA This unspoiled freshwater lagoon, which lies slightly past Pie de la Cuesta, is a bird sanctuary bordered by coconut palms and full of water hyacinths. The waters teem with catfish, mullet, and snook. The *Castillo del Rey León* beach club (see Pie de la Cuesta, above) offers a tour that includes transportation to and from Acapulco, a visit to a plantation, a short boat trip on the lagoon, lunch, and a few hours at the club (phone: 849905/6).

PARQUE PAPAGAYO On the grounds of the old *Papagayo* hotel, this delightful 60-acre park straddling Costera Miguel Alemán has cable cars, bumper cars, a Ferris wheel, a carousel, an artificial lake, boats, and a lakeside restaurant. Open daily. No admission charge (phone: 855244 or 856784).

CENTRO INTERNACIONAL ACAPULCO This former convention complex has become a major center of urban activity since its total renovation in 1994. Folkloric dance performances take place in the plaza on Wednesday and Saturday evenings year-round; admission usually includes dinner and an open bar (check with your hotel reservations desk for schedules and details). The center also has a movie theater, and there are occasional special productions in the *Teatro Juan Ruiz de Alarcón*. 4455 Costera Miguel Alemán (phone: 847050).

PARQUE CICI (CENTRO INTERNACIONAL DE CONVIVENCIA INFANTIL) On the beach, this small, well-maintained and recently remodeled amusement park (the name reflects its orientation toward children's activities, the remodeling means extra-clean facilities) has trained dolphins and seals, a pool with artificially made waves, two water toboggans, three dolphin shows daily, several bars and restaurants, a beach club, and jet skis. Open daily. Admission charge. Across the street from the *Embassy* hotel (phone: 841970/1).

CAPILLA DE LA PAZ (CHAPEL OF PEACE) At the tip of Las Brisas mountain, this modern structure contrasts dramatically with the flamboyant buildings around it. From its lofty perch, it commands an almost mystical view of the bay below. Beachwear not permitted. Open daily, with a midday (1 to 4 PM) closing (no phone).

PUERTO MARQUÉS About 8 miles (13 km) east of the center of the city, along the Carretera Escénica at the traffic circle just past *Las Brisas* resort (toward the airport), turn right and you'll find yourself in the fishing village of Puerto Marqués. The bay here is so calm it hardly shows a ripple. You can rent paddle, sail, and water-ski boats. Many seafood restaurants line the beach and the opposite side of the road. *Pipo's,* one of the best (see *Eating Out*), has a small marina with fishing boats for hire. Punta Diamante, the adjacent headland, is the site of the area's newest resort and condominium development, Acapulco Diamante. At press time, the *Camino Real Acapulco Diamante* and the *Vidafel Mayan Palace* were the only hotels open there (see *Checking In*), but plans include the construction of several more hotels, condominium complexes, a golf course, tennis and beach clubs, and commercial offices.

Sources and Resources

TOURIST INFORMATION

The *Procuraduría del Turista* (Tourist Protection Bureau), in the *Centro Internacional Acapulco* (see *Special Places;* phone: 844416), handles all kinds of tourist inquiries and helps to iron out disputes. It's open daily; at least one English-speaking staff member is always on duty. In the same building, the *Dirección de Turismo Municipal* (City Tourist Office; phone: 841625 or 847050, ext. 218/9) also is open daily, though staffing on Sundays is extremely limited. The *Secretaría de Fomento Turístico del Estado de Guerrero* (Guerrero State Secretariat for Promotion of Tourism; 187 Costera Miguel Alemán; phone: 843140 or 869171) also handles inquiries (closed weekends). In addition, several information kiosks line the Costera; they're open daily during high season, roughly mid-November through *Easter*.

LOCAL COVERAGE The tobacco shop in the *Acapulco Plaza* and most of the other large hotels sell the *International Herald Tribune,* the *Los Angeles Times, The New York Times, USA Today,* as well as *The News* and the *Mexico City Times,* both Mexico City–based English-language dailies. Newspapers are also available at *Sanborns* on Costera Miguel Alemán for considerably less than the hotels charge. *Acapulco News* and *Adventure in Acapulco,* local English-language weekly and monthly publications respectively, give tips on local happenings, as do three local Spanish-language dailies.

TELEPHONE The city code for Acapulco is 74. *Note:* Mexico's telephone company has embarked on a major expansion project that involves changing telephone numbers in many areas of the country. At press time, all numbers listed in this chapter were correct. However, if you have any difficulties reaching attractions listed here, contact the local tourist office.

CLIMATE AND CLOTHES Expect beach weather all year, with daytime temperatures ranging from the 80s F to the 90s F (27 to 37C) and nighttime temperatures averaging 10 degrees lower. Expect some rain, mostly in the form of afternoon showers, June through September. Whenever you come, bring lots of sunscreen. Dress is casual during the day. Upscale resortwear is de rigueur in most restaurants and nightclubs in the evening; Acapulco's nightspots do not look kindly on shorts, ratty jeans, or bare feet. Men are required to wear long pants and long-sleeved shirts (buttoned!) in the discos.

GETTING AROUND

AIRPORT Limos will carry up to five passengers to or from *Juan N. Alvarez International Airport* (phone: 852227 or 852332). Less expensive is an airport bus, which shuttles passengers between the airport and most hotels.

BOAT TOURS Several yachts and a catamaran make a three-and-a-half-hour cruise around the Bahía de Acapulco, Puerto Marqués, and La Quebrada; excursions generally include lunch or dinner, disco dancing, an open bar, a running commentary, and a show (in the evening). The *Bonanza* and *Fiesta Cabaret* (phone: 831803 or 832531) offer morning and afternoon trips, as well as three-hour starlight cruises that feature an open bar, music, and dancing; departure time is 7:30 PM. *Divers de México* (phone: 821397/8), owned by a very helpful American woman, runs a three-hour champagne sunset cruise with a show provided by the divers at La Quebrada, as well as a daytime *Buccaneer* cruise with the crew dressed up as pirates. Less expensive no-frills cruises depart at 11 AM and 4:30 PM. A four-hour ride (including food and an open bar) can be taken in the glass-bottom boats that leave Caleta all day long and pass over the *Virgen Submarina,* a bronze statue of Our Lady of Guadalupe, 13 feet under water. (Unfortunately, ocean debris obscures the statue except—usually—during winter months, when the water is more still.) Buy tickets for cruises at hotel tour desks.

BUS Inexpensive (1.40 pesos/about 19¢) buses run up and down the Costera all the way from Puerto Marqués to Caleta; service is irregular after midnight. With newer vehicles, service is much improved—but watch out for pickpockets when it's crowded.

CALANDRIA Decorated with brightly colored balloons, these two-passenger horse-drawn carriages run up and down the Costera. The standard ride is a tour of the town, but they also can be hired as taxis.

CAR RENTAL Most international agencies have offices at the airport and along the Costera. If you want to rent an air conditioned vehicle with automatic transmission, reserve well in advance. Jeeps and Volkswagen Beetles can be rented as well. *Saad* (phone: 843445 or 845325) rents only jeeps.

MOTORCYCLE Rent Honda Elites at *Parque CICI* (see *Special Places*) or next to the *Acapulco Plaza* (see *Checking In*) by the hour or day.

TAXI Acapulco cabs don't have meters, which means you have to agree on a price before getting in. There are cabstands in front of most of the hotels; rates are posted for major destinations. If you flag down a cab in the street, you'll have to haggle. At press time, no trip within Acapulco proper cost more than about 66 pesos (about $9); the fare is higher when the destination is Playa Revolcadero or Pie de la Cuesta, both a bit outside town.

SPECIAL EVENTS

The weeklong *Festival de Acapulco* (Acapulco Festival), held in May, features music and dance performances. *Día de los Muertos* (Day of the Dead; November 2) is an eminently Mexican holiday that combines a mocking attitude toward death and somber remembrances of departed relatives; activities usually begin the night before (see *Quintessential Mexico* in DIVERSIONS). The *Torneo Internacional de Pez Vela* (International Billfish Tournament) is held in late November or early December; an inter-club tournament (club participation varies) is held in February. December 1 marks the start of the 12-day *Torneo Internacional de Clavados* (International Diving Championship) at La Quebrada. *Día de la Virgen de Guadalupe,* December 12, a national holiday, is celebrated with special fervor. One day each month, the Bahía de Acapulco fills with sailboats participating in a regatta run by the *Club de Yates de Acapulco* (Acapulco Yacht Club).

SHOPPING

One of the most popular activities in Acapulco is buying things. Frequent visitors arrive with little more than a toothbrush, since resortwear and sports clothes are an Acapulco specialty. Stores and open-air markets also offer a wide selection of Mexico's best handicrafts, from handwoven serapes to native pottery and fine silver jewelry. The *Mercado Municipal* (City Market), about five blocks northeast of the *zócalo* at Mendoza and Constituyentes, is a good place to browse and bargain for handicrafts and curios, though you will find better prices at Pie de la Cuesta (see *Beaches,* above) or Puerto Marqués (see *Other Sights,* above).

For a productive shopping outing, stroll the Costera from the *Fiesta Americana Condesa* hotel to the *Plaza las Glorias Paraíso Acapulco.* The *Plaza Bahía* shopping mall, next to the *Acapulco Plaza* hotel, is air conditioned. The white-marble *Marbella* shopping center is on the Diana traffic circle, located east of town, halfway between the public golf course (see *Golf,* below) and *Parque Papagayo.* For some of Acapulco's more elegant shops, visit *La Vista* shopping center (Carretera Escénica, 2 miles/3 km before the *Acapulco Princess,* heading toward the airport). Most shops are open daily from 10 AM to 2 PM and 5 to 9 PM. Here are some of the better places:

Aca Joe It carries stylish casual T-shirts and togs for teens. 117 Costera Miguel Alemán (phone: 848643).

Artesanías Finas Acapulco Better known locally as *AFA,* it offers a vast selection of handicrafts, jewelry, leather goods, and clothing from all over Mexico. Av. Horacio Nelson, behind *Baby'O* (phone: 848049).

Benny A fashionable shop devoted to original designs in men's and women's clothing. Two locations: 114-7 Costera Miguel Alemán (phone: 841547) and *La Vista* (822228).

La Colección de Sergio Bustamante The world-renowned artist's fantastical eggs, animals, and people in ceramics, papier-mâché, and brass are displayed here. 711B Costera Miguel Alemán (phone: 844992).

Esteban High-fashion clothing for men and women. 2010 Costera Miguel Alemán (phone: 843084).

Galería Rudic Paintings and other works of art by top Mexican artists. Costera Miguel Alemán and Yañez Pinzón (phone: 844844).

María de Guadalajara High-quality designer swim- and beachwear, with a touch of Latino class. *Galería Plaza* shopping center, 143 Costera Miguel Alemán (phone: 855073).

Ronay If silver jewelry is your delight, this is the place. 999-1 Costera Miguel Alemán, below *Carlos 'n' Charlie's* restaurant (phone: 841007).

Rubén Torres Stunning sportswear for women and men. 1999 Costera Miguel Alemán (phone: 840786).

Suzett's Striking gold designs, especially in rings with precious stones. At the *Hyatt Regency* (phone: 842888).

Tane Silver jewelry, flatware, and objets d'art of impeccable design and quality. At the *Hyatt Regency* (phone: 846348) and *Las Brisas* (phone: 810816).

Taxco el Viejo A most imaginative silver shop that also sells items in gold, leather, wool, ceramics, and wood. A block from the cliffs from which the famous divers leap, at 830 La Quebrada (phone: 832571).

SPORTS

BOATING Sailing in the calm bay waters of Acapulco is easy, while navigating the more turbulent Pacific waves and currents requires greater expertise and skill. Small sailboats, good for bay cruising, can be rented at any of Acapulco's beaches, although landing them can be tricky. Catamarans and other boats of varying size are available for rent on all the bay beaches. The best places are Caleta and Puerto Marqués. *Divers de México* (see "Boat Tours" in *Getting Around,* above) rents private, chartered yachts by the hour.

BULLFIGHTING Established matadors perform Sundays at 5 PM from the beginning of December through *Semana Santa* (Holy Week). Hotel travel desks have the details and the tickets. The bullring is near Caleta.

FISHING The city's beaches are only slightly more crowded with people than its waters are crowded with fish. The Pacific waters abound with pompano, bonito, barracuda, yellowtail, red snapper, and shark, while the city's freshwater lagoons and the Río Papagayo have carp, catfish, and mullet.

Deep-sea charter boats leave about 8 AM and return around lunchtime. At Laguna Tres Palos (at Barra Vieja) and at Laguna Coyuca (see *Special Places* for both), you can rent small boats with awnings and angle for freshwater catfish. *Divers de México* (see "Boat Tours" in *Getting Around*) has nine American yachts, some air conditioned, all Coast Guard–approved and with uniformed crews. *Club de Esquíes Beto* (phone: 822034) rents fishing boats for four and speedboats from which five can fish.

Anglers can also make arrangements through their hotel or can try bargaining with boat captains face to face—not an uncommon practice and often advantageous, but be sure the price includes bait and beer. Most deep-sea boats dock downtown along the *malecón*.

GOLF Besides the courses listed below, Acapulco boasts the *Acapulco Diamante Country Club* (no phone), a par 72, 18-hole course near the Laguna Tres Palos in the Acapulco Diamante development. Though the course was not officially open at press time, visitors were allowed to use the greens if they brought their own clubs; ask at your hotel for details. Opened in 1995, the *Club de Golf Acapulco* has a plush nine-hole course next to the *Centro Internacional Acapulco* (see *Other Sights,* above; phone: 843545 or 843909). Tourists must pay a greens fee; equipment can be rented.

TOP TEE-OFF SPOTS

Acapulco Princess Ted Robinson designed this well-maintained, 6,359-yard, 18-hole course fraught with many water hazards. Wayne Sisson is the director, Manuel Martínez is the pro, and lessons are available. Non-guests are welcome; off-season fees are a bit lower than in the winter. Carretera Escénica, 12 miles (19 km) south of Acapulco (phone: 843100).

Pierre Marqués A member of the *Acapulco Princess* family, this par 72, 6557-yard, Percy Clifford course is one of the best on Mexico's Pacific Coast, with challenging, well-cared-for fairways. Reservations are accepted two days in advance. The 18-hole course is open year-round, but the official season is mid-December through mid-April. Wayne Sisson is in charge here, too; José Dominiquez is the pro. Guests can enter most of its many tournaments. Playa Revolcadero, down the road from the *Acapulco Princess* (phone: 842000).

In addition, two 18-hole courses have been completed at *Tres Vidas en la Playa* (phone: 621000; fax: 621003), a hotel under construction at the far southeast end of the *Vidafel Mayan Palace* complex (see *Checking In*). The complex's own golf club is set to open around the year 2000; nine holes of its projected 18-hole course are finished. There also is a nine-hole public course next to the *Centro Internacional Acapulco* on the Costera (phone: 840781/2).

HORSEBACK RIDING Playa Revolcadero is the place to go for a canter astride a pony. Ask for Mundo or Carlos—they'll take the time to find you the best mount. Horses also are available at Pie de la Cuesta.

JAI ALAI Not to be outdone by Miami and other resorts, Acapulco opened a massive jai alai fronton in 1994. It's across from the *Hyatt Regency* (phone: 843178 or 843195).

PARASAILING The next best thing to skydiving is going aloft in a parachute pulled by a speedboat. There's no trouble finding the boatmen—they are on every beach. *Be warned:* It can be dangerous.

SCUBA DIVING AND SNORKELING Diving is extremely popular here, though the water in the bay is never as clear as that of the seas along less-developed sections of the Pacific Coast or on the Caribbean. The best diving spot in Acapulco is off the shores of Isla la Roqueta (see *Special Places*).

Lessons and equipment are available at all major hotels. *Hermanos Arnold* (106 Costera Miguel Alemán; phone: 820788), in front of *Las Hamacas* hotel (see *Checking In*), is a school run by the Arnold brothers. Dive packages offered by *Divers de México* (see "Boat Tours" in *Getting Around*) include pool instruction and lunch. Lessons and equipment also are available at the entrance to Caleta. There is fine snorkeling at *Las Brisas* resort's private *La Concha Beach Club* (see *Checking In*).

TENNIS There are about 30 courts in town. Many of the best courts and best players are found at private clubs. You may have some difficulty reserving a court, so ask your hotel to make arrangements for you. Acapulco's best private clubs include the *Tiffany Racquet Club* (120 Av. Villa Vera; phone: 847949), with five clay courts (two lighted), and *Club de Golf Acapulco* (across from the *Malibu* hotel, on the Costera; phone: 843545 or 843909), with four cement courts (two lighted). In addition, several Acapulco hotels have fine tennis setups, and most courts are open to non-guests for a fee.

CHOICE COURTS

Acapulco Plaza Here are four lighted outdoor hard courts and one outdoor clay court atop a shopping center next door to the hotel. 123 Costera Miguel Alemán (phone: 859050).

Acapulco Princess It offers 11 courts (six clay, five Laykold), including two of the most lavish air conditioned indoor courts anywhere. Reservations are necessary. Private lessons are available from local pros Tomás Flores and Juan Téllez or from other instructors. Guests also may play at the adjacent *Pierre Marqués* hotel, run by the same management, with eight courts of its own (see below). Carretera Escénica, 12 miles (19 km) south of Acapulco (phone: 843100).

Las Brisas The five hard-surface courts (all lighted), pro shop, and tennis and backgammon club all are available to guests. Reserve in advance. 5255 Carretera Escénica, 8 miles (13 km) south of Acapulco (phone: 841580).

Hyatt Regency Acapulco Five lighted, hard-surface courts are available, plus a good pro shop. Guests who buy a tennis package can use the courts free of charge—don't forget to reserve playing time, though. 1 Costera Miguel Alemán (phone: 842888).

Pierre Marqués Here are eight courts, plus the tennis facilities of its sister hotel next door, the *Acapulco Princess* (see above). Carretera Escénica, 11 miles (18 km) south of Acapulco (phone: 842000).

Villa Vera The racquet club here has three lighted clay courts. 35 Lomas del Mar (phone: 840333).

WATER SKIING The calm waters of Caleta and Puerto Marqués are especially good for beginners. At Laguna Coyuca visitors can watch demonstrations of barefoot skiing. Boats are available at all major hotels. Champion waterskiers perform daredevil feats during the spectacular *Acapulco Water Ski Show,* held at the *Club de Yates de Acapulco* Tuesdays through Sundays at 9 PM. The best place to view the show is from the *El Colonial* restaurant (130-3 Costera Miguel Alemán; phone: 839107); the tourist office has more details.

WRESTLING Matches are held Wednesday nights at the *Coliseo Arena* (about three blocks northeast of the *zócalo*), which draws a rough crowd. There often is more fighting in the stands than in the ring. Boxing events (a tad more sedate) are held here Saturdays at 6 PM. Consult the newspapers for details (see *Local Coverage*).

NIGHTCLUBS AND NIGHTLIFE

Acapulco has its share of traditional Mexican fiestas, which usually feature mariachi music, folkloric dancing, a buffet, and an open bar. Fiestas at the *Centro Internacional Acapulco* and the *Marbella* shopping center frequently showcase the spectacular *Voladores de Papantla* (Flying Pole Dancers of Papantla). Check with your hotel for details. Javier de León's excellent folkloric ballet performs from mid-November through the week after *Easter* at the *Calinda* hotel (1260 Costera Miguel Alemán; phone: 840410). At *Las Brisas*'s *El Mexicano* restaurant (see *Checking In*), the festivities begin with a handicrafts market and end with a spectacular fireworks display. Make reservations through your hotel travel desk.

Acapulco really gets going well after dark. The discos don't get crowded until after 11 PM, so one way to get a table is to arrive around 10:30. One of Acapulco's hottest spots is *Baby'O* (22 Costera Miguel Alemán; phone: 847474), which looks like a stylized mud hut from the outside. The interior of *Le Dome* (402 Costera Miguel Alemán; phone: 841190), one of the port's original discos, is accented with a huge, ornate chandelier. Classy *Atrium* (30 Costera Miguel Alemán; phone: 841901) offers reproductions of the *Sistine Chapel* frescoes on the ceiling, while the music ranges from romantic to salsa. The aptly named *Extravaganzza* (next to *Los Rancheros,* on the Carretera Escénica; phone: 847154 or 847164) is big, modern, and posh, with an immense glass wall providing an awesome view of the bay. On the same street but up the hill from *Extravaganzza* is *Palladium,* which tends to attract a well-dressed, 20ish crowd and has one of the best light shows in town (phone: 810300). The selective door policy of the *Magic* disco (Costera Miguel Alemán at Fragata Yucatán; phone: 848815) has made it an "in" place. At *News* (12 Costera Miguel Alemán, across from the *Hyatt Regency;* phone: 845904), one of Acapulco's largest, most popular—and most casual—dance spots, it's not unusual to see people dancing on the tables.

Spanish-style *El Fuerte* (in *Las Hamacas* hotel—see *Checking In;* phone: 837709 or 837870) claims to have the best flamenco show this side of Seville. At *La Perla* (La Quebrada; phone: 831221 or 847254), the famed cliff divers provide the entertainment (for additional details, see *Special Places*). The Victorian decor and unobtrusive sound system at *Tiffany's* (*Acapulco Princess;* see *Checking In*) promote quiet conversation. World-famous female impersonators stage tasteful shows at *Tequila's Le Club* (29 Urdaneta, across from the *Centro Internacional Acapulco* and behind the *Gigante* supermarket; phone: 838236).

Best in Town

CHECKING IN

After a decade-long slump in hotel development, Acapulco began booming again in the mid 1990s (when the peso falls, more foreign tourists arrive). Most of the growth is in the Acapulco Diamante area, extending from *Las Brisas* out to the airport southeast of the bay. The newest addition is the *Vidafel Mayan Palace* complex (see below). In winter, expect to pay from $210 to $330 per night for a double room in a very expensive hotel, from $145 to $200 at an expensive one, about $100 at a moderate one, and $70 or less at an inexpensive one. All rooms have air conditioning, a TV set, and a telephone unless otherwise indicated. Note that rates from the second Monday after *Easter* through mid-November often are less than half of high-season prices. All telephone numbers are in the 74 city code unless otherwise noted.

We begin with our favorite havens (all very expensive), followed by recommended hotels, listed by price category.

ROOMS AT THE TOP

Acapulco Princess The exterior of the main building of this comprehensive resort resembles an Aztec pyramid, complete with balconies hung with exotic tropical blossoms. The interior looks like a sumptuous movie set, with floral hangings and ample marble. There's a championship 18-hole golf course, outdoor and (air conditioned) indoor tennis courts, parasailing facilities, five pools, a sauna, 1,019 rooms, seven restaurants (the *Hacienda* is the best), a disco, a nightclub, jeeps for rent, and even a bar under a waterfall. The traffic can get a bit hectic between lobby and lounge, but it's well run. The hotel also conducts classes in its *Gourmet Mexican Cooking School,* where, under the guidance of expert chefs, students learn to prepare Mexican fare and select wines, as well as how to use ancient utensils, many of which date back to pre-Columbian times. Week-long courses—held during the fall—are limited to 20 students; the cost, including accommodations, is about $600 a day, double occupancy. Surfing is possible at the beach here. The rate includes breakfast and dinner. Carretera Escénica, about 12 miles (19 km) south of Acapulco (phone: 843100; 800-223-1818; fax: 691015).

Las Brisas Just about the best resort address in Mexico since its opening in 1957, this pink hillside hideaway is among the most luxurious hotels anywhere. Three hundred semi-connected or solitary casitas and 10 four- to six-bedroom villas climb up the 750 acres of *Las Brisas*'s posh mountainside. There are 200 pools (shared and private), several condominium units, 150 pink-and-white-striped jeeps available for rent, five lighted tennis courts, water sports, and golf and fishing nearby. The rate includes membership in the hotel's private *La Concha Beach Club,* which serves some of the best ceviche in Mexico. The mountain-top view from the aptly named *Bella Vista* restaurant (see *Eating Out*) is among the most romantic on earth. The emphasis is on privacy and the recharging of human batteries. Among the special touches are complimentary continental breakfast, discreetly delivered each morning; jeep-borne room service (some guests prefer never to leave their casitas); and fresh hibiscus floating in the pools. The night spectacle of twinkling lights across the bay make this all well worth the price. 5255 Carretera Escénica, 8 miles (13 km) south of Acapulco (phone: 841650; 800-228-3000; fax: 842269).

Pierre Marqués The sister resort of the *Acapulco Princess* (a shuttle runs between the two), this jewel is the real royalty of the twosome. Built by the late J. Paul Getty, it is bordered by a palm-fringed, 18-hole golf course on one side and the Pacific on the other. It has gardens, terraces, lawns with bungalows, restaurants, bars, three pools, water sports and fishing gear, tennis, and shopping—and if that's not enough, the more frantic facilities at the adjacent *Acapulco Princess* are available, too. It's all surprisingly elegant and discreet, with 344 rooms, junior suites, and villas. Breakfast is included in the rate. Carretera Escénica, about 11 miles (18 km) south of Acapulco (phone: 842000; 800-223-1818; fax: 848554).

VERY EXPENSIVE

Camino Real Acapulco Diamante Located at the foot of a lush green hillside, all 154 units here have private lanai terraces overlooking the bay. There's a secluded beach, three pools, a spa–fitness center, a shopping arcade, a tennis court, and five restaurants. Nonsmoking rooms are available. Puerto Marqués, about 7 miles (11 km) east of the airport (phone: 812010; 800-7-CAMINO in the US; 800-90123 in Mexico; fax: 812700).

Hyatt Regency It offers 690 large, comfortable rooms, a 300-foot free-form pool, water sports on its beach, five lighted tennis courts, three restaurants, a coffee shop, two bars, and exercise classes. 1 Costera Miguel Alemán (phone: 691234; 800-228-9000 in the US; 800-00500 in Mexico; fax: 843086/7).

EXPENSIVE

Acapulco Plaza About half of the 1,008 rooms here are small; the rest are very comfortable suites. Facilities include four tennis courts, two pools, a fine beach, a shopping center next door, a health club, Jacuzzis, a sauna, four restaurants, and a coffee shop. The thatch-roofed bar is suspended from the roof, accessible via a wooden gangplank. Bear in mind that this is one of the liveliest resorts in town; consider requesting a room on an upper floor. Service at the front desk is not always friendly. 123 Costera Miguel Alemán (phone: 859050; 800-FIESTA-1 in the US; 800-50450 in Mexico; fax: 855285).

Continental Plaza Acapulco This landmark has a pool surrounding an island; its beach is enormous. It also features 390 rooms, three restaurants, a coffee shop, and a lobby bar with live music. Costera Miguel Alemán (phone: 840909; 800-88-CONTI; fax: 842081).

Fiesta Americana Condesa This 500-room property has two pools, social programs for kids during summer and *Christmas,* a lobby bar where live music attracts nighttime crowds, and a restaurant. On the beach at 1220 Costera Miguel Alemán (phone: 842828; 800-FIESTA-1 in the US; 800-50450 in Mexico; fax: 841828).

Sheraton Acapulco Set on a hillside on secluded Playa Guitarrón on the east end of the Bahía de Acapulco, it has 17 villas comprising 226 rooms and eight suites. Facilities include two pools (one with a swim-up bar), two restaurants, and a lobby bar with live music. 110 Costera Guitarrón (phone: 812222; 800-325-3535 in the US; 800-90325 in Mexico; fax: 843760).

Vidafel Mayan Palace The newest addition to Acapulco's hotel scene, this gargantuan complex has opened 380 of its eventual 2,400 suites. Gigantic replicas of Maya ruins are set in green marble niches throughout the grounds, which include an extensive stretch of Playa Revolcadero, a mile-long pool with waterfalls and boulders, two restaurants, a nine-hole golf course, 10 lighted clay tennis courts, and interconnecting water canals. The suites feature kitchens, dining rooms, and sitting areas. Future plans include the addition of six more restaurants, expansion of the golf course to 18 holes, a water park, and a monorail. 25 miles (40 km) east of town, off the Carretera Escénica at 22 Geranio (phone: 690201; 800-VIDAFEL; fax: 620008).

Villa Vera In this glamorous jet set favorite are a total of 80 spacious rooms, suites, and villas (many of which have private pools), an excellent restaurant, a large pool, a Jacuzzi, a fitness center, and three tennis courts. There's no beach, but a free shuttle takes guests to the beach at the *Maralisa,* some 3 miles (5 km) away. No children under 16 allowed. In town, at 35 Lomas del Mar (phone: 840333; 800-525-4800 or 800-223-6510; fax: 847479).

MODERATE

Boca Chica One of Acapulco's older places, right on the water, it has 45 units, two restaurants (one a sushi and oyster bar), and two pools. Snorkeling is at its best here. Rate includes breakfast and dinner. Playa Caletilla (phone: 836601 or 836741; fax: 839513).

Costa Club This 150-unit complex boasts a pool, a restaurant, a bar, and one of the best views of Mexico's Pacific Coast. Pie de la Cuesta (no direct phone; call the central phone exchange at 834379, 837148, or 837674 and ask for the hotel).

La Palapa All 340 suites here have balconies, indoor bars, and plenty of closet space. The hotel also has a large pool, a water sports center, a social program, live music nightly, and an electronic gameroom. 210 Fragata Yucatán, on Playa Icacos next to *Parque CICI* (phone: 845363; 800-334-7234; fax: 848399).

Plaza las Glorias El Mirador Besides the dramatic view of the cliffs and cliff divers from *La Perla* supper club, the hotel has three pools and 160 pleasant rooms with large bathrooms. It's best for those who don't need a beach at hand. 74 La Quebrada (phone: 831221; 800-342-AMIGO; fax: 824564).

Ritz In this modern 252-room high-rise is a pool, a restaurant, and even a video gameroom. 159 Costera Miguel Alemán, at Playa los Hornos (phone: 857336; fax: 857076).

INEXPENSIVE

Acapulco Dolphins An unpretentious hotel across from *Parque CICI,* it comprises 185 large, recently renovated rooms, a restaurant, a pool, a rooftop solarium with a Jacuzzi, and first-rate service. 50 Costera Miguel Alemán (phone: 846638 or 844441; fax: 843072).

Bali-Hai One of the advantages here is that guests can enjoy a quiet room in the back and still be right on the main strip. There is a restaurant and a pool. Near the *Acapulco Plaza,* at 186 Costera Miguel Alemán (phone: 856622; fax: 857972).

Las Hamacas Across from the beach on the strip, this 160-room hostelry offers a pool with bar, a garden dining room, and flamenco shows in its nightclub. The rooms off the pool are nicer and quieter, though they afford no view. 239 Costera Miguel Alemán (phone: 837746; 800-448-8355; fax: 830575).

Sands In the center of things, yet tranquil, it has a restaurant, two pools, a bar, two squash courts, 60 modest rooms, and 34 bungalows. The staff here is pleasant. 178 Costera Miguel Alemán, at Juan de la Cosa (phone: 842260; 800-422-6078; fax: 841053).

El Tropicano Two blocks from the beach, this place has 139 units, two pools, restaurants, a garden, and a disco. 510 Costera Miguel Alemán (phone: 841100; 800-528-1234; fax: 841308).

EATING OUT

Dining out here is relatively costly. For dinner for two, expect to pay from $65 to $80 at very expensive restaurants; from $50 to $60 at expensive ones; from $30 to $45 at moderate places; and $30 or less at inexpensive ones. Prices do not include drinks, wine, tax, or tip. Most restaurants below accept MasterCard and Visa, and a few also accept American Express and Diners Club; it's a good idea to call ahead and check. Unless otherwise noted, restaurants are open daily for lunch and dinner. All telephone numbers are in the 74 city code unless otherwise indicated.

VERY EXPENSIVE

Casa Nova With a wonderful view of the bay, this spot serves pasta, antipasto, and Italian renditions of shrimp and fish. Reservations necessary. 5256 Carretera Escénica, across from *Las Brisas* (phone: 846815/6).

Coyuca 22 This place looks like the set of a romantic Hollywood musical of the 1940s. The menu includes lobster thermidor. Closed for lunch and May through October. Reservations necessary. 22 Coyuca (phone: 835030 or 823468).

EXPENSIVE

Bella Vista Set atop a hill overlooking the entire city and bay, the prime eating place at *Las Brisas* hotel offers an eclectic choice of fare, ranging from Thai shrimp and bourbon beef tournedos to spicy duckling salad. Open for breakfast and dinner only. Reservations necessary. Carretera Escénica, 8 miles (12 km) south of Acapulco (phone: 841580).

El Campanario Well-prepared seafood dishes, colonial decor, and a panoramic view of Acapulco are the draws at this beautiful bell-tower dining room, set atop a mountain. After 10 PM, a romantic disco opens on the premises. Reservations advised. Calle Paraíso (phone: 848830).

Dino's Homemade bread and other Italian dishes are what make this place special, and dining on the terrace makes things even more pleasant. No reservations. 137 Costera Miguel Alemán (phone: 840037).

Embarcadero With a South Seas motif, it offers such temptations as charcoal-broiled mahimahi with rice and bananas. Closed Mondays in summer. Reservations advised. 25 Costera Miguel Alemán, near *Parque CICI* (phone: 848787).

Kookaburra This romantic spot specializes in seafood, steaks, and barbecue. There is also a wonderful ceviche bar. Closed for lunch. Reservations advised. Carretera Las Brisas (phone: 841448).

Madeiras With terrace dining and a view of the bay, this pretty place oozes sophistication. The prix fixe menu includes baby lamb chops, red snapper baked in sea salt, and frogs' legs. Closed for lunch and Sundays. Reservations advised. 33 Carretera Escénica, in *La Vista* shopping center (phone: 846921).

La Mansión In a colonial-style setting, it's famous for its steaks grilled tableside. Try the *lomo al jerez* (filet mignon marinated in sherry). Closed for lunch Mondays through Saturdays. Reservations advised. 81 Costera Miguel Alemán, across from the golf course (phone: 810796).

Miramar The view from the multilevel terraces is spectacular. Of the fine French fare offered, the *pato a la naranja* (crispy duck with orange sauce) is superlative. Closed Sundays in summer. Reservations necessary. In *La Vista* shopping center (phone: 847874).

Normandie Dine by candlelight in perhaps the best French restaurant in all of Mexico, run by a Frenchwoman, Nicole Lepine, and her daughter. Closed for lunch and May through October. Reservations advised. In town, at Costera Miguel Alemán and Malespina (phone: 851916).

Spicey Savor tasty dishes with a touch of Cajun, all in a tropical ambience featuring wood-paneled walls and lush hanging plants. Dinner only. Reservations necessary. Carretera Escénica, across from *Las Brisas* (phone: 81130 or 810470).

Suntory This fashionable place offers authentic Japanese food. Reservations advised. 36 Costera Miguel Alemán (phone: 848088).

Beto's Phenomenally popular for its breakfasts and lunches (though it serves good food at dinner too), live music, and good seafood. Reservations advised. 49 Costera Miguel Alemán, at Playa la Condesa (phone: 840473).

Carlos 'n' Charlie's A bit dreary of late, but it's still an Acapulco institution. Specialties include charcoal-broiled spareribs, stuffed shrimp, and sangria. Closed for lunch. No reservations. 112 Costera Miguel Alemán (phone: 840039).

Hard Rock Cafe Part of the ubiquitous chain, this is a combination rock 'n' roll hall of fame, bar, restaurant, dance hall, and boutique. The food, everything from shrimp *fajitas* to filet mignon, is tasty, and portions are generous. Live rock music is played from 11 PM to 2 AM. The popular boutique sells sportswear bearing the familiar logo. No reservations. 37 Costera Miguel Alemán, next to *Parque CICI* (phone: 846680).

Paradiso This fun beachside spot specializes in delicious red snapper. Reservations advised. Costera Miguel Alemán, right on Playa la Condesa (phone: 845988).

Tony Roma's Succulent ribs and other barbecued meats are the specialty at this gigantic eatery. Costera Miguel Alemán, in the *Continental Plaza Acapulco* (phone: 843348).

Villa Fiore Homemade fettuccine and other Italian dishes, including a must-try veal *piccata,* are served in this beautiful garden restaurant. Closed Mondays from the second Monday after *Easter* through mid-November. Reservations advised. 6 Av. del Prado, off the Costera (phone: 842040).

INEXPENSIVE

El Amigo Miguel Delicious ceviche and grilled grouper filets with crunchy garlic can be found here, in the bustling old section of the city. Take a table upstairs for the breeze, ambience, and view. No reservations. No credit cards accepted. One block off the Costera at 31 Benito Juárez (phone: 825195).

100% Natural Fresh vegetable sandwiches, exotic fruit drinks, and other organic goodies are served here. No reservations. No credit cards accepted. Costera Miguel Alemán, next to the *Banco Internacional Building* (phone: 853982).

Pipo's Each of the four branches looks raunchy, but regulars insist that they serve the best seafood on the Mexican Pacific—which makes up for the noise and less-than-adequate service. Across from the sport fishing docks, at 3 Almirante Bretón (phone: 822237); Puerto Marqués (Calle Managua; phone: 660098); 105 Costera Miguel Alemán (phone: 840165); and the oldest branch, on Carretera Escénica, about 4 miles (6 km) south of town (phone: 620126).

Los Rancheros Easy to overlook because of its hilltop location, this is a good place to sample authentic Mexican food while gazing out at the Pacific. Carretera Escénica, about 6 miles (10 km) south of town en route to *Las Brisas* (phone: 841908).

Cancún, Cozumel, and Isla Mujeres

(pronounced Kahn-*koon,* Ko-soo-*mehl,* and *Ees*-lah Moo-*hair*-ehs)

In the past 26 years, Mexico's Caribbean coast along the Yucatán Peninsula has been transformed from a secluded haven for divers and sun worshipers to a popular vacation spot for travelers from around the world. The region's biggest draw is Cancún, just off the peninsula's northwest coast. Once just an undeveloped and inaccessible spit of land, the quarter-mile-wide, 14-mile-long sandbar was transformed into a major tourist destination after computer analysis by *FONATUR,* Mexico's national tourist development agency, revealed that it had all the makings of a resort area: beautiful sea and some of the best diving in the world, adequate space, and proximity to the East Coast of the US as well as to the magnificent Maya ruins at *Chichén Itzá, Cobá* and *Tulum.* In addition to new hotels and resorts, a network of roads, transportation, and communications was built, connecting the resort area to important indigenous ruins and to the city of Mérida, so that visitors no longer had to choose between culture and carousal—though some tranquillity-seeking vacationers say the Cancún ambience tends too much toward the latter.

Shaped like an emaciated sea horse, Cancún island—also known as the *zona hotelera,* or hotel zone—is connected by a causeway at its nosepoint to Cancún City, the support city on the mainland, where some 340,000 people live. For most of the island's length, island and peninsula are separated by the unruffled Laguna Nichupté. Most of the island's resort hotels are scattered along the skinny east–west sand spit that forms the sea horse's head. Along its back, the Caribbean surf rolls in along a 12-mile length of shore with intermittent stretches of powdery white beach. (The crystalline Caribbean offers visibility to 100 feet, and the stretch of sea along the peninsula is world-famous for its plenitude of fish, coral, and wrecks.) Cancún City's handful of hotels attract mostly business-oriented and budget travelers; several are pleasant, with such amenities as swimming pools and free transportation to and from local beaches. In addition, the proposed $600-million, 330-acre Malecón Cancún project, which will include homes, shops, restaurants, offices, and a park overlooking the lagoon and Cancún's Hotel Zone, is still in the planning stages (Mexico's current economic woes are slowing its progress).

Cancún's growth—it now attracts more than three million visitors a year—has far outstripped that of its southern neighbor Cozumel, which had once been the preferred destination of travelers who wanted to explore Mexico's Caribbean beaches. Visitors to Cozumel, which lies 11 miles off the mainland coast and some 31 miles south of Cancún, tend to be more interested in the fabulous diving and fishing than in the glamour and glitzy nightlife up the coast.

Even more secluded is the 5-mile-long, ½-mile wide island of Isla Mujeres, located some 6 miles north of Cancún and 6 miles off the mainland. The Spanish gave the island its name, which means "Isle of Women," because they found many sculptures of females there. With its charming, fairly simple hotels and wide expanses of beach, the island has a small, but loyal, following of snorkelers, divers, and loafers. It's also a popular day-trip destination for visitors to Cancún.

Construction continues to change the face of the Yucatán's resort region, particularly in Cancún. Paseo Kukulcán (Kukulcán Boulevard), which runs from one end of Cancún to the other, has been expanded from two lanes to four. Currently there are more than 100 hotels in operation in both Cancún and Cancún City, plus condominiums, shopping centers, restaurants, and marinas scattered along Paseo Kukulcán. In a spirit of environmental awareness, the government has declared a moratorium on new hotel construction in Cancún—too late, some say. Cancún's weather and facilities are an authentic lure, but it is not the place for those who prize peace and privacy. Cozumel and Isla Mujeres, on the other hand, have managed to retain their slow pace and relaxed appeal.

Cancún, Cozumel, and Isla Mujeres At-a-Glance

SEEING THE CITY

The best way to get a bird's-eye view of Cancún is from the ultra-light seaplane owned by *Cancún Avioturismo* (phone: 98-830315), which takes off from Laguna Nichupté for a 15-minute flight over the island's Hotel Zone.

SPECIAL PLACES

Paseo Kukulcán is the only street on Cancún. In mainland Cancún City, Avenida Tulum is the main drag, but Avenida Yaxchilán is shaping up as the address of the more fashionable shops and restaurants. The village of San Miguel, on Cozumel, is about 10 blocks long and a few blocks wide; it's lined with many shops, restaurants, and boutiques. Isla Mujeres has a few fairly simple, charming, and reasonably priced shops and restaurants.

CANCÚN

PLAYA CHAC-MOOL This is the most popular public-access beach on the island. (All Cancún beaches are public, but access may be through hotel property; there are 12 public-access entries to beaches along the island.) There are several *palapa* (thatch-roofed) seafood restaurants here; dressing rooms and showers are open daily from 10 AM to 11 PM.

EL REY These modest Maya ruins on the lagoon at the southern end of the island are hardly impressive compared with those at *Tulum* or *Cobá,* but they are worth a visit. All of the structures that can be seen here today date from the 12th century. In the 1950s, when they were first excavated, the skeleton of a relatively large human male was discovered on top of the site's box-like central temple. Some anthropologists suggest that the skeleton was that of a chieftain (hence the name *rey,* which means king in Spanish). Unfortunately, there are too few surviving vestiges to determine with certainty just what purpose this temple served.

CENTRO DE CONVENCIONES (CONVENTION CENTER) Completely rebuilt in 1994 at a cost of $90 million, it accommodates up to 12,000 people and has facilities for theater performances, concerts, expositions, and conferences. The center also has a large shopping center, and future plans include the addition of an observation deck, a disco, and a revolving restaurant atop a 50-story "needle" tower. Km 9 of Paseo Kukulcán (phone: 98-830199).

COZUMEL

PLAZA The heart of Cozumel (and of San Miguel) is a wide plaza near where the ferry docks; most of the shops and restaurants are here. If you're traveling by motor scooter, find somewhere else to park: parking here is forbidden.

MUSEO DEL CARIBE (MUSEUM OF THE CARIBBEAN) Formerly the *Museo Cozumel,* this museum exhibits impressive 3-D models of tropical fish, of human-eating sharks, and of the underwater caves in the offshore reefs, plus historical and ethnographical exhibits. Other features are temporary exhibits, a library, a crafts shop, and a restaurant. Closed Saturdays. Admission charge. Av. Rafael E. Melgar between Calles 4 and 6, in San Miguel (phone: 987-21545).

LAGUNA CHANKANAB AND JARDÍN BOTÁNICO (CHANKANAB LAGOON AND BOTANICAL GARDENS) About 5 miles (8 km) south of town is a natural aquarium filled with multicolored tropical fish. Because suntan lotion collects in the water and harms the fish, swimming and snorkeling in the lagoon are sometimes prohibited, but they're always permitted at the nearby beach. The gardens boast more than 400 species of tropical plants. Open daily. Admission charge (no phone).

SAN GERVASIO The largest Maya ruin on Cozumel (a bit less than half the size of *Tulum*) is located just off the Carretera Transversal, the main road across the center of the island. A cluster of seven small temple groups, *San Gervasio* was occupied from the 4th century AD until the first contact with Spanish sailors in the 16th century. The site is said to have been the main ceremonial center for the worship of Ix-chel, the goddess of motherhood, pilgrimage, medicine, and weaving. Most of the stone buildings were scavenged by the Spanish invaders for building material; they have been partially restored. Visitors can hire an English-speaking guide at the entrance. Open daily. No admission charge on Sundays (no phone).

PLAYA SAN FRANCISCO On the southern tip of Cozumel, the island's most popular beach is accessible via a paved road, but it's also fun getting there aboard one of the vessels making the *El Zorro* cruise (phone: 987-20831). If your cruise doesn't provide lunch, try the *San Francisco* restaurant (see *Eating Out*).

PUNTA MORENA At this beach on the open Caribbean side of the island, the surf is rough, and swimming can be dangerous. Since the undertow can be tricky, check the currents first (plan to enter the water at one point, exit at another), and never swim alone. There's a sheltered lagoon nearby. If you get hungry, a beachside *palapa* restaurant serves grilled fish and beer.

ISLA MUJERES

EL GARRAFÓN The island's most famous attraction, this underwater national park (whose name means "The Jug") is located at the southern end. Its crystal-clear waters, coral reef, and great snorkeling are renowned. There's also a sea museum with an aquarium and pieces of wrecked historic galleons. The journey from the mainland (usually Cancún) to *El Garrafón* by boat is an adventure in itself—crew members catch fresh fish en route while passengers view schools of astonishingly tame tropical fish and turtles. The park and museum are open daily and charge separate admissions (no phone).

PLAYA NORTE This wide, beautiful beach (just one of many on Isla Mujeres) covers the entire northern end. Although the sunbathing here is fine, swimming is dangerous, and there are no lifeguards.

EXCURSIONS

ISLA CONTOY (CONTOY ISLAND) This undeveloped coral island, 25 miles north of Cancún, is a National Wildlife Reserve populated by gulls, pelicans, petrels, cormorants, herons, and other sea birds whose numbers are, unfortunately, diminishing. It traditionally has been popular with divers, picnickers, and bird watchers. It's also an important migratory point for other birds and an egg-laying spot for sea turtles. *Warning:* If you should happen upon a sea turtle, look, but don't touch! Disturbing these creatures is considered a very serious crime in Mexico, punishable by a long jail sentence. Several companies offer cruises between Cancún and the island (see *Cruises,* below).

PUERTO AVENTURAS About 49 miles (78 km) south of Cancún, this resort area features the largest marina in Mexico, an 18-hole golf course built around several pre-Columbian structures and a couple of ancient cenotes (sinkholes), a tennis club, and two fashionable waterfront hotels. The larger property, *Oasis Marina Mar* (phone: 987-23287 or 987-23376; 800-44-OASIS; fax: 987-23332) has 309 units, a beach, a pool, and two restaurants. A glimpse of the area's maritime history can be seen at the *Pablo Bush Romero Centro de Exploración de Arqueología* Km 98 of Route 307; no phone, but information is available from the *CEDAM* dive center at 987-35129), whose collection includes 18th-century silver goblets, gold coins, and other relics salvaged from the *Matanceros,* a Spanish merchant ship that sank off the coast of Akumal in 1741. The collection is closed Tuesdays; there's no admission charge. For a casual lunch in a safari-like atmosphere, try the *Papaya Republic* (Km 98 of Rte. 307; no phone); for more formal fare, try the nearby *Carlos 'n' Charlie's* (phone: 987-35131), a member of the ubiquitous chain.

AKUMAL AND OTHER COASTAL POINTS Once a private club run by undersea explorers, Akumal (59 miles/94 km south of Cancún) is now considered one of the best snorkeling and diving spots along Mexico's Caribbean coast. The town has two lovely hotels: The 61-room *Club Akumal Caribe* (phone: 987-22532; 800-351-1622 in the US; 95-800-351-1622 toll-free in Mexico) has a dive shop and a restaurant, and cannon recovered from the ancient wrecks are set on its grounds; the 81-room, 11-suite *Akumal Cancún* (phone: 987-22453; 98-842272 or 98-842641 on Cancún) offers water sports, a dive shop, two restaurants, and a disco.

Six miles (10 km) south of Akumal, a sign welcomes you to Chemuyil, a relatively unknown beach (sometimes crowded on weekends) that is about as close to a Paul Gauguin landscape as you can get in Mexico. Amenities here include a lively bar run by the Román family, as well as camping facilities, including 12 tents. At press time, 10 cabañas here that were destroyed in 1995 by Hurricane Roxanne were scheduled to be rebuilt. For more information, write to *Don Lalo Román Fideicomiso* (Xel-Ha, Tulum, QR 77500, México; no phone), the trust that maintains the beach.

Another 4 miles (6 km) south is Xel-Ha, a national park—really a series of lagoons—where you can snorkel. An intense conservation program has restored it to near-pristine beauty, best appreciated on weekdays when the park is less crowded. Across the road is the *Xel-Ha* archaeological zone, operated independently of the national park. The ruins here are interesting, if uninspiring. The main structure, a 10-minute hike over jagged limestone terrain, is the *Temple of the Birds,* where a faint image of Chac, the rain god, and several plumed flamingos can be discerned in the western wall. The park and the ruins are open daily; each has a separate admission charge (no phone).

SIAN KA'AN Beginning about 85 miles (136 km) south of Cancún and some 4 miles (6 km) south of the *Tulum* archaeological site (see *Extra Special*) is a 1.3-million-acre biosphere reserve, with tropical forests, mangrove swamps, palm-rimmed beaches, archaeological ruins, and coral reefs. It's a paradise for bird watchers and crocodile and butterfly lovers. There are two simple hotels on the reserve that cater to the fly-fishing crowd; both are at Boca Paila, about 6 miles (10 km) past the entrance: the pricey *Club de Pesca Boca Paila* lodge (represented by *Frontiers;* PO Box 959, Wexford, PA 15090-0959; phone: 987-21176 on Cozumel; 800-245-1950; book well in advance) and the even pricier *Pez Maya* cabins (no local phone; 305-664-4615 in Florida; 800-327-2880 elsewhere in the US). Unfortunately, the more rustic *palapa* establishments—including our favorite, the *Posada Cuzán*—were destroyed by Hurricane Roxanne in 1995; at press time, none had plans to rebuild. In Punta Allen, which lies some 24 miles (38 km) farther south, meals are available at Candy Guzmán's *Restaurant Candy,* an open-air, flower-filled *palapa*-style eatery on the road from the boat dock to the beach (no phone).

Arrangements can be made with one of the fishermen in Punta Allen to visit *los cayos* (the keys), which are groups of mangroves that lie in the mouth of the Bahía de Ascensión. For guided visits to the reserve, contact the *Amigos de Sian Ka'an* (Association of Friends of Sian Ka'an; Plaza Américas, Suite 50, 5 Av. Cobá, Cancún, QR 77500, México; phone: 98-849583; fax: 98-873080).

EXTRA SPECIAL

About 81 miles (129 km) south of Cancún are the Maya ruins at *Tulum.* On a cliff overlooking the fine white beaches and crystalline blue waters of the Caribbean, the compelling site is well worth the visit. It's open daily; there's no admission charge on Sundays (no phone).

Just south of *Tulum,* a road leads 26 miles (42 km) inland to *Cobá.* Like *Tulum,* it is thought to have been a major trading and religious center. The ruins are open daily; there's no admission charge on Sundays (no phone). For additional details on both sites, see *Mexico's Magnificent Archaeological Heritage* in DIVERSIONS.

Sources and Resources

TOURIST INFORMATION

The *Subsecretaría Estatal de Turismo* (Quintana Roo State Tourist Office) in Cancún is in the *FONATUR* building at Avs. Cobá and Nader (phone: 98-843238; fax: 98-843438); there's also a tourist information booth (Avs. Tulum and Tulipanes, near the *Mercado Ki-Huic;* phone: 98-848073). Both are in Cancún City and are open daily. The *Delegación Estatal de Turismo de Cozumel* (Cozumel Tourist Office) is in the *Plaza del Sol Building* (Av. Rafael E. Melgar and Calle 8; phone: 987-20972); it's closed weekends. There are also information booths at the tourist dock and at the airport; their hours coincide with plane and boat schedules. The *Delegación Estatal de Turismo de Isla Mujeres* (Isla Mujeres Tourist Office; 6 Hidalgo; phone: 988-70316) is closed weekends. Hotel personnel and travel desks are other good sources of information; there's also a toll-free, 24-hour tourist-information hotline (phone: 91-800-90392).

LOCAL COVERAGE *The News* and the *Mexico City Times,* both English-language dailies, are flown in from Mexico City. The best sources of tourist information in English on Cancún are a pocket-size, biannual booklet, *Cancún,* handed out free at the airport, and the quarterly *Cancún* magazine, found in many hotel rooms and on sale around town. On Cozumel, buy the English-language *Cozumel in One Day* or the *Blue Guide to Cozumel.* On Isla Mujeres, the English-language *Islander* tells you what's going on. In addition, we immodestly suggest that you pick up a copy of *Birnbaum's Cancún, Cozumel & Isla Mujeres 1997* (HarperCollins; $12.50).

TELEPHONE The city code for Cancún is 98; the city code for Cozumel and Isla Mujeres is 987. When calling from anywhere on Cancún, Cozumel, or Isla Mujeres to any other location on Cancún, Cozumel, or Isla Mujeres, simply dial the number without the city code. (For your information, however, all telephone numbers in this chapter do include city codes.) *Note:* Mexico's telephone company has embarked on a major expansion project that involves changing telephone numbers in many areas of the country. At press time, all numbers listed in this chapter were correct. If you have any difficulties reaching attractions listed here, contact the local tourist office.

CLIMATE AND CLOTHES Cancún boasts 200 rain-free days yearly and an average temperature of 80F (27C). Still, it can be chilly at night. Rain is most likely from mid-May to mid-June and in September. Dress is elegant but informal. Cozumel and Isla Mujeres are more casual than Cancún.

GETTING AROUND

BUS Cancún probably has the best municipal bus service in Mexico. Routes follow a straight line, and the vehicles are seldom crowded. Inexpensive vans that depart promptly and handle all luggage travel between the airport and hotels. From 6 AM to midnight, a flock of buses runs between Cancún City and the island's hotels and shopping area; the fare is 3 pesos (about 40¢ at press time). *FONATUR* buses—with reclining seats and air conditioning—travel a similar route; the cost is 5 pesos (about 65¢ at press time). *FONATUR* buses also go north to Puerto Juárez, where ferries leave for Isla Mujeres. *Autotransportes del Caribe* (*ADC;* phone: 98-841378) and *Autotransportes del Oriente* (*ADO;* phone: 98-843301) offer four departures daily from the downtown depot (Avs. Tulum and Uxmal) for Chetumal. Luxury *Expreso de Oriente* (phone: 98-234980) buses leave the depot daily for *Chichén Itzá,* Mérida, Playa del Carmen, *Tulum,* and other major Yucatán destinations.

CAR RENTAL Several agencies in Cancún City offer rental cars and jeeps: *Avis* (phone: 98-830803 or 98-860002); *Dollar* (phone: 98-844101 or 98-860165); *Econo-Rent* (phone: 98-841826); *Kokai Rent a Car* (phone: 98-843643); and *Monterrey Rent* (phone: 98-847843 or 98-860239). On Cozumel, *Rentadora Cozumel* (phone: 987-21120) rents jeeps—the best bet for local roads. There are no car rental agencies on Isla Mujeres.

CRUISES Numerous voyages depart from Cancún and nearby points. If you think getting there is half the fun, you might opt for a leisurely crossing to Isla Mujeres on the *Tropical Cruiser* (phone: 98-831488), which includes a full-day tour complete with a buffet lunch, soft drinks, a musical show, and a snorkeling trip to *El Garrafón*. It sails Mondays through Saturdays at 10 AM from *Playa Langosta Dock* in Cancún. The same company operates the *Tropical Cruiser Morning Express,* whose trips include snorkeling and a hearty buffet meal. Among the other vessels that cruise to Isla Mujeres from Cancún are the *Aqua Quin* trimaran (phone: 98-831883), which offers daily sails with a no-frills package of snacks and snorkeling; and the *Nautibus I and II* floating submarines (phone: 98-833552), which enable passengers to view underwater flora and fauna while comfortably seated inside a windowed keel. The more expensive *Atlantis* (phone: 98-833021) submarine tours submerge completely to explore natural coral reefs and sunken ships.

The *Cancún Queen* (phone: 98-852288 or 98-833007) paddle wheel steamer offers daytime cruises and steak-and-lobster dinner cruises from *AquaWorld* (see *Boating,* below) across Laguna Nichupté through a mangrove jungle. The *Dolphin Express* (phone: 09-831488) offers cruises that include snorkeling and a chance to see a dolphin show at the *Dolphin Discovery* facility in Pirates Village on Isla Mujeres. The *Galleon of Captain Hook* (phone: 98-833737) takes guests from the Embarcadero pier at Km 4.5 of Paseo Kukulcán to Isla Mujeres for daytime beach parties and dinner cruises with live entertainment; later in the evening it converts into a floating disco.

If you want to make an excursion from Cancún to Cozumel, *Aviomar* (phone: 98-846433; fax: 98-846935) offers an "Escape to Cozumel" tour via bus and water jet; it leaves Cancún's *Playa Linda Pier* daily at 9 AM. The day includes sightseeing, swimming, refreshments, and lunch on the beach. If you're already on Cozumel and want to go to Playa San Francisco—the best beach on the island, at the southern tip—try the *El Zorro* cruise (phone: 987-20831).

Cruises leave from Cancún and Isla Mujeres for the approximately two-and-a-half-hour journey to Isla Contoy, which is about 25 miles (40 km) north of Cancún. During the excursion, you'll have the opportunity to snorkel in the calm waters, or perhaps try your hand at fishing (equipment can be rented). The *Contoy II* (phone: 98-871862 or 98-871909 on Cancún) runs all-day trips to the island from the *Playa Linda Pier* in Cancún. The cruises, which include lunch, soft drinks, and alcohol, depart Mondays through Saturdays at 9 AM. The *Cooperativa Transporte Turística* (phone: 987-70274 on Isla Mujeres) offers prearranged package tours of Isla Contoy that leave daily at 9 AM from the waterfront docks on Isla Mujeres; the cost includes a light breakfast, lunch, and snorkeling equipment.

There are also many private boats, ranging in size from tiny fishing launches to seagoing 40-footers, which can be chartered for a fee. Check with your hotel travel desk for details (also see *Boating*).

FERRY Fifteen passenger ferries depart daily from a dock in Puerto Juárez (about 5 miles/8 km north of Cancún City) for Isla Mujeres every half-hour from 6 AM to 8:30 PM. Seven car ferries run by *Transportes Turísticos Magaña* (no phone) leave daily from Punta Sam (about 1 mile/1.6 km north of Puerto Juárez) for Isla Mujeres from 7:15 AM to 10 PM. Either way, it's a great day or overnight trip. The fares are reasonable, and the crossing takes 20 to 30 minutes. You don't need to make a reservation or buy tickets in advance; just go to Puerto Juárez or Punta Sam and get on the first boat that has room.

Billed as the world's largest water jets, the *México I, II and III* (phone: 987-21508 or 987-21588 in Cozumel) make a Playa del Carmen–Cozumel round trip 15 times daily. The older, slower *Cozumeleño* also ferries passengers to Cozumel from Playa del Carmen 8 times daily for about the same price. The crossing takes about 40 minutes; ferries leave every half hour from 5:30 AM to 7:30 PM. Car ferries leave for Cozumel from Puerto Morelos, but the wait is often quite long, with preference given to trucks and commercial transports, and the trip takes about three hours. Hiring a private fishing boat to take you to Cozumel is not a good idea, because the crossing can be fairly rough; however, the ride to Isla Mujeres is much calmer, and a trip on a fishing boat—generally lighter than a ferry—can be pleasant. Members of the local fishing cooperative wait for potential passengers at the docks in Puerto Juárez; bargain hard.

MOPED Small motorbikes are an easy way to get around and are available at many Cancún hotels, including the *Casa Maya* and the *Krystal Cancún* (see *Checking In*). On Cozumel, rent mopeds or bicycles at *Rentadora Cozumel* (172 Av. 10 Sur; phone: 987-21120 or 987-21503) or at the southern end of San Miguel at the *Plaza las Glorias* hotel (see *Checking In*). On Isla Mujeres, motorbikes give you maximum mobility at a low price; they're available from *Rent Me* (Av. Juárez at Calle Morelos, about 50 paces from the ferry dock; no phone).

TAXI Small green-and-white cabs are available at reasonable fares, according to zone, in the Cancún area. Taxis are abundant and usually available at all the island's hotels; if not, a doorman or bellman will call one quickly. In Cancún City there is a taxi stand on Avenida Tulum. On both Cozumel and Isla Mujeres, bright red taxis cluster around the ferry docks.

TOURS There are dozens of tour operators on Cancún, all of them with hotel offices on the island. Arrange excursions directly or through hotel travel desks. Boat, bus, and automobile tours are available.

SPECIAL EVENTS

Cozumel's annual *Carnaval* takes place during the period immediately preceding *Miércoles de Ceniza* (Ash Wednesday), which heralds the beginning of *Cuaresma* (Lent). The annual week-long *Regata del Sol al Sol,* organized by the *Isla Mujeres Yacht Club,* begins in St. Petersburg, Florida, and finishes at Isla Mujeres in April or May. The yearly spring *Regata Amigos*— which circles Isla Mujeres—takes place after the *Regata del Sol al Sol.* Every May, Cancún hosts an *International Jazz Festival.* The annual *Hacienda del Mar Sailfish Tournament,* held on Cozumel in May, attracts sports enthusiasts from all over. On the first day of spring and fall, more than 100,000 spectators gather at *Chichén Itzá* to watch an amazing phenomenon: Light and shadows strike *El Castillo* pyramid in such a manner that the snake god Kukulcán appears to be slithering down the side. The *Feria de Cancún* (Cancún Fair) takes place in November, with bullfights, cockfights, dances, and shows.

SHOPPING

Goods and handicrafts from all over Mexico (and the world) are sold in Cancún. The big and bustling *Mercado Ki-Huic* (Av. Tulum near Av. Cobá) in Cancún City is the municipal crafts market, featuring some 40-plus stalls with an occasional find but generally not the best prices in town. In the Hotel Zone, some of the most elegant shops can be found at the many shopping centers, all along Paseo Kukulcán: *Flamingo Plaza, Plaza la Fiesta, Plaza Kukulcán, La Mansión–Costa Blanca, Mayfair, El Parián, Plaza Caracol, Plaza Lagunas, Plaza Náutilus* and *Plaza Terramar. El Zócalo* (on Alcatraces, between Gladiolas and Tulipanes), an outdoor shopping center on the west side of the *zócalo* in downtown Cancún, is another fun place to shop.

On Cozumel, the work of some 200 first-rate Mexican artists is displayed and sold at *Bazar Cozumel* (Av. Juárez).

In a place as tiny as Isla Mujeres, it's hard not to hit every stall or stand that has something of interest to sell. Unless you are looking for seashell necklaces or hand-dyed T-shirts, it's probably better to make the trek to Cancún, where the selection is bigger and the prices are sometimes better. The one major exception—*Rachat & Romé*'s beautifully crafted jewelry.

In many places, shoppers are expected to bargain, which means a buyer really should know some basic Spanish, even if it's just a few numbers (though you can also use a pencil and paper to write out price offers). Don't bargain in shops that have the sign *"precios fijos"* (fixed prices), in government shops (often called *Artes Populares*), or in hotel shops.

Shops on all three islands generally are open daily from 10 AM to 2 PM and from 4 to 7 PM; most major stores on Cancún stay open until 9 PM. Hotel shops are generally open daily from 10 AM to 8 PM.

Visiting shoppers will notice that itinerant vendors—although technically outlawed in this part of Mexico—still manage to materialize on almost every beach and street. They can be persistent, but if you're not interested in their wares, respond with a firm "no."

CANCÚN

Anakena Maya temple rubbings, pre-Columbian reproductions, and unique jewelry. *El Parián* (phone: 98-830539).

Artland Rubbings, batik items, paintings, and jewelry, all inspired by Maya designs. *Plaza Terramar* (phone: 98-831562).

La Casita Arts, crafts, decorative items, leather, jewelry, and Mexican-inspired clothing. 115 Av. Tulum, Cancún City (phone: 98-841468).

Los Castillo Jewelry and art objects crafted from sterling silver and semi-precious stones by one of Taxco's best jewelers. *Flamingo Plaza* (phone: 98-850882).

Chantal Select pieces of hand-crafted silver jewelry. The shop has a stunning African motif. *Plaza Caracol* (phone: 98-830450).

Galerías Tableware with beautifully painted patterns, carved marble knickknacks, and chess sets. *Plaza Caracol* (phone: 98-830914).

Onyx and Handicrafts Good quality and prices for onyx pieces and other handicrafts. *Plaza Náutilus* (phone: 98-830699).

Ronay One of Mexico's most prestigious jewelers, specializing in gold designs. *Plaza Caracol* (phone: 98-831261).

Sebastián The very finest in designer silver jewelry. *Plaza Caracol* (phone: 98-831815) and *Plaza Náutilus* (phone: 98-831949).

Sybele High-quality imports from around the world, ranging from men's suits and women's lingerie to leather briefcases and fine perfume. 109 Av. Tulum, Cancún City (phone: 98-841181), and *Plaza Caracol* (phone: 98-831738).

Tane Silver and vermeil jewelry, tableware, and art objects—many with traditional pre-Hispanic designs. Others are antique reproductions. There are branches of this national chain in the *Camino Real* (phone: 98-830200) and *Hyatt Regency* (phone: 98-831349) hotels.

Xcaret An unusual and varied selection of some of the very best of Mexico's handicrafts—ceramics, textiles, papier-mâché—at reasonable prices. *Flamingo Plaza* (phone: 98-833256).

COZUMEL
All shops listed below are in San Miguel.

La Casita The parent of the Cancún store and the source of more smashing Mexican resort clothes, as well as Sergio Bustamante's imaginative animal and bird sculptures. Av. Rafael E. Melgar (phone: 987-20198).

Pama High-quality, duty-free imports, from jewelry and perfume to silk ties and women's fashions. 9 Av. Rafael E. Melgar (phone: 987-20090).

Plaza del Sol A nest of nearly a dozen art, crafts, jewelry, and import boutiques including *Los Cinco Soles,* which has a good selection of handicrafts from throughout Mexico. Av. Rafael E. Melgar at Calle 8 (no phone).

ISLA MUJERES

La Bahía Here's an upscale selection of beachwear, plus diving gear for rent. Near the ferry dock (no phone).

Rachat & Romé Outstanding jewelry designed and crafted by the friendly Cuban shop owner. In the flamingo-colored building steps from the ferry dock, at Av. Rueda Medina and Calle Morelos (phone: 987-70250).

SPORTS

BICYCLING A serpentine 6-mile path of pink brick bordered by garden plants and the seashore winds through Cancún, with *palapa*-topped rest stops along the way. In Cancún, rent bikes at the *Cancún* (two locations: *Plaza las Glorias,* at Km 3.5 of Paseo Kukulcán, and the *Sierra Cancún; see Checking In;* phone for both: 98-843299). On Cozumel, try *Rentadora Cozumel;* on Isla Mujeres, *Rent Me.* (See "Moped" in *Getting Around,* above, for both.)

BOATING Craft large and small, power and sail, crewed and uncrewed, are available on Cancún. Make arrangements at any hotel travel desk; at the *Royal Yacht Club* (Km 16.5 of Paseo Kukulcán; phone: 98-852360 or 98-852930); at *Marina Aqua Ray* (Km 10.5 of Paseo Kukulcán; phone: 98-833007 or 98-831763); *AquaWorld* (Km 15.2 of Paseo Kukulcán; phone: 98-852288 or 98-833007); or at the marinas of the *Camino Real, Club Lagoon,* or *Presidente Inter-Continental* hotels (see *Checking In*).

BULLFIGHTS Cancún's bullring, the *Plaza de Toros* (Av. Bonampak and Calle Sayil, in the south of Cancún City; phone: 98-848372) occasionally attracts major matadors. Corridas are held Wednesdays at 3:30 PM. The modern, three-tiered arena has a seating capacity of 6,000 and provides ample parking. Tickets are expensive—about 160 pesos (about $21) per person, compared to some 20 pesos (about $2.60) per person in Mérida.

FISHING Sailfish, bonito, and dorado (mahimahi) are in season from March through July; bluefin tuna in May; wahoo and kingfish, May through September; white marlin, April through May; and barracuda, red snapper, grouper, and mackerel, year-round. In Cancún, boats are available at *Aqua Tours* (Km 6.5 of Paseo Kukulcán; phone: 98-830227 or 98-830400), *Club Lagoon* (see *Checking In*), *Marina del Rey* (Km 15.5 of Paseo Kukulcán; phone: 98-831748), and the *Royal Yacht Club* (see *Boating,* above). Deep-sea charters (for up to six people), including crew, tackle, and lunch, are available, as are small outboards.

To charter boats on Cozumel, try *Aquarius Travel* (2 Calle 3 Sur; phone: 987-21092) or *Cozumel Angler's* 1 mile (1.6 km) south of town, at the *Club Náutico* (phone: 987-20118 or 987-21113). Here again, hotels can make all the arrangements. On Isla Mujeres, the *Cooperativa Transporte Turística* and *México Divers* (both at Av. Rueda Medina; phone: 987-70714) arrange four-person trips.

GOLF As befits a world class resort, Cancún can claim its own "designer" course.

TOP TEE-OFF SPOT

Club de Golf Cancún Though this famous club changed its name in the mid-1990s, everyone still calls it *Pok-Ta-Pok* (which means "stroke-by-stroke" in Maya). An 18-hole, par 72, Robert Trent Jones Jr.

course located on a small island in Laguna Nichupté, it offers gently rolling fairways bordered by palms, with the Caribbean breeze making play comfortable throughout the day. On the premises are a pro shop, a bar, and a restaurant. The club is open daily from 6 AM, and reservations are a must. The pro is Felipe Galindo; the director, Gustavo Escalante (phone: 98-831230).

There's also an 18-hole championship course at the *Caesar Park Beach and Golf Resort* (see *Checking In*). Less daunting nearby courses are the nine-hole course at the *Oasis* hotel and the 18-hole facility at the *Meliá Cancún* (see *Checking In*); both courses are open to non-guests for a fee. There's an extraordinary 18-hole course 61 miles (98 km) down the coast at Puerto Aventuras (Km 269.5 of Carretera Chetumal; phone: 987-22211 or 987-22233). It was designed by Tommy Lehman, who incorporated natural cenotes (sinkholes) and ancient Maya ruins into the layout.

HORSEBACK RIDING Rancho Loma Bonita (Km 49 of Rte. 307, between Puerto Morelos and Playa del Carmen; phone: 98-875465 or 875423) escorts riders through the jungle daily at 8 and 10:30 AM and 1:30 PM.

JET SKIING Laguna Nichupté is great for this water sport, which requires a minimum of learning time. Jet skis are available at *Marina Aqua Ray, AquaWorld,* and the *Royal Yacht Club* (see *Boating,* above, for all three).

SCUBA AND SNORKELING The clear, warm lagoons of the area teem with tropical fish and intricate, colorful coral deposits.

World famous for its exquisitely clear water and its proximity to Palancar Reef, Cozumel takes the diving honors among scubaphiles. But beware: Currents are strong on Cozumel. Don't dive without a guide. There are several dive shops along the waterfront in San Miguel on Cozumel, including *Aqua Safari* (phone: 987-20101), *Big Blue* (phone: 987-20396), *Dive House* (phone: 987-21953), and *Neptuno Divers* (phone: 987-20999). In addition, several shops based at local hotels—including *Casa del Mar* (located next to the hotel of the same name; phone: 987-21900), *Del Mar Aquatics* (at *La Ceiba* hotel), *Viajes y Deportes de Cozumel* (in the *Presidente Inter-Continental Cozumel*), and the dive shop at the *Plaza las Glorias* hostelry (see *Checking In* for details on hotels)—offer rental equipment, instruction, and dive trips to Palancar. Most hotels also have diving facilities at somewhat higher rates, but you may feel that the convenience is worth the added cost. Scuba classes range from pool instruction (about three hours) to four- or five-day seminars with a certified instructor that include theory, shallow shore dives, a boat dive to a shallow reef, and a full boat dive to Palancar Reef. Rent underwater cameras at *Cozumel Images* at the *Casa del Mar* hotel (on the waterfront; phone: 987-21944).

Isla Mujeres's transparent waters, coral reefs, and lagoons also are renowned among divers the world over. Rent equipment at *La Bahía* (see

Shopping) or the *Cooperativa Transporte Turística* (see *Fishing*), which also offers boats.

Cancún is perfectly situated for swimming and diving amid coral reefs, fish, and turtles. The waters change color from turquoise to indigo to emerald to tourmaline. Arrange diving trips and equipment rental through your hotel, *Aqua Tours* (see *Fishing*), or *Scuba Cancún* (Km 5.5 of Paseo Kukulcán, across from the *Casa Maya* hotel; phone: 98-831011).

Farther south along the coast, but worth the drive, are *Xcaret* and Akumal (see below).

BEST DEPTHS

Akumal With its large barrier reef, Akumal (18 miles/29 km south of Playa del Carmen) is a favored diving venue. The best diving spots are at *Club Akumal Caribe* and the *Akumal Cancún.* The waters have 200-foot visibility and stay at about body temperature all year. At 80 to 100 feet, divers can observe magnificent coral gardens, fish, and remnants of 15th-century shipwrecks. The teaching staff of the *Club Akumal Caribe* offers excellent instruction, and the club rents all kinds of diving equipment. (Also see *Special Places.*)

Punta Nizuc, Cancún The best scuba and snorkeling place on Cancún is in the waters off its southern point, Punta Nizuc. The government is towing shipwrecks from the 1988 hurricane here to create an artificial reef that will alleviate overcrowding of the natural coral reef.

Laguna Chankanab, Cozumel Another good spot, it swarms with reef fish. About ¼ mile to the north and south of the lagoon, elkhorn coral and a variety of tropical fish are visible. (Also see *Special Places.*)

Palancar Reef, Cozumel Off the southern tip of Cozumel, Palancar Reef is the second-largest coral atoll in the world and the largest in the Western Hemisphere, offering spectacular diving. Underwater visibility ranges up to 250 feet; the diving here is particularly good May through August.

Punta Paraíso (Paradise Point), Cozumel Off the beach at *La Ceiba* hotel (probably the best equipped for divers; see *Checking In*) lies the hulk of a C-46 aircraft that "crashed" here in the movie *Cyclone.* Moonlight diving escapades through the fuselage of this wrecked plane, which settled amid clusters of coral, are a celebrated nocturnal event.

El Garrafón, Isla Mujeres At the southern end of the island, this underwater national park has crystal-clear waters and lovely coral gardens. (Also see *Special Places.*)

Xcaret Inlet Just south of Playa del Carmen, about 50 miles (80 km) south of Cancún, this ecological park (pronounced Shka-*ret*) is a happy blend of ancient ruins and sun-kissed (often crowded) beach with an extra helping of cenotes (sinkholes) and underwater caves. A penned-in lagoon populated by dolphins offers visitors the opportunity to swim with nature's most intelligent aquatic mammals. However, only a limited number of people per day can do this, and you have to sign up on the spot, so make sure you're there right at 8:30 AM, when the gates open. Intrepid explorers also can swim along a "river" of sea water through a series of caves (the park provides life jackets, and snorkels and fins can be rented as well). *Xcaret* is open daily; there's one charge for the beach and an additional charge to swim with the dolphins (phone: 98-830654 or 98-830743).

There are no hotels at *Xcaret,* but if you bring your own sleeping bag, you can camp out near the ruins for a fee. There are extremely clean restrooms and shower facilities on the grounds.

SWIMMING AND SUNNING Besides those strands mentioned in *Special Places,* Cozumel features scores of beautiful, nearly deserted beaches that can be "discovered" by following dirt paths on either side of the island. Playa Chen Río, on the southern end of the Caribbean side, is protected from unpredictable, turbulent Caribbean currents by a ledge of coral that juts into the sea. Playa Punta Molas, on the northern end of the island, is accessible by boat or jeep and offers a pleasant day's journey. Many of the island's beaches are shaped into distinctive coves. Finally, don't overlook Playa del Carmen, the charming port town that serves as the departure point for the ferries to Cozumel. For details, see *Best Beaches off the Beaten Path* in DIVERSIONS and *The Yucatán Peninsula* in DIRECTIONS.

TENNIS Cancún and Cozumel are ideal tennis destinations, as many major hotels offer tennis facilities. On Cancún, there are courts at the *Aristos, Caesar Park Beach and Golf Resort, Calinda Beach Cancún, Casa Maya, Continental Villas Plaza, Fiesta Americana Condesa, Fiesta Americana Coral Beach, Hyatt Cancún Caribe, Krystal Cancún, Marriott Casa Magna, Meliá Cancún, Oasis, Presidente Inter-Continental, Sheraton Cancún* and *Villas Tacul* hotels and at the *Club de Golf Cancún* (see *Golf,* above; phone: 98-830871). (See *Checking In* for all hotels mentioned in this section.)

On Cozumel, courts are available at *La Ceiba, Club Cozumel Caribe,* the *Fiesta Americana Sol Caribe,* the *Fiesta Inn,* the *Holiday Inn Cozumel Reef,* the *Meliá Mayan Peradisus* the *Presidente Inter-Continental Cozumel,* and the *Villablanca* hotels. No courts are available on Isla Mujeres.

WATER SKIING Laguna Nichupté—behind the island of Cancún—is the ideal place to learn or perfect this exhilarating sport. Make arrangements at any island hotel, *Marina Aqua Ray* (see *Boating,* above), or at *Marina del Rey* (see *Fishing,* above).

WINDSURFING Lessons are available at several Cancún hotels, including the *Club Lagoon* (see *Checking In*). Boards are available for rent; several places offer weekly rates that include lessons. There are regattas Sundays at *Club Cancún* (Km 4.5 of Paseo Kukulcán; phone: 98-830855), a condominium complex with a private marina.

NIGHTCLUBS AND NIGHTLIFE

Reigning disco favorites are easily discernible by the crowds gathering outside before opening time (around 10 PM). Current hot spots are *La Boom* (Km 3.5 of Paseo Kukulcán ; phone: 98-831372); *Dady'O* and the adjoining *Dady Rock* (near the *Centro de Convenciones,* Km 9.5 of Paseo Kukulcán; phone: 98-833333); *Christine* at the *Krystal Cancún; Planet Hollywood* (in the *Flamingo Plaza* shopping center; phone: 98-850723) and the *Hard Rock Café* (phone: 98-832024) at the *Plaza Lagunas* shopping center. (See *Checking In* for details on hotels listed in this section.) *Carlos 'n' Charlie's* (on the marina; phone: 98-830846) is a good place for food, drink, dancing, and meeting people; it's open until midnight. *Batachá Tropical* in the *Miramar Misión* hotel (Km 10 of Paseo Kukulcán; phone: 98-831755) is a swinging disco that features live salsa music. *Daphny's* at the *Sheraton Cancún* is a popular video bar with live and taped music for dancing. *Sixties,* in the *Marriott Casa Magna,* plays dance music from the 1950s, 1960s, and 1970s. The *Camino Real* offers a nightly cabaret of Cuban music and dance. And be sure to try the world-famous hurricane cocktail (served in a 24-ounce glass) at *Pat O'Brien's Bar* (phone: 98-830418 or 98-830832) on Paseo Kukulcán across from the *Flamingo* hotel.

If you'd rather gamble the night away, there's nightly pari-mutuel betting on jai alai at *Jai Alai Cancún* (Km 4.5 of Paseo Kukulcán; phone: 98-833910 or 98-833916). On the same premises, *Super Book Cancún* (phone: 98-390004) is open 24 hours a day for off-track betting on horse races and other televised sports.

You can't miss the garishly painted *México Mágico* theme park (Km 12 of Paseo Kukulcán; phone: 98-834980), one of the few options in Cancún for family entertainment. Starting at 6 PM,, it offers six buffet dinner-theaters, in both English and Spanish, and an equal number of non-dinner shows. Each focuses on a different culture (Mexican fiesta, Italian opera, and so on), and features costumed dancers lip-synching to popular American and Mexican tunes. There are a number of dinner cruise ships to choose from, including the paddle wheeler *Cancún Queen* and the *Galleon of Captain Hook* (see *Cruises,* above), and the *Caribbean Carnaval Night Cruise* (phone: 98-843760), leaving from the *Fat Tuesday* dock at Playa Tortugas, Km 6.5 of Paseo Kukulcán. Without a doubt, however, the classiest act on the Mexican Caribbean waters is the *Columbus* (phone: 98-831488 or 98-833268), a motorized replica of a 15th-century Spanish galleon that departs the *Royal Yacht Club* each day at sunset and sails the lagoon. A steak-and-lobster dinner is included in the price.

A must-see is the *Ballet Folklórico de Cancún* at the *Centro de Convenciones,* presented nightly at 8 PM. Tickets include dinner and a complimentary cocktail. A torchlit beach, a delicious buffet, and exotic drinks make for a romantic evening at the *Hyatt Cancún Caribe*'s "Mexican Night," which takes place Mondays, Wednesdays, Fridays, and Saturdays at 7 PM. The *Sheraton Cancún* hosts a similar event Wednesdays at 7:30 PM; *Plaza las Glorias* offers one Tuesdays. There is a flamenco dinner show at *Gypsy's* (see *Eating Out*), with after-dinner dancing by the pier.

On Cozumel, *Scaramouche* (downtown, on Av. Rafael E. Melgar near Av. Dr. A. Rosario Salas; no phone) is lively and attempts sophistication. *Neptuno* (next to the *Acuario* restaurant on Av. Rafael E. Melgar; phone: 987-21537) also is popular.

Favorites on Isla Mujeres include *Jimbo's* (Av. Rueda Medina at Playa Norte; no phone), for salsa and reggae, and romantic *La Peña* (5 Calle Guerrero; no phone), which features live music and candlelight. Beach parties and night cruises complete the after-dark scene here.

Note: As is often the case in crowded discos and dance clubs, drinks may sometimes be watered and waiters may "forget" to bring you your change. Be insistent. In addition, beware of the *coscorrón* (literally "head-knocker"), also known as a "slammer" or a "muppet." Half tequila and half Sprite, it's blended in a covered shot glass by a couple of strong raps on the imbiber's table or head. It's usually made with the lowest-grade tequila on the market. Instead, try your tequila the traditional way, with a slice of lime and a lick of salt, or with *sangrita,* the traditional Mexican chaser made from orange juice and chilies. And make sure the tequila is a top-quality label, such as Sauza.

RED ALERT

Nearly every city in Mexico—except Mexico City—has a *zona de tolerancia.* Cancún's "tolerance zone," or red-light district, is just north of Cancún City, and it does a thriving business. The most obvious deterrent to sampling the wares these days is the threat of AIDS (*SIDA* in Spanish) and other sexually transmitted diseases. Men should bear in mind that many of the seemingly charming young girls are in fact young men in drag whose objective is to liberate their "clients" of cash and other valuables.

Best in Town

CHECKING IN

Cancún's hotels are relatively new, aspire to be lavish, and boast some of the highest prices in Mexico. Many of the hotels on the island fall within an area along Paseo Kukulcán known as the Hotel Zone. Travelers on a budget can find less costly accommodations in Cancún City, away from the major beaches. During high season (December through early May), expect to pay $150 to $300 per day for a double room in a very expensive hotel (the highest price would be for a two-bedroom villa); $80 to $150 in an expensive one; $40 to $75 in a moderate place; and $35 or less in an inexpensive one. Prices drop as much as 50% during the summer months. Although it has more than 24,000 hotel rooms, Cancún really does not have enough accommodations to meet the demand during the winter months, so it is best to go only with a confirmed, prepaid reservation.

Cozumel's more luxurious hotels are in either the North Zone or the South Zone, above and below the town of San Miguel. The in-town hostelries (most have neither beach nor pool) appeal most to budget travelers. Hotel prices on Cozumel are comparable to those on Cancún, and, as on Cancún, we recommend that you arrive with a confirmed reservation. Most hotel rates on Isla Mujeres fall into our moderate and inexpensive categories. All hotels listed have air conditioning and private baths unless otherwise indicated; virtually all hotels have satellite TV with remote control. *Note:* Parking can be a problem at some hotels.

We begin with our favorite (and rather pricey) haven, followed by recommended hotels, listed alphabetically by location and price category.

A SPECIAL HAVEN

Camino Real A ritzy pleasure palace, it has 381 rooms situated in two beautiful buildings, both affording magnificent views of the Caribbean. The older, main structure (designed by Ricardo Legoretta) reflects Maya architecture. The newer *Camino Real Beach Club Room* building offers 67 deluxe guestrooms and 18 suites, all with such amenities as concierge service, complimentary continental breakfast, and afternoon tea. All rooms have balconies and are decorated in a colorful Mexican design. A freshwater pool with a swim-up bar, a saltwater lagoon, three restaurants (including *Calypso;* see *Eating Out*), tennis courts, and plenty of water sports make this hotel one of the best around. On Punta Cancún, the northeast tip of the island (phone: 98-830100; 800-7-CAMINO in the US; 800-90123 in Mexico; fax: 98-831730).

CANCÚN

VERY EXPENSIVE

Caesar Park Beach and Golf Resort Run by the Westin group, this immense luxury property is sited on 240 well-landscaped acres. The main building is a modern, somewhat pyramidal structure containing 448 rooms and suites, an atrium lounge with a waterfall, a restaurant, a health club, and even a shopping mall. Nearby, the deluxe *Royal Beach Club* offers 80 rooms and two suites. All guestrooms have marble baths, private balconies with panoramic Caribbean views, mini-bars, and in-room safes; members of the *Royal Beach Club* receive complimentary continental breakfast and evening cocktails. A narrow white-sand beach (though the surf is rough for swimming), seven pools, an open-air eatery featuring seafood dishes and Japanese specialties, two lighted tennis courts, and an 18-hole championship golf course all combine to make this a true resort. Km 17 of Paseo Kukulcán (phone: 98-818000; 800-228-3000 in the US; 800-90223 in Mexico; fax: 98-818080).

Continental Villas Plaza Splendid is the only way to describe this 626-suite coral-toned complex that sprawls over seven blocks of oceanfront. Most rooms command a majestic view of the Caribbean; many also boast a private balcony with Jacuzzi. Among the amenities are seven restaurants, three pools, two tennis courts, and a private marina. Km 11 of Paseo Kukulcán (phone: 98-831022 or 98-851444; 800-88-CONTI; fax: 98-832270).

Fiesta Americana Condesa Each of its three towers has its own atrium lounge covered by a glass, *palapa*-shaped roof. The decor is mostly rattan complemented by fresh, vivid colors. There are 502 rooms—including 27 suites with Jacuzzis on private terraces—plus a split-level pool with a 66-foot waterfall, three indoor tennis courts (all air conditioned), a jogging track, a spa, a small beach, five restaurants, and a lobby bar where live music is played in the evenings. Km 15.5 of Paseo Kukulcán (phone: 98-851000; 800-FIESTA-1 in the US; 800-50450 in Mexico; fax: 98-851800).

Fiesta Americana Coral Beach Designed in Mediterranean style with a definite calypso accent, this super-luxurious, massive flamingo-pink complex is considered by many to be a true Mexican masterpiece. There are several restaurants and bars, a nightclub, a huge pool, tennis courts, and a gym. Km 8.5 of Paseo Kukulcán (phone: 98-832900; 800-FIESTA-1 in the US; 800-50450 in Mexico; fax: 98-833084).

Hyatt Cancún Caribe A graceful white arc a short walk from the *Centro de Convenciones,* this 198-room resort has 39 villas; several restaurants, including the superb *Blue Bayou* (see *Eating Out*); tennis courts; three pools; a Jacuzzi; water sports; and an art gallery in the lobby. There are also gardens spread out over 10 acres. Km 8.5 of Paseo Kukulcán (phone: 98-830044; 800-233-1234 in the US; 800-00500 in Mexico; fax: 98-831514).

Hyatt Regency Beautifully housed under a glass atrium, this hotel has 300 rooms, all with ocean views. There's also a pool, three bars, and three restaurants (the best is *Scampi;* see *Eating Out*). Paseo Kukulcán, on the northern tip of the island (phone: 98-831234; 800-233-1234 in the US; 800-00500 in Mexico; fax: 98-831349).

Krystal Cancún With lush, thick greenery outside and in, it offers 316 rooms and suites, tennis, and five fine restaurants (our favorites are *Bogart's* and

Hacienda 'el Mortero; see *Eating Out* for both). Km 9 of Paseo Kukulcán, on the northern tip of the island (phone: 98-831133; 800-231-9860; fax: 98-831790).

Marriott Casa Magna This six-story hostelry of contemporary design is stunningly decorated with Mexican textures and colors. All 450 rooms have balconies affording a view of either the Caribbean or the lagoon. On the premises are four restaurants, including a Japanese steakhouse; a nightclub; a pool; a Jacuzzi; and two lighted tennis courts. Km 14.5 of Paseo Kukulcán (phone: 98-852000; 800-228-9290 in the US; 800-90088 in Mexico; fax: 98-851731).

Meliá Cancún With a waterfall cascading over part of its entrance, this 450-unit marble-and-glass complex has a huge central atrium that looks and, unfortunately, *feels* like a tropical jungle. There is a full-service spa with exercise classes, massage, facials, and other beauty treatments. Other facilities include four restaurants, five bars, two pools, three tennis courts, and a small, par 54, 18-hole golf course. Km 15 of Paseo Kukulcán (phone: 98-851160; 800-336-3542; fax: 98-851263).

Meliá Turquesa A giant white pyramid sloping down to the beach, it offers 446 rooms decorated in soft colors and equipped with mini-bars and safe-deposit boxes. There also are two restaurants, three bars, a coffee shop, and two lighted tennis courts. Km 12 of Paseo Kukulcán (phone: 98-832544; 800-336-3542; fax: 98-851241).

Oasis Built in the tradition of an ancient Maya city, this 1,000-room complex of angled structures offers seven restaurants, nine bars, four tennis courts, a nine-hole golf course, and the longest swimming pool (nearly a third of a mile) in Cancún. Km 15 of Paseo Kukulcán (phone: 98-850867; 800-44-OASIS; fax: 98-833486).

Omni All 334 rooms here have large terraces; there also are 35 suites and 27 villas. Facilities include eight restaurants, bars, a gameroom, two lighted tennis courts, and a health center. There's not much of a beach, but guests seem to enjoy lounging and sipping tropical drinks on hammocks strung up by the sea. Km 16.5 of Paseo Kukulcán (phone: 98-850714; 800-THE-OMNI; fax: 98-850184).

Presidente Inter-Continental On the edge of the *Club de Golf Cancún* links (see *Golf,* above) and a peaceful lagoon, this stately, 298-room hostelry offers a tennis court, fishing, and water skiing—thus its popularity with sports enthusiasts. Its beach and location are among the best on Cancún. Four restaurants and a pool complete the picture. Km 7 of Paseo Kukulcán (phone: 98-830200 or 830202; 800-327-0200 in the US; 800-90444 in Mexico; fax: 98-832515).

Ritz-Carlton Cancún This super-luxury resort features 370 guestrooms (including 54 suites). All rooms offer private balconies with sea views, mini-bars, refrigerators, and two bathrooms. On premises: a health club, two pools, and three lighted tennis courts, plus three dining rooms. 36 Retorno del Rey, off Paseo Kukulcán (phone: 98-850808; 305-446-0776 in Florida; 800-241-3333 elsewhere in the US; fax: 98-851015).

Sierra Cancún The 261 rooms are elegantly decorated in a Southwestern style, with bright colors and tile floors. Formerly the *Sierra Radisson Plaza,* this ocean-front property features two restaurants, three lounges, two snack bars, an outdoor pool, a fitness center, two tennis courts, and plenty of water sports. Km 10.5 of Paseo Kukulcán (phone: 98-832444; 800-882-6684; fax: 98-833486).

Villas Tacul Each of the 23 Spanish-style villas in this colony has a garden, a patio, a kitchen, and two to five bedrooms. On a narrow but pleasant beach, it also offers a restaurant and two tennis courts. It's perfect for families or congenial two- or three-couple groups. Km 5.5 of Paseo Kukulcán (phone: 98-830000; 800-842-0193; fax: 98-830349).

Westin Regina Plaza In this complex are 385 rooms, each with an ocean or lagoon view; the 94 tower rooms have private balconies (as do some in the low-rise building). Facilities include five outdoor pools, two lighted tennis courts, a health club and recreation center, a water sports center, and a boat dock for access to evening cruises and water sports. There also are two restaurants and two lounges. Punta Nizuc, at the south end of the island (phone: 98-850086; 800-228-3000 in the US; 800-90223 in Mexico; fax: 98-850074).

EXPENSIVE

Calinda Beach Cancún Situated on the best beach on the island, between Laguna Nichupté and Bahía de Mujeres, this hostelry isn't as lavish as many of its neighbors, but it's nonetheless a favorite, as attested to by its loyal following. A restaurant, bars, tennis courts, and a gym also contribute to its popularity. All 460 rooms have ocean views. Km 4 of Paseo Kukulcán (phone: 98-831600; 800-228-5151 in the US; 800-90000 in Mexico; fax: 98-831857).

Casa Maya Originally built as condominiums, the 356 rooms and suites here are large, with immense walk-in closets, sinks the size of bathtubs, and tubs the size of swimming pools. Among the amenities are a pool, two lighted tennis courts, mopeds for rent, a restaurant, and cordial service. The place seems to be especially popular with families. Km 5 of Paseo Kukulcán (phone: 98-830555; 800-44-UTELL; fax: 98-831188).

Club Med Boasting one of the island's widest beaches, this is one of the prime places to stay on Cancún. The 410 rooms, each with two wide single beds and traditional Mexican decor, are set in three-story bungalows facing either the ocean or the lagoon. Windsurfing, sailing, snorkeling, and scuba diving (including scuba instruction) are included, as are all meals. Lunch and dinner include complimentary wine. There's entertainment nightly. Punta Nizuc, at the south end of the island (phone: 98-852929; 800-CLUB-MED; fax: 98-852900).

Fiesta Americana Each of the 281 rooms has rattan furnishings and a balcony overlooking the water. The pool area is nicely laid out, with a *palapa* restaurant and two bars, beyond which lies the aqua-blue bay. Snorkeling gear is available poolside. The fountain-filled lobby is a pretty place for before-dinner cocktails. Km 8 of Paseo Kukulcán (phone: 98-831400; 800-FIESTA-1 in the US; 800-50450 in Mexico; fax: 98-832502).

Playa Blanca A pioneer among Cancún's hotels (it opened in 1974), this link in the Best Western chain has 161 rooms, a pool, a small beachfront, and every water sport imaginable. Since it's next door to the marina, the boating facilities are excellent. There's also a restaurant. Km 3 of Paseo Kukulcán (phone: 98-830344; 800-528-1234; fax: 98-830904).

Royal Solaris Caribe A Maya pyramid–like structure that has annexed a neighboring high-rise hotel of nearly equal size, it offers 450 rooms, seven restaurants, a pleasant beach, a health club, social programs, and the largest swimming pool in Cancún. Km 23 of Paseo Kukulcán (phone: 98-850600; 800-368-9779; fax: 98-850975).

Sheraton Cancún This self-contained, 748-room gem is set apart on its own beach, which it shares with a small Maya temple. Other draws: six tennis courts, six pools, five dining rooms, *Daphny's* video bar (with live and taped music), aerobics classes, and scuba lessons. Km 12.5 of Paseo Kukulcán (phone: 98-831988; 800-325-3535 in the US; 800-90325 in Mexico; fax: 98-850083).

MODERATE

América At this pleasant place are 177 large rooms, each with its own terrace. Though it's not right on the beach, it does provide complimentary shuttle service to its own beach club. There's a pool, restaurant, bar, and coffee shop. Av. Tulum, Cancún City (phone: 98-847500; fax: 98-841953).

Aristos A friendly scale and typical Mexican hospitality make for easy comfort here. There are 222 smallish but pleasant rooms, an inviting pool area, a beach, two lighted tennis courts, and a restaurant. Km 9.5 of Paseo Kukulcán (phone: 98-830011; 800-5-ARISTOS; fax: 98-830078).

Club Lagoon On a quiet lagoon, this secluded collection of 89 adobe-type dwellings (the best face the lagoon), including rooms and two-level suites, is a real find. One picturesque courtyard opens onto another, with flowers playing colorfully against the white cottages. It also has two restaurants, two bars, and a nautical center. Laguna Nichupté (phone: 98-831111; fax: 98-834959).

Holiday Inn Express Club de Golf Cancún This no-frills, 120-room establishment adjoins the famous *Club de Golf Cancún* course (see *Golf,* above). Though the hotel has neither a restaurant nor a beach, it does boast a pool with two waterfalls, as well as complimentary transportation to a nearby beach club. It's one of the best values in the Hotel Zone. 21 Paseo Pok-Ta-Pok (phone: 98-832200; 800-HOLIDAY in the US; 800-00999 in Mexico; fax: 98-832532).

Plaza Caribe Downtown, across from the bus station, the 140 air conditioned rooms here fill up fast. Public buses will take you to the beach, 2 miles (3 km) away. Other facilities include a restaurant and a swimming pool. 36 Av. Tulum, Cancún City (phone: 98-841377; 800-528-1234; fax: 98-846352).

Plaza del Sol Shaped like a half-moon with two stylized canoes over its portals, it has 87 rooms, a pool, a restaurant, a bar, and complimentary transportation to and from the beach. 31 Av. Yaxchilán, Cancún City (phone: 98-843888; fax: 98-844393).

COZUMEL

VERY EXPENSIVE

Diamond Cozumel The newest (and most expensive) resort on the island, this property near Cozumel's relatively unpopulated southern tip combines luxury and ecotourism. Accommodations are in small thatch-roofed duplexes spread over the expansive, landscaped grounds. The 300 guestrooms are all two-story units, decorated in bright tropical colors and motifs. All have ceiling fans, but no air conditioning. The grounds, covered with scrub brush and palmetto, are great for bird watching and other nature exploration, and the hotel's location near Palancar Reef is convenient for snorkeling. However, the property is a long distance from town. There are two restaurants, a nightclub, and a private beach, and rental scooters and bicycles are available. Km 16.5, Carretera a Chankanab (phone: 987-23554; 800-858-2258; fax: 987-24508).

Club Cozumel Caribe A twisting, palm-canopied drive leads to this expansive 260-room beachfront property with attractive grounds. It offers tennis, a restaurant, and a bar. Unfortunately, it's so far removed from everything else on the island that you may have trouble getting a taxi to Palancar Reef or San Miguel. Playa San Juan (phone: 987-20100; 800-327-2254).

EXPENSIVE

Coral Princess Club A posh resort, it offers 70 units, each with kitchenette and private terrace. There's also a restaurant and video bar. On the north end of the island (phone: 987-23200 or 987-23323; 800-272-3243; fax: 987-22800).

El Cozumeleño This property has 80 large rooms, three restaurants, a bar, a tennis court, and a free-form pool. Playa Santa Pilar, on the north end of the island (phone: 987-20050; 800-437-3923; fax: 987-20381).

Fiesta Americana Sol Caribe A beautiful 322-room resort 'twixt beach and jungle, it has three tennis courts, good diving facilities, and a fine dining room. South Zone (phone: 987-20466 or 987-20700; 800-FIESTA-1 in the US; 800-50450 in Mexico; fax: 987-21301).

Holiday Inn Cozumel Reef In this inn are 165 guestrooms, three restaurants, two bars, two lighted tennis courts, a health spa, and a private boat dock. South Zone (phone: 987-22622; 800-HOLIDAY in the US; 800-00999 in Mexico; fax: 987-22666).

Meliá Mayan Peradisus Set on the isolated north end of the coast, this 12-story high-rise on the beach has 200 rooms and suites, two restaurants, an abundance of terraces, two tennis courts, a Mexican fiesta on Thursdays, and a Caribbean fiesta on Fridays. Playa Santa Pilar (phone: 987-20411 or 987-22109; 800-336-3542; fax: 987-21599).

Plaza las Glorias It's the only luxury hotel in town that is on the beach. A 170-room complex, each room has a private balcony and an ocean view. There are also a private marina, two restaurants, a lobby bar with live music, a scuba diving school, and a pool. South Zone (phone: 987-22000; 800-342-AMIGO; fax: 987-21937).

Presidente Inter-Continental Cozumel Cozumel's original luxury establishment (and still one of its best) offers 253 rooms, an excellent dining room, a nice pool, a pleasant beach, tennis, and water sports, including scuba diving, snorkeling, and game fishing. On the northern end of the island (phone: 987-20322; 800-327-0200 in the US; 800-90444 in Mexico; fax: 987-21320).

MODERATE

La Ceiba Well equipped and conveniently located for scuba divers, this 115-room hostelry has a spa, tennis, a restaurant, and a cocktail lounge. Punta Paraíso, south of town (phone: 987-20844; 800-777-5873; fax: 987-20064).

Fiesta Inn This three-story, colonial-style hostelry has 178 rooms and two suites. Surrounded by beautiful gardens, it's connected to the beach by a tunnel. Other pluses: a large pool, a tennis court, motorcycles for rent, a dive shop, a restaurant, a bar, and a coffee shop. Km 1.7 of the Costera Sur (phone: 987-22899; 800-FIESTA-1 in the US; 800-50450 in Mexico; fax: 987-22154).

Fontán Most of these 48 rooms face the lovely beach. There's also a pool, a restaurant, and a dive shop. North Zone (phone: 987-20300; 800-221-6509; fax: 987-20105).

La Perla Right on the beach, this four-story, 22-room hotel has its own swimming cove and a pier for private yachts. A pool, dive packages, a deli-bar, and a quiet, unpretentious atmosphere round out the amenities. Km 2 of Av. Rafael E. Melgar (phone: 987-20188; 800-852-6404; fax: 987-22611).

Playa Azul A family favorite, this member of the Best Western group offers 60 rooms and suites, a restaurant, a bar, and water sports. North of San Miguel, at Km 4 of the Carretera San Juan (phone: 987-20033; 800-528-1234; fax: 987-20066).

Sol Cabañas del Caribe Informal and friendly, this semitropical hideaway on one of the island's best beaches has 50 rooms, a small pool, and nine individual cabañas. There is a restaurant. Playa Santa Pilar (phone: 987-20072; 800-336-3542; fax: 987-21599).

Villablanca Though its draws—a tennis court, a pool, a dive shop, a boat for up to 60 divers, and classes in all water sports—compare with those usually found only at a resort hotel, this property has only 50 rooms and suites, some with Jacuzzis. Across the street, on the water's edge, is *Amadeus,* its restaurant/bar/beach club. Across from Playa Paraíso, south of town (phone: 987-20730; 800-DIVE-MEX; fax: 987-20865).

ISLA MUJERES

Cristalmar Tucked away on the inward coast, this 38-suite property has deluxe one-, two-, and three-bedroom units. The hotel also boasts its own secluded beach, a good restaurant, an excellent dive shop, and the nicest pool in town. Fraccionamiento Paraíso Laguna (phone: 987-70007; 800-622-3838; fax: 987-70509).

Cabañas María del Mar It has 55 units (including 12 cabañas), a restaurant, and a full-service 20-slip marina. The proprietors, the Limas, make everyone feel at home. At the north end of the island, on Av. Carlos Lazo (phone: 987-70179; fax: 987-70213).

Perla del Caribe This three-story hotel offers 120 rooms, most with balconies. There also are a restaurant and a pool. 2 Av. Madero (phone: 987-70444; 800-258-6454; fax: 987-70011).

Perla del Caribe II Under the same management as its relative on Avenida Madero (see above), this less expensive version contains 34 basic but pleasant rooms, all with a view. There's also a restaurant. Avs. Nicolás Bravo and Vicente Guerrero (phone: 987-70586/7).

Posada del Mar This pleasant 42-room hostelry is one of the best on the island, with palm-shaded grounds, a fine restaurant (*Los Pájaros;* see *Eating Out*), a bar, and laundry facilities. Across from the beach, at 15 Av. Rueda Medina (phone: 987-70212 or 987-70300; fax: 987-70266).

Rocamar Most of the 18 guestrooms in this modest hotel have terraces or balconies overlooking the sea and the rocky shore. A palm-lined courtyard with a thatch-roofed reception desk serves as the lobby. There is no restaurant. Av. Guerrero at Calle Bravo (phone/fax: 987-20101).

EATING OUT

Hotel food in the Cancún area is better than average. By all means try such Yucatecan specialties as *huevos motuleños* (black beans and fried eggs on a tortilla, with a spicy sauce on top) and delicious Yucatán lime soup, which also contains chicken, vegetables, and tortillas.

For a dinner for two, expect to pay $40 to $60 in expensive restaurants; about $20 to $40 in moderate places; and less than $20 in inexpensive ones. Prices do not include tax, tip, wine, or other drinks. Restaurant prices on Cozumel and Isla Mujeres are somewhat more moderate than those on Cancún. All restaurants below accept MasterCard and Visa, and a few also accept American Express and Diners Club; it's a good idea to call ahead and check. Unless otherwise noted, restaurants are open daily for lunch and dinner.

CANCÚN

EXPENSIVE

Augustus Caesar Seafood and traditional Italian dishes are served with panache in pretty surroundings. Live music is featured nightly from 8:30 PM to midnight. No shorts or T-shirts allowed. Reservations advised. *La Mansión–Costa Blanca* shopping center (phone: 98-833384).

Blue Bayou Customers nosh on Cajun and creole fare and sip specialty drinks in a multilevel dining area suspended among waterfalls and lush greenery. There's live jazz nightly. Closed for lunch. Reservations necessary. *Hyatt Cancún Caribe,* Km 8.5 of Paseo Kukulcán (phone: 98-830044, ext. 54).

Bogart's International dishes are served with quiet elegance in exotic Moroccan surroundings. No shorts or T-shirts allowed. Closed for lunch; dinner seatings are at 7 and 9:30 PM. Reservations advised. At the *Krystal Cancún,* Km 9 of Paseo Kukulcán (phone: 98-831183).

Calypso The decor at this dining spot combines elegance and a tropical exuberance, with fountains, pools, and live reggae music enhancing the romantic seaside ambience. The menu features first-rate Caribbean fare, with an emphasis on seafood—try the braised fish with lobster medallions and scallion sauce. Closed for lunch. Reservations advised. At the *Camino Real,* on the northeast tip of the island (phone: 98-830100, ext. 8060).

La Dolce Vita Modern decor supplies the backdrop for intimate dining here, where the sweet life is manifested in tasty pasta and seafood dishes. Reservations advised. 87 Av. Cobá, in Cancún City (phone: 98-841384).

Grimond's The mayor's former home has been gussied up with European furniture, Oriental rugs, English china, and French crystal. Diners choose from four sitting rooms, a dining room, and an upstairs piano bar, all duly elegant. The French chef recommends shrimp sautéed in a cherry wine sauce.

No shorts or beach sandals allowed. Closed for lunch. Reservations advised. 8 Pez Volador, next to the *Casa Maya* hotel (phone: 98-830438).

Gypsy's A touch of Spain in the Mexican Caribbean, this rustic-looking eatery specializes in Iberian fare (the paella is exceptional). Flamenco dancers entertain nightly. Closed for lunch. No reservations. Laguna Nichupté, across from the *Continental Villas Plaza* (phone: 98-832015 or 98-832120).

La Habichuela The place locals go for a night out and for *mar y tierra* (surf and turf) in a Maya garden replete with miniature ruins. Reservations advised. 25 Margaritas, Cancún City (phone: 98-843158).

Hacienda el Mortero A convincing copy of a hacienda in Súchil, Durango (complete with impressive stone fountain and lots of plants), it specializes in steaks and Mexican haute cuisine. The service is attentive, and there's live mariachi music in the evenings. Reservations advised. In the *Krystal Cancún,* Km 9 of Paseo Kukulcán (phone: 98-831133).

Iguana Wana This trendy spot—which bills itself as "a contemporary Mexican café and bar"—offers live jazz and a varied menu, including Tex-Mex chili and buckets of peel-your-own shrimp. No reservations. *Plaza Caracol* shopping center (phone: 98-830829).

Jaguari's Here's the place to sink your teeth into a thick, juicy steak. Run by a Brazilian, it offers premium beef cuts served with a South American–style *churrasquería* (barbecue) sauce. Reservations advised. Playa Gaviota Azul (phone: 98-832880).

Lorenzillo's Set under a giant *palapa* extending over Laguna Nichupté, this restaurant specializes in soft-shell shrimp and rock lobster. Casual dress is acceptable, but shorts and T-shirts are not allowed. Open daily for breakfast, lunch, and dinner. Reservations unnecessary. Km 10.5 of Paseo Kukulcán (phone: 98-833073).

Mikado Decorated with hardwood paneling and furnishings, this Japanese steakhouse offers *teppanyaki* fare in elegant surroundings. The chef will chop, prepare, and grill beef, seafood and vegetables at your table. One end of the restaurant looks out onto a courtyard landscaped in the style of a Japanese garden. Open daily for dinner. Reservations advised. At the *Marriott Casa Magna,* Km 14.5 of Paseo Kukulcán (phone: 98-852000).

El Pescador Perhaps the best seafood eatery in Cancún dishes up fresh lobster, shrimp, and red snapper on Mexican pottery. Don't miss the Yucatecan lime soup and the hot rolls, and try for a table outside on the fan-cooled terrace. Closed Mondays. Reservations unnecessary. 28 Av. Tulipanes, Cancún City (phone: 98-842673).

Scampi Superb northern Italian fare—delicious pasta, meat, and seafood—is served in a beautiful setting, with impeccable service. At the *Hyatt Regency,* Paseo Kukulcán, on the northern tip of the island (phone: 98-831234).

MODERATE

Bombay Bicycle Club Casual and comfortable, the menu is strictly US-style fare— good hamburgers, barbecued ribs, and calorie-filled desserts. The service is excellent and friendly. Open 7 AM to 11 PM. No reservations. Paseo Kukulcán, across from Playa Tortuga (98-831281).

Johnny Rockets Rock 'n' roll and a 1950s theme attract visitors to this hamburger eatery–video bar. The music is hot, the food even hotter. Definitely not a place for easy listening. No reservations. *Plaza Terramar* shopping center (phone: 98-833092).

Pizza Rolandi All kinds of Italian dishes are offered in an informal, outdoor setting. Reservations unnecessary. 12 Av. Cobá, Cancún City (phone: 98-844047).

Torremolinos Paella, crayfish, and crab prepared the Spanish way. No reservations. Av. Tulum and Calle Xcaret, Cancún City (phone: 98-843639).

INEXPENSIVE

Los Almendros Under the same management as its famous Mérida namesake, this eatery draws repeat customers for its authentic Yucatecan food. Reservations unnecessary. 60 Av. Bonampak, Cancún City (phone: 98-840807).

Amsterdam Bistro European dishes are served in this intimate bistro. The delicious bread is baked on the premises, and there is a huge salad and fresh fruit bar. Open for breakfast, lunch, and dinner; closed Mondays. Reservations unnecessary. 70 Av. Yaxchilán, Cancún City (phone: 98-844098).

100% Natural The menu consists of fresh fruit drinks, salads, sandwiches, and fruit and vegetable platters; there's live jazz music nightly. No reservations. Three locations: 6 Calle Sunyaxchen, downtown (phone: 98-843617); *Plaza Terramar* shopping center (phone: 98-831180); and *Plaza Kukulcán* shopping center (phone: 98-852904).

COZUMEL

EXPENSIVE

Acuario Once a real aquarium, it's now an elegant seafood restaurant, with entertainment provided by an immense tankful of exotic tropical fish in the middle of the room. Reservations advised. Av. Rafael E. Melgar at Av. 11 Sur, San Miguel (phone: 987-21097).

Donatello A premier Italian dining place with a New Orleans French Quarter ambience, it serves superb fresh pasta and offers a beautiful ocean view. Closed for lunch. Reservations advised. 131 Av. Rafael E. Melgar Sur, San Miguel (phone: 987-20090 or 987-22586).

Morgan's Lobster thermidor and special coffees are favorites at this comfortable, popular wood cabin. Good steaks and seafood also are served. Reservations advised. On the main plaza, in San Miguel (phone: 987-20584).

Pepe's Grill This romantic spot by the waterfront has excellent seafood and steaks. A variety of live music is featured nightly. Reservations advised. Av. Rafael E. Melgar, San Miguel (phone: 987-20213).

MODERATE

Mezcalito's Set on the surf-pounded Caribbean side of the island, this large open-air *palapa* serves up some of the tastiest grilled shrimp and fish on Cozumel. The atmosphere—white sand, ocean breezes, and friendly chatter—is unbeatable. A good spot, too, just to stop for a cold beer or a piña colada. No reservations. Punta Morena (no phone).

Las Palmeras Opposite the ferry dock, it's a great meeting place offering a varied menu for every meal, including breakfast. The homemade biscuits and French toast are a real treat. Reservations unnecessary. On the *malecón,* San Miguel (phone: 987-20532).

Pancho's Backyard The food is just what you would expect—good and plenty—served on hand-crafted ceramic pottery. Strolling mariachis give this place a certain *sabor mexicano.* No reservations. On the waterfront at Calle 8, San Miguel (phone: 987-22141).

INEXPENSIVE

Plaza Leza A sidewalk café, it prepares good Mexican snacks, charcoal-broiled steaks, and seafood. Reservations advised. 58 Calle 1 Sur, San Miguel (phone: 987-21041).

San Francisco The fare is—what else?—seafood (try the snail ceviche), and a band plays in the afternoons. Closed for dinner. Reservations unnecessary. A quarter mile from Playa San Francisco (no phone).

Sports Page If you can't survive without the *Super Bowl* or the *World Series,* stop in and watch the games on TV while munching on a burger and fries. No reservations. Av. 5, San Miguel (phone: 987-21199).

ISLA MUJERES

EXPENSIVE

Ciro's Lobster House A wide selection of Mexican wines accompanies the lobster and red snapper served here. Reservations advised. 11 Matamoros, in town (phone: 987-70102).

MODERATE

Gomar Lobster and fresh fish are best enjoyed on the romantic terrace, where tables sport bright, striped Mexican cloths during the day, elegant white tablecloths at night. You also can dine indoors. Reservations unnecessary. Avs. Hidalgo and Madero (phone: 987-70142).

Hacienda Gomar Exotic drinks and a good seafood buffet are what attract patrons to this eatery. Reservations unnecessary. On the west side of the island on the road to *El Garrafón* (no phone).

Mesón de Bucanero This quiet, wood-paneled restaurant in the heart of town offers a varied menu of fresh seafood (try the *huachinango asado*—red snapper, grilled whole), as well as Mexican regional cuisine, steaks, and a few traditional Maya dishes such as *pavo escabeche* (turkey in a spicy onion-and-orange sauce). Av. Hidalgo between Madero and Abasolo (phone: 987-70210).

Los Pájaros Facing the beach on the north end of town, this *palapa*-style eatery serves good Mexican fare. Reservations unnecessary. *Posada del Mar* hotel (phone: 987-70044).

INEXPENSIVE

Buho's Paradise Remaining open until the wee hours (a *buho* is a kind of owl), this nightclub/restaurant is great for late snacks. Reservations unnecessary. Next to *Cabañas María del Mar* at the island's northern tip (phone: 987-70179).

Pizza Rolandi Pizza cooked in a wood-burning oven and other Italian dishes are the attractions here. Reservations unnecessary. Av. Hidalgo, between Avs. Madero and Abasolo (phone: 987-70430).

Chihuahua

(pronounced Chee-*wah*-wah)

Chihuahua, the capital of Mexico's largest state (also called Chihuahua), sits on a plain almost 5,000 feet high, with the Sierra Madre to the west. The broad boulevards and convivial squares of this metropolis provide a welcome contrast to the arid, desolate plateau that stretches 232 miles from here to the US border at El Paso, Texas. Founded in 1709, the city was first called Real de San Francisco de Cuéllar, then San Felipe el Real de Chihuahua, later shortened to Chihuahua. It originally derived its wealth from surrounding cattle ranches and silver mines. No longer a major producer of silver, Chihuahua now depends on in-bond factories (assembly plants, or *maquilas,* for US products), cattle, and agriculture for its income. Today, the prosperous city claims almost one million inhabitants.

Two of Mexico's most famous revolutionary figures are closely linked with Chihuahua's violent history. It was here in 1811 that the Spaniards executed the father of Mexican independence, Padre Miguel Hidalgo, and his patriot conspirators. Chihuahua was also the home of General Pancho Villa, whose revolutionary army overthrew Porfirio Díaz in 1910 and won the civil war that followed. Chihuahua served as the country's capital in 1864 and 1865, when President Benito Juárez made the city his base during the French invasion of Mexico.

But Chihuahua is most famous for the tiny, hairless dogs, *perros chihuahueños,* first raised in the area. (Natives of Chihuahua are called *chihuahuenses,* and confusing the similar words constitutes a grave offense.)

The state of Chihuahua has some of the most beautiful scenery in Mexico. There is the Cascada de Basaséachic (Basaséachic Falls), a 980-foot-high waterfall set in a lush pine forest; and the awesome Barranca del Cobre (Copper Canyon), best reached via the *Ferrocarril Chihuahua al Pacífico* (Chihuahua-Pacific Railway), which runs along the canyon's rim, or the luxurious *South Orient Express,* which runs between the city of Chihuahua and Los Mochis on the coast. The desire to experience this spectacularly scenic trip is what brings many travelers to Chihuahua. For details on train trips, see *Extra Special,* below.

A surprise for many visitors is the presence of a substantial Mennonite population in the state of Chihuahua. In the 1920s, Mennonite farmers settled about 50 miles (80 km) southwest of the city, just outside Cuauhtémoc. The colony has since grown from about 2,000 to more than 55,000. The hardworking Mennonites are accomplished farmers, and their produce, especially their cheese, is prized throughout Mexico.

The indigenous Tarahumara, by contrast, are dwindling. Their extremely rugged existence involves roaming from the cool plateaus of the Sierra Tarahumara in the summer to the semitropical canyon floor in the winter, ingesting peyote during religious rites, and fishing and hunting for survival. (It is said that they are able to run so swiftly that they can catch deer; in fact, *tarahumara* means "running foot" in Nahuatl.) Weavers and potters, the Tarahumara can be easily recognized on the streets of Chihuahua by their roughly woven, red and white serapes and their long, flowing hair tied with narrow headbands.

Some may view Chihuahua primarily as a stopover on the long drive from Ciudad Juárez to Mexico City. But it should be considered on its own merits: a historical spot with unique attractions, as well as the jumping-off point for the spectacular Barranca del Cobre tour.

Chihuahua At-a-Glance

SEEING THE CITY
The best view of the town is from the *mirador* (lookout) on Santa Rosa hill. Just follow Avenida Venustiano Carranza.

SPECIAL PLACES
Because of its historic importance to Mexico and its own natural beauty, Chihuahua offers the visitor fascinating colonial and revolutionary landmarks, interesting museums, and afternoon or daylong treks into the countryside.

DOWNTOWN

CATEDRAL Dedicated to St. Francis of Assisi, the city's patron saint, this magnificent cathedral was built in an ornate Baroque style, out of pink quarry stone. Work was begun by the Jesuits in 1725 but not finished until 1825, by the Franciscans, because of frequent uprisings by the area's indigenous people. The façade is elaborately adorned with statues of St. Francis (below the clock) and the 12 apostles. The cathedral's *Museo de Arte Sacro* (Museum of Sacred Art) contains 18th-century works (closed weekends; no admission charge); its entry is at the west side of the cathedral. The Baroque pipe organ is considered one of the finest in the Western Hemisphere. Plaza de la Constitución (no phone).

PALACIO DE GOBIERNO (STATEHOUSE) Padre Miguel Hidalgo and Ignacio Allende, leaders of the 1810 uprising against Spain, were executed here by the Spanish in 1811; a plaque commemorates the spot on which Hidalgo died. Aarón Piña Morales's patio murals depict famous episodes in the history of Chihuahua. Open daily. No admission charge. On the east side of Plaza Hidalgo (phone: 160594).

PALACIO FEDERAL (FEDERAL BUILDING) This colonial structure contains the tower in which Hidalgo and his cohorts were imprisoned after their capture by the Spanish. The original building was a Jesuit college, built in 1717 for the education of the sons of leading Spanish families and of native *caciques* (chiefs). Largely destroyed by fire in 1941, the building was reconstructed according to the original plans. It now houses postal and telegraph offices, as well as a small museum. The museum is open daily; there's an admission charge. Plaza Hidalgo, across from the *Palacio de Gobierno* (phone: 151526, ext. 390).

IGLESIA DE SAN FRANCISCO The oldest church in Chihuahua was built by Franciscan monks in 1721. Adjoining it and connected by underground passageways is the *Capilla de San Antonio* (Chapel of St. Anthony). It was here, in 1811, that Padre Hidalgo's decapitated body was interred by the Franciscan fathers. They protected it until 1823, when independence was finally won, and then exhumed it and sent it to Mexico City. The tablet in the chapel that relates this gory tale omits the fact that directly after the execution, the head was sent to Guanajuato, where it was publicly displayed for the next 10 years. Plaza Zaragoza (phone: 103057)

STATUE OF HIDALGO This 45-foot, marble-and-bronze monument is dedicated to the heroes of the War of Independence. It features a life-size replica of Padre Hidalgo and smaller figures of his co-conspirators. Plaza Hidalgo.

QUINTA GAMEROS (REGIONAL MUSEUM) Ensconced in a resplendent Art Nouveau mansion, this museum is filled with blown-glass Italian chandeliers, carved-wood furniture, and gold leaf paintings on the walls and woodwork. Upstairs is a replica of the ruins at *Paquimé,* photos of old Chihuahua, and rooms devoted to the area's Mennonite community. Closed Mondays. Admission charge. 401 Bolívar (phone: 123834).

MUSEO DE ARTE POPULAR (MUSEUM OF FOLK ART) Small but extensive, it displays a typical Tarahumara home, along with textiles, pottery, toys, colorful clothing, musical instruments, masks, baskets, and cooking utensils. The shop sells crafts from the region. Closed Sundays and Mondays. No admission charge. 5 Reforma and Independencia (no phone).

QUINTA LUZ (MUSEUM OF THE REVOLUTION) This was once the home of Pancho Villa, a hero of the Mexican Revolution of 1910. One of his wives, Doña Luz Corral, lived here until her death in 1981. The museum is full of memorabilia, including the bullet-riddled car in which the general was assassinated in 1923. Open daily. Admission charge. 3014 Calle 10 (no phone, but information is available from the *Tarahumara* crafts shop across the street; phone: 152882).

MAUSOLEO DE PANCHO VILLA (PANCHO VILLA'S MAUSOLEUM) This architectural extravaganza, incorporating more than half a dozen styles, was built by Villa in 1913 as his final resting place. In fact, Villa was buried 200 miles to the south, where he was assassinated, and a couple of years later his body (minus his head, which had mysteriously been removed) was moved to Mexico City. The cemetery in which the empty mausoleum stands has metamorphosed into *Parque Revolución.*

ACUEDUCTO COLONIAL This impressive feat of engineering was begun in 1751. Although it is no longer used to transport water, it remains an interesting sight. The aqueduct is especially pretty at night by lamplight. A short section of it can easily be seen at Avenida Zarco and Calle 34.

TEATRO DE LOS HÉROES (HEROES' THEATER) This impressive modern structure replaced a landmark theater that burned in the 1950s. Theatrical performances, concerts, and exhibits are held here. División del Norte and Calle 23 (phone: 139794).

ENVIRONS

CASCADA DE BASASÉACHIC (BASASÉACHIC FALLS) At Mexico's highest waterfall, icy mountain water spills down more than 800 feet into a rapidly moving tributary of the Río Mayo. The canyon below is covered with beautiful jade-green pools, and there is a steep, narrow path through a pine forest leading from the rim of the canyon to the pools below. From Chihuahua, take Route 16 to Basaséachic. To see the entire waterfall, turn off Route 16 about 3½ miles (5 km) before reaching Basaséachic onto the road to San Juanito; the entrance to the *Parque Nacional* is marked. From here, there are three *divisaderos* (overlooks) accessible from the parking lot. If you want to stay overnight, *Cabañas Alma Rosa* (phone: 152049) offers modest—if expensive—cabins. (Be forewarned: There's no hot water.) Ocampo, the nearest town, also has rustic lodgings. Tours can be arranged through travel desks at the larger Chihuahua hotels.

CAMPOS MENONITAS (MENNONITE FARMING COMMUNITY) Eight miles (13 km) north of the small town of Cuauhtémoc (via Rte. 28) and a scenic hour-and-a-half drive west from Chihuahua, some 55,000 Mennonites live on and farm 123,500 acres of fertile land in the area that produces 90% of Mexico's apples. Traditionally a people who keep to themselves, the Mennonites have opened to the public one typical home, a cheese cooperative, and a hardware store (which sells handmade rolltop desks, wooden washing machines, and kerosene stoves, among other items). Visitors have the opportunity to buy handicrafts and sample the local cheese. Tours for a minimum of four people can be arranged through the *Rojo and Casavantes* travel agency in Chihuahua (1207 Calle V. Guerrero; phone: 155858). Although meals are not included in the tour, the group can arrange to dine simply at a Mennonite home. Tours also can be arranged through travel desks at Chihuahua's larger hotels. The only nearby lodging presently available is at *Posada del Sol* (phone: 158-23333), a little more than a mile (1.6 km) outside Cuauhtémoc.

EXTRA SPECIAL

One of the most extraordinary sights in all of Mexico, Barranca del Cobre (Copper Canyon) could easily swallow four Grand Canyons. The trip to this natural wonder takes about 12 hours via the *Ferrocarril Chihuahua al*

Pacífico (Chihuahua-Pacific Railway). Another option is to book a more leisurely five- or seven-day tour on the luxurious *South Orient Express,* which features comfortable passenger compartments and fine food in addition to the scenery. For additional details, see *Quintessential Mexico* in DIVERSIONS and *Ciudad Juárez to Mexico City* in DIRECTIONS.

Sources and Resources

TOURIST INFORMATION

The staff at the *Secretaría de Turismo del Estado de Chihuahua* (Chihuahua State Tourism Secretariat; in the *Palacio de Gobierno,* 1300 Calle Libertad and Calle 13; phone: 159124 or 162436) is very helpful. The office is open daily.

LOCAL COVERAGE No English-language newspapers or tourist publications are published in Chihuahua, although the tourist office does have pamphlets in English. The daily Mexico City *News* arrives at some downtown newsstands in the afternoon.

TELEPHONE The city code for Chihuahua is 14. *Note:* Mexico's telephone company has embarked on a major expansion project that involves changing telephone numbers in many areas of the country. At press time, all numbers listed in this chapter were correct. However, if you have any difficulties reaching attractions listed here, contact the local tourist office.

CLIMATE AND CLOTHES Chihuahua is cooler than other cities in Mexico, with temperatures sometimes dipping to 0F (-17C) December through January and reaching only the upper 70s F (upper 20s C) in summer. Some snow may fall December through February. The rainy season is July and August. Dress in this city is fairly informal.

GETTING AROUND

BUS Several bus lines go from one side of town to the other for a minimal sum, and some of them run until midnight. The fare is 1 peso (about 13¢). Light vans from *Transportadora Ares Acuario* (phone: 203366) travel between the airport and town for 35 pesos (about $4.70).

CAR RENTALS The leading car rental agencies are *Alpri* (phone: 125145); *Autorenta* (phone: 106048); *Avis* (phone: 141999); *Budget* (phone: 160909); *Dollar* (phone: 142171); and *Gamma Fast* (phone: 155981). All have offices at the airport.

TAXIS Your hotel can always call a cab for you, but it is easy enough to hail one on the street. Fares are quite reasonable, but agree on the price before you get in.

TOURS Travel desks at the larger hotels arrange city sightseeing, Barranca del Cobre (Copper Canyon) rail trips, and visits to the region's Mennonite community.

SPECIAL EVENTS

For the last two weeks in May, Chihuahua's colorful *Fiesta de Santa Rita*, in honor of the city's patron saint, is celebrated throughout town, with music, dancing, fireworks, parades, and food. There are also cattle fairs in June and October.

SHOPPING

Chihuahua has great buys on Tarahumara handicrafts, including handwoven and hand-dyed rugs and blankets, and stunning ceremonial masks. Two large indoor markets on Calle Aldama provide some interesting browsing. With about 20 stalls each, they are open daily (except at lunchtime); some sell Mennonite cheese, among other items. *Artesanías Mexicanas* (Calle 10, across from the *Quinta Luz*) is a good place to buy regional handicrafts; it also contains a rock shop with precious and semi-precious stones, along with a collection of fossilized stones that are not for sale. Most stores are open daily from about 10 AM to 2 PM and 4 to 6 PM.

SPORTS

BASEBALL AND BASKETBALL Both sports are popular here. There is no regular season or schedule for either the professional or university games, but most are played in May or June. Professional games take place at the *Universidad de Chihuahua* sports center (Av. Universidad; phone: 144292). Amateur games are played at the *Estadio General M. Quevedo* (Blvd. Díaz Ordaz; phone: 100558).

FISHING Freshwater angling is excellent at manmade lakes near Chihuahua. A favorite spot is the Presa Francisco I. Madero (Francisco I. Madero Dam) 52 miles (84 km) southeast of Chihuahua. Bass, carp, and catfish are all in good supply.

HUNTING The season runs approximately from November through January; the game is deer, coyote, squirrel, rabbit, wild sheep, peccary (a porcine mammal), turkey, quail, sandhill crane, duck, goose, and dove. Licenses are issued by Mexico's *Secretaría de Medio Ambiente, Recursos Naturales y Pesca* (Secretariat of the Environment, Natural Resources and Fisheries); see *Hunting* in DIVERSIONS for further information. To arrange an expedition, consult hotel travel desks. *Rancho La Estancia* (just north of Cuauhtémoc off Rte. 28; no local phone; phone in Chihuahua: 161657; fax in Chihuahua: 104688) offers lodging; for more information, see *Mexico on Horseback* in DIVERSIONS.

NIGHTCLUBS AND NIGHTLIFE

The action after dark is primarily at the discos. The top choices are *La Mina* in the *Victoria* hotel (Colón and Juárez; phone: 100548); *Medanos* in the *Sicomoro* hotel (see *Checking In*); *Robin Hood* (208 Av. Talavera; phone: 111975); *Los Primos* in the *Park Plaza Inn San Francisco* hotel (see *Checking*

In); and *La Puerta de Alcalá* (Av. Revolución; phone: 158393). *Hostería 1900*'s video bar (see *Eating Out*) attracts a good crowd. As is the case in many provincial towns, unescorted women—especially if scantily dressed—often have to contend with rude comments on the street.

Best in Town

CHECKING IN

Expect to pay $80 to $110 per night for a double room in an expensive hotel; about $50 to $75 in a moderate place; and $40 or less in an inexpensive one. Unless otherwise noted, the hotels listed have pools, private baths, air conditioning, TV sets, and telephones in the rooms. All telephone numbers are in the 14 city code unless otherwise indicated.

EXPENSIVE

Holiday Inn A 36-suite property with nice gardens and exceptional service. It's a favorite with overnight business travelers. All suites have kitchenettes; there's also a restaurant. 702 Escudero (phone: 143350; 800-HOLIDAY in the US; 800-00999 in Mexico; fax: 143313).

Park Plaza Inn San Francisco This cozy spot features wet bars and US television programming in each of its 140 rooms. There's a Sunday brunch and buffet in the popular restaurant. Centrally located, at 409 Calle Victoria (phone: 167770; 800-442-5991; fax: 153538).

Sicomoro Handsome and spacious, this property has 130 rooms, a pool shaped like the state of Chihuahua, the *Medanos* restaurant-bar-disco, a coffee shop, and a lively lobby bar. Three miles (5 km) from downtown. 411 Blvd. Ortiz Mena (phone: 135445; 800-448-6970; fax: 131411).

MODERATE

Casa Grande Here are 72 gray-and-white guestrooms, a restaurant, and a bar with live entertainment. On the outskirts of town on the road to Ciudad Juárez, at 4702 Av. Tecnológico (phone: 196633; 800-245-0272; fax: 193235).

Mirador Comfortable and well-kept, this place has 87 rooms, an inviting lobby, a restaurant, a bar, and free parking. A short drive from downtown, at 1309 Av. Universidad (phone: 132205; fax: 138906).

INEXPENSIVE

Parador de San Miguel This colonial-style hotel has only 45 rooms, plus a restaurant and a bar. 7901 Av. Tecnológico (phone: 170303; fax: 171500).

EATING OUT

Chihuahua is renowned for its steaks, but those who prefer other dishes won't be disappointed. Dinner for two at an expensive place will cost $40 to $50; in a moderate one, under $35. Prices do not include drinks, wine, tax, or tips. Most restaurants below accept MasterCard and Visa, and a few also accept American Express and Diners Club; it's a good idea to call ahead and check. All are open daily for lunch and dinner unless otherwise noted. All telephone numbers are in the 14 city code unless otherwise indicated.

EXPENSIVE

Chihuahua Charlie's This link in the ubiquitous Anderson's chain serves all the favorites, including a salad of bacon, watercress, and mushrooms, and "Oysters 444," a sampling of oysters prepared in a variety of ways. Reservations advised. 3329 Av. Juárez (phone: 157065 or 157589).

Club de los Parados First-rate steaks are served in a rustic setting. Reservations unnecessary. 3901 Av. Juárez (phone: 105335).

Los Parados de Tony Vega Under the same ownership as the *Club de los Parados,* this intimate colonial dining room with shuttered windows is a fine backdrop for great steaks. Check out the *Hunters Salon* upstairs. Reservations unnecessary. 3316 Av. Juárez (phone: 155656).

Salignac At this inviting place, international fare with a French influence predominates. Steaks with crayfish and dishes prepared with the region's famous black bass are especially good choices. There's also live entertainment. Reservations unnecessary. 3309 Av. Juárez (phone: 158616).

MODERATE

La Calesa One of the best steak places in Chihuahua. International dishes are also available, along with *puchero* (marrow soup with vegetables) and sea bass in garlic sauce. Reservations advised. Av. Juárez and Colón (phone: 160222).

Hostería 1900 The frontier decor and intriguing photographs provide an interesting backdrop for such unusual fare as wheat soup and *huitlacoche* crêpes (made with a corn fungus with a delicate mushroom-like taste). The video bar is open until 2 AM on Fridays and Saturdays. Reservations unnecessary. 903A Independencia (phone: 161990).

La Olla Housed in an old brewery with a copper *olla,* or vat, as its centerpiece, this dining spot specializes in beef dishes. No reservations. 3331 Av. Juárez (phone: 162220).

Los Vitrales Named for the tiny, diamond-shaped panes surrounding its dining room, this lovely restaurant with piano bar features a variety of Oriental and other international dishes. Reservations unnecessary. Av. Juárez at the corner of Colón (phone: 150676).

Cuernavaca

(pronounced Kwer-nah-*vah*-kah)

Among the topics likely to come up when professional travelers congregate is which city in the world has the best climate. Although it sounds like the kind of question around which battle lines are drawn and ideological splits develop, the topic actually engenders more consensus than conflict. For several centuries there has been one favorite with cognoscenti, from the Aztec kings and Hernán Cortés to the hundreds of American and European expatriates who live there right now. That is Cuernavaca, with a name like poetry and a climate that is simply perfect.

About an hour's drive south of Mexico City on the road to Acapulco (Rte. 95), Cuernavaca, with a population of nearly 300,000, is Mexico's oldest resort and the capital of the state of Morelos. The Aztec named it Cuauhnahuac, "Place of the Whispering Trees." The Spanish found the word unpronounceable when they arrived in 1521 and promptly changed the name to Cuernavaca ("Cow's Horn").

At 5,000 feet, the city has spring-like weather most of the year; when Mexico City (at more than 7,000 feet) is soaked in cold rain, the swimming pools of Cuernavaca glitter in the sun. Among its natural water sources are thermally heated springs and mineral waters, traditionally soothing for rheumatism and other ailments of the joints and incredibly relaxing and restorative to the spirit, even if one's elbows and knees are in perfect condition.

Despite its serene climate, Cuernavaca has at times been the scene of serious political controversy. After Mexico became independent in the early 19th century, the big sugar haciendas surrounding the city passed from rich Spaniards to equally rich Mexicans. These *hacendados* (landowners) often left their land in the hands of overseers, who treated native laborers like slaves. The haciendas soon became a visible symbol for the growing frustration of the peasants; during the 1910 revolution, this anger found perfect expression in leader Emiliano Zapata's battle cry "Land and liberty and death to the *hacendados!*" Indeed, during the revolution Zapata's ragtag army devastated every hacienda in the region. Zapata joined forces with the flamboyant bandit Pancho Villa in 1914, during the occupation of Mexico City; five years later, he was trapped by federal troops and shot. In Cuernavaca, Zapata is revered as a true folk hero.

When you visit Cuernavaca, you will undoubtedly be impressed by its flowers before you get any sense of its politics or history. Geraniums reach to rooftops; fuchsia and red and coral bougainvillea grow wild. Bluish-lavender jacaranda and flaming poinciana tint the air with color. Stretching into the distance outside town are fields of sugarcane, corn, beans, avocados, wheat, coffee, and peanuts. You'll also see groves of banana trees, mangoes, guavas, limes, and oranges. If you don't fall in love with Cuernavaca, you'll at least understand why it generates such intense passion in so many people.

Cuernavaca At-a-Glance

SEEING THE CITY

The best views of Cuernavaca are from Route 95, as you enter the town from Mexico City, and from the hills called Lomas de Cuernavaca, just east of Route 95.

SPECIAL PLACES

Cuernavaca is a little too big for walking around, although the *Palacio de Cortés* (Cortés's Palace) and *Jardín Borda* (Borda Gardens) are only four short blocks apart. The residential area south of the *zócalo* (main plaza) is pleasant to drive around in, because the gardens are not set behind walls, as they are on most Mexican properties. Note that the *Murales Siqueiros,* a vivid series of historical murals by famed Mexican artist David Alvaro Siqueiros on display at the *Casino de la Selva* hotel, have been closed to the public until the hotel completes an extensive remodeling project. Check with the tourist office for details.

ZÓCALO Cuernavaca is unusual in that it has two adjacent *zócalos*. One is Jardín Juárez (Garden of Juárez); the larger plaza is Jardín de los Héroes (Garden of Heroes), also called the Plaza de la Constitución. This is also one of the few towns where there is no church on the plaza. The *Palacio de Gobierno* (Statehouse) is here, though, and so are a number of sidewalk cafés. It's a favorite place for those who like to people watch and listen to lively band concerts (on Sundays).

CATEDRAL DE SAN FRANCISCO (CATHEDRAL OF ST. FRANCIS) Founded by Cortés in 1529, this is one of the oldest cathedrals in Mexico. It was originally part of a Franciscan monastery; during the colonial period, it housed missionaries en route to the Far East via Acapulco. The interior of the church was renovated in 1959. In the rear of the cathedral compound, the *Capilla de la Tercera Orden* (Chapel of the Third Order) has sculptures by indigenous artists. The mariachi mass at 11 AM and 7 PM on Sundays is famous all over Mexico, so if you want to hear the musicians, get here early. At the corner of Hidalgo and Morelos.

JARDÍN BORDA (BORDA GARDENS) The former estate of an 18th-century mining magnate boasts extensive landscaped gardens; art exhibits and concerts take place here frequently. Open daily. Admission charge. Across the street from the cathedral on Calle Morelos (phone: 120086).

MUSEO CUAUHNAHUAC (CUAUHNAHUAC MUSEUM) Intended by Hernán Cortés to be a fortress, this rather forbidding pile of stones housed state government offices for many years. It's now a state museum, with Diego Rivera murals depicting the history of the state of Morelos from the conquest to the 1910 revolution. The Spaniards invariably built their most important structures on top of existing Aztec constructions, and here you can see the *Pirámide de Tlauican* (a pyramid built by an indigenous group), which was buried until renovation efforts uncovered it. Closed Mondays. Admission charge. Southeast corner of Jardín de los Héroes (phone: 128171).

PIRÁMIDE DE TEOPANZOLCO The ruins of this pyramid—believed to date from the Aztec era—were discovered during the revolution of 1910, when cannon mounted on a hillside shook loose the soil. Closed Mondays. Admission charge. Near the railroad station, southeast of the market on Av. Vicente Guerrero (no phone).

PALACIO MUNICIPAL (CITY HALL) The murals on the second floor of this building depict Aztec rituals and scenes from the lives of Hapsburg rulers Maximilian and Carlota in mid-19th-century Mexico. Gallery exhibits change regularly. Closed weekends. No admission charge. Calle Morelos, across from the cathedral (phone: 120652).

SALTO DE SAN ANTÓN (ST. ANTHONY WATERFALL) A scenic waterfall cascades over a 100-foot-high ravine set in a pretty, landscaped area. At the top of the hill, you can buy local pottery; be sure to bargain for the best price. About 1 mile (1.6 km) west of downtown on Rte. 8.

CASA-MUSEO ROBERT BRADY (ROBERT BRADY HOUSE-MUSEUM) An expatriate American artist, Brady moved to Cuernavaca in 1961 and purchased this home, the *Casa de la Torre* (Tower House), originally part of a Franciscan convent. Brady lived and worked in Cuernavaca until his death in 1986, amassing a huge collection of Mexican and foreign works of art, pre-Columbian figures, Mexican colonial pieces, and fine examples of Mexican crafts, which now are displayed here. Closed Sundays through Wednesdays and Saturday afternoons. Admission charge includes a guided tour (available only in Spanish). 4 Nezahualcóyotl (phone: 143529).

MUSEO DE LA HERBOLARIA (HERB MUSEUM) Also known as *El Olvido,* this was Emperor Maximilian's refuge from court. In addition to the herb gardens and a museum of "traditional" medicine, the *Society of Friends of the Ethnobotanical Gardens* runs a small shop in which arts and crafts and naturally grown products are for sale. Open daily. No admission charge. 200 Matamoros (phone: 123108).

JUNGLA MÁGICA (MAGIC JUNGLE) Cuernavaca's spiffed-up playground features spring-fed canals that wind through 500 acres of lush tropical gardens, as well as vestiges of a 16th-century aqueduct on the hills. There's also a miniature train, an aviary and snake farm, a lake where rowboats and small-scale remote-control boats can be rented, children's games and amusement-park rides, a dolphin show, and a planetarium. Closed Mondays. Admission charge. Plan de Ayala and the Rte. 95D interchange (no phone).

XOCHICALCO About an hour east of town, this is a spectacular yet little-visited archaeological site whose features link it with the Olmec, Maya, Zapotec, Toltec, and Xochicalco civilizations. In one of the pyramids is a sunlit rooftop observatory used by ancient scientists to determine the date and time. (Also see *Mexico's Magnificent Archaeological Heritage* in DIVERSIONS.) Open daily. No admission charge on Sundays. The best way to get to *Xochicalco* is to have your hotel provide a guide-driver (no phone).

Sources and Resources

TOURIST INFORMATION

The *Secretaría de Turismo del Estado de Morelos* (Morelos State Tourist Secretariat; 802 Calle Morelos Sur; phone: 143794 or 143860) is very helpful. It's open daily.

LOCAL COVERAGE For maps and English-language guidebooks, newspapers, magazines, and even novels, go to *Librería las Plazas* (19 Centro las Plazas, off Jardín de los Héroes; phone: 188976).

TELEPHONE The city code for Cuernavaca is 73. *Note:* Mexico's telephone company has embarked on a major expansion project that involves changing telephone numbers in many areas of the country. At press time, all numbers listed in this chapter were correct. However, if you have any difficulties reaching attractions listed here, contact the local tourist office.

CLIMATE AND CLOTHES Cuernavaca's climate is warm and somewhat humid. It rarely gets colder than the 60s F (16–21C) or warmer than the low 80s F (27–28C), but the temperature can plunge as low as the mid-40s F (6–8C) during the infrequent *nortes* (north winds). The rainy season is June through September. Dress is casual.

GETTING AROUND

CAR RENTAL A car is a good idea here. *Hertz* (300 Plan de Ayala; phone: 143800) and *Rentacar Monroy* (Plaza Misión, 821-5 Av. Emiliano Zapata; phone: 183024) have decent selections.

TAXI You can pick up a cab at the *zócalo* and pay by the trip or by the hour. Establish the price before stepping into the vehicle; at press time, a ride within the city limits ranged from 15 to 20 pesos ($2 to $2.70).

SPECIAL EVENTS

The most unusual carnival in Mexico takes place the week before *Miércoles de Ceniza* (Ash Wednesday) in Tepoztlán, about a half hour from Cuernavaca. During the festival, the indigenous residents wear headdresses and perform folkloric dances. In April, the *Festival de las Flores* (Flower Festival) is held either at the *Jardín Borda* or in the *zócalo*.

SHOPPING

Cuernavaca is not particularly noted for any indigenous crafts, although the residents do make cane furniture (usually unvarnished), straw hats, and huaraches (sandals). The big local market that sells food, household items, and clothing also is the best place for hunting down local arts and crafts. To find it, walk five blocks north of the *zócalo* on Avenida Vicente Guerrero; turn right at the footbridge crossing a ravine, and you'll be at the market. There is an arcade with well-made crafts at the exclusive *Plaza los Arcos* shopping center (501 Plan de Ayala). Artisans set up stalls next to the *Museo Cuauhnahuac* (see *Special Places*), though bargain hunters may be disappointed. If you're looking for jewelry, go to a reputable shop—those "genuine" lapis lazuli beads sold at the market may turn out to be artfully painted plastic. Most stores in town open at 10 AM and close around 6 PM. Some close for lunch (or siesta) between 2 and 4 PM. Some shops to explore:

Bio-Art An outstanding selection of handicrafts, textiles, and decorative objects. Blvd. Díaz Ordaz and Alta Tensión (phone: 141458).

Cerámica de Cuernavaca Hand-painted dinnerware and objets d'art. 708 Plan de Ayala (phone: 100487).

Con Angel Only angels are displayed in a showroom in Patricia Garita's spectacular colonial-style home. They're made of clay, tin, copper, porcelain, glass, and papier-mâché. It's heavenly. Open Mondays through Saturdays, by appointment only. 410 Calle San Jerónimo (phone: 132208).

Harms Joyeros An exceptional selection of jewelry and handicrafts. Across from *Las Mañanitas* inn, at 12 Ricardo Linares (no phone).

Mieke Marten's Galería de Arte Mexican antiques and reproductions, as well as ceramics, furniture, lamps, and carved doors, are attractively displayed. There's also an art gallery. 5 Calle del Sol, in the Jardines de Cuernavaca area (phone: 157232).

SPORTS

GO-CARTS Races are held at the *Cuernavaca Track* (715 Av. Domingo Diez; phone: 132377).

GOLF The 18-hole, par 72, Joe Finger–designed *San Gaspar* course has a 280-yard practice tee. Open to the public, it's about 20 minutes southeast of Cuernavaca on the road to Cuautla (15 Av. Emiliano Zapata, Cliserio Alanís, Jiutepec; phone: 194424). Another good bet is *Los Tabachines Club de Golf* (Rte. 95; phone: 123845), designed by Percy Clifford. The well-maintained course is open to members and their guests. Juan Galindo is the pro; there are tennis courts and pools on the premises. The 18-hole course at the *Club de Golf Santa Fe* (Km 22.5 of Rte. 95D; phone: 739-12011) also is open to the public. The pro is Lázaro Domínguez; the manager is Jesús Contreras. And there is a nine-hole layout at the *Club de Golf*

Cuernavaca (1 Calle Plutarco Elías Calles; phone: 185946), the town's oldest and most beautiful course, and another nine-holer at *Hacienda de Cocoyoc* (see *Checking In*).

SWIMMING When Mexico City residents want to go swimming, they head for the Cuernavaca area, jamming many of the public pools on weekends. Among the facilities with large pools are *Agua Hedionda,* the most popular, in Cuautla (phone: 520044); *Oaxtepec,* about 35 miles (56 km) east of Cuernavaca (phone: 5-639-0071 or 5-639-4200), which can get particularly crowded on weekends; *Isstehuixtla,* a famous resort operated by the *Social Security Institute for Federal Employees (ISSSTE),* 28 miles (45 km) south of Cuernavaca (phone: 530-4278); *Balneario Hacienda de Temixco,* 3 miles (5 km) south of Cuernavaca in Temixco (phone: 127348), with 15 swimming pools and 10 wading pools; and *Hacienda de Cocoyoc* (see *Checking In*).

TENNIS The *Cuernavaca Racquet Club* (see *Checking In*) has nine clay courts (four lighted) terraced into hillside gardens; only overnight guests may use the courts. *Cuernavaca Track* (715 Av. Domingo Diez; phone: 132377) has six clay courts; *Tennis Palace* (903 Paseo del Conquistador; phone: 136500) has five synthetic courts; *Del Prado Cuernavaca* (58 Nardo; phone: 174000) has four lighted cement courts; *Club de Golf Santa Fe* (Km 22.5 of Rte. 95D; phone: 739-12011) has three hard-surface courts; and the *Villa Internacional de Tenis* (see *Checking In*) has 10 clay courts.

NIGHTCLUBS AND NIGHTLIFE

After dark on weekends, Cuernavaca is fairly lively. *Barbazul* (10 Calle Prado; phone: 139092) and *Marjaba* (1000 Sonora; phone: 162826) are two of the top discos; another favorite is *Ta'izz* (50 Bajada de Chapultepec; phone: 154060). Also popular is the *Samanna Dance Hall* (1522 Av. Domingo Diez; phone: 110445), which features live music, and *Los Quetzales,* a piano bar and restaurant in the *Villa del Conquistador* hotel (see *Checking In*).

Best in Town

CHECKING IN

Most hotels in Cuernavaca are small, with large, beautiful gardens set behind high walls. Most have heated pools, too. Make reservations at least a week in advance. Expect to pay $100 to $150 per night for a double room at expensive places; $65 to $95 at moderate ones; and $60 or less at the inexpensive spots. Unless otherwise noted, the hotels listed below have telephones, TV sets, and air conditioning in rooms, except for the moderate and inexpensive places, which do not have air conditioning. All telephone numbers are in the 73 city code unless otherwise indicated.

We begin with our favorite havens (all in the expensive category), followed by recommended hotels, listed by price category.

Hacienda de Cocoyoc Built in 1520, this beautifully restored estate, now a resort, has 289 rooms and 25 suites (some with private pools) furnished with Spanish colonial pieces. There is a nine-hole golf course plus access to an 18-hole course; two large pools, one framed by a historic stone aqueduct and waterfall; and five restaurants. Horseback riding and tennis are available. The American plan (all meals included) is offered. It's popular for meetings and conventions. On the road to Cuautla (phone: 735-62211; 5-550-6480 in Mexico City; 800-458-6888; fax: 735-61212).

Hostería las Quintas This dignified yet cozy place provides a relaxed atmosphere. There is a heated pool, an excellent restaurant with a bar, beautiful gardens, and a lovely display of bonsai trees. Originally a private home, the building has been operating as a hotel since the 1960s. Besides 10 rooms, there are 53 suites, 11 with fireplaces and all with private terraces overlooking a garden. Book well ahead for the busy winter months, when many Americans are in residence. 107 Av. Díaz Ordaz (phone: 183949; 800-99018 in Mexico; fax: 183895).

Las Mañanitas Perhaps the single most popular inn in Mexico, this refined hideaway can compete with the finest in Europe (it's a Relais & Châteaux member). In the winter, it's nearly impossible to get a room unless you make reservations *far* in advance, and it may even be difficult to get a table for lunch or dinner, since *Las Mañanitas* also happens to have what may be the best restaurant in town (see *Eating Out*). During high season, guests tend to stay for weeks, even months, and there are only two double rooms, 19 magnificent one-bedroom suites, and one rather astonishing two-bedroom suite to go around. The inn was constructed slowly, with the original turn-of-the-century mansion as its center and units added carefully and selectively over the years. Each room is different, finished with architectural elements salvaged from old houses in Puebla and furnished with real antiques and artful ersatz pieces. Each room also has its own private patio or terrace, and suites in the older section have individual fireplaces. The exquisite garden, sprinkled with Francisco Zúñiga bronzes, counts among its residents peacocks, cranes, flamingos, and parrots. Also featured are live music, alfresco dining, alert service from a staff of more than 100 (at an inn that sleeps perhaps only 45 guests!), and an air of simple but genuine luxury. No credit cards accepted. 107 Ricardo Linares (phone: 141466; fax: 183672).

EXPENSIVE

Camino Real Sumiya Formerly belonging to heiress Barbara Hutton, this opulent Japanese-style palace is now a hotel run by the Camino Real group. Its 157 rooms and six suites are impressively appointed and feature plenty of amenities, including mini-bars and satellite TV. There are also five restaurants (including the excellent *Sumiya*—see *Eating Out*), a swimming pool with a bar, and six tennis courts. In Jiutepec, about half a mile (1 km) past the CIVAC exit on Rte. 95 (phone: 209199; 800-7-CAMINO in the US; 800-90123 in Mexico; fax: 209142).

Cuernavaca Racquet Club A posh playground for the Beautiful People, it has 52 rooms. Those accustomed to the finer things in life can use the club's nine tennis courts, swim in the pool, and dine well. It's truly lovely. 100 Francisco Villa (phone: 112400; 800-228-5151; fax: 175483).

Hacienda Vista Hermosa This 102-room place attracts tour groups and hordes of day-trippers on Sundays, but it can be quite delightful midweek. It has a pool, tennis and squash courts, horseback riding facilities, a jogging track, a disco, and a restaurant. About 15 miles (24 km) south of Cuernavaca in Tequesquitengo (phone: 734-70492; 5-566-7700 in Mexico City; 800-70333 elsewhere in Mexico; fax: 734-70488).

Maximilian's Twenty-nine of its 62 cozy suites have fireplaces, and all have cable TV that picks up US channels. Other pluses: a large garden, two heated pools, a piano bar, friendly service, and a fine restaurant (see *Maximilian's* in *Eating Out*) specializing in international dishes. 125 Galeana, Colonia Acapantzingo (phone: 182010; fax: 183066).

Villa Béjar Antique cars transport guests and their luggage to these 67 deluxe suites. Two lovely pools, a tennis court, a beauty and health spa, boutiques, spacious gardens, impeccable service, and a good restaurant and bar with nightly entertainment make this place a favorite getaway for wealthy Mexicans. 2350 Av. Domingo Diez (phone: 113301 or 175000; 5-549-1560 in Mexico City; fax: 174953).

MODERATE

Hacienda de Cortés Built as a retirement home for the conqueror, this 16th-century plantation has 22 suites (no TV sets), plus lovely gardens, a pool, a Jacuzzi, and a good restaurant of the same name (see *Eating Out*) with live music. 90 Plaza Kennedy, Colonia Atlacomulco (phone: 160867; fax: 150035).

Posada Jacarandas The 85 rooms in this inn are set in spacious, manicured gardens, and most have porches (though no TV sets); there is also a "Love Nest" suite built high up in a tree. Meals are served on an enclosed terrace overlooking the gardens. Two tennis courts and swimming pools provide diversion. Rooms and dining facilities are separate for guests with and without children. 805 Cuauhtémoc (phone: 157777; 5-544-3098 in Mexico City; fax: 157888).

Posada San Angelo A 17-room colonial inn, it has a heated pool, lovely gardens, and a good dining room. 100 Cerrada de la Selva (phone: 141325; 800-99016 in Mexico; fax: 126604).

Del Prado Cuernavaca Large by Cuernavaca standards, this property has 200 rooms, a spacious garden, a pool, four tennis courts, social activities for adults and children, a restaurant, a bar, a snack bar, and a gym. 58 Nardo (phone: 174000; 800-336-5454; fax: 174155).

Villa del Conquistador This 39-room hostelry has a spectacular view of Cuernavaca, as well as a heated pool, tennis, squash, miniature golf, two restaurants, and a bar with live entertainment. 134 Paseo del Conquistador (phone: 131055; 5-516-0483 in Mexico City; fax: 132365).

Villa Internacional de Tenis There are 10 tennis courts for the 14 luxurious suites (five with air conditioning, two with satellite TV) at this lovely resort. Spacious gardens, a large pool, and a restaurant are among the other amenities. 702 Chalma, Colonia Lomas de Atzingo (phone: 130829 or 170611; fax: 173717).

INEXPENSIVE

Posada Primavera On a hill overlooking Cuernavaca, this 30-unit property offers a heated pool, a restaurant-bar, and a nightclub. 57 Paseo del Conquistador (phone: 138420; fax: 132793).

Posada de Xochiquetzal US expatriates run this 15-room colonial hotel, which has a lovely dining room with a fireplace, a large garden, and a pool. 200 Calle Leyva (phone: 120220 or 185767; fax: 129126).

Quinta las Flores All 20 rooms here overlook a charming garden (15 have telephones and TV sets). There is also a terrace spacious enough to accommodate a pool and dining room. Meals are served family-style, and breakfast is included in the rate. 210 Tlaquepaque (phone: 125769 or 141244; fax: 123751).

EATING OUT

Cuernavaca's restaurants offer a wide variety of international dishes. For a dinner for two, expect to pay $65 to $85 at an expensive place; $45 to $60 at a moderate one; and $40 or less at an inexpensive spot. Prices don't include drinks, wine, tax, or tip. Most restaurants below accept MasterCard and Visa, and a few also accept American Express and Diners Club; it's a good idea to call ahead and check. Unless otherwise noted, all restaurants are open daily for lunch and dinner. All telephone numbers are in the 73 city code unless otherwise indicated.

EXPENSIVE

Casa de Campo Ensconced in a former colonial home, this is one of Cuernavaca's most successful dining spots. *Camarones amorosos* (shrimp baked in a white sauce and served in a puff pastry shell) and the *princesa verde* (almond cake filled with raspberry jam) are two major reasons for its popularity. Reservations advised. 101 Abasolo (phone: 182635 or 182689).

Ma Maison A happy marriage of French cooking techniques and Mexican ingredients has produced such delicacies as filet of sea bass stuffed with *huitlacoche* (a corn fungus with a delicate mushroom-like flavor) and a pâté of smoked trout. Reservations advised. 58 Francisco Villa (phone: 131435).

Las Mañanitas In the hostelry of the same name, this is perhaps the best restaurant in town. Its international menu is complemented by fine service and seating on the terrace and in the garden. Reservations advised. No credit cards accepted. 107 Ricardo Linares (phone: 124646).

Prima o Poi Fine Italian dishes are served in this comfortable Mediterranean-style restaurant, where diners choose from a table in the wine cellar or on the mezzanine, which affords a panoramic view. Reservations advised. 1001 Av. Río Mayo, Colonia Vista Hermosa (phone: 163282).

Sumiya The late heiress Barbara Hutton's former Japanese-style palace (now the *Camino Real Sumiya*) is the splendid setting for the French and Japanese fare served here. Reservations advised. In Jiutepec, about half a mile (1 km) past the CIVAC exit on Rte. 95 (phone: 190033).

MODERATE

Le Château René In a venerable mansion of the same name, this restaurant offers well-prepared, thoughtfully served French and Swiss dishes. Reservations advised. 11 Calzada de los Reyes (phone: 172300).

Hacienda de Cortés This place—a favorite with locals—has an international menu, excellent service, and the romantic setting of a converted hacienda. Reservations unnecessary. 90 Plaza Kennedy, Colonia Atlacomulco (phone: 150035 or 158844).

Harry's Grill A lively crowd gathers at this link in the ubiquitous Carlos Anderson chain. Barbecued chicken and ribs are featured. Reservations advised. 3 Gutenberg (phone: 127679).

Maximilian's Fine international, Mexican, and even American-style cooking coexist here. Order the scrumptious *huitlacoche* (delicately flavored corn fungus) pâté in season (summer and fall). Reservations advised. 125 Galeana, Colonia Acapantzingo (phone: 182010).

El Vienés It's not fancy, but the food is excellent. Try the steak tartare and the lovely, soufflé-like Austrian dessert called *Salzburger nockerl.* Closed

Tuesdays. Reservations advised. 4 Lerdo de Tejada, a block north of Jardín Juárez (phone: 184044).

Vivaldi Set in a delightful converted house, this has become one of the most popular spots in Cuernavaca. Tasty European dishes—Hungarian goulash, beef Stroganoff, and Viennese pastries—are served in indoor and garden settings. No reservations. 102 Calle Pericón (phone: 180122).

INEXPENSIVE

La Parroquia This Mexican-sounding spot also dishes up Middle Eastern and other ethnic fare. Reservations unnecessary. On the *zócalo* (phone: 185820).

Ensenada

(pronounced En-se-*nah*-dah)

As a resort area, Ensenada may well be Southern California's best-kept Mexican secret. Although it claims the best beach and water sports section of the northern Baja coast, few people outside Los Angeles and San Diego know the city well. Ensenada is about 60 miles (96 km) south of the US-Mexico border at Tijuana, a short drive along the well-maintained four-lane scenic highway that connects the two cities. There is also regular bus service to Ensenada from San Diego and Tijuana.

Shipping is Ensenada's principal activity (it's the busiest port on the Baja peninsula). The city is larger than most visitors realize—in fact, with more than 350,000 inhabitants, it's the third-largest in the state. Concentrated in an area along or near the waterfront, the tourist attractions give Ensenada the appearance of a small, charming town when it is, in fact, a thriving port.

Bahía de Todos Santos (All Saints Bay) was named by Sebastián Vizcaíno in 1602, and it became a harbor of some note, although for centuries the settlement on shore remained small. Ensenada was a trading town for the handful of ranchers in the area and a supply point for some of the missions. Then, in 1870, gold was discovered at nearby Real de Castillo.

The gold rush that followed gave enough substance to the town that it was made the territorial capital. From Ensenada, settlers ventured into the vast, empty lands of Baja California, but the shortage of water doomed most efforts to failure. When the mines played out in Ensenada, and the capital was moved to Mexicali, the city went into decline.

Prohibition in the United States changed the city's fortunes. Bahía de Todos Santos became a safe harbor for rumrunners, and reckless film stars flew down in biplanes to drink and gamble at the old *Riviera Club*. When drinking again became legal in the US and gambling was declared illegal in Mexico, Ensenada might have withered once more, but its port facilities saved it. The Mexicali Valley, across the peninsula, had blossomed into a major cotton-growing area, and ships put in at Ensenada to pick up the bales for export.

Also important to the local economy is wine production, which began here two centuries ago and continues to thrive today. In fact, 70% of the wine and brandy consumed in Mexico is produced in Ensenada's Mediterranean climate. (Mexico is one of the world's largest consumers of brandy.) Fishing and the fish cannery industries are healthy industries here.

Multifaceted Ensenada also caters to ever greater numbers of tourists, many of whom pass through on longer trips through Baja on Route 1. As word gets out about its well-run hotels, excellent restaurants, varied shops and good bargains, lively nightlife, satisfying fishing, and appealing beaches, however, it is increasingly a popular destination on its own.

Ensenada At-a-Glance

SEEING THE CITY

To look out over Ensenada, follow Calle 2 up Chapultepec Hill, where there is an observation point marked *"Mirador."*

SPECIAL PLACES

Ensenada is full of nooks and crannies, some surprisingly large. Prime areas for strolling are Boulevard Costera and Avenidas López Mateos, Juárez, and Ruiz. The *malecón,* or boardwalk, along the waterfront, is a pleasant promenade.

AVENIDA LÓPEZ MATEOS Officially Avenida Adolfo López Mateos, named after the President of Mexico from 1958 to 1964, it is also known as Avenida Primera (First Avenue). This eminently walkable street is where almost all the hotels, numerous restaurants, and many of the better shops are located.

RIVIERA DEL PACÍFICO (PACIFIC RIVIERA) Once managed by Jack Dempsey and reputedly owned by Al Capone, this 1920s-era gambling casino brought in the jet setters before there were even any jets. It is now a social, civic, and cultural center. Blvd. Lázaro Cárdenas and Av. Riviera.

BODEGAS SANTO TOMÁS This winery, founded by the Dominicans in 1888, is one of the major producers of wine in Mexico. On view are the storage casks and the thousands of bottles that must be turned by hand to make sparkling wine. Usually there are three tours daily—at 11 AM and 1 and 3 PM—but it's a good idea to call ahead. Admission charge includes a sampling of wine and cheese. 666 Av. Miramar (phone: 82509 or 83333).

LA BUFADORA (BLOWHOLE) A dramatic sea geyser, La Bufadora is at Punta Banda on the southern arm of the bay. The ocean puts on a spectacular show here. The drive out takes about 30 minutes; be sure to wear comfortable shoes.

ISLA TODOS SANTOS (ALL SAINTS ISLAND) Some literary historians believe this was the inspiration for Robert Lewis Stevenson's *Treasure Island.* (The author, along with his mother and niece, lived in Ensenada for a year.) The island is visible from Playa La Jolla and *La Cueva de los Tigres* restaurant (see *Eating Out*), as well as from whale watching tour boats run by *Sportsfishing Charters* (phone: 82185)—also known as *Santa Mónica*—from December 26 until the end of the season (which lasts until late March or early April). Isla Todos Santos is not currently open to the public, though plans for tours and camping are in the works.

> ### EXTRA SPECIAL
> Drive across the peninsula on Route 3 to San Felipe, a fishing village on the Sea of Cortés (Gulf of California). The three-hour, 160-mile (256-km)

trip across the desert is memorable, for this is one of the last wilderness areas left in North America; on Route 3 you will feel very much alone. San Felipe's tourist office (phone: 657-71155) is at the corner of Avenida Manzanillo and Calle Mar de Cortés, and there are several places to stop for lunch. If you decide to spend the night, try *Las Misiones* hotel (phone: 657-71280; 800-6-MISIONES; fax: 657-71283) or *Las Palmas* (phone: 657-71333; fax: 657-71382), an elegantly remodeled property that is the town's oldest. You may want to take a different route for the return trip to California, via Mexicali or Tecate.

Sources and Resources

TOURIST INFORMATION

The *Chamber of Commerce* (693 Av. López Mateos; phone: 82322; fax: 82975) and the *Municipal Tourism Committee* (450 Blvd. Costero, at Teniente Azueta; phone: 82411 or 83675; fax: 88588) have helpful staffs; both offices are closed Sunday afternoons. The state tourist office and the office of the state attorney for tourist assistance are at the same location and share the same telephone numbers (Blvd. Costera between Las Rocas and Riviera Sts.; phone: 23022; 800-301-9687; fax: 23081). The state tourist office is open daily; the state attorney's office is closed weekends.

LOCAL COVERAGE The English-language monthly *Baja Sun,* available in hotels, is full of information and discount coupons for merchandise and drinks in local establishments. San Diego and Los Angeles newspapers are available at *Licores Baja* (on Av. López Mateos and Riviera).

TELEPHONE The city code for Ensenada is 617. *Note:* Mexico's telephone company has embarked on a major expansion project that involves changing telephone numbers in many areas of the country. At press time, all numbers listed in this chapter were correct. However, if you have any difficulties reaching attractions listed here, contact the local tourist office.

CLIMATE AND CLOTHES Ensenada shares Southern California's climate: It can be cool in winter and rainy in January and February. Dress is casual, but somewhat more conservative than in the US.

GETTING AROUND

Most hotels, restaurants, and shops are within walking distance of each other. Many visitors arrive in their own cars, and for those who don't, taxis are plentiful, though a bit expensive—about 66 pesos/$11 for a round trip to Playa Estero (see *Swimming and Sunning,* below). City buses are not efficient. A good local car rental agency is *Ensenada Rent-a-Car* (*Plaza Marina* shopping center, one block east of the state tourist office; phone: 81045). *Turismo Cenicenta,* also in *Plaza Marina* (phone: 81641) runs three-and-a-half-hour tours of the city and environs for a minimum of six persons. Several of the launches found at the harbor offer tours around the bay; they will take four or five people, though you don't have to be part of a group.

SPECIAL EVENTS

Something special always seems to be going on in Ensenada. The pre-*Lenten Carnaval,* or *Mardi Gras,* is one of the city's most colorful events. The *Feria de Tacos, Tamales y Mole* (Taco, Tamale, and Mole Fair), also known as the *Feria de Antojitos* (literally "Snacks Fair"), which features myriad Mexican finger foods, makes April a big party month. In April or early May, the *Regata Newport-Ensenada* (Newport-Ensenada Regatta), several thousand yachts strong, sets off for Ensenada from Newport Beach, California. In June the *Baja 500* (mile) off-road race gets off to a roaring start in Ensenada. The *Regata Todos Santos* (All Saints Regatta) is held every August. September brings the *International Chili Cook-Off,* followed by the *Feria Internacional de Mariscos* (International Seafood Fair) in October. In November, the *Baja 1,000* (mile) off-road race departs from Ensenada, and there is a large travel and handicrafts show. *Christmas* week is spiked with gaiety, as the town puts on traditional *posada* parties that continue through *Noche Vieja* (New Year's Eve). For details, call the tourist office (see *Tourist Information*).

SHOPPING

One of the most popular pastimes in Ensenada is buying things. The North American Free Trade Agreement has not changed things much here; Baja California is still a *zona franca* (free zone), and a great many items are imported untaxed. Many of the shops along Avenida López Mateos sell high-quality Mexican handicrafts at good prices. Most stores are open from 10 AM until 7 PM Mondays through Saturdays; they close at 5 PM on Sundays.

Artesanías Castillo Browse among silver necklaces, bracelets, earrings, and rings made by the renowned Castillo brothers of Taxco. 656 Av. López Mateos (phone: 82961).

Galería Anna Outstanding items in this jam-packed store include blankets, rugs, placemats, tablecloths, masks, furniture, and pottery. 821 Av. López Mateos (phone: 40704).

México Lindo A saddle shop that attracts real cowhands. It has good buys in belts, leather bags, hats, and chaps. 688 Av. López Mateos (phone: 81381).

La Mina de Solomon Home accessories; the engravings and pewter items are particularly noteworthy. 1000 Av. López Mateos (phone: 82836).

La Piel Stylish leather clothes for men and women. 720 Av. López Mateos (phone: 81294).

Swan Attractive leather handbags are sold here at what the store claims are factory prices. 668 Av. López Mateos (phone: 82829).

SPORTS

FISHING Yellowtail, in season May through November, is what most anglers go after, though sea bass, barracuda, swordfish, bonito, albacore, and halibut also inhabit the local waters. The best all-around fishing months are July through September, and daily charters are available. There are also open-ticket vessels, on which one individual can join an already existing group. Open-ticket vessels can also be hired by groups of two to four people. *Gordo's Sports Fishing* (phone: 83515) and *Sportsfishing Charters* (phone: 82185) are reliable outfits. Surf casting is popular south of town.

GOLF *Bajamar,* 20 miles (32 km) north of Ensenada, has 18 holes and some of the finest facilities anywhere in the area (phone: 615-50151; 800-BAJA-418).

HORSEBACK RIDING It's offered at the *Mona Lisa* campground (no phone), located 12 miles/20 km north of town off Rte. 1; and on the beach (at the end of Blvd. Costero). Escorted trail rides leave from *San Miguel Stables* at *Hacienda de los Rodríguez,* home of a former Mexican president (phone: 46767).

HUNTING The quail season is November through mid-January. The tourist office (see *Tourist Information*) takes reservations for *Ejido Uruapan,* a hunting ranch 26 miles (42 km) south of Ensenada. Hunters must bring their weapons with them, which involves *mucho* red tape. (For additional details, see *Hunting* in DIVERSIONS.)

SURFING The entire Pacific coast of the Baja Peninsula boasts ideal surfing conditions year-round. Hardcore surfers trek 8 miles (13 km) north of Ensenada to the village of San Miguel, where an abundance of rocks and sea urchins makes this a dangerous area for beginners. Surfing aficionados also go out to Isla Todos Santos (see *Special Places*); Playa Mona Lisa is recommended for novices.

SWIMMING AND SUNNING The premier beach resort of Baja California Norte boasts miles of shoreline. Estero, the area's best beach, is a hard sand strand that stretches for 10 miles south of the downtown area. It offers plenty of privacy and space for camping, and it's perfect for both sunning and bathing (go at low tide to avoid the undertow). Other possibilities for swimming and sunning are Playa La Jolla, Playa El Faro, and Playa Mona Lisa.

TENNIS Ensenada's private *Baja Tennis Club* (phone: 30220) has four lighted concrete courts; reservations must be made through hotels. Also check the *Estero Beach* and *Quintas Papagayo* hotels (see *Checking In*).

WATER SKIING The best facilities are at the *Estero Beach* hotel (see *Checking In*), which faces a sheltered lagoon south of town. Guests from other hotels are welcome.

NIGHTCLUBS AND NIGHTLIFE

Everybody in Ensenada either starts off the evening or ends it at *Cantina Hussong's* (113 Av. Ruiz; phone: 83210), a cow-town saloon left over from the gold rush days, and still wild and woolly. *Papas & Beer* (Av. López Mateos and Av. Ruiz; phone: 70125) features a folk band from the state of Sonora on some Thursday nights. If your taste runs to disco dancing or billiards, head for *Club de Tabi* (Calle Alvaro Obregón between Calles 2 and 3, which is 2½ blocks south of Av. López Mateos; phone: 82987).

Best in Town

CHECKING IN

Ensenada's hotels are busiest during the summer and on weekends. Always make reservations and try to arrive early in the day. Note that rates given here are for high season; in the low season, prices can drop by as much as 30%. Unless otherwise noted, the hotels listed have air conditioning, telephones, and TV sets in rooms. A double room in an expensive hotel costs $100 to $140 per night; in a moderate one, $50 to $100; and in an inexpensive one, $50 or less. All telephone numbers are in the 617 city code unless otherwise indicated.

EXPENSIVE

Las Rosas by the Sea A hotel and spa, this establishment offers 29 rooms and two suites, all with attractive decor, balconies, and ocean views (but no air conditioning). There is also a restaurant, a piano bar, a sauna, a spa with a Jacuzzi, and two pools. Two miles (3 km) north of Ensenada at Km 105.5 of Rte. 1 (phone: 44310 or 44320; fax: 44595).

MODERATE

Casa del Sol Best Western A pretty and hospitable property with 44 rooms, four suites, a bar, a large pool, and foreign currency exchange services. Continental breakfast is included in the room rate Mondays through Thursdays November through February. Av. Blancarte and Av. López Mateos (phone: 81570; 800-528-1234; fax: 82025).

Estero Beach This hostelry with 87 rooms and 20 suites (no air conditioning or in-room phones) is perfect for sports enthusiasts, boasting tennis, horseback riding from December through March, biking, sailing, water skiing, and fishing from June through September (but no pool). A restaurant and a bar are also on site. On the beach 6 miles (10 km) south of town (phone: 66235; fax: 66925).

Misión Santa Isabel A pretty, colonial-style place, it has 58 smallish rooms (no air conditioning) on only two floors; also available are a small pool, a restaurant, and a bar with live music on weekends. 1119 Castillo, corner of Av. López Mateos (phone: 83616; 619-259-0686 in San Diego; fax: 83345).

Punta Morro This elegant modern hotel overlooking the bay has 24 suites (21 have kitchens) with terraces and ocean views (but no air conditioning). All are equipped with refrigerators, and there's a restaurant, a nice pool, and a Jacuzzi. One mile (1.6 km) north of Ensenada on Rte. 1 (phone: 83507; fax: 44409).

Quintas Papagayo Most of the 26 suites and 20 cottages here have kitchens and ocean views (but there's no air conditioning, TV sets, or phones). Good seafood is served at *Hussong's El Pelícano & Oyster Bar* (see *Eating Out*), and there's also a pool, tennis courts, and a private beach. One mile (1.6 km) north of Ensenada on Rte. 1 (phone: 44980; fax: 44155).

San Nicolás Resort Lovely, with 141 rooms and seven suites decorated in colonial style, it has a view of the sea, a restaurant, two pools (one is huge), a bar, a disco, and security parking. Av. López Mateos and Guadalupe (phone: 61901; fax: 64930).

Travelodge In a rustic setting, it has 52 rooms with wet bars and in-room safes, a suite with a private Jacuzzi, a cozy restaurant and bar, a pool, and an outdoor Jacuzzi. 130 Av. Blancarte, corner of Av. López Mateos (phone: 81601; 800-578-7878; fax: 40005).

INEXPENSIVE

Bahía This casual place has 62 rooms with cable TV (but no air conditioning), a pool, a restaurant, two bars, music on weekends, and parking. Centrally located, at Av. López Mateos and Riveroll (phone: 82101, 82102, or 82103; fax: 81455).

Fiesta Inn It has 33 spacious rooms, seven with kitchens (but there's no air conditioning or phones). There's also a restaurant. Daily, weekly, and monthly rates are available, but reserve two to four weeks ahead for US holiday periods. One mile (1.6 km) south of downtown, at 237 Agustín Sanguines (phone: 61361).

EATING OUT

Quail, abalone, and Pacific lobster are the specialties to sample in Ensenada. Expect to pay more than $100 for a meal for two (including drinks, wine, tax, and tip) at an expensive restaurant; $50 to $100 in a moderate one; and $40 or less in an inexpensive one. Most restaurants below accept MasterCard and Visa, and a few also accept American Express and Diners Club; it's a good idea to call ahead and check. Unless otherwise noted, restaurants are open daily. All telephone numbers are in the 617 city code unless otherwise indicated.

La Cueva de los Tigres The "Tigers' Cave" claims Ensenada's most delightful setting—as well as the distinction of being one of the best restaurants in Mexico. Its abalone topped with shredded crab brings pilgrims from as far away as San Francisco and Seattle. Don't miss the sunset. Reservations advised. On the beach, 1½ miles (2 km) south of town by car (or a mile walking along the beach), on Av. Acapulco off Rte. 1; watch for the sign (phone: 66450).

El Rey Sol Not to be missed, Baja California's great French restaurant has become an Ensenada legend. The *medallones de camarones Doña Pepita* (shrimp prepared with bacon and capers) and the fabulous desserts are the stuff of which dining dreams are made. Reservations advised. Av. López Mateos and Blancarte (phone: 81733).

La Tortuga Popular selections here include breaded abalone, grilled lobster, and stuffed peppers—all served in a relaxed setting. No reservations. Downtown, at 800 Av. López Mateos (phone: 83075).

Casino Royal Run by the owners of *La Cueva de los Tigres* (see above), this dining star is ensconced in an old house with a lovely garden. The fare is continental, with specials like seafood gumbo and a complement of lamb and quail dishes. Reservations advised. Blvd. Las Lunas and Ondines (phone: 71480).

La Fonda Idyllically set above the Pacific on a flower-laden balcony, this eatery serves delightful Mexican food. No reservations. No credit cards accepted. In a pleasant rustic hotel of the same name, it's well worth the 19-mile (30-km) ride up-beach (or through the mountains) toward Tijuana, via Rte. 1 (phone: 66-287352 or 66-287353).

Casamar Seafood of all kinds is served here, and a soloist sings romantic ballads Wednesday through Saturday nights. No reservations. Across from the entrance to the harbor at 987 Blvd. Costero (phone: 40417).

Hussong's El Pelícano & Oyster Bar The excellent seafood dishes include squid in crabmeat sauce. Closed Mondays. No reservations. No credit cards accepted. In the *Quintas Papagayo* hotel, located 1 mile (1.6 km) north of town on Rte. 1 (phone: 44980).

Guadalajara
(pronounced Gwa-dah-lah-*ha*-rah)

Six major airlines fly into Guadalajara, making Mexico's second-largest city a top travel destination. Once proudly nicknamed the country's "biggest small town," Guadalajara has become sophisticated, cosmopolitan, and crowded. The city benefits from all the best of Mexican history and culture. During the reign of the Spaniards, Guadalajara was an important center for commerce, and the city's great wealth was lavished on superb colonial architecture. Spain's power eventually waned, but the beautiful buildings remain as a reminder of the city's past.

Guadalajara rests on a mile-high plain surrounded by rugged countryside, about 300 miles (480 km) west and slightly north of Mexico City. The city's relatively isolated site fostered its characteristic sense of independence, self-reliance, and pride.

The Spanish influence is as strong in Guadalajara, however, as in any city in the country. Following the conquest, orders were given to open an outpost of the empire in the West. The charter sent from Spain instructed the builders to use the finest materials in constructing the city: Streets were to be wide, and ample space was to be set aside for parks. Along with government buildings, there was to be a church, monastery, hospital, and market, all near the central plaza. During three centuries of colonial rule, those instructions served as a guide, and Guadalajara became "more Spanish than Spain." Its people are still known as *tapatíos,* a name thought to be derived from the word for the tasseled cape favored by Spanish gentlemen.

Though the 1990 census puts its population at nearly three and a half million (with unofficial figures even higher), Guadalajara has remained a city of parks and fountains, of monuments and flower-lined boulevards. Although it has been rapidly industrializing, erecting modern skyscrapers that rise above the city's traditional skyline, the city has managed to modernize its industrial facilities without altering its older, more historic areas or greatly endangering its way of life (though air pollution has in recent years become a problem).

Guadalajara is famed for its talented artisans, for the crafts of nearby Tlaquepaque (a village that has been absorbed by the sprawling city) and Tonalá, and for the tequila distilleries in the town of Tequila, about 35 miles (56 km) away. It is also the birthplace of José Clemente Orozco, one of this century's greatest artists, who did some of his best work here: For many people, his powerful murals at the *Instituto Cultural Cabañas* (Cabañas Cultural Institute) are reason enough to make a pilgrimage to this city.

This is also one of Mexico's most delightful areas for tourists. It has a marvelous climate—eternal springtime, with a rainy season for some three months during the summer. But most important in attracting visitors is its evocation of the graciousness and gentility of old Mexico.

Guadalajara At-a-Glance

SEEING THE CITY

The most superb views of the city are offered by the rooftop lounge of the *Calinda Roma* hotel (170 Av. Juárez between Calles Maestranza and Degollado; phone: 614-8650), from the hilltop perch of *El Tapatío* resort, and from the glass elevators of the 22-story *Fiesta Americana* hotel, Guadalajara's tallest building (see *Checking In* for *El Tapatío* and the *Fiesta Americana*).

SPECIAL PLACES

With a clearly marked map, you can easily drive around Guadalajara on your own; the traffic can get heavy, but it's manageable. If you want to really relax, however, hire a car and an English-speaking guide for a one-day tour. Many guides gather at the *Fénix Best Western* (see *Checking In*) at about 9 AM every day, but they also can be found at the "turismo" stands outside most of the major hotels.

DOWNTOWN

MUSEO REGIONAL DE GUADALAJARA In this 18th-century structure, which once served as a theological seminary, are outstanding Mexican and Spanish paintings, pre-Columbian relics, regional arts and crafts, portraits of dignitaries, colonial-period furniture, and even a carriage said to have belonged to Emperor Maximilian. Closed Mondays. Admission charge. Located at 60 Calle Liceo, across from the north side of the cathedral (phone: 614-2227).

CATEDRAL This is a strange hodgepodge of half a dozen architectural styles, including Gothic, Tuscan, Moorish, Mudejar, Corinthian, and even Byzantine. Construction was started in 1571; the church was consecrated in 1618. The cathedral houses many art treasures donated by Spain's King Fernando VII in appreciation of the financial support the city gave Spain during the Napoleonic Wars. Among the 11 ornate altars, the one dedicated to Our Lady of Roses is a standout. There's also a magnificent pipe organ. On Av. Alcalde (Av. 16 de Septiembre, but it changes names here), facing Plaza Guadalajara, which is also known as Plaza de los Laureles.

PALACIO DE GOBIERNO (STATEHOUSE) This historic structure, built in 1643, was the site of Padre Miguel Hidalgo's 1810 landmark decree abolishing slavery. The building features dynamic murals by Orozco. Open daily. No admission charge. Just southeast of the cathedral, on Av. Corona at Morelos, on the Plaza de Armas (phone: 614-5414).

PALACIO MUNICIPAL (CITY HALL) Of interest to visitors in this colonnaded, colonial-style building is a colorful mural depicting the founding of Guadalajara, as well as the *Galería Municipal,* which offers art exhibits. Open daily. No admission charge. Catercorner northwest of the cathedral, on Av. Hidalgo.

TEATRO DEGOLLADO (DEGOLLADO THEATER) Guadalajara's major cultural center, a lavishly beautiful 19th-century building decorated with rich reds, gold leaf, and crystal chandeliers, is the home of the *Orquesta Filarmónica de Jalisco* and the *Ballet Folklórico.* The latter performs on Sundays at 10 AM, and there are usually several performances of ballet, opera, the symphony, and other concerts during the week. The interior includes a notable mural depicting Dante's *Divine Comedy.* Located east of the cathedral, at the intersection of Calle Degollado and Av. Hidalgo (phone: 614-4773).

INSTITUTO CULTURAL CABAÑAS Built in 1803, this magnificent structure on Plaza Tapatía is now a center for the arts, housing—in addition to works of other artists—two of José Clemente Orozco's masterpieces, *Man of Fire* and *The Four Horsemen of the Apocalypse.* Closed Mondays. Admission charge. 8 Calle Cabañas (phone: 617-6734).

IGLESIA DE SAN FRANCISCO DE ASIS Dating from the early years of the conquest, this historic church is particularly notable for its elaborate façade. In *Parque San Francisco* on Av. Corona, six blocks south of Av. Juárez.

IGLESIA DE NUESTRA SEÑORA DE ARANZAZÚ (CHURCH OF OUR LADY OF ARANZAZÚ) Don't let the simple exterior fool you: Inside is one of Guadalajara's finest, most ornate altars. In *Parque San Francisco.*

IGLESIA DE SANTA MÓNICA A 250-year-old church with a lovely Baroque façade, it's located in a fascinating colonial neighborhood several blocks northwest of the *Palacio Municipal,* at the corner of Calle de Santa Mónica and Calle San Felipe.

SOUTH OF DOWNTOWN

MUSEO ARQUEOLÓGICO DEL OCCIDENTE DE MÉXICO (ARCHAEOLOGICAL MUSEUM OF WESTERN MEXICO) In this museum are ancient indigenous artifacts from the western states of Colima, Jalisco, and Nayarit. Closed Mondays. Admission charge. Av. 16 de Septiembre, across the street from the *Parque Agua Azul,* several blocks north of the railroad station (no phone).

PARQUE AGUA AZUL (BLUE WATER PARK) A delightful recreation area, with flower-filled gardens, an aviary, an orchid house, a screened-in tropical garden, and a children's park. On the edge are the *Instituto de la Artesanía Jalisciense* showroom (see *Shopping*) and the *Teatro Experimental* (Experimental Theater), which presents concerts and Spanish-language plays, including children's plays. The *Casa de Cultura de Jalisco* (Jalisco House of Culture), a venue for a variety of cultural events and exhibits, and a public library are across the street. Open daily. Admission charge. Calzada Independencia Sur and Calzada del Campesino.

NORTH OF DOWNTOWN

PARQUE NATURAL HUENTITÁN This park features a planetarium and a zoo that is not to be missed—with 1,500 animals in 27 special habitats. At the entrance are 17 columns, with a chimp by famed Guadalajara-born sculptor and potter Sergio Bustamante perched atop each, and a huge vertical fountain with 1,200 fantastical animal faces, also designed by Bustamante. The *Parque Zoológico de Guadalajara* (Guadalajara Zoo) has a four-story aviary, ponds filled with black and white swans, a children's zoo, and an enormous snake house. There's a magnificent view of the Barranca de Oblatos (see *Extra Special*), too. A walk through the park takes about two hours. For those with less time (or energy), there are four mini-trains. Make sure to wear a hat and sunscreen. Closed Mondays. Admission charge. At Calzada Independencia Nte. and Calzada Ricardo Flores Magón, on the edge of the Barranca de Oblatos, about 7 miles (11 km) northeast of downtown (phone: 674-4360, park; 638-4307, zoo).

NEARBY

TLAQUEPAQUE (pronounced Tla-kay-*pa*-kay) Formerly a distinct village and now enveloped by Guadalajara, this place is famous for its sophisticated handicrafts, including hand-painted pottery. There are also glass factories and artisans working in silver and copper, as well as indigenous weavers working at handlooms; see *Shopping* for details on particular stores in Tlaquepaque. The *Museo Regional de Cerámica* (Regional Ceramics Museum; 237 Independencia; phone: 635-5404) is also well worth a visit. It's closed Mondays; there's no admission charge. Visitor information is available at *Dirección de Turismo Tlaquepaque* (Tlaquepaque Tourist Office; 160 Donato Guerra; phone: 635-0238), which is closed weekends. About 5 miles (8 km) southeast of the city center on Rte. 80.

TONALÁ About 6 miles (10 km) east of Tlaquepaque, it's small-town Mexico, with none of the sophistication of Tlaquepaque. Dark, sienna-colored pottery and blown glass are the specialties here; Thursdays and Sundays are market days. Don't miss the *Museo Nacional de la Cerámica* (National Ceramic Museum; 104 Constitución; phone: 683-0494). The museum is closed Mondays; there's no admission charge. The tourist office (140 Av. Tonaltecas Sur; phone: 683-1740) is closed Sundays.

CHAPALA A town of about 25,700, it's on Lago de Chapala (Lake Chapala), Mexico's largest inland body of water (about 60 miles long and from 12 to 20 miles wide). The area has one of Mexico's largest retirement colonies of US citizens, complete with a large American Legion post. The suburb of Chula Vista is populated almost totally by US citizens. About 32 miles (51 km) southeast of Guadalajara on Rte. 44. For more information, see *The West Coast: Nogales to Mexico City* in DIRECTIONS.

AJIJIC (pronounced A-hee-*heek*) Populated largely by expatriate Americans, including a number of writers and artists, this picturesque village is wonderful for shopping, drinking, and generally lazing around. The village has some interesting little galleries and boutiques, and there are mineral baths in the nearby town of San Juan Cosalá. Ajijic is about 4 miles (6 km) west of Chapala, and San Juan Cosalá is 3 miles (5 km) past Ajijic. For more information, see *The West Coast: Nogales to Mexico City* in DIRECTIONS.

JOCOTEPEC (pronounced Ho-co-tay-*pake*) This pretty little fishing village with very few foreign residents is famous for its white serapes, which you'll see for sale everywhere. About 10 miles (16 km) west of Ajijic. (You can combine visits to Chapala, Ajijic, and Jocotepec in a one-day tour.)

TEQUILA The town where most tequila is produced. Cuervo, Sauza, Orendain, and Herradura are among the better-known distilleries. There's not much else to see, but it's a pretty trip, and the fields of blue agave (the type of maguey plant from which tequila is made) are memorable. Sauza offers free tours of its distillery—and cut-rate prices—Mondays through Saturdays. To arrange for a visit, contact the Sauza office in Guadalajara (phone: 647-8463). Tequila is about 35 miles (56 km) northwest of Guadalajara on Rte. 15. For more information, see *The West Coast: Nogales to Mexico City* in DIRECTIONS.

EXTRA SPECIAL

Barranca de Oblatos (Oblatos Canyon) is a 2,000-foot-deep gorge, lush with tropical vegetation and featuring steaming hot springs that spout from the canyon walls. Bear in mind that it's a steep climb. Seven miles (11 km) northeast of the city via Calzada Independencia.

Sources and Resources

TOURIST INFORMATION

The *Secretaría de Turismo del Gobierno del Estado de Jalisco* (Jalisco State Tourism Secretariat; 102 Morelos, on Plaza Tapatía; phone: 658-2222) has an English-speaking staff and excellent maps, as well as general information. It's open daily. The *Dirección de Turismo Municipal de Guadalajara* (Guadalajara City Tourist Office; phone: 616-3332 and 616-3335) is in *Los Arcos,* an Arc de Triomphe–like structure on Avenida Vallarta (Av. Juárez, which changes names in this part of the city), about a mile and a half west of downtown. There's also the *Oficina de Convenciones y Visitantes* (Convention and Visitors Bureau; 4095 Av. Vallarta, at Niño Obrero; phone: 647-9481). The second two offices are closed weekends.

LOCAL COVERAGE The English-language *Guadalajara Weekly* and the *Guadalajara Colony Reporter* have local coverage and arts and events listings, and *The News* and *Mexico City Times* publish both national and international news. The *Los Angeles Times, USA Today,* and the *Wall Street Journal* are available at the major hotels. The bilingual tourist publications *Let's Enjoy/Disfrutemos Guadalajara* and *Huésped* (Guest) are found in the rooms of major hotels.

TELEPHONE The city code for Guadalajara is 3. *Note:* Mexico's telephone company has embarked on a major expansion project that involves changing telephone numbers in many areas of the country. At press time, all numbers listed in this chapter were correct. However, if you have any difficulties reaching attractions listed here, contact the local tourist office.

CLIMATE AND CLOTHES The average daily maximum temperature is 73F (23C) in January, 85F (29C) in April, 79F (26C) in July, and 78F (26C) in October. Dress in Guadalajara tends to be slightly more conservative than in such tourist spots as Acapulco.

GETTING AROUND

Guadalajara is divided into four "sectors": Juárez, Hidalgo, Reforma, and Libertad, which in turn are divided into *colonias,* or neighborhoods. Most tourist sights, tourist shops, and large hotels are in Juárez or Hidalgo. Downtown, however, is called simply *el centro.*

BUS If you are adventurous and speak the language fairly well, you can take advantage of the dozens of buses crisscrossing the city. The fares range from 1 peso (about 13¢) to ride the older and slower local buses to 3 pesos (40¢) for the fast modern ones. Buses for the Lago de Chapala district leave every half hour or 20 minutes daily from the *Antigua Central Camionera* (Old Bus Terminal, which services such nearby destinations as the Chapala area and Tequila), at the corner of Av. 5 de Febrero and Av. Dr. R. Michel, north of the *Parque Agua Azul.* From the *Nueva Central Camionera* (New Bus Terminal, which mainly services long-distance destinations), you can take the Ciénaga de Chapala bus, which leaves about every 45 minutes. The New Bus Terminal is about 6 miles (10 km) southeast of town on the road to Zapotlanejo. More information is available from the tourist office (see *Tourist Information,* above).

Panoramex (phone: 610-5005 or 610-5057) offers a wide variety of tours. Passengers are picked up at *Parque San Francisco* and *Parque Los Arcos,* but the bus stops at hotels along the route on the way back. More information is available in hotel lobbies.

CAR RENTAL *Avis* (phone: 630-1750), *Budget* (phone: 613-0286), *Hertz* (phone: 647-8000, ext. 1054), *National* (phone: 614-7175), and *Dollar* (phone: 826-7959), as well as many local companies, have offices in town and at the airport.

TAXI Cabs are the most convenient way to get around town. Hail one in the street or get one outside your hotel; if you don't speak Spanish, write your destination on a slip of paper and hand it to the driver to avoid any misunderstanding. Though some taxis have meters, it is still common to set the fare with the driver before entering the cab; ask *"Cuánto cuesta a . . . ?"* ("How much to . . . ?"). Typical rates are posted in the lobbies of major hotels, and the tourist office can also give you advice.

SPECIAL EVENTS

The month-long *Fiestas de Tlaquepaque,* featuring handicrafts, food, drink, and folk dancing is usually held in Tlaquepaque in June. Fiesta time in Guadalajara comes in October, when there's a full schedule of activities—sporting events, theatrical presentations, daily bullfights, ballet, folk dancing, all known as the *Fiestas de Octubre* (October Festival). Countries from all over the world participate, with exhibits and performances. It is exciting but very crowded, and reservations must be confirmed months in advance. Another *Fiestas de Octubre* highlight is the traditional *paseo* (promenade) on Avenida Chapultepec in the evenings. During the day on Tuesdays and Sundays, there are old-fashioned *serenatas* (during which *charros* on horseback or in carriages ride around courting passing ladies) at the bandstand in the Plaza de Armas, across from the *Palacio de Gobierno.*

The most important religious celebration in the area occurs on October 12, when the statuette of the *Virgen de Zapopan* is returned to the *Basílica de Zapopan,* in the municipality of Zapopan on the outskirts of town, after touring most churches in Jalisco. Year-round at the Plaza de Armas, the *Banda del Estado* (Jalisco State Band) gives concerts on Thursday and Sunday evenings.

SHOPPING

Guadalajara is an excellent place to shop. Most stores in town don't bargain (you'll see signs stating *precios fijos,* which means "fixed prices"). Stores are usually open Mondays through Saturdays from 9:30 AM to 2 PM and 4 to 7 or 8 PM. Of particular interest are glass, pottery, serapes, and other handicrafts from the surrounding regions. Main shopping areas are on Avenida Juárez (which becomes Av. Vallarta as it heads west); also along Avenida Chapultepec and Avenida de las Américas. *Plaza del Sol* (Av. López Mateos Sur and Mariano Otero; open daily), one of Latin America's largest shopping centers, has some 200 shops. *Plaza México* (Av. México and Blvd. Homero), *Plaza Patria* (Av. Avila Camacho and Av. Patria Nte.), and *La Gran Plaza* (Av. Vallarta 3959, just east of the *Camino Real* hotel) also offer a good variety of stores. At the immense *Mercado Libertad* (Liberty Market; on Calzada Independencia at Juárez, downtown), you can haggle for everything from clothes and arts and crafts to food and even medicinal herbs. It's housed in a huge modern building occupying four square blocks, and it's open daily. *Expo Guadalajara,* the city's fairs and conventions center (two blocks southeast of *Plaza del Sol,* at Av. Mariano Otero and Av. de las Rosas; phone: 647-0055), is a showcase for national and foreign manufacturers.

Noteworthy stores in Guadalajara and its environs include the following:

Antigüedades Collignon Arts and artifacts from the viceregal era and early years of independence. 123 Calle Bernardo de Balbuena, Sector Hidalgo (phone: 616-0437).

Artecrisa High-quality glass at very reasonable prices; if you're going to be in the area long enough, the artisans will make up special orders in whatever color and design you want. They ship anywhere, but we recommend you carry the fragile objects home. 947 Tonalá, on the left side of the road from Tlaquepaque to Tonalá; watch carefully for the sign, because the street number is out of sequence and painted over (phone: 657-6731).

El Charro This is the place to buy elegant Mexican cowboywear, including sharkskin boots and classic hats. Three locations: 148 Juárez (downtown; phone: 614-9743), in the *Plaza del Sol* (phone: 121-5418), and *La Gran Plaza* (phone: 122-3258).

Galería del Calzado A great place to find shoes for the entire family—more than 50 shops under one roof. Av. México and Juan Palomar y Arias (but second street is still better known by its former name, Yáquis; phone: 647-6422).

Instituto de la Artesanía Jalisciense (Handicrafts Institute of Jalisco) An exhibition hall where you can buy choice items from glass blowers, weavers, potters, and jewelers. There's no haggling—all prices are fixed. 20 González Gallo, near the entrance to the *Parque Agua Azul* (phone: 619-4664). There's also a showroom in Ajijic, in the Lago de Chapala area, at Km 6.5, Carretera a Jocotepec (phone: 376-60548).

Museo de Arte Huichol (Museum of Huichol Art) This place—more of a shop than a museum—exhibits photographs of Huichol life, native costumes, and replicas of their dwellings. There are also handicrafts for sale. Located in the *Basílica de Zapopan,* to the right of the main entrance (no phone). The *Departamento de Turismo de Zapopan* (Zapopan Department of Tourism), located behind the basilica at 11 Calle Vicente Guerrero, can provide additional information (phone: 633-0571).

In nearby Tlaquepaque (see *Special Places*), many of the best shops are on Avenida Independencia. *Caoba* (No. 156; phone: 635-9770) carries an excellent selection of furniture typical of the area, as well as handicrafts and ceramics. For fine antiques, handicrafts, and furniture, try *Bazar Hecht* (No. 158; phone: 635-2241). Go to *El Zaguán* (No. 227; phone: 635-1683) for a wide selection of *equipales* (rustic furniture made of leather and wood) and crafts. *Sergio Bustamante* (No. 236; phone: 639-5519) carries wonderfully colorful sculptures of animals and imaginative jewelry in papier-mâché, copper, bronze, and tin. Check out *Antigua de México* (No. 255; phone: 635-3402; and in *Plaza Patria* shopping center; phone: 614-4069) for its unusual assortment of objets d'art, antiques, and made-to-order furniture. And *Casa Canela* (No. 258; phone: 635-3717) carries the best of nearly 600 suppliers of textiles, handicrafts, and furniture from all over Mexico.

Other worthwhile stores in Tlaquepaque include *El Palomar* (1905 Blvd. General Marcelino García Barragán, also known as Av. Tlaquepaque; phone: 635-5247), which has stoneware dishes made on the premises, plus outstanding jewelry, sculpture, and textiles; and *Ken Edwards de Tonalá* (70 Madero; phone: 635-2426), with beautifully crafted and colored stoneware in exclusive designs. Edwards's factory (phone: 683-0313), which is also open to the public, is at 184 Morelos in Tonalá.

SPORTS

BASEBALL The season roughly parallels that in the US. Games are played at the *Estadio de Beisbol* (Baseball Stadium, at Calzada Revolución and Calzada Olímpico in Sector Reforma, in southeastern Guadalajara) and at the *Parque Heliodoro Hernández Loza* in Tlaquepaque. Consult the tourist office for schedule and ticket information.

BOXING There are usually weekly matches at the *Arena Coliseo* (67 Medrano, in Sector Reforma). At times, though, there is more fighting among the spectators than in the ring. Consult the tourist office for schedule and ticket information.

BULLFIGHTING Guadalajara is the second major bullfight city in Mexico. During the season, which usually lasts from September through May, bullfights are held on Sundays twice a month (twice a week during the *Fiestas de Octubre*) at the *Plaza Nuevo Progreso* ring (on Calzada Independencia Nte., near the *Estadio Jalisco*). In *Cortijo la Venta* restaurant (725 Federación, Sector Reforma; phone: 617-1675), you can watch exhibitions of bullfighting with calves in a small ring as you dine and drink (but contrary to tradition, the animals are not killed). The restaurant is closed Mondays; it does not accept US credit cards. For more information, consult the tourist office.

CHARREADAS Mexican rodeos featuring elaborately dressed *charro* cowboys take place Sundays next to *Parque Agua Azul,* just north of the railroad station on Calzada Independencia Sur. Consult the tourist office for ticket information.

COCKFIGHTS Rooster rencounters, or contests, are held at the *Palenque Agua Azul* (in *Parque Agua Azul*) during the *Fiestas de Octubre* (see *Special Events*).

GOLF The 18-hole Joe Finger–designed *Club de Golf Atlas* (near the *El Tapatío* resort, at Km 6.5 of the Carretera a Chapala, also known as Blvd. Aeropuerto;

phone: 689-0085) is open to the public; Sixto Torres and Guadalupe Quezada are the pros. Larry Hughes designed the 18 holes at the *Santa Anita Golf Club* (a few minutes south of town on Rte. 15; phone: 686-0386), open to the public Tuesdays through Fridays. The manager is Juan Ramón Araiza, and the pro is John Hosterman. Also designed by Hughes, the *Las Cañadas Golf Club* (Km 14.5 of Rte. 54; phone: 685-0512) is a private course open only to members and their guests, though your hotel may be able to arrange special guest privileges. It's in a scenic valley just north of the city. At the 18-hole, par 72 *Guadalajara Country Club* (260 Mar Caribe; phone: 817-2858), guests of members may play Mondays through Fridays. The manager is Carlos Gutiérrez; the pro, Jesús Torres.

The *Chapala Country Club* (Vista del Lago, San Nicolás Ibarra; no phone) features a nine-hole course open to non-members with US golf club memberships, and it offers instruction. The nine holes at the *Chula Vista* (7 Paseo de Golf, Fraccionamiento Chula Vista; phone: 376-52281) are also open to non-members.

SOCCER Check the paper or with your hotel for where and when; usually on Wednesday nights and Sunday afternoons at *Estadio Jalisco* (Calzada Independencia Nte. at Calle Fidel Velázquez; phone: 637-0563, 637-0301, or 637-0299) and at the *Estadio 3 de Marzo* (1201 Av. Patria, in the *Universidad Autónoma de Guadalajara* complex (phone: 641-0568 or 641-2915).

TENNIS Mexico's second-largest city has ample opportunities for racquet enthusiasts.

CHOICE COURTS

El Tapatío The tennis facilities at this resort hotel (see *Checking In*) are among the most highly rated in Mexico, with 10 red clay courts (four lighted) and a pro shop. The tennis package, with instruction, is perhaps the best in the country. 4275 Blvd. Aeropuerto (phone: 635-6050).

Other hotels with tennis facilities (all described in *Checking In*): the *Camino Real* (one lighted concrete court); *Crowne Plaza* (two lighted concrete courts); and *Fiesta Americana* (two lighted artificial-grass courts).

Several golf clubs in and around town make courts available to the public for a fee, although certain conditions might apply. *Club de Golf Atlas* and *Santa Anita* allow anyone to use their courts, while *Las Cañadas Golf Club* and *Guadalajara Country Club* only allow members and their guests to use the golf and tennis facilities (see *Golf* for all four).

TRAP AND SKEET You can practice your shooting skills at the *Club Cinegético Jalisciense* (Rte. 15; no phone) on Sundays. Contact the tourist office for further information.

NIGHTCLUBS AND NIGHTLIFE

Guadalajara is rather sedate as nightlife goes, but there are a number of clubs and hotel bars that feature music and dancing. The *Caballo Negro* at the *Fiesta Americana; Jaguar* at the *Crowne Plaza;* and *La Diligencia* nightclub at the *Camino Real* have live music for dancing. For typical Mexican music (mariachis and trios), the place to head is *El Pueblito Cantina* at the *Hyatt Regency* (see *Checking In* for details on hotels). At *Peña Cuicacalli* (1988 Niños Héroes, just off the traffic circle of the same name; phone: 825-4690), live Latin American folk music can be heard Friday, Saturday, and Sunday nights; other types of music are featured Tuesdays through Thursdays. Popular discos include *Iceberg* at the *Hyatt, Romance Memories* at *El Tapatío, Video Disco Genesis* at the *Carlton* (Av. 16 de Septiembre and Niños Héroes; phone: 614-7272), and *Classic* at the *Motor Hotel Américas.* There's live tropical music and dancing at *Coco y Coco* at the *Fénix Best Western,* and live rock 'n' roll at the *Roxy Cultural Center* (80 Calle Mezquitán; phone: 658-0053). Jazz aficionados frequent *Copenhagen 77* (77 López Cotilla, across from *Parque Revolución;* phone: 825-2803).

Best in Town

CHECKING IN

Expect to pay $110 to $185 per night for a double room in a very expensive hotel; $70 to $100 at an expensive one; $40 to $60 at a moderate place; and less than $40 at an inexpensive one. Unless otherwise noted, the hotels listed have air conditioning, telephones, and TV sets in rooms. All telephone numbers are in the 3 city code unless otherwise indicated.

We begin with our favorite haven (in the very expensive category), followed by recommended hotels, listed by price category.

A SPECIAL HAVEN

Camino Real This is one of the most beautiful inland hotels in all of Mexico, a delightful enclave sheltered by high walls from the hustle and bustle of Mexico's second largest city. A sprawling, modern, 205-room place, it offers lovely gardens, huge shade trees, five heated pools, a putting green, a lighted tennis court, a bar, and the *Aquellos Tiempos* restaurant (see *Eating Out*). About 4 miles (6 km) from the center of town at 5005 Av. Vallarta (phone: 121-8000; 800-7-CAMINO in the US; 800-90123 in Mexico; fax: 121-8070).

VERY EXPENSIVE

Crowne Plaza Although the heavy traffic makes getting here a chore, the grounds (across from the *Plaza del Sol* shopping center) are beautiful. Most of the

300 rooms have balconies or terraces, and the facilities include a heated pool, two tennis courts, a putting green, three restaurants, and two bars (one with live entertainment). About 4½ miles (7 km) south of downtown, corner of Avs. López Mateos Sur and Mariano Otero (phone: 634-1034; 800-2-CROWNE in the US; 800-00999 in Mexico; fax: 631-9393).

Hyatt Regency This towering 414-unit property, built in a pyramid shape and offering an airy, 12-story atrium, boasts an outdoor pool on the 12th floor, a restaurant, a coffee shop, and a lobby bar. Rooms are decorated in rich earth tones. Occasionally the ballroom is turned into a nightclub offering top Mexican and international entertainers. There's also a *Tane* silver shop (a branch of the acclaimed Mexico City store) on the premises. Across from *Plaza del Sol,* at Avs. López Mateos Sur and Moctezuma (phone: 678-1234; 800-233-1234 in the US; 800-00500 in Mexico; fax: 678-1222).

Quinta Real This hacienda-style hostelry has 53 suites, all with fireplaces, and four with Jacuzzis. There is an excellent restaurant (see *Eating Out*), a lobby bar, pretty gardens, an outdoor Jacuzzi, and a pool. 2727 Av. México, at Av. López Mateos Nte. (phone: 615-0000; 800-445-4565; fax: 630-1797).

EXPENSIVE

Fiesta Americana One of the most striking modern luxury hotels in Mexico. Guests may enjoy its coffee shop, Mexican-style restaurant, and elegant lobby bar, plus a large pool and two tennis courts. There are 391 rooms. 225 Aurelio Aceves, on the Minerva traffic circle (phone: 825-4848 or 825-3434; 800-FIESTA-1 in the US; 800-50450 in Mexico; fax: 630-3725).

El Tapatío High on a hillside outside of town, this may be the most complete resort hotel in inland Mexico. Each of the large, comfortable 120 rooms and suites contains a stocked mini-bar and has a private balcony. There is a large heated pool, fine tennis on 10 clay courts, a jogging track, a sauna, a bar, and a restaurant. Shopping and crafts enthusiasts will enjoy the proximity to Tlaquepaque (see *Shopping,* above), and golf is available at the nearby *Club de Golf Atlas* (see *Sports,* above). However, maintenance is not always what it should be, and air pollution in this part of town can be bothersome. Four miles (6 km) south of the city at 4275 Blvd. Aeropuerto (phone: 635-6050; 800-227-0212 in the US; 800-36180 in Mexico; fax: 635-6664).

Vista Plaza del Sol Among the amenities offered at this 354-room property are a heated pool, a restaurant, a bar with entertainment, and secretarial services. In *Plaza del Sol,* at 2375 Av. López Mateos Sur (phone: 647-8890; fax: 622-9685).

MODERATE

Fénix Best Western This downtown hotel has 260 rooms, the *Coco y Coco* nightclub (see *Nightclubs and Nightlife,* above), a worthwhile restaurant, and

De Mendoza Centrally located, this hotel has 110 rooms, a pool, and a fine restaurant. Just north of the *Teatro Degollado,* at 16 Venustiano Carranza (phone: 613-4646; 718-253-9400 in New York City; 800-221-6509 elsewhere in the US; 800-36126 in Mexico; fax: 613-7310).

Posada Guadalajara Colonial-style, with 172 rooms built around a patio; there's also a pool and a restaurant. 1280 Av. López Mateos Sur (phone: 121-2022; fax: 122-1834).

Vista Aranzazú Business travelers favor this downtown property, which has a friendly staff. The 500 rooms are quite nice; facilities include a coffee shop, a bar, a nightclub, and a restaurant. 110 Av. Revolución, at Degollado (phone: 613-3232; fax: 614-5045).

INEXPENSIVE

Francés Guadalajara's oldest hostelry has been designated a national monument. The 60 rooms are pleasant, and there is a good restaurant—*Molino Rojo* (see *Eating Out*)—plus *Maxim's* disco. Downtown, several blocks south of the *Teatro Degollado,* at 35 Maestranza (phone: 613-1190; fax: 658-2831).

Motor Hotel Américas In addition to the 24 suites with kitchenettes and 87 double rooms, this place has a pool, a disco, and a restaurant. 2400 Av. López Mateos Sur, across from *Plaza del Sol* (phone: 631-4415; fax: 631-1237).

Posada Regis Many of the 19 guestrooms in this 18th-century colonial mansion overlook a lovely courtyard with lush green plants and trees. There's a dining room that serves breakfast and lunch, but not dinner. The downtown location (on a side street six blocks south of the cathedral) is especially convenient. 171 Av. Corona (phone/fax: 613-3026).

EATING OUT

There are many excellent restaurants in Guadalajara. Expect to pay $40 or more for dinner for two at the expensive places, $25 to $35 at the moderate ones, and under $25 at the inexpensive ones. Prices do not include drinks, wine, tax, or tips. Most restaurants listed below accept MasterCard and Visa; several also accept American Express and Diners Club. Unless otherwise noted, all restaurants are open daily for lunch and dinner. All telephone numbers are in the 3 city code unless otherwise indicated.

EXPENSIVE

Aquellos Tiempos At lunchtime, the appetizers are Mexican, but the main dishes at this posh spot are international, with fresh salmon steak in mango sauce the most popular selection. The dinner menu is more formal (and more

THE CITIES GUADALAJARA

139

expensive), with some French specialties. Reservations advised. In the *Camino Real* hotel, 5005 Av. Vallarta (phone: 121-8000).

Artur's Though the decor is British and clubby, the steaks served here are American cuts and quite good. Reservations advised. 507 Av. Chapultepec Sur, at Calle Mexicaltzingo (phone: 825-6510).

La Fuente A very popular place in a chic neighborhood, offering a wide selection of international dishes and live piano and violin music. Closed Sundays. Reservations advised. 1899 Plan de San Luis, in Colonia Chapultepec Country (phone: 824-0454).

Quinta Real Mexican and international fare is prepared to perfection in an exquisite, formal setting. The Sunday buffet is outstanding. Reservations necessary. In the *Quinta Real Hotel,* 2727 Av. México (phone: 615-0000).

Suehiro At this authentic Japanese restaurant, dishes are prepared right at your table. Reservations advised. 1701 Av. de la Paz (phone: 826-6833).

MODERATE

El Delfín Sonriente The name translates as "the grinning dolphin," an appropriate moniker for a place that features good seafood, frogs' legs, and a few Japanese specialties. Reservations unnecessary. 2239 Av. Niños Héroes (phone: 616-0216).

La Destilería Billing itself as a museum of tequila as well as an eatery, this bilevel establishment displays tools of the trade and antique photographs of the tequila-making process. The cuisine is Mexican with a nouvelle twist: shrimp crêpes with *huitlacoche* (corn fungus with a mushroom-like flavor) in *poblano* chili sauce and spicy chicken breast stuffed with cheese are two of the tasty selections. 2916 Av. México, about five blocks west of the *Quinta Real* hotel (phone: 640-3440).

Restaurant with No Name The sign on the door says "Restaurant, Art Gallery, and Music." An indoor-outdoor spot, its fine offerings include filet of beef in nut sauce, and *pipián,* a Yucatecan dish made with pork and a pumpkin seed–flavored sauce. The paintings on display are for sale. In the afternoons, a trio plays classical music; in the evenings, music is provided by a troubadour. Reservations advised. 80 Madero in Tlaquepaque (phone: 635-4520).

Riscal Especially good paella is served here every day, in addition to a wide variety of international dishes. Reservations advised. 1751 López Cotilla (phone: 616-8677).

INEXPENSIVE

La Chata *Tapatío* fare (food typical of Guadalajara) predominates here—try the hearty *pozole* (a hominy-based broth usually containing pork). There's live piano music at lunch and Mexican music in the evening. Reservations unnecessary. Three locations: 2277 José Francisco Zarco (616-9553); Av. López Mateos Sur and Av. Mariano Otero (phone: 632-1379); 126 Av. Corona, downtown (phone: 613-0588). The Zarco locale is the original—and the best.

Los Itacates Delicious Mexican food is served in this charming traditional dining spot, complete with carved wooden chairs and attractive tile floors. Most main dishes are also available as tacos—a great way to try something new in small portions. Open daily 8 AM to 11 PM. 110 Av. Chapultepec Nte. (phone: 825-1106). There's a branch at 3363 Av. Mariano Otero, across from the *Plaza de la Luna* shopping center, near *Plaza del Sol* (phone: 121-2216).

Molino Rojo Under the same management as *The Restaurant with No Name* (see above), this place features an eclectic decor and an informal atmosphere. The menu might include anything from salads or hamburgers to cactus leaves stuffed with ham and cheese. Reservations unnecessary. In the *Francés Hotel*, 35 Maestranza (phone: 613-1190).

Los Otates y Algo Más The excellent Mexican food offered here has made this eatery a favorite for more than 40 years. Reservations unnecessary. Two locations: 1835 López Cotilla (phone: 615-3338) and 2455-2 Av. México (phone: 630-2855).

Oui Café This casual and pleasant place serves a large selection of interesting salads and a variety of coffees. Open daily 8 AM to 11 PM. Reservations advised. 2171 López Cotilla, several blocks southeast of *Los Arcos* (phone: 615-0614).

Recco Dine on Italian fare in an Italian villa where the pasta is prepared to perfection. Reservations advised. 1981 Libertad (phone: 825-0724).

Guanajuato
(pronounced Gwah-nah-*wah*-toe)

Considered one of Mexico's most beautiful cities, Guanajuato (pop. 122,000) is certainly its most European. Built into the mountainous terrain of the Sierra Madre at the bottom of a narrow canyon, the town was established in 1559 along the banks of the Río Guanajuato. This meandering river created a ground plan of winding, labyrinthine streets, and the result is a hilly confusion occasionally opening up into small plazas and fading again into narrow alleys or steep stairways. With this layout, and the Spanish and Moorish architecture imported by the founding families, Guanajuato looks as if it might have been transported directly from the hills of Andalusia.

Shortly after the town's founding, silver was discovered in the surrounding mountainside; as more and more veins were unearthed, Guanajuato soon became the richest city in Mexico. The newly wealthy Spanish mine owners built opulent mansions in Guanajuato and also provided the town with a number of elegant and very well funded churches.

In 1732, the Jesuits added another amenity to the thriving city in the form of a university intended for the wealthy sons of the mining families. The Jesuits themselves were evicted soon after, but the institution has survived under one authority or another ever since. The result has been an emphasis on culture and learning that adds a European sensibility to the flavor of the city. The local tradition of *estudiantinas* (troubadour groups) also lends the city a cultivated air: Male university students, dressed in colorful 16th-century costumes and armed with mandolins and guitars, serenade women throughout town, winning as their reward some token of appreciation—a ribbon or flower—which is then proudly displayed on their capes. This tradition is still practiced today, and the young students, dressed in britches and ruffled sleeves, wandering past colonial buildings, through narrow streets, and across tiny courtyards, make an enchanting picture. The large student population, some 50,000 strong, also gives Guanajuato a youthful, stylish flair.

While many of its buildings are large and impressive, Guanajuato's streets are often little more than narrow, cramped lanes or *callejones* (alleyways), which are so steep that many have stairs built into the sidewalks. Lined with flowerpot-trimmed houses, these streets bear quaint names such as the Tumbler, the Four Winds, the Five Gentlemen, the Backbone, the Monkey Jump, the Blowpipe, and, most famous of all, the Kiss. (This last is so named because one can lean from a balcony on one side of the street to exchange a kiss with someone on the balcony across the way.)

Guanajuato's largest and most forbidding building is the *Alhóndiga de Granaditas* (Grain Warehouse), which played an important role in the city's most exciting historical episode. It was to this place that the wealthy mine-

and land-owning patriarchs fled in 1810, when Padre Miguel Hidalgo and his ragtag army of angry farmers and miners invaded the city during the War of Independence against Spain. The building was instantly transformed into a seemingly impregnable fortress, and, with balls of fire flying from the parapets onto the attacking army below, the battle seemed decided in favor of the Spanish mine owners. But in the face of gunfire and hurling flames, a miner named Juan Martínez—known by the nickname El Pípila—made his way to the massive wooden door of the stone fortress and set it on fire. The revolutionaries poured into the structure, killing their enemies and taking the city. They did not hold it for long, however, and soon after, Hidalgo, Allende, Aldama, and Jiménez—the four leaders of the revolt—were executed in Chihuahua. Their heads were sent back to Guanajuato, where they were impaled on hooks at the corners of the granary and displayed for the next 10 years. The hooks still remain as grim reminders of the passions of the time.

Another reminder of earlier days is Guanajuato's subterranean highway system. Running the 2-mile length of the town, this channel was originally built as a flood drain. With the coming of the automobile, it was discovered that Guanajuato had such narrow streets that two cars traveling in opposite directions usually could not pass each other. The solution was a one-way system aboveground and a conversion of the subterranean waterway into a two-way, rapidly moving thoroughfare. Lighted at night and surrounded by the foundations of ancient buildings, this sunken road provides an eerie ride unlike any other.

This adaptation of the waterway is one of the few concessions Guanajuato has made to contemporary living. Such trappings of modernity as gas stations and bus depots are restricted to the edge of town, posing no threat to the architectural integrity of the town's center. The entire town has been declared a national monument (it has also been declared an international treasure by *UNESCO*), which means that any restoration work or new building must conform strictly to the old Spanish style.

Guanajuato At-a-Glance

SEEING THE CITY

The scenic drive following the hills along the south side of Guanajuato offers several beautiful vantage points; from along this route the red, coral, gold, green, and blue façades of buildings constructed with the lovely *cantera* stone from the surrounding hills make Guanajuato look like a Cubist painting in pastel hues. Stop at the statue honoring El Pípila, Guanajuato's independence war hero; this spot offers magnificent views. Both Paseo de la Presa and Route 45 toward Irapuato lead to the drive. The statue can also be reached on foot from town via a strenuous climb up a long set of steps.

The *Faro* (Lighthouse) is another fine spot from which to see the city; the bus marked "Presa-Estación" will take you most of the way, leaving only a short walk uphill behind the dam. Route 110, also known as the Carretera Panorámica and leading to the *Mina Valenciana* (Valenciana Mine), also commands some spectacular views.

SPECIAL PLACES

IN THE CITY

ALHÓNDIGA DE GRANADITAS (GRAIN WAREHOUSE) Built in 1718, this massive stone building—now a museum—was the scene of the first battle in Mexico's War of Independence, which began in 1810. Of particular interest are the murals by Chávez Morado in the stairwells and a chamber dedicated to the Heroes of Independence, lit by an eternal flame. There are exhibitions of local costumes, arts and crafts, and photography. Closed Mondays. Admission charge. Calle 28 de Septiembre (phone: 21112).

PARROQUIA (PARISH CHURCH) Also known as the *Basílica de Nuestra Señora de Guanajuato* (Basilica of Our Lady of Guanajuato), this church dates to 1671. Here is housed the famous wooden image of the Virgin Mary, the *Virgen de Santa Fe de Guanajuato,* which was sent from Granada in 1557 as a gift from Philip II of Spain. It is considered the oldest piece of Christian art in all Mexico. Plaza de la Paz.

JARDÍN DE LA UNIÓN (GARDEN OF THE UNION) Known affectionately as the *Pedazo de Queso* ("Piece of Cheese") because it's shaped like a wedge of cheese, this central plaza is the most active *zócalo* in town. Among its features are an old-fashioned bandstand, tiled pavements, hedgelike *trueno* trees, and ornate wrought-iron benches. Concerts take place here Tuesdays and Thursdays at 7 and 9 PM and Sundays at noon and 1:30 PM. Avs. Juárez and Allende.

IGLESIA SAN DIEGO (CHURCH OF ST. JAMES) This church was built in 1663 and almost destroyed by floodwaters about a century later. It was rebuilt in the Churrigueresque vernacular, the Baroque Spanish architectural style introduced to Mexico in 1750. Its highly ornate doorway in particular exemplifies the Mexican adaptation of the Churrigueresque style. Jardín de la Unión.

TEATRO JUÁREZ (JUÁREZ THEATER) A fine example of Mexican Churrigueresque, this elaborate structure was begun in 1872 and was continually refurbished after its 1878 opening (a testament to the greatest of Guanajuato's mining booms, 1873–1903). The exterior, crowned with eight carved muses, is Doric; the interior, a riot of graceful Art Nouveau railings, gilt carvings, and velvet fabrics, is a harmonious marriage of French and Moorish design. The first performance here was of *Aïda,* in l903; today, the theater welcomes all the great opera, theater, and dance companies of Europe. Closed Mondays. Admission charge. Jardín de la Unión (phone: 20183).

MUSEO DIEGO RIVERA (DIEGO RIVERA MUSEUM) What is now a lovely museum was the birthplace of Diego Rivera, one of Mexico's greatest muralists. Period furniture, including the brass bed in which Rivera was born in 1886, fills the ground floor; on the second floor are nearly 100 of the artist's works, including a large sketch for his mural in New York City's Rockefeller Center; the third floor houses temporary exhibitions. Closed Mondays. Admission charge. 47 Calle Pocitos (phone: 21197).

UNIVERSIDAD DE GUANAJUATO (UNIVERSITY OF GUANAJUATO) The descendant of the Jesuit school opened in 1732, this is now one of the most important seats of learning in Mexico. While it no longer is affiliated with the Jesuits, the school has been in continuous operation for more than 250 years; it became a state university in 1945. The main wing is especially beautiful, with its glass roof and grand staircase. The university serves as a cultural focal point for the city, offering symphony recitals, theater performances, a radio station, a choir, a library, and a movie club. It also is the center of the famous student *entremeses* (short farces; also see *Nightclubs and Nightlife*). Ask at your hotel or check the newspapers for program information. 5 Calle Lascurraín de Retana (no phone).

IGLESIA DE LA COMPAÑÍA DE JESÚS (CHURCH OF THE SOCIETY OF JESUS, OR JESUITS) Many a camera has been trained on this lovely 18th-century church—often referred to as *La Compañía*—with its pink stone Baroque façade and cupola reminiscent of St. Peter's Basilica in Rome. Near the university, on Calle Lascurraín de Retana.

TEATRO PRINCIPAL (MAIN THEATER) Most of the cultural activity in Guanajuato takes place here; exhibitions of contemporary art and international films are always on the agenda. The imposing building has a two-level façade with Tuscan columns. Ask at your hotel or check the newspapers for program information. Calle Ayuntamiento, next to the university (no phone).

MUSEO ICONOGRÁFICO DEL QUIJOTE (QUIJOTE ICONOGRAPHIC MUSEUM) Works of art, some bordering on kitsch and all inspired by Cervantes's *Don Quixote de la Mancha,* are displayed here. (Quijote is an alternate spelling for the name of the legendary "knight.") The entire collection—including works by Salvador Dalí and well-known Mexican artists Rafael and Pedro Coronel—was donated by Eulalio Ferrer, a Spanish expatriate who fought against Franco during the Spanish Civil War and now heads one of Mexico's most important advertising agencies. Closed Mondays. No admission charge. San Francisco and Manuel Doblado (phone: 26721).

ENVIRONS

VALENCIANA This suburb of Guanajuato is well worth the trip because of its beautiful church and incredibly rich working silver mine, the *Mina Valenciana.* The town church, the *Iglesia de San Cayetano* (in the center of town; also known as simply *La Valenciana*), was built by the owner of the mine. His plans for the church were so grandiose that jealousies were aroused in Guanajuato, so he agreed to a compromise stipulating that only one of the towers would be completed so that the church would not be perfect. It is rumored that the church's patron had silver dust mixed into the cement that binds the stones of the foundation. True or not, he certainly spared no expense in decorating the interior. The ornate altars, heavily trimmed in gold leaf, are fine examples of Mexican chromatic art, and the pulpit came from China. In daily use since its completion in 1788, the church also hosts the celebrations honoring the *Fiesta de la Purísima* (Feast of the Immaculate Conception) every December 8.

The *Mina Valenciana* was once the largest and richest silver mine in Mexico. Until the early 19th century it was estimated that one-third of the world's silver came from this one source, and today one can still see the miners at work extracting its incredible wealth out of the earth. The mine and church are 3 miles (5 km) northwest of Guanajuato on the road to Dolores Hidalgo (Rte. 110), with spectacular views along the way. No formal tours of the mine are offered, but most major hotels will help you arrange for a car and a driver to take you around the area. The mine is open daily; there's an admission charge (no phone).

CERRO DEL CUBILETE Crowning this 9,442-foot peak is a monument to *Cristo Rey* (Christ the King), visible to travelers long before they reach Guanajuato. The 82-foot-high statue marks what is said to be the geographical center of Mexico. The view of the Bajío (Mexico's central plateau region) from here is magnificent, with agriculturally rich lands dotted by lakes and smaller mountain peaks visible in all directions. Ten miles (16 km) west of Guanajuato on Rte. 110.

PRESA DE LA OLLA (OLLA DAM) AND PARQUE DE LAS ACACIAS (ACACIA PARK) The construction of this dam in the 18th century created not only a reservoir to hold the city's water supply but also a lake and surrounding park area. You can purchase food in the restaurant or eat at the designated picnic areas. Right in the center of the park are beautiful flower gardens and a large statue of Padre Miguel Hidalgo. At the end of "La Presa" bus line, Calle de la Presa; pick up the bus underground by the stairway at Jardín de la Unión or in front of the *Mercado Hidalgo*.

EX-HACIENDA DE SAN GABRIEL DE BARRERA This beautifully restored hacienda is furnished with colonial-period antiques and graced by 17 manicured gardens, each featuring plants and decorations from a different country. The modern *San Gabriel de Barrera* hotel also is on the grounds (see *Checking In*). Closed Mondays. Admission charge. About 1 mile (1.6 km) on the road to Marfil (phone: 20619).

PRESA LOS SANTOS (LOS SANTOS DAM) Across the top of this dam are stone statues of saints. It's located in the community of Marfil, a played-out mining area that is enjoying a renaissance as an American retirement community.

Two miles (3 km) south of Guanajuato on Rte. 110; local buses and taxis make the trip here very inexpensive.

EXTRA SPECIAL

Perhaps due to the dryness of the air, bodies left in the crypt of Guanajuato's *Panteón,* or municipal cemetery, do not decompose; they mummify. They are displayed in the glass cases lining the walls of the museum at the cemetery's entrance. One can almost reach out and touch the hollow-socketed bodies—with skin, tongues, and hair intact—of about 50 men, women, and children, dating anywhere from the mid-1800s to the 1990s. The compelling collection is best avoided by anyone prone to nightmares. Take the "Presa Panteón" bus. The museum is open daily; there's an admission charge (no phone).

Sources and Resources

TOURIST INFORMATION

The tourist office (14 Plaza de la Paz; phone: 20086 or 21574) is helpful, but the map it supplies is as confusing as the winding, unmarked streets it purports to depict. Fortunately, the map is supplemented by a detailed explanation (available in English) of how to get where you want to go. The tourist office is open daily.

LOCAL COVERAGE Next door to *Casa Valadez,* at Jardín de la Unión, is a small shop that sells a handy booklet, *Guide and Legends to Know Guanajuato,* that includes three walking tours; the broken English is charming.

TELEPHONE The city code for Guanajuato is 473. *Note:* Mexico's telephone company has embarked on a major expansion project that involves changing telephone numbers in many areas of the country. At press time, all numbers listed in this chapter were correct. However, if you have any difficulties reaching attractions listed here, contact the local tourist office.

CLIMATE AND CLOTHES The temperature hovers around the low 70s F (21–23C) except during the rainy season in late summer and early fall, when it can dip to 60F (16C). Dress is consistently casual but conservative.

GETTING AROUND

Guanajuato is extremely hilly, and while the city is small enough to get around on foot, it often is easier and more relaxing to ride.

BUS There are three routes of interest to tourists. One, "Presa-Estación," follows the one-way system from one end of town to the other. The second, "Centro-Valenciana," goes from the *Alhóndiga de Granaditas* up the hills, past the hotels bordering Route 110 to the *Mina Valenciana,* and then to Dolores

Hidalgo. The third, "Presa-Panteón," takes you to the mummies. The fare is 1.5 pesos (about 20¢).

CAR RENTAL There is a local car rental agency at the *Real de Minas* hotel (see *Checking In*). Alternatives are the *Quick* agency at the *Calzada* hotel (107 Calzada de los Héroes; phone: 471-64500) and *Hertz* (108 Calzada de los Héroes; phone: 471-66020), both in León (about an hour away).

TAXI Aqua-and-white taxis cruise the streets and can also be found at the bus station. They are available for trips to specific destinations and can be rented by the hour for more general cruising. *Taxis Alhóndiga* (phone: 25209) and *Taxis Hidalgo* (phone: 21445) both offer 24-hour service throughout town.

TOURS Tours are a practical and rewarding way to get to most of Guanajuato's places of interest. *Transportes Turísticos de Guanajuato Microbus Azul* (2 Bajos de la Basílica; phone: 22134 or 22838) is a reliable source for a hired car and English-speaking guide.

SPECIAL EVENTS

Guanajuato's religious festivals, which feature regional dances, fireworks, and occasional parades, include several events during *Semana Santa* (Holy Week), including *Viernes Santo* (Good Friday), on which decorative altars are constructed to honor *Nuestra Señora de las Minas* (Our Lady of the Mines, the patron saint of miners). There's also the *Fiesta de la Virgen de Guanajuato* (Feast of the Virgin of Guanajuato; May 22–31); various saints' days from June 15 to June 24, ending with *Día de San Juan* (St. John's Day); the annual dam-opening ceremony at *Presa de la Olla* on the first Monday in July; the *Fiesta de San Ignacio* (Feast of St. Ignatius), also known as *Día de la Cueva,* because prayers are held inside the *Mina de San Ignacio* (San Ignacio mine, about 2 miles/3 km west of town; July 31); *Día de los Muertos* (Day of the Dead; November 2), which begins on the last day of the weeklong *Feria de Alfeñique,* a festival of candy creations held in the Plaza de la Paz; the *Fiesta de la Purísima* (Feast of the Immaculate Conception; December 8); and the *Día de la Virgen de Guadalupe* (Feast Day of the Virgin of Guadalupe; December 12).

Among Guanajuato's secular events are the *Festival Internacional Cervantino* (International Cervantes Festival), held the last week in October in honor of the author of *Don Quixote.* The town fills up for this famous festival, which features theatrical presentations and draws some of the best performing artists from around the world; make hotel reservations several months in advance. Performances—some indoor and some out—take place at the *Teatro Juárez, Teatro Principal, La Compañía,* and the *Alhóndiga de Granaditas.* The festival office in Guanajuato is on Avenida Mineral de Cata (phone: 20959); for more information, write to the *Festival Internacional Cervantino* (273 Av. Alvaro Obregón, Fourth Floor, Colonia Roma, México DF 06140, Mexico; phone: 5-533-4123 in Mexico City).

SHOPPING

Among the limited number of noteworthy shops in Guanajuato is the government-run handicrafts shop (Plaza del Agora, next to Jardín de la Unión). The central *Mercado Hidalgo* (Hidalgo Market; Av. Juárez) is a huge, vaulted, iron-and-glass building with elaborate grillwork. The vast ground floor contains mostly stalls selling produce, meat, and poultry; upstairs is a range of pottery, baskets, copper from nearby Santa Clara, and some clothing. The exquisite (and pricey) majolica pottery designed by Guanajuato's most famous contemporary craftsman, Gorky González, is available at considerable savings from his studio on Calle Huerta de Montenegro (phone: 24326). Most shops in Guanajuato are open daily from 10 AM to 6 PM, with some closing for lunch (or siesta) between 2 and 4 PM.

Capelo Exquisite pottery made in a local workshop is offered for sale here. 57 Carcamanes (phone: 22268).

Casa del Sol Beautiful reproductions of antique jewelry. 10 Calle Luis González Obregón (phone: 28919).

Cerámica Telpatl Handmade rustic pottery. *Plaza Mayor* shopping center, at Plaza de la Paz (no phone).

El Cubilete This sweets shop sells an interesting array of candies, including some shaped like mummies. 188 Av. Juárez (phone: 25934).

La Valenciana Prices are reasonable and the service is friendly at this shop chock-full of local crafts. Next to *La Valenciana* church at 4 Calle Mineral, Valenciana (phone: 22734).

SPORTS

SWIMMING There are pools at several of the major hotels, including *Castillo de Santa Cecilia, Paseo de la Presa Best Western,* and *Real de Minas* (see *Checking In* for all).

TENNIS Courts are at the *Paseo de la Presa Best Western, Real de Minas,* and *San Gabriel de Barrera* (see *Checking In* for all).

NIGHTCLUBS AND NIGHTLIFE

Guanajuato does not have a particularly vibrant nightlife. There are cocktail lounges in *Castillo de Santa Cecilia, Hostería del Fraile, Parador de San Javier, Real de Minas,* and *San Diego* (see *Checking In* for details on hotels listed in this section). The disco scene is pretty much confined to weekends, with most of the action at *La Galería* in the *Parador de San Javier;* the *Paseo de la Presa Best Western; El Pequeño Juan* (Rte. 110 and Calle Guadalupe; phone: 22308); *La Calle* (on the road to Marfil; phone: 21086); and *Sanchos,* in the Mineral de Cata neighborhood (Av. San Luis; phone: 21976).

On weekend evenings, *estudiantinas* (troubadour groups) entertain at the bar in the *Castillo de Santa Cecilia;* they also perform occasionally at the *Posada Santa Fe*. Also on weekends, university students attired in period costume act out *entremeses* (short farces originally performed between plays in the 17th century); most performances take place outdoors at the Plazuela San Roque.

Best in Town

CHECKING IN

While most of the hotels in Guanajuato date from after World War II, the decor tends to be Spanish colonial. The larger, newer hotels are not downtown, so if a convenient location is important, reserve early. Expect to pay $90 to $120 per night for a double room in an expensive hotel, $50 to $80 in a moderate hotel, and $35 to $45 in an inexpensive one. Unless otherwise noted, the hotels listed below have air conditioning, TV sets, and telephones in the rooms. All telephone numbers are in the 473 city code unless otherwise indicated.

We begin with our favorite haven, followed by recommended hotels, listed by price category.

A SPECIAL HAVEN

Hacienda de Cobos This former *hacienda de beneficio* (a mill where silver and gold ore was crushed and washed) dates from 1765; it was rebuilt and converted into an inn in 1972. It is a pleasure to find this refuge, shut off from the bustle outside by walls and gates. Guests enter the private compound from Padre Hidalgo or through a gate and down a cobblestone drive leading from Avenida Juárez. Either way, they find a large, stone courtyard surrounded on all sides by walls and rooms. There are 40 rooms in all (five suites, six double-bedded rooms, and 29 standard rooms), all of which are rather plain, clean, and chilly (there are no fireplaces). The interesting restaurant, built against an original old wall of the estate with a high, domed ceiling, serves simple, good food. There are sitting rooms and TV rooms in what were once the stables; bar service and comfortable lounging areas are in the courtyard, which is highlighted by huge trees, the old well that once provided the water to wash the precious ore, and two giant millstones. Things are decidedly pleasant—and moderately priced—here, only 15 minutes from the central plaza. 3 Padre Hidalgo (phone: 20350; fax: 20143).

EXPENSIVE

Gran Plaza An elaborate resort and business hotel, this establishment opened in 1995 and boasts 140 posh rooms, a swimming pool, coffee shop, restaurant,

lobby bar, business center, and four meeting rooms for groups of 20 through 100. Km 6, Carretera Guanajuato–Juventino Rosas, on the southeast edge of town (phone/fax: 31990/1/2; phone: 5-535-8824 in Mexico City).

La Abadía Here are 43 spacious rooms, a coffee shop, a bar, and a pool. There are four floors but, unfortunately, no elevator. The rate includes breakfast. Downtown, at 50 San Matías (phone: 22465; fax: 22464).

Castillo de Santa Cecilia This walled, turreted, medieval-style castle has a heated pool, restaurants, and a nightclub. A prayer chapel was opened in 1996. Some of the 88 rooms afford an excellent view of the city. Located 1½ miles (2 km) northeast of town on Rte. 110, the road to Valenciana (phone: 20485; fax: 20153).

Hotel Museo Posada Santa Fe This ideally situated hostelry in a colonial-era building has 50 rooms, a popular outdoor café, a must-see collection of paintings depicting early Guanajuato, and a delightful lounge–piano bar. US senior citizens with identification receive a 15% discount. 12 Jardín de la Unión (phone: 20084; fax: 24653).

Parador de San Javier Set on the lovely grounds of a 17th-century hacienda, this hotel has 117 units, a heated pool, a cocktail lounge with live entertainment, a disco, and even a bullring and rodeos. There are also four meeting rooms whose capacity ranges between 50 and 200 people. One and a half miles (2.5 km) northeast of town on Rte. 110, at 92 Plaza Aldama (phone: 20626; fax: 23114).

Paseo de la Presa Best Western In this modern hostelry are 60 rooms, all with commanding views; most have balconies. Facilities include a pool, a tennis court, a disco, and a restaurant. The rate includes breakfast. About 2 miles (3 km) south of town, on Route 110, near the statue of El Pípila (phone: 23761; 800-528-1234; fax: 23224).

Real de Minas This quiet hacienda-style property has a heated pool, a tennis court, a gameroom, a cocktail lounge with nightly entertainment, and TV sets that receive some US channels. Some of the 175 rooms have private balconies; others have fireplaces. The service is good. 17 Nejayote, at the entrance to town on Rte. 110 (phone: 21460; 800-90220 toll-free in Mexico; fax: 21508).

San Diego Originally a 17th-century convent, this hotel has 55 rooms, a restaurant, and a very popular bar with live music. Garage parking is a block away. Right in the center of town, at 1 Jardín de la Unión (phone: 21300; fax: 25626).

San Gabriel de Barrera A comfortable modern hotel, it offers 139 intimate rooms, a restaurant, a pool, and a tennis court, all on the grounds of the former hacienda of the same name (see *Special Places*). One and a half miles (2.5 km) south of town, on the road to Marfil (phone: 23980; fax: 27460).

El Carruaje Offering a panoramic view, beautiful gardens, a pool, and *El Asomadero* bar—where you sit in saddles as you sip drinks and nibble hors d'oeuvres—this 50-room hostelry is a good choice. The restaurant specializes in traditional Guanajuato fare, such as *enchiladas mineras* (fried enchiladas). Km 1 on Rte. 110 toward Dolores Hidalgo (phone: 22140).

Las Embajadoras This near-hideaway hotel has a garden filled with trees, flowers, fountains, and parrots; it also has 27 rooms and an atmospheric restaurant of the same name (see *Eating Out*). At the intersection of Paseo Madero and Embajadoras, near *Parque Embajadoras* (Embajadoras Park), just outside town en route to the *Presa de la Olla* (phone: 20081).

Guanajuato Offering a beautiful view of the town and the surrounding countryside, this motel has 50 units with showers, plus a pool, a restaurant, and a bar. Two miles (3 km) northeast of town on Rte. 110 (phone: 20689).

Hostería del Fraile This tranquil 37-room hostelry retains its original 17th-century ambience. There also is a dining room–bar with a fireplace. Just north of the *Teatro Juárez,* at 3 Sopeña (phone: 20188; fax: 21179).

Socavón de la Mina Another colonial-style place, it is decorated in earth tones and has 37 large rooms, with equally roomy bathrooms, set around a courtyard; there's also a cheery restaurant-bar. A 10-minute walk north of central Guanajuato, at 41A Alhóndiga (phone: 24885).

Villa de la Plata With eight rooms and 28 condo suites and villas (some available for rent), this spot also features a playground, an indoor heated pool, a tennis court, a bar, a coffee shop, a restaurant, a gameroom, and a steambath. Km 3 on Rte. 110, northeast toward Dolores Hidalgo (phone/fax: 25200).

EATING OUT

Many of the best restaurants in Guanajuato are found in the hotels. Dinner for two at a moderate restaurant will run $35 to $45; at an inexpensive one, $30 or less. Prices do not include drinks, wine, tax, or tip. Most restaurants below accept MasterCard and Visa, and a few also accept American Express and Diners Club; it's a good idea to call ahead and check. Unless otherwise noted, all are open daily for lunch and dinner. All telephone numbers are in the 473 city code unless otherwise indicated.

La Antorcha Come here for a lovely view of the city, and sample such international specialties as mushrooms in garlic butter and *chicharrones de pollo* (super-crisp chicken pieces). Closed Mondays. Reservations advised. About 2 miles (3 km) south of town at the intersection of Route 110 and Callejón de Guadalupe, near the statue of El Pípila (phone: 22308).

Casa Valadez This simple eatery serves sandwiches and Mexican dishes. A tasty specialty is pork knuckles in spicy adobo sauce. Grab a window seat. Reservations unnecessary. Across from the *Teatro Juárez,* at 3 Jardín de la Unión (phone: 21157).

4 Ranas Good Mexican and international fare—particularly meat specialties—and a nice selection of domestic wines draw repeat customers here. Reservations unnecessary. 24 Plazuela San Fernando (phone: 20301).

Guanajuato Grill Here the setting is relaxed; the menu, international. The specialty is *crepas de huitlacoche* (crêpes filled with a surprisingly tasty corn fungus). Reservations unnecessary. Downtown, at 4 Alonso (phone: 20287).

Las Palomas Foreigners gravitate here for Mexican dishes; the *licuados* (fruit drinks) are excellent. Reservations unnecessary. Behind *La Parroquia,* at 19 Ayuntamiento (phone: 24936).

El Retiro This popular café boasts good lunch specials, king-size tacos, tasty *molletes* (sliced rolls topped with beans and melted cheese), and delicious *campechanas* (puff pastry glazed with honey). Reservations unnecessary. No credit cards accepted. Down the street from the *Teatro Juárez* at 12 Sopeña (phone: 20622).

La Venta Vieja Quiet and romantic, it has only 11 tables, laden with fresh flowers and set against large, curving windows. The fare is traditional Mexican. Closed Sundays. Reservations unnecessary. 1 Plaza San Javier (phone: 21434 or 20626).

INEXPENSIVE

Las Embajadoras The bill of fare is traditional Mexican food, including a variety of shrimp dishes. Don't pass up the dessert cart, with its flans, puddings, and pies. Reservations unnecessary. In *Las Embajadoras* hotel, on a drive off the *Parque Embajadoras* en route to the *Presa de la Olla* (phone: 20081).

Huatulco

(pronounced Wa-*tul*-co)

Buoyed by the success of Cancún, Ixtapa-Zihuatanejo, Los Cabos, and Loreto, *FONATUR* (Mexico's national tourism development fund) has ventured into Huatulco, a project price-tagged at $200 million and expected to surpass Cancún in size and total visitors by its scheduled completion date in 2024.

Set on the Pacific Coast in the state of Oaxaca, about 65 miles east of Puerto Escondido, Huatulco (its full name is Las Bahías de Huatulco, or the Bays of Huatulco) encompasses 18 miles of cove-jagged coastline on nine lovely bays. The complex is absolutely stunning: Beach after white-sand beach is framed by the ominous, jagged, gray-black peaks of the Sierra Madre del Sur and cerulean blue water.

Until its decline around the end of the 16th century, tiny Huatulco was apparently a pretty exciting place. It was an important Zapotec, and then Mixtec, settlement before the Spanish conquerors arrived. Because of its strategic location, it had become the most important port on the Pacific by 1579. That was the year that Sir Francis Drake attacked Huatulco; eight years later, the infamous English navigator-pirate Thomas Cavendish also invaded the town. Furious at finding little of value in the homes of the humble villagers, Cavendish ordered his men to destroy the wooden cross that stood on a nearby beach. But according to local lore, the sacred cross—the Santa Cruz de Huatulco—remained mysteriously untouched by their axes and saws. When even fire failed to harm it, Cavendish tried—in vain—to haul the cross out of the ground by tying ropes around it and pulling it with one of his vessels. In 1612, Bishop Juan de Cervantes carried part of the cross to the city of Oaxaca and used that piece to make a copy of the original, which stands today on the main altar of the cathedral there. Another piece of the cross was set in silver and sent to the Vatican.

Phase One of the development of Huatulco—the addition of 1,300 hotel rooms on Bahías Tangolunda, Chahue, and Santa Cruz—was completed in the early 1990s. *Club Med Huatulco* is attracting a European crowd; the *Sheraton Huatulco,* the *Royal Maeva,* the *Crowne Plaza,* and the *Omni Zaashila* hotels have opened their doors as well. Huatulco's airport receives daily flights from Mexico City, Acapulco, and Puerto Escondido.

The region is gearing up for more major development over the next 20 to 30 years: Plans call for a total of about 21,000 hotel rooms by 2020, although the country's economic woes may put a crimp in these projects. The overall plan includes villas, condominiums, and homes, and the local population is expected to exceed 300,000. All this means that the resort is currently being blasted and scraped from the base of the Sierra Madre, and the nine relatively undeveloped, lovely bays are on their way to becoming major tourist attractions. The pure tranquillity that used to be Huatulco's main draw may not last too long under these conditions.

However, Huatulco still has a way to go before it reaches the popularity and bustling atmosphere of Cancún. Nightlife remains largely confined to the hotels, although there are several seafood restaurants in the Bahía de Santa Cruz area and a couple of discos in town. Shopping is fairly limited. But the calm waters of the bays are perfect for swimming and snorkeling, the fishing is excellent, and there's plenty of sunshine. Oaxaca, with its Zapotec ruins and mouth-watering mole sauces, is only a half-hour flight away (for detailed information about that city, see *Oaxaca* in THE CITIES). In the same way that a stay in Cancún or Cozumel is enhanced by a few days in Mérida, a vacation that combines paradisiacal Huatulco and colonial Oaxaca provides the best of both worlds.

Huatulco At-a-Glance

SEEING THE CITY

If you're flying into Huatulco from Oaxaca, try to sit on the left-hand side of the aircraft, the best vantage point for a comprehensive view of the nine bays of Huatulco.

SPECIAL PLACES

Huatulco currently comprises three distinct sections—Tangolunda (the Hotel Zone), Santa Cruz (with more modest lodgings, the marina, and several restaurants), and La Crucesita (the town created to house the resort's employees and their families). There's little sightseeing in this sand-and-sea resort.

ZÓCALO (MAIN SQUARE) This spiffy plaza encompasses an outdoor theater, a handicrafts market, and a cultural center. Blvd. Benito Juárez, Santa Cruz.

BAHÍA CONEJOS Reputedly named for the large population of *conejos* (rabbits) that used to romp here, this is still a picturesque bay where pelicans stand sentry on the rocks, butterflies flit among the trees, and porpoises frolic in the sea. Right next to the Hotel Zone, the wide beach is perfect for swimming, sunbathing, and shelling. Although it's still relatively untouched, in the last few years there have been vague plans in the works to construct several hotels here—so enjoy it while it lasts. Playa Bocana stretches from Bahía Conejos to the Río Copalita. Though swimming here is hazardous, the delightful beach is lined with *palapa* (thatch-roofed) restaurants that specialize in seafood, beans, and homemade tortillas. Access is by boat only.

BUFADORA (BLOWHOLE) The water spouts like a whale at this natural geyser. Between Bahías Entrega and Organo; access by boat only.

Sources and Resources

TOURIST INFORMATION

The *Secretaría de Turismo* (Secretariat of Tourism; phone: 10388) is located in the Hotel Zone on Paseo de Tangolunda, across the street from the *Sheraton Huatulco;* it's closed weekends. The publication office of *Huatulco Espacio 2000* (see below) is another source of tourist information (Calle Guamuchil near the *zócalo;* phone: 70027); it's closed Sundays. Information also is available from hotel desks.

LOCAL COVERAGE The local publication *Huatulco Espacio 2000,* available at most hotels, provides a good map and listings in English and Spanish for visitors.

TELEPHONE The city code for Huatulco is 958. *Note:* Mexico's telephone company has embarked on a major expansion project that involves changing telephone numbers in many areas of the country. At press time, all numbers listed in this chapter were correct. However, if you have any difficulties reaching attractions listed here, contact the local tourist office.

CLIMATE AND CLOTHES Huatulco is blessed with the idyllic climate typical of most of Mexico's Pacific Coast, with year-round temperatures averaging 82F (28C). From October through June, it seldom rains. As for clothes, anything goes, as long as it's lightweight. Don't forget to pack plenty of sunblock— you'll need it even when you're not intentionally soaking up the sun.

GETTING AROUND

Huatulco's three sections are accessible to one another only by bus, car, or van.

BUS Very inexpensive minibuses run among the three sections of Huatulco, but we don't recommend taking them, since service is extremely sporadic. Buses operated by *Cristóbal Colón* (Calle Ocotillo; phone: 70261) and *Gacela* (Palo Verde; phone: 70103) run frequently between Huatulco and Puerto Escondido, and *Gacela* also has service to Acapulco.

CAR RENTAL *Budget* and *Dollar* cars can be rented at the airport. *Dollar* has another office at the *Sheraton Huatulco* (phone: 10055, ext. 787) and the *Castillo Huatulco* (phone: 70126); *Budget* has offices at the corner of Calles Ocotillo and Jazmín in La Crucesita (phone: 70010). The *Dollar* office at the *Castillo Huatulco* also rents Honda Elite motorcycles, available at hourly and daily rates.

TOURS *Servicios Turísticos del Sur,* which operates out of the *Sheraton Huatulco* (see *Checking In*) and the *Castillo Huatulco* (phone: 70572) hotels, offers full-day excursions to the Laguna Chacahua and to Puerto Escondido, as does *Turismo Tangolunda,* with offices in the *Royal Maeva* hotel (phone: 10000) and at the corner of Oaxaca and Zoquiapan in Santa Cruz (phone:

70272). They also offer three-hour tours of the bays, with a stop for swimming and snorkeling. In addition, *Servicios Turísticos del Sur* runs an interesting tour to Tehuantepec, a town famous for having the only matriarchal society in the country. (For additional information on Tehuantepec, see the *Mexico City to the Guatemala Border* route in DIRECTIONS.)

VAN It's better to take a van than a taxi to your hotel from the airport. *Transporte Terrestre* (phone: 10308) has vans that meet arriving flights, and hotels will arrange transportation to the airport by van for departing guests. At press time, the one-way fare between the airport and the hotels was 30 pesos (about $4) per person.

SHOPPING

Because shopping options in Huatulco are rather limited, most people combine a stay here with a visit to the city of Oaxaca, one of Mexico's premier shopping destinations. Some hotel boutiques carry a selection of handicrafts along with beach- and resortwear. There also are some stalls on the square in La Crucesita and around the dock in Santa Cruz; though they sell mostly junk, with patience you can find some colorful embroidered dresses and shirts and a small selection of black Oaxacan pottery.

SPORTS

BOATING The *Sociedad Cooperativa Turística de Tangolunda* (phone: 70081) rents boats at the beach of Santa Cruz; the group also offers trips to the various bays on a glass-bottomed boat. If asked, the captain will offer some local lore.

FISHING These waters are superb for deep-sea fishing, and the sailfish bite year-round. (Getting a permit is not difficult; see *Fishing Mexico's Rich Waters* in DIVERSIONS for more information.) You can charter a boat from the *Sociedad Cooperativa Turística de Tangolunda* (see *Boating*), but it's advisable to bring your own gear. *Triton Dive Center* at the *Castillo Huatulco* hotel (phone: 70055) operates a 27-foot motor launch that accommodates five passengers (four lines). *Club Med Huatulco* (see *Checking In*) takes members on excursions to its own fishing spot, La Pêche au Gros.

GOLF The 18-hole *Huatulco* golf course (near the *Sheraton Huatulco;* phone: 10059) is open to the public.

HORSEBACK RIDING *Servicios Turísticos del Sur* (see *Tours,* above) offers morning and afternoon outings across the mountains to the Río Copalita. The four-hour morning trip includes a stop for a swim at Playa Magueyito.

SAILING *Club Med Huatulco* and the *Royal Maeva* (see *Checking In* for both) have sailboats for unlimited use by guests. Room rates include lessons.

SCUBA DIVING AND SNORKELING *Marina Bahías de Huatulco,* the water sports center at the *Sheraton Huatulco* (see *Checking In*), rents snorkeling equipment.

Snorkeling enthusiasts should head for Bahía Tangolunda, where the great reef (just below the surface) is made up partly of giant cauliflower-shaped coral, and friendly tropical fish dot the underwater world with color. Visibility is good down to 20 feet. Another good coral reef is at Playa Entrega, a beach where snorkeling equipment and snacks are available. *Club Med Huatulco* (see *Checking In*) provides gear for its guests. *Triton Dive Center* (see *Fishing*) offers diving and snorkeling trips and allows non-diving companions to go along. A minimum of three divers is required for a scuba trip; for snorkeling trips, the minimum is six people. All trips include a boat, equipment, a guide, and soft drinks. *Triton* offers several diving courses as well.

SWIMMING AND SUNNING Dozens of white, sun-swept beaches span this stretch of the coast. The beaches outside *Club Med Huatulco,* the *Sheraton Huatulco,* the *Omni Zaashila Resort,* and the *Royal Maeva* (see *Checking In* for all) are good for swimming, since all have calm waters. Bahía Maguey is the only beach in the bay area with fine sand; you'll recognize it by the maguey plants jutting up out of the stone surrounding the beach. If you yearn for privacy, adjacent Bahía Organo is quiet, but beware of the undercurrent. There's good shelling and big waves at Bahía Conejos (see *Special Places*).

TENNIS Among the hotels and clubs that offer tennis facilities are *Club Med Huatulco* (11 synthetic-surface courts, six lighted); the *Crowne Plaza* (one lighted hard-surface court); the *Sheraton Huatulco* (four lighted synthetic-surface courts); the *Royal Maeva* (two lighted concrete courts); the *Omni Zaashila Resort* (one lighted synthetic surface court); and the *Huatulco* golf course (four lighted hard-surface courts). See *Checking In* for additional details on hotels.

WINDSURFING This is one of the many water sports available to guests at *Club Med Huatulco,* the *Omni Zaashila Resort,* and the *Royal Maeva;* it's also available on the beach at the *Sheraton Huatulco* (see *Checking In* for all).

NIGHTCLUBS AND NIGHTLIFE

Generally, nights in Huatulco are quiet, unless you're staying at the *Royal Maeva* or at *Club Med Huatulco,* where the *gentils organisateurs* (GOs) enthusiastically demonstrate how to dance to salsa, and a string of yellow beads buys *muchas* margaritas. The *Sheraton Huatulco* is the venue for nightly mariachi serenades, as well as a Friday-evening Mexican fiesta— with a buffet dinner, marimba music, and folkloric dances. (See *Checking In* for details on hotels.) Otherwise, nightlife is limited to the *Magic Circus* (Blvd. Benito Juárez and Calle Oaxaca, in Santa Cruz; phone: 70017), a disco about two blocks from the *Binniguenda* hotel, and the *Savage* disco (phone: 10111) at the *Punta Arena* shopping center, near the *Sheraton Huatulco.* For a quieter evening, take a walk on the beach or count the seemingly endless number of stars in the sky.

Best in Town

CHECKING IN

Expect to pay up to $300 per night for a double room at an expensive hotel; about $150 at a moderate place; and $100 or less at an inexpensive place. Rates go down by about 30% between *Easter* and January. Note that rates at *Club Med Huatulco* and the *Royal Maeva* include most activities and all meals. Unless otherwise indicated, the hotels listed have air conditioning, telephones, and TV sets (with at least a few English-language programs) in all rooms. All telephone numbers are in the 958 city code unless otherwise indicated.

We begin with our favorite haven (in the expensive range), followed by recommended hotels, listed by price category.

A SPECIAL HAVEN

Marco Polo This exquisite 25-suite property is perched atop a cliff overlooking Tangolunda Bay, in the middle section of the Hotel Zone. The rooms are large and airy, with pale yellow walls trimmed with white, original artwork, beautiful Oaxacan crafts, marble floors, and luxurious bathrooms. All suites have private terraces (ask for one with a garden); a few even have Jacuzzis. Other amenities include a pool, a delightful restaurant (also called *Marco Polo;* see *Eating Out*), and a lobby bar. Steps lead down to an almost private beach. 1 Balcones de Tangolunda, Tangolunda (phone: 10202/3; fax: 10102).

EXPENSIVE

Club Med Huatulco The largest Club Med village in the Western Hemisphere, it has 475 no-frills rooms—each with a private terrace and hammock—set in casita clusters on Bahía Tangolunda. The club offers a full range of water sports on four isolated coves, and there are three pools and 11 tennis courts (six lighted). Unfortunately, the hotel's four small beaches are only fair. In addition to the main cafeteria-style eatery, there's an excellent Moroccan restaurant, a seafood place, a Mexican restaurant, a fancy Italian restaurant, and a disco. *Club Med* operates nonstop charter flights from New York, Chicago, Houston, and Los Angeles. Tangolunda (phone: 10081; 800-CLUB-MED; fax: 10101).

Omni Zaashila Resort It would seem that no expense was spared in creating this spectacular resort that spans 27 beachfront acres landscaped with tropical gardens, fountains, and waterfalls. The 120 rooms and 64 one- and two-bedroom suites are clustered in Mediterranean-style villas. All have private balconies, ocean views, and Italian marble floors; in addition, 41 rooms and 24 suites have private splash pools. Other amenities include a 100-meter free-form pool, a beach club, two restaurants, a poolside snack bar, a lounge with live music nightly, a lighted tennis court, and most water sports. Playa Rincón Sabroso, Bahía de Tangolunda (phone: 10460; 800-THE-OMNI; fax: 10461).

Royal Maeva Features at this all-inclusive beachfront hotel include 300 rooms, two restaurants, a coffee shop, bars and lounges, a pool, two tennis courts, gardens, and a playground. Paseo de Tangolunda, Tangolunda (phone: 10000; 10048, or 10064; 800-GO-MAEVA; fax: 10220).

MODERATE

Crowne Plaza Tiered on a hill overlooking Bahía Tangolunda, this impressive property offers 135 large suites, 24 of them with Jacuzzis. Facilities include two restaurants, two pools, a wading pool, a lighted tennis court, a playground, a gym, and a beach club with water sports. 8 Blvd. Benito Juárez, Tangolunda (phone: 10044; 800-2-CROWNE in the US; 800-00999 in Mexico; fax: 10221).

Sheraton Huatulco Set on a wide, crescent-shaped beach at the end of Bahía Tangolunda, this contemporary Mexican-style resort is furnished throughout with Oaxacan crafts. All 347 rooms have bay views, terraces, mini-bars, safes, and 24-hour room service. There also are two restaurants, a coffee shop, two bars, shops, a health club, and four tennis courts. Paseo de Tangolunda, Tangolunda (phone: 10055; 800-325-3535 in the US; 800-90325 in Mexico; fax: 10113).

INEXPENSIVE

Binniguenda Huatulco's first hostelry, set about 530 yards from Bahía Santa Cruz, features 75 rooms, a lobby bar, and a restaurant. There's no beach, but a pool and gardens are on the grounds. 5 Blvd. Benito Juárez, Santa Cruz (phone: 70077; 800-336-5454; fax: 70284).

Castillo Huatulco With the *Triton Dive Center* on the premises, this is the perfect place for those who prefer scuba, snorkeling, and other water activities to just swimming and sunning. There are 107 cheerful rooms, a pool, a restaurant, and a very efficient and helpful staff. A block from the dock, on Blvd. Benito Juárez, Santa Cruz (phone: 70051; fax: 70131).

EATING OUT

Expect to pay $60 for dinner for two at an expensive place and about $35 at a moderate one; there are no truly excellent inexpensive eateries here. Prices don't include drinks, wine, tax, or tips. Most restaurants we list accept MasterCard and Visa, and a few also accept American Express and Diners Club; it's a good idea to call ahead and check. Unless otherwise noted, the restaurants listed below are open daily for lunch and dinner. All telephone numbers are in the 958 city code unless otherwise indicated.

EXPENSIVE

Cavendish This is a pretty place with pink tablecloths and lots of plants. Try the filet of fish stuffed with crab and served with a béarnaise sauce. Reservations advised. In the *Punta Tangolunda* shopping center, Tangolunda (phone: 10146).

Marco Polo The emphasis is on Italian and Swiss specialties at this gorgeous hotel restaurant. The sweeping view of Bahía Tangolunda is truly magnificent. Reservations advised. In the *Marco Polo*, 1 Balcones de Tangolunda, Tangolunda (phone: 10202/3).

1/2 Carlos 'n' Charlie's Part of the popular Anderson's chain, it offers the standard casual setting, zany waiters, and tasty food. The items on the menu include ribs, oysters, and shrimp with beer. Closed for lunch and Sundays. Reservations advised. Calles Carizal and Flamboyán, La Crucesita (phone: 70005).

La Pampa Argentina Head here for excellent meat, prepared Argentine-style and served with the traditional vinegar-based *chimichurri* sauce. Other popular items are the pasta dishes and the fresh salads. Reservations advised for dinner. Across from the *Huatulco* golf course, Tangolunda (phone: 10001).

MODERATE

Avalos "Doña Celia" At this simple, open-air waterfront eatery, ask for a two-kilo lobster accompanied by a *michelada* (beer with ice, lime, and salt). No reservations. Santa Cruz (phone: 70128).

Ixtapa and Zihuatanejo

(pronounced Eeks-*tah*-pah and See-wah-tah-*nay*-ho)

Mexico's immensely long Pacific Coast is blessed with port towns, fishing villages, and resort cities for every taste. Among the newer of these resort areas are the neighboring towns of Ixtapa and Zihuatanejo, 150 miles northwest of Acapulco, in the state of Guerrero. Though Ixtapa is only about 4 miles from Zihuatanejo, they have very little in common; side by side, they provide a look at two contrasting moods of Pacific Mexico.

Though its status as a popular resort is fairly recent, Zihuatanejo has a long history. Long before Columbus was born, the village (which was known then as Zihuatlán, "Place of Women," because the local society was matriarchal) was chosen by the Tarascan as a royal bathing resort. The figurines, ceramics, and stone carvings (including stelae) that continue to be found in the area attest to the presence of many civilizations dating back to about 3000 BC, including the Chichimec, Cuitlatec, Olmec, and Aztec, as well as the Tarascan, who dominated the area the longest (from around 1400 to 1500). European influence in the region began in 1527, when Spanish conquistadores launched a trade route from the Bahía de Zihuatanejo to the Orient. Galleons returned with silks and spices and, from the Philippines, the first coconut palms to arrive in the Americas. Because the Spaniards did little colonizing in this region, Zihuatanejo remained a tiny fishing village for centuries, virtually undiscovered by tourists—until the advent of Ixtapa in the 1970s.

Ixtapa was carved out of an immense, lush coconut plantation when *FONATUR* (Mexico's national tourism development fund) realized the area had excellent resort potential. The $50-million development project included the construction of a new highway from Acapulco; sewage, electrical, and communications systems for Zihuatanejo; a recreational and residential complex; and the *Ixtapa-Zihuatanejo International Airport.* Ixtapa's ecology-sensitive master plan called for controlled, limited growth, and the area's strict adherence to the plan's high nature-to-cement ratio is obvious. Even today, there is no need for any traffic signals in either town (honestly). While Zihuatanejo remained essentially untouched, Ixtapa sprouted luxury hotels, high-tech discos, two 18-hole golf courses, a yacht marina, and village-like shopping centers, as well as acres of manicured landscapes.

In contrast with glamorous Ixtapa, Zihuatanejo is a delightful place just to poke around. The town is charming, with many good handicrafts shops, bars, and restaurants. Fishing still is a way of life here, and this is a good place to eat fresh lobster, snapper, and clams, as well as game fish such as tuna, marlin, and sailfish. Restaurateurs from both Zihuatanejo and Ixtapa gather at the Playa Principal (Town Beach) every morning to purchase the fresh catch from the local fishermen returning from a night at sea. The beachside basketball court, which doubles as the main plaza, also is the locale for fiestas and open-air dances on Sunday nights.

In total, the "dual resort" area runs along 16 miles of tropical coastline with dozens of sandy beaches, scalloped coves, lagoons, and inlets. The surrounding foothills of the Sierra Madre Sur, dotted with mango, papaya, lemon, and tamarind trees, provide a panoramic backdrop.

The attractions here are sun and sea. Hotel guests usually are content to enjoy the sand at their doorstep, but those who enjoy exploring will find pristine beaches and even jungle treks to isolated lagoons vibrant with birds and other wildlife. Scenic scuba diving and snorkeling are possible, and both light-tackle and deep-sea fishing are outstanding. There are also boat trips to Isla Ixtapa (see *Extra Special*).

The final major step in Ixtapa's master plan—the development of the 430-acre Marina Ixtapa recreational and residential complex, fashioned out of a mangrove lagoon north of Playa del Palmar (the Hotel Zone beach)—was completed in mid-1994. There are several restaurants along the waterside promenade, and *El Faro,* an 82-foot lighthouse topped by a delightful bar, towers over the marina, which can accommodate 600 yachts up to 100 feet long. Running between the yacht marina and the northern end of the Hotel Zone is an 18-hole Robert Trent Jones Jr. golf course crisscrossed by canals.

Though Marina Ixtapa promises to attract even more resort-loving travelers, the area's lush natural beauty, scenic beaches, and plentiful fishing and diving opportunities—along with the small-town charm of Zihuatanejo—continue to make it a tranquil and inviting vacation spot.

Ixtapa and Zihuatanejo At-a-Glance

SEEING THE CITY

The approach to Ixtapa from the airport affords a dramatic hilltop view of the resort below. You also can admire the sweep of Ixtapa from the aerial tramway that runs from the south end of Playa del Palmar to the cliff-top *El Faro* restaurant at the *Club Pacífica* condominium complex (phone: 31027; not to be confused with *El Faro* in Marina Ixtapa). For a panoramic vista of the Bahía de Zihuatanejo, stop at the roadside *mirador* (lookout) on the way to Playa la Ropa. The oyster-shaped bay, only 1.6 miles wide, is one of the Mexican Pacific's most scenic. Sunsets are spectacular.

SPECIAL PLACES

PLAYA QUIETA Just up the coast from Ixtapa's Hotel Zone, its name means "quiet beach," but the *Club Med* next door makes it pretty lively. Sailing and windsurfing are popular, and boats leave from here for nearby Isla Ixtapa (see *Extra Special*).

PLAYA DEL PALMAR Named for the palm groves out of which Ixtapa was fashioned, this 2-mile stretch of beach fronts Ixtapa's Hotel Zone. Numerous water sports are available here, and the beach is popular with joggers. Several *morros* (jagged rock formations) offshore create dramatic silhouettes against the fiery sunsets.

MUSEO ARQUEOLÓGICO DE LA COSTA GRANDE (ARCHAEOLOGICAL MUSEUM OF THE GREAT COAST) This beachside museum features close to 1,000 pieces of art and artifacts, some dating to the Olmec era, discovered at nearby sites. The objects are complemented by illustrated maps and murals with written explanations (in Spanish). Closed Mondays. Admission charge. Paseo del Pescador at Plaza Olof Palme, Zihuatanejo (phone: 32552).

PLAYA LA ROPA *Ropa* means "clothes" in Spanish, and this beach is said to be so named because centuries ago clothing, apparently the cargo of a wrecked ship, washed up here. The main beach for the Zihuatanejo hotels, this is one of the longest and most beautiful, and the most popular. Sheltered within the bay, the sandy beach has no surf, but all kinds of water sports, including water skiing, parasailing, windsurfing, jet skiing, and banana-boat riding, are available. Along the beach are several good seafood restaurants, including *Punta Marina* (phone: 43347) and *La Gaviota* (see *Eating Out*).

PLAYA LAS GATAS This beach along the Bahía de Zihuatanejo lies slightly south of Playa la Ropa, on the bay side of a small peninsula that juts into the water. It's best reached by boat from Zihuatanejo's pier; buy a ticket from the *Cooperativa de Lanchas de Recreo y Pesca Deportiva* (Recreational and Fishing Boat Cooperative; phone: 42056) booth at the beginning of the pier. The *gatas* (nurse sharks) the beach was named for disappeared from here long ago. The long row of hand-cut rocks serves as a breakwater; no one is sure exactly who made it or why. The prevailing theory is that a Tarascan king built it to shelter his daughter's private swath of sand. There is a small dive shop, and modest *palapa* (thatch-roofed) restaurants serve fresh seafood (*Chez Arnoldo* is one of the best; see *Eating Out*). This is a great place to go for lunch and a swim or snorkel. The last boats return at 5 PM.

BARRA DE POTOSÍ A small fishing village surrounded by grapefruit, coconut, papaya, mango, and tamarind orchards, it lies 12½ miles (20 km) south of Zihuatanejo. This is where the Laguna Potosí (great for birding) meets the Pacific, at the southern end of the vast, pristine beach known as Playa Blanca. Several *palapa* restaurants here serve seafood dishes, including a local delicacy called *pescado a la talla* (thin strips of fish marinated in spicy—though not hot—adobo sauce).

EXTRA SPECIAL

Isla Ixtapa, also known as Isla Grande, is a favorite destination for a boat trip and a good place for a day's—or a half-day's—excursion. Reached by cruise tours from Ixtapa and Zihuatanejo, or just a five-minute boat ride from Playa Linda, the small, wooded island is great for sunning, snorkeling, and eating. The island has delightful beaches, and diving here is great.

The main beach, Cuachalalate, is lined with *palapa* eateries serving fresh seafood. At the opposite end of the beach from the small boat dock, *Nacho's Dive Shop* (no phone) rents snorkel and scuba gear. A five-minute walk to the island's west side takes you to Playa Varadero; *El Marlin*, a *palapa* seafood restaurant here, has delicious food. Windsurfing equipment, banana boats, and aquacycles are available on Playa Cuachalalate and Playa Varadero. The last boats return to the mainland daily at 5 PM from docks on both beaches.

Sources and Resources

TOURIST INFORMATION

In Ixtapa, the local branch of the *Secretaría de Turismo del Estado de Guerrero* (Guerrero State Tourism Secretariat) is across from the *Presidente Ixtapa* hotel at *La Puerta* shopping center (phone: 31967/8). In Zihuatanejo, the municipal *Oficina de Turismo de Zihuatanejo-Ixtapa* is on the south side of the *zócalo* (phone: 42001, ext. 120). Both offices are closed Sundays. All Ixtapa hotels and the larger ones in Zihuatanejo have travel desks. In Ixtapa, all hotel personnel that work with the public speak English; this is not the case in Zihuatanejo.

LOCAL COVERAGE *The News* and the *Mexico City Times,* both English-language daily newspapers, are available at most Ixtapa hotels. Major hotel newsstands also carry various US magazines and some US newspapers, including *The New York Times* (a day late). Available free everywhere, the monthly bilingual guide *Que Hacer, a Donde Ir* (What to Do, Where to Go) provides tourist information, including listings of shops, restaurants, hotels, and special events. The bilingual newspaper *Diario 17 Ixtapa-Zihuatanejo,* also free, features local news and tourist information.

TELEPHONE The city code for Ixtapa-Zihuatanejo is 753. *Note:* Mexico's telephone company has embarked on a major expansion project that involves changing telephone numbers in many areas of the country. At press time, all numbers listed in this chapter were correct. However, if you have any difficulties reaching attractions listed here, contact the local tourist office.

CLIMATE AND CLOTHES Temperatures here average in the 80s F (27–32C) year-round; the humidity often is tempered by a breeze after sundown. The rainy season is June through October, but even then the sun shines most of the day. Dress is casual, but not shocking.

GETTING AROUND

BUS Minibuses run between Ixtapa and Zihuatanejo about every 20 minutes until 11 PM. The fare is 1.5 pesos (about 20¢), and the trip takes about 15 minutes. *Colectivo* vans provide transportation between Ixtapa and the airport for 20 pesos (about $2.70) per person and between Zihuatanejo and the airport for 16 pesos (about $2.15) per person. For *colectivo* information, call 42046 or 42785. Purchase tickets at the airport or through your hotel desk. Frequent, inexpensive first class buses bound for inland destinations, as well as towns along the Pacific Coast such as Acapulco, depart from the *Estación de Autobuses* (Bus Station) in Zihuatanejo (20 Calle Ejido; phone: 43477).

CAR RENTAL Most major international firms are represented at the airport, as well as at Ixtapa hotels and in Zihuatanejo. A good local agency is *Quick* (*Westin Brisas Resort Ixtapa;* phone: 31830), which will deliver and pick up cars at the airport.

CYCLES Rent scooters or small motorcycles by the hour or by the day in Ixtapa at *Hola Renta Motos* (no phone), in *La Puerta* shopping center across from the *Presidente* hotel. In Zihuatanejo, cycles are available from *Renta de Motos Michelle* (Calle Galeana; phone: 42102).

TAXIS Rates are standardized, and cabs are unmetered. For an idea of the taxi fares, check at the lobby of any major hotel: The rates usually are posted. Most drivers will take up to three passengers. The trip between Ixtapa and Zihuatanejo usually takes about 10 minutes.

TOURS *MTA* (in the *Sheraton Ixtapa;* phone: 31379; fax: 31296); *Paseos Ixtapa* and *American Express* (both in the *Krystal Ixtapa;* see *Checking In*) offer tours, as do travel desks at other hotels. Typical outings include trips into the backcountry, one-day excursions to Acapulco, and cruises, as well as bird watching, sport fishing, and diving expeditions.

SPECIAL EVENTS

The *Torneo de Pez Vela* (Swordfish Tournament) is held in May and December. Hundreds of athletes from around the world participate every November in the *Triatlón Internacional Ixtapa* (Ixtapa International Triathlon), a combination swimming, bicycling, and running race.

SHOPPING

Though area stores have been buffeted by the country's economic woes, there are still some 300 shops distributed among Ixtapa's seven shopping malls, which include *Los Patios* (Paseo Ixtapa), *Plaza las Fuentes* (Paseo Ixtapa), and *La Puerta* (Paseo Ixtapa, across from the *Presidente Ixtapa* hotel). The shops in the *Westin Brisas Resort Ixtapa* hotel (see *Checking In*) are fine for beachwear and silver. Paseo del Pescador and Pasaje Agustín Ramírez, Calle 5 de Mayo, Cuauhtémoc, and Pedro Ascencio in Zihuatanejo are good shopping streets.

The area's municipal and handicrafts markets, while not as grand and colorful as the markets of Guadalajara or Oaxaca, still offer plenty to delight visitors. Zihuatanejo's main municipal market, located on the east side of Benito Juárez between Calles González and Nava, sells food, clothing, and household goods. Local crafts can be found at *mercados de artesanía* (open-air handicraft markets), which are held across the street from the *Sheraton* hotel in Ixtapa, and along Calle 5 de Mayo and alongside Playa la Ropa in Zihuatanejo. In general, shops are open daily from 10 AM to 7 PM (later in high season, roughly *Christmas* through *Easter,* as well as July through August). Some stores close between 2 and 4 or 5 PM.

IXTAPA

Chiquita Banana Unusual handicrafts and folk art from all over Mexico, including silver serving spoons, ceramic serving dishes, jewelry, and Panama hats (but no bananas). *Los Patios* shopping center (no phone).

Ferrioni Collection Colorful, top-quality beach- and casualwear, including a line for children. *La Puerta* shopping center (phone: 32343).

La Fuente An imaginative selection of handicrafts and folk art, as well as accessories for interior decor, from various regions of Mexico. *Los Patios* (no phone).

Galería San Angel Among the Mexican arts and crafts featured here are sculptures depicting fantasy and quasi-religious subjects produced by some of Mexico's finest artisans, including the renowned Sergio Bustamante. *Los Patios* (phone: 30392).

Kos Women's bathing suits and beachwear from Europe. Blvd. Ixtapa, across from the *Dorado Pacífico* hotel (no phone).

Mic-Mac Fine native art and handicrafts, knickknacks, and fun, folkloric men's and women's apparel. *La Puerta* (phone: 31733).

Roberto's Silver jewelry and ornamental pieces from Taxco. *Plaza las Fuentes* shopping center (no phone).

Scruples Fashions from Christian Dior, Nina Ricci, and Bill Blass. *La Puerta* (phone: 31493).

Tanga Bikini Shop A large selection of the latest in beachwear for the whole family, including Mexican designs and imports from Israel, Brazil, and Spain. *Los Patios* (no phone).

ZIHUATANEJO

Byblos The best shop in the area for bilingual books and maps, plus a small selection of recorded music. 5 Pasaje Agustín Ramírez (phone: 42281).

Casa Marina Five fascinating folk art and handicraft shops all under one roof. Rugs, weavings, wooden ritual masks, regional costumes and crafts, and silverwork, plus a good selection of colorfully embroidered clothing. 9 Paseo del Pescador (phone: 42373).

Cecilia's Silver jewelry at good prices. 19 Calle Nicolás Bravo (phone: 43192).

Deportes Náuticos Sportswear and sporting gear for men and women. Calles Nicolás Bravo and Vicente Guerrero (phone: 44411).

Galería Maya Folk art, leather goods, crafts, and other unique items, many from Oaxaca. 31 Calle Nicolás Bravo (phone: 44606).

D'Xochitl Hand-embroidered cotton clothing for women, including designs from Suceso, Opus I, and Girasol. Calles Ejido and Cuauhtémoc (phone: 42131).

SPORTS

FISHING Before Ixtapa was a gleam in anyone's eye, anglers came to Zihuatanejo to fish for marlin, sailfish, yellowfin tuna, and dorado (mahimahi). Closer to shore, there is grouper, wahoo, swordfish, and bonito. Arrange fishing excursions through *Ixtapa Fishing Charters* (6 Paseo del Pescador; phone: 44426; 717-424-8323 in the US; fax: 717-424-1016 in the US). *Aeroméxico Vacations* (phone: 800-245-8323), the airline's in-house tour program, offers comprehensive sport fishing packages from the US to Ixtapa and Zihuatanejo. Beware of individuals who approach you on the street and offer deep-sea fishing deals that sound too good to be true—they usually are.

GOLF The 18-hole, par 72 *Ixtapa Golf Club* (phone: 31062), designed by Robert Trent Jones Jr., was built during Ixtapa's initial development by *FONATUR.* It extends from lush jungle areas to the south end of the Hotel Zone beach, or Playa del Palmar. The course and surrounding land are home to many local varieties of birds, and alligators inhabit some of the natural lake-like water hazards. Caddies or carts are required. Clubhouse facilities include a restaurant, a bar, a pro shop, five lighted tennis courts, and a large pool with a congenial lounge area.

For a more challenging game, try Ixtapa's newest venue, the 18-hole, par 72 *Marina Ixtapa Golf Course* (phone: 31410; fax: 30825) at the Marina Ixtapa development. Designed by Robert von Hagge, the course measures about 6,900 yards from the back tees and is traversed by 2 miles of canals, providing delightful transportation within the marina area via canoes and small, silent, electric motorboats. Golf carts are required, as players are not allowed to walk the course. Also on the grounds is the *Marina Ixtapa Clubhouse,* which features tennis courts, a pool, a gym, and a restaurant.

HORSEBACK RIDING Guided tours on horseback leave from Playa Linda, a 15-minute taxi ride north of Ixtapa. Hotel tour desks can make arrangements a day in advance; otherwise, just show up in the morning or early afternoon.

PARASAILING While wearing an open parachute, you are pulled by a speedboat racing across the bay at Ixtapa or the Bahía de Zihuatanejo; at a certain speed, you become airborne, flying above the Pacific. Parasailing is offered daily by outfits along the Hotel Zone beach in Ixtapa, and on Playa la Ropa in Zihuatanejo. Be careful: Accidents are rare, but they do happen.

SAILING Catamarans and other boats are available with or without crew; charter yachts and sailboats through the *Marina Ixtapa Clubhouse* (phone: 31410). Sailing is popular at Playa Quieta, up the coast from Ixtapa. In Zihuatanejo, rent windsurfers on Playa la Ropa. (See *Special Places* for details on both beaches.)

SCUBA AND SNORKELING The undersea scenery is breathtaking here. There are at least 28 dive sites in the area, ranging from shallow corals to jagged underwater canyons 100 feet deep. All are rated for beginner, intermediate, or expert divers. Isla Ixtapa (see *Extra Special*) has powdery white beaches and clear waters perfect for snorkelers and divers; equipment for both is available from *Nacho's Dive Shop* (no phone) on the island. Another good snorkeling spot nearby is Playa Manzanillo, down the coast from Playa las Gatas (make advance boat reservations at the booth on the *Zihuatanejo Pier*). Los Morros de Potosí, rock formations located a three-minute boat ride from Barra de Potosí (see *Special Places*), offer extraordinary underwater experiences for expert scuba divers.

Equipment, instruction, *NAUI* certification courses, and snorkeling and scuba excursions are offered by the *Zihuatanejo Scuba Center,* with facilities at *Puerto Mío Marina* (phone: 42748) and a dive shop (3 Calle Cuauhtémoc, across from Banamex; phone: 42147). The center also offers morning classes in the pools of the *Sheraton Ixtapa, Presidente Ixtapa, Dorado Pacífico,* and *Holiday Inn* hotels (see *Checking In* for all). Those wishing to combine a vacation with a certification course should take the written and pool segments before departing from home, leaving the ocean-dive part for Ixtapa-Zihuatanejo.

SURFING Surfers try to keep their favorite spots as secret as possible. One of them, however, is Troncones, at the south end of a long, isolated beach and named for the large tree trunks found there; it's about a 20-minute drive up the coast northwest of Ixtapa. There are no rentals in Ixtapa or Zihuatanejo, so bring your own equipment.

SWIMMING AND SUNNING The Bahía de Zihuatanejo is naturally sheltered, so the water is tranquil, with few or no waves on Playa Principal, Playa la Madera (southeast of downtown, next to the pier), Playa la Ropa, or Playa las Gatas (see *Special Places* for additional details on the latter two beaches). Playa Quieta and Isla Ixtapa (see *Special Places* for both) also have no surf. Playa del Palmar (Ixtapa's Hotel Zone beach) does have waves; be especially careful when red flags go up on the hotel beaches. Each of Ixtapa's major beachfront hotels has a lifeguard on duty throughout the day.

TENNIS The *Ixtapa Golf Club* and the *Marina Ixtapa Clubhouse* (see *Golf*) have lighted courts open to the public for a fee. All the beachfront Ixtapa hotels (except for the *Omni Ixtapa*), as well as the *Villa del Sol* in Zihuatanejo, have lighted tennis courts for guests only. Most have resident pros and tennis clinics.

WINDSURFING Playa Quieta in Ixtapa is a favorite windsurfing spot. In Zihuatanejo, rent windsurfers on Playa la Ropa in front of the *Villa del Sol* hotel.

NIGHTCLUBS AND NIGHTLIFE

After-dark action centers around the hotels, especially those in Ixtapa, which make sure that guests don't get bored. Mexican fiestas—with buffets offering regional fare, handicraft bazaars, and colorful folkloric dance shows—take place at different hotels on certain nights; the best is at the *Dorado Pacífico* on Tuesdays (see *Checking In*). *Christine* at the *Krystal Ixtapa* hotel (see *Checking In*) is a high-tech favorite. Some of the Ixtapa hotels, such as the *Krystal Ixtapa* and *Sheraton Ixtapa* (see *Checking In* for both) have bars or restaurants with live music and dancing; reservations are recommended in season. The nightly impromptu dance parties on a raised platform by the beach at *Carlos 'n' Charlie's* (see *Eating Out*) always draw a crowd.

Nightlife in Zihuatanejo is more casual. *Coconuts* restaurant offers live music and dancing nightly in a tropical garden under the stars, and the *Bay Club* restaurant features live jazz every night on its outdoor patio (see *Eating Out* for both). At the *Villa del Sol* (see *Checking In*), there's a Mexican fiesta on Friday nights, with an elaborate buffet and a folkloric singing ensemble.

Best in Town

CHECKING IN

Most of Ixtapa's hotels are luxury resorts located on the beach. Zihuatanejo's hostelries are older, cozy, and homey, except for the deluxe *Villa del Sol, Puerto Mío,* and *La Casa Que Canta.*

Julia Ortiz Bautista, the owner of *JOB Representaciones* (*Villas del Pacífico*, Edificio C, Despacho 01, Zihuatanejo 40880, Guerrero, México; phone/fax: 44374), arranges rentals of villas, bungalows, apartments, and condominiums in Zihuatanejo and Ixtapa. Prices range from $50 to $500 per day; weekly and monthly rates also are available.

Expect to pay $200 or more per night for a double room at a very expensive hotel; $140 to $190 in an expensive one; $85 to $120 in a moderate place; and $80 or less in an inexpensive one. Unless otherwise noted, all rooms have air conditioning, a TV set, and a telephone. Rates often are 30% to 40% lower June through August. All telephone numbers are in the 753 city code unless otherwise indicated.

We begin with our favorite havens, followed by recommended hotels, listed by location and price category.

A REGAL RESORT AND A SPECIAL HAVEN

Villa del Sol This low-key (but expensive) Zihuatanejo inn is on the best beach in town, with 36 deluxe units (ranging from split-level junior suites to two-bedroom beach suites) nestled amid palm trees and tropical gardens. In the middle of the complex are a small pool and a large *palapa* (thatch-roofed shelter) that houses the bar and open-air dining area. There's also a multi-story dining room next door (also called *Villa del Sol;* see *Eating Out*). Another pool has a swim-up bar, and the hotel offers all water sports. This is one of only two hotels in Mexico that are members of the prestigious Relais & Châteaux group (*Las Mañanitas* in Cuernavaca is the other). High season rates include breakfast and lunch or dinner. Children under 14 are not accepted during the winter (November 15 through April). Playa la Ropa, Zihuatanejo (phone: 42239; 800-223-6510; fax: 42758).

Westin Brisas Resort Ixtapa Surrounded by acres of palm trees and tropical flowers, this pricey resort—designed by Ricardo Legorreta—faces its own secluded cove, just a three-minute taxi ride from the Hotel Zone. The exterior resembles the side of a colossal Aztec pyramid. All 428 rooms (including 18 suites) have unobstructed ocean views and private terraces complete with hammocks. The *Ixtapa Golf Club* (see *Golf*) is minutes away, and the hotel's four lighted tennis courts are near a complex of multilevel pools and waterfalls. The restaurant, *Portofino* (see *Eating Out*), is superlative. Playa Vista Hermosa, Ixtapa (phone: 32121; 800-228-3000 in the US; 800-90223 in Mexico; fax: 30751).

IXTAPA

EXPENSIVE

Club Med A 15-minute drive up the coast from the Hotel Zone on a secluded 21-acre estate, this 375-room property is one of Club Med's best-run resorts. Geared toward families, with supervised activities for children from four months to 12 years of age, it also offers boat trips to Isla Ixtapa, 12 tennis courts, horseback riding, water sports, and even a computer workshop. Rates include all meals and most sports. Playa Quieta (phone: 30944; 800-CLUB-MED; fax: 30393).

Dorado Pacífico With 285 spacious, balconied rooms, this place offers some of Ixtapa's loveliest accommodations. All rooms open onto an airy pyramidal atrium with glass elevators. There are three restaurants, including *Pancho Villa* (see *Eating Out*), four bars, and a coffee shop. The large cloverleaf-shape pool has a water slide and a swim-up bar alongside a *palapa* restaurant; drinks and snacks also are served on the hotel's beach. Hotel Zone, on Blvd. Ixtapa (phone: 32025; 800-44-UTELL; fax: 30126).

Holiday Inn Formerly the *Plaza Ixtapa,* this impressive 14-story property on Playa del Palmar offers 287 beautifully decorated rooms and suites. The lobby, built around a courtyard filled with flowers, also presents a striking appearance. Facilities include an elegant restaurant, a snack bar–coffee shop, a pool, two tennis courts, and meeting space. Blvd. Ixtapa (phone: 31066; 800-HOLIDAY in the US; 800-00999 in Mexico; fax: 31991).

Krystal Ixtapa Set amid luxuriant gardens, this striking, white, flatiron-shape structure juts out toward the sea. Besides 256 rooms, there are two restaurants, including *Bogart's* (see *Eating Out*); a coffee shop; a snack bar; a gym; racquetball courts; a bar; and the *Christine* disco. Hotel Zone, on Blvd. Ixtapa (phone: 30333; 800-231-9860; fax: 30216).

Omni Ixtapa It boasts 306 units, plus a presidential suite with a private pool. Other draws: a gymnasium, a huge pool, restaurants, a coffee shop, a lobby bar, and a *palapa* bar. At the northern end of the Hotel Zone, on Blvd. Ixtapa (phone: 30003; 800-THE-OMNI; fax: 31555).

Presidente Ixtapa Rates at this beachfront hotel include meals, most sports, arts and crafts classes, and cooking lessons. The "Chicqui Club" offers activities for children—even Spanish classes. The 400 rooms (including 11 junior suites), many with garden balconies, are set in colonial-style villas and a tower with outside glass elevators. Also on the premises are two restaurants, a snack bar, a lobby bar with music nightly, and two pools (one with a swim-up bar). Of the two separate beachside pool areas, one has all the activities, while the other stays quiet and tranquil. Hotel Zone, on Blvd. Ixtapa (phone: 30018; 800-447-6147; fax: 32312).

Sheraton Ixtapa One of Ixtapa's most luxurious properties has 354 units surrounding an immense atrium, the fine *La Fonda* restaurant serving Mexican food, and a lobby bar with live music. The beachside pool is huge. Blvd. Ixtapa, at the south end of the Hotel Zone (phone: 31858; 800-325-3535 in the US; 800-90325 in Mexico; fax: 32438).

Villa del Lago Located in a quiet residential area, this exquisite six-suite bed and breakfast establishment overlooks the lake and the lush, green fairways of the *Ixtapa Golf Club*. Several golf packages are offered, with free transportation to the clubhouse. On the grounds of the property is a terraced pool and, beside it, a restaurant; there's also a small indoor dining room. 4 Retorno de las Alondras (phone: 31482; fax: 31542).

ZIHUATANEJO

VERY EXPENSIVE

La Casa Que Canta "The house that sings" is a mix of old-fashioned charm and modern luxury that blends right into a rocky cliffside next to Playa la Ropa (see *Special Places*). Furnished in Mexican colonial style, the 18 private, balconied one-bedroom suites boast a stunning view of the Bahía de Zihuatanejo. There are two pools (one freshwater, one saltwater); in addition, two suites each have their own pool. Other amenities include a restaurant of the same name (see *Eating Out*), and a lounge with a bar. Camino Escénico a Playa la Ropa (phone: 42722; 800-525-4800; fax: 42006).

EXPENSIVE

Puerto Mío On its own secluded cove just inside the Bahía de Zihuatanejo, this property has 25 units in a colonial-style mansion, plus six separate bungalows—and all units have bay views. The mansion has its own pool; there is a second pool with underwater stools for bay watching. Two restaurants are on the premises, one with great sunset views (also called *Puerto Mío;* see *Eating Out*). The hotel has its own small marina, which is the headquarters of the *Zihuatanejo Scuba Center*. 5 Paseo del Morro (phone/fax: 42748).

MODERATE

Bungalows Pacíficos A loyal clientele frequents this hospitable hillside inn—and for good reason. Each of its six spacious apartment-style units has a ceiling fan (no air conditioning), a fully equipped kitchenette, and a large private terrace affording a sweeping panorama of the Bahía de Zihuatanejo. (There are no TV sets or phones, however, and there is no restaurant.) Each unit has access to Playa la Madera. Located between Playa la Ropa and the center of Zihuatanejo, from which it's a four-minute walk via a night-lit bayside footpath (phone/fax: 42112).

Catalina-Sotavento Two old favorites, the *Catalina* and the *Sotavento,* are next to each other and under the same management. Together, they comprise 121 spacious rooms (request one with a view) on eight terraced hilltop levels, with hammocks on the balconies. All rooms have ceiling fans but no air conditioning; there are no private phones or TV sets. On the grounds are three restaurants. Be careful of the steep, meandering steps here. Playa la Ropa (phone: 42074; fax: 42975).

Villas Miramar This well-run beachside hotel offers 17 attractive private villas with modern furnishings and views of the beach and the bay. There are two pools and a restaurant-bar. A short taxi ride from downtown, at Playa la Madera (phone: 42106; fax: 42149).

INEXPENSIVE

Avila With 27 rooms, it boasts a delightful location on the town beach. Rooms on one side of the hotel overlook Playa del Pescador and the Bahía de Zihuatanejo, while the others overlook the town. The only guest phone is in the lobby. *Tata's* restaurant specializes in Mexican fare and seafood. 8 Calle Juan N. Alvarez (phone: 42010; fax: 43299).

Las Urracas Guests drive through a stone entryway into grounds filled with trees, plants, and paths connecting 16 bungalows, each with a living room, bedroom, and kitchen. Two bungalows face the beach. There is no restaurant.

The management caters to longtime repeat guests. A minimum three-day stay is required. No credit cards accepted. Playa la Ropa (phone: 42053).

Zihuatanejo Centro In this pleasant and modern four-story property are 69 rooms with balconies; the decor is highlighted by interesting murals by local artist Alejandro Honda. There's a restaurant. In the heart of town, close to the Playa Principal, at 2 Pasaje Agustín Ramírez (phone: 43661; fax: 42669).

EATING OUT

There are some excellent dining choices in Ixtapa and Zihuatanejo—in both formal and casual atmospheres. Dinner for two costs $75 or more at an expensive restaurant; between $40 and $75 at a moderate one; and $20 or less at an inexpensive place. Prices do not include drinks, wine, tax, or tip. Most restaurants below accept MasterCard and Visa, and a few also accept American Express and Diners Club; it's a good idea to call ahead and check. Unless otherwise noted, restaurants are open daily for lunch and dinner. All telephone numbers are in the 753 city code unless otherwise indicated.

IXTAPA

EXPENSIVE

Beccofino This Mediterranean-style waterfront eatery, with both a dining room and an outdoor café, features fine Italian food and wines. Reservations advised. Marina Ixtapa (phone: 31770).

Bogart's Choose from an international menu in an exotic Moroccan atmosphere. Closed for lunch. Reservations advised. *Krystal Ixtapa Hotel,* Hotel Zone, Blvd. Ixtapa (phone: 30333).

Bucaneros The large-paned windows here provide a fine view of the yacht slips at Marina Ixtapa; the specialties are seafood and continental fare. Reservations advised. Marina Ixtapa (phone: 30916).

Casa Club de Marina Ixtapa This spacious restaurant has terraces overlooking the canals and fairways. The fare is international, with an emphasis on seafood. Open daily from 7 AM to 8 PM for breakfast, lunch, and snacks; December through March and during *Semana Santa* (Holy Week), the restaurant is open for dinner as well. Reservations advised. *Marina Ixtapa Clubhouse* (phone: 31410).

El Galeón With appropriately nautical decor, this waterfront spot serves seafood specialties and tacos *al pastor* (with meat and cooked on a large, vertical spit) and quesadillas *con huitlacoche* (the usual cheese filling includes delicately flavored corn fungus). Open daily from 10 AM to 2 PM. Reservations advised. Marina Ixtapa (phone: 31410).

Pancho Villa The *Dorado Pacífico*'s mezzanine-level eatery offers excellent pre-Hispanic and Mexican dishes, plus live piano music nightly. Closed for lunch. Reservations advised. Hotel Zone, on Blvd. Ixtapa (phone: 32025).

Portofino Romance is in the air at the *Westin Brisas Resort Ixtapa*'s intimate, excellent eatery. Two favorites from the Italian menu: veal *piccata* in marsala wine sauce and lobster in basil sauce. Reservations advised. Hotel Zone, on Blvd. Ixtapa (phone: 32121).

Villa de la Selva What was once the cliff-top vacation home of Luis Echeverría Alvarez, a former President of Mexico, is now one of Ixtapa's most fashionable restaurants, serving seafood, as well as Mexican, continental, and flambéed dishes. It's wonderful for sunset cocktails and dinner, and special nighttime lighting makes it possible to have a lovely view of the ocean directly below even after sundown. Closed for lunch. Reservations advised. Beyond the *Westin Brisas Resort Ixtapa* on Paseo de la Roca (phone: 30362).

MODERATE

Da Baffone Fine pasta is the hallmark of this Italian eatery. Reservations unnecessary. *La Puerta* shopping center (phone: 31122).

Cactus Under the same management as Zihuatanejo's *El Patio* (see below), this restaurant-bar serves Mexican dishes and seafood. Closed for lunch; open until midnight. Reservations unnecessary. Blvd. Ixtapa, across from the *Holiday Inn SunSpree Resort Ixtapa* (no phone).

Carlos 'n' Charlie's It's part of the ribs 'n' beer chain, though more sophisticated than most. There's dancing nightly on an elevated beachside platform. No reservations. Beachfront location next door to the *Posada Real* hotel (phone: 30085).

Los Mandiles Good appetizers, *flautas, fajitas,* and spicy Mexican specialties like chicken *chipotle* (grilled chicken in a smoky red chili sauce) are the draws here. Reservations unnecesary. Behind *Las Galerías* shopping center (phone: 30379).

INEXPENSIVE

El Bocadito Delicious *antojitos* (typical Mexican specialties) such as tacos, *chiles rellenos,* and enchiladas are served at this eatery, whose name means "the little mouthful." No reservations. Blvd. Ixtapa, across from the *Omni Ixtapa* hotel (no phone).

Mamma Norma's Come in the morning for standard breakfast fare—scrambled eggs or beans and tortillas—or later in the day for pizza. Delivery service available. Open daily from 7 AM to 11 PM. No reservations. *La Puerta* shopping center (phone: 30274).

ZIHUATANEJO

La Casa Que Canta In the hotel of the same name, this multilevel restaurant is topped by a huge *palapa;* the decor features chairs painted with vivid Frida Kahlo motifs. The fare is local-catch seafood, often prepared with fruit. Reservations required. Camino Escénico a Playa la Ropa (phone: 42722).

Puerto Mío There actually are two seaside dining areas here: a casual open-air restaurant-bar just above the pool and a genteel dining room just above the restaurant-bar. The food is continental with Mexican touches. Reservations advised. 5 Paseo del Morro (phone: 42748).

Villa del Sol In the hotel of the same name, this is the perfect place for a candlelit alfresco dinner, complete with strains of Beethoven wafting through the seaside palms. The menu often features Mexican dishes and fresh seafood, prepared Mexican-European style. Open for breakfast, lunch, and dinner. Reservations necessary. Playa la Ropa (phone: 42239 or 43239).

MODERATE

Bay Club At this lively eatery, the menu is continental and the management specializes in making sure guests have a good time. A jazz band performs nightly on the patio, where there's also a beautiful view of the bay. Open daily from 5 PM to 1 AM. No reservations. A 10-minute drive south of town on the Carretera Playa la Ropa, at Playa la Madera (phone: 44844).

Café Marina Right in town, this down-to-earth little eatery offers truly inventive dishes by Swiss chef "Paul." His memorable creations include oyster mushrooms and quail. Two blocks north of the *Iglesia de Nuestra Señora de Guadalupe,* on Calle 5 de Mayo (phone: 42185).

Casa Elvira A pleasant and unpretentious place, it has served consistently excellent seafood and Mexican specialties since 1956. Reservations advised. Paseo del Pescador, between the pier and the basketball court (phone: 42061).

Coconuts This terrace eatery with small, hand-painted parasols for lampshades is a favorite with the local café society for its good seafood, pâté, and black bean soup. Reservations advised. 1 Pasaje Agustín Ramírez (phone: 42518).

La Gaviota Try the *filete de pescado mexicano* (fish filet cooked with tomatoes, onions, and mild peppers) at this rustic, yet romantic, place, just a few yards away from the surf. Reservations unnecessary. South end of Playa la Ropa (phone: 43677).

El Mesón del Cabrito Right in town, this alfresco restaurant features several succulent varieties of *cabrito* (kid), farm-raised in northern Mexico. No reservations. 24 Calle Ejido (phone: 43344).

El Patio An open-air patio set in a lovely garden and an indoor dining room both offer a delightful ambience, fine Mexican fare, and amiable service. A quintet plays wonderful Andean folk music nightly. Reservations advised for dinner. 3 Calle 5 de Mayo (phone: 43019).

Rossy This friendly, open-air eatery serves some of the best seafood around. Try the succulent brochette of shrimp with slices of pineapple and bell pepper. Open for breakfast, lunch, and dinner. No reservations. Right on the beach, at the south end of Playa la Ropa (phone: 44004).

La Sirena Gorda Near the town pier, this casual alfresco spot features tasty fish-kebab tacos and truly delicious seafood dishes. A whimsical mural of a rotund *sirena* (mermaid) hangs over the bar. Open for breakfast, lunch, and dinner; closed Wednesdays. No reservations. 20A Paseo del Pescador (phone: 42687).

Ziwok The compound name indicates that this place is the only stir-fry restaurant in "Zihua." Vegetable dishes, as well as sushi and sashimi, are served. Desserts are good, too. Reservations unnecessary. Behind *La Sirena Gorda*, on Calle Juan N. Alvarez. (phone: 43136).

INEXPENSIVE

Las Brasas There's prime people watching on the pedestrian mall, inexpensive barbecue and chicken mole on the menu, and a shrine to the Virgin of Guadalupe in the corner. Reservations unnecessary. 13 Calle Cuauhtémoc (phone: 42577).

Chez Arnoldo It's worth the boat trip to savor Arnoldo's artistically prepared seafood at this simple beachside eatery. No reservations. Playa las Gatas (no phone).

El Deli Go for bagels with smoked salmon for breakfast and big deli-style sandwiches at lunch and dinner. There's sidewalk seating on the Cuauhtémoc pedestrian mall. Reservations unnecessary. 12 Calle Cuauhtémoc (phone: 43127).

Garrobos Consistently good seafood, including octopus and squid, paella (request in advance; earlier that day will do), and the best homemade flan around are the attractions here. Open for breakfast, lunch, and dinner. No reservations. At the *Raul Tres Marías* hotel, 52 Calle Juan N. Alvarez (phone: 42977).

Nueva Zelanda This simple diner serves good *tortas* (sandwiches on a baguette-like roll) and an array of healthful fresh-fruit cocktails and juices. No reservations. 23 Calle Cuauhtémoc (phone: 42340).

Pizzería Emilio's A tiny, friendly place, it offers the best pizza in town, baked in a wood-burning oven. The dozen toppings range from succulent shrimp to potent jalapeño and *chipotle* chilies. No reservations. 5 Calle Vicente Guerrero (phone: 45270).

Tamales y Atoles "Any" Here are the best tamales and *atole* (a sweet, cornstarch-based beverage in various flavors, served hot) in the area. Any, the owner, also serves other Mexican specialties such as *pozole,* a thick, mildly spicy stew. No reservations. 33 Calle Nicolás Bravo (phone: 32709).

LOCAL COLOR

For a sampling of local fare and a glimpse of the "real" Zihuatanejo, stroll down the brick-paved beachfront Paseo del Pescador from the main pier to the *Museo Arqueológico de la Costa Grande* (see *Special Places*). Locals gather here, children skip by after school, and strolling musicians serenade at the little restaurants. Stop for a snack at *Casa Arcadia* (no phone), next to the museum; no reservations or credit cards are accepted. At night, the walkway's extension to Playa la Madera is illuminated by lamplight.

Los Cabos

(pronounced Los *Kah*-bos)

The *real* southern California lies a full thousand miles south of San Diego, at the tip of the Baja Peninsula. Known as Land's End, this area possesses all the remoteness and mystery that its name suggests, and the two towns there—together called Los Cabos, Cabo, or the Capes—combine with desert, rocks, and sea to create a compelling destination.

Cabo San Lucas, often called simply Cabo, was "discovered" in 1537 by Francisco de Ulloa, Hernán Cortés's navigator. In time, it served as a regular port of call for the oceangoing *Nao de China* on its voyages between Manila and Acapulco. When the local pirates got wind of this schedule, word of profitable buccaneering potential spread quickly, and they hid in nearby caves to ply their bloody trade. San José del Cabo, the smaller of the two towns, was founded in 1730 as a Jesuit mission on the banks of the Río San José estuary.

Times have certainly changed since the days of marauders and missionaries. Indeed, Los Cabos is one of the fastest-growing resorts in Mexico. Today, the two towns have some 4,250 hotel rooms and a combined population of 54,000; these numbers are expected to swell to 8,000 hotel rooms and 120,000 people by the year 2000.

San José del Cabo is the more established of the two resort areas. It has a wide, landscaped boulevard, a nine-hole golf course, and a hotel strip, all creations of *FONATUR,* the national fund for tourism development, currently in the midst of promoting an extensive project to develop the 7-square-mile area. With its central plaza, low-lying houses, and dream-like quality, San José del Cabo reflects Old Mexico more than any other place in Baja. It feels forgotten by time, yet it is an important commercial, agricultural, and cattle raising center. It's also more spacious and considerably more sedate than Cabo San Lucas, attracting visitors who prefer to spend most of their time lolling by the pool or lingering over a good meal.

Modern Cabo San Lucas, on the other hand, resembles a smaller, trendier Ensenada, with plenty of shopping, watering holes, and sport fishing—as well as a lot of (US) Californians. The area around the marina is crowded with hotels, and Boulevard Marina hums with activity. San Lucas is a bustling, energetic place, with restaurants and bars that never seem to close, more T-shirt shops than any town could possibly need, and a flourishing nightlife.

In between the two towns, the Palmilla and Cabo del Sol developments have sprung up, both with championship golf courses designed by Jack Nicklaus; the *Grand Hyatt Los Cabos* is slated to open at Cabo del Sol at the end of 1997. The Cabo Real development, about 11 miles (18 km) north of San Lucas, built around a Robert Trent Jones Jr.–designed golf course, one day will comprise hotels, condominiums, and shopping areas. Already completed are the *Meliá Cabo Real* and the *Westin Regina Los Cabos* hotels (see *Checking In*). And travel between the two towns has been facilitated by a four-lane superhighway that runs along the ocean.

Los Cabos already ranks fourth—after Cancún, Puerto Vallarta, and Acapulco—among Mexico's leading beach destinations, and it could easily replace any one of them. The area gets a lot of sun, and in winter many Northerners come to thaw out and to view the great whales that congregate in these waters during their December-through-March mating season. And with its many championship courses, Los Cabos is gearing up to become one of the premier golf resorts in all of Mexico.

Los Cabos At-a-Glance

SEEING THE CITY

The best view of San José del Cabo is from the terrace of the *Da Giorgio* restaurant, a 10-minute drive south of town on Route 1 (see *Eating Out*). The *Finisterra* hotel affords a panoramic look at Cabo San Lucas, the *Marina San Lucas,* the market, and the Pacific. The view of Land's End through the arch-like stone formations near the *Meliá San Lucas* hotel is a photographer's dream. (See *Checking In* for details on both hotels.) Or ride a horse up to the hilltop condos of Pedregal, where there are stunning harbor views (see *Horseback Riding*). Just follow the arrows to a cluster of rocks and a spectacular view of the ocean, bluffs, and the old and new lighthouses.

SPECIAL PLACES

Most of what there is to see and do here involves sheer natural beauty—beaches, desert, rocks, and bluffs. But there's more for those who want to explore.

SAN JOSÉ DEL CABO

PARROQUIA (PARISH CHURCH) Consecrated in 1940, this simple building was erected on the site of a far older church, built in 1734. The painted tiles above the door depict several scantily clad indigenous inhabitants pulling the just-murdered Padre Nicolás Tamaral (a founder of the town) through the desert by a rope. Plaza Mijares.

PLAYA BARCO VAREDO "Shipwreck Beach" gets its name from the remains of a Japanese vessel found here. Transparent tide pools along the shore, as well as rock formations (which make for good hiking and exploring), are the main attractions. There are no restaurants or rental facilities. Turn into the road marked "Barco Varedo" at Km 9 of Route 1.

PALACIO MUNICIPAL (CITY HALL) The 1730 inscription on the tower of this yellow colonial building reminds passersby of the founding of the town. The interior now houses offices, including that of the local tourism organization (see *Tourist Information,* below). Blvd. Mijares, between Calles Zaragoza and Av. Manuel Doblado.

CABO SAN LUCAS

LAND'S END The rugged, mysterious rock formations at the very tip of Baja are what make this place so special. Sea lions and pelicans lounge in the sun nearby. Near the arch here are two unusual underwater cascades of sand discovered by Jacques Cousteau; the spot is very popular with scuba divers.

PLAYA DEL AMOR (LOVERS' BEACH) This charming cove at Land's End faces both the Sea of Cortés and the Pacific; locals cynically call its turbulent, unswimmable Pacific side "Divorce Beach." There are no vendors or restaurants, so you should pack your own food, drinks, and snorkeling gear. Accessible by walking from the *Solmar* hotel toward the arch (see *Checking In*) or by taking a boat taxi from the *Marina San Lucas* or Playa Médano.

PLAYA MÉDANO Right in town, this long strip of sand sweeps north of the *Hacienda Beach* hotel (see *Checking In*). It's the best beach for swimming and people watching. Lounge chairs, kayaks, jet skis, and big seagoing tricycles are available for rent. Glass-bottom boats bound for Land's End also leave from here.

PLAYA SANTA MARÍA The most secluded beach in the area, and probably the nicest overall, is good for swimming, snorkeling, diving, and collecting beach flora. Park in the lot of the *Twin Dolphin* hotel (see *Checking In*), and walk to the left and down the hill; it will take about 10 minutes to get there. About 7½ miles (12 km) from San Lucas.

PLAYA CHILENO Small and clean, with crystal-clear water, this strand is perfect for swimming, snorkeling, and scuba diving. *Cabo Acuadeportes* (phone: 30117; 713-680-2090 in the US), which rents water sports equipment, has an office here, by the *Cabo San Lucas* hotel (see *Checking In*). Six miles (10 km) from San Lucas.

EXTRA SPECIAL

Set aside a morning to explore southern Baja's rare, remote beauty; it's worth renting an automobile (see "Car Rental" in *Getting Around,* below). Drive north on Route 1 to the quiet little town of Todos Santos. The hourlong drive is actually more impressive than the town: The road hugs the coast and flirts with the ocean, then swings away and passes a scattering of ranches; narrow dirt roads entice the driver into taking a closer look at secluded beaches; butterflies drift effortlessly across the road; and it's often necessary to brake for the ubiquitous burro or occasional cow. Todos Santos was founded in 1734 by the Jesuits and destroyed by Indians a couple of years later (it eventually recovered somewhat). The town's modern-day inhabitants trace their ancestry back to a particular Dominican priest who, it's said, took fathering rather seriously. These days, the economy of Todos Santos is based primarily on agriculture and livestock. And in recent years, the town has become a favorite residence for artists. Stop for a bite at the *Santa Fe* restaurant (Centenario and León; phone: 40340), which serves the best Italian food in the area. The town still has some dirt streets, as well as a little park, a church, a hotel, and bed and breakfast accommodations; for information, consult the tourist offices in Los Cabos (see *Tourist Information*).

Return to Los Cabos along Route 1. Diehard drivers may add another few hours to the itinerary by making a circuit: Head north via El Triunfo, then south again, still on Route 1, via the picturesque towns of San Antonio, Santiago, and Miraflores. In the latter, leather goods are sold in houses designated *taller* (pronounced ta-*yehr*); stop in at the big white house on the way into town. For a refreshing swim en route, stop at Buena Vista or La Rivera, two pleasant beaches located about 45 miles (72 km) north of San José.

Sources and Resources

TOURIST INFORMATION

For the best service, go to the *Fondo Mixto Pro Turismo* (Matching Funds For Tourism, a combined federal, state, and local effort) office in Cabo San Lucas (Calle Madero between Calles Guerrero and Hidalgo; phone: 32211). It's closed Sunday. In San José del Cabo, the tourist office in the *Palacio Municipal* (City Hall; phone: 20377; see *Special Places*) has limited information and a very erratic schedule. Hotel desks are much more helpful. The information booth (separate from the desk) in the lobby of the *Finisterra* hotel in San Lucas is particularly useful to first-time visitors (see *Checking In*). Car rental agencies can provide maps, as can *FONATUR* (Rte. 1, around the corner from San José's Hotel Zone, which runs along the Sea of Cortés; phone: 20383). *FONATUR* is closed weekends.

LOCAL COVERAGE Free local publications in English—*Los Cabos News, Baja Sun,* and *Los Cabos* guide magazine—are good sources of current information about Los Cabos. They are all available at newsstands, the tourist office, and most hotels.

For general reading on the history of the area, drop by the library on Plaza Mijares in San José del Cabo, which has some English-language books. For news of home, pick up a copy of the *Los Angeles Times* or *USA Today* at any of the larger hotels listed in *Checking In.*

TELEPHONE The city code for Los Cabos is 114. A call from Cabo San Lucas to San José del Cabo, or vice versa, is charged as a long-distance call, though it is not necessary to dial 91 and the city code first. *Note:* Mexico's telephone company has embarked on a major expansion project that involves changing telephone numbers in many areas of the country. At press time, all numbers listed in this chapter were correct. However, if you have any difficulties reaching attractions listed here, contact the local tourist office.

CLIMATE AND CLOTHES There are 350 sunny days a year here, with an average temperature between 70 and 75F (21 and 24C). August and September are the hottest months. *Chubascos* (tropical storms), which come through from August to early October, can cause cancellations of fishing trips for a day or two. Winter temperatures dip to the mid- to high 50s F (approximately 12 to 15C) at night. While dress is casual, short shorts are considered inappropriate in downtown areas and out of place in a disco.

GETTING AROUND

BUS The bus stations in San José (Calle Valerio González; phone: 21100) and Cabo San Lucas (Calles Zaragoza and 16 de Septiembre; phone: 30400) are little more than storefronts. Buses make trips every 40 minutes between the two towns, from 6 AM to 10 PM daily, for 7 pesos (about 95¢) each way. There are 14 daily departures from San José (considerably fewer from San Lucas) to La Paz. Both the western (coastal) route and the eastern (mountain) route are scenic.

CAR RENTAL Most international firms are represented at the airport and in town. Parking in Los Cabos is informal; anywhere's fine unless the curb is painted red.

MOTORCYCLE In San Lucas, rent from *Dollar Moto Rent* (at *Plaza las Glorias* hotel; phone: 32050); in San José, try *Dollar* at either Calles Zaragoza and Guerrero (phone: 20100) or at the *Presidente Forum Resort* hotel (see *Checking In*).

SEA EXCURSIONS Glass-bottom boats depart from the beach in front of *El Galeón* restaurant overlooking the marina in San Lucas every hour on the half hour from 9:30 AM to 2:30 PM. *Cabo Acuadeportes* (Playa Chileno, next door to the *Cabo San Lucas* hotel; phone: 30117; 713-680-2090 in the US) takes one to four passengers to Playa del Amor. The *Pez Gato* catamaran (phone: 32458 or 33797) goes on a four-hour swimming-and-snorkeling excursion to Playa Santa María; breakfast and lunch are included in the rate. It departs from the pier in Cabo San Lucas daily at 10 AM.

TAXI Cabs are stationed in San José and San Lucas; they rarely cruise the streets. In San José, there's a large taxi stand on Plaza Mijares facing the church and one in front of the *Presidente Forum Resort* hotel. In San Lucas, it's catch-as-catch-can downtown, though you may find cabs on the main plaza and at the *Plaza Arambaro* and *Plaza Bonita* shopping centers. The set fare for a one-way ride between the two towns is 90 pesos (about $12). Less expensive *colectivos* (vans) take groups of up to eight passengers to and from the airport and between and around both towns.

TOURS Most hotel lobbies have tour desks that help arrange for visitors staying in San José to visit San Lucas and vice versa. A tour by minibus takes about five hours. *Dollar Moto Rent* (see *Motorcycle*) has a three-hour all-terrain-vehicle tour to Cabo Falso, a beach area that features the *Faro Viejo,* the remains of a 19th-century lighthouse. The excursion passes through untamed desert country filled with cactus and many kinds of animals, including snakes; the view of the ocean at Cabo Falso is breathtaking. Departures are at 9 AM and 12:30 and 4 PM.

SPECIAL EVENTS

Día de San José (St. Joseph's Day) is March 19, and *Día de San Lucas* (St. Luke's Day) is October 18; both are accompanied by a two-week celebration. In October and November, the *Torneo Internacional de Marlín* (International Black and Blue Marlin Fishing Tournament) is held at the *Hacienda Beach* resort (see *Checking In*).

SHOPPING

In recent years, more and more chic shops have sprung up in Los Cabos, purveying a good selection of beachwear, accessories, and womenswear. Other popular items available here include T-shirts, silver jewelry, and a limited assortment of crafts from all around the country. Baja's only noteworthy indigenous product is damiana, an amber liquor made from an herb of the same name that grows wild on the peninsula; it's also used to make tea. Both drinks are said by some to be aphrodisiacs. Most shops open at 10 AM, close from 1 to 4 PM, and then stay open as late as 8 PM; most close Sundays.

CABO SAN LUCAS

Boulevard Lázaro Cárdenas and Hidalgo are the major shopping streets in town, and the large open-air market beside the marina should not be overlooked. Merchandise and prices are about the same in most places, making comparison shopping unnecessary. In the tiny *Plaza Arambaro* shopping center (Blvd. Marina), visit *Local #4* for men's tropical shirts and *Bulnes Barrera* for fine ceramics. *Plaza Bonita* (Blvd. Marina), the most fashionable shopping center in Los Cabos, has the area's nicest shops, as well as several pleasant restaurants.

Dupuis An exclusive collection of icons, rustic furniture, decorative objects in pewter and ceramics, blown glass, and embroidered pillows. *Plaza Bonita* (no phone).

Galería del Arco Paintings, sculptures, and prints by contemporary Mexican artists. Across from the *Marina San Lucas* at Blvd. Cárdenas and Calle Zaragoza (phone: 30551).

Mamma Eli's One of the best stores in San Lucas, with high-quality glassware from Guadalajara, silver jewelry, baskets, crafts, and Mexican clothing in unique designs. On the main plaza (phone: 31616).

Temptations A most unusual selection of clothes and accessories for women, including some one-of-a-kind resortwear. *Giggling Marlin Building,* Blvd. Marina and Calle Matamoros (phone: 31015).

SAN JOSÉ DEL CABO

Here, the main streets for shopping are Calle Zaragoza, running east; Avenida Manuel Doblado, which runs west; and Boulevard Mijares, running north and south. Our favorite San José shop is *Coppal* (Calle Zaragoza; no phone), filled with fine silver jewelry, tableware, ceramics, and some antiques.

SPORTS AND FITNESS

CANOEING It's possible to rent a canoe or ocean kayak from *Cabo Acuadeportes* (see *Sea Excursions,* above). Try canoeing over to Playa del Amor for a look at Pelican Rock, a pretty spot where sea lions congregate.

FISHING The Sea of Cortés is famous for the large variety of fish in its waters; blue and striped marlin are the trophies most sought after by anglers here. About 40,000 marlin are hauled out of "Marlin Alley" waters every year, and visitors are likely to witness this event repeatedly at the pier in Cabo San Lucas. The best season for large marlin, black or blue, runs from November through January, though some big ones have been pulled in during the off-season. Sailfish are the main bounty in spring, with some swordfish. Striped marlin are abundant year-round. While a catch-and-release policy is strictly enforced, fishing fleets are allotted a certain number of fish per day that can be taken home.

Fishing is equally popular in San José del Cabo and Cabo San Lucas. The famous Gordo (Fat) Bank, 7 to 10 miles off the coast of San José, is a particularly prolific spot. *Pangas,* 22-foot outboard skiffs, carry a maximum of four people (including the captain, whose presence is required by law)] and are perfect for fishing for dorado, wahoo, and yellowfin. In Cabo San Lucas, *pangas* are for rent at Playa Palmilla and at *Cabo Acuadeportes* (see *Sea Excursions*); a 38-foot boat for a maximum of six people is also available. A custom-made, air conditioned twin screw (a type of two-propeller boat) that bunks 10 people can be rented through *Fleet Solmar* at the *Solmar* hotel in San Lucas or through *Victor's* in the lobby of the *Presidente Forum Resort* hotel in San José (see *Checking In* for both).

Rather than renting a boat on your own, you can save money by asking to be teamed with other people who want to fish, or by buying a single ticket for a spot on a boat. Check with *Fleet Solmar* (see above) or *Tortuga Fleet* (in the *Finisterra* hotel; see *Checking In*), both in Cabo San Lucas.

Hotels and some restaurants can supply box lunches for a day's outing; with advance notice, restaurants will often prepare the catch and serve it with rice and vegetables. Hotels may provide freezing service as well. Pack fish in a plastic, *not* Styrofoam, chest for air transport home. Do-it-yourselfers in need of fishing tackle can check with *Cabo Acuadeportes* (see *Sea Excursions*).

GOLF Los Cabos is being developed as a world class golf resort, and it boasts some of the most playable links in all of Mexico.

TOP TEE-OFF SPOTS

Cabo Real Robert Trent Jones Jr. designed this 18-hole, par 72 course with ocean, desert, and mountain views. The challenging layout features mainly desert terrain, with plenty of sand traps, but there's one hole right on the water. The course is located in the Cabo Real development, which will eventually include hotels, condominiums, shopping areas, and even a shooting range (though completion dates are uncertain). The golf club features a pro shop, a driving range, and a clubhouse with a bar and restaurant. Bobby Glover and Todd Branson are the pros. Km 19 of Rte. 1, 11 miles (18 km) north of Cabo San Lucas (phone: 40000, ask for golf extension; 800-336-3542).

Cabo San Lucas Country Club Roy Dye designed this 18-hole, par 72 venue, yet another addition to the rapidly growing roster of courses in the area. Nine holes opened in 1996, adding to the nine holes already constructed. A clubhouse, 10 tennis courts, and 2,000 residential units are in the works as well. Lázaro Cárdenas, 1 mile (1.6 km) from Cabo San Lucas (phone: 31120; fax: 34322).

Cabo del Sol Designed by Jack Nicklaus, this relatively new, par 72 public layout is situated on an 1,800-acre resort site on the ocean. Seven of this course's 18 holes are right on the water. Future plans include the addition of 2,000 hotel rooms, two more golf courses, shopping centers, and a tennis club. Eight miles (13 km) east of Cabo San Lucas, in the Cabo del Sol development (phone: 33990; 800-FUN-GOLF).

Palmilla Jack Nicklaus's first course in Latin America is considered to be the premier golf facility in the area, if not in all of Mexico. Offering desert, ocean, and mountain views, the 18-hole, par 72 course is complemented by a clubhouse, pro shop, and dining area; an additional nine-hole course is expected to be ready in 1998. The director of operations is Rick Renick; the pro is Brad Wheatley. Five miles (8 km) west of San José del Cabo, near the Cabo Real development (cellular phone: 114-88525; 800-637-CABO).

In addition, the interesting nine-hole golf course at the *Los Cabos Country Club* in San José del Cabo (phone: 20905) is open to the public. There is a clubhouse, and clubs and carts can be rented (but no caddies are available).

HORSEBACK RIDING Horses are for hire, with a guide, from *Ramón's Horse Rentals,* in front of the *Cabo San Lucas* hotel. Juan and Jesús Angel rent horses from 6 AM to 6 PM in front of the *Presidente Forum Resort* in San José; they are not employed by the hotel. No prior riding experience is necessary.

SAILING AND WINDSURFING Rent Sunfish, catamarans, or windsurfers from *Cabo Acuadeportes* (see *Sea Excursions*).

SCUBA DIVING Dive sites around Cabo San Lucas include Pelican Rock, Grand Sand Fall and Little Sand Fall (underwater cascades of sand near Land's End), North Wall, South Wall, Shepherd's Rock, Sea Lion Colony, the Pinnacle, and the Shipwreck. *Cabo Acuadeportes* (see *Sea Excursions*) rents equipment, sells disposable underwater cameras, and offers a three-day diving package. Dive trips, lessons, and equipment are also available from *Amigos del Mar,* a *PADI* international dive center at the *Solmar* hotel (see *Checking In;* phone: 30505; 800-344-3349). Diehards with a car head about an hour north of San José, past La Playita and Punta Gorda, to two shipwrecks; 6 AM is the best time to go.

SNORKELING Playas Chileno, Santa María, and del Amor are all good choices; you can rent gear at Playas Médano, Chileno, and Palmilla. The brain coral and tropical fish, plus 60 to 70 feet of visibility, make Playa Chileno most popular; park by the fence and walk in (it's not far). Another favorite spot lies between Km 9 and 10 of Route 1, where there is a lot of beach camping; turn off on the only suggestion of a road. Check with hotel travel desks for tours, or contact *Cabo Acuadeportes* (see *Sea Excursions*).

SURFING Head for Costa Azul, also known as Acapulcito ("little Acapulco"), just below the lookout between San José and San Lucas. Another fertile spot is about 4 miles (6 km) north of La Playita. Signs point the way.

SWIMMING AND SUNNING In addition to the strands mentioned in *Special Places,* there are many unmarked beaches in this part of the world. Enjoy their beauty, but remember that many are unsafe for swimming because of the dangerous undertow. A prime example is Playa Buenos Aires, an inviting sweep of sand between San José and San Lucas. Adventurous travelers should take the Camino Rural Costero, just off San José's main drag, west to a 60-mile (96-km) stretch of little-known coastline with some pretty, unspoiled beaches: Cabo Pulmo and Los Frailes are just two good choices. We recommend making this journey in a four-wheel-drive vehicle, as it's easy to get stuck in the soft sand of the unpaved, rural roads.

TENNIS The courts at *Los Cabos Country Club* (see *Golf*) are open to the public for a fee; there are lighted courts for night play. In San José del Cabo, tennis facilities are available at the *Palmilla* (two hard-surface courts), *Posada Real Best Western* (two lighted cement courts), *Meliá Cabo Real* (two lighted artificial-grass courts), and *Presidente Forum Resort* (two lighted cement courts) hotels. In San Lucas, try the *Hacienda Beach* (one cement court),

Meliá San Lucas (two lighted artificial-grass courts), *Twin Dolphin* (two lighted hard-surface courts), *Calinda Cabo San Lucas* (two lighted concrete courts), or *Cabo San Lucas* (two cement courts). (See *Checking In* for details on hotels.)

NIGHTCLUBS AND NIGHTLIFE

Evening entertainment in San José del Cabo centers around *Eclipse* (no phone); *Iguana* (phone: 20266); and *Tropicana* (phone: 20907), all on Boulevard Mijares.

Much more goes on at night in Cabo San Lucas. First, take in the sunset at the *Whale Watchers* bar at the *Finisterra* hotel. *Cabo Wabo* (Calles Guerrero and Lázaro Cárdenas; phone: 31188) has become a popular dance spot. There's also dancing—from 10:30 PM to 3 AM—at *El Squid Roe* (Blvd. Marina, across from *Plaza Bonita;* phone: 30655), and live music and dancing at the *Giggling Marlin* (Blvd. Marina and Calle Matamoros; phone: 31182). Also try *Carlos 'n' Charlie's* (20 Blvd. Marina; phone: 31280) and the upscale *Hard Rock Café* (Blvd. Marina, across from *El Squid Roe;* phone: 33806).

In high season (November through April), colorful Mexican fiestas are presented on Friday nights at the *Palmilla* hotel near San José del Cabo, and on Saturday nights at the *Fiesta Inn San José del Cabo.* In Cabo San Lucas, the fiestas are at the *Hacienda Beach* and the *Meliá San Lucas* hotels, usually Friday and Saturday nights. Fiestas usually include a lavish buffet of Mexican dishes, folk dances, mariachis, fireworks, and piñatas. (See *Checking In* for details on hotels.)

Best in Town

CHECKING IN

Most of the larger hotels in and between San José and San Lucas have extensive water sports facilities and tour desks. Reserve one to two months ahead for rooms during high season (November through April); for the *Christmas–New Year* vacation period, think in terms of two to three *years* ahead at the major resorts. The newest addition to the hotel scene here will be the *Grand Hyatt Los Cabos,* which is due to open in the Cabo del Sol development in late 1997. The beachfront hotel will offer 316 rooms and suites and several restaurants; for more information, call 800-233-1234. Rates given here are for high season; they may drop as much as 40% during the off-season. Expect to pay $200 or more per night for a double room at a very expensive hotel; $125 to $195 at an expensive one; $75 to $120 at a moderate place; and $70 or less at an inexpensive one. Unless otherwise noted, all rooms have air conditioning, TV sets, and telephones. All telephone numbers are in the 114 city code unless otherwise indicated.

We begin with our favorite haven, followed by recommended hotels, listed by location and price category.

A SPECIAL HAVEN

Twin Dolphin So private it doesn't even have a shingle out front, this is the classiest operation in the area. It's the pet project of American oil millionaire and ecologist (thus the "dolphin" theme) David Halliburton, who limited its size to 44 spacious rooms and six suites, each with an ocean view and private balcony. There is a big pool with a swim-up bar; a rocky beach that's lovely to look at, though a little difficult for swimming (another, safer swimming beach is close by); two lighted tennis courts; an 18-hole putting green; and deep-sea fishing boats. Most of the hotel's food is imported from the US, and meals are just fine. Not a swinging place, it nonetheless offers relaxing luxury in a remote spot. The air of exclusivity here is heady. Rates (in the very expensive category) include two or three meals daily; a no-meals option is available June through October. At Km 12 of Route 1, it's about 28 miles (45 km) from the Cabo San Lucas airport and 6½ miles (10 km) north of Cabo San Lucas (phone: 30256; 213-386-3940 in California; 800-421-8925 elsewhere in the US; fax: 30496; 213-380-1302 in the US).

SAN JOSÉ DEL CABO

VERY EXPENSIVE

Meliá Cabo Real Built of glass and marble, this pyramid was the first hotel to open in the Cabo Real development. On the premises are 286 rooms, 14 suites, two tennis courts, a huge pool, a fitness center, three restaurants, a water sports center, and a bar. Arrangements can be made for fishing trips and golf. On the Golfo de Cortés, Km 19.5 of Rte. 1 (phone: 30967; 800-336-3542; fax: 31003).

Palmilla This Mexican Eden basks on a secluded bluff, and its 62 oversize rooms, eight suites, one five-bedroom villa, charming restaurant, and grounds impart the spirit of Old Mexico. There's tennis, croquet, a pool, an open-air lounge, and even a picturesque chapel where weddings sometimes take place. Two beaches are nearby as well. Rates include three meals a day (box lunches are made on request). The hotel is in the middle of the 900-acre Palmilla development, which features an 18-hole, Jack Nicklaus—designed golf course and a putting green; another nine-hole course is scheduled to open in 1998. The resort will eventually comprise a shopping and entertainment village with restaurants, boutiques, a European-style health spa, and a movie theater. Three miles (5 km) south of San José on Rte. 1 (phone: 20583; 800-637-CABO; fax: 714-851-2498 in the US).

Westin Regina Los Cabos One of the Cabo Real development's two hotels (the *Meliá Cabo Real* is the other), it has 229 rooms, 14 suites, three restaurants, and a bar. There are also three outdoor pools, two lighted tennis courts, and a fitness club. Arrangements can be made for golf, hunting trips, and horseback riding. On the Golfo de Cortés, Km 22.5 of Rte. 1 (phone: 29000; 800-228-3000 in the US; 800-90223 in Mexico; fax: 29010).

EXPENSIVE

Presidente Forum Resort Formerly the *Presidente Inter-Continental* and still under the same management, the hotel is now all-inclusive and has 237 recently renovated rooms and suites, some with patios and others with balconies. All rooms overlook gracefully landscaped grounds and the turbulent sea beyond (better not to swim here). The hotel serves as the sprawling social center for San José, with nonstop activities that include lobby and poolside games, tennis, and horseback riding on the beach. There's also a restaurant and an estuary that offers spectacular bird watching. Hotel Zone (phone: 20211; 800-447-6147 in the US; 800-90444 in Mexico; fax: 20232).

MODERATE

Fiesta Inn San José del Cabo This friendly place is set right on the beach. There are 90 rooms, 21 suites, a restaurant, and a bar. A five-minute drive south of San José, on Malecón San José (phone: 20701; 800-FIESTA-1 in the US; 800-50450 in Mexico; fax: 20480).

Posada Real Best Western Landscaped grounds, 150 comfortable rooms and suites, a pool, tennis, volleyball, a restaurant, and a congenial, if noisy, lobby bar are highlights here. The place is relatively unassuming, but guests return again and again. Across the street from the golf course in the Hotel Zone (phone: 20155; 800-528-1234; fax: 20460).

INEXPENSIVE

Colli Think of it as a bed and breakfast establishment, but without the breakfast. It's right downtown, with 12 tidy rooms (no telephones or TV sets). There are three drawbacks, however: It's often full, it doesn't have a restaurant, and it doesn't accept credit cards. Hidalgo between Calle Zaragoza and Av. Manuel Doblado (phone: 20725).

CABO SAN LUCAS

VERY EXPENSIVE

Meliá San Lucas Decorated with white marble, modern wood furniture, and cool colors, the 142 rooms and three suites here have private terraces and ocean views. Amenities include two pools, two tennis courts, a restaurant, a coffee shop, and a bar. Situated over a wide strip of beach facing the arch at Land's End, on Playa Médano (phone: 34408; 800-336-3542; fax: 30420).

Pueblo Bonito In this beautiful Mediterranean-style complex are 148 suites, the beachside *Cilantro's* restaurant, a health club, and a free-form pool with a waterfall in the center. Playa Médano (phone: 32900; 800-262-4500 in the US; 800-654-5543 in Canada; fax: 31995).

EXPENSIVE

Cabo San Lucas This 2,500-acre resort is known locally as *El Chileno* because of its location on Playa Chileno. Along with attractive flowered patios, it has 75 rooms in 25 low-slung buildings as well as 14 villas with two to seven bedrooms each. It also boasts a pretty sea view, five pools, two tennis courts, a hunting club, a fishing fleet, outstanding shops, and good food and service. Rte. 1, 6 miles (10 km) north of Cabo San Lucas (phone: 33457/8; 213-655-2323 in California; 800-SEE-CABO elsewhere in the US; fax: 213-655-3243 in the US).

Calinda Cabo San Lucas The Land's End rock formations can easily be admired from the poolside terrace or outdoor Jacuzzis. A congenial place with a restaurant and lobby bar, it has a Mexican fiesta with mariachis on Thursday nights and live music on Friday and Saturday nights in season. The 125 suites are spacious, and service is attentive. Rte. 1, about 3 miles (5 km) north of Cabo San Lucas (phone: 30045; 800-228-5151 in the US; 800-90000 in Mexico; fax: 30077).

Finisterra Perched atop a cliff, it commands a sweeping view of the town, the marina, and the Pacific. The establishment has 195 atractive colonial-style rooms, four two-bedroom cottages with kitchenettes, two tennis courts, a beach club with an enormous stretch of sand at the base of the cliff, three pools, a restaurant, and a charming shop. Downtown, across from the marina (phone: 33333; 714-476-5555 in California; 800-347-2252 elsewhere in the US; fax: 30590).

Hacienda Beach A secluded property, it features 112 comfortable rooms, including 30 cabañas and 12 suites, in buildings connected by palm thickets and stone walkways. Guests can enjoy a kidney-shaped pool or the only swimming beach in downtown San Lucas; its water sports center is tops. On the premises are shops selling high-quality merchandise, a tennis court, and a good restaurant. On the beach (phone: 30122/3; 800-733-2226; fax: 213-852-0821 in the US).

Plaza las Glorias This Mediterranean-style hostelry forms part of the *Marina San Lucas*. It has 287 rooms, two restaurants and a snack bar, a lobby bar, a pool, a beach club, a disco, and a variety of shops. In the heart of town, on Blvd. Marina (phone: 31220; 800-635-8483; fax: 31238).

Solmar Closest to Land's End, the water is too rough for swimming here, but the view, especially at sunset, and the sound of waves as you drift off to sleep are mesmerizing. This casual, low-key place with 94 junior suites, a restaurant, a bar, a fleet of fishing boats, and a car rental desk attracts a young crowd and fishing enthusiasts. About a half mile (1 km) southwest of downtown (phone: 33535; 800-344-3349; fax: 30410).

INEXPENSIVE

Marina This small place is worth a try if everything else is booked. It has 24 rooms, seven nice suites, a tiny pool, and a restaurant-bar with satellite TV, but no telephones or TV sets in the rooms. No credit cards accepted. Near the marina, on Blvd. Marina at Calle Guerrero (phone: 32484 or 31499).

EATING OUT

Seafood dishes get top billing on most Baja menus, but it's possible to get good Mexican and continental fare as well. If it rains hard in San José, many restaurants close their doors until their patios dry out. If this happens, diners can still depend on *Damiana* (see below). As a rule, hotel restaurants are best avoided. Dinner for two, without drinks, wine, tax, or tip, will cost $60 to $90 in expensive places; $40 to $55 in moderate places; and $35 or less in inexpensive places. Most restaurants below accept MasterCard and Visa, and a few also accept American Express and Diners Club; it's a good idea to call ahead and check. Unless otherwise noted, all restaurants below are open daily for lunch and dinner. All telephone numbers are in the 114 city code unless otherwise indicated.

SAN JOSÉ DEL CABO

EXPENSIVE

Damiana In this restored, romantic 18th-century house, specialties include charcoal-broiled lobster, shrimp, steaks, and abalone in garlic sauce. Try the damiana liquor to determine if it really is an aphrodisiac. Reservations advised. Downtown, on Plaza Mijares (phone: 20499).

MODERATE

Le Bistrot French fare—including filet of beef in green peppercorns or béarnaise sauce and bouillabaisse—is served in a cozy atmosphere. Closed Mondays. Reservations unnecessary. No credit cards accepted. 4 Calle Moreles (phone: 21174).

Da Giorgio The most romantic spot in Los Cabos is Italian through and through. Diners can watch bread baking in the wood-burning oven. Even if there's a wait, ask to dine on the terrace under the stars. The bread is soft pizza crust; the salad bar, a dieter's delight. Reservations advised. Km 25 of Rte. 1, a 10-minute drive south of San José (phone: 21988).

INEXPENSIVE

Bing's Ice Cream Shop Remember the days of the single scoop for 50¢? It still exists here. There are banana splits and sundaes, too. No credit cards accepted. Two locations: Blvd. Mijares (no phone) and Blvd. Marina, next to *El Squid Roe* (no phone).

CABO SAN LUCAS

EXPENSIVE

Las Palmas *The* place to eat in Cabo San Lucas for good food, attentive service, and atmosphere. The menu touts shrimp, lobster, quail, and frogs' legs in season, topped off with a Kahlúa parfait or amaretto cake. Don't believe anyone who says the less expensive places are as good as this. Reservations advised. Playa Médano, near the *Meliá San Lucas* hotel (phone: 30447).

MODERATE

Alfonso's Nouvelle cuisine is offered in the dining room and on the patio of a comfortable, colonial-style house that has become something of a landmark. Closed for lunch. Reservations advised. Playa Médano, near the *Hacienda Beach* hotel (phone: 32022).

Cascadas Le Club Excellent chicken, meat, and seafood are served in a tropical beach setting. Live music is featured nightly in winter. Reservations advised for dinner. Located 1½ miles (2 km) northeast of San Lucas off Rte. 1 on the beach at the *Club Cascadas de Baja* (phone: 30728).

Cilantro's Good food and lots of fun can be had at this spot specializing in mesquite-grilled seafood and Mexican dishes. Reservations advised. On the beach, at the *Pueblo Bonito* hotel (phone: 32500).

See Señor This brand-new place has already cultivated a devoted local following for its fish burgers, chili, and other hearty, simple dishes. The atmosphere is fun and friendly. Open for breakfast and lunch only. Reservations unnecessary. No credit cards accepted. Playa Médano, near the *Office* restaurant (phone: 30401).

Señor Sushi and Tai Won On Bar Despite its name, this place doesn't serve sushi anymore, but the menu does offer plenty of other seafood, including grilled mahimahi and sea bass stuffed with deviled shrimp. There is also beef teriyaki. Closed Tuesdays. Reservations unnecessary. Blvd. Marina, across from *Plaza las Glorias* (phone: 31323).

INEXPENSIVE

Giggling Marlin You'll always find hordes of people hanging out at this landmark. The menu includes seafood, *fajitas,* and surprisingly good hamburgers. Opens for breakfast at 8 AM. No reservations. Calle Matamoros and Blvd. Marina (phone: 30606).

Manzanillo

(pronounced Mahn-sa-*nee*-yo)

The small, slow-moving Pacific Coast port town of Manzanillo was positioned to become one of Mexico's foremost vacation spots in the mid-1960s, when the late Bolivian tin tycoon Antenor Patiño decided to build a fairy-tale resort just outside town. The result was the 1974 opening of *Las Hadas*—a magnificent, sprawling, whitewashed complex of villas and bungalows that vaguely resembles a Moorish village.

Manzanillo has yet to blossom into a bustling resort center, but *Las Hadas* ("the fairies") attained legendary status and, for some, it remains the one real reason to come here. The Camino Real group (which bought the property in 1993) finished a $3-million restoration in 1995 that included a complete remodeling of all the rooms. Today, *Las Hadas* shares its prime location on the north shore of Bahía Manzanillo (Manzanillo Bay) with only a few gated condominium developments.

Manzanillo was chosen by the conquering Spanish as a port because of its natural harbor, provided by two large, scallop-like bays. Cortés visited twice and directed early shipping expeditions from Manzanillo's beaches. (The port's name comes from the *manzanilla,* or chamomile, plant, common in Colima state, that was found at the site where the first dock was built.) In November 1564, the expedition led by Miguel López Legazpi set sail from nearby Navidad harbor to conquer the Philippines for the Spanish crown. The ships were built by native peoples and Spaniards on the beaches of Salahua, not far from where *Las Hadas* now sits.

These days, Manzanillo continues to be a major port, a chief conduit for Guadalajara's industrial activity and one of Mexico's most important doors to the Orient. The docks are downtown, and the railroad tracks to the wharves cut across the main street. Although most of the harbor is fenced off and heavily patrolled, it is possible to observe some fishing boat activity from a couple of harborfront restaurants. The state government has announced a $50-million project for a downtown marina complex, projected to include a cruise-ship dock, a shopping center, a hotel, and slips for 240 yachts, though nothing is off the ground yet.

Tourist development stalled in Manzanillo due to a series of devastating earthquakes between October and December 1995, giving second thoughts to potential visitors and investors alike, and—at press time—putting out of commission some of our favorite hostelries, including *Plaza las Glorias* and *Tenisol.* (The *Bel-Air,* another top choice, was due to reopen as we went to press.) The area's natural beauty virtually guarantees a revival of tourism; in the meantime, Manzanillo may be the biggest beachfront bargain in Mexico.

If you take a morning flight from Mexico City to Manzanillo, about 40 minutes away, you'll fly to one side of the Nevado de Colima, an extinct volcano that is one of Mexico's highest mountains, and its active twin, the Volcán de Fuego, Mexico's most active volcano. Steam and yellow fumes can sometimes be seen rising from the top, and its sides are covered with a fine, black volcanic sand. A river runs near the base, cutting its way through the Sierra Madre Occidental in an example of the power of river erosion.

Your jet will slip over the coastal hill terrain and suddenly zoom out over the blue Pacific. On the right is an airstrip that, from the plane, looks too small to land on. It isn't. The plane takes a wide clockwise sweep over the ocean and comes in from the north end of the runway on one of the few beachfront landing strips in Mexico. Breaking waves are to your right; coconut groves sway on your left; a memorable visit to Manzanillo lies just ahead.

Manzanillo At-a-Glance

SEEING THE CITY

Groves of coconut palms, avocados, and mangoes line the highway on the way south from the airport. First, the road crosses a wide tidal lagoon and you get an eyeful of hundreds of herons; then the bay comes into view. Manzanillo is on the eastern side of the bay; on the far western shore are exclusive resorts and yacht basins. For a great coastline view, you can drive from the western shore to the top of the steep hill above. A narrow, nearly continuous strip of beachfront development runs between the western and eastern shores, with accommodations becoming less luxurious and more affordable the closer you come to the city. The road into downtown Manzanillo is often clogged with port traffic, providing plenty of time to look at cargo ships, navy patrol boats, and the Petróleos Mexicanos tank yard.

SPECIAL PLACES

A long, 500-foot-high ridgeline of solid rock splits Manzanillo into two sections: the harborfront zone, encompassing the main square and public buildings, and the public market district, to the south of the rock formation, entered by car on Calle Felipe Carrillo Puerto and on foot on Avenida México, an opposing one-way street. The rock formation is covered with small hillside homes reached by a labyrinth of narrow stairways. Ambitious sightseers who climb from the market to the top of the rock are rewarded by a spectacular view of the city and the bay. Descending the stairway on the other side of the rock puts you one or two blocks north of the *zócalo*.

ZÓCALO While most of Manzanillo's downtown area is dusty and tired, the *zócalo* (main plaza) is worthy of note. Located across the street from the waterfront, it's lined with old globe-shaped, cast-iron street lamps and graced with two fountains that, when functional, spout water via recirculating pumps. Between the fountains is a gingerbread cast-iron bandstand topped by a brass weather vane. In the middle of the *zócalo,* busts of Padre Miguel Hidalgo and Benito Juárez face each other across the lawn.

PLAYA AZUL One of Manzanillo's best beaches, it starts at *La Posada* hotel (see *Checking In*) and curves northwest to the river at *Las Hadas* hotel. Residents say the surf is calmest around *La Posada,* gets rougher toward the river, and then is calm again in the bay area protected by the Península de Santiago. The sea is relatively calm all along the beach from December through May.

PLAYA LAS HADAS If you are not a guest at *Las Hadas,* or at any of the complexes that are part of the development, it will be difficult to gain access to this lovely beach in its own private cove. On the beach there are small tents that look as though they came from the deserts of Morocco. Playa las Hadas is definitely for sunning, but not for hard-core swimming, since the beach is small and there's very little surf. Other beaches in the area have better waves.

PLAYA LA AUDIENCIA This is the favorite beach of residents, set in a compact cove on the west side of the Península Las Hadas.

PLAYA SANTIAGO This beach starts at the *Playa de Santiago* hotel (northwest of town) and continues west around Bahía Santiago. It is one of the best beaches in the area and the largest close to town. Waves on the open bay can be rough, but the inlet in front of Playa Santiago is shallow, with small waves and no undertows. On this and other beaches, you can buy a drink of *tuba,* a sweet, slightly fermented beverage made locally from the sap of the coconut palm and sold by roving vendors who pour the liquid out of a gourd on a string.

PLAYA MIRAMAR In the western extreme of Bahía Santiago, about 7 miles (11 km) northwest of Manzanillo, this is another excellent beach.

NEARBY ATTRACTIONS

CUYUTLÁN About 30 miles (48 km) southeast of Manzanillo is Cuyutlán, where the surf is similar to that of southern California beaches in the US. Legend has it that in April or May comes the *ola verde* (green roller), an immense wave of green water that continuously rolls in from the Pacific at heights of up to 30 feet and smashes on the white beach. The wondrous wave has to be seen to be believed, but there aren't many around who have seen it. Modest beachside accommodations are available.

BARRA DE NAVIDAD/SAN PATRICIO Some 37 miles (59 km) northwest of downtown Manzanillo—but only half that distance from the airport—Bahía Melaque (Melaque Bay) shelters the adjacent fishing villages of Barra de Navidad and San Patricio (also known as Melaque). Curio shops and family-run seafood restaurants have sprung up along the villages' cobblestone streets, but this less-known destination still offers a delightful alternative to Manzanillo for those who prefer their beachfront hideaways traffic-free and quaint. For more information, see *Best Beaches off the Beaten Path* in DIVERSIONS.

COLIMA The state capital, founded in 1523, is about two hours inland from Manzanillo, via Route 110. One of its attractions is the *Museo de las Culturas de Occidente* (Museum of Western Cultures; phone: 331-23155), with about 750 native archaeological pieces, housed in the *Casa de la Cultura* (Calzada Galván Norte and Av. Ejército Nacional). It's closed Sundays and Mondays; there's no admission charge. The *Museo Universitario de Culturas Populares* (University Museum of Folk Culture; phone: 331-26869), which boasts a large collection of masks and handicrafts, is in the *Instituto de Bellas Artes* (Fine Arts Institute; 27 de Septiembre and Manuel Gallardo). It's closed Mondays; there's an admission charge. Philatelists will enjoy the stamp collection in the *Museo Regional de Historia de Colima* (16 de Septiembre and Reforma; phone: 331-29228). It's closed Sundays and Mondays; there's an admission charge.

In Comala, about 5$\frac{1}{2}$ miles (9 km) northwest of Colima, there's a crafts school and factory where colonial furniture, ironwork, art, tooled leather, and other items are sold.

Sources and Resources

TOURIST INFORMATION
The *Coordinación General de Turismo de Colima* (Colima State Tourist Office; 4960/Km 9.5 Boulevard Miguel de la Madrid; phone: 32277 or 32264). The staff will give you a map of Manzanillo and a list of sights in Colima, the capital. The office is closed weekends.

LOCAL COVERAGE *Costa Azul* (Blue Coast), available free at hotels and the airport, offers information on what to see and do in Manzanillo. Another good resource is the *Manzanillo Riviera Guide,* an English-language monthly newspaper. The *Los Angeles Times* and the English-language dailies Mexico City *News* and *Mexico City Times* are sold at local newsstands and in the gift shops of the larger luxury hotels.

TELEPHONE The city code for Manzanillo is 333. *Note:* Mexico's telephone company has embarked on a major expansion project that involves changing telephone numbers in many areas of the country. At press time, all numbers listed in this chapter were correct. However, if you have any difficulties reaching attractions listed here, contact the local tourist office.

CLIMATE AND CLOTHES The best time to visit Manzanillo is mid-November through May. The rainy season is usually June through September. Temperatures hover around 80F (27C), with an average low of 70F (21C). At the big resorts, dress is casual. Women may wear slacks, shorts, swimsuits, or less by day; at night evening slacks or skirts are standard attire. Men can wear informal sports clothes and can forget about coats and ties (except at the restaurant at *Las Hadas,* where jackets are required).

GETTING AROUND

AIRPORT Since the airport is 27 miles (43 km) north of Manzanillo, visitors must rent a car, take a minibus, or hire a cab. *Colectivos* (minibuses), whose fares are regulated, go into town for about 21 pesos ($2.80) per person.

CAR RENTAL *Autorentas de México* (phone: 32580), *Avis* (phone: 31590), and *National* (phone: 30611) have offices in the airport. *Hertz* (phone: 30595) has desks at *Las Hadas* and *Club Maeva* (see *Checking In* for information on both hotels.)

TAXI Cabs are abundant and are the easiest way to get into *Las Hadas* and *Club Maeva,* which have gate controls. Local cabbies, known by sight and name, zip through.

TOURS *Bahía Gemelas* travel agency (phone: 31000) arranges for city tours, trips to Colima, and excursions to Barra de Navidad, an unspoiled fishing village about an hour away. It also handles horse rentals, fishing boat charters, and reservations for sunset cruises, as well as ground transportation to and from the airport. An agreeable way to watch the sunset is on a two-hour tour of the bay on the *Verano,* which sets sail daily at 5 PM. The boat leaves from *Las Hadas* hotel (phone: 42000).

SPECIAL EVENTS

Manzanillo celebrates *Carnaval* for a week before *Miércoles de Ceniza* (Ash Wednesday). A queen is crowned, and there are dances, floats, parades, and general merrymaking. Most events are held in the *zócalo.* Hundreds of people appear for the annual *Regata San Diego–Manzanillo,* which usually takes place in February or March. That race is followed the next day by a regatta known as the *Circuito Mexorc,* which departs from Manzanillo to other ports on the Pacific Coast. In late March of odd-numbered years, Manzanillo also cohosts a regatta that begins in Marina del Rey, California. The *Fiestas de Mayo* are held May 1 through 10, with dancing in the plaza and lots of food and drinks. (The celebration commemorating the incorporation of Manzanillo as a city is held on May 8.) The *Torneo Internacional de Pez Vela* (International Sailfish Tournament) is held in November. From December 1 through 12, young children, especially girls, are dressed in native costumes and make pilgrimages to all the churches to pay homage to the *Virgen de Guadalupe.*

SHOPPING

Except for a few shops in the downtown area that carry a similar and decidedly uninspired collection of Mexican crafts, shops don't seem to fare well in Manzanillo. There are, however, a few exceptions. Stores are generally open from 10 AM to 2 PM and from 5 to 8 PM; closed Sundays.

Bugatti A casual-to-dressy selection of chic resortwear for women. At the restaurant of the same name (see *Eating Out*). Cruce las Brisas (phone: 32999).

Centro Artesanal Las Primaveras The most interesting selection of hand-crafted items in town, with blown glass, papier-mâché, stoneware, paper flowers, and leather goods. *Plaza Santiago* shopping center (phone: 31699).

Tane A tiny branch of the Mexico City–based shops, carrying a small selection of jewelry and objets d'art by Mexico's premier silversmiths. Puerto Las Hadas (phone: 32350).

SPORTS

FISHING Manzanillo is renowned as the sailfish capital of the world. Although mid-October through March is the big fishing season—when the large bill-fish run—dorado, sea bass, skipjack, and mackerel are caught all year. Fishing trips can be arranged through the *Cooperativa de Prestadores de Servicios Turísticos de Manzanillo* (phone: 21031). *Flota Lori*, with four fishing boats, is also highly recommended (phone: 31323 or 20297).

GOLF *La Mantarraya,* the course at *Las Hadas* (see *Checking In*), was designed by Roy and Pete Dye and is considered among the best in Mexico. It's open to the public; Rafael Belmont is the pro.

HORSEBACK RIDING *Club Maeva* (see *Checking In*) arranges for rides on the beach or in the mountains.

HUNTING If you can bear to leave the beaches, there are grebe, deer, peccary, and migratory ducks in the area. But be sure you have gotten the necessary permits first (see *Hunting* in DIVERSIONS).

SNORKELING AND SCUBA DIVING *Las Hadas* has a wide variety of equipment for rent, as does the *Club Med Playa Blanca* and most of the other major hotels (see *Checking In*).

SURFING The best virgin surfing beaches in the world are along the dirt road running some 30 miles (48 km) south of Manzanillo. There are also excellent waves of all types, good for all levels, off the beaches around town. Camping is common among the surfing crowd, which is not large here.

SWIMMING AND SUNNING Manzanillo's beaches offer varied types of surf, from docile to dangerous. In addition to the strands described in *Special Places,* Boca de Apiza, about 25 miles (40 km) south of town, has calm and clear waters, ideal for swimming. Better yet is Playa los Pascuales, an idyllic beach at the mouth of the Río Armería, a few miles farther south from Manzanillo on Route 100. Costa Careyes (Turtle Coast), a series of small coves north of Manzanillo, has a few superb beaches, such as those at the *Club Med Playa Blanca* resort and at the *Bel-Air* hotel (see *Checking In* for both; the *Bel-Air* was scheduled to reopen as we went to press).

TENNIS Many of Manzanillo's hotels have tennis facilities, including *Club Maeva* (12 courts, six lighted); *Las Hadas* (10 lighted courts, eight hard-surface, and two clay); *Club Med Playa Blanca* (five synthetic-surface courts, four lighted); and *Bel-Air* (two synthetic surface courts, scheduled to reopen as we went to press). See *Checking In* for more information.

NIGHTCLUBS AND NIGHTLIFE

The best nightspots are *Cartouche* disco at *Las Hadas,* and *Boom Boom* disco at *Club Maeva.* (For details on hotels, see *Checking In.*) Other good places are *Oui* (Km 9 of the Carretera Manzanillo-Santiago; phone: 32333) and *Solaris* (in the *Vista Playa de Oro,* at Km 12.5; phone: 32540). *Enjoy* (phone: 32839) is a little farther out, just before Miramar. The hottest nightspot is *Vog* (at Km 9.2 of the Carretera Manzanillo-Santiago; phone: 31875). During high season, the *Sierra Manzanillo* hotel (see *Checking In*) is the venue for a lively Sunday-night Mexican fiesta, with a Mexican buffet, folkloric ballet, mariachis, and dancing. And everyone should spend at least one evening in the cozy *Legazpi* piano bar at *Las Hadas.*

Best in Town

CHECKING IN

During the high season, expect to pay about $180 to $250 per night for a double room in a very expensive hotel (sometimes meals and activities are included in that price); $90 to $175 in an expensive place; $50 to $90 in a moderate place; and less than $45 in an inexpensive one. The luxury 60-villa *Bel-Air Tamarindo,* located 40 minutes north of the Manzanillo airport, was scheduled to open as we went to press; for information, call 800-457-7676. Off-season, rates in and around Manzanillo drop about 30% and ambience about 95%. Most hotels have air conditioning, TV sets (with some English-language channels), and telephones in the rooms. All telephone numbers are in the 333 city code unless otherwise indicated.

VERY EXPENSIVE

Bel-Air This elegant property—the former *Costa Careyes* hotel, purchased in 1994 by the Bel-Air hotel group—closed after sustaining damages in the 1995 earthquakes but was scheduled to reopen as we went to press. The 60 rooms and suites are decorated in warm colors and have private terraces (several have Jacuzzis). Other features include a restaurant with indoor or alfresco dining, a bar with live entertainment, a full-service health and beauty spa, a tennis court, an equestrian center, yacht moorings, a jogging trail, a large pool, a water sports center, movies, a library, shops, and a polo club. Located on Costa Careyes in the neighboring state of Jalisco, about an hour north of the Manzanillo airport (phone: 335-10000; 800-457-7676; fax: 335-10100).

Camino Real las Hadas The Camino Real hotel group, which bought this once-leg-endary property in 1993, has undertaken a $3-million renovation that has resulted in refurbished rooms and suites (a total of 220) and the addition of a new lobby. Throughout the hotel's decline and renaissance, however, its restaurant, *Legazpi* (see *Eating Out*), has remained superb. Rincón las Hadas, on the Península de Santiago between Bahías Manzanillo and Santiago (phone: 30000; 800-7-CAMINO in the US; 800-90123 in Mexico; fax: 30430).

Club Maeva With 514 one- and two-bedroom villas (some with kitchenettes), this vacation village across the road from its own section of Playa Santiago seems to have everything—12 tennis courts, one of the largest swimming pools in Latin America (with plants, waterfalls and a swim-up bar), horseback rid-ing, water sports, a boutique, a disco, and even a supermarket. There's a good social program, too. Two restaurants are on the property. The rate includes three meals a day and most activities. Playa Santiago (phone: 30595; 800-GO-MAEVA; fax: 30783).

Club Med Playa Blanca Daytime activities range from sailing and scuba diving to tennis, circus classes, and an intensive English horseback riding program; nighttime diversions include dancing and entertainment. Guest accom-modations are in 300 rooms, distributed among red brick bungalows. There's a good beach, too. Rate includes all meals and most activities. (Guests must buy the Club Med package here.) From December 15 through April 30 a minimum stay of one week is required. About 54 miles (90 km) north of town, on Costa Careyes, Jalisco (phone: 335-10001/2/3 and 335-10005; 800-CLUB-MED; fax: 335-10005).

EXPENSIVE

Sierra Manzanillo The 351 rooms and suites at this beachfront hotel—formerly the *Radisson Sierra Plaza Manzanillo*—are tastefully decorated in soft pastels and colorful Mexican crafts, and all offer balconies and a view of the ocean. There are four lighted tennis courts, restaurants, bars, a pool, and a repro-duction of a typical Mexican plaza. The place tends to attract a young, party-oriented crowd. Rates include meals and recreational equipment. Playa la Audiencia (phone: 32000; 800-882-6684; fax: 32272).

MODERATE

Condotel Arco Iris Twenty one- and two-bedroom bungalows with private baths and maid service are offered here. There's a swimming pool and an attrac-tive garden. On the beach in the Salahua section of Manzanillo (phone/fax: 30168).

Fiesta Mexicana Popular with families, this place has 186 cheerful rooms, a pool, a restaurant, a bar, and horses for rent. Playa Azul (phone: 32181; fax: 32180).

Villas la Audiencia This three-story hotel built around a courtyard swimming pool has 26 units. Most are two-bedroom suites, but there are a few single rooms that can be added to a suite as a third bedroom. The decor is a bit tacky (for instance, the furniture is upholstered in plastic), but each suite has a full kitchen. There's no restaurant. Located 7 miles (11 km) north of downtown, at Av. La Audiencia and Av. Las Palmas (phone: 30861; fax 32653).

INEXPENSIVE

Hotel Colonial The only decent downtown lodging, this stately old hotel is a still a bit musty. The 38 rooms are plain and minimally furnished (some have air conditioning, but none have phones or TV sets). But the location is perfect for anyone who wants to stay right in the heart of town; it's a block west of the *zócalo* and a five-minute walk from the public market district. There is a restaurant and a bar. 100 Av. México (phone: 21080).

Parador Marbella A real find, this 54-room beachfront place has a pool and *Marbella*, a good restaurant (see *Eating Out*). Km 9.5 on the Carretera Manzanillo-Santiago, across the street from the Social Security hospital (phone/fax: 31103).

Playa de Santiago Its 105 units, including the penthouse suite, all have private balconies, a bay breeze, and ceiling fans. Amenities include a swimming pool, a so-so tennis court, a restaurant, a bar, shuffleboard, and a boat launching ramp. The beach, in a protected cove, is excellent. Covered parking is available for guests. On the west side of the Península de Santiago (phone: 30270 or 30055; fax: 30344).

La Posada A small, pleasant place with its own beach, 23 rooms, a pool, a coffee shop, and parking. A full breakfast is included in the rate. Playa Azul (phone/fax: 31899).

EATING OUT

For dinner for two, expect to pay $50 to $60 in an expensive restaurant; $30 in a moderate place; and $10 in an inexpensive one. Price ranges do not include drinks, wine, tax, or tips. Most restaurants below accept MasterCard and Visa, and a few also accept American Express and Diners Club; it's a good idea to call ahead and check. Unless otherwise noted, the restaurants listed are open daily for lunch and dinner. All telephone numbers are in the 333 city code unless otherwise indicated.

EXPENSIVE

Bugatti A continental spot, with Italian dishes a specialty, and good salads. A guitarist plays at lunchtime, and there's live music for dancing at night. The restaurant also has a chic womenswear boutique (see *Shopping*). Reservations advised. Cruce las Brisas, the intersection of the Carretera Manzanillo-Santiago and the road to Las Brisas (phone: 32999).

Kitzia's Candlelight, fresh flowers, and a beautiful garden set the stage at one of Manzanillo's newer restaurants. The international menu includes shrimp in tequila and filet mignon. Reservations advised. Km 10.5 on the airport road (phone: 31414).

Legazpi This is as elegant as Manzanillo gets. Soft tones and candlelight complement the indoor and outdoor setting. The food, prepared with French techniques and Mexican ingredients, is excellent, and the service is nearly perfect. Jackets required for men. Closed Sundays, Mondays, Wednesdays, and Fridays. Reservations advised. At *Las Hadas Hotel,* Rincón las Hadas, on the Península de Santiago between Bahías Manzanillo and Santiago (phone: 30000).

L'Récif Take a dip in the barside pool, enjoy a spectacular view, and savor the fine seafood prepared by the French chef-owner. In the winter, a champagne brunch is served on Sundays. Closed September 15–30. Reservations advised. At the Vida del Mar resort complex, along the road to Naranjo (phone: 30624).

MODERATE

Ly Chee This establishment has about 20 tables with an excellent view of port activity. The food is Cantonese, with some emphasis on fish dishes. Reservations unnecessary. 397 Calzada Niños Héroes (phone: 21103).

Rosalba's Good, hearty Mexican dishes are served with homemade tortillas in a double *palapa* that's next to the gas station in Santiago. Reservations unnecessary. Km 13 on the Blvd. Miguel de la Madrid (phone: 30488).

El Vaquero Charcoal-broiled steaks and chops are the specialty here. Beef is cut in the American manner and may even be ordered by the kilo (2.2 pounds!). Reservations advised. Cruce las Brisas, the intersection of the Carretera Manzanillo-Santiago and the road to Las Brisas (phone: 31654).

INEXPENSIVE

Juanito's Americans congregate here to watch the big sports games. Favorites from both sides of the border are served—fried chicken, ribs, burritos, tacos, and the like. The management allows customers to make long-distance phone calls and send faxes from here. No reservations. No credit cards accepted. Carretera Manzanillo-Santiago (phone: 31388).

Marbella A simple, cozy place with overhead fans but no air conditioning. The fare is international, with good paella and roast lamb. No reservations. At the *Parador Marbella,* Km 9.5 on the Carretera Manzanillo-Santiago, across the street from the Social Security hospital (phone: 31103).

Mazatlán
(pronounced Ma-saht-*lahn*)

Just south of the Tropic of Cancer, in the state of Sinaloa, is one of the most popular resorts and active ports in all of Mexico. Mazatlán rests on a peninsula jutting into the Pacific Ocean, with a bay sprinkled with tiny islands and a natural sheltered harbor. At the same latitude as the south end of the Baja Peninsula and Honolulu, this beautiful spot offers the same idyllic weather conditions.

While Mazatlán's attractions are primarily water-oriented, it differs from Mexico's two other major west coast resorts—Acapulco and Puerto Vallarta—in several respects. It is much closer to the US-Mexico border, and although four direct international flights are available (from Denver, Los Angeles, San Francisco, and Seattle), the majority of its tourist trade arrives by car, much of it via the four-lane highway from Nogales, on the Arizona-Mexico border. Mazatlán is also less expensive than its southern counterparts; many visitors are sports enthusiasts who come for extended stays and watch their pennies more closely than the one-week suntan-seeking pilgrims to Acapulco. Because it is so thoroughly imbued with the sporting spirit, Mazatlán is exhaustively equipped for fishing and, to a lesser degree, hunting (primarily duck) expeditions. But fishing is what Mazatlán is mostly about. Located at the mouth of the Sea of Cortés (also known as the Gulf of California), the port offers some of the world's greatest sport fishing. Marlin bite from November through May; sailfish, from May through November.

The name Mazatlán, from the Nahuatl word meaning "Place of the Deer," refers to the large herds that once migrated along the coast. While game is still abundant in the surrounding countryside, migration patterns have changed, with animals avoiding the immediate Mazatlán area and its flourishing tourist attractions.

Once the home of the ancient Totorame civilization, Mazatlán was later frequented by Pacific-based pirates who, according to legend, buried their treasure in the coves and inlets that dot the coast near the city. A few Spaniards settled here in the early 1600s, but the town was not incorporated until 1806 and had no municipal government until 1837. It was left to a group of enterprising Germans to develop Mazatlán as a port so they could import agricultural equipment to Mexico. By the end of the 19th century, Mazatlán was heavily involved in trade with countries in Europe and Asia.

Today the city, with a population of 500,000, is the home port of the nation's largest shrimp fleet: Tons of shrimp are processed here each day and shipped to the US, Mexico's major customer. Cruise ships and freighters from a multitude of countries are usually moored at the docks, and ferry boats run daily across the Sea of Cortés to La Paz, Baja's largest southern city.

Blessed with a plethora of beautiful beaches, ocean water that hovers around 75F (24C) in the summer, and a full complement of fishing opportunities, Mazatlán has become a favorite spot for travelers seeking an alternative to more crowded and increasingly urban resorts like Acapulco. With its long stretch of large beachfront hotels, seafood restaurants, nightclubs, and bright lights, Mazatlán is truly striking.

Mazatlán At-a-Glance

SEEING THE CITY

The traditional way to see the city's lovely ocean vistas is aboard a *pulmonía,* a taxi that looks something like a golf cart with open sides. On land, the best spot from which to get a panoramic view of Mazatlán and the surrounding waters is atop Cerro del Crestón (Summit Hill), also the location of *El Faro,* a massive lighthouse. Once separated from the mainland and now connected by landfill, this strip of land and its crowning lighthouse mark the entrance to the busy harbor. The lighthouse—the second-highest in the world—stands more than 500 feet above sea level, and its light is visible from as far as 50 miles out to sea. The view from the top of the hill is magnificent: To one side lie the Pacific, the beaches, and Hotel Row; on the other side is the harbor.

Valentino's disco (in the *Valentino* shopping complex; phone: 136212), with its lofty window wall, affords a mesmerizing view of the sea crashing against the rocks below and the curving beaches of Mazatlán beyond.

SPECIAL PLACES

Mazatlán offers plenty of entertainment, from its busy harbor to the bustling activity around the *zócalo* and along the *malecón* (seawall) boulevard; however, beaches are the first priority for most visitors.

BEACHES

PLAYA CAMARÓN Beginning below *Valentino's* at Punta el Camarón, this snug little beach with coarse yellow sand is quite popular for swimming and bodysurfing. The surf can be dangerous at times, though, and there are no lifeguards.

PLAYA LAS GAVIOTAS A 15-minute drive north from downtown, its soft, smooth, golden sand and gentle surf make this lovely beach a pleasant place to swim. Between Playa Camarón and Playa Sábalo.

PLAYA NORTE This moderately wide stretch of pale yellow sand is not as exclusive as Playa Sábalo or Playa las Gaviotas, but many people consider it more fun. It's Mazatlán's largest beach, catering primarily to the local population. Lockers, showers, beach chairs, and umbrellas are for rent here. It extends 6 miles (10 km) north of the *malecón*.

PLAYA OLAS ALTAS The name means "high waves," which says it all. It's popular for surfing, but the tide can be tricky and there are no lifeguards. Olas Altas is popular with the younger set and is a good place to enjoy those magnificent sunsets.

PLAYA SÁBALO Starting around *El Cid* resort and extending a mile to the rocks of Punta Sábalo is the sheltered, quiet, and quite fashionable Playa Sábalo. Don't be put off by all the expensive hotels along here: You can still walk between (or even through) them to the beach, which—like all beaches in Mexico—is open to the public.

OTHER SITES

MALECÓN Starting at Playa Olas Altas, north of El Mirador, this seaside boulevard marks the beginning of Mazatlán's swimming beaches. Several of the city's better shops and restaurants, plus older hotels, are here. From Olas Altas, the *malecón* stretches north past Paseo Claussen, a rocky beach good for shell collecting but not for swimming; on to Playa Norte; and finally to Playa Avenida del Mar, a wide strip of sand bordered by several newer hotels. Farther north are Playas las Gaviotas and Sábalo.

EL MIRADOR This lookout point above Playa Olas Altas, along the *malecón,* is used for high dives by the town's young daredevils. Almost anytime the tide is in, you can see young men jump from the top of this rock into the shallow, fast waters below. Contributions are collected before the dive is attempted—just in case. Paseo Claussen and Olas Altas.

TEATRO ANGELA PERALTA Named in honor of the internationally renowned Mexican diva, Mazatlán's recently renovated opera house also hosts pop concerts, plays, and a variety of other performances. Set in Mazatlán Viejo (Old Mazatlán), it has been declared a historical monument. The other historic buildings around the *zócalo,* which date to the late 19th and early 20th centuries, are currently undergoing major restorations. The theater is open to visitors daily from 9 AM to 6 PM. No admission charge. On Calle Carnaval, a block west of Plazuela Machado (phone: 153334).

MUSEO DE ANTROPOLOGÍA This small museum contains a collection of pre-Hispanic artifacts and exhibits of contemporary art. Closed Mondays. Admission charge. 76 Sixto de Osuna (phone: 153502).

ACUARIO (AQUARIUM) Filled with fish and kids, this aquarium has 250 species (of fish) on display. There is a small sea museum, an auditorium where Spanish-language documentary films are shown, and, outside, a small botanical garden. Don't miss the dolphins, turtles, moray eels, and sharks. Open daily. Admission charge. 111 Av. de los Deportes, just off Av. del Mar (phone: 117815).

LA GRUTA DE CERRO DEL CRESTÓN (CAVE OF SUMMIT HILL) Beneath the craggy peak on which *El Faro* (The Lighthouse) stands, separating the ocean from the harbor, is a small cave. It is said that pirates used this secret hollow— revealed only at low tide—to store their stolen treasure. Approaching the cave is dangerous, but it is fun to note in passing, especially for those with active imaginations.

EXTRA SPECIAL

Several islands in the bay off Mazatlán's harbor are perfect destinations for day excursions. Palmito de la Virgen, a bird watcher's paradise, is accessible by a boat that makes the trip daily; your hotel or the tourist office can provide the current schedule and rates. Seashell collectors and snorkel fans can take an amphibious boat to Isla de los Venados (Deer Island) for an afternoon; in the evening, it is the venue for torchlit beach parties. The *Tiburón* and the *Ocean Express* leave from the beach at *El Cid* resort (see *Checking In*).

Those who have had enough "resort living" and are looking for something out of the ordinary should take the jungle tour to the town of San Blas in the state of Nayarit. The trip includes a ride down the river in a dugout canoe, a swim, a visit to Padre Eusebio Kino's mission, and a short tour of San Blas. Take a good supply of insect repellent. For more information on San Blas, see *The West Coast: Nogales to Mexico City* in DIRECTIONS.

About 40 miles (64 km) southeast of Mazatlán, over a spectacularly scenic road, is Copalá, a truly authentic and historically rich Mexican pueblo of only 600 inhabitants (among them several Americans). For more details, see *Reynosa to Mazatlán* in DIRECTIONS.

Sources and Resources

TOURIST INFORMATION

The *Oficina de Informacíon Turística Regional Mazatlán* (Mazatlán Regional Tourist Information Office; 1300 Av. Olas Altas at the corner of Mariano Escobedo; phone: 151221 or 151220) provides helpful brochures and maps. Many of the staff speak English. The office is closed weekends.

LOCAL COVERAGE The English-language *Mazatlán Pacific Pearl*, published locally, is available free in hotels, restaurants, and other tourist locations. *Mazatlán Inside*—available for free at the airport and tourist office—contains a comprehensive list of activities and an excellent city map. A very helpful map is also published by the *Mazatlán Arts and Crafts Center;* it's free at most hotel travel desks. The *Mexico City Times* and *The News,* Mexico's only English-language daily newspapers, are sold throughout Mazatlán. *The*

New York Times, USA Today, and the *Los Angeles Times,* which are flown in daily, are usually available after noon.

TELEPHONE The city code for Mazatlán is 69. *Note:* Mexico's telephone company has embarked on a major expansion project that involves changing telephone numbers in many areas of the country. At press time, all numbers listed in this chapter were correct. However, if you have any difficulties reaching attractions listed here, contact the local tourist office.

CLIMATE AND CLOTHES Mazatlán's idyllic climate—especially its mild and sunny winters—make it attractive to escapees from the north. The temperature is usually in the 70s F (21–26C), with an all-time low of 52F (11C). The water is close to air temperature, and there is little or no rain. The summers are slightly hotter and more humid. While it may rain briefly in the afternoon, or at night, from June through October, it's never much of an inconvenience. Dress is casual: a bathing suit, hat, and sunglasses for the beach, resortwear in town.

GETTING AROUND

While Mazatlán is easily navigated on foot, the variety of noteworthy sights and sites beyond the city makes alternative modes of transport a necessity.

BUS Mazatlán has several bus lines, which are easily found on all major streets; the destination of each bus is clearly marked on its front. The fare ranges from 1 to 2 pesos (13¢ to 27¢). Service is good along Avenida Camarón Sábalo/Avenida del Mar, a single street that runs along the shore where most of the hotels are located. Minibus transportation from the airport costs 20 pesos (about $2.65) per passenger (phone: 115554).

CAR RENTALS *Budget* (phone: 132000), *Hertz* (phone: 150345, airport; 134955, downtown), and *National* (phone: 136000) have offices at the airport and in town. *Rent Me!* (between the *Quijote* and *Caravelle* hotels; phone: 146433) rents replicas of old-fashioned cars by the hour.

FERRY Large ferries make the 18-hour trip between Mazatlán and La Paz in Baja California. Although they can transport your car or RV, don't even consider it during high season. Commerical vehicles are given priority, so private cars are often bumped off the ferry; waits of several days are not uncommon. You're better off leaving your car in Mazatlán. Fares vary widely, and reservations should always be made well in advance. The ferry leaves the main pier at Prolongación Carnaval daily at 3 PM; for up-to-date schedule and fare information, call 117020.

MOPED An excellent way to get around, mopeds are available from *María's Mopeds* (1666 Av. Camarón Sábalo and Río Ibis; no phone). There's a limited supply, so rent in the morning.

SEA EXCURSIONS A three-hour "Fiesta Cruise" of the harbor and bay is a lovely excursion. The boat leaves from the sport fishing pier near the ferry terminal around 11 AM. English-speaking guides point out various places of interest along the way, including the fishing harbor, *El Faro,* the pirate caves of Cerro de Crestón, and a seal rock (the seals arrive in November and leave in May, although some have made Mazatlán their permanent home). Musical entertainment is provided by a marimba player, and drinks and cocktails are included. Tickets, schedules, and departure locations can be obtained from most hotel travel desks, or contact the tourist office (see *Tourist Information*).

TAXI There are two types of cabs in Mazatlán. The first is the usual taxi that can be called to your hotel or hailed on the street. The second, known as a *pulmonía,* can only be hailed on the street. *Pulmonías,* open-air vehicles resembling golf carts, offer a comfortable, breezy ride—perfect for this hot place. You can bargain with drivers of both types of cabs; check at your hotel desk for prices.

SPECIAL EVENTS

Mazatlán's annual *Carnaval*—the largest in Mexico—is held during the week before *Miércoles de Ceniza* (Ash Wednesday). The festivities include balls, dances, ballets, plays, *charreadas* (Mexican rodeo), a poetry contest, beauty pageants, and other kinds of merriment. Finally, on the night before *Lent* begins, the celebration ends with a colorful parade of floats and fireworks.

The *Fiesta Cultural de Sinaloa* draws Mexico's top musicians, who perform in concerts and at other cultural events throughout November. December 8 is *Día de la Purísima* (Feast of the Immaculate Conception), the city's most important religious fiesta. A statue of the Virgin Mary is paraded through the streets, and there is a huge display of fireworks in the evening.

SHOPPING

While Mazatlán is by no means a shopper's paradise, some stores do stock an ample selection of handicrafts from the rest of Mexico. Expect to pay more than you would in the area where the items were made, but less than in the US. Early afternoon is a pleasant time to shop. Most stores are open daily from 9 AM until 8 PM, with no afternoon siesta break.

Aca Joe A great place to buy T-shirts and sportswear. Av. Camarón Sábalo and Gaviotas (phone: 141212).

La Carreta Here is an excellent selection of well-made Mexican handicrafts—brass and tin objects, paper flowers, clay pots, candles, furniture, rugs, and more. Two locations: *El Cid* resort (phone: 133333) and the *Costa de Oro* hotel (phone: 135344).

Casa Roberto Roberto has tasteful gifts, from rugs and accessories for home decorating to original artwork. At the *Playa Mazatlán* hotel (phone: 138320).

The Leather House An attractive, air conditioned shop featuring boots, handmade leather jackets, skirts, slacks, belts, and handbags. Some items are made of snakeskin and other exotic materials. 203 Rodolfo T. Loaiza, across from the *Los Sábalos* hotel (no phone).

Maya del Pacífico Decor here is fully Maya, with replicas of ancient artifacts on display and a full reproduction of a wall from *Bonampak*. What's for sale are high-quality jackets, shoes, and boots made of snakeskin and eelskin, all custom-made in the back of the store (footwear takes five days, clothing, about three). 411 Rodolfo T. Loaiza, across from the *Los Arcos* hotel (no phone).

Mazatlán Arts and Crafts Center A cooperative of about 20 shops with some craftspeople working on the premises. Woodcarvings, metal sculptures, and paper flowers are among the more tempting items. 417 Rodolfo T. Loaiza, in Plaza Tres Islas (phone: 135022).

Mr. Indio Gold and silver jewelry is the specialty here. Two locations: across from the *Playa Mazatlán* hotel, at 311 Rodolfo T. Loaiza (phone: 134923) and at 206 Angel Flores Pte. (phone: 113753), where artisans may be seen at work in their shops.

Sea Shell City Two floors of seashells, some gawdy, others simply gorgeous. Don't miss the shell mosaics upstairs. 407 Rodolfo T. Loaiza (phone: 131301).

Tane A branch of Mexico's most prestigious and costly silver shop, it carries jewelry, flatware, and decorative items. In the *Camino Real* hotel (phone: 131111).

The Tequila Tree Crafts, women's clothes—including María de Guadalajara casuals—and wonderful items for kids; there's also a men's shop with very nice sandals and beachwear. No tequila, though. 1000 Av. Camarón Sábalo (no phone).

SPORTS

BASEBALL Mazatlán's professional Triple-A league team, *Los Venados* (the Deer), is in the *Mexican Pacific Coast League,* where Fernando Valenzuela and other big leaguers got their start. The season runs October through January; the stadium is just a five-minute taxi ride from most hotels. Call the tourist office (see *Tourist Information*) for schedules.

BOATING Motorboats, sailboats, banana boats (long and narrow, with one sail), water skiing, and parasailing are available at all the northern beaches.

BULLFIGHTING From *Christmas* through *Easter,* bullfights are held every Sunday at the *Plaza de Toros Monumental* (Calzada Rafael Buelna) or at *El Toreo* (Av. Camarón Sábalo). Inquire at the tourist office for schedule and ticket information.

CHARREADAS The *Lienzo Charro* in the Juárez section of town is where rodeos are held each Sunday year-round. Contact the tourist office for additional details.

FISHING Some of the most exciting game fishing in the world is done in the waters off Mazatlán. While November through May is the most popular time, fishing here is good all year. Marlin are most plentiful from November through May; sailfish from May through November. Both types of fish often weigh in at over 100 pounds. Mazatlán is considered the best billfishing port on the Pacific Coast, and there are also plenty of sea bass, tuna, bonito, red snapper, and many other varieties.

There are 10 sport fishing fleets in operation in Mazatlán, with more than 75 cruisers designed to take two to six passengers. Most of the better boats come equipped with refrigerators, ship-to-shore radios, tackle, and bait; any hotel or travel agent can make charter arrangements before you arrive. If you are planning to visit in the winter, it is wise to reserve a boat when you make your hotel reservation. *Mike's Sportfishing* (phone: 112824) at the *Marina Flota Faro* and *Bill Heimpel's Star Fleet* (phone: 122665) are both reliable.

Light tackle fishing, feasible along the inland lagoons, is equally challenging. The trophies may not be as impressive as giant billfish, but, if anything, the little fighters require more skill to land. Gilberto Aviles (phone: 113640) provides good guides. José Jiménez, who runs the *Copalá* travel agency (2313 Calle Belisario Domínguez; phone: 128326), is also an excellent fishing guide.

GOLF The 18-hole course at *El Cid* resort (see *Checking In*) was designed by Larry Hughes. José Avelar is the pro; Lucy Reina is the manager. There also is a nine-hole course at *Club Campestre de Mazatlán* (Rte. 15; phone: 147494).

HORSEBACK RIDING Horses may be rented at *Rancho Guadalupe* on Playa las Gaviotas (phone: 141266) or on the beach at Avenida Camarón Sábalo.

HUNTING Doves and ducks are plentiful in season (about October through April). Palmito de la Virgen (see *Extra Special,* above) has great duck shooting, as do the surrounding marshes and fields. Trips that include a guide, guns, licenses, and transportation can be arranged through all hotels or through Roberto Aviles (phone: 113728 or 116060).

SCUBA DIVING Diving is decent at Isla de los Venados, Isla Dos Hermanos, and Isla los Cardones. Venados is best for beginners; Hermanos is only for the experienced. *Aqua Sport,* at *El Cid* resort (see *Checking In*), offers trips, including equipment and guides; a half-hour preparatory class is available for non-certified divers.

SKEET SHOOTING Mazatlán has its own skeet club, and visitors are welcome. Hotel travel desks can make all arrangements.

SURFING Many surfers agree that Mazatlán has some of the best surfing waters in North America. The beaches north of town—Las Gaviotas, Camarón, and Sábalo (see *Special Places*)—attract the most surfers. Punta Cañones, in front of the *Freeman* hotel, and Punta Lupe, 1½ miles (2 km) south of the *Playa Mazatlán* hotel (see *Checking In*), are particularly good spots; the latter offers ideal waves for beginners. At the mouth of the harbor, just after entering Mazatlán, there is an excellent spot for advanced surfers.

SWIMMING, SUNNING, AND SNORKELING In addition to Mazatlán's better-known strands (see *Special Places*), the beaches extending north from the center of town for about 12 miles are all open to the public for swimming and snorkeling. Piedra, a relaxing but rustic beach off Mazatlán, offers long flat stretches of sand, clear blue-green waters, and thatch-palm umbrellas.

TENNIS *El Cid* resort has 13 courts (four clay, nine Laykold), two of them lighted; the *Costa de Oro,* three lighted cement courts; *Los Sábalos,* two lighted cement courts; and the *Camino Real,* two lighted cement courts atop a small bluff next to the surf (see *Checking In* for details on hotels; the courts are open to non-hotel guests for a fee). In addition, *Las Gaviotas Racquet Club* (Calles Ibis and Río Bravo; phone: 135939 or 113182) has seven cement and clay courts, and the *Club Reforma* (Calle Rafael Buelna next to the *Plaza de Toros Monumental;* phone: 131000) has eight cement courts. Both clubs are open to the public.

WATER TOBOGGANING Kids will especially like the giant toboggan down the 100-foot Kamikaze water slide at *Acuático Mazagua,* on Playa Cerritos (phone: 140622).

NIGHTCLUBS AND NIGHTLIFE

The disco scene is very big in Mazatlán, and the leading hotels all have their own spots. (See *Checking In* for all hotel addresses and phone numbers.) The discos take reservations, and during the winter it's wise to call ahead. The spectacular setting at *Valentino's* (in the *Valentino* shopping complex; phone: 136212), which clings to a bluff above the sea at Punta el Camarón, draws big crowds. Other dancing spots include the *Chiquita Banana* restaurant in the *Camino Real* hotel; *Caracol Tango Palace* at *El Cid* resort; *Fandangos* in *Las Palmas* shopping center (phone: 137363); and *Frankie O's* (Av. del Mar; phone: 125800). *Bora Bora* (phone: 136212), a *palapa* (thatch-roofed) bar on the beach at the *Valentino* complex, has disco dancing from noon until 4 AM. *Aleluya's Republic* (406 Av. Camarón Sábalo; phone: 132040), a combined steakhouse and disco, has an all-day happy hour and a pit for dancing. *La Guitarra* disco at the *Hacienda Mazatlán* hotel has live music Wednesdays through Sundays.

Great fun are the Mexican fiestas held at the *Playa Mazatlán* hotel on Tuesdays and Saturdays; the *Inn at Mazatlán* (6291 Av. Camarón Sábalo; phone: 135500) and the *Riviera Mazatlán* hotel on Wednesdays; the *Plaza Maya* (414 Rodolfo T. Loaiza; no phone) nightly; the *Fiesta Piñata* at the

Océano Palace hotel Tuesdays and Fridays; and the *Mazatlán Arts and Crafts Center* (417 Rodolfo T. Loaiza; phone: 132031) Wednesday and Thursday nights, where the shows include performances by the *Voladores de Papantla* (Flying Pole Dancers of Papantla).

A more prosaic, if equally enjoyable, evening can be had at *Mickey's No Name Café* (at the *Mazatlán Arts and Crafts Center;* 417 Rodolfo T. Loaiza; phone: 132031), the *número uno* sports bar in town, with 18 TV sets. The atmosphere is relaxed, and the food—barbecued ribs, chicken, prime ribs, and turkey—is not bad. At *Señor Frog's* (Av. del Mar; phone: 151110 or 121925), a bar and grill that's part of the popular Carlos Anderson chain, there's music and dancing at night.

Best in Town

CHECKING IN

Two main areas of Mazatlán have accommodations. One is in town, near the center of the city and along Avenida Olas Altas, which borders the more southerly beaches. The other is farther north, along the beaches that have been developed during Mazatlán's growth as a resort. Older and less expensive hotels are more likely to be in the first location, while the newer, more luxurious ones are along Playa Norte, Playa las Gaviotas, and Playa Sábalo, to the north. If you want to visit during *Carnaval* season, be sure to make hotel reservations at least six months in advance (and be prepared to pay through the nose—perhaps as much as twice the normal rate). All hotels listed below have air conditioning, private baths, and telephones and TV sets in the rooms. Expect to pay $100 or more per night for a double room in an expensive hotel; $60 to $90 in a moderate place; and $55 or less in an inexpensive one. Rates may drop as much as 40% in the summer. All telephone numbers are in the 69 city code unless otherwise indicated.

We begin with our favorite haven (which is, we must admit, rather pricey), followed by recommended hotels, listed by price category.

A SPECIAL HAVEN

Camino Real On a small hill overlooking Playa Sábalo, the best-situated property in town has 170 rooms, three restaurants, three bars with live music, a beach club, a social program, shops, two lighted tennis courts, terraces, a heated swimming pool and a wading pool, and lots of class. The management will provide tips on the best places to fish, on bullfights and *charreadas* (traditional rodeos), on where to rent boats to go to Laguna Maimero or into the deeper parts of the Pacific for deep-sea fishing, on surfing, on duck hunting, and on practically anything else. About 7 miles (11 km) northwest of town on Av. Camarón Sábalo (phone: 131111; 800-7-CAMINO in the US; 800-90123 in Mexico; fax: 140311).

El Cid This impressive 800-acre property comprises three hotels: the *Granada Country Club* and the *Castilla Beach,* with a total of 600 rooms and suites, and the 402-unit, 25-story *El Moro.* On the premises are a health spa; more than 70 shops, boutiques, and galleries; 11 restaurants and lounges; and a rooftop heliport. The three hotels share a disco, an 18-hole golf course, 13 tennis courts, squash and racquetball courts, five pools, a gym, a jogging path, and Sinaloa's only legal betting parlor. Arrangements can be made for a full complement of water sports, fishing, horseback riding, and skeet shooting. About 5½ miles (9 km) north of downtown on Av. Camarón Sábalo (phone: 133333; 310-827-1148 in Los Angeles; 800-446-1069 elsewhere in California; 800-525-1925 elsewhere in the US; fax: 141311).

Costa de Oro Well situated on Playa Sábalo, it has 360 rooms and suites. Amenities include a pool, two restaurants, a bar, and three lighted tennis courts. Av. Camarón Sábalo (phone: 135344 or 135366; 800-342-2431; fax: 144209).

Pueblo Bonito A low-rise condo/hotel forming a horseshoe around a pretty garden and large pool, it has 240 suites. A fine Italian restaurant (*Angelo's;* see *Eating Out*), a coffee shop, a good beach, and several bars complete the facilities. One block from the *Camino Real* hotel at 2121 Av. Camarón Sábalo (phone: 143700; 800-262-4500; fax: 141723).

Los Sábalos On the beach, this property with 185 beautifully decorated rooms and a sparkling white façade is awash with wicker and colorful flowers. Facilities include a health club, tennis courts, and a restaurant. 100 Rodolfo T. Loaiza (phone: 143700; 800-528-8760; fax: 141723).

Las Casitas Each of the 12 two-bedroom, two-bathroom apartment units here has a kitchen and cable TV, and is decorated in a rustic Mexican style. There's no restaurant, but the friendly, English-speaking owners, who live on the premises, often invite guests into their home for dinner or cocktails (all gratis). On Playa las Gaviotas, at 777 Av. Camarón Sábalo (phone: 135609; fax: 130169).

Fiesta Inn Here are 100 modern, attractive rooms and 7 suites. Built on the beachfront, it also offers a swimming pool and wading pool, a restaurant specializing in international cuisine, a snack bar, and a lobby bar. 1927 Av. Camarón Sábalo (phone: 190100; 800-FIESTA-1 in the US; 800-50450 in Mexico; fax: 190130).

Holiday Inn Sunspree Resort Contemporary Mexican in decor, the 204 large rooms here all face the ocean. Set within attractively landscaped gardens are two restaurants, a lobby bar with live music, a swimming pool, a fitness center, one lighted tennis court, and a beach club. 696 Av. Camarón Sábalo (phone: 132222; 800-HOLIDAY in the US; 800-00999 in Mexico; fax: 141287).

Océano Palace Designed for the young, this former disco has 200 refurbished rooms, two pools, a restaurant, and a bar with live music nightly. Guests receive complimentary tennis passes to *Las Gaviotas Racquet Club.* About 7 miles (11 km) northwest on Av. Camarón Sábalo (phone: 130666; 800-352-7690; fax: 139666).

Playa Mazatlán All the Americans in Mazatlán seem to gravitate here, if not to the hotel, then to its terrace bar. This vast complex has 435 rooms, a heated pool, a whirlpool bath, social programs, fishing, boating, water skiing, skin diving, nightly outdoor dancing, and a dining room. The place borders on the frenetic at times. Four and one-half miles (7 km) northwest on Playa las Gaviotas (phone: 134444; fax: 165125).

Riviera Mazatlán With one building on the beach and another across the street, it has 244 rooms and suites (some with kitchenettes), a restaurant, a bar, and a gym. Guests have access to the tennis courts at *Las Gaviotas Racquet Club.* 51 Av. Camarón Sábalo (phone: 134822; fax: 144532).

Solamar Inn It resembles an ancient villa, with 56 spacious rooms (all with kitchenettes). There's also a restaurant and a pool. Across the street from the beach, at 1942 Av. Camarón Sábalo (phone: 136666; fax: 138211).

Suites las Flores This casual beachside high-rise has 110 suites with kitchenettes, perfect for an extended stay; it also has 14 double rooms (without kitchenettes). Pluses include a popular bar, lively beachfront, pool, and restaurant. On Playa las Gaviotas, across from Isla de los Venados (phone: 135100; 800-252-0327 in California; 800-421-0787 elsewhere in the US; fax: 143422).

Suites las Palmas This property has 178 rooms and 12 suites in a cluster of six attractive three-story buildings. There's a restaurant and a lobby bar with live music. Two blocks from the beach, at 305 Av. Camarón Sábalo (phone: 134366; fax: 143477).

INEXPENSIVE

De Cima One of Mazatlán's first beach hotels—and still popular—with 140 rooms, a good piano bar, a pool, and a restaurant. 48 Av. del Mar near downtown (phone: 127300; fax: 127311).

Hacienda Mazatlán Each of the 95 rooms has a balcony, a beach view, and a large bathroom. There is also a pool, sauna, dining room, cocktail lounge, and nightclub. One and one-half miles (2 km) northwest of town, on Av. del Mar (phone: 127000; fax: 151579).

Posada Don Pelayo Although it's not on the beach, it's still popular. Some of the 175 rooms have balconies, refrigerators, and/or kitchenettes. There's a pool and tennis court, plus free transportation to *Chico's* beach club. 1111 Av. del Mar (phone: 131818; fax: 140799).

Puesta del Sol Accommodations here include 22 bungalows with kitchenettes, plus 115 rooms. There's also a pool, a restaurant, and a bar. Av. Camarón Sábalo (phone: 135522; fax: 143381).

Sands Across the street from the beach, this low-key place has 87 comfortable rooms equipped with satellite TV and refrigerators. There's also a pool, a Jacuzzi, and a restaurant. Av. del Mar (phone: 120000; fax: 151025).

EATING OUT

Since Mazatlán still boasts Mexico's largest shrimp fleet, *camarones* are a major attraction virtually everywhere. A dinner for two will run up to $75 at expensive restaurants; $30 to $40 at moderate establishments; and $25 or less at inexpensive places. Drinks, wine, tax, and tip are extra. Most restaurants below accept MasterCard and Visa, and a few also accept American Express and Diners Club; it's a good idea to call ahead and check. Unless otherwise noted, all restaurants are open daily for lunch and dinner. All telephone numbers are in the 69 city code unless otherwise indicated.

EXPENSIVE

Angelo's A very pretty place decorated in pastels, it specializes in fine Italian and international dishes. Open for dinner only; closed Sundays. Reservations advised. At the *Pueblo Bonito Hotel*, 2121 Av. Camarón Sábalo (phone: 143700).

Casa Loma This secluded spot features excellent international fare and impeccable service. Closed in the summer. Reservations necessary. No credit cards accepted. 104 Av. Gaviotas (phone: 135398).

Miyiko Set in a Japanese garden with a small stream, it offers excellent Japanese fare. Reservations advised. 70 Av. del Mar (phone: 116590).

Señor Pepper One of Mazatlán's most elegant dining spots, it offers candlelit dinners, live music, and dancing. Lobster and steaks cooked over a mesquite grill are the specialties. Open for dinner only. Reservations necessary. Across the street from the *Camino Real,* Av. Camarón Sábalo (phone: 140101).

MODERATE

Anifanti It's hard to miss a place like this, where an airplane sticks out over the front door. The interior is more subdued, and the Italian food is very tasty. Try the lamb au jus. Reservations unnecessary. 550 Av. Camarón Sábalo (phone: 142000).

El Jardín This eatery serves shrimp, fish, hamburgers, and salad in a traditional Mexican setting. Open for breakfast and lunch only; closed Mondays. Reservations unnecessary. In the *Plaza Gaviotas Hotel,* across from the *Playa Mazatlán Hotel* (phone: 134322).

Mamucas Some say this is the best seafood restaurant in all Mexico, though few tourists know about it. The ambience is unpretentious and family-oriented, with the tables pushed close together. Everything from the kitchen is great, but the specialty is *parrillada de mariscos* (seafood for two, grilled in an earthen pot). Closed Mondays. No reservations. Downtown at 404 Simón Bolívar Pte., two blocks from Paseo Claussen (phone: 113490).

El Marinero Stop at this popular place for a fresh seafood lunch or, in the evening, for dinner and a mariachi serenade. Dinner is often cooked tableside on a charcoal brazier. The friendly waiters will offer good advice on what to eat and what to see. Reservations advised. Near the harbor, at 530 5 de Mayo Nte. (phone: 117682).

El Parador Español Spanish dishes are the specialty in this dining spot with a charming outdoor terrace. Reservations advised. Av. Camarón Sábalo, next to *El Cid* resort (phone: 130767).

El Patio The rustic decor in this intimate, cozy eatery includes a bale of hay and a collection of oversize wooden spoons hanging from the ceiling. A good place to start the evening with a cocktail, followed by some seafood. A real find. Reservations advised. 30 Av. del Mar (phone: 117301).

El Shrimp Bucket Something of a national shrine, this is where the late Carlos Anderson (of *Carlos 'n' Charlie's* fame) got his start. It's a trifle more sedate than some of his other places: There's dancing to a marimba band on the patio and romantic music indoors. Reservations unnecessary. In *La Siesta Hotel,* 11 Av. Olas Altas (phone: 116350 or 128019).

INEXPENSIVE

La Cueva A large, family-style place where the grilled fish is the hands-down favorite. Open for breakfast, lunch, and dinner. Reservations advised. 2002 Av. del Mar (phone: 127802).

Doney's Good Mexican food is served in this rambling old house, a local favorite. Open for breakfast, lunch, and dinner. Reservations advised for groups of eight or more. 610 Mariano Escobedo (phone: 112651).

Lario's A good choice for Mexican food, especially seafood chowder. Reservations advised for groups of eight or more. 413 Rodolfo T. Loaiza (phone: 141767).

Pekin Here you'll find the best Chinese food in town. Reservations advised. Near the cathedral at 4 Benito Juárez Nte. (phone: 113330).

Mérida

(pronounced *May*-ree-dah)

The capital of the state of Yucatán and, with about a million people, the only city of significant size on the peninsula, Mérida was founded on January 6, 1542, by Spanish nobleman Don Francisco Montejo. After he razed the Maya city of T'Ho, Montejo salvaged the debris and quarried the local pyramids for stone to construct a "Christian" settlement on the same site, modeled in the Romanesque style of his birthplace: Mérida, Spain. In June of the same year, 250 Spaniards fought off between 40,000 and 60,000 Maya who were laying siege to the six-month-old city, a battle that marked the end of the Maya era and signaled the beginning of a system in which large tracts of land were owned by the Spanish and worked by native inhabitants. It wasn't until the 1930s that a more equitable system of distribution attempted to give the Yucatán's indigenous inhabitants a fairer stake in the land their families had lived on for centuries. (As can be seen from the protests and uprising that began in southern Mexico in January 1994 and still continue today, the question of equitable land distribution in Mexico is far from settled.)

Mérida is an excellent base for excursions to the Maya ruins of *Chichén Itzá, Uxmal, Sayil,* and *Kabah,* which are among the world's most remarkable testimonies to a historic civilization. (See *Archaeological Zones,* below, and the *Yucatán Peninsula* route in DIRECTIONS.) The Maya were heir to the Olmec culture, the first Mesoamerican civilization. The Olmec, who lived along the southern gulf coast in what is now the state of Tabasco, mysteriously appeared around 1200 BC. Known for their ability to move giant 10-ton stones over long distances by water, they built giant temples, were sculptors of great facility—carving giant basalt heads as well as intricate jade miniatures—and devised the Mexican calendar later used by the Maya, Toltec, Aztec, and others. At its height, the Olmec influence reached from the Valley of Mexico in the north to the land that is now Guatemala and El Salvador, but by the time of Jesus Christ, they disappeared as mysteriously as they had emerged.

The Maya culture spanned the centuries between the disappearance of the Olmec and the coming of the Spanish. They were the most advanced of the pre-Columbian Mexican civilizations, with a highly developed social structure, a vast knowledge of astronomy and mathematics, and a system of hieroglyphics. Their amazing accomplishments include the erection of immense terraced pyramids and other places of worship, whose walls, portals, and stairways were embellished with frescoes and stone carvings. By the 8th century, the Maya controlled the entire Yucatán Peninsula.

The Maya culture flourished until the 10th century, when the Toltec, a militaristic branch of the Nahuatl, seized control of the peninsula. The brutality of the Toltec was expressed in their art and their warfare. *Chichén Itzá* reveals dramatic evidence of this fierce stylistic influence in sculptures with jaguar motifs, feathered serpents, birds of prey holding human hearts in their claws, and frescoes depicting human sacrifice. The invaders and inhabitants of the area around Mérida became more integrated between the 10th and 13th centuries, however, and a new culture emerged: the Maya-Toltec. The excavations of *Chichén Itzá,* begun in 1923, have yielded a great deal of information on the merging of the two cultures. After three centuries of serving as the chief ceremonial center for the Maya-Toltec, *Chichén Itzá* was abandoned; within the next hundred years, the Maya-Toltec civilization declined, although people of Maya descent still live in the region.

With various good hotels and restaurants, excellent museums, a plethora of charming colonial buildings, and proximity to so many compelling archaeological ruins, Mérida is in some ways the ideal Mexican city, offering the visitor a full range of modern amenities while at the same time affording insight into the area's Maya heritage and its colonial past.

Mérida At-a-Glance

SEEING THE CITY

An enjoyable way to get a sense of the city is to take a ride around town in a *calesa,* or horse-drawn buggy (see *Getting Around*).

SPECIAL PLACES

Except for a few main boulevards, most streets in Mérida are numbered rather than named. It's helpful to remember that all east-west streets have odd numbers; north-south streets have even numbers. To get a feeling for the city, start at the *zócalo,* Plaza de la Independencia. The most interesting sites, shops, hotels, and restaurants are within three blocks of the *zócalo,* and walking is pleasant and easy.

DOWNTOWN

PLAZA DE LA INDEPENDENCIA (ZÓCALO) Mérida's main plaza has a wheel-and-spokes pattern and carefully tended hedges. It is especially inviting at sunset, a good time to sit on a bench and people-watch.

CASA DE MONTEJO Now a bank, this lovely 16th-century Spanish colonial home was the residence of the Montejo family. It originally covered an entire block, and even though only a section remains, it is still impressive. The large rooms were built around two patios and furnished with imported European furniture. Most telling is the stone carving around the entrance door of the Montejo coat of arms, flanked on each side by a conquistador with a foot on the head of a Maya. The figures on top are of Adelantado Montejo, his wife, Beatriz, and their daughter Catalina. Closed afternoons and weekends. On the south side of the plaza.

CATEDRAL This majestic twin-towered church, completed in 1598, was designed by Juan Miguel de Agüero, the architect of *Morro Castle* in Havana, Cuba. Above the entrance is the royal coat of arms of Spain; inside is the *Capilla del Cristo de las Ampollas* (Chapel of Christ of the Blisters), with a replica of a statue reputed to have been carved in the early 17th century from the wood of a tree that burned all night but was found untouched the next morning. (The original statue was destroyed when the cathedral was burned during the Mexican Revolution of 1910.) On the east side of the plaza (no phone).

PALACIO DE GOBIERNO (STATEHOUSE) Absolutely not to be missed. Walk into the courtyard and up the back stairs; all the murals lining the walls are by Francisco Castro Pacheco, a leading contemporary *yucateco* artist. On the second floor of the building is the *Sala de Historia* (Hall of History), the most handsome room in all of Mérida. Open daily. No admission charge. On the north side of the plaza at the corner of Calles 60 and 61 (no phone).

IGLESIA FRANCISCANA DE LA ORDEN TERCERA (FRANCISCAN CHURCH OF THE THIRD ORDER) Frequently used for fashionable weddings, this is perhaps the prettiest church in town. East side of Calle 60 at the corner of Calle 59 (no phone).

LA ERMITA DE SANTA ISABEL (HERMITAGE OF ST. ISABEL) This tiny travelers chapel, built in 1742, is notable for the Maya statuary in its gardens. Its small interior botanical garden is a wonderful place to relax. Four blocks from the plaza between Calles 66 and 64 (no phone).

PASEO DE MONTEJO Wealthy 19th-century residents built splendid homes along this wide faux-Parisian boulevard, which is lined with trees, small palaces, chalets, and extravagant monuments. Most of the old mansions have been converted to hotels, restaurants, or banks. Make sure you stop at the giant *Monumento a la Patria* (literally "Monument to the Homeland"), which depicts Mexico's history from the pre-Columbian era to the 20th century.

MUSEO DE ANTROPOLOGÍA E HISTORIA One of the finest provincial museums in Mexico, it beautifully depicts the Maya lifestyle. A visit here prior to touring the ruins helps bring Maya history into focus. The museum is housed in the *Palacio Cantón,* the largest and perhaps loveliest of the mansions on the Paseo de Montejo and the former residence of Yucatán's governors. Closed Mondays. Admission charge. Entry is on Calle 43 (phone: 230055).

LOS ARCOS (THE ARCHES) Mérida was once a walled city with 13 Moorish arches, of which only three remain today. One is the *Arco de San Juan* (Arch of St. John), about five blocks south of the plaza on Calle 64 in *Parque San Juan* (San Juan Park), which has a statue of Rachel at the well near its central fountain. This arch leads to *La Ermita de Santa Isabel* (see above). The *Arco del Dragón* (Dragon Arch) is near the Dragones military regiment headquarters at Calles 50 and 61. The third, *Arco del Puente* (Bridge Arch), is at Calles 50 and 63.

MUSEO NACIONAL DE ARTE POPULAR (NATIONAL FOLK ART MUSEUM) This small museum is worth the hike from downtown. On display are masks, pottery, clothing, and other examples of *yucateco* arts and crafts. Upstairs there is an excellent—though completely unorganized—collection of folk art from all over the country. The shop on the first floor boasts incredibly reasonable prices. Closed Sundays and Mondays. No admission charge. On Calle 59 between Calles 48 and 50 (no phone).

ARCHAEOLOGICAL ZONES

CHICHÉN ITZÁ Some of the most dramatic ruins in all of Mexico, these cover 7 square miles. Plumed serpents, carved in stone, appear everywhere in this place, whose name means "at the mouth of the well of the Itzá" (a Maya tribe). Open daily. No admission charge on Sundays. About 100 miles (160 km) east of Mérida on Route 180 (no phone). For additional details, see *Mexico's Magnificent Archaeological Heritage* in DIVERSIONS.

UXMAL (pronounced Oosh-*mal*) Not as large as *Chichén Itzá* but equally fascinating, this was the major site of the Classic period of the Maya civilization. Open daily. No admission charge on Sundays. About 50 miles (80 km) south of Mérida on Route 180 (no phone). For additional details, see *Mexico's Magnificent Archaeological Heritage* in DIVERSIONS.

DZIBILCHALTÚN (pronounced Zee-beel-chal-*toon*) This archaeological site is believed to have been inhabited longest by the Maya—from about 500 BC until the arrival of the conquistadores around AD 1500. The *Temple of the Seven Dolls* is especially interesting during the spring and autumn equinoxes, when light is reflected through parts of this strange structure. The cenote (sinkhole) can be used for a welcome dip. Open daily. No admission charge on Sundays. About 13 miles (21 km) north of Mérida, just off the road to Progreso (no phone).

KABAH This ceremonial center was built in the same architectural style as *Uxmal,* 14 miles (23 km) to the northwest. Now undergoing extensive restoration, *Kabah* is most notable for its *Palace of the Masks,* whose façade is covered with carved masks of the rain god Chac. Also here is the great arch, gateway to the ancient causeway linking this city with *Uxmal.* Open daily. No admission charge on Sundays (no phone).

SAYIL AND LABNÁ Little of either of these two ceremonial centers has been restored, but it is still possible to appreciate the fine sculpture and carvings that decorate the façades of their palaces. Both sites are open daily. No admission charge on Sundays. *Sayil* is 20 miles (32 km) southeast of *Uxmal* via a paved road; *Labná* is 5 miles (8 km) farther (no phone for either site).

GRUTAS DE LOLTÚN The largest known cave in the Yucatán was inhabited by hundreds of Maya people from as far back as 4,000 years ago until the late 1800s. Access is via a guided tour (available in English, Spanish, and German). The high points include ancient petroglyphs, rock paintings, stalactites that produce musical notes when struck, and a strange subterranean forest called *"El Mundo Perdido"* (the lost world), lit only by a small ray of sunlight shining through a hole in the ceiling. The cave is located 9 miles (15 km) east of *Labná* on the paved road off Route 261. It's open daily; there's no admission charge on Sundays (no phone). There's an additional charge for the guided tour.

ALSO OUTSIDE MÉRIDA

HACIENDA YAXOCOPOIL Twenty miles (32 km) south of Mérida, this was once one of the most important *henequén* (sisal) plantations in the Yucatán, covering more than 22,000 acres and maintaining 1,000 head of cattle. Though much smaller now, the plantation is still in operation, and visitors can watch *henequén* being processed. Part of the main house has been converted into a museum, which is open daily. No admission charge (no phone).

PROGRESO Twenty-three miles (37 km) north of Mérida on the Gulf of Mexico, this shipping port is the hub of the Yucatán's international commerce. The 2-mile-long pier—the longest in the world—accommodates large freighters and cruise ships. Progreso also has miles of golden, sandy beaches offering swimming, water skiing, and fishing, as well as many good seafood restaurants. Until only a few years ago, the town was known only by *meridiños* and a handful of US expatriates, but its fame as a quiet place to get away from it all is spreading fast.

CELESTÚN This nature preserve is located 58 miles (93 km) west of Mérida on Route 281. It is the home of the *National Center for the Study of Aquatic Birds,* and about 230 species of waterfowl live here. A boat and guide can be hired for a two-and-a-half-hour tour of the marshes to the flamingos' feeding grounds. During the mating season (April through May), there can be as many as 100,000 flamingos at any given site. As they fly through the air, the birds create a huge, awe-inspiring pink cloud that sails gracefully overhead.

EXTRA SPECIAL

The *Grutas de Balankanchén* (Balankanchén Caverns), only 5 miles (8 km) from the ruins at *Chichén Itzá,* lay sealed for 500 years. Their beauty is impressive, and entering them today gives one the feeling of stepping into sacred space. In fact, the Maya once held religious ceremonies here. The passageways are narrow and steep, and even small children have to stoop sometimes; those prone to claustrophobia stand forewarned. At the end of the caves is a perfectly clear pool; looking into it gives the impression of peering into a canyon. Groups are limited to a minimum of three and a maximum of 15 (oxygen gets scarce fast). Tours in English, which last 45 minutes, are given to groups of five or more by local guides from 9 AM to 4 PM, with a break from noon to 2 PM, or can be arranged through travel agencies in Mérida. Open daily. Admission charge (no phone).

Sources and Resources

TOURIST INFORMATION

The best source of information about Mérida is your hotel's travel desk or desk clerk or the tourist information center in the *Teatro Peón Contreras* (59 Calle 60; phone: 249290), which is open daily. A city-run program called *Mérida a Domingo* (Mérida on Sunday) sponsors entertainment at all parks and plazas, including an antiques fair at *Parque Santa Lucía;* events schedules are posted on the bulletin board at the *Casa de la Cultura* (Calle 63 between Calles 64 and 66; phone: 285576 or 285707).

LOCAL COVERAGE The free local publication *Yucatán Today* provides tips on what to see and do, information on local history and customs, and good maps of the downtown area; it's available at hotels and the tourist office. Surprisingly, another good city map is the placemat in the coffee shop of *Los Aluxes* hotel (see *Checking In*).

TELEPHONE The city code for Mérida is 99. *Note:* Mexico's telephone company has embarked on a major expansion project that involves changing telephone numbers in many areas of the country. At press time, all numbers listed in this chapter were correct. However, if you have any difficulties reaching attractions listed here, contact the local tourist office.

CLIMATE AND CLOTHES It is almost always hot in Mérida, with daytime temperatures ranging between 85F and 95F (29C to 35C) and nighttime temperatures between 70F and 80F (21C and 27C). During January and early February, you may need a sweater, especially at night. The weather is generally tropical, with high humidity; the rainy season is in the summer. Dress is casual, though shorts are not typical attire. When visiting the ruins, be sure to wear slacks and sturdy shoes.

GETTING AROUND

BUS Routes are marked on the front of the buses, which stop at every corner; the fare is 1 new peso (about 13¢). Buses to the archaeological zones leave from the terminal at Calle 69. First and second class service is available to *Uxmal.* A special express bus to the sound-and-light show leaves at 5:15 PM and returns when the last show is over. Deluxe buses to *Chichén Itzá* depart at 6:30 and 8:30 AM. Buses to the nearby port of Progreso leave from Calle 62 between Calles 65 and 67 every half hour.

CALESA These quaint horse-drawn buggies can be hired to take you around town. Pick one up at the plaza. A ride to Paseo de Montejo or *Parque Centenario,* the large westside city park that houses the zoo, and back should take about an hour. Be sure to bargain with the driver before getting in.

CAR RENTAL *Avis* (phone: 283152), *Budget* (phone: 272708), *Hertz* (phone: 249187 or 242834), and *National* (phone: 259855) all have offices at the airport.

TAXI Cabs can be rented by the hour or on a per-trip basis; settle the price before starting. *Colectivos* (jitneys) travel set routes, picking up and depositing passengers along the way. They cost 3 pesos (about 40¢) to travel anywhere within the city limits.

TOURS Mérida's numerous tour operators provide a good way to see the archaeological ruins and other sights; make arrangements through your hotel travel desk.

SPECIAL EVENTS

Parades, dancing, and musical events take place during the week of *Carnaval,* leading up to *Miércoles de Ceniza* (Ash Wednesday). A fiesta in honor of *Nuestra Señora de Guadalupe* (Our Lady of Guadalupe) in the San Sebastián parish runs from December 12 through 14.

SHOPPING

The most popular native crafts are bags and placemats made of sisal, an agave fiber. Yucatecan hammocks made of fine cotton thread (check the weave—the more threads per inch, the better the hammock) are a great buy; another is the *jipi,* a fine version of the Panama hat, made by hand of palm fiber near Mérida. *Guayaberas* (tailored men's dress shirts with embroidered fronts), *huipiles* (embroidered dresses worn by Maya women), huaraches (braided sandals), mosquito netting, silver, and gold filigree can be found in shops throughout Mérida.

The *mercado* (public market) on the corner of Calles 56 and 67 is a good place to find local crafts. The *García Rejón* handicrafts market (Calles 65 and 62) is usually less expensive than most places in town, provided you have the patience to bargain. (Stores usually have fixed prices, so you can't bargain.) At the *Plaza Internacional* (Calle 58 at Calle 59; phone: 248060), you'll find a dozen small shops, including fashion boutiques, art galleries, arts and crafts boutiques, and a bookstore, all housed in a stately 300-year-old mansion two blocks north of the *zócalo.* The main shopping streets are Calles 57 and 59 in the 10-block area between Calles 54 and 64. Most shops open between 8 and 9 AM, close for lunch and a siesta from 1 to 4 PM, and then reopen until 8 or 9 PM. Most stores, except those in shopping malls, are closed on Sundays. Some shops to explore:

La Canasta This unusual little boutique specializes in locally designed dresses and shirts made from Indonesian-like batik with Mexican motifs. Good quality and reasonable prices. 500 Calle 60, at Calle 61 (phone: 281978).

Casa de las Artesanías There is no bargaining at this government-run store, which offers consistently high-quality handicrafts. 503 Calle 63, between Calles 64 and 66 (phone: 235392).

Casa de los Jipis This is the place to buy a handmade *jipi* Panama hat. Many street vendors in town sell straw imitations of the *jipi* for about $5, but if you want the real McCoy, shop here and expect to pay between $20 and $70 (depending on the quality of the fiber and the weave). 526 Calle 56, at Calle 65 (phone: 213002).

Fábrica de Guayaberas Jack Variations on the traditional *guayabera;* the best are 100% cotton. 507 Calle 59, between Calles 60 and 62 (phone: 215988).

México Lindo Hand-crafted silver jewelry, many pieces with a Maya theme. Worth browsing through even if you aren't planning to buy. 486G Calle 60, between Calles 55 and 57 (no phone).

Rolly's A good selection of ceramic stoneware, papier-mâché, onyx, and other typical handicrafts at reasonable prices. 527 Calle 59, between Calles 64 and 66 (phone: 234065).

SPORTS

BASEBALL The baseball season runs from March through August. The baseball stadium is in *Parque Kukulcán;* local company-sponsored teams play here. Consult the tourist office for additional details.

BULLFIGHTING Bullfights are held on Sundays throughout the year, but the big-name matadors usually perform only from January through March. The *Plaza de Toros Mérida* is on Paseo de la Reforma, a block from Avenida Colón. Consult the tourist office for additional details.

GOLF F. Mier y Terán designed the par 72, 18-hole course at *Club de Golf La Ceiba,* 9 miles (14 km) north of Mérida at Km 14 of Rte. 261 (phone: 247525). There's a greens fee, and clubs—but not electric carts—are available for rent.

SWIMMING Almost all the hotels have small swimming pools. There are nice beaches, with good water skiing, 23 miles (37 km) north, at Progreso (see *Special Places*) and Telchac Puerto.

TENNIS The *Holiday Inn* has one court (see *Checking In*); non-guests may play here for a fee. *Club Campestre de Mérida* (phone: 271100) has 16 clay and synthetic lighted courts, and there are several courts at *Club de Golf La Ceiba* (see *Golf,* above).

NIGHTCLUBS AND NIGHTLIFE

The municipal government sponsors concerts and dance performances at various sites around the city every night but Saturday; for the current schedule, check at the tourist office (see *Tourist Information*). The *Calinda Panamericana Mérida* (see *Checking In*) has a Mexican fiesta Friday and Saturday evenings and regional dances other nights. *Los Tulipanes* (462-A Calle 42; phone: 272009) has performances of native and Cuban-style dancing. The *Trovador Bohemio* (550 Calle 55; phone: 230385) and the *Peregrina Piano Bar* (by *Parque Santa Lucía;* no phone) both offer drinks and relaxed entertainment, including guitar music. The *Holiday Inn*'s nightclub (see

Checking In) is also popular, as is *Studio 58* in the *Maya Continental* hotel (483 Calle 58; phone: 235395).

Best in Town

CHECKING IN

For a double room, expect to pay $100 to $160 per night in an expensive hotel; $60 to $95 in a moderate place; and $55 or less in an inexpensive one. Unless otherwise noted, the hotels listed below have air conditioning, TV sets, and telephones in the rooms. All telephone numbers are in the 99 city code unless otherwise indicated.

EXPENSIVE

Fiesta Americana Mérida The city's newest and most luxurious hotel has 350 spacious rooms equipped with mini-bars, marble baths, terry cloth robes, fresh flowers, and in-room, pay-per-view movies. The building is a larger version of the Paseo de Montejo mansions of the 1920s (see *Downtown,* above), and the restaurant serves continental fare. Av. Colón at Paseo de Montejo (phone: 421111; 800-FIESTA-1 in the US; 800-50450 in Mexico; fax: 421112).

Holiday Inn A colonial-style hotel, it features 213 rooms and suites, all equipped with mini-bars, satellite TV, and views of either the swimming pool or a large fountain. The "Executive Class" rooms on the top floor also boast such amenities as nightly turndown service, terry cloth robes, hair dryers, and valet service. Facilities include a tennis court, a nightclub, and a restaurant. Off Paseo de Montejo at 498 Av. Colón and Calle 60 (phone: 256877; 800-HOLIDAY in the US; 800-00999 in Mexico; fax: 257755).

Hyatt Regency The tallest building in town, this 17-story establishment features ultra-elegant contemporary styling, from its vast polished stone and brass lobby to the 299 large, luxuriously appointed guestrooms. A favorite of politicians visiting the capital of the state of Yucatán, the hotel features conference facilities and business-oriented services. There is an elegant restaurant. Av. Colón at Av. 60 (phone: 420202; 800-228-9000 in the US; 800-00500 in Mexico; fax: 257002).

MODERATE

Los Aluxes An impressive and modern 109-room hostelry with an outdoor pool and poolside bars, a dining room, and a cheerful coffee shop. 444 Calle 60, between Calles 49 and 51 (phone: 242199; 800-782-8395; fax: 233858).

Calinda Panamericana Mérida A Quality Inns property, it has 110 modern rooms, a restaurant, and a bar. Downtown, at 455 Calle 59 (phone: 239111; 800-228-5151 in the US; 800-90000 in Mexico; fax: 248090).

El Castellano With 170 rooms, it's one of Mérida's largest and sleekest hotels. Amenities include shops, a restaurant, a bar, and a pool. 513 Calle 57, between Calles 62 and 64 (phone: 230100; fax: 230110).

D'Champs In this 88-room property are two restaurants, a pool, and numerous small boutiques. 543 Calle 70 (phone: 248655; fax: 236024).

Del Gobernador Tidy and tasteful, this 61-room spot offers a good restaurant, live music several times a week, and a very small pool. All rooms have ceiling fans and most have air conditioning. 535 Calle 59 at Calle 66 (phone: 237133; 800-223-4084; fax: 281590).

María del Carmen The modern-looking exterior of this 100-room Best Western property belies its charmingly colonial interior. Among its draws are a garden courtyard, a very good dining room, a bar, and a gift shop. 550 Calle 63 between Calles 68 and 70 (phone: 239133; 800-528-1234; fax 239290).

Mérida Misión Park Inn The 147 rooms are located in a modern tower. There's a good restaurant and a popular piano bar. Three blocks from the *zócalo,* at 491 Calle 60 (phone: 239500; 800-44-UTELL; fax: 237665).

Montejo Palace This is a quiet place, with 90 rooms, some with small balconies. In addition to a dining room and a good coffee shop, there is a popular cocktail lounge and a pool. 483C Paseo de Montejo (phone: 247644; 800-221-6509; 718-253-9400 in New York City; fax: 280388).

Paseo de Montejo A modern establishment under the same management as the neighboring *Montejo Palace,* it has 92 rooms, a restaurant, a bar, and a pool. 482 Paseo de Montejo (phone: 239033; fax: 280388).

Residencial This flamingo-toned, *Gone with the Wind*–style mansion has 66 spacious rooms, plus an elegant dining room and a large pool. 589 Calle 59 at Calle 76 (phone: 243899 or 243099; 800-826-6842; fax: 240266).

INEXPENSIVE

Gran Hotel This replica of a turn-of-the-century French hotel has elaborate ceilings, columns, and 31 large, old-fashioned rooms (some are air conditioned). The five-story building centers around a delightful patio. There is a good dining room. In *Parque Cepeda Peraza* (Cepeda Peraza Park), also known as *Parque Hidalgo,* 1½ blocks north of the *zócalo* (phone: 99-247730; fax: 99-247622).

Posada Toledo This small (20 rooms) hotel was built at the turn of the century as the home of a prominent local politician. The rooms, which open onto a courtyard overgrown with flowering plants, vary from dark and cramped to palatially elegant. Ask to see the room before agreeing to rent it. All rooms have ceiling fans, but do not have air conditioning, TV sets, or telephones. Calle 58 at Calle 57 (phone: 232256; fax: 231690).

EATING OUT

Very little chili pepper is used in *yucateco* cooking, although it is served alongside the main dish as a sauce. Pickled and charcoal-broiled meat is a Yucatecan specialty. Try the *panuchos* (open-face tortillas topped with chicken and pickled onion); *cochinita* or *pollo pibil* (pork or chicken, respectively, baked in banana leaves); or *papadzul* (a tortilla filled with chopped hard-boiled eggs and topped with a sauce of ground pumpkin seeds).

Expect to pay up to $40 for a meal for two in an expensive restaurant; about $15 to $25 at a moderate one; and under $15 at an inexpensive one. Prices do not include drinks, wine, tax, or tip. Reservations are advised at midday for all expensive places. In the evening, reservations are unnecessary unless otherwise noted. Most restaurants below accept MasterCard and Visa, and a few also accept American Express and Diners Club; it's a good idea to call ahead and check. Unless otherwise noted, all restaurants are open daily for lunch and dinner. All telephone numbers are in the 99 city code unless otherwise indicated.

EXPENSIVE

Alberto's Continental Patio This lovely colonial mansion with outdoor and indoor dining areas features first-rate Lebanese dishes and very friendly service. 482 Calle 64 (phone: 212298).

La Casona There's an interior courtyard with a lovely fountain, plus an inside dining room, whose bar sports antique barber's chairs. Italian food, including homemade pasta, is the highlight; the steaks and seafood rate, too. There's a good wine list. 434 Calle 60 at Calle 47 (phone: 238348).

Château Valentín In an elegant converted 18th-century home, this establishment serves such well-prepared regional specialties as *pollo pibil* and *pzic venado* (a venison dish) as well as international fare. 499D Calle 58-A (phone: 256367).

Le Gourmet Once an elegant home, it specializes in French and creole cooking and is where the local gentry go for their big nights out. 109A Av. Pérez Ponce (phone: 271970).

Pancho's The owner is Canadian and the menu is continental, with lots of flambéed dishes prepared tableside. With its old photos and Victrola, it resembles an antiques store. There's live music and dancing Wednesdays through Saturdays. Open for dinner only. 509 Calle 59, between Calles 60 and 62 (phone: 230942).

Picadilly's The decor in this English-style pub is elegant, but dress is casual (ties and jackets are not required), and the fine food—ribs, onion rings, pasta, grilled beef, and cherry cheesecake—is strictly American. There's live music and dancing Friday and Saturday evenings. 118 Av. Pérez Ponce (phone: 265280).

Yannig Named after its inspired chef, this sophisticated spot delivers well-prepared, appetizingly presented dishes, among them crêpes with a mild Roquefort sauce, New Orleans–style chicken, and *kermor* (fish and mushrooms in a pastry shell). Closed Mondays. Reservations advised. 105 Av. Pérez Ponce (phone: 270339).

MODERATE

Los Almendros This is one of the best places to sample the finest *cochinita* or *pollo pibil, panuchos, papadzul,* and other Yucatecan delicacies. Service is slow, so be prepared to spend a long time here. 493 Calle 50-A, between Calles 57 and 59, across from the Plaza de Mejorada (phone: 212851).

El Pórtico del Peregrino This low-key place has a chapel-like setting, with meals served in romantic courtyards and dining rooms. The atmosphere is enhanced by such dishes as shrimp grilled in garlic, chicken liver shish kebab, baked eggplant casserole with chicken, delicious desserts, and homemade sangria. Calle 57 between Calles 60 and 62 (phone: 216844).

La Prosperidad A local favorite, it serves Yucatecan dishes in a large, thatch-roofed dining room. A variety of appetizers accompanies each meal. Entertainment is live and lively, as is the ambience. 456 Calle 56 (phone: 240764).

El Tucho In this rustic, thatch-roofed restaurant, diners can savor some of the finest Yucatecan dishes in town, as well as several Cuban specialties (the chef is from Havana). There is live entertainment day and night; occasionally, it takes on a cabaret atmosphere, but mostly there's Cuban music or a Yucatán folk dance group. 482 Calle 60, between 55 and 57 (phone: 242323).

INEXPENSIVE

El Faisán y El Venado Now in its fifth decade, this rustic place has become a Mérida tradition. The decor includes a giant (albeit crude) replica of the main pyramid at *Chichén Itzá,* cement Maya figures, and glyphs along the cracked walls. Some of the best Yucatecan food in the city is served here. There's also live organ music all day and night. Night owls will appreciate the daily 7 AM to 3 AM schedule. 618 Calle 59 (phone: 286362).

Mexico City

To describe Mexico City is to describe much of Mexico. It is the political, cultural, social, and economic center of the country, a city whose metropolitan area includes anywhere from 18 million to 22 million people (estimates vary widely) and whose population within official city limits may be the world's largest. Everything that is Mexican originates or is represented here, and Mexicans call it simply Mexico, just as Americans refer to New York City as New York. In fact, the city gave its name to the country when, after independence, the colonial designation New Spain was dropped. It is the one destination that virtually all visitors to Mexico share, the common terminus of the major north-south highways, and the best place from which to start tours of the Yucatán Peninsula, the jungles of Chiapas, and the southern reaches of Mexico's long Pacific Coast.

Mexico City is one of the oldest continuously inhabited areas in North America. Some 20,000 years ago the entire Valle de Anáhuac (now called the Valley of Mexico), an 883-square-mile plain more than 7,000 feet above sea level and ringed by mountains rising some 3,000 feet higher, was no more than a series of lakes dotted with islands and divided by masses of spongy land. (Indeed, *anáhuac* is Nahuatl—the Aztec language—for "land by the water.") Around those lakes and islands grew small, independent villages whose inhabitants developed a relatively sophisticated agricultural lifestyle.

In 1325 (1321 in some accounts), the Aztec, seeking a site for a permanent home, were said to have wandered into the valley and to have seen an eagle perched on a cactus while devouring a snake. (The same image now appears on the flag of Mexico.) The Aztec built their city on the surrounding site, calling it Tenochtitlán, and built a temple on the spot where the eagle appeared. Directly adjacent, in the area that became Mexico City's *zócalo,* or central square, was built the palace of Montezuma (or Moctezuma, as the Aztec emperor is called in Nahuatl and in Spanish).

Within two centuries, the aggressive Aztec had managed to conquer all the surrounding territory, and they extracted taxes in the form of produce, slaves, and precious metal from tribes as far away as Veracruz and Guatemala. In 1519, when Hernán Cortés entered the city, he found a metropolis of some 500,000 people spread across several islands with subtly engineered bridges and sluices, wide avenues, great temples, marketplaces, and public buildings that rivaled any in Europe. Bernal Díaz del Castillo, whose journals record Cortés's conquest, declared that Tenochtitlán was a more impressive city than Venice. Nevertheless, the Spanish, who ruled Mexico for the next three centuries, tore down all of the city's monuments and virtually leveled the rest of Tenochtitlán, often building churches and government buildings in the very spots where ancient temples had stood. In effect, they created a European clone on what had been the most glorious city in the Western Hemisphere.

But the city the Spanish built was spectacular in its own right. Most of Mexico City's important colonial landmarks are still standing. During Emperor Maximilian's reign (1864–67), the Paseo de la Reforma was laid out in a frank imitation of the Champs-Elysées in Paris. A walk down the Reforma, or from Eje Central Lázaro Cárdenas east to the *zócalo* along Avenida Francisco I. Madero (often shortened to Avenida Madero), offers an overview of much of the city's Spanish and other European heritage— from the ancient *Iglesia de San Francisco,* built by Cortés with stones taken from the Aztec temple that stood on the site, to the *Palacio de Iturbide,* the wonderfully preserved Baroque mansion of Agustín de Iturbide, Mexico's first ruler after independence from Spain.

The *zócalo* is still the very heart of the city—and of the country. Flanked by the *Palacio Nacional* (presidential office building), the two buildings that make up the city hall, the *Catedral Metropolitana,* and the *Monte de Piedad* (National Pawnshop), the *zócalo* has seen revolutions, coronations, and even Mexico's first bullfight. Over the years, the city simply spread out from the *zócalo,* Los Angeles–style. (The region comprising Mexico City is called the *Distrito Federal*—or Federal District, abbreviated "DF" in Spanish—which is governed through a mayor, or chief, appointed by the president.) In the last couple of decades high-rises have begun poking their penthouses into the smoggy clouds. The old suburbs, such as Coyoacán and San Angel to the south, have retained their identities, but they are surrounded by neighborhoods that all too often are concrete slums.

Anyone flying into the Valley of Mexico today is struck by the thick haze of smog hovering above the city. Much of it comes from Mexico City's vehicular traffic, a snarling mess at best. There are three million cars in use here—new, old, functioning, and only half-functioning—pouring noxious fumes into the thin air. The streets are seldom deserted in the metropolitan area: Traffic slacks off between 1 and 4 AM, but by 5 AM the buses are out in full force and the streets are clogged once again. The government has taken much-needed steps to improve Mexico City's air quality, although it remains among the world's most polluted cities. Restrictions on driving have been imposed, and in 1991 the government closed the city's largest government-run oil refinery, which is to be rebuilt outside the city.

Considering its size, it's not surprising that Mexico City is an easy place in which to get lost. Walking is perplexing; driving is downright maddening. Streets change names as they cross from one *colonia* (neighborhood) into another; only one, Insurgentes, keeps the same name as it runs the entire length of the city. Adding to the confusion are the many curving and diagonal streets, which run obstacle courses around the city's many small squares, parks, and traffic circles and create three- and five-sided blocks.

While Mexico City residents are justly considered demons behind the wheel of a car, on foot they revert to type. They stroll, often stopping in the middle of the sidewalk to talk. No green space is left empty, no park bench totally unoccupied. Constant nibblers, they have turned the coffee break into a sidewalk-sitting art. And who can blame them? Mexico City is a place to be studied, a city that assails the senses with everything from the smell of corn tortillas to the barking of street vendors and the cheery sight of flowers everywhere (even the dividing lanes of major highways have blooming garden plots).

Mexico City comes vibrantly alive on Sundays, the ideal day to explore. The best place to start is the floating gardens of *Xochimilco* (see *Special Places*). Sunday is also the best day for bullfights and for the big sidewalk art fair at *Parque Sullivan* (Sullivan Park), where Paseo de la Reforma crosses Avenida Insurgentes. There's a wide variety of paintings—not by nationally known artists (not yet, anyway), but often of high quality nevertheless. Best of all, the prices are right, the atmosphere festive. Sundays also bring the *Mercado Tepito* (often called the Thieves' Market in English), next to the *Mercado de la Lagunilla* (Lagunilla Market), where you can find anything from antique keys to carpets. There also are concerts and other types of live entertainment on Sundays in *Bosque de Chapultepec* (Chapultepec Park), a favorite picnicking and strolling venue for thousands of Mexican families.

Above all, Mexico City is resilient. In the face of pollution, overcrowding, and such natural disasters as the 1985 earthquake—which destroyed large parts of the city and necessitated massive reconstruction of the area around the *Alameda Central* (Alameda Park)—the city radiates an unstoppable verve and an appeal all its own. With all the splendor of antiquity, the wrenching sadness of poverty, and the glitter of modern times, Mexico City is a place that every traveler should experience at least once.

Mexico City At-a-Glance

SEEING THE CITY

The best view of Mexico City is from the observation deck of the 44-story *Torre Latinoamericana* (Latin American Tower) on the southeast corner of Eje Central Lázaro Cárdenas and Avenida Madero. One floor below is the *Muralto* restaurant and bar (phone: 510-3610 or 521-7751), where you can relax and enjoy the view. The *Majestic* hotel's rooftop restaurant, *La Terraza* (73 Av. Francisco I. Madero, just east of the *zócalo;* phone: 521-8601), offers a great view of the central square. The rooftop lounge of the *Sevilla Palace* (see *Checking In*) also provides a spectacular view, as do the terraces and rooftop garden of the *Castillo de Chapultepec* in *Bosque de Chapultepec* (see *Special Places*).

SPECIAL PLACES

Mexico City's top tourist attractions are for the most part concentrated in several distinct areas, each of which could be explored in a day or so.

Foremost is the historic area surrounding the *zócalo;* for shopping, there's the Zona Rosa (Pink Zone; see *Shopping*); for relaxation and museum-going, there's *Bosque de Chapultepec;* north of the city are the pyramids of Teotihuacán; and south are the strikingly beautiful *Universidad Nacional Autónoma de México* and the floating gardens at *Xochimilco.* Most museums and archaeological sites in Mexico City don't charge admission on Sundays and holidays.

ZÓCALO AND ENVIRONS

The true heart of the city, the *zócalo* is the second-largest square in the world (only Red Square in Moscow is larger). Completely restored over the past few years, this area has been officially designated the *Centro Histórico de la Ciudad de México* (Historic Center of Mexico City). It's now one great outdoor museum, as most of the buildings have been declared national monuments and have plaques telling something of their history. Paving blocks have replaced asphalt, and many streets are closed to cars. Turn-of-the-century electric globes now illuminate the neighborhood, and store merchants are toning down their more garish signs.

PALACIO NACIONAL Originally Cortés's headquarters, this structure later became the official residence of the Spanish viceroys. Emperor Maximilian had his offices here during his short reign, and so have all the presidents of Mexico since then. The building also houses the *Museo Benito Juárez* (Benito Juárez Museum), which displays many of Juárez's personal possessions and other memorabilia concerning this 19th-century politician who masterminded many of Mexico's economic and educational reforms. The museum is closed weekends; there's an admission charge (phone: 522-5646).

Of the *Palacio Nacional*'s three patios, only the center one, with its magnificent murals by Diego Rivera, is open to the public. Rivera used murals to illustrate the country's history of violence and social repression, as well as to expose its contemporary political and social problems. Typical of his work, the murals in the *Palacio Nacional,* which stretch over three walls, portray only two kinds of people: the good (the natives and the workers) and the evil (the Spanish conquerors—especially Cortés—the church, and the rich and powerful). For example, Cuauhtémoc, the last Aztec emperor, is shown as an idealized youth; Cortés as a demented syphilitic. The mural on the north wall represents Rivera's vision of pre-Hispanic life. The west wall depicts scenes from Mexico's colonial and modern history, including slavery, the Inquisition, the evangelizing of Catholic priests, the intervention of France and the United States, the dictatorship of Porfirio Díaz, General Santa Anna, independence, and, finally, the 1910 revolution. A huge portrait of Karl Marx, Rivera's idol and hope for the future, dominates the south wall.

Over the center portal hangs the historic bell of the church in the town of Dolores Hidalgo, which Padre Miguel Hidalgo rang in 1810 to rally his followers, the event that marked the beginning of the struggle for independence. Try to go in the late afternoon to see the changing of the guard. The central patio is open daily. No admission charge. East side of the *zócalo* (no phone).

CATEDRAL METROPOLITANA (METROPOLITAN CATHEDRAL) Its cornerstone was laid in 1562, but it took 250 years to complete this imposing edifice. As a result, it reflects the most popular architectural styles of the 16th, 17th, and 18th centuries. Several of the 14 chapels are done in the wildly ornamental Baroque style known as Churrigueresque, a word derived from the name of the Spanish artisan José Churriguera. The façade of the *sagrario* (chapel) next door is considered the finest example of Churrigueresque architecture in Mexico City. Extensive renovations, currently in progress, are likely to continue through 2006, but visitors are welcome inside during the process. North side of the *zócalo*.

MUSEO DE LAS CULTURAS (MUSEUM OF CULTURES) Here is a widely varied collection of artifacts and art objects from Southeast Asia, ancient Greece, Africa, Oceania, Japan, Israel, Egypt, northern Europe, and all the Americas. The 22 exhibition rooms surround a beautiful patio. Closed Mondays and holidays. Admission charge. North of the *Palacio Nacional*, at 13 Calle Moneda (phone: 542-0187).

MONTE DE PIEDAD (NATIONAL PAWNSHOP) Literally translated, the name means Mountain of Pity. Established in 1775 by Pedro Romero de Terreros, who was made a count in honor of his generous gifts to the King of Spain, the pawnshop still offers low-interest loans on personal property. Of particular interest is the large corner room, which has jewelry, and a smaller room on the inside passageway, which has antiques. Closed Sundays. Across from the cathedral, on the northwest corner of the *zócalo* (phone: 518-2013).

TEMPLO MAYOR (GREAT TEMPLE) In 1978, the *Templo Mayor* was discovered under the streets of the city by electric-company workers. Once the holiest shrine of the Aztec empire, it contained a wealth of artifacts, which can be seen in the fascinating *Museo del Templo Mayor*.

In an attempt to reproduce the concept of the temple itself, the spectacular museum is divided into two sections. The south wing is dedicated to Huitzilopochtli, the Aztec god of war. It provides background on how Tenochtitlán was settled, offering insights into the religious, political, and social structure of the Aztec, as well as the importance of war and sacrifice, tribute and commerce. The *Sala de Monolitos* (Hall of Monoliths) contains impressive sculptures found during the excavations, including the *Guerreros Aguila* (Eagle Warriors). The north wing, dedicated to the rain god Tlaloc, contains a reproduction of part of the temple, a scale model of the sacred city, an exhibit of the fauna found in the offerings, and another on aspects of daily life. Finally, one room presents versions of the conquest as depicted and related by the native inhabitants and by Hernán Cortés. Guided English-language tours of the site and the museum are available by appointment. Closed Mondays. Admission charge. 8 Av. Seminario, northeast of the cathedral and just north of the *Palacio Nacional* (phone: 542-0606).

PLAZA DE LAS TRES CULTURAS (PLAZA OF THE THREE CULTURES) The site of the final defeat of the Aztec, this plaza is in the middle of the Tlaltelolco housing development, much of which was destroyed by the 1985 earthquake. It now features the remains of a pre-Columbian pyramid, a Spanish colonial church, and the tall, modern *Secretaría de Relaciones Exteriores* (Foreign Relations Secretariat, or Foreign Ministry) building—three cultures standing side by side. Near the *Mercado Lagunilla,* about eight blocks north of Av. Madero.

EL CENTRO (DOWNTOWN)

PALACIO DE BELLAS ARTES (PALACE OF FINE ARTS) Construction of this Italian marble structure, which combines Maya, Mixtec, Art Nouveau, and Art Deco motifs, was started in 1900 under the regime of Porfirio Díaz. It was finished 34 years later at the then-staggering cost of $20 million. The structure is so heavy that it has sunk 18 feet into the city's spongy subsoil. Housed here is Mexico's best collection of works by Mexican artists David Alfaro Siqueiros, José Clemente Orozco, Rufino Tamayo, Juan O'Gorman, Miguel Camarena, and Diego Rivera, as well as works of major contemporary international artists. Most notable is Rivera's replica of his controversial mural for Rockefeller Center in New York City. Among other things, the mural featured a portrait of Lenin, which so horrified the Rockefellers that they ordered it painted over.

The *Ballet Folklórico* performs in the palace's opulent 3,500-seat theater, which contains a striking Tiffany stained glass curtain. The fern-filled bistro off the lobby is a delightful place for a meal or a snack. The art collection is closed Mondays and holidays. Admission charge to special exhibits only. Corner of Av. Juárez and Eje Central Lázaro Cárdenas (phone: 512-3633).

MUSEO NACIONAL DE ARTE (NATIONAL MUSEUM OF ART) Constructed during the Díaz administration, this magnificent building houses an excellent museum with paintings, sculpture, and graphics covering the history and development of Mexican art from its inception to the present. The collection includes works by landscape painter José María Velasco—Diego Rivera's teacher—that are considered among his best. Closed Mondays and holidays. Admission charge. 8 Calle Tacuba, a few steps from Eje Central Lázaro Cárdenas (phone: 512-3224).

CASA DE LOS AZULEJOS (HOUSE OF TILES) The story behind this handsome house, built in 1596, is interesting: The son of one of the Counts of Valle de Orizaba was considered a ne'er-do-well by his father, who once chastised him with the remark "You will never have a house of tiles," that is, "You will never make good." The son set to work and became very wealthy, and when he acquired this lovely house, he had every square inch of the façade covered with white and blue tiles. It's now occupied by *Sanborns,* a good retail chain that sells silver, crafts, and gift items. There's also a restaurant. Open daily. 4 Av. Francisco I. Madero (phone: 510-9613).

IGLESIA DE SAN FRANCISCO (CHURCH OF ST. FRANCIS) This church was built by Cortés with stones taken from the ruins of the Aztec temples. At one time the church was part of a vast Franciscan monastery, which was destroyed in the 1860s. Av. Madero, across from the *Casa de los Azulejos.*

MUSEO JOSÉ LUIS CUEVAS Here is the personal art collection—mostly Mexican and other Latin American works—of one of Mexico's most controversial contemporary artists. Dominating the central patio is Cuevas's gigantic bronze sculpture of an Amazonian woman bearing on her right knee a likeness of Cuevas's face—a "manifestation" that he said appeared by itself just days before the opening of the museum. Closed Mondays. No admission charge. 13 Calle Academia (phone: 542-8959).

PALACIO DE ITURBIDE (ITURBIDE PALACE) This beautiful 18th-century structure was the home of Agustín de Iturbide during his brief reign as Emperor of Mexico (1822–23). Later it became a hotel, then an office building. It is now used by Banamex (the largest bank in Mexico) as a museum for temporary exhibits. Open daily during exhibits only. No admission charge. 17 Av. Francisco I. Madero (phone: 255-3535).

MUSEO DE LA CIUDAD DE MÉXICO (MUSEUM OF MEXICO CITY) Once the mansion of the Count of Santiago, this striking building, with an intricately carved façade, now houses fine exhibits of the history of Mexico City. Graphic prints and maps depict early indigenous settlements and cities, and there are models of monuments, costumes, and furniture of past eras. One entire room off the courtyard is devoted to the history of transportation in Mexico City, while the second floor has wonderful photographs and portrayals of revolutionary leaders and of present-day life in the city. The third floor features the works of Mexican Impressionist painter Joaquín Clausell. Closed Mondays and holidays. Admission charge. 30 Calle Pino Suárez, at Calle República de El Salvador (phone: 542-0671). It's across the street from the *Iglesia de Jesús el Nazareno* (Church of Jesus of Nazareth), where Hernán Cortés was buried in 1547.

MUSEO EL BORCEGUÍ (SHOE MUSEUM) One of the few museums of its kind in the world (the name is an old Spanish word for "boot"), it contains miniatures in gold, silver, porcelain, wood, ivory, and candy, as well as music boxes, pincushions, and other items, all in the form of footwear. There's a total of 15,000 pairs of shoes here, dating from the 17th century to modern times. Closed Sundays. No admission charge. Located, appropriately enough, over Mexico's oldest and most successful shoe store, also called *El Borceguí,* at 27 Calle Bolívar (phone: 512-1311).

PLAZA DE SANTO DOMINGO Surrounded by historical buildings, this is one of the oldest and most beautifully preserved plazas in the city. *Evangelistas* (public scribes) and small printing operations set up their "offices" under the arches, typing out love notes and business letters for the illiterate. The building on the northeast corner of the plaza, now the *Museo de la Herbolaria* (Museum of Herbal Medicine), once served as the *Palacio de la Inquisición* (Headquarters of the Inquisition); the museum is closed Mondays, and there's no admission charge (no phone). Three blocks north of the *zócalo* at Calle República de Venezuela.

HOSPITAL DE JESÚS (HOSPITAL OF JESUS) This, the oldest continuously functioning hospital in the Americas, was founded by Cortés in 1527. Calles República de El Salvador and Pino Suárez.

ALAMEDA CENTRAL (ALAMEDA PARK) The charm of this gracious colonial park belies its former identity as the "Burning Place," where victims of the Inquisition were burned at the stake. The centerpiece of the park is the *Hemiciclo Juárez* (Juárez Hemicycle), a handsome marble monument built in 1919 to commemorate 100 years of independence. North side of Av. Juárez between Eje Central Lázaro Cárdenas and Paseo de la Reforma.

MUSEO DE LA ALAMEDA (MUSEUM OF THE ALAMEDA) The highlight here is the huge Diego Rivera mural called *Dream of a Sunday Afternoon in the Alameda,* which illustrates changes in the park through the centuries, as well as memories of the artist's youth. Closed Mondays. No admission charge. On the western edge of Jardín de la Solidaridad (Solidarity Plaza), facing Av. Juárez (phone: 521-1016).

MUSEO FRANZ MAYER The magnificently restored 16th-century *Ex-Hospital de la Mujer* (Former Women's Hospital) houses the awesome personal collection of Franz Mayer, a German-born financier. Mexican, European, and Oriental applied arts (silver, ceramics, textiles, furniture, and ivories) from the 16th to the 19th centuries, plus a model of an 18th-century pharmacy, make up most of the collection. There are Dutch, Flemish, and Italian Renaissance paintings, plus a library that contains 770 different editions of *Don Quixote.* Closed Mondays. Admission charge. Behind the *Alameda Central* on Plaza Santa Veracruz, at 45 Av. Hidalgo (phone: 518-2265).

MUSEO DE SAN CARLOS (MUSEUM OF SAN CARLOS) This restored mansion is Mexico's European art museum. The building was a wedding gift from Emperor Maximilian to Marshal Bazaine, then the commander of the French army in Mexico; it subsequently served as a cigarette factory, school, national lottery building, and post office. It now houses a superb collection of European paintings and sculptures, many of them donated by King Carlos III of Spain. Among its treasures are notable works by Peter Paul Rubens, Franz Hals, Tintoretto, Titian, El Greco, Van Dyck, Velázquez, Rembrandt,

Brueghel, Gainsborough, and Pissarro. Closed Tuesdays and holidays. Admission charge. 50 Calle Puente de Alvarado (phone: 592-3721).

MUSEO DE SAN ILDEFONSO (MUSEUM OF SAINT ILDEFONSO) Established in 1751 by the Jesuits as a preparatory school for children of wealthy Spanish colonists, this building later served as a medical school until 1864. The walls are decorated with works by some of Mexico's most important muralists, including Diego Rivera, David Alfaro Siqueiros, and José Clemente Orozco. Be sure to visit the *Salón Generalito,* where the original 16th-century wooden chairs are displayed. Closed Saturdays. Admission charge. 16 Justo Sierra, just behind the *Templo Mayor* (phone: 789-2505).

SECRETARÍA DE EDUCACIÓN PÚBLICA (SECRETARIAT OF PUBLIC EDUCATION) The walls and stairwells literally are covered with nearly 100 gloriously colorful murals by Diego Rivera and some of his disciples. The murals depict the various regions of Mexico, the sciences, and many national heroes. Rivera did the murals shortly after studying in Europe, which helps explain their resemblance to works of Picasso and Cézanne. Closed weekends. No admission charge. At Calles República de Argentina and República de Venezuela (phone: 510-4766).

MUSEO DE LA CHARRERÍA (RIDING MUSEUM) *Charro* means "gentleman rider," and in this colonial building is a large collection of saddles, spurs, firearms, suits, and other trappings of this supremely Mexican pastime. Closed weekends. No admission charge. 108 Calle Isabel la Católica (phone: 709-4838).

PINACOTECA VIRREINAL (VICEREGAL PAINTING MUSEUM) Art of the 16th, 17th, and 18th centuries is displayed in what was once the *Iglesia de San Diego,* built in 1591. Closed Mondays and holidays. Admission charge. 7 Calle Dr. Mora (phone: 510-2793).

BOSQUE DE CHAPULTEPEC (CHAPULTEPEC PARK)

Comprising three sections, this huge "people's playground" has museums, restaurants, and a large zoo with natural habitats for the animals (it's home to the surviving female of the original pair of pandas given to Mexico by the People's Republic of China, plus her "babies," born in captivity). Other features are a children's zoo, a lake for boating, lovely fountains and walkways, plenty of picnic grounds, and a large amusement park (closed Mondays) with a frighteningly high roller coaster. There also is the flashy *Auditorio Nacional* (National Auditorium), where top Mexican and international artists perform. *Chapultepec* has been a recreation center ever since it was the royal preserve of the Aztec kings. It is a definite must-see, especially on Sundays, when the place is alive with activity.

MUSEO NACIONAL DE HISTORIA (NATIONAL MUSEUM OF HISTORY) The 18th-century *Castillo de Chapultepec* (Chapultepec Castle) has an interesting history: Originally chosen as the site for Montezuma's country residence, it was used as a military academy and fortress during the Mexican-American

War (a handful of teenage cadets threw themselves from the tower rather than surrender to the Americans in 1847), and was converted into the residence of Emperor Maximilian and Empress Carlota in 1866. After Maximilian's execution, the castle was the official presidential residence until the administration of Lázaro Cárdenas in the 1930s; since then, it has been a museum and a center for ceremonial events. On display are the formal gardens designed by Carlota and the elegantly furnished quarters that she and the emperor occupied. Besides a collection of valuable jewels, Gobelin tapestries, furniture, ceramics, paintings, statues, and other historical relics, the castle has two rooms dedicated to the independence and the revolution of Mexico, with murals by O'Gorman and Siqueiros. It's a pretty steep climb up the hillside, but the castle itself, and the spectacular view of the city from its terraces, makes the hike worthwhile; on the lower terrace, you can see Maximilian's elegant royal coach. Closed Mondays. Admission charge (phone: 286-0700).

MUSEO DEL CARACOL (MUSEUM OF THE SNAIL) Great moments in Mexico's struggle for liberty are depicted in three-dimensional displays with light and sound. The museum's official name is *Galería de Historia—"La Lucha del Pueblo Mexicano por Su Libertad"* (Gallery of History—"The Mexican People's Fight for Liberty"), but everyone calls it the *Museo del Caracol* because of its spiral shape. Closed Mondays. Admission charge. West of the castle, on top of the hill (phone: 286-3971 or 553-6311).

MUSEO NACIONAL DE ANTROPOLOGÍA (NATIONAL MUSEUM OF ANTHROPOLOGY) Hands down, this is one of the world's outstanding museums. Architect Pedro Ramírez Vázquez used the grandeur of an Aztec temple as the inspiration for his design. The heart of the complex is a huge patio sheltered by an immense aluminum umbrella-like structure supported by a single column, covered in reliefs and sheathed by a cylinder of water. The surrounding interconnected galleries, which open onto the central patio, contain murals by some of Mexico's most renowned artists and are a fitting showcase for the splendor of Mexico's past.

The exhibit halls are divided into displays representing the Mesoamerican, prehistoric, pre-classic, and Teotihuacán-Mexica eras. Among the many treasures are the sun stone, more commonly known as the Aztec calendar stone; a fascinating reproduction of the Tlatelolco market; treasures from the Palenque tombs; and a reproduction of the Maya paintings at *Bonampak* (the originals, deep in the jungles of the state of Chiapas, are not easily viewed). Ground-floor exhibits include every conceivable relic, from jewelry, musical instruments, stone carvings, pottery, lavish ornaments, tapestries, costumes, and footwear to medicinal herbs, gourds, feather and shell crafts, temple decor, burial offerings, gold and alabaster bowls, and figurines. The second floor is devoted to displays of how indigenous peoples live in Mexico today. The restaurant on the premises is pleasant. Bilingual guides are available, and the gift shop sells an excellent, if expensive, English-language guidebook. Closed Mondays. Admission charge. On the Reforma in *Bosque de Chapultepec* (phone: 553-6386).

MUSEO DE ARTE MODERNO (MUSEUM OF MODERN ART) In this spectacular, circular, dark glass structure are some of the most celebrated works of José María Velasco, Diego Rivera, José Clemente Orozco, Juan O'Gorman, David Alfaro Siqueiros, Rufino Tamayo, Miguel Covarrubias, and Francisco Icaza. Separated from the main building by a statue-filled garden is another gallery, which houses rotating collections of current artists and visiting exhibitions. Closed Mondays and holidays. Admission charge. At Paseo de la Reforma and Calzada Gandhi (phone: 553-6233).

CENTRO CULTURAL DE ARTE CONTEMPORÁNEO (CULTURAL CENTER FOR CONTEMPORARY ART) This atrium was created 10 years ago with monies from the *Fundación Cultural Televisa,* a nonprofit organization funded by Mexico's private television monopoly. (It was originally built as a press center for the 1986 *World Cup* soccer championship.) Permanent exhibits include paintings, sculptures, graphics, and decorative art, both Mexican and international; a 1,400-piece photographic collection selected by Mexico's grand master of photography, Manuel Alvarez Bravo; and a 400-piece collection of pre-Hispanic art. There are temporary shows, too. Don't miss the museum shop. Closed Mondays. Admission charge. Next to the *Presidente Inter-Continental* hotel at Av. Campos Elíseos and Calle Jorge Elliot (phone: 282-0355).

PAPALOTE MUSEO DEL NIÑO (PAPALOTE CHILDREN'S MUSEUM) The colorful exhibits contained in this massive blue-tiled complex run the gamut from remote control–activated airplanes to a five-story maze. One of the most interesting exhibits is an ugly plaster figure called the "nightmare-eating monster"; children can write their nightmares on slips of paper and get rid of them by dropping them into its mouth. Films in the Imax wide-screen cinema change monthly. The $15-million museum is based on the premise that kids learn most from hands-on activities; displayed everywhere are signs that say *"Se puede tocar"* (Touching Permitted). But be warned: any adult wishing to visit the *Papalote* (the word means "butterfly" in Nahuatl and "kite" in Spanish) must be accompanied by a responsible child. Closed Mondays; additional hours on Thursday evenings from 7 to 11 PM—a much less crowded time to visit. Admission charge. 269 Av. Constituyentes in *Bosque de Chapultepec,* next to the *periférico,* or beltway (phone: 237-1700).

MUSEO RUFINO TAMAYO (RUFINO TAMAYO MUSEUM) In this striking structure are two groups of exhibition salons linked by ramps and built around a central sculpture-filled courtyard. They contain the personal collection of Rufino Tamayo, who was one of the country's greatest painters; included are works by more than 165 other modern artists, such as Picasso and Ernst. Closed Mondays and holidays. Admission charge. Paseo de la Reforma, between the *Arte Moderno* and *Antropología* museums in *Bosque de Chapultepec* (phone: 286-5889).

POLIFORUM CULTURAL SIQUEIROS (SIQUEIROS CULTURAL POLYFORUM) The impact and incredible scope of this large cultural center, which includes a number of exhibition and performance spaces for various art forms, is a fitting tribute to David Alfaro Siqueiros, the great, prolific Mexican artist whose impassioned political and social conscience permeated his work. On the third level is the pièce de résistance—*La Marcha de la Humanidad* (The March of Humanity), a powerful, 27,000-foot mural depicting Mexican workers. Open daily. No admission charge. Av. Insurgentes Sur and Calle Filadelfia, Colonia Nápoles, about a 40-minute drive from downtown (phone: 536-4521/2/3/4/5).

MUSEO FRIDA KAHLO (FRIDA KAHLO MUSEUM) This colonial-style building was the home and studio of Frida Kahlo, whose fascinating work has won her something of a cult following. Many of her imaginative paintings are on display, as are unique pieces of popular art and furniture and mementos of her marriage to Diego Rivera. The lovely patio-garden is a perfect spot to stroll and take in the atmosphere. Closed Mondays and holidays. Admission charge. 247 Calle Londres, Coyoacán, about a 45-minute drive from downtown (phone: 554-5999).

MUSEO LEON TROTSKY The Russian revolutionary's last home is now a museum filled with his furnishings and memorabilia. One of the more unusual exhibits is a collection of photographs of Trotsky with other famous figures of the 1930s. Perhaps more interesting than the museum itself is the story behind the house: Forced into exile from the USSR in 1929, Trotsky eventually came to Mexico on the suggestion of Diego Rivera. He took up residence in a house owned by Rivera's wife, Frida Kahlo, with whom he had an affair. His friendship with Rivera subsequently ended, and Trotsky had to find other living quarters. With its high walls and towers, this house seemed the perfect refuge from the Stalinists who continued to pursue him. But in 1940, Ramón Mercader, a Spanish Stalinist, stabbed Trotsky to death while he was at work at his desk. Closed Mondays. Admission charge. 45 Calle Viena, Coyoacán, about a 45-minute drive from downtown (phone: 658-8732).

MUSEO NACIONAL DE CULTURAS POPULARES (NATIONAL MUSEUM OF FOLK CULTURES) Fascinating and imaginative hands-on exhibits about Mexico's folk traditions and popular modern trends are found here. Closed Mondays and holidays. No admission charge. 289 Calle Hidalgo, Coyoacán, about a 45-minute drive from downtown (phone: 554-8848).

MUSEO DE LAS INTERVENCIONES (MUSEUM OF FOREIGN INTERVENTIONS) The *Ex-Convento de Santa María* (Former Convent of St. Mary) is the setting for this predominantly military museum. It was here that General Anaya surrendered to General Winfield Scott in 1847, during the Mexican-American War. The simple coach used by Benito Juárez is on display. Closed Mondays.

Admission charge. Calles 20 de Agosto and Xicoténcatl, Coyoacán, about a 45-minute drive from downtown (phone: 604-0981).

ANAHUACALLI This striking pre-Aztec-style (less geometric and grandiose than Aztec art) structure designed by Diego Rivera contains more than 60,000 treasures from Mexico's ancient indigenous cultures as well as some of Rivera's masterful murals. Upstairs is a replica of his studio, with artwork ranging from his first sketch (a drawing of a train done when he was three years old) to the canvas he was working on at the time of his death. Closed Mondays and holidays. No admission charge, but donations are welcome. 150 Calle del Museo, off División del Norte, Coyoacán, about a 45-minute drive from downtown (phone: 617-3797).

CASA DEL RISCO (HOUSE OF PORCELAIN) The formal name of this attraction is the *Centro Cultural Isidro Fabela* (Isidro Fabela Cultural Center), but it's better known by its nickname, which comes from the *riscos* (pieces of porcelain) that decorate it. For many years it was the home of Don Isidro Fabela, the famous jurist, statesman, and art collector. Its centerpiece is the unusual fountain in the central patio, made from sets of porcelain dishes and pieces of ceramics. Fabela's extensive library and art collection are on view upstairs. Closed Mondays. No admission charge. 15 Plaza San Jacinto, San Angel, almost an hour's drive from downtown (phone: 616-2711).

CONVENTO DEL CARMEN Combine a stop at this picturesque 17th-century convent, now a museum of colonial-era paintings, with an excursion to the *Casa del Risco.* And don't miss the crypt in the basement, home to well-preserved mummies attired in the clothes of their era. Closed Mondays. Admission charge. 4 Av. de la Revolución on the Plaza Carmen, San Angel, almost an hour's drive from downtown (phone: 616-2816).

MUSEO ALVAR AND CARMEN T. DE CARRILLO GIL This museum has an outstanding permanent collection of works by Orozco, Rivera, and Siqueiros. There also are temporary exhibitions of contemporary artists. Closed Mondays and holidays. Admission charge. 1608 Av. de la Revolución, San Angel, almost an hour's drive from downtown (phone: 548-7467).

MUSEO ESTUDIO DIEGO RIVERA (DIEGO RIVERA STUDIO MUSEUM) The home and studio of the artist has been turned into a museum filled with his accoutrements—brushes and paint, and letters and photographs of friends—and his collection of *judas,* which are colorful figures representing the devil and, more generally, the concept of evil (several are figures of politicians). The model for the restoration work was a Rivera painting, *The Painter's Studio,* which itself is on view. The two-story structure was designed by his friend and fellow artist Juan O'Gorman. It may seem uncomfortably small for a person of Rivera's girth, but he lived here happily for 24 years. Closed Mondays. Admission charge. Av. Altavista and Calle Diego Rivera, Colonia

San Angel (next to the *San Angel Inn*), almost an hour's drive from downtown (phone: 548-3032).

CIUDAD UNIVERSITARIA (UNIVERSITY CITY) The *Universidad Nacional Autónoma de México* (*UNAM,* or National Autonomous University of Mexico) was founded here in the mid-16th century, making it one of the oldest institutions of higher learning in the Western Hemisphere—although you wouldn't know it from the look of its daring, contemporary architecture. The buildings are notable for their vivid exterior murals, including ones by Diego Rivera (on the stadium) and David Alfaro Siqueiros (on the *rectoría,* or dean's office building). Most famous of all is the 10-story wraparound mosaic by Juan O'Gorman covering the façade of the library. Approaching the *periférico* (beltway), on both sides of Av. Insurgentes Sur, at Calle Copilco, about a 45-minute drive from downtown (phone: 616-1936).

SALA NEZAHUALCÓYOTL (NEZAHUALCÓYOTL HALL) Its outstanding acoustics place this concert hall among the world's greatest. The architecture is stark and modern, so unadorned it's striking. Av. Insurgentes Sur, past the Ciudad Universitaria, in Pedregal de San Angel, about a 90-minute drive from downtown (phone: 655-1344).

CUICUILCO This archaeological site is noted for its unusual circular pyramid. Astronomically oriented, it is considered the earliest urban center in the Valley of Mexico. Open daily. No admission charge. Av. Insurgentes Sur, just south of the *periférico* (beltway) and across from the *Villa Olímpica* (Olympic Village), at least a 90-minute drive from downtown (no phone).

XOCHIMILCO (pronounced So-chee-*meel*-co) Mexico's famous floating gardens are laced with 124 miles of interconnected canals. When the Aztec empire began to expand, the small amount of farmland in the valley (which was mostly islands and lakes) disappeared. The ever-resourceful Aztec solved the problem by building dirt-covered rafts on which they planted their crops. Those *chinampas* (floating islands) have long since taken root in the shallow waters, but *Xochimilco* continues to be an important producer of flowers and vegetables for Mexico City. Ignore the self-styled guides at the entrance to the canal area; instead, go directly to the main docks (*Embarcadero Nuevo Nativitas*) on Calle Mercado. Here you can have a gondolier pole you around the floating gardens in a *trajinera* (flower-bedecked boat). The flower vendors and the floating mariachi bands add to the experience. *Xochimilco* is lively and great fun on Sundays; it's somewhat quieter the rest of the week. Take Calzada Tlalpan to the traffic circle at the *Estadio Azteca* (Aztec Stadium), and follow the signs to the left, or take Avenida Insurgentes Sur all the way south to the *periférico* (beltway), and then continue about five more minutes into the park. Either way, expect at least a 90-minute drive from downtown. If you haven't rented a car, a cab is the easiest way to get here.

While you're visiting *Xochimilco,* don't pass up the *Museo Dolores Olmedo* (5843 Av. México; phone: 676-1166). As a tribute to Diego Rivera, Dolores "Lola" Olmedo, a close friend of the artist, converted her magnificent private home (originally a 16th-century monastery) into a museum displaying a fine collection of his work. Along with Rivera's paintings are some remarkable pieces by the artist Frida Kahlo, who was Rivera's wife. The museum also houses Mexican folk art and pre-Columbian pieces. It's closed Mondays; there's an admission charge.

In the town of Santa Cruz Acalpixcán, about 2 miles (3 km) west of Xochimilco, street vendors sell colorful, locally produced seed candies. A candy fair is held in June, but the candy "factories" (residents' homes) may be visited at any time and can be reached by car or *trajinera* from *Xochimilco.* Also in the town is the *Museo Arqueológico de Xochimilco* (Archaeological Museum of Xochimilco; on the Xochimilco-Tulyehualco Hwy. at the corner of Calle Tenochtitlán; no phone). The collection includes more than 2,300 pieces from the Teotihuacán and Aztec cultures. The museum is closed Mondays; there's no admission charge.

NORTHERN MEXICO CITY AND NORTH OF THE CITY

BASÍLICA DE LA VIRGEN DE GUADALUPE (SHRINE OF THE VIRGIN OF GUADALUPE)

Catholics consider this place one of the most holy in the Americas. Catholic heads of state, such as Charles de Gaulle and John F. Kennedy, paid homage here during visits to Mexico, and Pope John Paul II said mass at the shrine in 1979. It is said that on this spot in 1531, the Virgin Mary—with dark skin, like the indigenous people—appeared before a native farmer and asked him to have a church built in her honor. The farmer passed the request on to the bishop, who, not believing him, sent him away. The Virgin appeared to the farmer again, this time directing him to a barren, stony place where she said he would find roses growing. He wrapped the roses in his cloak and brought them to the bishop. When he unwrapped the roses, he discovered the image of the Virgin imprinted on the cloak. Unfaded by time and something art experts admit they cannot explain, the cloak is exhibited on the main altar of the shrine. The apparition marked a great upturn in the conversion rate of the indigenous peoples, and the Virgin of Guadalupe quickly became the patron saint of all Mexico. There actually are two basilicas: The old shrine, where the cloak had been on display for about 250 years, was closed to the public in 1976 because it had been badly damaged over the years by earthquakes and was sinking into the spongy subsoil; today it serves as a museum of religious art. The new basilica, designed by Pedro Ramírez Vázquez (the architect of the *Museo Nacional de Antropología*), was inaugurated in 1976 and stands right next to the old shrine. The shrine is perpetually engulfed with pilgrims (some of whom enter the church on their knees), especially in December. Both buildings are open daily. Admission charge to the museum. Near the northwest outskirts of the city, about a 45-minute drive from downtown, off Av. Insurgentes Nte. (phone: 577-6088).

TENAYUCA This excellently preserved stepped pyramid rests on a base 223 by 250 feet. Started by the Toltec, it was taken over by the Aztec in the 15th century and is considered one of the finest examples of Aztec architecture extant. On the northwest outskirts of the city via Calzada Vallejo, about a 90-minute drive from downtown. Closed Mondays. Admission charge (no phone).

ACOLMAN Construction of this imposing monastery-fortress started in 1538. On the façade are stone carvings of the Augustinian shield and figures of St. Peter, St. Paul, and the Virgin Mary, as well as of natives with baskets on their heads. Now a national monument, the partially restored site depicts how monks lived during the colonial era. Closed Mondays. Admission charge. About an hour from downtown, on the road going out of Av. Insurgentes Nte., which connects with the toll road to the *Pirámides de Teotihuacán* (see *Extra Special*), another 6 miles (10 km) ahead (no phone).

EXTRA SPECIAL

Only 31 miles (50 km) northeast of Mexico City are the *Pirámides de Teotihuacán* (Pyramids of Teotihuacán), compelling testaments to a mysterious culture that flourished in the area before the Aztec arrived. For more details, see *Mexico's Magnificent Archaeological Heritage* in DIVERSIONS. The pyramids are open daily; there's no admission charge on Sundays. Take Avenida Insurgentes Norte, which connects with the toll road to Teotihuacán (phone: 595-60188). There also is regular bus service from the *Central de Autobuses del Norte* (Av. Cien Metros) in Mexico City. The trip takes between 60 and 90 minutes.

Sources and Resources

TOURIST INFORMATION

The best general source of information is the *Secretaría de Turismo* (Tourism Secretariat; in the Polanco district, 172 Av. Presidente Mazarik; phone: 250-0027, 250-0123, 250-0151, 250-0493, or 250-8604), which has numerous English-speaking staff members. The *Infotur* office in the Zona Rosa (54 Calle Amberes, at Calle Londres; phone: 525-9380/1/2/3/4) has information on sites throughout the Federal District. Both offices are open daily.

LOCAL COVERAGE *The News* and the *Mexico City Times,* both Mexico City–based English-language dailies, keep visitors informed about world events, what's at the movies, what's on TV, and a great deal more. The *Daily Bulletin* and the *Gazer,* available free in hotel lobbies, list restaurants, nightly entertainment, and other data of note. Another excellent resource is the *Guía Roji* map and street guide, which is available at any newsstand or bookshop and includes all the city streets and *colonias,* with routes, bus lanes, and subway and streetcar lines marked. *USA Today, The New York Times,* the

Los Angeles Times, and the *Miami Herald* are available at most large hotels and at newsstands.

TELEPHONE The city code for Mexico City is 5. *Note:* Mexico's telephone company has embarked on a major expansion project that involves changing telephone numbers in many areas of the country. At press time, all numbers listed in this chapter were correct. However, if you have any difficulties reaching attractions listed here, contact the local tourist office.

CLIMATE AND CLOTHES The capital has an average year-round temperature of 65F (18C). From October through May, days are dry and sunny; from June through September, expect afternoon rains. Carry a light jacket or wrap at night. Dress casually during the day (but no shorts) and more formally for the evening. (Men often must wear jackets and ties at the more expensive restaurants.)

GETTING AROUND

BUS Buses and minibuses run along the main avenues and arteries known as *ejes viales.* They are impossibly crowded during rush hours, but at other times service is fair to good. The fare on older buses is 40 centavos (about 5¢); newer, bright-red vehicles charge 1 peso (about 13¢) and offer a more comfortable ride. *Peseros*—VW vans with a horizontal stripe around them and marked with a triangle—operate like buses, cramming in as many people as will fit and following set routes. The fare—usually about 1.5 pesos (about 20¢)—depends on your destination, which you should tell the driver when you board. Tourists are fond of taking the *peseros* that run along Reforma, but be careful: Only some go to the *zócalo.* Even if you don't speak Spanish, you can ask: *"Zócalo?"* If the van drives off without you, it's not going there. *A word of warning:* Pickpockets are frequent passengers.

CAR RENTAL Since driving in crowded Mexico City can be difficult, in most cases we recommend taking taxis when exploring the city and its environs. That said, cars can be picked up from most international firms at the airport and at numerous locations around the city. One reliable local franchise that is considerably less expensive than the larger international agencies is *Romano Rent a Car* (195 Thiers, Colonia Anzures; phone: 250-0055 or 545-5722).

Mexico City's pollution controls, a welcome and necessary restriction, affect resident and visiting drivers alike. Laws prohibit drivers from using their cars on certain days, depending on their automobile's license plate number—and this includes rental cars. Do not drive on Mondays if your license plate ends with 5 or 6; on Tuesdays if it ends with 7 or 8; on Wednesdays, with 3 or 4; on Thursdays, with 1 or 2; and on Fridays, with 9 or 0. The laws often are suspended on major holidays, while they may be extended to a second day if pollution levels are very high—check the local papers for details. At press time, the fine for driving on a prohibited day was 400 pesos (about $53).

METRO Mexico's subway is clean, fast, and efficient. The surprisingly quiet cars have rubber tires, and classical music is piped in over the sound system in the stations. It is also incredibly inexpensive, at 1 peso (about 13¢) per ride ticket. Some two million people ride the metro daily, and it has relieved some of the traffic congestion. It is possible to ride the entire system on one ticket, but note that luggage is not allowed. The interestingly decorated stations have numerous shops and restaurants. The ultramodern *Pino Suárez* station even houses an Aztec pyramid that was discovered during the construction of a subway line. As when riding the buses, keep a good grip on your purse or wallet.

TAXI In front of larger hotels, there usually is a taxi stand with perhaps two types of vehicles. The larger and more comfortable are distinguishable only by their blue license plates and the letters *SET (Servicio Especial de Turismo)* at the bottom, and are driven by bilingual guides. A guide with no client at the moment will work as a hackie. By Mexican standards, the fee will be high, but the mere fact that you can communicate in English may make it worthwhile. There also are white and red-orange or white and maroon cars at the hotels and at taxi stands at key points around the city. The colors indicate that these are *sitio* cabs; that is, they work from a cabstand and supposedly cannot cruise for passengers. They, too, charge relatively high rates, but they're often worth the price, especially when less expensive cabs are unavailable. *Sitio* cabs often don't bother with their meters, so be sure to ask the price before getting in. Many of the drivers at hotel stands understand at least some English.

White and yellow taxis and green and light gray cabs have meters and are supposed to cruise for passengers. There are thousands of these taxis, and they charge less than *SET* and *sitio* cabs do. Taxi fares are set by the city government, and rate hikes usually lag well behind increases in the cost of living. Drivers tend to use their meters for some time after a fare increase, but when inflation catches up, the meters "break" and drivers charge whatever they like. The way to handle this is to ask, *"Cuánto cuesta a . . . ?"* ("How much to . . . ?") and give your destination. If the driver points to the meter, the charge will be what the meter registers. If the driver names a flat rate that you find reasonable, get in.

Tourists frequently believe that they have been overcharged (residents get overcharged, too). If you want to dispute any charges, take down the cab's number and call 250-0123, the tourism secretariat hotline. They will tell you how to file a formal complaint.

TOURS The central tourism office provides information on a variety of tours offered throughout the city (see *Tourist Information,* above).

SPECIAL EVENTS

The *Festival del Centro Histórico de la Ciudad de México* (Festival of the Historic Center of Mexico City), with ballets and concerts in the cathedral and in other downtown venues, is held for two weeks in March. The season around *Semana Santa* (Holy Week, the week leading up to *Easter*) is marked by numerous celebrations, ranging from solemn religious processions to wild fiestas. On May 1, a huge parade of more than 150,000 workers from various unions marches through the *zócalo* in observance of *Día del Trabajo* (Labor Day). But the biggest event of the year is *Día de la Independencia* (Independence Day), celebrated September 15–16. Every September 15 at 11 PM, the president rings the bell at the *Palacio Nacional* to signal the start of the festivities, an event accompanied by an elaborate fireworks display. The *zócalo* below is filled with celebrating Mexicans (the crowd can get pretty rough at times). The best way to see the ceremony is to take a table in the open-air *La Terraza* restaurant atop the *Majestic* hotel (73 Av. Francisco I. Madero, just east of the *zócalo*; phone: 521-8601) or reserve a room facing the *zócalo* at the *Howard Johnson Gran* (see *Checking In*). At 11 AM the next day, a huge military parade proceeds from the *zócalo* to the *Auditorio Nacional,* in front of the *Presidente Inter-Continental* hotel, arriving at about 2 PM.

Día de la Revolución (Revolution Day) on November 20—the anniversary of the start of the Revolution of 1910—is marked with huge celebrations and a parade dominated by participants from various governmental agencies, as well as members of military squadrons and athletic clubs and teams, who frequently perform short routines. The procession follows a route similar to that of the *Día de la Independencia* parade. December 12, the *Día de la Virgen de Guadalupe,* Mexico's patron saint, is the most important religious holiday in Mexico. Numerous celebrations take place from *Navidad* (Christmas) through the *Día de los Reyes Magos* (Three Kings Day) on January 6. In addition, there are so many smaller fiestas—including the one on March 19 that's celebrated by anyone named José—that you're bound to run into at least one during your trip.

SHOPPING

If you like to shop, Mexico City is your kind of place. The best, most concentrated shopping area is the Zona Rosa, a 12-square-block district bounded by Reforma on the north, Niza on the east, Chapultepec on the south, and Florencia on the west. Though its traditionally chic ambience is fading somewhat, the neighborhood is still full of boutiques, jewelry stores, leather goods shops, antiques stores, and art galleries, plus dozens of great restaurants and coffee shops. It is always busy—you can run into a traffic jam even at 2 AM, between shows at the nightclubs.

The wealthy Polanco area is fast surpassing the Zona Rosa as a classy shopping neighborhood. Three of Mexico City's major hotels (the *Nikko México, Presidente Inter-Continental,* and *Camino Real*) are located here (see *Checking In*), turning what was once an elegant residential area into a hubbub of activity. The *Pabellón Polanco,* near the *Nikko México* and *Presidente Inter-Continental* hotels, is a comfortable and compact shopping center filled with fashionable shops and restaurants. Hundreds of equally good stores line Avenidas Insurgentes and Juárez and the streets of San Angel, Coyoacán, and *El Centro* (the old downtown area).

La Merced (Circunvalación, one block north of Fray Servando Teresa de Mier), a central produce market, is one of the city's busiest shopping areas. Also try the *Mercado Tepito* (known as the "Thieves' Market" in English), which spreads all over the streets of Rayón on weekends. It's adjacent to the *Mercado de la Lagunilla* (Lagunilla Market, between Calles Allende and Chile, about eight blocks north of Av. Madero). You'll find genuine and (mostly) fake antiques, lots of old books (some of them in English), new power tools, antique keys, odds and ends of china, crystal bottle stoppers, cheap plastic toys, copper and brass articles, old and new clothes, carpets, and furniture. This is where Mexicans went to buy contraband products before the days of free trade. *Warning:* The English moniker of "Thieves' Market" is appropriate. Watch your wallet!

In general, department store prices are considerably higher in Mexico than in the US. The major department store chains are *Liverpool, Suburbia,* and *Palacio de Hierro.* Convenient branches of *Liverpool* are in Colonia del Valle (1310 Av. Insurgentes Sur; phone: 524-9424) and Polanco (425 Av. Mariano Escobedo; phone: 531-3440). There are *Suburbia* stores in Polanco (203 Av. Horacio; phone: 250-6055); Colonia Condesa (180 Calle Sonora; phone: 584-4399); and Colonia Nápoles (1235 Av. Insurgentes Sur; phone: 563-7766). And there's a branch of *Palacio de Hierro* in Colonia Roma (230 Calle Durango; phone: 511-7227). The posh and pricey *Perisur* mall is on the southern edge of the city near where the *periférico* (beltway) meets Avenida Insurgentes. Department stores generally are open from 10 AM to 7 PM Mondays, Tuesdays, Thursdays, and Fridays, and from 10 AM to 8 PM Wednesdays and Saturdays.

FONART, the government bureau dedicated to promoting Mexican crafts, has four stores in Mexico City: downtown (89 Av. Juárez; phone: 521-0171); in the Zona Rosa (136 Calle Londres; phone: 525-2026); in Coyoacán (115 Calle Presidente Carranza; phone: 554-6270); and in Colonia Mixcoac (three blocks northeast of the *Mixcoac* metro stop, at 691 Av. Patriotismo; phone: 563-4060). All are open Mondays through Saturdays from 10 AM to 7 PM. Many other handicrafts stores are open daily. Most shops in general are open daily from 10 AM to 6 PM, though many stay open as late as 9 PM.

Following is a list of stores and markets, by area, to get you started.

CITYWIDE

Aca Joe T-shirts and beachwear from the reliable chain. Two locations: 19 Calle Amberes, Zona Rosa (phone: 525-2718), and 318 Av. Presidente Mazarik, Polanco (phone: 281-3213).

Aries One of Mexico's finest leather stores, including suede ready-to-wear, luggage, and handbags. Two locations: 14 Calle Florencia, Zona Rosa (phone:

533-2509), and in the *Plaza Polanco* shopping center, 11 Jaime Balmes (phone: 395-2745).

Los Castillo Considered by many to be Taxco's top silversmiths, they create fine ceramics inlaid with silver. Two locations: 41 Calle Amberes, Zona Rosa (phone: 511-6198), and in the *Nikko México* hotel, Polanco (280-1111).

Dupuis An impeccable selection of furniture, icons, and gifts. Two locations: 180B Av. de las Fuentes, in Pedregal (phone: 595-4307), and 240 Paseo de las Palmas, in Lomas de Chapultepec (phone: 540-0074).

Feders Great hand-blown glass and Tiffany-style lamps. Two locations: 67 Lago Moritz, Colonia Anáhuac (phone: 260-2958), and in the *Bazar Sábado,* at 11 Plaza San Jacinto in San Angel (phone: 550-7944; see below).

Galería de Sergio Bustamante On display here are the famous artist's fantastical creatures of papier-mâché, metal, and ceramic, as well as his equally imaginative jewelry. Two locations: 11 Calle Amberes, Zona Rosa (phone: 525-9059), and in the *Nikko México* hotel, Polanco (phone: 282-2638).

Misrachi Paintings, sculptures, lithographs, and prints by such top Mexican artists as Tamayo, Cuevas, and Siqueiros. Two locations: 20 Calle Génova, Zona Rosa (phone: 533-4551), and Calle la Fontaine and Av. Homero, Polanco (phone: 250-4105).

Platería Ortega Fine jewelry, decorative objects, and serving pieces in sterling silver. Two locations: 18 Calle Florencia, Zona Rosa (phone: 207-5612), and 13 Av. 5 de Mayo, downtown (phone: 512-6069).

Tane A treasure trove of superb silver and gold, ranging from museum-quality reproductions of antique pieces to bold new designs by young Mexican silversmiths. The main store is in the Zona Rosa, at 70 Calle Amberes (phone: 533-3662); there are several other branches in the city and other parts of the country.

CENTRO (DOWNTOWN)

American Bookstore The city's largest and best selection of English-language publications. Closed weekends. 25 Av. Francisco I. Madero (phone: 512-7284).

Avalos Glass Factory Glass blowers can be seen at work in the mornings here. Goblets, serving pieces, and entire sets of dishes are for sale. (They're very fragile, so it's best to buy a few more than you think you need.) Two blocks north of *La Merced,* at 5 Calle Carretones (phone: 522-5311).

Bazar del Centro Tasteful shops selling Taxco silver, handicrafts, stoneware, and art are set around a lovely patio in a 17th-century building. 30 Calle Isabel la Católica (phone: 521-1923).

Dulcería Celaya A candy lover's dream or a dieter's nightmare, this charming little shop carries colorful and very sweet sweets from all over the country. 39 Av. 5 de Mayo (phone: 521-1787).

De la Fuente Bustillo Exclusive gold jewelry and antiques. 28 Av. Francisco I. Madero (phone: 512-3460).

Galería Reforma This handicrafts collection—including furniture, jewelry, ceramics, clothing, and brass and copper items—is probably Mexico's largest. 575 Paseo de la Reforma Nte., at Calle Gonzalo Bocanegra (phone: 526-6800).

Mercado Abelardo Rodríguez This market is especially interesting at *Christmas,* when there's a great selection of piñatas, nativity scenes, and toys. It's located in an interesting area filled with lovely Spanish colonial buildings. Calle Venezuela between Calles Carmen and Argentina (no phone).

Mercado de la Ciudadela Almost 200 artisans exhibit their works at this wonderfully labyrinthine complex of one-story buildings. Calle Balderas between Calles Ayuntamiento and Emilio Dondé (no phone).

Mercado San Juan Artisans and merchants from all over the country display popular arts and crafts in this modern building, where a spiral ramp links all the floors. Calle Ayuntamiento between Calles Buen Tono and Aranda (phone: 510-4801).

Mercado Sonora This market offers a wide variety of herbs for cooking and medicinal use, as well as poultry and other foods. There's a huge toy market here at *Christmas.* South of *La Merced* at Av. Fray Servando Teresa de Mier and San Nicolás (no phone).

Museo Nacional de Artes e Industrias Populares A government-run shop with an exceptionally good selection of textiles and pottery, as well as a huge crafts map of Mexico in the front room. There's also a handicrafts museum whose entrance is around the corner. 44 Av. Juárez (phone: 521-6679).

Víctor Artes Rare lacquerware, high-quality ceramics, and traditional indigenous jewelry. 8 and 10 Av. Francisco I. Madero, Room 305 (phone: 512-1263).

ZONA ROSA

Colección de Felgueres A diminutive shop filled with diminutive things, from dollhouse furniture and lead soldiers to miniature nativity scenes. 130 Calle Hamburgo (phone: 514-1405).

Currier The best chocolate shop in Mexico, hands down. 77 Calle Guadalquivir (phone: 525-2232).

Flamma A fantastic array of candles in a beautiful townhouse. Calles Hamburgo and Florencia (phone: 511-8499).

Galería Arvil Art by established older artists and promising newcomers. 9 Cerrada de Hamburgo, between Calles Florencia and Estocolmo (phone: 207-2647).

Mercado Insurgentes A neighborhood market where, besides artistically arranged stalls piled with meat and produce, there is a wide selection of handicrafts, embroidered clothing, and silver. Prices are fairly good, but there always is room to negotiate. Entrance on 154 Calle Londres or 167 Calle Liverpool (no phone).

Tamacani Handwoven wool rugs in original and unusual designs. 51 Calle Varsovia (phone: 533-5155).

Tapetes Mexicanos Oriental-style handloomed wool rugs, including ones from Temoaya in the state of México, incorporating Mexican motifs and colors. 235 Calle Hamburgo (phone: 207-4991).

POLANCO AND ENVIRONS

Arte Zapoteco Creditable gold and silver facsimiles of the jewelry discovered at *Monte Albán,* plus copies of colonial-era pieces and much more. In the *Presidente Inter-Continental* hotel (phone: 327-7700).

Galería Estela Shapiro Works by internationally known Mexican artists, as well as young aspirants. 72 Calle Victor Hugo, Colonia Anzures (phone: 525-0123).

Girasol A wonderful shop famous for superb handloomed fabrics and delightful hand-embroidered gowns and skirts. 258 Calle Francisco Petrarca (phone: 203-6597).

Lo Que el Viento Se Llevó "Gone with the Wind" is an outstanding collection of Mexican colonial furniture and decorative objects. Two locations: 56 Calle Victor Hugo (phone: 254-4327) and 89 Calle Julio Verne (phone: 545-7923).

La Paloma Carefully chosen pottery from Oaxaca, Puebla, and Guanajuato, marvelously colorful wooden animals from Oaxaca and Guerrero, and red glassware from Guadalajara. They can be relied on to ship your purchases home. 191 Av. Presidente Mazarik (phone: 280-3670).

Pladi The draw here is beautifully designed jewelry and decorative items. Calle la Martine between Avs. Newton and Horacio (phone: 203-4569).

Populartes With many unique items, it's probably the most exceptional collection of Mexican handicrafts in the city. 103 Av. Campos Elíseos (phone: 254-2236).

SOUTHERN MEXICO CITY

Bazar Sábado (Saturday Bazaar) In this 17th-century convent, more than 200 top artisans display their creations—many of them available nowhere else in Mexico. Visitors can soak up the atmosphere at the wonderful restaurant on the patio. The art show (outside, in front) and the sidewalk vendors add to the festive, joyous bustle. While haggling with the vendors outside is common, the artisans inside consider it an insult. Open Saturdays only. 11 Plaza San Jacinto, in San Angel (phone: 550-7944).

SPORTS

AUTO RACING Speedsters head for the *Autódromo Hermanos Rodríguez,* near the airport (phone: 649-8700), where the *Grand Prix Formula I* race is held in May.

BASEBALL The season runs from mid-April through mid-August. Mexico City has two home teams, the *Diablos Rojos* (Red Devils) and the *Tigres* (Tigers). Weeknight games are generally held at 7 PM and Sunday games at 11 AM at the *Parque Seguro Social* (Social Security Park; Av. Cuauhtémoc and Obrero Mundial; phone: 639-4076).

BOXING AND WRESTLING Both take place regularly downtown at the *Arena Coliseo* (Colosseum Arena; 77 Perú; phone: 526-1687). The atmosphere is very rough: Don't be surprised if a lit cigarette butt lands in your lap or a firecracker explodes over your head.

BULLFIGHTING Twelve corridas *formales* (with veteran matadors) are held promptly at 4 PM on Sundays November through January in the *Plaza México* (241 Calle Augusto Rodín; phone: 563-3959/60/61). Although you can purchase tickets at any of the half dozen box offices at the stadium, we recommend asking the travel desk at your hotel to get them for you; otherwise, you may end up with a bad seat in the blazing sun. Tickets for *novilladas* (bullfights with novice matadors), held April through June, are much less expensive than those for main season events.

GOLF The city has no public golf courses, but there are several excellent private country clubs. Some of the major hotels can arrange temporary memberships for guests, but usually on weekdays only. Exchange privileges are available for members of US country clubs; you can also apply for guest privileges through your hotel. Unless otherwise indicated, the courses listed below are open daily. The long 18-hole and the short 18-hole course at the *Club de Golf México* (San Buenaventura, in the southern Tlalpan district, about 30 minutes from downtown; phone: 573-2000) were both designed by Percy Clifford. The *Mexico City Country Club* (also in Tlalpan, about 25 minutes from downtown; phone: 549-3040, ext. 208) has an 18-hole course and a par 3 layout, both designed by George Brademus. *Club de Golf Chapultepec* (425 Av. Conscripto; phone: 589-1200), in the wealthy eastern suburb of Lomas de Sotelo near the *Hipódromo de las Américas* racetrack, about 40 minutes from downtown, is the site of the *Mexican Open* in November. About an hour's drive from downtown are *Bellavista,* in the northeast suburb of Ciudad Satélite (phone: 398-9707); *Hacienda,* in the northern suburb of Tlalnepantla (phone: 379-0033); and *Vallescondido,* in the eastern suburb of Atizapán de Zaragoza (Av. Club de Golf; phone: 308-0092/3, 308-1101, or 308-2131). Also about an hour to the east is the large *Coral Golf Resort* (in Ixtapaluca, Km 29.8 on the old Puebla Hwy.;

phone: 597-20276/7), which is closed to the public on Mondays; there are two 18-hole Larry Hughes courses.

HORSE RACING The beautiful *Hipódromo de las Américas* (Av. Industria Militar, Colonia Lomas de Sotelo; phone: 557-4100) is closed for the last two weeks in December. Races take place on Tuesdays and Thursdays at 3 PM, Fridays at 5 PM, and weekends at 2:30 PM. If you make a killing, there are no IRS agents waiting to take your name and address, but the Mexican equivalent of the IRS takes a big bite.

There are several dining spots on the premises; some of the more exclusive hotels can arrange a visit to the elegant *Jockey Club* on the top level. Below the *Jockey Club* on the second tier is the *Gay Dalton Club* (Gay Dalton was a famous stakes-winning horse in Mexico). Anyone can enter, but you may have to slip the waiter a few dollars and spend some time at your table. Don't despair if you can't get in; there's also the *Nuevo Laredo Turf Club,* the *Derby,* the *Handicap,* and the *Palermo.*

Peseros (jitney cabs) to the *Hipódromo* leave from the terminal at the *Chapultepec* metro station (see *Getting Around*).

JAI ALAI At the famous *Frontón México* (northwest corner of Plaza de la República, No. 17; phone: 546-5369), there's betting throughout each game, but unless you're familiar with the complicated system, you're better off just being an interested spectator. There are three games nightly, Tuesdays through Saturdays beginning at 7 PM and Sundays at 5 PM. Be warned: The crowd here has become somewhat rowdy in recent years.

SOCCER Called *fútbol,* this is the most popular sport in Mexico. The season runs through the summer and fall. Most games are played in the huge *Estadio Azteca* (Aztec Stadium; 3465 Calzada Tlalpan; phone: 677-7198). Weekday games usually begin at 8:45 PM, Saturday games at 5 PM, and Sunday games at noon. Matches also take place in the *Estadio Olímpico* (Olympic Stadium, in Ciudad Universitaria; phone: 548-9791) on Saturdays at 5 PM. Make arrangements through your hotel for tickets. Both stadiums are in southern Mexico City.

SWIMMING If your hotel does not have a pool, the manager can usually make arrangements for you to use the pool at a nearby hotel, or can set up guest privileges at a private sports club.

TENNIS *Club de Tenis Reyes* (34 Calle José María Tornel; phone: 515-6004) in the San Miguel Chapultepec district has four lighted indoor cement courts, which are open from 7 AM to 10 PM. Reservations are required to play, and lessons are available.

A number of private golf clubs (see *Golf*) have courts and accept visitors on weekdays; your hotel can make arrangements. Or ask at your hotel about court availability at one of the following private clubs: *Chapultepec Sports Club* (665 Av. Mariano Escobedo; phone: 511-4848); the *French Club* (75 Av. Francia; phone: 524-0424); the *Israeli Sports Club* (620 Blvd. Manuel

Avila Camacho; phone: 557-3000); the *Italian Tennis Club* (185 Av. Santa Ursula; phone: 573-1174); the *Junior Sports Club* (3 Sindicalismo; phone: 277-7666); the *Spain Club* (2390 Av. Insurgentes Sur; phone: 550-3488); and the *Swiss Sports Club* (840 San Borja; phone: 559-3320).

There also are courts in many Mexico City hotels, including the *Camino Real* (four lighted Laykold tennis courts); the *Nikko México* (three indoor Laykold courts and a practice court); and the *Sheraton María Isabel* (two lighted asphalt courts); however, you must be a hotel guest to play. (See *Checking In* for details on the hotels.)

THEATER AND MUSIC

The city offers several interesting cultural attractions, including one that's world-renowned.

TOP TROUPE

Ballet Folklórico de México This wonderful dance company is known around the world for its brilliantly staged and costumed presentations. They perform Wednesday evenings at 9 PM and Sundays at 9:30 AM in the *Palacio de Bellas Artes* (corner of Av. Juárez and Eje Central Lázaro Cárdenas; phone: 512-3633) and Sundays at 9 PM in the *Teatro Hidalgo,* right behind the *Palacio de Bellas Artes* (12 Av. Hidalgo; phone: 709-3111, ext. 149). For additional details, see *Quintessential Mexico* in DIVERSIONS.

In addition, first-rate Mexican and international theatrical and musical performers, including David Copperfield, Sting, and Plácido Domingo, appear at the showy *Auditorio Nacional* (National Auditorium) in *Bosque de Chapultepec* (phone: 520-9060). The *Ollin Yoliztli* (phone: 655-3611) and *Nezahualcóyotl* (phone: 665-1270) concert halls (both near the *Perisur* shopping center) and *Teatro de la Ciudad de México* (36 Donceles, downtown; phone: 510-2197), just a few blocks north of the *Palacio de Bellas Artes,* also offer excellent concerts by local and international orchestras and concert artists.

NIGHTCLUBS AND NIGHTLIFE

Mexico City has a lively after-dark scene. Plan to spend at least one evening at Plaza Garibaldi (a few blocks south of Paseo de la Reforma Nte.), where you can sit on a bench and people watch while the mariachi bands play. Among the well-known bars on the plaza are *Guadalajara de Noche* (phone: 526-5521); *Tenampa* (phone: 526-6176); and *Plaza Santa Cecilia* (phone: 529-1102), which offers a good Mexican fiesta. For terrific mariachi music in more elegant surroundings, try *La Mancha* at the *Aristos* hotel or the *Jorongo Bar* in the *Sheraton María Isabel.* (For details on the hotels listed in this section, see *Checking In.*)

The beautiful brass-and-glass lobby bar in the *Sheraton María Isabel* is a lovely place for a quiet drink. *Las Sillas,* at the *Fiesta Americana Reforma* hotel, is another good spot to enjoy an early evening cocktail. Other nightspots in the *Fiesta Americana Reforma* are *Stelaris,* a rooftop supper club, and *Barbarella,* a dance hall featuring the latest musical groups. The music and people watching are best at the lobby bars of the *Nikko México* and *Presidente Inter-Continental;* for music and dancing with a view, try *Torre de Oro* in the *Sevilla Palace. Yesterday's* at the *Aristos* is another popular nightclub.

The clubs with the best floor shows include the *Premier* (190 Av. San Jerónimo; phone: 548-9723 or 652-6933); *Maquiavelo* in the *Krystal Zona Rosa* hotel; and *Señorial* (188 Calle Hamburgo, in the Zona Rosa; phone: 511-9778). The top discos are *Cero-Cero* at the *Camino Real* hotel; *Disco Club* at the *Presidente Inter-Continental; Zazzy* at the *Nikko México; Taizz* at the *Sevilla Palace; News* (225 Av. San Jerónimo; phone: 395-1353); and *Quetzal* at the top of the *International Trade Center* (Av. Insurgentes and Viaducto Miguel Alemán, Colonia Nápoles; no phone). *Lipstick,* at the *Aristos,* has good rock groups and the best popcorn in town. The Polynesian show at the *Mauna Loa* restaurant (see *Eating Out*) has been popular for years. There's also live music, dancing, and a disco, *El Corsario,* downstairs. The *Focolare* restaurant (87 Calle Hamburgo, Zona Rosa; phone: 511-2679) has a fun Mexican fiesta Fridays and Saturdays. On Saturdays, there's also a good fiesta on the patio of the historic *De Cortés* hotel. Other old favorites include *El Patio* (9 Calle Atenas; phone: 535-3905) and *El Hijo del Cuervo* (17 Jardín Centenario, in Coyoacán; phone: 658-5306).

Salsa is king at *Antillano's* (78 Calle Francisco Pimental in Colonia San Rafael; phone: 592-0439), and there's a great belly dancer at *Adonis* (424 Av. Homero in Polanco; phone: 250-2064), a Lebanese restaurant-nightclub. *A note of warning:* It's a good idea to leave valuables at your hotel and keep a good grip on whatever you do take with you; pickpockets and thieves enjoy Mexico City's nightlife, too.

Best in Town

CHECKING IN

At times, every hotel in Mexico City fills up, so it's a good idea to confirm your reservation. Expect to pay $200 or more per night for a double room at very expensive hotels, $150 to $200 at expensive ones, $80 to $140 at moderate ones, and $70 or less at inexpensive ones. Unless otherwise noted, the hotels listed below have air conditioning, telephones, and TV sets in the rooms. All telephone numbers are in the 5 city code unless otherwise indicated.

We begin with our favorite havens (we admit that they're pricey), followed by recommended hotels, listed by price category.

A REGAL RESORT AND A SPECIAL HAVEN

Camino Real A true resort, even if it is in the middle of one of the most crowded cities in the world. Designed by Ricardo Legorreta, the 716-room hotel's bold architecture—sloping exterior walls and, indoors, spacious lobbies adorned with murals, paintings, and sculpture—calls to mind an Aztec temple. Among the more prosaic attractions are two pools, a spa, bars, gorgeous gardens, and even rooftop tennis. There are several restaurants on the premises, including a branch of *Fouquet's* of Paris and *Azulejos* (see *Eating Out* for both). A complete, self-contained gem, it's impeccably sited near *Bosque de Chapultepec,* at 700 Av. Mariano Escobedo (phone: 203-2121; 800-7-CAMINO in the US; 800-90123 in Mexico; fax: 254-4332).

De Cortés Few would expect to find an inn as small, charming, tranquil—even romantic—as this in Mexico City. Perhaps even more surprising is that the 19-room, eight-suite hotel is in a former Augustine monastery. Now a national monument and part of the Best Western chain, the monastery has functioned as a hotel since 1943. Its somber, fortress-like façade features a crumbling sculpture of St. Augustine. Inside, beyond the registration desk, is a spacious, plant-filled courtyard surrounded by two floors of rooms. With high ceilings and massive wood beams, the rooms are simply but tastefully decorated and usually adorned with fresh flowers. The meter-thick walls shelter guests from otherwise inescapable traffic noises. Meals are served at tables set around the courtyard or, if the weather is bad, inside a small, cheery dining room. The kitchen's reputation is good enough to attract even fussy Mexico City businesspeople for breakfast and lunch. Dinner is served by candlelight; Saturday evenings there is an elaborate fiesta. Right on the *Alameda Central,* one block east of the *Palacio de Bellas Artes,* at 85 Av. Hidalgo (phone: 518-2181/2/3/4/5; 800-528-1234; fax: 512-1863).

VERY EXPENSIVE

Four Seasons Mexico City The newest luxury hotel in Mexico City (opened in 1995), has 240 rooms and suites, two restaurants, a bar, a lobby lounge, a health club, and a business center, all housed in a posh, pink-stone structure. The most striking feature is the center patio, featuring a stunning fountain. 500 Paseo de la Reforma, near *Bosque de Chapultepec* (phone: 230-1818; 800-332-3442 in the US; 800-268-6282 in Canada; fax: 230-1817).

Marco Polo Here are 60 tastefully furnished, comfortable rooms and four penthouse suites. All the suites have a Jacuzzi, and the largest also affords a spectacular view of the Paseo de la Reforma and the *Angel de la Independencia* monument (a column topped by a golden angel, symbolizing Mexico's independence). Pluses include valet parking and a small restaurant-bar. Bilingual secretarial service is available. 27 Calle Amberes, in the Zona Rosa (phone: 207-0299; 800-223-9868 in the US; 800-90060 in Mexico; fax: 533-3727).

Marquis Reforma Excellent service and facilities are the main draws at this pink-and-blue Art Deco palace. The 125 rooms and 84 suites feature all the comforts, including original artwork, mini-bars, personal safes, and electronic door locks. There is a good restaurant, a coffee shop, a lobby bar, an indoor jogging track, a spa, and an executive center. 465 Paseo de la Reforma, Zona Rosa (phone: 211-3600; 800-235-2387 in the US; 800-90176 in Mexico; fax: 211-5561).

Nikko México This hotel boasts 750 stylish rooms, including 20 suites, all equipped with an ultramodern security system. Among the many amenities are a French and a Japanese restaurant, a disco, three tennis courts and a practice court, and an athletic club with an indoor pool. One floor is for female guests only. 204 Av. Campos Elíseos, Polanco (phone: 280-1111; 800-NIKKO-US in the US; 800-90888 in Mexico; fax: 280-9191).

Sheraton María Isabel Large (752 rooms) and luxurious, this property offers a restaurant and a coffee shop, an impressive lobby bar, two other bars featuring entertainment, and a solarium and heated rooftop pool. 325 Paseo de la Reforma, Zona Rosa (phone: 207-3933; 800-325-3535 in the US; 800-90325 in Mexico; fax: 207-0684).

EXPENSIVE

Century This elegant 142-room hotel has sunken marble bathtubs, a restaurant, a heated pool, and a nightclub. 152 Calle Liverpool, Zona Rosa (phone: 726-9911; 800-344-1212; 800-70111 in Mexico; fax: 525-7475).

Fiesta Americana Reforma The facilities at this large (607-unit) property include three dining rooms and five bars. It's an excellent spot for nightlife. 80 Paseo de la Reforma, downtown (phone: 705-1515; 800-223-2332 in the US; 800-50450 in Mexico; fax: 705-1313).

Imperial This historic turn-of-the-century landmark—topped by a gilt cupola—has 65 units, including 10 suites, all comfortably furnished and equipped with safes and all the other usual amenities. There also is a restaurant, a coffee shop, a lobby bar with live music in the evenings, and parking. 64 Paseo de la Reforma, downtown (phone: 705-4911; fax: 703-3122).

Krystal Zona Rosa With 302 rooms, this excellently run hostelry offers fine facilities, including a heated pool, two restaurants, a lobby bar with live music, and a popular nightclub. 155 Calle Liverpool, Zona Rosa (phone: 228-9928; 800-231-9860; fax: 511-3490).

Presidente Inter-Continental This popular 683-unit hostelry has several restaurants, including a branch of *Maxim's* of Paris (see *Eating Out*), plus shops on each level. The lobby bar, with live classical music and jazz, is a congenial place to meet people. Right on the edge of *Bosque de Chapultepec,* at 218 Av. Campos Elíseos (phone: 327-7700; 800-327-0200 in the US; 800-90444 in Mexico; fax: 327-7789).

Westin Galería Plaza In this spacious property are 434 rooms and two executive floors. The excellent food and drink at the *Ile de France* restaurant (see *Eating Out*) and at the congenial *tapas* bar make up for the somewhat surly service. There also is a lobby bar and a coffee shop. 195 Calle Hamburgo at Calle Varsovia, Zona Rosa (phone: 211-0014; 800-228-3000 in the US; 800-90223 in Mexico; fax: 207-5867).

MODERATE

Aristos This active place features a gym and nightclub, as well as a sauna to take the kinks out the following morning. There are 353 rooms, plus two restaurants, a nightclub, and a rock music club. 276 Paseo de la Reforma, Zona Rosa (phone: 211-0112; 800-5-ARISTO; fax: 514-4473).

Calinda Geneve A popular old favorite run by Calinda Quality, it features 320 rooms. On the premises are a restaurant-bar, a drugstore, and a gift shop. 130 Calle Londres, Zona Rosa (phone: 211-0071; 800-228-5151 in the US; 800-90000 in Mexico; fax: 208-7422).

Emporio This property has 150 rooms, all with Jacuzzis. There's a restaurant and a bar with live music. Midway between downtown and *Bosque de Chapultepec,* at 124 Paseo de la Reforma (phone: 566-7766 or 627-0272; fax: 627-0272).

Howard Johnson Gran Truly a grand hotel, it's architecturally sophisticated, charming, and gracious, though in need of some exterior renovation. The façade belies the beauty of its Art Nouveau interior: a magnificent stained glass domed ceiling, a monumental wrought-iron French-style staircase, cage elevators, and singing birds in brass cages. The 124 rooms are in very good condition. There is valet parking, a baby-sitting service, a gift shop, and two restaurants. On the corner of the *zócalo,* at 82 Calle 16 de Septiembre (phone: 510-4040; 800-456-4656 in the US; 800-50549 in Mexico; fax: 512-2085).

Ritz A quiet, 126-room Best Western property, it has been a favorite of wealthy Mexicans for years. There is a solarium and restaurant-bar. Near the *zócalo,* at 30 Av. Francisco I. Madero (phone: 518-1340; 800-528-1234; fax: 518-3466).

Sevilla Palace Here are 414 rooms, a restaurant, a coffee shop, a covered rooftop pool, a health club with a Jacuzzi, a disco, and a terraced rooftop lounge affording a spectacular view of the city. 105 Paseo de la Reforma, near downtown (phone: 705-2800; 800-732-9488; fax: 535-3842).

Bristol Very pleasant, with 154 rooms, a restaurant, and a bar, this hostelry is located in an interesting neighborhood not far from the Zona Rosa and Paseo de la Reforma. 17 Plaza Necaxa, Colonia Cuauhtémoc (phone/fax: 208-1717).

Polanco This is a real bargain, with 75 smallish but pleasant rooms and four junior suites. A good Italian restaurant, *La Bottiglia,* also is on the premises (see *Eating Out*). 8 Calle Edgar Allan Poe, Polanco (phone: 280-8082; fax: 280-8066, ext. 101).

EATING OUT

Mexico City is a sophisticated, cosmopolitan metropolis that abounds with restaurants of every ethnic stripe. Most of the restaurants listed here have English-speaking waiters. To play it safe, order bottled water, even in the finest restaurants. Remember that you'll have most restaurants pretty much to yourself if you go for lunch before 2 PM or for dinner before 9 PM.

Restaurants in the very expensive category charge $100 or more for dinner for two; in the expensive category, about $75; in the moderate category, about $50; and in the inexpensive category, about $30. Prices do not include drinks, wine, tax, or tip. Most restaurants below accept MasterCard and Visa, and a few also accept American Express and Diners Club; it's a good idea to call ahead and check. Unless otherwise noted, all restaurants are open daily for lunch and dinner; some may close between lunch and dinner. All telephone numbers are in the 5 city code unless otherwise indicated.

Les Ambassadeurs This restaurant's setting resembles the patio of a hacienda, and the emphasis is on upscale Mexican fare. A spectacular aquarium adorns one of the walls. Reservations necessary. Downtown, at 12 Paseo de la Reforma (phone: 566-3587).

Chez Wok Luxuriate in the posh ambience while feasting on the best of Chinese culinary tradition, including tasty dishes from Canton, Szechuan, Shanghai, and Beijing. Renowned specialties include "lacquered duck," cooked in a caramel sauce that forms a glossy coating, shark's-fin soup, and more than 40 varieties of dim sum, which here are Chinese ravioli (round, stuffed rice pasta). Reservations necessary. 117 Tennyson, corner of Av. Presidente Mazarik, Polanco (phone: 281-3410 or 281-2921).

Fouquet's This branch of the famous dining place in Paris serves some of the finest French food in the city. Ties are required for men. Closed Saturday lunch and Sundays. Reservations necessary. In the *Camino Real Hotel,* 700 Av. Mariano Escobedo (phone: 203-2121).

La Galvia Especially popular with Mexico's advertising crowd, this spot features exquisitely presented dishes like Norwegian monkfish, venison in blackberry sauce, and chicken in watercress sauce. Jacket and tie are required for men except on Saturdays. Closed Sundays. Reservations necessary. 247 Av. Campos Elíseos, Polanco (phone: 281-2310).

Ile de France For nearly impeccable service and fine French dishes prepared imaginatively, be sure to visit this lovely spot. Closed Sundays. Reservations advised. At the *Westin Galería Plaza Hotel,* 195 Calle Hamburgo at Calle Varsovia (phone: 211-0014).

Los Irabién This excellent restaurant houses a superb collection of art that has been passed down for generations in the old-money family that owns the place. The nouvelle Mexican dishes include steaks smothered in strawberry and black pepper sauce, pistachio soup, and lobster baked in tequila. The service is excellent. Open for breakfast, lunch, and dinner; closes Sundays at 6 PM. Reservations necessary. 45 Av. de la Paz, San Angel (phone: 550-8662 or 550-1182).

Isadora Nouvelle cuisine and traditional continental fare with a decidedly Mexican influence are served in this elegant restaurant. The superlative appetizers and soups alone make up for the at-times-underwhelming main courses and desserts. Closed Sundays. Reservations necessary. 50 Calle Moliere, Polanco (phone: 280-1586 or 280-5586).

Maxim's The French food and atmosphere here are nearly as wonderful as those in its parent restaurant in Paris. Jacket and tie required for men. Closed Saturday lunch and Sundays. Reservations necessary. At the *Presidente Hotel,* 218 Av. Campos Elíseos (phone: 281-0249 or 281-3687).

Sir Winston Churchill's The food and atmosphere are very British in this restored Tudor mansion. The house specialty is roast beef with Yorkshire pudding. Closed Sundays. Reservations advised. 67 Blvd. Manuel Avila Camacho, Polanco (phone: 280-6070).

Suntory Japanese food is featured; the beautiful gardens create a lovely atmosphere. Reservations advised. Two locations: 14 Torres Adalid, Colonia del Valle (phone: 536-9432), and 535 Calle Montes Urales and Paseo de la Reforma, Lomas de Chapultepec (phone: 202-4711).

EXPENSIVE

Antigua Hacienda de Tlalpan Set in a beautifully restored 18th-century hacienda on two acres of gardens where peacocks roam freely, it features fine Mexican and international fare. Reservations advised. 4619 Calzada Tlalpan, in the Tlalpan district (phone: 573-9933).

Azulejos This pleasant, cheerful spot offers especially well prepared Mexican dishes. An excellent buffet is served on Sundays. Don't waste your calorie quota on the disappointing desserts, though. Reservations advised. In the *Camino Real Hotel,* 700 Av. Mariano Escobedo (phone: 203-2121).

Bombay Palace Specializing in *moghlai* cuisine of northern India, this spacious, informal restaurant is part of a quality international chain with branches in Budapest, London, and Kuala Lumpur. The tandoori chicken—cooked with saffron in a wood-burning oven—is outstanding, and there's a daily buffet at lunch. 43 Amberes, Zona Rosa (phone: 525-3856 or 514-4497).

Cicero Centenario The crowd is fun and the food tasty at this restored New Orleans–style mansion. Carnivores will love the roast beef. Reservations advised. 195 Calle Londres, in the Zona Rosa (phone: 533-4276).

Delmonico's This eatery is justly famous for its excellent Mexican, American, and international fare. The weekend brunches here are works of art. Reservations advised. 91 Calle Londres, in the Zona Rosa (phone: 207-4949).

Estoril With a menu of first-rate Mexican and continental dishes, the specialties here include fried parsley, mole, and *huitlacoche* (a corn fungus that has a mushroom-like flavor) crêpes. Reservations advised. Two locations: 75 Calle Génova, Zona Rosa (closed weekends; phone: 208-6418), and 24 Calle Alejandro Dumas, Polanco (closed Sundays; phone: 280-3632).

Hacienda de los Morales One of the most beautiful restaurants in Mexico City is located in an impressive, meticulously restored 16th-century hacienda. The international menu is superb, but it is especially famous for its traditional Mexican dishes. Reservations advised. 525 Calle Vázquez de Mella, Colonia Morales (phone: 281-4554).

Lago Chapultepec This elegant, architecturally spectacular restaurant overlooks the lake in the newer section of *Bosque de Chapultepec.* International fare is served in a dressy, formal atmosphere; there's also a bar and dancing. Reservations necessary. Lago Mayor, segunda sección (second section), *Bosque de Chapultepec* (phone: 515-9586).

Mauna Loa Extravagant Polynesian decor and excellent Cantonese and international cooking are featured here. There is a stage show and music for dancing, as well as a disco downstairs. Reservations advised. 240 Av. San Jerónimo, Pedregal (phone: 616-2902).

Mazurka Wonderful Polish dishes are presented in a very European atmosphere; owner Tadeusz Podbereski was Pope John Paul II's personal chef during his visit to Mexico. A string quartet plays Thursday through Saturday evenings; there's a pianist Monday through Wednesday evenings. Closed Sunday dinner. Reservations advised. 150 Calle Nueva York, Nápoles (phone: 523-8811 or 543-4509).

Mesón del Cid Delicious Spanish food, perhaps the best in Mexico, is served here. Suckling pig and spring lamb are among the recommended entrées. On Saturday nights, there's a medieval dinner with live music, jugglers, and jesters providing entertainment during the meal. Reservations necessary Saturday nights; advised other nights. 61 Calle Humboldt, downtown (phone: 521-1940).

Rozendaal Warm service and outstanding, beautifully presented food are the draws here. The menu changes with the seasons, but the *magret de canard "Croustillant Lilián"* (crisp duck in a light sweet-and-sour sauce) and the *tortilla azul rellena de camarones en crema de cilantro* (shrimp-filled blue tortilla in a cilantro cream sauce) are excellent choices when they're available. Closed for dinner Sundays through Wednesdays. Reservations advised. 27 Calle Praga, near the Zona Rosa (phone: 525-2800).

Toscana Come here for classy Italian fare served in elegant, medieval-style surroundings, including marble walls adorned with frescoes. The house specialty is *gnocchi al formaggi,* a potato pasta in a mouth-watering cheese sauce, and the lasagna is outstanding. On Thursday nights, a string quartet and operatic soprano serenade diners. Reservations advised. 2374-H Av. Insurgentes Sur, Colonia Chimalistac (phone: 550-7169).

MODERATE

Arroyo Sample the best of regional Mexican cooking: lamb steamed in maguey leaves; *huauzontles* (broccoli-like flowerettes strung along a slender stem stuffed with cheese and fried); *nopales* (cactus) salad; and more. There's a folkloric show every day; call for schedule. Open daily from 8 AM to 8 PM. Reservations advised. 4003 Av. Insurgentes Sur, Tlalpan (phone: 573-4344).

Bellinghausen At this delightful patio, try one of the exceptional fish dishes. It's especially good for lunch. No reservations. 95 Calle Londres, in the Zona Rosa (phone: 207-4978).

La Bottiglia Beautifully prepared Italian dishes and a cozy, unpretentious ambience have made this spot one of the most popular in the area. Reservations necessary, especially for lunch. In the *Polanco* hotel, 8 Calle Edgar Allan Poe (phone: 280-0609).

Café de Tacuba Very old and traditionally Mexican, it's great for lunch, particularly for its many varieties of enchiladas. Reservations unnecessary. Two locations: 28 Calle Tacuba, near the *zócalo* (phone: 518-4950), and 88 Av. Newton, Polanco (phone: 250-2633).

La Cava This spacious, beautifully decorated eatery offers Spanish, Mexican, and international dishes. Request a seat on the lovely patio. *Huitlacoche* (corn fungus with a mushroom-like flavor) crêpes are among the specialties. Reservations advised. 2465 Av. Insurgentes Sur, San Angel (phone: 616-0052 or 616-1376).

Chalet Suizo Not surprisingly, great fondues and other Swiss and German dishes are the draws here. Although it's popular and crowded, you rarely have to wait more than a few minutes for a table. Reservations advised. 37 Calle Niza, in the Zona Rosa (phone: 511-7529).

Fonda Casa Paco For Mexican cooking at its best, try the squash soup here, which is served inside a small squash. The squash-blossom and *huitlacoche* (corn fungus with a mushroom-like flavor) crêpes are light and delicate. Closed Sundays. Reservations advised before 9 PM; necessary afterward. 126 Calle Velázquez de León at Antonio Caso, Colonia San Rafael (phone: 546-4060).

Fonda del Recuerdo Popular and festive, this place attracts a crowd that likes loud, live Veracruz music (two groups often play at the same time). Try a *toritos,* a tequila-based drink that has the punch of nitroglycerin, and the house *botana* (an appetizer of guacamole, fried pork rinds, and roast pork served in earthenware bowls). Reservations advised. 37 Calle Bahía de las Palmas, Colonia Anzures (phone: 260-2045).

La Gondola At one of the best Italian eateries in the neighborhood, many dishes are prepared at the table. Reservations advised. 21 Calle Génova, in the Zona Rosa (phone: 514-0743).

La Lanterna Stop counting your cholesterol long enough to sample Italian dishes like *filete a burro nero* (filet of beef in black butter). Closed Sundays. Reservations advised. 458 Paseo de la Reforma, Zona Rosa (phone: 207-9969).

Loredo Hamburgo Try the *carne asada* (broiled steak with a spicy sauce) or *sábana* (a sheet of thin steak that covers the entire plate). There's excellent seafood, too. Reservations unnecessary. 29 Calle Hamburgo, Zona Rosa (phone: 566-3636).

Las Mercedes This is a great spot for fancy Mexican cooking: Order the lamb baked in maguey leaves or shrimp baked with cheese. Reservations advised. Two locations: 113 Calle Leibnitz at Darwin, Colonia Anzures (phone: 254-5000 or 254-8211), and 91 Calle Río Guadalquivir, Colonia Cuauhtémoc (phone: 254-5044).

Mesón del Caballo Bayo Set in a restored hacienda, this beautiful restaurant is the place for *barbacoa* (lamb steamed in maguey leaves) and other Mexican specialties. Very popular with the "Beautiful People," it's usually packed at midday and on weekends. Reservations advised. Near the racetrack, at 360 Av. del Conscripto (phone: 589-3000 or 589-1384).

Mesón del Perro Andaluz This is one of the Zona Rosa's most popular indoor-outdoor cafés for people watching, sangria sipping, and appetizer munching. Reservations unnecessary. 26 Calle Copenhague (phone: 533-5306).

Mi Lomita Hefty portions of good meat are prepared Argentine-style here. Reservations advised. 52 Av. Presidente Mazarik, at Torcuato Tasso, Polanco (phone: 250-2522).

La Opera This lively cantina was once an all-male domain (in fact, a bullet hole in the ceiling was the work of Pancho Villa). Now, however, both sexes are welcome to sample the Spanish and international fare. Try the enchiladas, steak tartare, or roast kid—and don't forget the tequila. Closed Sundays. Reservations advised. Near the *zócalo,* at 10 Av. 5 de Mayo (phone: 512-8959).

Piccadilly Pub A good change of pace, this spot serves such hearty Anglo fare as roast beef and Irish stew, plus the best cherries jubilee in town. Reservations advised. 23 Calle Copenhague, in the Zona Rosa (phone: 514-1515).

INEXPENSIVE

El Caminero Tacos filled with broiled meat and melted cheese, accompanied by grilled *cebollitas* (scallions), are the specialty here. No reservations. Behind the *Sheraton María Isabel* at 138 Calle Río Lerma (phone: 514-5615).

Fonda el Refugio Locals come to this wonderful little place for such Mexican staples as *carne asada* (thin filet of beef broiled and served with beans, enchiladas, and guacamole). Closed Sundays. Reservations advised. 166 Calle Liverpool, in the Zona Rosa (phone: 207-2732).

Hostería de Santo Domingo In business for almost 150 years, this spot offers fine Mexican food and colorful decor. There is lively music at noon. No reservations, but on weekends be prepared for a long wait unless you arrive before 2 PM. Near the *zócalo,* at 72 Calle Belisario Domínguez (phone: 510-1434).

Los Panchos The best *tacos de carnitas* (roast-pork tacos) in town always taste better eaten at the street stand than in the restaurant in back, but they are actually the same. No reservations. 315 Calle Moliere, Colonia Anzures (phone: 203-8803 or 203-8870).

Monterrey

(pronounced Mon-te-*ray*)

Mexico's third-largest city (with a population of about 3.5 million) is the capital of the state of Nuevo León and the country's main industrial center. Beautifully situated in a 1,767-foot valley in the Sierra Madre Oriental, Monterrey is flanked by the hulking 7,809-foot Cerro de la Mitra (Mitre Peak) to the west and the distinctive 5,703-foot Cerro de la Silla (Saddle Peak)—the city's emblem—to the east.

Often referred to as "the Sultan of the North," Monterrey is second only to Mexico City as a commercial center. *Regiomontanos* (natives of Monterrey) have a reputation for aggressive business practices and hardheaded accounting, as is evident in an old folktale. According to the legend, Cerro de la Silla's saddle-shaped crest was formed when a local resident lost a peso on the topmost ridge of the mountain and kept digging frantically until he recovered it.

Monterrey was founded in 1596 by a group of Spanish families, led by Don Diego de Montemayor. The town was named Villa de Nuestra Señora de Monterrey in honor of the Conde de Monterrey, the Viceroy of New Spain at the time. The early settlers were frequently attacked by Apache and Comanche warriors, but they survived and eventually prevailed. The city is a natural crossroads for anyone traveling north or south through eastern or central Mexico, including just about every army that has marched through the country: Both the Spanish and the revolutionaries held the city at one time during the 1810–21 struggle for independence; a century later, when Pancho Villa began the 1910 revolution in the north, Monterrey's citizens were once again embroiled in battle. In 1847, during the Mexican-American War, Monterrey, like Mexico City and Veracruz, was invaded and occupied by the forces of General Zachary Taylor, who stayed in the city until a peace treaty was signed. One of the most bitter battles of the war occurred on the hill crowned by Monterrey's *Obispado* (Bishop's Palace), where the Mexican army held out for two days after the city below had surrendered.

Eventually, however, Monterrey's strategic mountain-pass location became more of an advantage than a liability. Just as armies found it a convenient stopover, so have millions of travelers over the years. With the city's excellent train service and the highway running from Laredo via Monterrey to Mexico City, practically everything and everybody traveling to Mexico from the part of the US and Canada east of the Rocky Mountains come through here.

Nevertheless, Monterrey did not develop into an industrial center until after 1888, when the Mexican government granted tax exemptions to new industries here. From then on the city boomed, and today iron and steel, beer, cement, tiles, glass, cigarettes, chemicals, textiles, and construction materials are manufactured in Monterrey. John Deere, Chrysler, and General Electric all have factories here.

Still, interest in Monterrey is not limited to the historian or the business-minded. It is also a big college town, with seven universities, among them the main campus of the *Instituto Tecnológico de Monterrey,* which is the *MIT* of Mexico and also has branches around the country. The state *Universidad de Nuevo León* and the private *Universidad de Monterrey* attract medical students from the US. The college crowd, along with most everyone else, strolls through the Gran Plaza in the evenings, until midnight in summer.

The city has a noticeably large collection of modern sculpture, much of it on the Gran Plaza. Among the most outstanding pieces are Rufino Tamayo's striking *Homage to the Sun* and Gabriel Ponsarelli's celebratory *The Children and Monument to Youth.* More controversial are Luis Barragán's orange *Beacon of Commerce,* with its piercing green laser, and the unwieldy *Fountain of Life* by Luis Sanguino. Near the plaza in the Garza García district, on the south bank of the Río Santa Catarina on Avenida Gómez Morín, is a prominent 100-foot-high sculpture, known locally as *Los Tubos* (The Pipes), by Xavier Meléndez.

Among the attractions of Monterrey's environs are the *Grutas de García* (García Caverns), among the largest and most beautiful caverns in Mexico, and Huasteca Canyon, a 1,000-foot gorge with striking rock formations.

Monterrey At-a-Glance

SEEING THE CITY

Cerro de Chepe Vera (Chepe Vera Hill), where the *Obispado* (Bishop's Palace) stands, commands a panoramic view of the city; on the west side of town, it's reached via Calle Padre Mier. Sunsets are lovely from atop the Mesa de Chipinque (Chipinque Mesa), the ridged plateau 12 miles (19 km) southwest of the city. Closer to home, the tower of the *Palacio Federal* (Old City Hall), at the northern end of the Gran Plaza, and the second floor and the roof of the *Palacio Municipal* (New City Hall) at the southern end (ask a guard for permission to look) provide sweeping views of what lies in between.

SPECIAL PLACES

The intersection of Juárez and Aramberri is the orientation point in Monterrey: The numbers start here and ascend as you get farther away. Direction orientation also begins from here: Streets running north and south are designated *Norte* (Nte.) and *Sur;* those going east and west, *Oriente* (Ote.) and *Poniente* (Pte.).

GRAN PLAZA Also known as Plaza Macro, it's one of the largest town squares in the world. Abounding with fountains, flowers, walkways, modern sculpture, a theater, and an underground shopping mall, it is also where the action is most evenings, with band concerts on weeknights in summer. The south end incorporates verdant Plaza Zaragoza, the site of the *Palacio Federal,* the cathedral, and the towering *Beacon of Commerce.* (The stately building with the winding stair leading to the front entrance is the *Monterrey Casino,* a private social club.) Bounded by Washington, Constitución, Zaragoza, and Dr. Coss.

CATEDRAL Construction of this cathedral began in 1635 and continued until 1791. The richly carved Baroque façade, the Catalonian bell tower, and the murals by Mexican painter Angel Zárraga depicting the life of the Virgin Mary are all notable. Calles Zuazua and Ocampo.

PALACIO DE GOBIERNO (STATEHOUSE) This decrepit but endearing red sandstone structure, with eight Corinthian columns in front, houses the offices of the governor and other state officials. Of interest inside are the pigeon-riddled colonial-style patio, the plaque commemorating the meeting between Franklin D. Roosevelt and Mexican President Manuel Avila Camacho, and the historical exhibition in the red reception room that includes the guns used by the firing squad to execute Emperor Maximilian. Open weekdays. No admission charge. Zaragoza and 5 de Mayo.

PALACIO FEDERAL (OLD CITY HALL) Now housing the telegraph and postal services, this building at the northernmost end of the Gran Plaza has a lovely 16th-century courtyard complete with wrought-iron lamps and tiled arches. The *Iglesia del Sagrado Corazón de Jesús* (Sacred Heart of Jesus Church) is next door. Open weekdays. No admission charge. Zaragoza and Washington.

EL OBISPADO (BISHOP'S PALACE) Built in 1788 as the residence of a bishop, this strategically located palace served as a fort during the 1846 Mexican-American War. French forces attacked it during their invasion, and Pancho Villa used it during the 1910 revolution. The battle-scarred exterior tells the story; the small museum inside elaborates on it. Closed Mondays. Admission charge. On the west side of town atop Cerro de Chepe Vera. Take Calle Padre Mier to Calle México, then take the next left (phone: 346-0404).

IGLESIA DE LA PURÍSIMA (CHURCH OF THE IMMACULATE CONCEPTION) This church, designed by Enrique de la Mora y Palomar, draws architecture fans from all over the world. An impressionistic bronze sculpture of Christ and the apostles adorns the façade of the cruciform shell. The simple bell tower features a terra cotta sculpture depicting the Immaculate Conception. The small wooden statue of the Virgen Chiquita (Little Virgin), sitting on the main altar, is said to have prevented the Río Santa Catarina from flooding the city during a violent storm in 1756. Corner of Serafín Peña and Av. Hidalgo Pte.

SANTUARIO DE GUADALUPE (SANCTUARY OF GUADALUPE) This modern church resembles a giant tepee—incongruously flanked by statues of the Virgin of

Guadalupe and Pope John Paul II—set against the skyline. (The older, original church stands off to one side.) Jalisco and Libertad, in Colonia Independencia.

CUAUHTÉMOC BREWERY COMPLEX Two brands of beer—Bohemia and Carta Blanca—are produced in this complex, one of the largest breweries in Mexico. The original brewery, also on the premises, was converted into the *Museo de Monterrey,* one of Mexico's finest museums of contemporary art. It houses works by Bartolomé Murillo, José Orozco, David Alfaro Siqueiros, Diego Rivera, and Rufino Tamayo, among others. In addition, some of the old brewery's huge wooden barrels and copper vats are exhibited.

Also here is the *Salón de la Fama* (Hall of Fame), which honors national and international baseball greats, as well as other athletes. Tours of the brewery, given Tuesdays through Fridays, include free samples. Further, the grounds of the brewery contain pools, tennis courts, baseball diamonds, basketball courts, soccer fields, an amphitheater for cultural events, a clubhouse with table tennis and billiards, bowling alleys, a library, a movie theater, and even a ballroom. All facilities are open to the public. Closed Mondays. No admission charge. 2202 Av. Universidad Nte. (phone: 328-5355, brewery; 328-5844, museum).

MUSEO DE ARTE CONTEMPORÁNEO (MUSEUM OF CONTEMPORARY ART) Designed by Ricardo Legorreta, one of Mexico's leading architects, this striking museum is dedicated to displaying works by artists from the Americas. The huge bronze sculpture of a dove at the entrance is the work of Jalisco artist Juan Soriano. In addition to 14 exhibition halls surrounding a covered central patio, facilities include a restaurant and coffee shop, a library, and an auditorium. Closed Mondays. Admission charge. Gran Plaza, next to the cathedral, Calles Dr. Coss and Ocampo (phone: 342-4820).

MUSEO DE HISTORIA MEXICANA (MUSEUM OF MEXICAN HISTORY) This most recent addition to Monterrey's cultural scene uses high-tech video and sound effects and interactive exhibits to explore Mexico's fascinating history. Built around a central hall with displays about the country's ecosystems, its four galleries highlight pre-Hispanic, colonial, 19th-century, and modern Mexico. Closed Mondays. No admission charge. 455 Calle Dr. Coss, on the Gran Plaza (phone: 345-9898).

CENTRO CULTURAL ALFA (ALFA CULTURAL CENTER) A striking science museum that resembles a tin can set at an angle in the ground, it features hands-on exhibits. The planetarium includes a giant-screen Omnimax theater. Closed Mondays. Admission charge. Free transport to and from *Parque Alameda* (Alameda Park), at Villagrán and Washington. 1000 Av. Roberto Garza Sada Sur (phone: 356-5165).

CASA DE LA CULTURA (HOUSE OF CULTURE) For art and railroad lovers alike, it offers changing exhibitions of modern art, housed in a Tudor-style train station trimmed with beautiful woodwork. Open daily. No admission charge. 400 Colón Nte. and Carranza (phone: 374-2612).

ENVIRONS

CHIPINQUE MESA A short drive up the pine-covered slopes of the Sierra Madre ends in this ruffle-ridged, 5,000-foot plateau, surely a relation—if distant— to the New Jersey Palisades. It is also a resort area, with the usual summer homes and cabins, a restaurant, a hotel, and picnic facilities. Eight miles (13 km) southwest of Monterrey, off Rte. 40 toward Saltillo.

CAÑÓN DE HUASTECA (HUASTECA CANYON) This 1,000-foot gorge with massive rock formations framing the stark ravines is great for an outing, particularly of a photographic nature. At noon, what appears to be the image of the Virgin of Guadalupe can be discerned in the rocks. Follow Route 40 toward Saltillo beyond the Chipinque turnoff to the village of Santa Catarina; then go 2 miles (3 km) south (left) on Huasteca. Signs are posted.

COLA DE CABALLO (HORSETAIL FALLS) The area surrounding the natural pool below the triple cascades (also known as the Three Graces) is an ideal picnic spot. Climb the three-quarters of a mile from the parking lot to the base of the falls (a rather arduous trip) or ride a horse to the top. About 22 miles (35 km) south on Rte. 85 to El Cercado, then 4 miles (6 km) west to the falls. Open daily. Admission charge.

SALTILLO A one-and-a-half-hour drive west from Monterrey, Saltillo is a fairly small city (pop. 310,000) with much to offer, including great shopping, sophisticated dining, and charming accommodations. For additional details, see the *Nuevo Laredo to Mexico City* route in DIRECTIONS.

EXTRA SPECIAL

The *Grutas de García* (García Caverns), among the largest and most beautiful in the country, are set high inside a mountain, one of only five such sets of caverns in the world. A cable car inches up 3,700 feet to the entrance of the cavern, where 90-minute tours (in English and Spanish) are conducted over well-lighted passageways that meander ever higher inside the mountain. The caverns comprise four huge grottoes and 12 smaller ones. The more than 20 rock formations are labeled in Spanish and English. Closed December 12. Admission charge. Thirteen miles (21 km) on Route 40 and then 15 miles (24 km) north to Villa de García.

Sources and Resources

TOURIST INFORMATION

For up-to-the-minute information in English on entertainment and special events in Monterrey, as well as general information and brochures, call or visit the helpful people at the state *Infotur* office on the ground floor of the *Congreso del Estado* building (corner of Calles Matamoros and Zaragoza; phone: 345-0870 or 345-2438; 800-235-2438). On Mondays, when *Infotur* is closed, the staff at the state tourist bureau's administrative offices can help you (*Kalos Building,* at Constitución and Zaragoza, Level A-1, Suite 137; phone: 240-1080; 800-235-2438).

LOCAL COVERAGE The English-language *Spot Light* magazine, with highlights of timely goings-on, is available in most hotels. Pick up a useful *Guía Roji* map of the city at any *Sanborns.*

TELEPHONE The city code for Monterrey is 8. *Note:* Mexico's telephone company has embarked on a major expansion project that involves changing telephone numbers in many areas of the country. At press time, all numbers listed in this chapter were correct. However, if you have any difficulties reaching attractions listed here, contact the local tourist office.

CLIMATE AND CLOTHES Monterrey enjoys (or suffers through, depending on your perspective) all four seasons, though winter and summer are shorter here than in the US. In August, it's not uncommon for the temperature to reach 95F (35C); in December and January, it can drop to 20F (-7C), and it often snows. Visitors dress casually, according to the season.

GETTING AROUND

Having a car in Monterrey can be a boon, particularly if you want to explore beyond the city limits, but it also can be vexing because of heavy traffic, narrow streets, and few parking lots downtown.

CAR RENTAL All major US firms are represented at the airport and the major hotels; among them are *Avis* (phone: 344-5680), *Budget* (phone: 340-4101), *Dollar* (phone: 342-0503), and *National* (phone: 344-6136). *Hertz* has two offices (at the airport and at 814 Garibaldi Sur; phone: 345-6136).

TAXI Prices for the 12-mile (19-km) trip to and from the airport in yellow and white cabs are fixed; other prices are not—ask before getting in. Taxis can be flagged down on the street; they're also available at *sitios* (taxi stands) on Avenida Hidalgo (opposite the *Camino Real Ambassador* hotel) and at the corner of Padre Mier and Escobedo. For pick-up service to the airport, call *Transportes Montrans* (1612 Av. Hidalgo Pte.; phone: 345-7398) or *Autotransportes Aeropuerto* (117 Corona Nte.; phone: 340-5416).

TOURS *Osetur* (phone: 347-1799) runs two tours daily Tuesdays through Saturdays, and one tour on Sunday mornings, to such places as the Gran Plaza, the *Kristaluxus* crystal factory, Chipinque Mesa, and *Grutas de García.*

SPECIAL EVENTS

The Mexican *Día de la Independencia* is commemorated with special fervor in Monterrey, beginning with fireworks on the night of September 15 and followed by a parade the next morning. Celebrations for the *Día de*

Nuestra Señora de Guadalupe (Day of Our Lady of Guadalupe, December 12)—dances, parades, and processions—begin in early December.

SHOPPING

Monterrey boasts few locally produced crafts, except for leather goods and crystal; however, the many factories in town and the discounts they offer make shopping here really worthwhile. *Kristaluxus* (400 José María Vigil, between Guerrero and Zuazua; phone: 329-1530) is Latin America's largest glass factory, and its crystal store has markdowns of 30% to 50%. Factory tours are given weekdays from 9 AM to 1 PM and from 2:30 to 6:30 PM. Many other factories are open for tours; inquire at the tourist office (see *Tourist Information*). The best shops for leather are concentrated on Plaza Hidalgo; many items feature Mexican designs embossed into the leather. Most stores are open from 10 AM to 8 PM and are closed on Sundays.

Casa de las Artesanías de Nuevo León (Dr. Coss and Allende; phone: 345-5817) and *Carápan* (305 Av. Hidalgo Ote. and Galeana; phone: 345-4422) are good places for crafts. For a vast selection of tiles, try *Cerámica Regiomontana* (Km 335 of Blvd. Díaz Ordaz; phone: 336-0047), where tours may be arranged.

There are enough stores to satisfy even the most indefatigable shopper in *Plaza Morelos* (located beneath the Gran Plaza) and *Galerías Monterrey* (at Gonzalitos and P.A. González). The latter, one of Mexico's largest shopping centers, houses a branch of *Tane* (phone: 333-6824), a link of the prestigious national chain of silver shops.

For some of the best baked goods in town, stop in *Mary Lu–La Baguette* (250 Paseo La Victoria and 204 *Galerías Monterrey;* phone: 338-5593, 338-5592, or 338-2577).

SPORTS

The dry bed of the Río Santa Catarina is the site of 2 miles of sports facilities, including tracks, courts, soccer fields, and baseball diamonds. There is also a sports complex—open to the public—at the *Cuauhtémoc Brewery Complex* (see *Special Places*).

BASEBALL The city's team, the *Sultanes de Monterrey,* is a member of Mexico's professional Triple-A league; games are played March through July. Check with the tourist office (see *Tourist Information*) or your hotel desk for the schedule.

BULLFIGHTS The popular spectacles are held each Sunday, March through November, at 4 PM at the *Plaza de Toros Monumental* (Av. Universidad; phone: 374-0505). Obtain tickets at the bullring or from your hotel travel desk.

CHARREADAS Mexican cowboys—some of them businessmen and professionals in "real life"—compete in rodeo exhibitions most weekends, usually on

Sundays. The venue changes from week to week; check with your hotel travel desk.

COCKFIGHTS Popular at fairs and fiestas, and the betting runs high. A less bloody, bladeless version of the sport can be witnessed at *La Fe Palenque* restaurant (see *Eating Out*).

GOLF Monterrey has half a dozen private golf courses, and visitors usually can obtain temporary memberships through their hotel travel desk. The *Club de Golf Valle Alto* (7 miles/11 km south of Monterrey; phone: 317-8400) has an 18-hole course.

HIKING Do as the local folks do and climb up Chipinque Mesa: Follow Gómez Morín past the *Los Tubos* sculpture and proceed up the mountain to a tollbooth and parking lot. From there, take a footpath straight up. The climb takes more than an hour.

NIGHTCLUBS AND NIGHTLIFE

Most late-night action in Monterrey centers around the downtown hotels (see *Checking In* for details on the ones listed below). Popular discos include *Sherezada* in the *Days Inn Granada* and *Scaramouche* in the *Monterrey Crowne Plaza*. Other hot dance clubs are *Koko Loco* (849 Pino Suárez Sur; phone: 345-1231); *Excess* (350 Pino Suárez Sur; phone: 344-5065); and *Disco Bar Onix* (201 Enrique C. Livas Pte.; no phone).

The *Pavillón Bar* of the *Camino Real Ambassador* hotel has live jazz nightly; the lobby bar of the *Gran Hotel Ancira* has jazz nightly except Sundays. Latin American music is performed at *La Milpa de Valerio* in Colonia del Valle (200 Gómez Morín; no phone), and the *Monterrey Crowne Plaza* presents a variety of musical performers in the evenings.

If your preferences are more family-oriented, visit *Parque Plaza Sésamo* (Sesame Street Park), a theme park whose offerings include extensive water games, swimming, amusement park games and rides, a restaurant and snack bars, and live entertainment featuring all the beloved Sesame Street characters. It's a 10-minute drive north of downtown, at 3700 Av. Agrícola, in Colonia Agrícola. The park is closed Mondays; there's an admission charge (phone: 354-5400).

Best in Town

CHECKING IN

Monterrey has a variety of excellent modern hotels, most with air conditioning and heating, color satellite TV, in-room phones, and pools. Expect to pay $150 or more per night for a double room at a very expensive hotel; $100 to $140 at an expensive one; $70 to $90 at a moderate place; and $65 or less at an inexpensive one. All telephone numbers are in the 8 city code unless otherwise indicated.

Fiesta Americana Monterrey An ultramodern property with 288 rooms and suites, a gym, a tennis court, a heated indoor pool, a restaurant, a 24-hour coffee shop, and two bars. Located in one of the city's most exclusive neighborhoods at 300 Av. Vasconcelos Ote. (phone: 368-6000; 800-FIESTA-1 in the US; 800-50450 in Mexico; fax: 368-6040).

Quinta Real Monterrey The slogan of this recently opened world class property is "Your new home away from home," indicating its commitment to providing a comfortable, friendly atmosphere. The decor throughout is elegant and plush, particularly in its 125 well-appointed suites, and the service is professional and attentive. Facilities include a fine continental/Mexican restaurant, a bar, a grand ballroom, a health club, and a business center. Located in the western part of the city, at 500 Diego Rivera (phone: 368-1000; 800-445-4565; fax: 368-1070).

EXPENSIVE

Camino Real Ambassador This beautifully renovated, *gran turismo* property has 240 large, tastefully furnished rooms, a heated pool, an indoor tennis court, a health club, two restaurants, including *Le Pavillón* (see *Eating Out*), a coffee shop, and a bar. Request an odd-numbered room for a mountain view. 310 Ocampo Ote. (phone: 342-2040; 800-7-CAMINO in the US; 800-90123 in Mexico; fax: 345-1984).

Gran Hotel Ancira Built in 1911, this 240-room Monterrey landmark—formerly the *Radisson Ancira Sierra Plaza*—has retained its Old World charm. Amenities include a small pool, a popular restaurant, and a lobby bar with live music, as well as a smaller bar that recalls a Toulouse-Lautrec haunt. Plaza Hidalgo (phone: 345-7575; fax: 344-5226).

Holiday Inn Monterrey Norte Attractive gardens are a plus at this 195-unit motel, as are its restaurant, bar, nightclub, pool, shops, and two lighted tennis courts. Six miles (10 km) north on Rte. 85 at 101 Av. Universidad Nte. (phone: 376-2302; 800-HOLIDAY in the US; 800-00999 in Mexico; fax: 332-0565).

Monterrey Crowne Plaza This spacious, businesslike 390-room hotel has a bar, a tennis court, a pool, a solarium, aerobics, a popular disco, and a good restaurant. 300 Av. Constitución Ote. (phone: 319-6000; 800-2-CROWNE in the US; 800-00999 in Mexico; fax: 344-3007).

Monterrey Gran Plaza Here is an imposing hotel with 197 rooms, as well as a good dining room and bar with nightly entertainment. The hotel overlooks the Gran Plaza. Morelos and Zaragoza (phone: 343-5120; 800-221-2222; fax: 344-7378).

MODERATE

Antaris A comfortable establishment, with striking black lacquer furniture and 44 small rooms with wet bars. There is a restaurant and a pool. However, it's at the top of a very steep hill, and to get a taxi you must usually walk a half mile to the bottom. 400 Río Danubio Ote., Garza García (phone/fax: 378-9966).

Days Inn Granada A 163-room hotel with a pool, a restaurant, a bar, and a popular disco. In Colonia Lomas del Roble, on Av. Jorge del Morral and Almazán (phone: 352-7453; fax: 352-7484).

Fiesta Inn Valle Conveniently located for both business travelers and tourists, this modern downtown hostelry offers 176 spacious—if cookie-cutter—rooms and suites, meeting rooms, a restaurant, and a bar with live music. 327 Av. Lázaro Cárdenas, Garza García (phone: 399-1500; 800-FIESTA-1 in the US; 800-50450 in Mexico; fax: 363-6895).

Río This property has 395 rooms, a pool, a cocktail lounge, and a dining room. Padre Mier and Garibaldi, seven blocks west of the Gran Plaza (phone: 344-9040; 800-421-0767; fax: 345-1456).

Royal Courts A modern colonial-style hostelry with 80 rooms, a heated pool, and a restaurant. Six miles (10 km) north of town at 314 Av. Universidad (phone/fax: 376-2710; 800-528-1234).

INEXPENSIVE

El Paso Autel Although less centrally located than most places, this hotel offers a pleasant environment and good value, with 64 rooms, a coffee shop, and a pool. Near the *Palacio Federal,* at 130 Zaragoza Nte. (phone: 340-0690; fax: 344-4647).

EATING OUT

Several restaurants in town specialize in *norteño* (northern-style) cooking, which means charcoal-broiled steaks, *cabrito* (kid), and thin wheat-flour tortillas. The beef, which comes from Chihuahua and points west, is known for its tastiness. Expect to pay $55 to $75 for a full dinner for two at expensive places; about $45 at moderate places; and $40 or less at inexpensive places. Prices do not include drinks, wine, tax, or tips. Most restaurants below accept MasterCard and Visa, and a few also accept American Express and Diners Club; it's a good idea to call ahead and check. Unless otherwise noted, all restaurants are open daily for lunch and dinner. All telephone numbers are in the 8 city code unless otherwise indicated.

EXPENSIVE

Gambrino's *Filete Gambrino* (filet of beef stuffed with *huitlacoche,* a delectable corn fungus that has a mushroom-like flavor) and mole *poblano* are delicious specialties offered at these elegant eateries. Reservations advised. Two locations: 265 Gómez Morín (phone: 378-9719) and in *Galerías Monterrey,* at Gonzalitos and P.A. González (phone: 333-0752).

Luisiana Downtown's poshest dining room features high-quality continental dishes, plus a smattering of eclectic offerings (rattlesnake steaks occasionally appear on the menu). Tuxedoed waiters and soft piano music add to the elegant ambience. Reservations necessary. 530 Av. Hidalgo Ote. (phone: 343-1530).

Le Pavillón Very refined decor, service, and food—Mexican and international—characterize this restaurant. Closed Sundays. Reservations necessary. In the *Camino Real Ambassador Hotel,* 310 Ocampo Ote. (phone: 340-6390).

Résidence An elegant, old-fashioned townhouse has been converted into an impressive international restaurant where movers and shakers convene to enjoy prime ribs and a *menú de degustación,* with samplings of seven dishes. Reservations necessary. 605 Degollado Sur at Matamoros (phone: 342-7230).

El Tío A landmark for more than 60 years, this traditional eatery—decorated with bullfighting paraphernalia—specializes in roast kid and also offers great steaks. Eat indoors or outside on the patio. Reservations advised. Downtown, at 1746 Av. Hidalgo Pte. (phone: 346-0291).

MODERATE

Casa Grande It offers mostly Mexican food and a view of Chipinque Mesa from its lamplit garden. Reservations advised. In Garza García, at 152 Vasconcelos Pte. (phone: 338-6044).

La Fe Palenque The strictly Mexican fare served at this huge establishment (it seats 400) is accompanied by cockfights. Contrary to tradition, however, no blades are attached to the cocks' claws, so the spectacle is colorful, but less bloody. (No betting allowed.) Live Mexican music is also featured. Reservations unnecessary. 2525 Av. Morones Prieto Pte. (phone: 345-1347).

El Molcas Everything in this establishment is pure Mexican, including the lively music performed daily and on Saturday and Sunday nights. The buffet is a real bargain, but there are plenty of à la carte selections, too. Reservations advised. Two locations: 2778 Av. Roberto Garza Sada Sur (phone: 359-5900) and next door to the *Fiesta Americana Monterrey* hotel at 601 Monte Rocalloso (phone: 363-4451).

INEXPENSIVE

El Pastor This simple corner eatery with the *cabrito* (kid) roasting in the window was one of the first places to serve this local specialty. It's still the best place for *cabrito,* and you can order it prepared several different ways (*al pastor* means roasted). No reservations. 1067 Madero Pte., five blocks west of Pino Suárez (phone: 374-0480).

Morelia

(pronounced Mo-*ray*-lyah)

Stately and regal, Morelia is among the gems in Mexico's colonial highlands. It's a wonderfully relaxing place and a rewarding base from which to explore the towns and villages of the lovely state of Michoacán, of which it is the capital. The city (pop. more than 500,000) is about midway between Guadalajara and Mexico City—roughly three and a half hours from Mexico City and three from Guadalajara, thanks to a highway that opened in 1994—and sits on a 6,368-foot-high plateau.

Antonio de Mendoza, Mexico's first viceroy, founded the city in 1541 and named it Nueva Valladolid, in honor of his hometown in Spain. It kept the name through 300 years of Spanish rule; after independence, the Mexicans renamed the town Morelia to honor a local hero of the War for Independence, José María Morelos.

The indigenous Tarasco, who lived in the area before the Spaniards arrived, successfully resisted the Aztec, and those who remain in the region have not allowed the modern world to encroach too much on their culture. They live in the villages surrounding the town and on the nearby island of Janitzio, in Lago de Pátzcuaro (Lake Pátzcuaro). Although tourism is the main source of income on the island, the Tarasco there generally go their own way—making pottery, woodcarvings, and serapes and raising just enough food for themselves—much as they did in pre-Columbian times.

As in most Mexican towns, Morelia's *zócalo* (main plaza), shaded by trees, surrounded by colonnades, and lined with cafés, is the focal point of town life. (Note the characteristic rose-colored *cantera* stone of which many buildings are constructed.) As part of a "Family Sundays" program, concerts and cultural programs are held on the plaza. Don't be surprised if someone offers to sell you a guitar or violin: Both instruments are made by hand in nearby villages and generally are reasonably priced.

This region is particularly famous for its folk art, due in large part to the efforts of Vasco de Quiroga, Michoacán's first bishop. He traveled to the nearby villages, encouraging the artisans by helping them to find markets for their work. It was in nearby Pátzcuaro, in fact, that Quiroga established the *Colegio de San Nicolás* (University of St. Nicholas), the oldest university in Latin America.

The best-known crafts of the region are woodcarvings and pottery, produced in a great variety of styles—the different colors and painted designs usually indicate in which village the work was created. One popular pattern is a light beige background with brown line drawings of people, fish, and other animals. You can buy a complete dinner set for reasonable prices. The only drawbacks are the high lead content of the clay and glaze (unless fired at adequately high temperatures, they're best used as decoration only) and the fragility of the products, which don't always survive the trip back home.

Another local craft is elegant, Oriental-looking lacquerware, which is exquisite, though expensive. You'll find trays, plates, and delicate boxes decorated by a process known as inlay: Tiny grooves are etched into the wood and filled with gold leaf to form a design, and the whole surface is lacquered to preserve the pattern. To tell if an item has been inlaid, run your fingertips lightly over the work. If it is perfectly smooth, it has only been painted; if it feels slightly bumpy, then it is legitimate lacquerwork.

Morelia At-a-Glance

SEEING THE CITY

For a good overview of the city, follow Calle Galeana about 2 miles (3 km) off Route 15 to the hills of Santa María, to the west of town.

SPECIAL PLACES

In Morelia, some street names are followed by the designations Pte., Ote., Nte., and Sur, which mean, respectively, *poniente* (west), *oriente* (east), *norte* (north), and *sur* (south).

PLAZA DE LOS MÁRTIRES (PLAZA OF THE MARTYRS) Filled with fountains and flowers, Morelia's *zócalo* is the focal point of downtown socializing and the best place to start a sightseeing tour. Free concerts take place here Sundays at 6 PM.

CATEDRAL (CATHEDRAL) Begun in 1640 by Vasco de Quiroga, it was not finished until a century later. The building is one of the best examples in Mexico of the Plateresque style, with its perfectly proportioned towers, rose stone façade (given a thorough cleaning in 1994 to bring out the lovely color), and colonial portal. East side of Plaza de los Mártires.

ACUEDUCTO (AQUEDUCT) If you drive into Morelia from Mexico City, you will pass this remarkable engineering feat—an 18th-century masonry aqueduct 30 feet high with 253 arches. You'll know you're here when you see a large fountain with a sculpture of three striking, half-clad Tarasco women (a real Tarasco woman would never appear in public in such attire, let alone pose for an artist). Walk along the Calzada de Fray Antonio de San Miguel, shaded by centuries-old trees. Also stop in at the *Santuario de Guadalupe*. Inside, native *retablos*—altarpieces—in this case, paintings that depict the life of monks who settled in Nueva Valladolid (the name originally given to what is now Morelia). The sanctuary also is of interest because of its brightly colored clay ornamentation. Av. Tatavasco on *Jardín Morelos*.

MUSEO CASA MORELOS (MUSEUM OF THE HOME OF JOSÉ MARÍA MORELOS) One of the homes of the famed Mexican patriot houses a museum with manuscripts and memorabilia, including the blindfold Morelos wore when he was executed. (His birthplace is nearby, at the intersection of Corregidora and García Obeso.) Closed Mondays. Admission charge. Calle Aldama and Av. Morelos (phone: 132651).

MUSEO REGIONAL MICHOACANO (REGIONAL MUSEUM OF MICHOACÁN) Indigenous artifacts from the Michoacán region, as well as colonial weapons, furniture, and paintings, are on display at this 18th-century palace. Cantú's mural *The Four Horsemen of the Apocalypse,* on the second floor, is the museum's most celebrated work. Closed Mondays. Admission charge. Near the main plaza, at 305 Calle Allende and Abasolo (phone: 122407).

COLEGIO DE SAN NICOLÁS (UNIVERSITY OF ST. NICHOLAS) Originally founded by Vasco de Quiroga in Pátzcuaro, the university was moved to its present site in 1580 and is now a high school. Don't miss the interesting murals on the walls of the patio. Closed Sundays. No admission charge. A block west of the plaza, on Av. Madero.

MUSEO DE ARTE CONTEMPORÁNEO (MUSEUM OF CONTEMPORARY ART) In a very "unmodern" building (a 19th-century house, in fact), this lovely museum features 13 galleries of changing exhibitions. Closed Mondays. No admission charge. 18 Av. Acueducto and *Parque Cuauhtémoc* (phone: 125404).

MUSEO DE ARTE COLONIAL (MUSEUM OF COLONIAL ART) An interesting collection of Christ figures made from sugar and corn cane pulp, and several colonial paintings are displayed in this converted 18th-century home. Especially noteworthy is the Miguel Cabrera painting in the charming interior patio. Closed Mondays. No admission charge. 240 Av. Benito Juárez (phone: 139160).

PARQUE ZOOLÓGICO BENITO JUÁREZ (BENITO JUÁREZ ZOO) On about 60 beautifully landscaped acres of wooded land, the zoo contains more than 3,000 mammals, reptiles, and birds, including species that cannot be seen anywhere else in Mexico. There's a restaurant on the premises. Open daily. No admission charge. Avs. Benito Juárez and Las Camelinas (phone: 140488).

CASA DE LA CULTURA (HOUSE OF CULTURE) One of Morelia's oldest and most impressive structures was built in 1619 as a Carmelite monastery and is now part school, part museum. It contains the interesting *Museo de la Máscara* (Mask Museum), a small archaeology museum, and changing exhibitions of photography, painting, and sculpture. Open daily. No admission charge. Av. Morelos Nte. near Plaza de Carmen (phone: 131059).

CENTRO DE CONVENCIONES (CONVENTION CENTER) Besides convention facilities, this modern complex has a hotel, a bookstore, a small handicrafts shop, and the *Teatro Morelos,* which stages plays and concerts. There also is a lovely wooded area with an orchid house (open daily) and a small planetarium with shows Fridays and Saturdays at 7 PM and Sundays at 5 and 7 PM. Admission charge to the planetarium. Calzada Ventura Puente and Av. Las Camelinas (phone: 146202).

MUSEO DEL ESTADO DE MICHOACÁN (MUSEUM OF THE STATE OF MICHOACÁN) Once the home of Mexico's only native-born emperor, Agustín de Iturbide, this stately mansion is now a museum dedicated to the traditions of Michoacán. One room houses Michoacán's first drugstore. Open daily. No admission charge. Calles Guillermo Prieto and Santiago Tapia (phone: 130629).

EXTRA SPECIAL

Little more than an hour's drive southwest of Morelia via Route 15 or 120 is Pátzcuaro, the heart of Tarasco country. Lago de Pátzcuaro, about 1½ miles (2 km) north of town on Calzada de las Américas, is one of the highest lakes in the country. You can take a boat ride out to the island of Janitzio (pronounced Ha-*neet*-see-o), whose inhabitants live pretty much the way they have for centuries. In Janitzio, the year's biggest event is *Día de los Muertos* (Day of the Dead; November 2), when all-night vigils take place starting on the evening of November 1. (For additional details, see *Special Events,* below.) About an hour west of Pátzcuaro is Uruapan (pronounced Oo-roo-*ah*-pahn), where you can find the most beautiful lacquerware made in the area, see the extinct Paracutín Volcano, and visit the Tzararacua (pronounced Tsah-rah-*rah*-kwah) waterfall. For more details on Pátzcuaro, Janitzio, and Uruapan, see *The West Coast: Nogales to Mexico City* in DIRECTIONS.

Sources and Resources

TOURIST INFORMATION

The *Oficina del Turismo del Estado* (State Tourist Office; 79 Nigromante, near Av. Madero; phone: 120415) is an excellent source of information and maps of Morelia and its environs. Open daily, it's worth visiting just to see the splendid colonial mansion that houses it.

TELEPHONE The city code for Morelia is 43. *Note:* Mexico's telephone company has embarked on a major expansion project that involves changing telephone numbers in many areas of the country. At press time, all numbers listed in this chapter were correct. However, if you have any difficulties reaching attractions listed here, contact the local tourist office.

CLIMATE AND CLOTHES Morelia's weather is moderate, with winter temperatures in the 60s F (16 through 21C) and summer readings rarely exceeding 90F (32C). Dress casually and for comfort, and in the summer—the rainy season—carry an umbrella.

GETTING AROUND

Several points of interest in Morelia are within walking distance of Plaza de los Mártires; you can reach the others by car or taxi.

BUS Local buses are a good way to see the city if you don't have a car. The fare ranges from 1 to 1.5 pesos (about 13¢ to 20¢ at press time), and exact change is required. Buses marked "Directo" and "Alberca" travel to the *Plaza de las Américas* shopping center, the *Calinda Morelia* hotel, and several good restaurants nearby. The bus marked "Santa María" goes to the Santa María area, where the *Villa Montaña* hotel and several restaurants can be found, and it passes the zoo en route. All of these buses can be picked up downtown at Plaza Melchor Ocampo on Calle Santiago Tapia; they run daily from 6 AM to 9 PM. Ask about other bus routes at the tourist office.

CAR RENTAL Agencies with offices at the airport and in town include *Dollar* (676 Av. del Campestre, across the street from the *Plaza de las Américas* shopping center; phone: 153050) and *Quick Rent-a-Car* (1454 Av. Las Camelinas; phone: 154466).

TAXI Plentiful and inexpensive, cabs can be hired by the ride, hour, or day. If you can't get one at the main plaza, walk to the bus station, at Calles Eduardo Ruiz and Valentín Gómez Farías, where there's always a string of them, or call 166130.

SPECIAL EVENTS

Morelia's cathedral, with its extraordinary 19th-century organ, is the site of an international organ festival that takes place annually for about 10 days in May. *Día de los Muertos* (Day of the Dead) on November 2 (but with exhibits and observances beginning at least a day or two earlier) is the biggest event of the year in nearby Pátzcuaro and Janitzio (see *Extra Special,* above). Candlelight processions visit the cemeteries to decorate the graves in an all-night celebration beginning November 1. If you want to attend, make hotel reservations well in advance.

SHOPPING

There are stores throughout the city, but many are downtown, especially sweets and handicrafts shops. Most stores are open daily from 10 AM to 6 or 7 PM, though some close an hour or two earlier on Sundays. A few small shops close between 2 and 4 PM.

Casa de las Artesanías In the former *Convento de San Francisco* (Convent of St. Francis), this museum-like shop features handicrafts from all over Michoacán. There's also a small crafts museum. Part of the proceeds help establish and support regional arts schools. Plaza Valladolid, Humboldt and Fray Juan de San Miguel (phone: 122486).

La Casona An extraordinary selection of crafts from all over the state. 293 Av. Madero Ote. and Belisario Domínguez (phone: 130998).

Exportaciones Guare Hand-crafted furniture, hand-lacquered in blooming colors. 421 Av. Héroes de Nocupítaro (phone: 125763).

Fabrica Señal Exceptionally beautiful hand-crafted colonial-style furniture, plus an extensive selection of high-quality folk art. 134 Ramón López Velarde, in the Santa María area, behind the *Villa Montaña* hotel (phone: 142438).

Mercado de Dulces (Candy Market) A candy lover's dream; be sure to try the area's specialty, *ate,* a very sweet jellied fruit that comes in a variety of flavors. Behind the state tourist office on Calle Valentín Gómez Farías and Av. Madero Pte. (no phone).

Mercado Independencia (Independence Market) Behind the *Iglesia de las Capuchinas* (Church of the Capuchin Sisters), it offers Tarasco products, including natural cures for nerve, kidney, and liver ailments. About seven blocks south of the *zócalo,* on Av. Lázaro Cárdenas (no phone).

SPORTS

Club Campestre (Av. del Campestre; phone: 141203), a private nine-hole golf course, extends playing privileges to tourists. Fishing is good at Lago de Pátzcuaro (pick up a permit beforehand at the local tourism office). Those seeking to confine their recreation to one locale can avail themselves of the pool, the tennis, basketball, and volleyball courts, and other facilities at the *Centro Deportivo Venustiano Carranza* (Venustiano Carranza Sports Center; phone: 141332), located where the aqueduct ends. About 10 miles (16 km) north of Morelia via Avenida Acueducto is the *Balneario Cointzio* (Cointzio Spa; 45 Av. Morelos Sur; phone: 137954), with thermal waters, two pools, lockers, and a snack bar. It's closed Mondays.

NIGHTCLUBS AND NIGHTLIFE

Most social activity takes place along Avenida Las Camelinas. The *Calinda Morelia* hotel (see *Checking In*) has live music in its stylish lobby bar, and *Canta Bar* (2225 Av. Lázaro Cárdenas; phone: 155354) attracts a lively crowd for rock 'n' roll. Some of the bigger hotels, such as the *Gran Hotel Centro de Convenciones* (see *Checking In*), have cocktail lounges with entertainment, at least on the weekends. *Dali's* (100 Av. del Campestre; phone: 155514) is a private dance club that extends guest privileges to tourists.

Best in Town

CHECKING IN

Expect to pay from $100 to $150 per night for a double room in an expensive hotel; from $50 to $100 in a moderate place; and $45 or less in an inexpensive one. Prices may be lower in the summer. Unless otherwise noted, rooms in the hotels listed have telephones and TV sets (some with cable or satellite channels) but no air conditioning. All telephone numbers are in the 43 city code unless otherwise indicated.

We begin with our favorite havens (both in the expensive range), followed by recommended hotels, listed by price category.

SPECIAL HAVENS

Villa Montaña This appealing hostelry has been built in stages, with bits and pieces added continually since its 1958 opening, all radiating from the original hacienda estate building. There is a maze of terraces, brick walks, serendipitous gardens, stone columns and carvings, and connected stuccoed cottages in several separate buildings. A small patio adjoins the dining room, which is in the original house (along with a piano bar with a fireplace). There's a patio bar, and a colonial sitting room with an unbeatable view of the city. The pool and tennis court also afford a wonderful vista. The seven rooms and 33 suites range from fine to great. No two are alike, but all boast broad beams, authentic colonial furniture, and fireplaces (some suites have *three* fireplaces). Private patios abound. The food is well prepared, though the menu is limited (see *Villa Montaña* in *Eating Out*). The hotel levies a 10% service charge in lieu of tipping; the rate includes three meals daily. Children under eight are discouraged during high season. On the city's southern outskirts, in the Santa María area, at 201 Calle Patzimba (phone: 140231; 800-223-6510; fax: 151423).

Virrey de Mendoza City records confirm that the ground floor of this inn dates from sometime before 1565. Later, probably around 1744, a second floor was added, and then, in 1938, when the place was turned into a hotel, the third floor was constructed. The building's growth has followed the original colonial plan—a large courtyard and two smaller patios surrounded by rooms on all sides. Broad staircases (and Morelia's first elevator) lead upstairs, past an authentic suit of armor and other intriguing objets d'art. The lobby is now located in the glassed-over courtyard. The 39 rooms and 15 suites are squeaky-clean and furnished extravagantly in colonial style, with very high ceilings and gleaming modern baths; however, the amplified piano music played nightly in the lobby carries everywhere. There's also a café. On the *zócalo,* at 16 Portal de Matamoros (phone: 120633; fax: 126719).

EXPENSIVE

Bugambilias Morelia This modern property has 48 guestrooms. The overall atmosphere is light and airy, with lots of plants; there are a restaurant, a bar, and an outdoor Jacuzzi. On the southern outskirts of town, at 3325 Av. Las Camelinas (phone: 155356; 800-448-8355; fax: 155410).

Calinda Comfort Inn A colonial-style hostelry, it has 80 rooms built around an interior patio with a pool. Guests may use the facilities at its sister hotel, the

Calinda Morelia (see below), just two blocks away. 5000 Av. Las Camelinas (phone: 157100; 800-228-5151 in the US; 800-90000 in Mexico; fax: 157257).

Calinda Morelia Beautiful and modern, this 126-room establishment has a tennis court, a pool, a Jacuzzi, a pleasant restaurant, and a spacious lobby bar with piano music every night but Monday. 3466 Av. Las Camelinas, across from the *Plaza de las Américas* shopping center (phone: 143111; 800-228-5151 in the US; 800-90000 in Mexico; fax: 145476).

Gran Hotel Centro de Convenciones Comfortable and modern—but somewhat sterile—it offers 253 rooms, a restaurant, a lobby bar with live music at night, a pool, and two tennis courts. On the lovely grounds of the *Centro de Convenciones*—see *Special Places*—at Calzada Ventura Puente and Av. Las Camelinas (phone: 150023; 800-45005 toll-free in the rest of Mexico; fax: 150281).

MODERATE

Alameda Sedate and rather bland, this hostelry has 116 rooms (36 in a newer section), two restaurants, two lobby bars, and a cafeteria. Friday and Saturday nights, performances are given of the "Danza de los Viejitos," a famous and funny folk tradition in which masked dancers pretend to be old men with canes. In the heart of the city, one block west of the *zócalo,* at 313 Av. Madero Pte. (phone: 122023; fax: 138727).

Catedral This colonial-style place offers 44 comfortable, rustic rooms equipped with large bathrooms. Facilities include a cozy lobby, a restaurant, a bar with live entertainment, and medical services. On the north side of the *zócalo,* at 37 Ignacio Zaragoza (phone: 130467; fax: 130783).

Mansión de la Calle Real A lobby restaurant and 266 cheery rooms draw guests to this congenial place. Between the main plaza and the aqueduct, on the east side of town, at 766 Av. Madero Ote. at Isidro Huarte (phone: 132856; fax: 121408).

De la Soledad Most of the 60 rooms in this converted monastery have wood-beam ceilings; more modern amenities include a restaurant (see *Eating Out*) and a bar. Downtown, at 90 Ignacio Zaragoza (phone: 121888; fax: 122111).

INEXPENSIVE

Posada Vista Bella Set in the Santa María hills, this motel has 16 apartments available on a monthly basis, as well as 42 rooms for overnight accommodations. On the premises are a pool and a restaurant. Two miles (3 km) off Rte. 15, on the city's southern outskirts and down the street from the *Villa Montaña* (phone/fax: 140284).

EATING OUT

The best food in Morelia is served at the more exclusive hotel dining rooms and at some of the spots that have sprung up along Avenida Las Camelinas, on the south side of town. At restaurants in the moderate category, dinner for two will cost from $40 to $55; at inexpensive restaurants, expect to pay $35 or less. Prices do not include drinks, wine, tax, or tips. Most restaurants below accept MasterCard and Visa, and a few also accept American Express and Diners Club; it's a good idea to call ahead and check. Unless otherwise noted, all restaurants are open daily for lunch and dinner. All telephone numbers are in the 43 city code unless otherwise indicated.

MODERATE

La Cabaña de Vic An attractive, greenery-filled place, it serves good Mexican food and steaks, including the *Vic especial*—grilled beef and pork with bacon and mild chilies, topped with melted cheese. Closed Mondays. Reservations advised. 1535 Av. Las Camelinas (phone: 140979).

Cenaduría Lupita A Morelia tradition for more than 40 years, the fare at this simple family eatery centers on local specialties. Try the *pollo placero* (chicken with potatoes and other vegetables in a spicy red sauce) or the renowned *enchiladas morelianas,* filled with cheese and onions and topped with potatoes. On weekends at lunchtime, a small combo sings love songs, usually accompanied by guitar. Reservations unnecessary. 1004 Sánchez de Tagle, one-half block north of Avenida Lázaro Cárdenas and 10 blocks east of the *zócalo* (phone: 121340).

La Pasta Nostra Surprisingly tasty homemade pasta and pizza are served here; they'll deliver pizzas, too. The Sunday brunch and lunch buffet is excellent. Reservations advised. 2276 Av. Lázaro Cárdenas (phone: 152810). There's a branch at 944 Av. Madero (phone: 123148).

La Posta del Gallo A warm welcome, immaculate surroundings, excellent grilled meat, generous drinks and salad bar, and efficient service are the draws here. Reservations unnecessary. 1036 Blvd. García de León (phone: 148935).

El Solar de Villagrán This pretty place framed by gardens serves good Mexican and international food. There is live music afternoons and evenings. Closed Mondays. Reservations unnecessary. 13 Av. del Campestre and Rincón de las Comadres, near the *Calinda Morelia* (phone: 145647).

De la Soledad Well-seasoned, home-style meals are offered in the austere dining room of this former monastery. The prix fixe luncheon menu is a real bargain, and on Saturdays there's a Mexican brunch and lunch buffet with live music. Reservations unnecessary. In the hotel of the same name, at 90 Ignacio Zaragoza (phone: 121888).

La Tórtola At this cozy wood cabin, the fare is light but tasty, including *corundas* (similar to tamales, but not filled), *buñuelos* (crisp fried cakes served with heavy syrup), and hot chocolate. Tortillas here are still made by hand. Reservations unnecessary. 477 Francisco Márquez (phone: 146033).

Villa Campestre Located in an elegant wooded garden, this posh dining spot offers French-style dishes (prepared by a French-trained chef) and a well-stocked wine cellar. Open daily for breakfast, lunch, and dinner. Jacket and tie, or *guayabera* (a tailored dress shirt, usually embroidered) required for men. Reservations advised. 465 Av. del Campestre (phone: 240006 or 240010)

Villa Montaña This small dining room is striking, with black and white tablecloths ablaze with bright orange carnations and napkins. The limited fixed-price menu changes daily. Reservations necessary. At the lovely *Villa Montaña*, 201 Calle Patzimba (phone: 140231).

INEXPENSIVE

Los Comensales A popular spot for Mexican fare, it includes local dishes such as chicken mole and fried chicken with enchiladas. Also try the house specialty, *pollo placero* (chicken with vegetables and tortillas). Reservations advised. No credit cards accepted. 148 Ignacio Zaragoza (phone: 129361).

Monterrey Surrounding an interior courtyard on the plaza, this pleasant place is the local choice for grilled *cabrito* (kid). The mixed grill also is delicious. Reservations unnecessary. 149 Portal Galeana (phone: 130867).

Las Viandas de San José This, the second venture of the owners of *Los Comensales* (see above), offers the same regional favorites, plus a wide selection of other Mexican dishes. Open daily from 8 AM to 10:30 PM. Reservations advised. No credit cards accepted. 263 Alvaro Obregón (phone: 123728).

Oaxaca
(pronounced Wah-*ha*-kah)

Located 5,070 feet above sea level, the charming colonial city of Oaxaca is surrounded by the Sierra Madre del Sur mountains and nestled in a fertile valley. Nicknamed "the Green City" because many of its buildings were constructed from green volcanic stone, Oaxaca is 338 miles (546 km) south of Mexico City. Despite the automobiles on its streets, the atmosphere of the city is reminiscent of the 18th and 19th centuries.

The state of Oaxaca, of which the city of Oaxaca (pop. 214,000) is the capital, is endowed with vast geographic, historic, and ethnic diversity. Together with Chiapas (the state bordering on the east), Oaxaca has the largest indigenous population in Mexico, which explains the richness and variety of its handicrafts, folklore, culture, and gastronomy. *Oaxaqueños,* as the natives are called, are mostly descendants of the Zapotec and Mixtec peoples. Eight distinct languages and 52 dialects are spoken; for many, Spanish is their second language.

The great Zapotec and the Mixtec civilizations, which flourished 2,000 years ago, left magnificent ruins at nearby *Monte Albán, Mitla,* and *Yagul.* All within a 25-mile radius of the capital, these rich archaeological zones attest to the advanced development of these societies. Although well versed in astronomy, architecture, agronomy, and medicine, they were no match for the warlike Aztec, who conquered the area (then called Huexayácac, which means "gourd tree forest" in Nahuatl) in the late 1400s. The Aztec were conquered in their turn by the Spaniards, who founded the city of Oaxaca in 1529. Hernán Cortés liked this part of Mexico so well that he claimed 7,200 square miles of the region for himself; later he assumed the title of Marqués del Valle de Oaxaca. His descendants kept the land in their possession until 1910.

Oaxaca's history is filled with illustrious names. For example, it is the birthplace of two of Mexico's most influential presidents, Benito Juárez and Porfirio Díaz. A Zapotec who received no formal education as a child, Juárez eventually studied law and then went into politics, holding several public offices during his meteoric rise to the presidency, which he attained in 1858. As president, the iconoclastic Juárez divested the Catholic church of its considerable power, a policy that ignited the Reform War. With French help, the conservatives set Maximilian up as emperor and almost drove Juárez from the country. In the end Juárez triumphed, the French forces fled, and Emperor Maximilian was executed. Porfirio Díaz, a Mixtec and the antithesis of Juárez, became president in 1876 and ruled Mexico with an iron fist, banning the free press and organized labor. Beholden to foreign interests, he presided over a quasi-feudalistic society until he was forced out by the Mexican Revolution of 1910. Some of Mexico's leading artists, such as Rufino Tamayo, Rodolfo Morales, and Francisco Toledo, also were born in Oaxaca.

Today, this city is amazingly unspoiled—a colonial gem that offers 16th-century architecture, magnificent churches, excellent museums, a colorful outdoor market, and fascinating side trips to archaeological ruins and indigenous villages. If we had to choose just one place to represent the essence of Mexico, it would be Oaxaca.

Oaxaca At-a-Glance

SEEING THE CITY

Cerro del Fortín, the hill north of Oaxaca that rises 350 feet above the city, offers the best overview of the area. On its lower slope is an open area with a good lookout spot. Slightly farther up a short dirt road at the top of the hill is a pyramidal monument to the flag of Mexico, which also offers a magnificent view. To reach Cerro del Fortín, take Route 190 about a mile (1.6 km) east of the Avenida Madero turnoff. The hill directly south is *Monte Albán,* which is also a fine place from which to see the area and the city (see *Special Places*).

SPECIAL PLACES

As in most Mexican towns, life in Oaxaca begins in the *zócalo,* and many of the city's most compelling sights and sites are situated nearby.

PLAZA DE ARMAS (ZÓCALO) Oaxaca's lovely main plaza is filled with grand old trees and many paths, which lead to its centerpiece, a delicate white wrought-iron gazebo. The *zócalo's* charm is enhanced by its several fountains, shaded benches, and the presence of folks of every description—hawkers, *evangelistas* (public letter writers), *oaxaqueños,* tourists, and students. Concerts are held here Mondays through Saturdays at 7 PM and on Sundays at 12:30 PM, and wandering street musicians can be heard here almost all the time. The ideal place to view the lively comings and goings is from one of the sidewalk cafés under the Spanish colonnades around the square. The tempo picks up in the evening, and whenever there's a big band concert, the whole town seems to turn up.

BASÍLICA DE LA SOLEDAD (BASILICA OF SOLITUDE) This house of worship, with its façade of green cantera (a type of volcanic stone) carved to resemble a Baroque altarpiece, was constructed in 1682. It contains the stone statue of *La Virgen de la Soledad* (the Virgin of Solitude), the patron saint of Oaxaca, who is believed to have great healing powers. The legend attending her arrival in the city is represented on glass panels in the museum at the rear of the church. In the 17th century a pack train arrived in town with one more mule than the muleteer could account for. When the train got to what became the site of the basilica, the extra mule suddenly fell down and died. It was found to be carrying the statue of the Virgin, and the people immediately set about building a church to commemorate the miraculous event. The statue's forehead is graced with a large hanging pearl; the torso is robed in a jewel-encrusted black velvet cloak. The museum also has an eclectic collection of offerings from devotees of the Virgin; its walls are covered with *ex-votos,* paintings that tell the story of various miracles attributed to her. The museum is closed Sundays. No admission charge. Calle Independencia, on the Plaza de la Danza (phone: 67566).

CATEDRAL DE OAXACA The cathedral was built in 1535, and its original lovely Baroque façade remains intact despite various alterations. The clock, a gift to the city from King Fernando VI of Spain in 1755 and made with all wooden works, still keeps good time. Plaza de Armas.

IGLESIA DE SANTO DOMINGO Founded by Dominican priests in 1570, this vast church is an exquisite example of Baroque art. While the outside is certainly worth a close look, the interior is truly exceptional. Covered in gold scroll and polychrome reliefs set against a white background, with paved tile floors and massive gold chandeliers, the church has 11 chapels, including the lovely *Capilla de la Virgen del Rosario* (Chapel of the Virgin of the Rosary), which is off to the right as you enter. This unique site should not be missed. At Calles Gurrión and Macedonio Alcalá.

MUSEO REGIONAL DE OAXACA Of particular interest in this small but formidable museum is the large collection of priceless objects—made of silver, jade, turquoise, bone, and crystal—discovered in a tomb at *Monte Albán* in 1932; they are on the second floor, behind a heavily vaulted door. Other exhibits include a fascinating display of regional arts and crafts, costumes, and archaeological relics. Closed Mondays. No admission charge on Sundays. In the converted convent attached to the *Iglesia de Santo Domingo.* Calle Macedonio Alcalá (phone: 62991).

MUSEO RUFINO TAMAYO DE ARTE PRE-HISPÁNICO The famous *oaxaqueño* artist Rufino Tamayo and his wife, Olga, donated to their native city their 2,000-piece collection of pre-Hispanic art; they also completely restored and decorated the 16th-century mansion that houses it. Archaeological pieces trace the development of art in Mexico from 1250 BC to AD 1500. Each of the seven galleries features works from a specific culture: Olmec, Totonac, Zapotec, Mixtec, Maya, Nayarit, and Teotihuacán. The patio has a huge fountain and beautifully landscaped gardens. Closed Tuesdays. Admission charge. Calle Morelos, four blocks from northwest of the *zócalo* (phone: 64750).

MUSEO DE ARTE CONTEMPORÁNEO DE OAXACA This museum features the work of local artists, including Rufino Tamayo, Francisco Gutiérrez, Rodolfo Nieto, and Francisco Toledo. Closed Tuesdays. No admission charge, but donations are welcome. 202 Calle Macedonio Alcalá (phone: 68499).

FUENTE DE LAS SIETE REGIONES (FOUNTAIN OF THE SEVEN REGIONS) An impressive tribute to the natives of Oaxaca, it includes six statues of women in regional garb and is topped by a figure of a male dancer from the nearby indigenous village of Teotitlán del Valle wearing a plumed headdress. Calzada Porfirio Díaz, past the *Misión de los Angeles* hotel.

ENVIRONS

ARBOL TULE Standing 4 miles (6 km) southeast of Oaxaca in Santa María el Tule, this huge ahuehuete cypress is estimated to be between 2,500 and 3,200 years old, making it very likely the oldest tree in the world. El Tule, some 140 feet in height and 136 feet in circumference, is still growing today. Its roots have extended so far down that it is difficult to get enough water to them; since the 1950s, an English company has compensated for this deficiency by pumping water to the roots. Rte. 190, en route to Mitla.

MONTE ALBÁN Once an important Zapotec and Mixtec religious city with more than 50,000 inhabitants, it is now one of the most magnificent archaeological sites in all Mexico. Covering 25 square miles, it's 5½ miles (9 km) southwest of Oaxaca. (For more information, see *Mexico's Magnificent Archaeological Heritage* in DIVERSIONS.) Buses to *Monte Albán* leave Oaxaca from the *Mesón Mina del Angel* (518 Calle Mina; phone: 66666). Check schedules at the tourist office (see *Tourist Information*). During the high season, get there an hour early to get the bus you prefer; try to sit on the right-hand side for the best views. Most of the drive is straight up, tortuously slow, and splendidly scenic. If you prefer to drive, take Calle García Vigil, cross the *zócalo,* and continue on Miguel Cabrera to the *periférico* (beltway). Cross the bridge and take the right fork. The site is open daily, but closes earlier in the day during the rainy season (roughly mid-May through mid-October). No admission charge on Sundays (no phone).

MITLA Located 27 miles (46 km) southeast of Oaxaca on Route 190, *Mitla* was first settled by the Zapotec, and was subsequently taken over by the Mixtec. (For more information, see *Mexico's Magnificent Archaeological Heritage* in DIVERSIONS.) A trip to the site can be nicely combined with a stop at the *Arbol Tule* (see above) and the *Museo de Arte Zapoteco Frissell,* just off the plaza in the town of Mitla. This museum houses a fine collection of artifacts—all labeled in English—that clearly traces the development of the Zapotec-Mixtec empires. The museum is open daily; there is an admission charge (no phone). About a half mile (1 km) from the museum, the ruins can be reached by following the main, paved street, which is lined with small clothing shops. Adjoining the ruins is a small handicrafts market. Second class buses leave Oaxaca every half hour from the terminal next to the *Central de Abastos* (Central Market, across from the *periférico,* or beltway, southwest of the city); pay the driver directly. The trip takes one hour each way. The ruins are open daily, but close earlier in the day during the rainy season (roughly mid-May through mid-October). Admission charge (no phone).

TLACOLULA DE MATAMOROS (TLACOLULA CHAPEL) About 23 miles (38 km) from Oaxaca on the road to Mitla, this chapel testifies to the creativity of the native artists of the colonial era. It was built in 1523, and its walls are adorned with frescoes graphically depicting the grisly deaths of some of the saints—one is pictured with an ax plunged into the top of his head; another is in a vat of boiling oil.

YAGUL About 19 miles (30 km) southeast of Oaxaca on the road to Mitla (Rte. 190) is yet another group of ruins. Not as elaborate as *Monte Albán, Yagul* is nonetheless beautiful and interesting enough to be worth the trip. This city is predominantly a fortress that's set slightly above a group of palaces and temples; the site includes a ball court and more than 30 uncovered underground tombs. Open daily. Admission charge (no phone).

Sources and Resources

TOURIST INFORMATION

The public information office of the *Secretaría de Desarollo Turístico del Estado de Oaxaca* (Oaxaca State Tourist Development Secretariat) is at Calle 5 de Mayo and Avenida Morelos (phone: 64828; fax: 61500). There also are information booths (no phones) at the airport and in front of the *Museo de Arte Contemporáneo* (202 Calle Macedonio Alcalá); both the office and the information booths are open daily. *Amistad International,* a local tourist organization, operates an extremely helpful office in the *Palacio Municipal* (Independencia at García Vigil; phone: 63810); closed weekends.

TELEPHONE The city code for Oaxaca is 951. *Note:* Mexico's telephone company has embarked on a major expansion project that involves changing telephone numbers in many areas of the country. At press time, all numbers listed in this chapter were correct. However, if you have any difficulties reaching attractions listed here, contact the local tourist office.

CLIMATE AND CLOTHES Oaxaca's altitude keeps the temperature pleasant all year. Daytime temperatures are usually in the high 60s to mid-70s F (19–24C); it cools at night to the low- to mid-60s F (16–19C). Oaxaca has rainy and dry seasons typical of the tropics; the rainy season starts in May and usually lasts through October, with showers in the afternoons and occasional days of nonstop rain in July and August. The nicest time to visit Oaxaca is the dry season, which is between November and May. The city is very casual. Be sure to have a sturdy pair of walking shoes for exploring the ruins.

GETTING AROUND

BUS Several inexpensive bus lines cross Oaxaca; all run fairly frequently (service ends at midnight) and post their destinations clearly on the front. The fare is 1 peso (about 13¢). Buses also go to all of the major archaeological sites.

CAR RENTAL *Budget* (phone: 50330), *Dollar* (phone: 66329), *Hertz* (phone: 62434), and other firms have desks at the airport and offices in downtown Oaxaca.

TAXI Oaxaca has about 700 taxis, which may be hired by the trip or by the hour; rates should be pre-arranged. Cabs can be called (phone: 62190), and they are always lined up at the *zócalo. Transportación Terrestre Aeropuerto* (phone: 44350) offers service to and from the airport.

TOURS There are several sightseeing agencies in Oaxaca, and almost every hotel can arrange guided tours to the archaeological sites as well as to colorful markets in nearby towns.

SPECIAL EVENTS

Known for its lively fiestas, Oaxaca often fills to capacity during holiday times. One of the city's most popular events is *Guelaguetza,* a festival celebrated to ensure a good harvest. Held in July and highlighted with dances from seven regions of the state, it dates back to a pre-Hispanic ceremony honoring Centéotl, the god of rain and fertility. Later, Spanish missionaries appropriated the ceremony in the name of the Virgin of Carmen. The dances are performed on the last two Mondays in July, but other events are held as well during that week, including the selection of the goddess Centeocihuatl, who presides over festivities; a pageant dedicated to Centéotl, featuring music, magnificent costumes, and dances; and a reenactment of events from Oaxaca's past, including the Aztec and Spanish conquests and the battle between the Zapotec and the Mixtec in which Donaji, the last Zapotec princess, was taken hostage and decapitated. The events take place in a vast open-air auditorium on the Cerro del Fortín (on Rte. 190, 1 mile/1.6 km east of the Av. Madero turnoff) and in the city itself. Reservations are necessary for the main performances and can be arranged through travel agents in the US; book no later than May.

As part of the celebration of the *Día de los Muertos* (Day of the Dead, November 2), a colorful altar-making contest is held in the *zócalo* on November 1 and 2. The fiesta for *La Virgen de la Soledad,* held at the *Basílica de la Soledad* December 16 through 18, marks the beginning of *Navidad* (Christmas) celebrations. The highlight is the *posada,* the procession from inn to inn that reenacts Joseph and Mary's quest for lodgings in Bethlehem; it is held in a different church every night December 18 through 22. On December 23, *Noche de los Rábanos* (Night of the Radishes), the entire *zócalo* is set up with booths from one end to the other. Each booth features imaginative "tableaux" or sculptures carved from the knobby, misshapen radishes grown in the region. The subjects of the sculptures range from religious figures and nativity scenes to buildings, plants, and anything else conceivable. On *Nochebuena* (Christmas Eve), there are processions from the various churches of Oaxaca to the *zócalo,* with decorated floats, music, dancing, a colorful piñata contest, and the inevitable fireworks.

SHOPPING

The famous dark green pottery of the nearby village of Atzompa is available at excellent prices in Oaxaca, as are the Miró- and Picasso-inspired wall hangings from Teotitlán del Valle and the black unglazed pottery of Coyotepec. Cotton and woolen shawls, blouses, bags, blankets, heavy serapes, and hammocks are all well made in this area, as are baskets and fine steel hunting knives and machetes with ornate hand-carved handles and engraved blades. Many pieces of jewelry on sale in Oaxaca are reproductions of pieces found at *Monte Albán*—including necklaces, earrings, and pendants of gold, jade, and seed pearls.

Saturday is the big market day in town, and merchants from all the neighboring communities, wearing native clothing and speaking various dialects of Zapotec, come to sell their wares at the arts and crafts *tianguis* (street markets) outside the *Central de Abastos* (across from the *periférico,* or beltway, southwest of the city). All the different types of mole are available in the *Veinte (20) de Noviembre* market (at Calles 20 de Noviembre and Aldama). Considered one of the most colorful and interesting of all Mexican markets, it is worth a visit. Behind the market is a chocolate mill, *Mayordomo,* where Oaxacan chocolate can be specially blended with almonds, sugar, and cinnamon. All the small towns in the region have their own market days as well; check with the tourist office (see *Tourist Information*) for a list. Another way to shop in Oaxaca is simply by sitting at a table of a sidewalk café or on a bench in the *zócalo.* The vendors will come to you: men with serapes over their arms; women balancing rebozos (shawls) on their heads; and young children offering everything from chicks to lottery tickets. For more ambulatory shopping, Oaxaca has many marvelous stores. Shops are generally open daily from 10 AM to 2 PM and 4 to 7 PM; market stalls from 8 AM to 3 or 4 PM.

Aripo Ten rooms are filled with rugs, pottery, weavings, and ornaments, primarily from Oaxaca. You can watch weavers work at wooden looms. Two locations: 809 García Vigil (phone: 69211) and 200 Av. 5 de Mayo (no phone).

Arte Mexicano Paintings and prints by contemporary Oaxacan artists, imaginative animal figures, and tin mirrors are sold. In the *Palacio de Santo Domingo,* across from the *Iglesia de Santo Domingo.* 407 Calle Macedonio Alcalá (phone: 43815).

Artesanías Cocijo Pottery, wood, and tinware, at very reasonable prices. The proprietor is a walking encyclopedia of Oaxacan crafts. 117 Calle Leona Vicario (phone: 68081).

Artesanías Mendoza Here, one of the region's master weavers, Emiliano Mendoza, creates rugs and tapestries in traditional and contemporary designs, using pure wool, most of it dyed with natural colors. There's an excellent restaurant, *Flamanalli,* on the premises (see *Eating Out*). In Teotitlán del Valle, some 18 miles (29 km) east of Oaxaca. 39 Av. Juárez (phone: 956-20255).

Casa Brena This handicrafts shop has ceramics and weaving workshops on the premises. Walk to the rear—listen for the slapping of the looms—to see workers spinning yarn, weaving, and dyeing cloth. Visitors are also welcome to watch the potters at work. 700 Calle Pino Suárez (phone: 50222).

Galería de Arte de Oaxaca A wonderful collection of works by contemporary Mexican artists, some well-known and some yet to be discovered. Downtown, at 102 Calle Trujano (phone: 69719).

La Mano Mágica An art gallery–handicrafts boutique featuring the best of regional artists and artisans. Rugs and tapestries are woven on the premises. 203 Calle Macedonio Alcalá (phone: 64275).

Mercado de Artesanía A market with well-displayed crafts, where weavers can be seen at work. Some items cost 50% less than elsewhere, but you can bargain them down still further. Corner of Calles J. P. García and Zaragoza (no phone).

El Oro de Montealbán Reproductions of pre-Hispanic jewelry made on the premises. Two locations: Plazuela Adolfo C. Gurrión (phone: 64528 or 64946) and *Palacio de Santo Domingo,* 407 Macedonio Alcalá (phone: 43813).

El Palacio de las Gemas Regional gold jewelry with pearl and coral inlays as well as a large collection of semi-precious stones. Corner of Calles Morelos and Alcalá (phone: 69596).

Productos Típicos de Oaxaca This group of shops set around a sculpture garden is packed with quality pottery, textiles, handmade toys, and tin figures. They will ship items too big to carry. 602 Av. Belisario Domínguez (phone: 52263).

Tianguis A wide selection of native handicrafts. Portal de Clavería, on the *zócalo* (phone: 69266).

SPORTS

CHARREADAS Mexican-style rodeos are held in the *Lienzo Charro* in the village of San Lorenzo Cacaotepec, about 22 miles (35 km) north of the city, on Route 132. If you're not driving, take a *taxi colectivo* (jitney) from the bus station next to the *Central de Abastos* (Central Market, across from the *periférico,* or beltway, southwest of the city). Rodeo events are well advertised around town.

TENNIS *Club de Tenis Brenamiel* (Km 539.5 of Rte. 190; phone: 41815) has 10 lighted, hard-surface courts, which are open to visitors for a fee. The *Misión de los Angeles* has two courts, and the *Victoria* has one (see *Checking In* for both hotels).

NIGHTCLUBS AND NIGHTLIFE

The *Victoria* hotel has a lovely bar with live music and an excellent view over the city; the lobby bar at the *San Felipe* is another popular spot. *El Corcel Negro* at the *Fortín Plaza, Rojo Caliente* at the *Misión de los Angeles,* and *Candela* (211 Allende; phone: 67933) have live music for dancing. There's also the *zócalo,* where music can be heard from 7 to 8:30 PM nightly. People promenade, and lively socializing continues until 11 PM. *El Sol y La Luna* restaurant and coffeehouse (409 Margarita Maza; phone: 62933) is a lively gathering place with music every night. Popular discos are *NBC Studio Rock* (103 Escuela Naval Militar; phone: 31170) and *Snob* (811 Calzada Héroes de Chapultepec; phone: 53204). The *Monte Albán* hotel, on the north side of the *zócalo,* has a very fine nightly show of regional dances; it's free to guests (cover charge for non-guests; phone: 62777). On Thursdays at 8 PM the *Misión de los Angeles* features folkloric dancing. A celebration dedicated to the god of rain and fertility, along with a lavish Oaxacan buffet, is presented Fridays at 7 PM at the *Camino Real Oaxaca.* (See *Checking In* for information on all hotels listed above.)

Best in Town

CHECKING IN

Expect to pay $125 to $175 per night for a double room in an expensive hotel; $50 to $125 in a moderate place; and $25 to $45 in an inexpensive one. All hotels listed have TV sets and telephones in the rooms; the mild climate makes air conditioning unnecessary, though several places have ceiling fans. All telephone numbers are in the 951 city code unless otherwise indicated.

EXPENSIVE

Camino Real Oaxaca Though housed in a restored 16th-century convent, this 91-room jewel boasts a reasonable complement of modern conveniences, including a heated pool, an excellent restaurant (*El Refectorio;* see *Eating Out*), and a cocktail lounge. This place is worth a visit even if you don't spend the night; particularly noteworthy is the *Patio de los Lavaderos* (Patio of the Washbasins) at the rear of the building, where about a dozen stone basins fed by a central fountain are clustered under a charming cupola. Jazz is played in the bar every night but Tuesdays. 300 Av. 5 de Mayo (phone: 60611; 800-7-CAMINO in the US; 800-90123 in Mexico; fax: 60732).

Victoria Surrounded by terraced grounds and well-kept gardens, this sprawling, salmon-colored complex is perched on a hill overlooking the city. Amenities include *El Tule,* a very good dining room (see *Eating Out*), a tennis court, a heated pool, and picture-perfect bougainvillea vines. A total of 37 rooms, 34 villas, and 56 junior suites are available; ask for one with a view. Km 545 of Rte. 190 (phone: 52633; 800-44-UTELL; fax: 52411).

MODERATE

Fortín Plaza Located near the Cerro del Fortín, this modern, somewhat sterile 100-room, six-story hostelry affords a magnificent view of the city. There's a pool, a bar, a coffee shop, and a restaurant. Av. Venus and Calzada Héroes de Chapultepec (phone: 57777; 800-622-4009; fax: 51328).

Hacienda la Noria An 85-room hostelry south of the *zócalo,* it has two pools, a restaurant, and ample grounds. *Periférico* (beltway) at 100 Calle La Costa (phone: 67555; fax: 65347).

Hostal de la Noria Located in a restored colonial building one block from the *zócalo,* this recent addition to Oaxaca's hotel scene is owned by the proprietors of *Hacienda la Noria* (see above) and offers the same friendly service. There are 52 junior suites, with rustic wood furniture and ceiling fans; there's also a restaurant, a bar, and a solarium. 918 Av. Hidalgo (phone: 47844; fax: 63992).

Misión de los Angeles A pleasant, 15-unit hostelry with spacious gardens, a pool, two tennis courts, a dining room (*Antequera;* see *Eating Out*), the popular *Rojo Caliente* with live music and dancing, a gameroom, and a coin-operated laundry. It's a fine walk from here along Avenida Juárez to the Fuente de las Siete Regiones (see *Special Places*). 102 Calzada Porfirio Díaz (phone: 51500; fax: 51680).

San Felipe This luxurious property boasts 160 rooms and suites—many with views of the city—a pool, a restaurant, and a lobby bar with live music. Southwest of town, and well worth the 10-minute trip. 15 Jalisco Sur, in San Felipe del Agua (phone: 35050; fax: 35744).

INEXPENSIVE

California This modern hotel has 32 rooms with balconies, good food, and friendly service. Near the *Misión de Los Angeles,* at 822 Calzada Héroes de Chapultepec (phone/fax: 53628).

Gala A few steps south of the *zócalo,* this hotel has 36 tastefully furnished rooms with large tiled bathrooms. There's a restaurant on the premises. 103 Calle Bustamente (phone: 42251; fax: 63660).

Las Golondrinas The 28 rooms here are spacious, but simply furnished. Breakfast is served outside, under the trees, but there's no restaurant. Corner of Palacios and Calle Allende (phone: 68726; fax: 42126).

Mesón del Rey A nice little surprise of a hotel, near the *zócalo,* it offers 27 rooms, a cozy lobby, a dining room, and a cordial staff. No credit cards accepted. 212 Calle Trujano (phone: 60033; fax: 61434).

Parador Plaza This attractive downtown property has 59 rooms surrounding a delightful patio. The decor is modern Mexican, and there's a restaurant. A real find. 103 Calle Murguía (phone: 64900; fax: 42037).

Señorial One of the most conveniently located hostelries in Oaxaca, it has a pool, a roof garden, a restaurant, and a bar that's open until 10 PM. The one drawback is the thin walls between its 127 rooms. Right on the *zócalo,* at 6 Portal de las Flores (phone: 63933; fax: 63668).

EATING OUT

Oaxacan specialties are among the finest in Mexico, so don't miss the opportunity to enjoy them. Mole (pronounced *mo-*lay) is a spicy, multi-ingredient sauce that takes days to prepare. The ingredients, which often include chocolate, are pulverized, then added to the simmering mixture according to a strict timetable; it is served over chicken or pork. Oaxaca is also famous for its cheese, tamales, chocolate, and mezcal, a volcanic alcoholic brew made from the sap of the maguey plant. The bottle often contains a *gusano* (worm), which aficionados nibble as they drink. Expect service to be slow. Dinner for two can cost $45 or more in expensive spots; $25 to $40 in moderate ones; and under $25 in inexpensive places. Prices do not include drinks, wine, tax, or tips. Most restaurants below accept MasterCard and Visa, and a few also accept American Express and Diners Club; it's a good idea to call ahead and check. Unless otherwise noted, all restaurants are open daily for lunch and dinner. All telephone numbers are in the 951 city code unless otherwise indicated.

EXPENSIVE

El Asador Vasco Basque and Oaxacan dishes are the specialties here. Try the steamy black mole or the *cazuelas*—small casseroles of baked cheese, mushrooms, and shrimp in garlic. Dining is elegant, the bar comfortable, and the service friendly. Warning: It's easy to order too much. Reservations advised, especially if you want a table overlooking the plaza. One flight up at Portal de las Flores, on the *zócalo* (phone: 69719).

El Refectorio The refectory of the original convent and the adjoining patio have been combined into a charming setting for continental and Oaxacan dishes. On Fridays, there's a Oaxacan buffet in the chapel. Reservations advised. At the *Camino Real Oaxaca,* 300 Av. 5 de Mayo (phone: 60611).

El Sagrario An elegant colonial residence with a spiffy modern interior—the downstairs bar, the pizza parlor on the main floor, and the upstairs restaurant are all built around a covered patio. Live music from the bar can be heard throughout the place. The steaks in particular are excellent. Reservations advised. 120 Calle Valdiviesco (phone: 40303).

El Tule A hotel dining room with excellent continental and Oaxacan fare (chicken served with mole is a specialty) and a fascinating view of the city below (mist-shrouded in the morning; streetlight-sprinkled at night). Reservations advised. In the *Victoria Hotel,* Km 545 of Rte. 190 (phone: 52633).

Del Vitral In this lovely mansion complete with European chandeliers and stained glass windows, specialties include traditional Oaxacan mole and such exotic regional specialties as *nido de grillo*—a basket of tortillas, fried grasshoppers, and guacamole. There's live music in the afternoons and evenings. Reservations advised. 201 Calle Guerrero (phone: 63124).

<h3 align="center">MODERATE</h3>

Alameda The good food (mole and Oaxacan-style stuffed peppers), service, and decor (especially the indoor patio), as well as the reasonable prices, make this a very agreeable place to dine. Reservations unnecessary. Two blocks from the *zócalo* at 202 Calle J. P. García (phone: 63446).

Antequera Set in the *Misión de los Angeles* hotel, it features a pleasant dining room. Get here before 10 PM for dinner. Reservations advised. 102 Calzada Porfirio Díaz (phone: 51500).

La Casita Many consider this the best place to enjoy true Oaxacan cooking. The dishes are displayed, so you can see what your food looks like before you order it. It's especially famous for *chapulines* (grasshoppers), but there are also more conventional local dishes such as chicken enchiladas and the ubiquitous mole. Try to get a table by the window. Reservations advised. One flight up at 612 Calle Hildalgo, on the south side of the *zócalo* (phone: 62917).

Flamanalli Here, where members of the Mendoza family weave and sell their renowned rugs (see *Shopping*), one can sample delicious regional dishes; many of the recipes are pre-Hispanic in origin. Try the Zapotec soup, made with young corn and squash vines. Open from 1 to 5 PM. Reservations unnecessary. 39 Av. Juárez, Teotitlán del Valle (phone: 956-20255).

La Morsa A large, open-air *palapa* (thatch-roofed building) serving excellent seafood and steaks. Closed Sundays. Reservations advised. 240 Calzada Porfirio Díaz (phone: 52213).

Los Pacos A local favorite for well-prepared regional dishes, including mole and *chiles rellenos de picadillo* (*poblano* peppers stuffed with ground meat flavored with fruits and nuts). Open from 8 AM to 8 PM. Reservations advised. 108 Av. Belisario Domínguez (phone: 53573).

<h3 align="center">INEXPENSIVE</h3>

El Biche Pobre The hands-down favorite for local dishes (there are about seven types of mole) and Oaxaca's famous tamales. Closed Wednesdays. Reservations unnecessary. Mártires de Tacubaya and Abasolo (no phone).

Casa Elpidia Simple but clean, this place is where *oaxaqueños* flock for good regional food. No reservations. No credit cards accepted. 413 Calle Miguel Cabrera (phone: 64292).

La Flor de Oaxaca One block west of the *zócalo,* this is where locals come for breakfast, lunch, and dinner—or simply for a snack. It's an especially good place to sample a true Oaxacan breakfast of tamales and hot chocolate. Reservations unnecessary. 311 Calle Armenta (phone: 65522).

CAFÉ SOCIETY

Many inexpensive sidewalk cafés offering good Mexican fare line the *zócalo*. Among the best are *El Jardín* and *Del Portal* (neither has a phone).

Puebla

(pronounced *Pwe*-blah)

At one time, Puebla was the most Spanish city in Mexico. Unlike most colonial towns, which were built on the ruins of native centers after the fall of the Aztec, Puebla was established on uninhabited territory, about 80 miles (128 km) east of modern Mexico City. It was thus one of the first places in New Spain in which the burgeoning Spanish-Mexican culture could take root without striking the chalk and bones of the mighty indigenous civilization that preceded it, and that it destroyed.

Puebla was founded in 1531 by the Spanish as a fortress town, midway between the defeated Aztec capital of Tenochtitlán and the east coast. According to legend, the bishop of nearby Tlaxcala dreamed of two angels laying out a perfect city on a beautiful expanse of land covered with flowers and trees and surrounded by tall volcanic peaks. The bishop set out in search of his vision, finding the exact spot in a 7,000-foot-high valley surrounded by mountains, with 17,872-foot Popocatépetl (Smoking Mountain) and 17,454-foot Iztaccíhuatl (White Lady) rising to the southeast.

The city was settled mostly by immigrants from Spain's Talavera region—famous for its tiles and pottery—who brought whole families to establish new lives. In this they were very different from the average Spaniards in New Spain, most of whom had come to the new country for mercenary purposes. The *poblanos* (as residents are called) came to stay; their fortunes were the fortunes of the city and the country. But they were very Spanish, and Puebla was strongly pro-Spanish during Mexico's colonial period and consequently a stronghold of the Catholic church. *Poblanos* claim that a church was built for every day of the year in Puebla and its environs. Catholicism is still a strong influence here; when Pope John Paul II visited Mexico in 1979, he held a conference of Latin American bishops in Puebla.

Puebla's greatest moment occurred on May 5, 1862, when a makeshift Mexican army under the command of General Ignacio Zaragoza repulsed the first French contingent sent to Mexico by Napoleon III after Mexico stopped paying indemnities to France. The victory itself was not nearly so important as what it symbolized—the halting of French intervention. Today, the *Cinco de Mayo* (Fifth of May) is a national holiday.

These days, the city has taken on a more cosmopolitan air than at any time during its history, due in great part to an influx of foreign residents—US students at the *Universidad de las Américas* (University of the Americas) and German workers at the Volkswagen plant. (According to the 1990 government census—the most recent—the city's population was 1.2 million, though the *Secretaría de Turismo,* or Secretariat of Tourism, calculates it at closer to 2.5 million.) Change started in the early 1970s with the arrival of the university, Mexico's only US-style college and an institution that continues to draw hundreds of US students every year. Only a two-hour drive from Mexico City, Puebla—a uniquely Spanish-Mexican town—is a wonderful destination for first-time visitors to Mexico.

Puebla At-a-Glance

SEEING THE CITY

Fuerte de Loreto (Fort Loreto) stands outside town on a hill that commands an excellent view of the city in the valley below and the surrounding mountains, including the two volcanic peaks. It's 2 miles (3 km) northeast of the *zócalo* (main plaza) via Calzada de los Fuertes.

SPECIAL PLACES

Everything in Puebla starts at the *zócalo,* and many of the beautiful colonial buildings, old churches, and famous shops are nearby. The streets are laid out in a grid system, but they are not numbered consecutively, as streets in the US often are. Calle Reforma Manuel A. Camacho runs along the north edge of the *zócalo;* streets north of it have even numbers, and streets to its south have odd ones. Calle 16 de Septiembre (which becomes Avenida 5 de Mayo as it runs north of the *zócalo*) is perpendicular to Calle Reforma Manuel A. Camacho; streets west of it are odd-numbered, while streets to its east are even-numbered. Most addresses (especially on numbered streets) feature a directional, so if you learn four words of Spanish, you'll be able to find almost anything in Puebla: *Sur* means south; *Norte* (Nte.), north; *Poniente* (Pte.), west; and *Oriente* (Ote.), east.

IN TOWN

ZÓCALO (MAIN PLAZA) This large square is flanked on the east by the cathedral and on the other sides by the handsome portals of colonial buildings, shops, and souvenir stalls. Tall trees shade the area, and parterres of tropical flowers are laid out around fountains and a bandstand. Many of the park benches and nearby buildings are made of Talavera tile. In the center of town at Calle 16 de Septiembre, Av. 2 Sur, and Calle 3 Ote.

CATEDRAL DE LA INMACULADA CONCEPCIÓN (CATHEDRAL OF THE IMMACULATE CONCEPTION) Construction of this twin-towered, tile-domed cathedral started in 1575 but was not completed until 1649. The altar, designed by Manuel Tolsá and made of Puebla onyx and marble, is particularly fine; the woodcarvings by Pedro Muñoz on the doors and choir stalls also are notable; and the 14 highly embellished chapels contain valuable religious paintings. There are usually a couple of English-speaking guides who will explain the fine points for a modest tip. On the south side of the *zócalo.*

MUSEO AMPARO (AMPARO MUSEUM) Mexican banker and philanthropist Manuel Espinoza Yglesias restored a beautifully proportioned colonial mansion, filled it with his impressive collection of pre-Hispanic and colonial art, and named it for his wife, Amparo. Excellent explanations of each piece are provided in Spanish and English, and additional information about the archaeological displays is available on computerized monitors in every hall. Headsets that offer commentary in English can be rented at the front desk. Closed Tuesdays. Admission charge. A few blocks south of the *Catedral de la Inmaculada Concepción,* at 708 Calle 2 Sur (phone: 464646).

MUSEO JOSÉ LUIS BELLO Y GONZÁLEZ (JOSÉ LUIS BELLO Y GONZÁLEZ MUSEUM) Fine collections of ornate furniture, paintings, ironwork, glassware, and gold and silver articles from the colonial period are exhibited. Closed Mondays. Admission charge. 302 Calle 3 Pte. (phone: 329475).

MUSEO JOSÉ LUIS BELLO Y ZETINA (JOSÉ LUIS BELLO Y ZETINA MUSEUM) Not related to the similarly named institution described above, this rich collection includes furniture, ivories, sculpture, and crystal. Also on exhibit are a number of 16th- through 18th-century European and Mexican paintings—including a Goya drawing and a piece by Miguel Cabrera. Closed Mondays. No admission charge. Next to the *Iglesia Santo Domingo* (see below), at 409 Av. 5 de Mayo (phone: 324720).

CASA DE ALFEÑIQUE (HOUSE OF THE ALMOND CAKE) The highly detailed façade of this structure that houses the regional museum of Puebla looks something like the frosting on a cake, hence its name. Inside are historical exhibitions, colonial furnishings, and some archaeological artifacts. Closed Mondays. Admission charge. Calle 4 Ote. and Av. 6 Nte. (phone: 324296).

IGLESIA SANTO DOMINGO (CHURCH OF ST. DOMINIC) Puebla's most lavishly decorated church is famous for its extravagant *Capilla del Rosario* (Rosary Chapel) and the gold leaf-covered carvings and sculptures that adorn every inch of wall, ceiling, and altar space. Av. 5 de Mayo and Calle 4 Pte.

SANTA ROSA What was once Puebla's largest convent is now a museum of sorts. Mole sauce was first created here in the beautifully tiled kitchen, and the elaborate arts and crafts found throughout the building include a six-foot earthenware candelabrum, handmade leather goods, and regional costumes. Closed Mondays. Admission charge. 1203 Calle 3 Nte. (phone: 462271).

MUSEO DE ARTE RELIGIOSO (MUSEUM OF RELIGIOUS ART) In 1857 the Mexican government confiscated all church property and outlawed monasteries and convents, in effect driving underground Puebla's *Convento de Santa Mónica* (Convent of St. Monica). With its hidden staircases, doors, and passageways, it remained undiscovered until 1934. Today it is one of Mexico's more unusual museums, with an extensive collection of paintings, sculptures, and religious articles and clothing. One exhibit here traces the stages and tasks of convent life. Closed Mondays. Admission charge. Near *Santa Rosa,* at 103 Calle 18 Pte. and Av. 5 de Mayo (phone: 320178).

BIBLIOTECA PALAFOX (PALAFOX LIBRARY) An absolute must for bibliophiles, this library built in 1646 contains more than 50,000 volumes and maps from the 17th and 18th centuries, as well as the 1493 *Nuremberg Chronicle,* illustrated with some 2,000 engravings. The spacious, high-ceilinged room with carved cedar bookshelves, red tile floors, and inlaid onyx reading tables creates an atmosphere of peace and a sense of the permanence of the written word. Closed Mondays. Admission charge. Second floor of the *Casa de la Cultura* (House of Culture) at 5 Calle 5 Ote. (phone: 465354).

TEATRO PRINCIPAL (PRINCIPAL THEATER) This restored theater is among the oldest in the Americas. It's open only during concerts and scheduled events, but you can peek inside in the mornings, when the cleanup crew is working. Calles 8 Ote. and 6 Nte. (phone: 326085).

FUERTE DE LORETO AND FUERTE DE GUADALUPE (FORT LORETO AND FORT GUADALUPE) The site of the historic battle of May 5, 1862, Loreto now is a military museum commemorating the event. The prize of its collection is a photograph of Maximilian comforting the tearful priest who came to give him last rites before his execution. The forts form part of the *Centro Cívico 5 de Mayo* (Cinco de Mayo Civic Center) complex, along with the *Museo de la Historia Natural* (Museum of Natural History; phone: 353419) and the *Planetario* (Planetarium; phone: 352099). The museums and planetarium are closed Mondays. Admission charge. Two miles (3 km) northeast of the *zócalo* (reached via the bus marked "Maravillas" or taxi).

ENVIRONS

AFRICAM This zoo-cum-park is Puebla's answer to the *Lion Country Safaris* in the US. About 3,000 animals—including lions, elephants, giraffes, zebras, camels, tigers, llamas, and rhinoceroses—roam free within the park's 15,000 acres. On the grounds are a restaurant, a snack bar, a gift shop, and restrooms. Drive your own car, or take one of the zebra-striped *Africam* buses that leave from the bus terminal at Boulevards Norte and Tlaxcala three times a day on weekdays and four times a day on weekends and holidays. Open daily. Admission charge. Blvd. Valsequillo, 9 miles (14 km) south of downtown (phone: 361212).

CHOLULA Once among the most important religious centers in Mexico, this site flourished at the same time as *Teotihuacán* (the pyramid site outside Mexico City). Open daily. No admission charge Sundays (no phone). Five miles (8 km) northwest of Puebla on Rte. 190. To get there, pick up a *combi* (Volkswagen van) in front of the *Museo Nacional del Ferrocarril* (National Railroad Museum; Calles 11 Nte. and 12 Pte.), or join an excursion through your hotel's travel desk. For additional details on *Cholula,* see *Mexico's Magnificent Archaeological Heritage* in DIVERSIONS.

TONANTZINTLA This town is home to the *Iglesia de Santa María* (Church of St. Mary), which has a wonderful cupola and walls decorated with vivid paintings of fruits, flowers, and images of the indigenous workers who built the church. A few miles farther south is one of the most beautiful churches in the state, the *Iglesia de San Francisco Acatepec* (Church of St. Francis of Acatepec), an ornate 18th-century building covered in bright Talavera tiles. Tonantzintla is 6 miles (10 km) south of Puebla via Route 190.

HUEJOTZINGO (pronounced Way-ho-*tseen*-go) The specialty here is a reasonably priced, bubbly apple cider known as *sidra*. The small town's Franciscan convent, on the main square, dates from 1570 and is one of the first in the Americas. It contains a magnificent altarpiece covered in gold leaf. A few miles south of Tonantzintla on Rte. 190.

Sources and Resources

TOURIST INFORMATION

The *Dirección de Turismo del Estado de Puebla* (Puebla State Tourism Office; 3 Calle 5 Ote.; phone: 461285) is open 365 days a year.

LOCAL COVERAGE There are no local English-language publications here, but *The News* (from Mexico City) and the *Mexico City Times*—both published daily—are widely available.

TELEPHONE The city code for Puebla is 22. *Note:* Mexico's telephone company has embarked on a major expansion project that involves changing telephone numbers in many areas of the country. At press time, all numbers listed in this chapter were correct. However, if you have any difficulties reaching attractions listed here, contact the local tourist office.

CLIMATE AND CLOTHES Puebla's climate is similar to the capital's, with relatively mild summers and winter temperatures in the 60s F (16–21C). Carry an umbrella in the summer, which is the rainy season. Dress is generally casual.

GETTING AROUND

BUS Buses that go to the forts can be found at the *zócalo*. The fare is 80 centavos (about 10¢); buses run until 11:30 PM.

CAR RENTAL *Rente Ford Budget* has an office in town (2927 Av. Juárez; phone: 303976).

TAXI Hail a cab—which, like a city bus, will take you to the forts—at the *zócalo*. Negotiate the fare with the driver before getting in; a ride within town should cost between 20 and 30 pesos ($2.70 to $4).

TOURS Hotel travel desks arrange sightseeing trips in town and excursions to *Cholula* (see *Special Places,* above). Licensed guides can be found at the tourist office and around the corner from the cathedral; their hourly rate does not include transportation.

SPECIAL EVENTS

Carnaval (just before *Lent*) in nearby Huejotzingo (see *Special Places*) is spectacular, particularly the mock battles between Moors and Christians. On May 5, all kinds of celebrations and frivolity commemorate the *poblanos'* 1862 defeat of the French. The *Feria de Puebla* (Puebla Fair), during which some interesting cultural events are scheduled, also takes place in May. Fireworks mark the *Fiesta de San Agustín* (Feast of St. Augustine) on August 28. On the last Sunday in September, the town of Atlixco (15 miles/25 km southwest of Puebla) celebrates the *Fiesta de San Miguel Arcángel* (Feast of St. Michael the Archangel), noted for its fine presentation of regional dances.

SHOPPING

Puebla is best known for its local onyx, Talavera tiles, and pottery, as well as *dulce de camote,* a sweet-potato candy that comes wrapped in tissue paper. A special treat for the senses is the *Mercado Victoria* (on Calle 6 Pte., between Av. 5 de Mayo and Av. 3 Nte.), the local produce market, with beautifully arranged fruits, vegetables, flowers, and dozens of varieties of black mole paste. *El Parián,* a mall of handicrafts shops right near the *Iglesia de San Francisco,* is a good place to bargain for onyx and other crafts. On Sundays, the Plazuela de los Sapos (Calle 7 Ote., near Calle 4 Sur) turns into a huge flea market.

Best bets for tile and pottery are *Talavera Uriarte* (911 Calle 4 Pte.; phone: 321598) and *Casa Rugerio* (111 Calle 18 Pte.; phone: 323843), where they still use techniques dating from the 16th century. Antiques, both originals and reproductions, are available at *Galería Chapis* (312 Calle 6 Sur; phone: 421155; and 404 Calle 7 Ote.; phone: 321352) and at many other shops along Calle 6 Sur. You can see local artists at work in their studios in *Barrio de las Artistas* (Calle 8 Nte., between Calles 4 and 6 Ote.; no phone). Most shops are open Mondays through Saturdays from 10 AM to 2 PM and 4 to 7 PM; market stalls are open from 8 AM to 4 PM, though some handicrafts stalls stay open an hour or two later.

SPORTS

GOLF Puebla's one 18-hole course, the *Club Campestre de Puebla* (7319 Prolongación 11 Sur; phone: 284813), is open to visitors who are members of a US golf club.

SOCCER The local team, *Los Pericos de Puebla,* plays at the *Estadio Cuauhtémoc* (Cuauhtémoc Stadium) at the *Unidad Deportiva* sports complex in the northern part of the city (Av. Ignacio Zaragoza and the road from Puebla to Mexico City; phone: 363746).

SWIMMING Several miles before the *Club Campestre de Puebla* (see above), the *Agua Azul* complex (Prolongación 11 Sur; phone: 431330) has a series of pools and artificial lakes. On weekends, as might be expected, it is crowded, but it's quite pleasant midweek.

TENNIS The *Club Britania* (8 Calle Santa Fe; phone: 490099) has 18 courts, a pool, and a squash court available to members and their guests. The *Club Campestre de Puebla* (see *Golf*) has four courts, which are open to members of US golf clubs. There also are tennis facilities at *El Mesón del Angel* and *Villa Arqueológica* hotels (see *Checking In*).

NIGHTCLUBS AND NIGHTLIFE

Mariachis stand around in the Plaza de Santa Inés waiting to be hired, so don't expect to see them strolling through the crowds singing. The Plazuela de los Sapos (Calle 7 Ote., near Calle 4 Sur) also draws mariachis and nighttime strollers. The top discos are *Paradise* (158 Prolongación Monterrey, in front of the *El Mesón del Angel* hotel; phone: 240432); *News* (31 Poniente, at Blvd. Atlixco; phone: 311330); and *Baby'O* (5513 Prolongación Chignahuapan; phone: 482440). Other popular spots for dancing are *Sr. Frog's* (78 Calle Teziutlán Sur; phone 488786) and *Porthos* (Rte. 190, also called Av. Recta a Cholula; phone: 473024), between Puebla and the ruins of *Cholula*. Two bars, *Huapango* (2105 Av. Juárez; phone: 483184) and *El Camote* (1918 Av. Juárez; phone: 483184), attract lively crowds, especially on weekends.

Best in Town

CHECKING IN

A double room for a night will cost $100 to $175 in an expensive hotel; $65 to $95 in a moderate place; and $60 or less in an inexpensive one. The deluxe *Camino Real Puebla* was scheduled to open as we went to press; for more information, call 800-7-CAMINO. Unless otherwise noted, all hotels listed below have TV sets and telephones in each room; some have air conditioning. All telephone numbers are in the 22 city code unless otherwise indicated.

EXPENSIVE

De Alba Popular with those for whom excellent service and a friendly, efficient staff are important, this local favorite has 208 modern rooms and suites (all with mini-bars). A pool, three restaurants, including *Don Paco* (see *Eating Out*), a coffee shop, a bar, tennis courts, a business center, and even a golf course are added incentives. In southern Puebla, at 141 Av. Hermanos Serdán (phone: 486055; fax: 487344).

Aristos A heated indoor pool, 120 rooms, a restaurant, a coffee shop, and a central location—where Avenida Reforma and Calle 7 Sur meet—make this hotel an attractive option (phone: 320565; 800-5-ARISTO; fax: 325982).

Condado Plaza This first class establishment offers 68 attractively decorated rooms and suites that feature plenty of amenities, including cable TV, in-room safes, mini-bars, and electronic locks. There are two restaurants, two bars, and a business center. Privada 6B Sur and Calle 31 Ote. (phone: 372733; fax: 379305).

El Mesón del Angel Set on nicely landscaped grounds, this property offers 192 rooms with refrigerators and terraces; some rooms have fine views of the volcanoes. Recreational facilities include two pools and a tennis court; there also are two bars and two restaurants. On the northern edge of town, at 807 Av. Hermanos Serdán (phone: 243000; fax: 242227).

Real de Puebla Formerly the *Misión Park Plaza Puebla,* this modern high-rise has 225 rooms, a pool, a garden, a restaurant, three bars (including a nice lobby bar), and a health club. Downtown, at 2522 Calle 5 Pte. (phone: 489600; fax: 489733).

MODERATE

Lastra A pleasant place to spend the night, it has 53 units, a garden, a pool, a good restaurant, and a bar. 2633 Calzada de los Fuertes, near the forts (phone: 359755; fax: 351501).

Del Portal With 100 units, this colonial-style hotel offers a restaurant and a bar. Just off the *zócalo,* at 205 Maximino Avila Camacho (phone: 460211; fax: 467511).

Posada San Pedro This colonial-style hostelry has 80 rooms; there are also two restaurants, a bar, and a pool. Downtown, at 202 Calle 2 Ote. (phone: 465077; fax: 465376).

Villa Arqueológica The 40 rooms at this Club Med property offer spartan comfort. Amenities include tennis, a pool, and French fare. It's not necessary to buy the all-inclusive vacation package here. 601 Calle 2 Pte., at the *Cholula* archaeological zone (phone: 471966; 800-CLUB-MED; fax: 471508).

INEXPENSIVE

Campestre Los Sauces In this colonial-style hotel are 47 rooms, a pool, gardens, and a bar with entertainment. Midway between Puebla and *Cholula* on Km 122 of Rte. 190 (phone/fax: 471011).

Palacio San Leonardo This attractive 80-room hostelry has a restaurant, a bar, and a pool. Centrally located, at 211 Calle 2 Ote. (phone: 460555; fax: 421176).

EATING OUT

Poblanos are proud of their excellent local specialties, which are distinct from those found in other parts of the country. Mole (pronounced *mo*-lay), the unique spicy sauce, was first concocted in Puebla. Another original creation is *chiles en nogada,* a *chile poblano* filled with spiced ground beef and almonds, topped with a white sauce of ground walnuts, cream cheese, and pomegranate seeds—all representing the white, red, and green of the Mexican flag. You can sample mole anytime; mid-August through mid-October is the season for *chiles en nogada.*

The area on Avenida Juárez known as the Zona Esmeralda ("Emerald Zone") is where you'll find the newer restaurants. Several of these places have a fairly sophisticated ambience, with the menu more international than Mexican. Expect to pay $60 to $80 for a dinner for two in expensive restaurants; $40 to $55 in moderate ones; and $35 or less at inexpensive places. Prices do not include drinks, wine, tax, or tips. Most restaurants below accept MasterCard and Visa, and a few also accept American Express and Diners Club; it's a good idea to call ahead and check. Unless otherwise noted, all restaurants are open daily for lunch and dinner. All telephone numbers are in the 22 city code unless otherwise indicated.

EXPENSIVE

Las Bodegas del Molino Set in a remodeled 16th-century hacienda furnished with antiques, it serves fine Mexican and international food. Reservations advised. At the edge of town, at Molino de San José del Puente (phone: 490399).

MODERATE

La Bola Roja That Mexican delicacy known as *gusanos de maguey* (fried worms, or, more precisely, cactus maggots) is served here, as well as less esoteric dishes such as *arroz a la poblana* (rice cooked with garlic, tomatoes, peas, and onions) and, naturally, mole *poblano.* Reservations unnecessary. Three locations: 1305 Calle 17 Sur (phone: 437051); in the *Plaza Dorada* shopping center, at 3510 Av. 5 de Mayo (phone: 407582); and in the *Plaza Loreto* shopping center, at 366 Calle I. Zaragoza (phone: 361422).

Charlie's China Poblana One of Carlos Anderson's many outposts, this place has a strong following among both residents and tourists. The varied menu features international and Mexican fare. Especially notable are the shrimp dishes, the filet of beef *arriero* (prepared in banana leaves), and the famous spinach-and-mushroom house salad. Reservations advised. 1918 Av. Juárez (phone: 463184).

Don Paco The specialty here is hearty Spanish fare, including paella, *lechón* (suckling pig), and *fabada* (bean, pork, and sausage stew). There's dancing to live music Friday and Saturday nights. Reservations advised. In the *De Alba* hotel, 141 Av. Hermanos Serdán (phone: 486055).

Donato Camarano Here's a good place for steaks, pasta, pizza, and charcoal-broiled kid. Reservations unnecessary. 1221 Calle 22 de Septiembre (phone: 453169).

Fonda de Santa Clara Try the delicious mole over chicken and enchiladas, washed down with an *horchata* (a drink made from ground cantaloupe seeds).

Reservations unnecessary. Two locations: 307 Calle 3 Pte. (phone: 422659), closed Mondays, and 920 Calle 3 Pte. (phone: 461919), closed Tuesdays.

La Hacienda de San Pedro The decor is Mexican ranch, but the fare is strictly US-style steaks. A trio plays here Friday and Saturday nights. Reservations advised. 2504 Av. Juárez (phone: 490843).

El Tejado The service is excellent at this good steakhouse. Reservations unnecessary. Two locations: 2302 Calle 16 de Septiembre (phone: 401853) and Blvd. Héroes del 5 de Mayo, between Calles 2 Sur and 16 de Septiembre (phone: 406297).

Vittorio's Pasta and pizza are prepared *a la poblana* (with mole and other local seasonings) in this café. Reservations unnecessary. On the *zócalo,* at 106 Portal Morelos (phone: 327900).

INEXPENSIVE

El Cortijo The Spanish ambience and dishes such as paella, *fabada,* and snails make for a pleasant dining experience. Reservations unnecessary. 506 Calle 16 de Septiembre (phone: 420503).

Puerto Escondido

(pronounced *Pwer*-toe Es-con-*dee*-doe)

True to its name, which means "hidden port," Puerto Escondido—a town on the Pacific Coast in the state of Oaxaca—remains one of the lesser known but most beautiful, unspoiled, and unsophisticated hideaways of southern Mexico. At one time, *FONATUR*, the government agency responsible for the development and improvement of Mexico's tourist sites, had very big plans for the area. Fortunately for lovers of unspoiled and unsophisticated hideaways, however, the plans seem to have been significantly scaled down in favor of the larger development farther south at Huatulco.

Puerto Escondido was established as a port in 1928 to facilitate the shipment of coffee beans grown on the lush slopes of the Sierra Madre del Sur mountains. The construction of the coastal highway (Route 200) in 1967 made getting here from other parts of the country a lot easier. Soon, vacationers were flocking to the area, attracted by its sandy beaches, hidden coves, rough surf, low prices, and absolute peace and quiet. Today, Puerto Escondido can be reached directly by jet from Mexico City as well as by car.

While this town of about 10,000 is no longer the lazy fishing village it was in the 1960s, it retains its secluded atmosphere. Despite Puerto Escondido's growing popularity as a tourist destination, it still offers plenty of long stretches of beach where visitors can find a spot to claim for themselves, with no one else in sight. And though there are a handful of good hotels, it will probably be some time—if ever—before rows of hotels line Playa Zicatela, as once was predicted.

About 95% of Puerto Escondido's population is of indigenous descent, and most make their living from fishing or farming. Even with the onslaught of significant tourism, it's still possible to feel like an intruder here. Inhabitants are not hostile or cold—it's just that they're gracious without being purposefully ingratiating, which can be a shock if you're used to the effusive welcomes offered visitors in other parts of Mexico. Service is inevitably slow (sometimes almost nonexistent), and there just isn't much for tourists to *do*. Unless, of course, you want to relax on the pristine, quiet beaches, swim in the Pacific or the bay, snorkel over fantastical coral reefs, dine on fresh seafood in the town's handful of restaurants, and watch the local fishermen pulling into the harbor in their colorful boats, mending their nets, and unloading the day's catch. If all this sounds like heaven to you, Puerto Escondido is the perfect place to unwind.

Puerto Escondido At-a-Glance

SEEING THE CITY

A lovely, sweeping vista of Puerto Escondido and its beaches can be enjoyed from the Carretera Costera (Route 200). The *faro* (lighthouse), a 15-minute walk from the main street, offers another panoramic view. The Camino del Faro sign points the way to the red and white tower. It is open daily; no admission charge.

SPECIAL PLACES

Though Puerto Escondido lacks museums, historic landmarks, parks, and churches, it has some of the most beautiful beaches in the world, and because the resort is relatively undiscovered, they tend to be blissfully uncrowded.

PLAYA PRINCIPAL This half-mile stretch of beach that curves around La Bahía (The Bay) is the center of most activities—fishing, swimming, and sunning. The water at the western end is so calm that locals refer to it as the "Bathtub" or "Kiddie Cove."

PLAYA ZICATELA The path around Los Marineros (The Sailors), the rocky outcroppings at the east end of La Bahía, leads to a 2-mile stretch of off-white sand pounded by powerful waves. Surfers consider this one of the best beaches in the world (see *Surfing*). This is not a place for casual swimming (or novice surfing), as the undertow here is treacherous and deadly, but joggers and hikers find this beach very enjoyable. An hour's stroll up and down the shore, followed by breakfast at the *Santa Fe* (see *Eating Out*), is a fine way to start any day. Zicatela Point, at the far end of the beach, is a haven for pelicans, seagulls, sandpipers, and other winged species, as well as for beach- and sunset-loving Homo sapiens.

ENVIRONS

PUERTO ANGELITO "Port of the Little Angel" is a small, picture-perfect blue bay that is sheltered from the sea by coral reefs. Its two golden beaches are attractive to swimmers for their calm waters, and to snorkelers and divers for the legions of colorful fish that inhabit the reefs. Boats can be hired at La Bahía for a tour of the bay, which includes a stop for swimming and snorkeling. To get here by car, take Route 200 north toward the airport, and about 1½ miles (2 km) from town, turn left at the sign for Puerto Angelito. The bay also can be reached on foot or by taxi.

PLAYA BACOCHO Located 2 miles (3 km) west of town, this narrow, isolated beach with windswept sand and thundering waves is the place to wallow in solitude and contemplate the open sea. (Don't swim here; the undertow is too dangerous.) The *Best Western Posada Real* hotel (see *Checking In*) provides a stunning view of this beach.

LAGUNA MANIALTEPEC Some 15 miles (24 km) west of Puerto Escondido, this lagoon is brimming with tropical birds and surrounded by thick, luxuriant vegetation. Two travel agencies working out of the same office, *Hidden Voyages Ecotours* and *Turismo Rodimar* (see *Tours*), offer dawn and sunset wildlife tours of the lagoon, in addition to other excursions.

PUERTO ANGEL This small fishing community, about 50 miles (80 km) southeast of Puerto Escondido, lacks the charm and ambience of its neighbor, but its superb beaches make up for it. The main attractions are Playa del Panteón (Cemetery Beach), which has a small graveyard with brightly painted tombstones perched above it, and Playa Zipolite, about 5 miles (8 km) out of town, the only nudist beach in Mexico (beware of the undertow). At the far end of Playa Zipolite is Playa del Amor (Love Beach), a tiny, secluded haven for lovers and others. The best bet for lodging here is the *Posada Cañón Devata,* about 100 yards uphill from Playa del Panteón (phone/fax: 958-43048), an intimate hotel with a good vegetarian restaurant and ecologically conscious owners.

EXTRA SPECIAL

Parque Nacional Chacahua makes for a wonderful day trip out of Puerto Escondido. This entrancing 50-square-mile retreat has fine sandy beaches and inviting inlets and coves, all populated by every kind of bird and fish known to the tropical Pacific. Three tiny fishing villages complete the serene landscape. *Turismo Rodimar* (see *Tours*) arranges eight-hour tours.

Sources and Resources

TOURIST INFORMATION

The *Oficina de Turismo del Estado de Oaxaca* (Oaxaca State Tourist Office; Calle 5 Pte. and Rte. 200; phone: 20175) offers a very good map and information on hotels and prices. The office is closed weekends.

LOCAL COVERAGE Inquire at the tourist office about a guide to Puerto Escondido called *Por la Costa* (Along the Coast), available in English. English-language magazines can be found at *Acuario Comercial* on Avenida Pérez Gazga. *The News* and the *Mexico City Times,* both dailies published in Mexico City, are available at *Lupita's,* a grocery store near the *Bananas* restaurant.

TELEPHONE The city code for Puerto Escondido is 958. *Note:* Mexico's telephone company has embarked on a major expansion project that involves changing telephone numbers in many areas of the country. At press time, all numbers listed in this chapter were correct. However, if you have any difficulties reaching attractions listed here, contact the local tourist office.

CLIMATE AND CLOTHES Puerto Escondido enjoys a hot, dry climate. Average temperatures range between about 70F and 90F (21C and 32C), with the hottest days occurring from May through August, the coolest in January. Dress is casual; shorts and sandals usually suffice, even in town.

GETTING AROUND

The town is small enough to be seen easily on foot, and most of the important spots are within easy walking distance of one another. To tour Puerto Escondido's beautiful environs, however, some form of motor transportation is necessary.

BUS Five long-distance bus lines provide daily service; the best are *Cristóbal Colón* (phone: 20284) and *Estrella Blanca* (phone: 20427 or 20086). Buses run frequently to Pochutla, where connections to Huatulco or Puerto Angel can be made. *Cristóbal Colón* buses travel between Puerto Escondido, Tuxtla Gutiérrez, and San Cristóbal de las Casas in the state of Chiapas, as well as to the city of Oaxaca. (*Note:* Chiapas has calmed considerably following the anti-government uprising in 1994, but it's still a good idea to check with tourism authorities before traveling there.) *Estrella Blanca* travels the route to Acapulco. The station for both lines is just uphill from the *crucero,* the only traffic light in town.

CAR RENTAL *Budget* (in the *Best Western Posada Real;* phone: 20312 or 20315) is represented here.

TAXI Cab drivers are willing to drive anywhere, and it is possible to negotiate reasonable hourly rates. Taxis cruise along Avenida Pérez Gazga; they also can be summoned by phone.

TOURS *Turismo Rodimar* (906 Av. Pérez Gazga; phone: 20737 or 20734) arranges all-day excursions by car, minibus, or bus (depending upon the number of passengers) to Huatulco, and half-day excursions to Puerto Angel, which include a visit to the nudist beach, Playa Zipolite. *Hidden Voyages Ecotours* (same address and phone as *Turismo Rodimar*) offers beach, lagoon, and mountain tours, as well as dawn and sunset wildlife excursions. Minne Dahlbert, the German-Canadian owner of the *Mayflower* hotel (see *Checking In*), organizes private tours to nearby sites.

SPECIAL EVENTS

The town has only two noteworthy events during the year. Each August, Puerto Escondido stages the *Torneo Internacional de Surfeo* (International Surfing Tournament), which attracts expert surfers from all over the world. On November 4, the town's biggest bash, *Noviembre en Puerto Escondido* (November in Puerto Escondido) features such events as polo "burro" matches (polo played on burros and using brooms), a fishing tournament, exhibitions of parachuting and ballooning, a surfing contest, and several cultural events.

SHOPPING

Shopping in Puerto Escondido is limited: There are only a few shops along Avenida Pérez Gazga—*Tanga's* (no phone) is the best for beachwear; *Tamar* (no phone) is the best for handicrafts. While most handicrafts lack distinction, there are some excellent buys in locally crafted baskets and red and white coral jewelry. On Saturday, the big market day, vendors stream in from surrounding communities to sell their produce—particularly tropical fruits, such as pineapples, bananas, and *zapotes* (sapodillas)—at the *Mercado Benito Juárez* downtown market. In general, shops are open from 10 AM to 2 PM and 4 to 8 PM daily.

SPORTS

FISHING The *Turismo Rodimar* travel agency (see *Tours*) rents fishing boats for up to four people (three-hour minimum), including rods and bait.

HORSEBACK RIDING Horses can be rented at Laguna Manialtepec, Playa Zicatela, and in nearby Barra de Colotepec. The *Turismo Rodimar* travel agency (see *Tours*) makes arrangements. A typical half-day trip takes in the full range of Mexican scenery, from river crossings and thick jungle undergrowth to stark rock formations and hot springs.

SNORKELING AND DIVING Dive trips are available, but they don't include equipment, which is available for rent at the various destinations. There's good snorkeling at Puerto Angelito, but the best diving areas are in the coves near Puerto Angel.

SURFING The surf's great in this part of Mexico.

WONDERFUL WAVES

Playa Zicatela From sunup to sundown, a dozen or so surfers match their skills against the waves at Playa Zicatela, while spectators watch enthralled from the beach. This beach boasts some of the best surfing waves in the world. It is particularly famous for its "pipelines," a term that refers to giant waves that curl in on themselves and form tunnels through which an intrepid surfer can ride. Since the undertow is so strong, however, only the most skillful should attempt to surf here. No surfboard rentals are available.

Good left-point waves for beginners can be found about 1½ miles (2 km) south of town, while excellent beach breakers for advanced surfers crash along the shore just south of town. There also is excellent surfing on the pristine beaches to the north and south of Puerto Escondido, which can be reached by four-wheel-drive vehicles (available for rent in town or at the airport) or by boat.

TENNIS The *Fiesta Mexicana* hotel (see *Checking In*) has a lighted artificial grass court open to the public.

NIGHTCLUBS AND NIGHTLIFE

Puerto Escondido has little nightlife; in fact, if the town had sidewalks, they would roll up very early. But for those who aren't satisfied with just counting stars, there's *Bacocho* (45 Tehuantepec; no phone); *Pauline* at the *Fiesta Mexicana* hotel (see *Checking In*); *El Sol y la Rumba* (Av. Pérez Gazga; no phone); *Tequila Boom Boom* (Av. Marina Nacional and Av. Pérez Gazga; no phone); and *El Tubo* (no phone), a sleazy disco on the main beach that's lots of fun if you like that kind of thing. It's usually open daily—except when it's not. There's live rock and dancing at *Coco's* restaurant and beach club at the *Best Western Posada Real* hotel (see *Checking In*).

Best in Town

CHECKING IN

For such a small town, Puerto Escondido has a fair number of hotels. Expect to pay $75 to $90 per night for a double room in an expensive hotel; $50 to $70 in a moderate place; and $45 or less in an inexpensive one. During the off-season, summer through fall, rates drop about 25%. Unless otherwise noted, all hotels listed below have air conditioning, telephones, and TV sets in the rooms. All telephone numbers are in the 958 city code unless otherwise indicated.

EXPENSIVE

Best Western Posada Real This resort-style hotel isn't as quaint as some of the others in town, and guests must walk down a cliff to get to the beach, but the staff is friendly and helpful. There are 100 rooms, *Coco's* restaurant and beach club (see *Eating Out*), three bars, two pools, and lovely grounds. Blvd. Benito Juárez (phone: 20237 or 20185; 800-528-1234; fax: 20192).

Villa Sol One of Puerto Escondido's newer hostelries, it offers 72 rooms, 24 junior suites, and 12 two-bedroom master suites, as well as a pool, a restaurant, a bar, and complimentary transportation to the beach. Fraccionamiento Bacocho (phone: 20402 or 20061; fax: 20451).

MODERATE

Fiesta Mexicana This modern two-story, 90-room hotel offers three restaurants, a lighted tennis court, three swimming pools, the *Pauline* disco (see *Nightclubs and Nightlife,* above), and an attentive staff. Blvd. Benito Juárez (phone: 20150; fax: 20125)

Santa Fe The front door opens onto La Bahía, and the back door leads to Playa Zicatela. There are 40 rooms with authentic Mexican decor, plus eight bungalows with kitchenettes, a small pool, and a fine dining area overlooking sand and surf (see *Eating Out*). Calle del Morro (phone: 20170; fax: 20260).

Mayflower This spotless, colonial-style hostelry has 12 fan-cooled rooms with balconies (but no phones or TV sets), plus three dormitories (shared bath)—and costs about $8.50 per night at press time. There's no restaurant. About a block from the beach, on Andador Libertad (phone: 20367; fax: 20486).

Nayar Two blocks uphill from the beach, here are 36 rooms with TV sets (some with balconies) and a pool. The seafood restaurant affords diners a lovely view of the town. No credit cards accepted. 407 Av. Pérez Gazga (phone: 20113; fax: 20547).

Las Palmas It's simple, but clean and comfortable, with 40 rooms with ceiling fans (no phones or TV sets), a pleasant palm-filled courtyard, and a restaurant (see *Eating Out*). Boats to Puerto Angelito can be rented right out front. Av. Pérez Gazga (phone: 20230).

Posada Loren Clean, and basic, it has 24 rooms with fans (no phones or TV sets). There's no restaurant. 507 Av. Pérez Gazga (phone: 20057; fax: 20448).

Rincón del Pacífico This small, well-maintained place on the beach offers 24 rooms decorated cheerily in yellow and white, as well as four junior suites with air conditioning, TV sets, and refrigerators. There's also a restaurant (see *Eating Out*). 900 Av. Pérez Gazga (phone: 20056; fax: 20101).

Villa Marinero Situated close to the beach, this property has 16 bungalows, each with a bedroom with a fan, a small living room, and a kitchenette (but no TV sets or phones). Carretera Costera, Colonia Marinero (phone: 20180).

EATING OUT

Puerto Escondido is not known for elaborate dinners or polished service, but the seafood is almost always good. Expect to pay up to $30 for a meal for two in a moderate place, and less than $15 at an inexpensive spot. Prices do not include drinks, wine, tax, or tip. Most restaurants below accept MasterCard and Visa, and a few also accept American Express and Diners Club; it's a good idea to call ahead and check. Unless otherwise noted, all restaurants are open daily for lunch and dinner, and reservations are unnecessary. All telephone numbers are in the 958 city code unless otherwise indicated.

Coco's This informal restaurant and beach club set in an open-sided *palapa* (thatch-roofed building) on the beach features seafood and a spectacular view. In the *Best Western Posada Real,* Blvd. Benito Juárez (phone: 20185 or 20137).

La Fonda del Gourmet A huge warehouse decorated with 15-foot oars, anchors, shells, and fishing nets. Specialties include shrimp in orange sauce, steaks, and a seafood brochette. Open for breakfast, lunch, and dinner; closed Sundays. Reservations advised. Av. Marina Nacional (phone: 20791).

Hostería del Viandante There is sometimes a wait for a table at this little *palapa*-topped pizzeria, one of the most popular spots in town. The menu includes a dozen varieties of pizza, as well as typical pasta dishes. Rock 'n' roll music sets an upbeat mood. Av. Pérez Gazga (phone: 20671).

Junto al Mar Gregoria Silva has been preparing tasty seafood and Mexican specialties in this *palapa* "next to the sea" since 1958. Av. Pérez Gazga and Av. Marina Nacional (phone: 20286).

Restaurant Posada de Loren Shaded by palm trees, this beachside restaurant specializes in brochettes of jumbo shrimp and lobster. It's also a great place to take in seaside goings-on. Not connected with the *Posada Loren* hotel. Open daily from 3 to 11 PM. Av. Pérez Gazga (phone: 20448)

Santa Fe Those tired of *huevos rancheros* for breakfast might drop by this gracious restaurant for a vegetarian treat of homemade yogurt with granola or tofu hotcakes with fruit. Seafood is offered as well. Open for breakfast, lunch, and dinner. In the *Santa Fe Hotel,* Calle del Morro (phone: 20170).

Sardina de Plata A popular place well known for tasty seafood and good steaks. Reservations advised. Av. Pérez Gazga, Fraccionamiento Bacocho, next to the *Rocamar* hotel (phone: 20328).

Spaghetti House The best Italian food in town, hands down. What better way to enjoy your pasta than with a spectacular view of the ocean and a bottle of Mexican chianti-style wine? Be sure to try the cheese-garlic bread. Andador Azucenas on the main beach (phone: 20005).

INEXPENSIVE

Bananas Everyone in Puerto Escondido seems to congregate here to watch international newscasts on cable TV in air conditioned comfort. Good sandwiches and tacos are served. Av. Pérez Gazga (phone: 20005).

Los Crotos The service may be the slowest in town, but the prices and the food—*camarones con frutas* (shrimp and fruit in a cream sauce) and *pescado con camarones* (fish smothered in shrimp)—are worth the wait. On Av. Pérez Gazga, next to the long-distance phone service booth (phone: 20025).

Las Palmas This seafood restaurant is as clean and pleasant as the hotel in which it's located. The tables are on an open-air terrace with a view of the bay. In *Las Palmas Hotel,* Av. Pérez Gazga (phone: 20230).

Rincón del Pacífico In the hotel of the same name, with the same pleasant atmosphere and service. Seafood, naturally, and steaks are on the bill of fare. 900 Av. Pérez Gazga (phone: 20056 or 20193).

Siete Regiones This huge place specializes in typical Oaxacan fare from, as the name implies, the seven regions of the state. There's no extra charge for the fine view. On Av. Pérez Gazga, near *Los Crotos* (phone: 20551).

Puerto Vallarta

(pronounced *Pwer*-toe Va-*yar*-tah)

A small and remote agricultural village until the early 1960s, Puerto Vallarta is today one of the fastest-growing seaside resorts in North America. Its resident population (which includes many foreigners) is approximately 250,000, a figure that swells when tourists fill its 14,000-plus hotel rooms at the height of the season.

In the state of Jalisco, Puerto Vallarta lies between the rugged Sierra Madre to the east and 25 miles of white sand beaches along the beautiful Bahía de Banderas (Banderas Bay) on the west. For US citizens suffering winter blues, it is an ideal spot for a summer vacation in February. Puerto Vallarta is also the perfect headquarters for deep-sea expeditions. The area is well suited to both fishing and scuba diving; the marine population includes sailfish, marlin, bonito, tuna, squid, shark, and porpoise.

In the mid-19th century, a sailor named Guadalupe Sánchez began frequenting Puerto Vallarta (then known as Las Peñas) in his small boat in order to deliver salt to be transported to inland mines for refining silver. In Sánchez's wake, settlers came to raise corn, beans, bananas, and tobacco. After the Revolution of 1910, the town was incorporated.

By the late 1950s, a number of Americans had discovered Puerto Vallarta, building homes along the hills that drop down to the Río Cuale in the neighborhood that came to be known as Gringo Gulch. In the early 1960s, director John Huston chose Puerto Vallarta as the locale for his film *The Night of the Iguana*. Reporters flocked here to keep abreast of the daily dallyings of the star, Richard Burton, and his not-yet wife Elizabeth Taylor, who had flown in to keep him company. Suddenly, Puerto Vallarta was appearing regularly in newspapers around the world.

The first person to cash in on the town's new fame was a foresighted Russian immigrant named Suña Gershenson, who, even before the movie people arrived, had begun constructing the town's first luxury hotel, the *Posada Vallarta* (now the *Krystal Vallarta*). Others followed his lead, and *Playa de Oro* (now part of the Vista chain), a Westin property (now the *Camino Real*), and a *Holiday Inn* (now the *Ramada*) soon went up. The government pushed a highway through the mountains, bringing with it telephone lines, and an international airport was opened. In the early 1970s, the government put in water and drainage works, patched up the streets, and spruced up the town for its future role as a resort.

The Río Cuale splits Puerto Vallarta into northern and southern sections. About two-thirds of the city is on the northern side, near the older hotels and commercial district; the more residential southern end leads to some of the larger modern resorts on the edge of town. The *malecón* (seawall and waterfront avenue) runs north-south along the bay, and most of the town extends no farther than five or six blocks into the eastern hills. Between the docks and the airport is Marina Vallarta, a resort complex with an 18-hole golf course and several hotels. Nuevo Vallarta, a relatively new development with a vast, beautiful beach, waterways, magnificent homes, villas, and condos, is 10 miles (16 km) to the north, just over the state line in neighboring Nayarit. Flamingo Club Estates, another development in Nayarit, is next to Nuevo Vallarta.

In the middle of the Río Cuale is a small rock island with an archaeological museum, a cultural center, restaurants, bars, and shops. Here, native women beat their laundry on the rocky shore, one of the few reminders of Puerto Vallarta's past. But, for the most part, the Puerto Vallarta of yesterday is just a glimmer of a memory. Today, a visit to Puerto Vallarta is much more likely to produce visions of horseback riding on the beaches; parasails alighting on the calm waters of the bay; motorboats, sailboats, and cruise ships pulling into their moorings; and sophisticated restaurants, luxury hotels, chic shops, and nightclubs.

Still, the place hasn't lost its charm. The locals are friendly, the red-tile-roofed houses still appear to tumble down the streets to Bahía de Banderas, and most of the furor of activity is concentrated at Playa de los Muertos. Sometimes traffic clogs the narrow streets, and there are many more shops and restaurants than truly necessary, but, happily, the town's sunny personality perseveres.

Puerto Vallarta At-a-Glance

SEEING THE CITY

Puerto Vallarta's downtown area is perfect for strolling. To get the lay of the land, follow the *malecón,* which runs parallel to the waterfront in the heart of the city, and then go up any hill for a panoramic view of the bay.

SPECIAL PLACES

In theory, the beaches are what lure people to Puerto Vallarta, but beaches are only part of the scene in this most picturesque resort.

LOS ARCOS These oddly eroded rocks form arches that jut more than 80 feet out of the water of the bay south of town. Home to brilliantly colored tropical fish, the area is a popular snorkeling and diving destination.

IGLESIA DE GUADALUPE The church was begun in 1920 and work continued, in fits and starts, until 1963, when the crown atop it, now Puerto Vallarta's most distinctive landmark, was put in place. 370 Hidalgo.

MALECÓN The waterfront avenue looking out over Bahía de Banderas is Puerto Vallarta's most interesting street. There are several nice shops and restaurants, and it's a lovely place to stroll at sunset.

RÍO CUALE AND GRINGO GULCH The Cuale, which runs deep during the summer rainy season but becomes more of a stream in winter, cuts through Puerto Vallarta; many of the lovely houses along the hills here are occupied by foreigners in a neighborhood known as Gringo Gulch.

CASA KIMBERLY Formerly the hideaway of Richard Burton and Elizabeth Taylor and most recently a bed and breakfast establishment, the building is now a Taylor-Burton museum with original furnishings, photo exhibits, and memorabilia from *The Night of the Iguana*. Open daily. Admission charge. 445 Zaragoza (phone: 21336).

ISLA RÍO CUALE This small island at the mouth of the Río Cuale is a nice place to stroll. It offers shops, restaurants, refreshment stands, and a small archaeological museum (closed Mondays; no admission charge; no phone). At one end is *Le Bistro* (phone: 20283), a handsome restaurant and bar where taped jazz is played. Just outside is a statue of film director John Huston.

MARINA VALLARTA A mega-project set on a flat, 445-acre site at the northernmost end of Puerto Vallarta (between the cruise ship docks and the airport), this development has $1\frac{1}{2}$ miles of beachfront, a marina with slips for 300 boats, an 18-hole golf course, tennis and beach clubs, a spa, restaurants, bars, and a shopping center. In addition to several luxury hotels (including the *Marriott Casa Magna Puerto Vallarta, Velas Vallarta, Bel-Air,* and *Westin Regina Resort;* see *Checking In*), there are private homes, villas, condominiums, and time-sharing units. Marina Vallarta is as different from traditional Puerto Vallarta as night is from day. Traditional Vallarta is quaint and picturesque; Marina Vallarta is flat, modern, and somewhat gaudy. It's almost a city in itself; in fact, you could easily spend two weeks here without ever having to leave the grounds. The hotels fronting the marina and beach are spectacular— with massive lobbies, marble floors, and glamorous pools—but they all hide the splendid sea view from everyone except their guests.

PLAYA DE LOS MUERTOS For years, city officials tried to change the name of this beach (Dead Men's Beach) to Playa del Sol (Sunny Beach), but to no avail. Supposedly it got its grim name eons ago from pirates, but today the only bodies found here are those of tourists soaking up the sun or recovering from a night on the town. Although some find it grubby—especially at the height of the season, when it's filled with fun seekers—it's definitely where the action is. There are restaurants, snack stands, cocktail bars, waterskiers, gigolos, and parasailers. Music can be heard everywhere, from strolling mariachis to children playing instruments made from empty tin cans and dried gourds. This beach is also the setting of a mobile marketplace; you can buy items as varied as bathing suits, serapes, and even watches from Taiwan without leaving your spot on the sand.

The northern and southern ends of the beach are less crowded because the grading is steep. Beware: Just a few steps into the water, and you'll be in over your head. On rough days, the waves can top six feet. Most people opt for the safer, shallower part of the beach, between the *Tropicana* and *San Marino Plaza* hotels.

TO THE SOUTH

MISMALOYA Seven miles (11 km) south of Puerto Vallarta, just after Los Arcos on the highway to Barra de Navidad (Rte. 200), is this paradise, where John Huston made *The Night of the Iguana*. At the base of towering, palm-studded cliffs, between clear green waters and thick clusters of tropical foliage, are *La Jolla de Mismaloya* hotel (see *Checking In*), high-rise condominium complexes, and many *palapa* (thatch-roofed) restaurants serving grilled fish.

Combis (minibuses) bound for Mismaloya frequently leave from Calle Olas Altas in front of *Daiquiri Dick's* restaurant (see *Eating Out*); the fare is 1.10 pesos (about 15¢). The fun way to get here, though, is to rent a car or a jeep. In addition, *taxi acuático* (launch) service is provided from Playa de los Muertos and the marina; you'll find current schedules and rates at the desk of your hotel or at the tourist office (see *Tourist Information*).

If you'd rather go by boat, motor launches can be rented in Puerto Vallarta from the *Cooperativa Progreso Turística Vallarta* (Paseo Díaz Ordaz; phone: 21202) for fishing and snorkeling trips, or just to transport you to quieter beaches farther south along the coast—Boca de Tomatlán, Las Animas (great for snorkeling and diving), Quimixto, and Yelapa. Except for Boca de Tomatlán, these beaches are only accessible by boat. Excursions range from one hour to several hours, with longer trips for up to six passengers including stopovers of several hours at one of the beaches. In addition, canoes can be rented and scuba diving arranged at the *Cooperativa Progreso Turística Vallarta* for exploring the nearby lagoon above and below the water's surface.

BOCA DE TOMATLÁN This small village 2½ miles (4 km) south of Mismaloya at the mouth of Río los Horcones has a few good places to eat, including *Chico's Paradise* (see *Eating Out*) and *La Roca,* a beachfront seafood eatery (no phone). *Pangas* (motor launches) depart from here for Playas las Animas, Quimixto, Mismaloya, and Yelapa.

PLAYA LAS ANIMAS Las Animas is the first beach south of Boca de Tomatlán (about 10 minutes by boat). The water is clear, the waves calm. The few beachfront restaurants here offer the usual seafood fare.

YELAPA A popular day-trip destination, Playa Yelapa has an open-air beach restaurant and a small hotel. To get here, you'll have to go by boat from Puerto Vallarta or Boca de Tomatlán; the journey takes about an hour. For additional details, see *Best Beaches off the Beaten Path* in DIVERSIONS.

TO THE NORTH

NUEVO VALLARTA On one of the most beautiful strips of beach in the area, Nuevo Vallarta (New Vallarta, 10 mi/16 km north of Puerto Vallarta, in the neighboring state of Nayarit) is the site of a busy marina, some magnificent villas, condominiums, and deluxe hotel properties. Here are *Jack Tar Village,* an all-inclusive hotel (phone: 329-70100; fax: 329-70160); the *Sierra Nuevo Vallarta* (see *Checking In*); the *Diamond Resort* (phone: 329-70400; 800-858-2258; fax: 329-70082); and the latest addition, *Paradise Village* (phone: 329-70770; 800-995-5714 or 714-837-1798; fax: 70782; 714-837-1298), as well as a well-maintained beach club with a restaurant-bar, lockers, tennis courts, a small museum and gift shop, and water sports equipment available for rent.

BUCERÍAS The name may not be as familiar as Mismaloya, but it offers beautiful beaches and spectacular views of beachfront homes. Probably the best reason to visit Bucerías (17 miles/27 km north of Puerto Vallarta) is to enjoy oysters sold fresh from the shell at roadside stands. City buses leave every hour beginning at 9 AM from the *Autobús del Pacífico* station on Avenida Insurgentes. If you don't want to go back on the bus, there are *combis* (minibuses) that can take up to 15 passengers back to Puerto Vallarta.

PUNTA MITA AND ENVIRONS About 22 miles (35 km) north of Puerto Vallarta, at Km 136 of the Tepic Highway (Rte. 200), is the turnoff to the Punta Mita road, 13½ miles (22 km) of sharp curves. At Punta Mita you can enjoy the seafood at the popular *Miramar* restaurant (Km 20, La Cruz de Huanacaxtle; no phone) and the calm waters of the beach. Playa Destiladeras, with its soft, beige sand, long, rolling waves, and an open-air beachfront restaurant, is about 4 miles (6 km) farther on. Punta del Burro, 4 miles (6 km) from Destiladeras, is a lovely, unspoiled beach; the next beach, La Manzanilla, is shaded by manzanilla trees. At El Anclote, a short distance past the entrance to the town of Punta Mita, the water is ideal for surfing and there's a good seafood restaurant. The arid northern point of Bahía de Banderas, also called Punta Mita, was recently purchased by Japanese resort developers who have closed the area to the public pending future construction. At Santa Cruz Huanacaxtle, a small town on the north side of Bahía de Banderas, you can hire a *panga,* or motor launch, to take you out to Las Islas Marietas (see *Sea Excursions* below). The water at the islands is somewhat colder, but it is almost as clear as the Caribbean.

SAN SEBASTIÁN Nestled in the Sierra Madre northeast of Puerto Vallarta, this former mining boomtown is now a popular hiking and horseback riding destination. The town, built around a central plaza, has a cantina, two tiny *misceláneas* (general stores), and a 300-year-old church. San Sebastián can be reached by car (four-wheel-drive is recommended) in about three hours; there is some spectacular scenery along the route. Take the Ixtapa–Las Palmas road through about 6 miles (10 km) of jungle to Subida de las Huacas, where the climb up the Sierra Madre begins (*subida* means climb). The road cuts through a few *rancherías* (tiny towns)—Arroyo de las Canoas, Potrero de Secas, and El Balcón—to Rancho Cieneguillas. Farther on is

La Estancia de Landeros, the largest town in the San Sebastián region; the next town is San Sebastián. *Aero Taxis de la Bahía* (phone: 22049) has air service to San Sebastián on Tuesdays, Thursdays, and Saturdays. Accommodations are available at *Hacienda Jalisco* (no phone), a mansion that has been restored as a charming hotel. For additional details, consult the tourist office (see *Tourist Information,* below).

Sources and Resources

TOURIST INFORMATION

The *Delegación Regional de Turismo* (Regional Tourism Office) is downtown, in the *Palacio Municipal* (City Hall; Calle Juárez; phone: 20242/3). Its English-speaking staff offers maps, brochures, guides, and hotel information. The office is closed Sundays.

LOCAL COVERAGE *Vallarta Today* is an English-language daily with a good rundown of what's going on in town. Other good sources of information are *Lifestyles,* a local English-language quarterly with excellent maps, and the *Guadalajara Colony Reporter*'s Puerto Vallarta section. *The News* and the *Mexico City Times,* two English-language newspapers flown in daily from Mexico City, are sold at hotel newsstands and many local kiosks, as is the *Los Angeles Times.*

TELEPHONE The city code for Puerto Vallarta is 322. *Note:* Mexico's telephone company has embarked on a major expansion project that involves changing telephone numbers in many areas of the country. At press time, all numbers listed in this chapter were correct. However, if you have any difficulties reaching attractions listed here, contact the local tourist office.

CLIMATE AND CLOTHES Puerto Vallarta's weather is splendid—clear, warm days and mild nights year-round, though during the rainy season (from late June through early October), you might need a sweater. Otherwise, bring lightweight, comfortable sports clothes.

GETTING AROUND

BUS One bus line runs from the town of Ixtapa (east of the airport) to Playa Olas Altas. Another goes from Olas Altas to Boca de Tomatlán. Service is frequent; it's an easy and inexpensive way to get around. The fare is 1 new peso (about 13¢).

CAR RENTALS All the major agencies have offices at the airport and will deliver a car to your hotel. In town, call *Avis* (phone: 11112), *Budget* (phone: 26766), *Dollar* (phone: 31434 or 11001), *Hertz* (phone: 40055 or 11399), or *National* (phone: 21107 or 11226).

SEA EXCURSIONS The *Sarape* (phone: 44777, 10262, or 10415) departs every morning for Yelapa, spends two-and-a-half hours in port, and returns around 4

PM; it also makes a sundown cruise with snacks, an open bar, music, and dancing. The *Princesa Vallarta* (phone: 44777) offers daily all-day tours around the bay, stopping at Los Arcos for a half hour of snorkeling, and then going on to Playa las Animas for lunch at a beach restaurant and swimming. Equipment, lunch, and an open bar (on the way back only) are included. The *Bora Bora* (phone: 43680 or 45484) offers daylong cruises to Playa las Animas, including breakfast, lunch, and an open bar. Other boats go to Quimixto, where passengers can hike up to the waterfalls. The catamaran *Simpático* (phone: 40202, ext. 2700, or 41251) makes stops for swimming and snorkeling at Los Arcos and Playa las Animas. Tickets and schedules are available at hotel travel desks or at Playa de los Muertos; boats leave from the sports boat dock just north of Playa de Oro (see *Swimming and Sunning*). Cruises to Las Islas Marietas—an island wildlife sanctuary 3 to 6 miles (5 to 10 km) southwest of Punta Mita, where gray whales may be seen in winter and dolphins, sea turtles, and manta rays are plentiful year-round—are offered by *Zodiac Adventures* (phone: 329-80060; fax: 329-80061).

TAXIS Plentiful here, cabs can be hailed in the street or called from a hotel. A list of fixed rates is posted at the hotels, though it's always a good idea to ask, *"Cuánto cuesta a…?"* ("How much to…?") before you get in.

TOURS Various agencies in town and hotel travel desks will arrange bay cruises, sightseeing in the backcountry, horseback excursions, and plane trips to Mexico City and Guadalajara. *Amex* (*Villa Vallarta* shopping center; phone: 46876/7) is a reputable agency offering a variety of tours in and around Puerto Vallarta. They also offer day cruises to several destinations, including Mismaloya. Guided mountain bike tours through the jungle east of town are offered by *SunBike* (381 Basilio Badillo; phone: 20080) and *Bike Mex* (361 Calle Guerrero; phone: 31680).

SPECIAL EVENTS

A regatta from Marina del Rey, California, takes place in February of odd-numbered years. For information, call the *Marina del Rey Yacht Club* (phone: 310-822-9082 in the US). During the entire month of May, the residents of Puerto Vallarta honor their city with a festival that features parades, a bullfight, soccer games, a windsurfing regatta, fireworks displays, dancing, and street music. The *Torneo Internacional de Pesca* (International Fishing Tournament), held the first week of November, attracts fishing buffs from around the world; the first prize is a new car. The festivities for the *Virgen de Guadalupe* begin on November 28 and last until December 12, her feast day.

SHOPPING

Browsing and buying are nearly as popular in Puerto Vallarta as swimming and sunning. Most shops are small, with the owner doing the selling. The favorite purchase is resortwear, although art can be as good a buy as clothing. Several galleries in the heart of Puerto Vallarta offer a wide range of local and other artworks, from sculpture, paintings, and photographs to bead and yarn creations of the Huichol (an indigenous group native to northern Jalisco and neighboring areas of the states of Nayarit and Zacatecas). There are also dozens of handicrafts shops offering unusual, well-crafted items from all over Mexico: Taxco silver, Oaxaca pottery, and ceramics and glass designs made in the Guadalajara suburb of Tlaquepaque. Good Mexican tequila is a smart buy here, too—most of it is made in the town of Tequila, also in the state of Jalisco. Many local artists and craftsmen exhibit and sell their work daily at the south end of the *malecón*.

The *Mercado Publico* (Municipal Market, now commonly called the Flea Market, between Calles Matamoros and Miramar, near the bridge) bulges with Mexican and Guatemalan crafts. Puerto Vallarta shopping centers include *Plaza Malecón*, on Paseo Díaz Ordaz; *Plaza del Río*, on Hidalgo at the Río Cuale; *Villa Vallarta*, a modern shopping center on the road to the airport in front of the *Plaza las Glorias* hotel; and *Plaza Marina*, an ultra-modern, air conditioned mall at Marina Vallarta. Isla Río Cuale, the island in the river of the same name, is also a good place to shop. Several stalls on the island sell local crafts, and the *Katy Boutique* (phone: 47909) offers some of the most interesting women's clothing in town. Stores are generally open daily from 10 AM to 2 PM and 4 to 8 PM. The following are among Puerto Vallarta's better shops:

Aca Joe Beach Best known for T-shirts and tank tops telling the world where you've been. 588 Paseo Díaz Ordaz, facing the bay (phone: 22454).

Alfarería Tlaquepaque Native art and pottery from Guadalajara's famous crafts center, as well as a complete selection of *equipales* (rustic chairs made of leather and wood). 1100 Av. México (phone: 20488).

Arte de las Américas Contemporary paintings and sculpture by Mexico's finest artists, including local expatriates from the United States, are the focus of this chic gallery. *Marina las Palmas II* shopping center, in Marina Vallarta (phone: 11985).

Bezán The artist's gallery-studio-home, where he displays his paintings and sculptures among his exquisite collection of fine art and objects. Even the bathroom, with its tiled tub, is a work of art. 756 Guadalupe Sánchez (phone: 23012).

La Colección Unusual jewelry, hand-painted wearable art, accessories, ceramics, stained glass lamps, Huichol art, and ceremonial masks. 263 Calle Juárez (phone: 20290).

Fiesta A supermarket of crafts, with quality ranging from the truly exquisite to junk. *Villa Vallarta* shopping center (phone: 46116).

Galería Indígena Masks, sculptures, yarn-and-bead art of the Huichol, pre-Hispanic reproductions, lacquerware, and extraordinary engraved gourds. 270 Calle Juárez (phone: 23007).

Galería Pacífico Here are the works of some of Mexico and Latin America's finest artists, including limited-edition graphics by Rufino Tamayo, Francisco Zúñiga, Luis Filcer, and Francisco Toledo. 109 Av. Insurgentes (phone: 21982).

Galería Uno A selection of painting and sculpture by some of Mexico's best artists, including Vladimir Cora, plus Mexico-inspired works of several foreign artists. In an old-fashioned home, the gallery itself is a showplace. 561 Morelos (phone: 20908).

Galería VallARTa Sharing space with *La Colección* handicrafts store (see above), this gallery features works by Rufino Tamayo, José Luis Cuevas, and Francisco Toledo. 263 Calle Juárez (phone: 20290).

Huarachería Lety Huaraches (sandals made of interwoven leather) originally were a Puerto Vallarta specialty; the tradition continues here. There's a wide selection; custom work is done as well. 472 Calle Juárez (phone: 21417).

Joyas Finas Suneson Beautifully designed and crafted sterling silver jewelry and decorative items. 593 Morelos (phone: 25715).

María de Guadalajara Easy-to-wear dresses made from crinkly cottons in soft earth tones and pastels. 550 Morelos (22387).

Nelly's One of the best-known resortwear shops in town, with a selection of hand-embroidered dresses inspired by traditional Mexican costumes. At the *Fiesta Americana Puerto Vallarta* hotel (phone: 42010).

Nina & June June creates the clothing, fashioned from handloomed fabrics, while Nina designs the unique line of jewelry. 227-8 Hidalgo, upstairs (no phone).

Olinalá Gallery The knowledgeable proprietor, Nancy Erickson, seeks out the finest pieces of artwork by native peoples. Among the unusual items are ritual masks, beaded art, lacquerware from Olinalá, and lapidary. 274 Lázaro Cárdenas (phone: 24995).

Querubines High-quality folk art, native hand-embroidered clothing for men and women, rustic furniture, ceramics, pewter, and some antiques. Calles Juárez and Galeana (phone: 23475).

Ric Carefully crafted, unusual silver jewelry from Taxco. Good quality at about half the comparable stateside prices. Two locations: the *Pueblo Viejo* shopping center (phone: 30143) and the *Villa Vallarta* shopping center (phone: 44598).

La Rosa de Cristal Blown-glass plates, goblets, and platters made in the owners' Tlaquepaque workshop. 272 Av. Insurgentes (phone: 25698).

Sergio Bustamante Whimsical animal sculptures and a line of jewelry made by the imaginative Guadalajara-area artist. 275 Calle Juárez (phone: 21129).

Sucesos Hand-painted fabrics and trendy designs for women, plus unique jewelry. 233 Calle Libertad, at Hidalgo (phone: 26374).

Tabu Creations by Patti Gallardo, one of Puerto Vallarta's best-known fashion designers, are shown at this boutique, which also carries accessories for the home and sculptures by local artisans. 28 Isla Río Cuale (phone: 23528).

Tane A branch of the store owned by Mexico's most prestigious silversmith, with sterling silver serving pieces, art objects, tableware, and jewelry. Many pieces are combined with vermeil. At the *Camino Real* hotel (phone: 30124).

SPORTS

Puerto Vallarta offers just about every kind of water sport you might want and a few you probably never even considered. In addition, a number of large hotels have facilities for the land-bound athlete, and there are miles of undeveloped countryside for the hiker and horseback rider.

BASEBALL On many Sundays year-round, local teams play at the ball field just north of the city on Rte. 200 (no phone).

BOATING Canoes, sailboats, motorboats and the accompanying water skis, scuba diving equipment, and snorkels can all be rented by the hour along the beaches, on the *malecón,* at Marina Vallarta, and at any major hotel. *Island Sailing International* (phone: 10880, ext. 119), at the *Plaza Iguana Marina Resort* (see *Checking In*), offers introductory three-hour sailing lessons, plus hourly or daily sailboat rentals. Also at Marina Vallarta, *Sail Vallarta* (phone: 10096 or 10097) rents sailboats with or without crews. Daily morning and afternoon sails on the *Ehecatl* (four-passenger minimum) leave from Deck B of the *Club de Tenis Puesta del Sol* in Marina Vallarta (behind the *Vidafel* hotel; phone: 10096 or 10097). The excursion price includes a captain and crew, an open bar, snorkeling equipment, lunch, and snacks. The most popular route is south to Playas Yelapa, Quimixto, or Las Animas, with a stop for snorkeling at Los Arcos. For those who enjoy more active sailing, the rougher northern route includes a stop at Punta de Mita.

BUNGEE JUMPING This exciting (but rather dangerous) sport, which has become very popular here in recent years, involves jumping from a great height with a bungee (elastic cord) tied around your ankles. Thrill-seekers can practice their bungee technique by jumping off a high crane at *Salto al Pacifico* (no phone), located 2 miles south of Puerto Vallarta off Route 200.

FISHING Bordered by rich fishing waters, Puerto Vallarta is an outstanding departure point for deep-sea expeditions. Catches include sailfish, marlin, bonito, tuna, red snapper, and shark; the season extends throughout the year. Numerous charter companies have headquarters at the northern end of the *malecón;* arrange a rental yourself or have your hotel do it for you. We recommend *Island Sailing International* (phone: 10880, ext. 119) or *Cooperativa Progreso Turística Vallarta* (phone: 21202). Freshwater bass fishing at *Rancho el Aguacate* can be arranged through *Viva Tours* (Maritime Terminal building, between the *Playa de Oro* hotel and the *Westin Regina Resort;* phone: 40410 or 48026).

GOLF Puerto Vallarta boasts two "designer" golf courses.

TOP TEE-OFF SPOTS

Club de Golf Marina Vallarta This 18-hole course was designed by Joe Finger. The manager is Tim Tallman; the pro, Billy Sitton. Guests of the *Marriott Casa Magna Puerto Vallarta, Bel-Air, Camino Real, Plaza las Glorias, Plaza Iguana Marina Resort, Velas Vallarta,* and *Sheraton Buganvilias* hotels have access to the links (see *Checking In* for all). At the Marina Vallarta complex (phone: 10171).

Los Flamingos This beautiful, challenging Percy Clifford 18-holer has full rental facilities and a clubhouse, all open to the public. Eduardo Pérez is the pro; Héctor Almeida is the manager. In Flamingo Club Estates, just north of Nuevo Vallarta (phone: 20379).

HIKING The most popular route is the 2-mile (3-km) hike from the *Sheraton* to the *Krystal Vallarta* hotels; another option is from Playa del Sol to Playa Conchas Chinas. From Nuevo Vallarta (12 miles/20 km north of Puerto Vallarta), you can hike north to Bucerías (6 miles/10 km) or south to the jetty (2 miles/3 km). There are rocky areas here, so be sure to wear rubber-soled shoes. An option for serious hikers is the 24-mile (38-km), mostly uphill trek to the town of San Sebastián (see *Special Places*).

HORSEBACK RIDING With beautiful trails surrounding the city and along the shore, riding is very popular in Puerto Vallarta. Horses can be rented by the hour at most of the major public beaches, as well as at the beaches of several of the larger hotels, including the *Krystal Vallarta, Playa de Oro* (see *Checking In* for both), and the *Ramada* (2½ miles/4 km north on the road to the airport).

Rancho Charro (895 Francisco Villa; phone: 40114) offers a variety of horseback riding packages, including three-hour excursions that leave at 10 AM and 3 PM, and botanical tours—including lunch—led by a professor of natural sciences from the United States. The company also sponsors eight-day trips to San Sebastián from October through May for groups of six or more riders. The trips include two nights at the *Molino de Agua* hotel in Puerto Vallarta, horses, camping equipment, five nights at the *Hacienda Jalisco* hotel in San Sebastián, and all meals.

Riding excursions sponsored by *Rancho Ojo de Agua* (227 Cerrada de Cárdenas; phone: 40607) follow trails through forests and fruit trees, past small villages, and into the mountains; they also include a swim in the Río Pitillal. There are two guided, three-hour rides, at 10 AM and 3 PM daily. *Rancho Ojo de Agua* also offers six-hour rides to the mountains, including guide and lunch, and riding classes (English-style).

In addition, *Rancho Ojo de Agua* organizes a five-day trip for a minimum of six riders to *Rancho la Soledad* in the Sierra Madre, a six-hour horseback ride from Vallarta. This trip is offered during the last week of every month, but with prior notice it can be taken at a group's convenience. Large tents are provided for sleeping, and there are sanitary facilities (including showers) and swimming pools fed by springs along the route. From *Rancho la Soledad,* participants make daily trips to the surrounding areas, including visits to *El Limbo,* an unrestored archaeological site, and nearby thermal baths. The trip is recommended only for experienced riders and includes a guide, meals, excellent mounts, and riding and sleeping gear. To make arrangements, write to Mari Torres de González (Cerrada de Cárdenas 227, 48240 Puerto Vallarta, Jalisco, México).

Viva Tours (see *Fishing*) offers horseback riding excursions for riders of all skills in *Rancho el Aguacate.* One tour includes transportation to the ranch, overnight accommodations, and meals. *Note:* Never venture out on one of these trails without a guide.

PARASAILING This sport is a big favorite here. Pulled by a speedboat and wearing an open parachute, the rider is lifted into the air like a kite and eventually descends gracefully (in theory, anyway). Hotels disclaim responsibility for injuries (which can be serious), but they do provide information through their sports or tour desks. The *Krystal Vallarta, Camino Real,* and the *Ramada* (2½ miles/4 km north on the road to the airport) have parasailing facilities on their beaches.

SCUBA DIVING AND SNORKELING *Chico's Dive Shop,* which has three branches—next to *Carlos O'Brian's* restaurant on the *malecón* (phone: 21895), and at the *Continental Plaza Vallarta* and *Marriott Casa Magna Puerto Vallarta* hotels (see *Checking In*)—offers snorkeling and scuba trips Mondays through Saturdays to Los Arcos (see *Special Places*), plus twice-weekly excursions to Las Islas Marietas (see *Punta Mita and Environs,* and *Sea Excursions,* above). *Chico's* also has one-day scuba lessons, four-day certification programs, and equipment for rent and for sale.

At Mismaloya, it's easy to arrange for snorkeling and scuba diving guides and tours, but visiting divers must bring their own equipment.

SOCCER When there are no baseball games, there is a Sunday afternoon soccer game every week at the local ball field (see *Baseball*).

SWIMMING AND SUNNING Besides the strands mentioned in *Special Places,* Puerto Vallarta boasts miles of shoreline. Playa las Palmas, just north of town, is quieter and less cluttered than Playa de los Muertos; Playa Conchas Chinas, south of town, is also very nice. Also within city limits is Playa las Amapas, a small stretch of sand between Playa de los Muertos and Playa Conchas Chinas, and Playa de Oro, which stretches from the airport to the *Krystal Vallarta* hotel.

TENNIS The following tennis facilities are open to visitors for a fee.

CHOICE COURTS

Club de Golf los Flamingos There are four lighted clay courts here; reserve through local hotels. Just north of Nuevo Vallarta (phone: 329-20379).

Continental Plaza Tennis Club Features four indoor and four outdoor clay courts, with classes and clinics designed by Wimbledon champion John Newcombe. Next to the *Continental Plaza Vallarta* hotel (see *Checking In;* phone: 40123).

Los Tules Here are two cement and three asphalt courts, all lighted. Next to the *Fiesta Americana Puerto Vallarta* hotel (see *Checking In;* phone: 44560, ask for the tennis courts).

In addition, most of the large hotels have courts for guests, many illuminated for night games. The following hotels have tennis facilities: *Camino Real* (two lighted composition courts); *Krystal Vallarta* (two lighted clay courts); *Marriott Casa Magna Puerto Vallarta* (three lighted synthetic grass courts); *Sheraton Buganvilias* (four cement courts, two lighted); *Westin Regina Resort* (three lighted synthetic grass courts); and *Playa de Oro* (three lighted cement courts). (See *Checking In* for details on hotels.)

WINDSURFING AND WATER SKIING Two-day windsurfing courses are offered on the beach in front of the *Ramada* (2½ miles/4 km north on the road to the airport; phone: 41700, ask for the travel desk); reservations required. There are also schools at the *Iguana Beach Club,* next to the *Westin Regina Resort* (phone: 10062) and at *Las Palmas Beach,* the *Fiesta Americana Puerto Vallarta,* and *Krystal Vallarta* hotels (see *Checking In*). Water skiing can be arranged at *Las Palmas Beach* hotel and at most of the beaches.

NIGHTCLUBS AND NIGHTLIFE

Puerto Vallarta has a little of everything for fun after dark. Start with the *Sarape* sunset cruise (see *Sea Excursions*), or, for the best no-frills view of the sunset, head for the beach at Punta Mita, the northernmost point of Bahía de Banderas. Sunsets are also particularly impressive from the *El Nido* bar atop *Los Cuatro Vientos* hotel; the *Azulejos Bar* in the *Camino Real; El Faro* (The Lighthouse) at the *Royal Pacific Yacht Club* in Marina Vallarta (phone: 10541); and the *Krystal Vallarta*'s *Seven Columns Terrace* poolside. (See *Checking In* for details about hotels listed in this section.)

The *Krystal Vallarta* hotel hosts a Mexican fiesta—including mariachis, folkloric dancing, drinks, and an all-you-can-eat buffet—Tuesday and Saturday nights. During high season, many other hotels, including the *Camino Real* and the *Plaza las Glorias Pelícanos,* organize similar Mexican fiestas. At *La Iguana* (167 Lázaro Cárdenas; phone: 20105), there are fiestas Thursdays and Sundays, year-round. There's dancing nightly in the *Sixties Disco* bar at the *Marriott Casa Magna Puerto Vallarta*.

The lively, popular *Friday López's Karaoke Bar* (phone: 42010) at the *Fiesta Americana Puerto Vallarta* hotel gives everyone a chance to be a singing star; *Christine,* in the *Krystal Vallarta* hotel, features a laser light show set to disco music and is another hot spot. *La Ballena* (at the entrance to the Nuevo Vallarta development; phone: 329-10154), has dancing until dawn. Tables are removed and the live rock music for dancing begins at 11 PM at the *Hard Rock Café* (652 Paseo Díaz Ordaz; phone: 25532), one of Puerto Vallarta's most popular spots for eating, drinking, and dancing. *Carlos O'Brian's* (see *Eating Out*) is still one of Vallarta's most popular restaurant-nightclubs. *Collage,* an entertainment complex at Marina Vallarta (phone: 10500), is everything its name implies—plain-to-fancy dining spots, a bowling alley, a *karaoke* bar, a disco, even a large-screen video golf game. In Mismaloya, don't miss *Iggy's* at *La Jolla de Mismaloya*.

Best in Town

CHECKING IN

The winter season is when Puerto Vallarta is at its best—and also when the hotels are jammed. Wherever you decide to stay, make a reservation, with a confirmation from the hotel itself. Don't depend solely on a travel agent's voucher; request proof of confirmation.

We've listed hotels charging $150 or more a day for two as very expensive; $75 to $150 as expensive; $40 to $75 as moderate; and under $40 as inexpensive. In the more costly categories, rates drop considerably from May through November. Most hotels in the expensive and moderate categories have air conditioning and TV sets unless otherwise noted; all hotels have telephones in the rooms. All telephone numbers are in the 322 city code unless otherwise indicated.

We begin with our favorite (but pricey) havens, followed by recommended hotels, listed by price category.

REGAL RESORTS AND SPECIAL HAVENS

Las Alamandas Although it's about an hour and three-quarters from Puerto Vallarta, this small, exclusive hideaway is well worth the drive. Situated on 70 acres on what is known as the Mexican Riviera are 11 guest units with private terraces and large, tiled bathrooms. The decor features brightly colored rattan furniture, antiques, and Mexican folk art. Two of the units also have full-size living and dining rooms and fully equipped kitchens. There's a tennis court, pool, restaurant, and gym. In Quemaro, Municipio de la

Huerta, south of Puerto Vallarta via Rte. 200 (phone: 333-70259 or 333-70147; 5-540-7657 in Mexico City; 800-223-6510; fax: 333-70161; 5-540-7658/9 in Mexico City).

Camino Real An elegant resort with lush grounds and a nearly private beach, it offers 348 deluxe accommodations (250 rooms and five suites in the main tower and 87 rooms and six suites in the *Royal Beach Club* tower). The 11 suites in the two towers each have a private pool. There are also three restaurants (including *La Perla*—see *Eating Out*), beach facilities, two tennis courts, a pool with swim-up bar, a spa, organized social programs for adults, a playground, and a great weekly Mexican fiesta. One and one-half miles (2 km) south on Rte. 200, on Playa las Estacas (phone: 15000 or 30123; 800-7-CAMINO in the US; 800-90123 in Mexico; fax: 30070).

Krystal Vallarta As much a secluded village as a hotel, this place was designed in a lovely classical Mexican fashion, complete with gaslit cobblestone walkways. There are 468 rooms, suites, and villas, most with clay tile floors and whitewashed walls. All rooms have mini-bars. The huge lobby bar features live Mexican music (and dancing, if you wish); there also are 42 pools (37 of them private, in the villas section) and three children's pools. Sunsets at the *Seven Columns Terrace* pool—complete with fountains, waterfalls, and a swim-up bar—are truly special. There are two clay tennis courts; water skiing, scuba diving, horseback riding, and parasailing are available. Each guest has a personal *palapa* (small thatch-roofed hut) on the beach. There are six restaurants, including *Bogart's* (see *Eating Out*), plus *Christine's* disco, which draws a young, energetic crowd. Located 2 miles (3 km) north of town on Av. de las Garzas (phone: 40202; 800-231-9860; fax: 40222).

Posada Río Cuale It's rare to find a true inn in Mexico that's near the sea, but this one qualifies. The place is pleasant, quiet, and friendly, and popular with US and Canadian travelers. There's a decent-size pool and an eye-pleasing hacienda-like design. What's more, the location is perfect for seeing Puerto Vallarta, since most good downtown restaurants, bars, discos, and shops are only a few steps away, and it's also only half a block from a very good beach. All of the 25 well-furnished, clean rooms fetch the same price—although no two are alike. There are three levels, lots of brick and whitewash, spiral staircases outside, and plenty of greenery. Downstairs (next to the pool) is a large, open, and justifiably respected dining room called *Le Gourmet* (see *Eating Out*). All in all, it's very relaxed—a nice change from the typical high-rises that dominate Puerto Vallarta. 242 Aquiles Serdán (phone: 20450).

VERY EXPENSIVE

Bel-Air An elegant pink-and-white mansion set near the golf course in Marina Vallarta, this hostelry has 42 suites and 25 one- and two-bedroom villas furnished with antiques and original works of art. The *El Candil* restaurant is here (see *Eating Out*), plus a bar, a pool, and two tennis courts. 311 Pelícanos, Marina Vallarta (phone: 10800; 800-457-7676; fax: 10801).

Coral Grand Surrounded by a beautiful garden complete with cascading waterfalls, this beachfront property has 120 suites, a tennis court, a free-form pool, and three restaurants. About 10 minutes south of downtown Vallarta at Km 8.5 on Rte. 200 (phone: 30507; fax: 30216).

Fiesta Americana Puerto Vallarta A fine hotel with a gigantic, *palapa*-domed lobby, 291 luxurious rooms, and 35 suites. Tennis, a pool, a beach, fine food, and a *karaoke* bar are among the draws here. On Playa los Tules, about 1.5 miles (2.5 km) north of downtown (phone: 42010; 800-FIESTA-1 in the US; 800-50450 in Mexico; fax: 42108).

La Jolla de Mismaloya This luxury property features a popular seafood restaurant of the same name (see *Eating Out*) and *Iggy's,* one of the area's most enduring discos. There are 303 suites, three pools, two Jacuzzis, two lighted tennis courts, and a gym. Located on a small bay in Mismaloya, about 7 miles (11 km) south of downtown Puerto Vallarta (phone: 30660; 800-322-2344; fax: 30500).

Marriott Casa Magna Puerto Vallarta One of several hostelries in Marina Vallarta, this one has 433 rooms and 29 suites, all with private balconies. Facilities include three tennis courts, a health club, a pool, several restaurants, and a disco. Marina Vallarta (phone: 10004; 800-228-9290 in the US; 800-90088 in Mexico; fax: 10760).

Sierra Nuevo Vallarta This all-inclusive resort (formerly the *Radisson Sierra Plaza*) offers 350 spacious, luxuriously appointed rooms with balconies and ocean views. It has a contemporary feel—no local color here—and a bustling atmosphere. There are three restaurants and three connected pools, and various activities are available, including tennis, bicycling, horseback riding, kayaking, scuba diving, and windsurfing. Meals, drinks, tips, and sports are included in the room rate. Nuevo Vallarta (phone: 329-71300; 800-882-6684; fax: 329-71094).

Westin Regina Resort This luxury beachfront place has 280 units, all with balconies. Amenities include two restaurants, two bars, four outdoor pools, tennis courts, and a fitness center. Ask for a room with an ocean view. 205 Paseo de la Marina Sur, Marina Vallarta (phone: 11100; 800-228-3000 in the US; 800-90223 in Mexico; fax: 11141).

EXPENSIVE

Continental Plaza Vallarta This establishment, right on the ocean, has 359 rooms, 79 suites, and the eight-court *Continental Plaza Tennis Center,* with classes and clinics designed by Wimbledon champion John Newcombe. On the beach, at Playa las Glorias (phone: 40123; 800-888-CONTI; fax: 45236).

Plaza las Glorias A pretty and comfortable place with an atrium lobby, 389 rooms and villas, two restaurants and bars, and two pools, around which there's a Mexican fiesta every Tuesday night. On the beach, at Playa las Glorias (phone: 44444; 800-342-AMIGO; fax: 46559).

Plaza Iguana Marina Resort Overlooking the marina, this establishment has 104 suites with tiled floors and hand-carved Mexican furniture. There also is a pool, a restaurant, and a disco. Marina Vallarta (phone: 10880 through 10887; fax: 10889).

Sheraton Buganvilias Lavish, with greenery everywhere, it has 501 oceanfront rooms, plus three buildings with 169 suites. There are four tennis courts, a beach, two pools, and several bars and restaurants. On the beach north of town (phone: 30404; 800-325-3535 in the US; 800-90325 in Mexico; fax: 20500).

Velas Vallarta This all-suite property offers its guests a fine view of the beach and an intimate atmosphere. All 362 suites are decorated with floral prints and Mexican tiles and have full kitchens, living rooms, and terraces. There are two restaurants, three pools, and three bars. Along with use of the hotel's four lighted tennis courts, guests have access to Marina Vallarta's golf course. Marina Vallarta (phone: 10091; 800-659-8477; fax: 10755).

MODERATE

Buenaventura Colonial-style, with 209 unrenovated but clean rooms, this place is within walking distance of town. Its large, *palapa*-roofed lobby boasts an archaeological exhibit; there's also a restaurant, pool, and beach club. The location and affordable prices attract both noisy young travelers and more mature bargain hunters. On the beach, at 1301 Av. México (phone: 23737; fax: 46400).

Casa Panorámica Part or all of this delightful seven-bedroom villa can be rented. Built up in the hills just south of town, this place offers a dramatic view of Bahía de Banderas. There are several terraces, a pool, and bars. Breakfast is included in the rate. Km 1 of Rte. 200 toward Mismaloya (phone: 23656; 800-745-7805; 213-396-7855 in California).

Hacienda Buenaventura A short walk from the beach, this attractive colonial-style place has 154 rooms, a pool, gardens, a restaurant, a bar, and meeting rooms. Paseo de la Marina, next to the *Krystal Vallarta* (phone: 23737; 800-223-6764; fax: 46400).

Molino de Agua Right in town, this rustic and romantic little hostelry has 62 small, terraced rooms with river and ocean views. The bar has live music in the evening during winter, and there are two pools, a Jacuzzi, and a restaurant. Ignacio Vallarta, at the corner of Aquiles Serdán, at the river's edge (phone: 21907; 800-423-5512; fax: 26056).

Las Palmas Beach In this spacious beachfront resort complex, whose floors are linked by an interesting network of interior wooden bridges, most of the 165 units have balconies and beach views. There also are a pool, a restaurant, and a bar. Located about 1.5 miles (2.5 km) north of town, at 50 Cerrada las Palmas (phone: 40650; 800-995-8584; fax: 40543).

Playa de Oro Immense, with 340 balconied units, this is an ideal choice for sports lovers: Besides three tennis courts, two pools, and beach facilities, there's scuba diving, snorkeling, fishing, and water skiing. A Jacuzzi, four restaurants (including coffee shops), and five bars complete the hedonistic setup. Three miles (5 km) north, just off the road to the airport on Av. de las Garzas (phone: 46868; 800-882-8215; fax: 40348).

Plaza las Glorias Pelícanos It has 186 rooms, 15 villas (each accommodating up to eight people), and three pools. Located on a nice beach, at Km 2.5 on the road to the airport (phone: 41010; 800-342-AMIGO; fax: 41111).

Quinta María Cortez This eclectic villa has six one-bedroom suites, some with terraces and telephones, and all with kitchenettes and imaginatively decorated baths. Each suite is cluttered with antiques, interesting "junque," and original paintings. No air conditioning or ceiling fans here, but the breeze is delightful. There are no TV sets, either—just the beach and a pool. No children under five. Playa Conchas Chinas (phone: 21317 or 21184; fax: 23928).

San Marino Plaza Formerly the *Oro Verde,* this establishment has 134 rooms and 28 suites, a restaurant, and a pool. Centrally located and right on the beach, at 111 Rodolfo Gómez (phone: 21555; fax: 22431).

INEXPENSIVE

Los Cuatro Vientos This charming place is a longtime Vallarta favorite. There are 16 simple but comfortable rooms and suites, without air conditioning, ceiling fans, or TV sets, but with a lovely breeze. There's also a small pool, the excellent *Chez Elena* restaurant (see *Eating Out*), and a bar. The rate includes continental breakfast. Up the hill behind the *Iglesia de Guadalupe* at 520 Matamoros (phone: 20161).

Posada de Roger Simple and basic, it boasts 50 rooms (some air conditioned), a delightful bar, *El Tucán,* a pool—and the lowest rates in Puerto Vallarta. There's no restaurant. 237 Badillo (phone: 20836; fax: 30482).

Rosita Built in the late 1940s, this is one of the city's oldest hotels. There are 90 rooms around a central courtyard and 10 two-bedroom suites overlooking the fishing activity on the beach. Amenities include a restaurant, a pool, and a beauty salon. Located on the north end of the *malecón* at 901 Paseo Díaz Ordaz (phone: 21033).

EATING OUT

While it's hard to have a bad meal in Puerto Vallarta, it's also tough to happen upon a great one. The service in most places is exceptionally friendly and good. Dinner for two will cost $40 to $60 in an expensive restaurant; $20 to $40 in a moderate one; and under $20 in an inexpensive one. Prices do not include drinks, wine, tax, or tip, and are considerably lower off-season. Most restaurants below accept MasterCard and Visa, and a few also accept American Express and Diners Club; it's a good idea to call ahead and check. Unless otherwise noted, all restaurants are open daily for lunch and dinner. All telephone numbers are in the 322 city code unless otherwise indicated.

EXPENSIVE

Le Bistro Specialties include chicken and apple salad, *Bistro* brochette (shrimp, chicken, and steak), shish kebab, jumbo shrimp, and a variety of tasty crêpes. The handsome bar and recorded jazz make this a good place to relax after dinner. Closed Sundays. Reservations advised. Just off Av. Insurgentes on Isla Río Cuale (phone: 20283).

Bogart's Inspired by the film *Casablanca,* the menu features French-continental fare in an exceptionally posh and romantic setting, with fountains and pools, stark white decor, booths, velvet foot pillows for female guests, and piano music. The very friendly waiters dress in Moroccan attire, and the bar walls are decorated with Bogart memorabilia. Open for dinner only; seatings at 6 and 9 PM. Reservations advised. At the *Krystal Vallarta,* Av. de las Garzas (phone: 40202, ext. 2609).

Café des Artistes This place is elegant and romantic. The chef prepares French nouvelle cuisine with a heavy Mexican accent, serving such dishes as roast duck in honey-and-soy glaze with lime sauce, and squash-flower soup served in a small pumpkin shell. Open for dinner only; closed Sundays. Reservations necessary. Leona Vicario and Guadalupe Sánchez (phone: 23228).

El Candil This lovely, pink-and-white dining room features such dishes as rack of lamb and ceviche *"tres puertos"* (prepared Acapulco-, Veracruz-, and Puerto Vallarta–style). Reservations advised for dinner. In the *Bel-Air Hotel,* 311 Pelícanos, Marina Vallarta (phone: 10800).

Chef Roger The Swiss chef at this outstanding European-style bistro makes imaginative use of Mexican ingredients in creating an interesting selection of international dishes. Open for dinner only. Reservations advised. 267 Agustín Rodríguez (phone: 25900).

La Jolla de Mismaloya This popular restaurant with a glorious view of the bay is casual during the daytime but has a candlelit, elegant atmosphere in the evening. The menu features Mexican and international dishes; the crab-meat enchiladas have attracted quite a following. Reservations advised for dinner. In the *La Jolla de Mismaloya Hotel,* Mismaloya, about 7 miles (11 km) south of downtown Puerto Vallarta (phone: 30660).

La Perla An outstanding dining spot specializing in innovative contemporary fare (salmon prepared with pasta, crab, and lime sauce), as well as more traditional dishes and excellent desserts. At the *Camino Real Hotel,* 1½ miles (2 km) south on Rte. 200, on Playa las Estacas (phone: 30123).

Señor Chico's This dining spot prides itself on a dish named *tres amigos* (lobster, shrimp, and scallops), as well as a spectacular view from the hills of Conchas Chinas. There's live music nightly from 8 to 11 PM. Reservations advised. 377 Púlpito (phone: 23570).

MODERATE

Adobe Café The Santa Fe–style decor is elegant yet unpretentious, and the food, which ranges from Tex-Mex to nouvelle Mexican, is excellent. Reservations advised. 252 Basilio Badillo (phone: 26720).

Andale Near Playa de los Muertos, this informal eatery is a favorite among locals and visitors for an afternoon beer (or two). Specialties include scallops with fettuccine, a tasty chicken in wine sauce, and mouth-watering garlic bread dripping with melted butter. Reservations advised. 425 Paseo de Velasco (phone: 21054).

Archie's Wok Archie, this popular restaurant's namesake, was the late John Huston's chef. Now Archie's widow carries on, offering the same sampling of dishes from several Asian countries. Reservations advised. 130 Francisca Rodríguez (phone: 20411).

Balam There's zero atmosphere, but fresh lobster, giant shrimp, oysters, octopus, and several varieties of fish are served here in a variety of ways, including ceviche. Reservations advised. 425 Basilio Badillo (phone: 23451).

La Ballena A restaurant-bar-club—dance hall that's spacious, noisy, and lots of fun. The food—nachos, *fajitas,* tacos, and burgers—is simple and good. Open until 4 AM. At the entrance to Marina Vallarta (phone: 10154).

Carlos O'Brian's Another member of the Carlos Anderson chain, it serves lunch and dinner in a lively, upbeat atmosphere. There is a bar, a grill, and everything from ribs to "Chato Brian" (chateaubriand) for two. Closed on *New Year's Day.* No reservations. On the *malecón,* at 786 Paseo Díaz Ordaz (phone: 21444).

Las Cazuelas Reminiscent of the dining room of a hacienda, this family-run place is known for its Mexican fare prepared from family recipes. There's also a good choice of seafood dishes. Open for dinner only. Closed July and August. Reservations advised. 479 Basilio Badillo (phone: 22498).

Chez Elena Established nearly 40 years ago, this spot offers traditionally prepared regional fare, including a memorable mole, and the Yucatecan specialty *cochinita pibil* (pork baked in banana leaves), accompanied by tortillas that are freshly made by hand on the patio. Also featured are fish and shellfish entrées, and a few vegetarian dishes. There's live music, too. Reservations advised. In *Los Cuatro Vientos Hotel,* 520 Matamoros (phone: 20161).

Chico's Paradise Set amidst lush foliage on a spot where two river canyons meet in a breathtaking formation of rocks and natural pools, this is a delightful spot to spend the afternoon and enjoy a tasty meal of black bean soup, crawfish, and coconut pie. Reservations advised for large groups. About 12 miles (19 km) south of town along Rte. 200 toward Manzanillo (phone: 20747).

Daiquiri Dick's Enjoy lunch and dinner on the terrace overlooking the beach. Both the decor and food are California *à la mexicana.* Reservations advised. 314 Olas Altas (phone: 20566).

El Dorado A popular spot for years, this place is good for snacks and Mexican food. It's especially well known for its *pescado El Dorado* (fish topped with melted cheese). A prime location for wave watching, it's busiest at lunchtime. Reservations advised. Amapas and Púlpito (phone: 21511).

Le Gourmet A local favorite with a truly delightful setting. Lobster bisque, *huachinango* (red snapper), and pepper steaks are among the specialties. There is even espresso and a good choice of wines; mariachis perform Thursday and Saturday nights. Reservations advised. In the *Posada Río Cuale,* 242 Aquiles Serdán (phone: 20450).

Mama Mía This branch of the famous San Miguel de Allende eatery specializes in Mexican and international dishes; 14 varieties of coffee are available. There's live music nightly. No reservations. Paseo Díaz Ordaz and Allende (phone: 23544).

Moby Dick's The menu here centers around seafood (what else?) in simple, pleasant surroundings. Reservations advised. North end of the *malecón,* near the *Rosita* hotel (phone: 20655).

El Nuevo Panorama A delightful, *palapa*-style place right on a beautiful beach, its menu features seafood, excellent meat, tacos, and sandwiches. No reservations. At the beach club at Nuevo Vallarta (no phone).

El Ostión Feliz (The Happy Oyster) No view and no frills, but the service is friendly and the seafood is luscious. Reservations advised for large groups. 177 Libertad (phone: 22508).

Las Palomas A variety of flags out front make it easy to spot this lively open-air place on the *malecón,* where the Mexican fare and seafood are simple and satisfying. Reservations unnecessary. Paseo Díaz Ordaz and Aldama (phone: 23675).

Red Onion A very popular place, with lively Mexican decor and such Mexican dishes as *chiles rellenos* (*poblano* chilies stuffed with cheese). It also offers steaks and fresh fish. Open daily for breakfast, lunch, and dinner. Reservations necessary for large groups only. No credit cards accepted. 822 Paseo Díaz Ordaz (phone: 21087).

Ristorante Deli Romano A standout amid Puerto Vallarta's abundance of Italian restaurants, this cozy eatery run by an Italian chef and an expatriate restaurateur from New York features fresh pasta, homemade breads, and tantalizing combination plates. Reservations unneccessary. 419 Basilio Badillo (phone: 20725)

Santos Decorated with paintings and sculptures by local artists, this delightful place presents international and Mexican dishes as well as original creations by Santos, the owner and chef. A special dessert is a deep-fried tortilla served with ice cream and Kahlúa. Closed Mondays. Reservations advised. 136 Francisca Rodríguez (phone: 25670).

El Set On the cliffs overlooking the beaches, it is chock-full of *ambiente*. Specializing in seafood, the place is fun at lunchtime, perfect for cocktails, and lovely at dinner. Reservations advised. On the highway to Manzanillo, $1\frac{1}{2}$ miles (2 km) from town (phone: 15342).

INEXPENSIVE

The Corner Bar The sports bar, good music, good food (Mexican and deli), and fair prices make this a favorite hangout for expats. No reservations. Vallarta and Cárdenas (phone: 24100).

Dugarel Playa There's indoor and terrace seating, great seafood, and a panoramic view of Bahía de Banderas. No reservations. Av. del Pacífico, in Bucerías (no phone).

Pancake House Puerto Vallarta's favorite breakfast spot, also known as "Casa de los Hotcakes," also offers typical US diner fare (meat loaf, pot roast, fried chicken, cakes, and pies) at lunch and dinner. No reservations. No credit cards accepted. 289 Basilio Badillo (phone: 26272).

San Miguel de Allende

(pronounced Sahn Mee-*gel* day A-*yen*-day)

In the Bajío region of Mexico, San Miguel de Allende sits at an altitude of 6,135 feet, surrounded by rich farmland, pretty lakes, and the beautiful Sierra Madre. Once the center of rebellion and the War of Independence, the town is today Mexico's most celebrated artists' colony. Founded in 1542 by a Franciscan friar, Juan de San Miguel, San Miguel was settled by a group of native people to whom he had taught European techniques of weaving and agriculture. The friar also marked off the streets, parceled out land, and established a tradition of artisanship and an artistic sensibility that survive to this day.

In the 18th century, the wealthy Spaniards who owned the lucrative silver mines in nearby Guanajuato built elegant colonial palaces in San Miguel. The town soon was surrounded by vast estates, or haciendas, also controlled by wealthy Spaniards. At that time, the town was known as San Miguel el Grande, to distinguish it from the other communities in the area also named in honor of St. Michael. The Bajío region in those days seethed with rebellion. The *criollos* (Creoles, or Spaniards born in the colony rather than in Spain itself) were second class subjects of the king, while the mestizos (of mixed Spanish and native ancestry) and pure-blooded native peoples were considered an even lower class. First the American and then the French Revolution sparked the notion that matters might be improved. Napoleon's invasion of Spain, which brought his brother to the throne, catalyzed those colonists who would not rebel against the legitimate king but had fewer qualms about taking up arms against a usurper.

The independence movement was led by Padre Miguel Hidalgo, a parish priest in the nearby town of Dolores, and Ignacio Allende, formerly of a royalist regiment. They defeated the Spanish garrison in Guanajuato in 1810, but a year later both men were captured by the royalists in Chihuahua and beheaded. Nevertheless, the movement they initiated lived on, and when Mexico achieved independence in 1821, it honored its heroes, naming the town of Dolores "Dolores Hidalgo" and changing San Miguel el Grande to "San Miguel de Allende."

A full century after Hidalgo's call to arms, the Mexican Revolution began. One of its results was the breaking up and destruction of many of the huge plantations and palatial manor houses, some of which today stand only as ruins. Others have been restored as private residences or hotels. In 1938, US artist Stirling Dickinson founded an art school on one estate, which was taken over in 1951 by Nel and the late Enrique Fernández (she's from the US; he was Mexican). They created the *Instituto Allende,* intended as a place of study for US residents. At first, the institute attracted mostly ex-soldiers funded by the GI Bill; today, still run by Nel Fernández, it attracts both young and old: college students picking up a few extra credits and pensioners taking courses ranging from sculpture to photography. Because of the institute, San Miguel de Allende has a large community of US expatriates that includes many artists and writers: Almost any social gathering will include a painter, a musician, or an actor or two. In fact, with many of the former US residents sporting 1960s-style long hair and love beads, the town has an odd, time-warp atmosphere.

The countryside around San Miguel is famous for health spas with hot springs. In the town itself, many beautiful Spanish buildings and colonial-era cobblestone streets remain. Houses are close to the street, with tall windows covered by elaborate metal grilles. There are beautiful hand-carved wood doors and stone coats of arms on many of the buildings. Declared a national monument in 1926, San Miguel is protected from any new construction that is not in the colonial style. Today, 100,000 people live in the area.

The center of town is the Plaza Allende, where every evening the charming custom of the *paseo,* or promenade, is carried out: The young women walk in one direction and the young men in the other, admiring and meeting one another. (It's a Mexican teenager's equivalent of cruising through a shopping mall.) On Sundays, the city's band provides musical accompaniment. Hundreds of people congregate to watch, to stroll, and to socialize.

San Miguel de Allende At-a-Glance

SEEING THE CITY

There are two exceptional spots from which to see San Miguel and the surrounding countryside. Up a long flight of stone steps behind the *Instituto Allende* and *Parque Benito Juárez* (Benito Juárez Park) is the Cerro del Chorro (Hill of Springs). Named for the clear springs that surface here, the hill provides all of the drinking water for the city. A refreshment stand and benches await those who undertake the climb.

El Mirador (The Lookout) offers another magnificent panorama of the city and its environs. It is accessible by foot via Calle Real, an old cobblestone street, or by car via the road to Querétaro. It's only a block away from the *Posada la Ermita* hotel (phone: 20787), where you can stop for a poolside drink.

There is also a commanding view of the whole valley from the dining room of the *Hacienda de las Flores* hotel (see *Checking In*).

SPECIAL PLACES

LA PARROQUIA (PARISH CHURCH) Dominating San Miguel's skyline, this unusual pink-stone, Gothic-spired church was built less than 100 years ago. The architect, Ceferino Gutiérrez, was a self-educated stonemason who found his inspiration in picture-postcard reproductions of European churches.

Inside, take time to look at the murals depicting local history and culture, and to visit the crypt. Closed Wednesday mornings. South side of Plaza Allende.

PARQUE BENITO JUÁREZ (BENITO JUÁREZ PARK) Filled with fountains, flowers, and young lovers, this small park has picnic tables, playground equipment, basketball courts, and a stream meandering through untamed woods. White lilies bloom here in the spring. On the southeastern outskirts of town, at the foot of Cerro del Chorro (see *Seeing the City*), between Calle de Tenerías and Puente de Animas.

LA CASA DE IGNACIO ALLENDE The birthplace of Allende, a military leader in Mexico's struggle for independence, now houses temporary art exhibits, mainly work done by the indigenous Otomí. Closed Mondays. No admission charge. 1 Cuna de Allende, just off Plaza Allende (phone: 22499).

PALACIO DE LOS CONDES DE LA CANAL (HOUSE OF THE COUNTS OF DE LA CANAL) The most imposing colonial building in all San Miguel was constructed by a wealthy 18th-century mining family named de la Canal. It now houses a branch of Banamex, and can be seen during banking hours (weekdays from 9 AM to 1:30 PM). An art gallery is open to the public Tuesdays through Fridays. Northwest corner of Plaza Allende facing Calle Canal (phone: 21004, bank).

INSTITUTO ALLENDE This converted 1735 hacienda on the southern edge of town houses the school responsible for changing the population, economy, and way of life of San Miguel. Year-round, courses are given in the arts and in Mexican and other Latin American literature; summer programs for teachers and MA and MFA degrees are also offered. The classes, taught in English, are well attended by US students. The beautiful building and grounds are worth a visit even for those not interested in taking courses. An exhibit room features the work of students and teachers, much of it for sale. 20 Ancha de San Antonio (phone: 20190).

CENTRO CULTURAL IGNACIO RAMÍREZ (IGNACIO RAMÍREZ CULTURAL CENTER) This branch of the *Instituto de Bellas Artes* (Fine Arts Institute) of Mexico City offers courses in music, art, dance, weaving, ceramics, and metalwork. Once a convent, the buildings now offer lectures, concerts, theatrical performances, and dance recitals. The complex is known locally as "Las Monjas" ("The Nuns"). There are two galleries with changing exhibits, a number of murals, a café, a lovely patio, and a bulletin board in English with up-to-date local announcements of happenings around town. If the room housing the unfinished David Alfaro Siqueiros mural is closed, ask permission to see it. Closed Sundays. No admission charge. 75 Calle Hernández Macías (phone: 20289).

JARDÍN DE LAS ORQUÍDEAS (ORCHID GARDEN) Well worth the strenuous uphill walk east from town along Calle Correo, Sterling Dickinson's gardens seem truly secret, a riot of entangled plants—orchids, irises, cacti, fruit trees—through which a stream flows. October and November are the months to see the most flowers. Closed Sundays. No admission charge. 38 Prolongación Santo Domingo (no phone).

EL CHARCO DEL INGENIO This ecological preserve, which comprises more than 100 acres, is home to a wide range of plant life, including oak forests of the high mountains, cacti and other succulents of the semi-arid lowlands, and the tropical foliage surrounding the pools at the bottom of the canyon. The park belongs to a nonprofit organization dedicated to the study and preservation of the area. Open daily. Admission charge. Northeast of town, at 211 Sollano (phone: 22990).

TEATRO ANGELA PERALTA San Miguel's historic concert hall is one of the most beautiful and acoustically perfect in all of Mexico. For schedule information, call the tourist office (see *Tourist Information*). Calle Hernández Macías at Calle Mesones.

SANTUARIO DE ATOTONILCO (SHRINE OF ATOTONILCO) Native peoples from all over Mexico have been making pilgrimages to this religious center since the 18th century, when it was built. It was here that the rebel army led by Allende and Hidalgo made its first stop. They seized a banner of the Virgin of Guadalupe, declared it their flag of liberation, and carried it into battle. The choice of this popular religious figure brought the natives decisively into the insurrection on the side of the rebels. Inside the sanctuary, frescoes and sculptures provide a glimpse of Mexican popular art dating from the 18th century. About 8 miles (13 km) north of San Miguel, on Rte. 51 (no phone).

Sources and Resources

TOURIST INFORMATION

The *Secretaría de Turismo del Estado* (State Tourism Secretariat; on the *zócalo* (main plaza), next to the *Terraza* restaurant; phone: 21747) has an English-speaking staff that will provide maps and pamphlets on the city and surrounding area, plus listings of local doctors, cultural and sporting events, and hotels and restaurants. The office is open daily.

LOCAL COVERAGE The weekly English-language newspaper *Atención San Miguel* offers a good rundown of what's going on in town; it can be found, along with English-language books and magazines, at *La Conexión* (1 Aldama; phone: 22312); *El Pegaso* (6 Corregidora; phone: 21351); and *El Colibrí* (30 Sollano; no phone). *The News* and the *Mexico City Times,* both English-language dailies that cover national and international news, are available throughout town.

TELEPHONE The city code for San Miguel de Allende is 415. *Note:* Mexico's telephone company has embarked on a major expansion project that involves changing telephone numbers in many areas of the country. At press time, all numbers listed in this chapter were correct. However, if you have any difficulties reaching attractions listed here, contact the local tourist office.

CLIMATE AND CLOTHES The average monthly temperature in San Miguel is about 70F (21C), with evenings slightly cooler than days. If you visit during the rainy season—roughly from July through September—bring rainwear and insect repellent. Dress is informal; remember to pack a sturdy pair of walking shoes, because all the streets (and most of the sidewalks) are foot-pounding cobblestone.

GETTING AROUND

San Miguel's streets are narrow and steep, and while it is possible to drive around with very little competing traffic, walking is by far the most rewarding way to explore the city.

BUSES Five bus lines run through town. The bus terminal at Calzada de la Estación is pleasant, clean, and safe. The fare is 1.5 pesos (about 20¢); call 20084 for schedule information. Buses run until about 10:30 or 11 PM nightly.

CAR RENTALS The local firm *Gama* (phone: 20815), with offices on the plaza, has a small rental fleet. There are larger agencies in the nearby towns of Celaya and Querétaro.

TAXI Call *Sitio Allende* (phone: 20192 or 20550) or *Sitio Terminal* (phone: 21795). Be sure to set the price before getting in.

TOURS The *Centro de Crecimiento,* a school for disabled children, organizes three-hour "Saturday Sojourns" to interesting places outside of San Miguel, such as working ranches, a monastery, a cheese factory, old haciendas, and an equestrian center. Ticket proceeds go toward the school's upkeep. The bus leaves the *Centro de Crecimiento* on Saturdays at 10:30 AM; tickets are available at the school (6 Zamora Río; phone: 20318), *Casa Maxwell* (14 Calle Canal, at Calle Umarán; phone: 20247), or *El Colibrí* (30 Sollano; no phone). Every Sunday at noon, a small group leaves from the *Biblioteca Pública de San Miguel* (San Miguel Public Library; 25 Calle de los Insurgentes; phone: 20293) to tour some of the beautiful homes and gardens of San Miguel; refreshments and a talk are included. Tickets are available in the library, as well as around the *zócalo,* during regular business hours and half an hour before the tour leaves.

SPECIAL EVENTS

In San Miguel, *Semana Santa* (Holy Week) is celebrated with processions, religious displays in the windows of private homes, colorfully decorated churches, and a sunset procession on *Viernes Santo* (Good Friday). The national holidays, especially *Día de la Independencia* (Independence Day, September 16—but the celebrations start at 11 PM on September 15) and *Día de la Revolución* (Revolution Day, the anniversary of the start of the

1910–21 Revolution; November 20), are quite special here, with *charro* (rodeo) horsemen joining marching bands. On October 12, the city celebrates *Día de la Raza* ("Day of the Race") to commemorate the arrival of Columbus, who foretold the arrival of Spaniards who would have children with native women, thereby creating a new race; a civic ceremony is held at the *Iglesia de San Francisco* (Calles San Francisco and Juárez), and a celebration is held in the evening at the bullring.

San Miguel de Allende also has a few of its own holidays. *Veintiuno de Enero* (January 21) celebrates the birth of San Miguel's secular patron, the independence hero Ignacio Allende. It consists mostly of civic ceremonies, a large parade through town, and the usual music and dancing on every square and street corner. About the middle of June, thousands of local boys and girls dress up in crazy ("loco") costumes to celebrate the *Fiesta de los Locos,* which also honors St. Anthony of Padua. The *Festival Internacional de Música de Cámara* (International Chamber Music Festival), held during the first half of August, features acclaimed groups from around the world. From September 29 to about October 4, the *Fiesta de San Miguel* (Feast of St. Michael the Archangel) celebrates San Miguel's patron saint, with a fair featuring games, fireworks, a bullfight, plenty of food, and much music and dancing.

San Miguel is chock-full of charitable organizations, and it seems that some event is always being held to raise funds for a worthy cause. Attending one of them is a good way to get to know the town's many interesting and friendly residents. A sad note: Pickpockets work overtime on holidays in San Miguel.

SHOPPING

A shopping spree is often the highlight of a visit to San Miguel de Allende, and most of the galleries and stores in the *zócalo* (main plaza) area carry high-quality paintings, sculpture, clothing, ceramics, tin, and wrought-iron items. Distinctive cloth goods—many of them handloomed and embroidered—are also an excellent buy. Shops are generally open daily from 10 AM to 2 PM and 4 to 6 PM.

Antigua Casa Canela Handicrafts, textiles, and art are sold in this museum-like setting, which includes replicas of a model colonial home, a chapel, a neighborhood store, and a cantina. 20 Calle Umarán (phone: 21880).

Artesanías Chela Handsome tin and brass sconces, mirrors, and other decorative pieces. 6 Calle Correo (phone: 23166).

Beckman A wide collection of silver and jewelry, including silver-plated decanters, fine, heavy ladles, and *Christmas* ornaments. 105 Calle Hernández Macías (phone: 21613).

La Calandria A tasteful collection of authentic antiques and reproductions. 5 Calle San Francisco (phone: 22945).

Casa Canal Locally designed colonial furniture is the highlight here, as well as Josefa clothing designs, which are adorned with embroidery and appliqués. 3 Calle Canal (phone: 20479).

Casa Maxwell Built in 1810 as the home of the insurgent Juan de Umarán, this place houses a vast collection of local crafts; shipping can be arranged. A block from the plaza, at 14 Calle Canal and Calle Umarán (phone: 20247).

Casas Coloniales Wool rugs, curtains, pillows, bed and table linen, fabric and trim, and some home furnishings—all in interesting textures and wonderful colors. 36 Calle Canal (phone: 20286).

David David Pérez fashions marvelous silver jewelry; he will take orders for special pieces. 53 Calle Zacateros (phone: 20056).

Galería Atenea Once a lovely home, now it's an attractive gallery filled with select crafts and contemporary paintings, sculpture, and photographs. The same owner runs *Galería Sergio Bustamante* (see below). 15 Calle Cuna de Allende (phone: 20785).

Galería San Miguel San Miguel's most popular gallery has a good selection of paintings, watercolors, and prints. On the *zócalo* (phone: 20454).

Galería Sergio Bustamante Fantastical sculptures by the well-known artist. 15A Calle Cuna de Allende (phone: 20785).

Girasol Colorful women's clothes inspired by Mexican folk costumes, with an abundance of tiny pleats, ribbons, and appliqués, and a definite European flair. 6 Calle Umarán (phone: 20951).

Josefa Wrought-iron garden furniture, fountains, benches, and handicrafts fill this attractive shop. 16 Calle Canal (phone: 20216).

Josh Klingerman Gallery In what was once the stable of the Allende home, this gallery has an interesting selection of contemporary art. The proprietor, an expert on Mexican art, gives free lectures Thursday afternoons. 6 Calle Umarán (phone: 20951).

Llamas The assortment of tin and brass goods here includes beautiful lamps, chandeliers, mirrors, and picture frames. Three locations: across from the *Instituto Allende,* at 5 Ancha de San Antonio (phone: 21904); 11A Ancha de San Antonio (phone: 21264); and 11 Calle Zacateros (phone: 21232).

Ono Imaginative and educational toys, hand-painted textiles, archaeological reproductions, and unusual crafts. Two locations: 38 Calle Mesones (phone: 21311) and 10 Portal de Guadalupe (no phone).

El Pegaso This lovely shop is a hangout for local US expatriates, with original clothing, jewelry, crafts, and a few tables to sit and sip coffee, including the best cappuccino in town. It's a good information center. Across from the post office, at 6 Calle Corregidora (phone: 21351).

Zarco A wide selection of hand-painted plates, tiles, and tin and brass items. 24 Sollano (phone: 20323).

SPORTS

BULLFIGHTS There is no set corrida season; bullfights are scheduled occasionally (check with the tourist office). The bullring is on Calle Recreo.

GOLF *Club de Golf Malanquín* (Km 3 of the Carretera a Celaya, heading south of town; phone: 20516) has a good nine-hole course (no carts).

HORSEBACK RIDING Horses are available for guests at the *Hacienda Taboada* and the *Rancho el Atascadero* hotels (see *Checking In* for both).

SWIMMING Many of the hotels have pools, and near the *Hacienda Taboada* hotel there is a large public pool with a playground and picnic area. *Club de Golf Malanquín* (see *Golf*) has an Olympic-size pool. Non-guests of the *Aristos San Miguel* (see *Checking In*) can join the hotel's "Amigos Club," which grants access to the pool and other facilities for a monthly fee.

TENNIS Courts are available at *La Unidad Deportiva* (across from the *Misión de los Angeles* hotel; see *Checking In*; no phone). The *Rancho el Atascadero* and *Quinta Loreto* hotels have tennis courts (see *Checking In*), and there are four clay courts at the *Club de Golf Malanquín* (see *Golf*).

NIGHTCLUBS AND NIGHTLIFE

San Miguel de Allende is rife with nightspots that go strong into the wee hours of the morning. Though official closing time is 1 AM, the rule is often relaxed to accommodate the clientele. The current hot spot is *Edoardo's* (146 Carretera Querétaro; no phone), which has a large gay following. The *Ring* (25 Calle Hidalgo, a block north of Plaza Allende; phone: 21998) is a popular discotheque with loud music. *Laberintos* disco (across from the *Instituto Allende;* no phone), which attracts mainly a local crowd, is also loud and has a cover charge. *Disque Disco* draws big crowds to the *Hacienda Taboada* (see *Checking In* for details on hotels listed in this section). *La Fragua* (3 Calle Cuna de Allende; phone: 20958) has a lovely patio and true Mexican flavor and occasionally features a variety show. *Mama Mía* (8 Calle Umarán; phone: 22063) has live music, from Andean folk to jazz, on its patio nightly except Tuesdays. *La Princesa* (5 Calle Recreo; phone: 21403) is a favorite early evening spot for a drink and to listen to music. Aficionados of honky-tonk bars should not miss the *Cucaracha* (22 Zacateros; phone: 20196), with its good jukebox. *La Mancha,* in the *Aristos San Miguel* hotel, always has a good mariachi group.

If discos and clubs aren't your thing, there's a bar and movie theater Mondays through Thursdays at the *Villa Jacaranda* hotel; Saturday night there's *karaoke,* popular with the local American expatriates.

Best in Town

CHECKING IN

The going rate per night for a double room with bath in a very expensive hotel ranges from $100 to $150; in an expensive place, $75 to $90; in a moderate place, $45 to $65; and in an inexpensive place, under $40. Some hotels include one to three meals a day. Most hotels do not have air conditioning; some have TV sets and phones in rooms. All telephone numbers are in the 415 city code unless otherwise indicated.

We begin with our favorite havens (all in the very expensive range), followed by recommended hotels, listed by price category.

SPECIAL HAVENS

Casa de Sierra Nevada Once an archbishop's residence, this 18th-century building is by far the best posada in town. The 18 suites and three rooms are distributed among the original building and the four houses next to and across the street from it. Each room has its own individual decor and furnishings, but all are spacious, with high ceilings, and full of antiques. Most have at least one fireplace, some have two baths, and most have telephones. Suite 2 is decorated in peach, with a travertine marble bathroom and a large terrace overlooking the cathedral. Suite 7, with gray and yellow furnishings, is intimate and romantic. The wonderful *Sierra Nevada* dining area (see *Eating Out*) is narrow and long, at once charming, homey, and a bit formal. Guests may use the tennis courts, pool, and nine-hole golf course at the *Club de Golf Malanquín*. There is a garden area, with a heated pool, a sun deck, a spa, and a beauty center. Some credit cards are accepted; personal checks accepted by prior arrangement. Centrally located, at 35 Calle Hospicio (phone: 20415; 800-223-6510; fax: 22337).

Villa Jacaranda If you're in the mood for intimate and quiet cordiality, you've come to the right place. This romantic inn is surrounded by gardens and furnished with local crafts and art; hand-painted Mexican tiles hang on the bathroom walls. All 16 units (including 12 suites) have cable TV and fireplaces; most have private or semiprivate patios and terraces. There is a Roman plunge bath and a Jacuzzi in the central patio, a cinema-bar where the latest movies (in English) are shown, and an internationally acclaimed restaurant (see *Eating Out*) that is a favorite of San Miguel residents. Three blocks southeast of Plaza Allende, at 53 Calle Aldama (phone: 21015 or 20811; fax: 20883).

Villa Santa Mónica This, one of San Miguel's prettiest inns, has eight rooms, no two alike (No. 4 is completely independent from the rest, with a separate entrance). All guestrooms have fireplaces and private patios. There is also a restaurant, a massage room and sauna, and a small oval pool. Guests with dinner reservations in the restaurant receive free cocktails. The rate includes breakfast. In a secluded area across from *Parque Benito Juárez* (see *Special Places,* above), one of the most delightful spots in town. 22 Calle Baeza (phone: 20427 or 20451; fax: 20121).

VERY EXPENSIVE

Hacienda de las Flores The ambience is elegant without being imposing at this hostelry with five double rooms and six junior suites. On the premises are a fine restaurant with a panoramic view of the valley, a boutique, and a poolside bar where free films are shown. Breakfast is included in the room rate. 16 Calle Hospicio (phone: 21808; fax: 21859).

Hacienda Taboada This 64-room spa offers a full complement of sports, plus thermal baths for après-sport soaking. For additional details, see *Spa-Hopping Special* in DIVERSIONS. Six miles (10 km) north of town on Rte. 51, with free bus service into San Miguel (phone: 20850 or 20888; 800-447-7462; fax: 21798).

La Puertecita Boutique Twenty very private suites nestled in the woods. Amenities include pools, golf, tennis privileges at a nearby club, private Jacuzzis, direct-dial phone service, 24-hour complimentary transportation to and from town, and game, billiards, and music rooms. Learning workshops and land cruises of colonial Mexico, as well as language and cultural packages, are offered. Eight suites are reserved for nonsmokers. The owners and staff are extremely attentive. On the east side of town, at 75 Calle Santo Domingo (phone: 22250; 800-336-6776; fax: 25505).

EXPENSIVE

Real de Minas It has 65 air conditioned rooms, all with satellite TV. There's also a large pool, lovely gardens, a restaurant, and a bar–dance club with live music on weekends. A five-minute drive south from downtown, on Calle Ancha de San Antonio (phone: 22626; fax: 21727).

MODERATE

Aristos San Miguel This pleasant place has 100 rooms, 10 four-bedroom villas, a pool, and a lovely garden setting. There's also a cocktail lounge and a popular restaurant. Next to the *Instituto Allende* (formerly its dormitory), at 2 Calle Cardo (phone: 20149 or 20392; 800-527-4786; fax: 21631).

Mansión del Bosque A real home away from home; the rate at this 24-room guest-house includes breakfast and a family-style dinner of "international home cooking," from chop suey to borscht. A one-month minimum stay is required from December through February; summer sees a younger clientele. 65 Calle Aldama (phone: 20277).

Misión de los Angeles Overlooking Allende Dam, it has 60 rooms with vaulted ceilings (some with king-size beds), a bar with a fireplace, a pretty restaurant, a pool, and table tennis. About a mile (2 km) south of town on the Carretera a Celaya (phone: 22099; fax: 22047).

Parador del Cortijo Formerly the *Clínica Naturista Agua Maravillosa* spa, this small (only 19 rooms) inn offers two swimming pools, a Jacuzzi, a restaurant, and massages (book in advance). North of town, at Km 9 on Route 51 (phone: 21700).

La Puertecita Centro Ideal for extended stays, this guesthouse is owned by the proprietors of *La Puertecita Boutique* (see above). The six tastefully decorated, spacious rooms have large closets and splendid bathrooms with skylights and hand-painted tiles. Guests have access to a comfortable living-dining area, a restaurant, a rooftop terrace, and a Jacuzzi. Continental breakfast is included in the rate; cultural and language packages are available. No minimum stay required. Four blocks west of *La Parroquia* (see *Special Places,* above), at 2 Cerrada de Pila Seca (phone: 22118; 800-336-6776; fax: 20424).

Rancho el Atascadero This converted hacienda offers 51 rooms with fireplaces, one of the few tennis courts in town, a sauna, a swimming pool, jai alai, a dining room that features a good Sunday brunch, and extensive grounds that make you feel you're in the country. A hotel shuttle bus provides transportation into town. A mile (1.6 km) east of town on Prolongación Santo Domingo (phone: 20206 or 20337; fax: 21541).

Suites el Patio Under capable management, this small (only seven rooms), comfortable hotel has a good restaurant and a bar with live music in the evenings. Convenient downtown location, at 10 Calle Correo (phone: 21647; fax: 23180).

INEXPENSIVE

Posada Carmina Best known locally for its restaurant (see *Eating Out*), this simple but clean 10-room hotel attracts return guests primarily because of Señora Carmina García, the consummate hostess. It's a real find. Just west of the *zócalo,* at 7 Calle Cuna de Allende (phone: 20458).

Quinta Loreto Surrounded by gardens, it has 30 rooms in the older section, eight rooms in a new wing, and a few apartments that are almost always rented. There's a pool, a tennis court, and a good restaurant (see *Eating Out*). A real bargain. On the northeast side of town, at 15 Calle Loreto (phone: 20042; fax: 23616).

EATING OUT

Dinner for two in San Miguel de Allende will cost from $50 to $60 in an expensive restaurant, between $30 and $45 in a moderate one, and $25 or less in an inexpensive place. Prices don't include drinks, wine, tax, or tip. Most restaurants below accept MasterCard and Visa, and a few also accept American Express and Diners Club; it's a good idea to call ahead and check. Unless otherwise noted, all restaurants are open daily for lunch and dinner. All telephone numbers are in the 415 city code unless otherwise indicated.

EXPENSIVE

La Bodega Set in a dimly lit 18th-century wine cellar, it serves Chinese, Italian, Mexican, and American food. Closed Wednesdays. Reservations advised. No credit cards accepted. 34 Calle Correo (phone: 21481).

El Campanario Solicitous service, excellent specialties—such as filet of beef in Roquefort sauce and lobster thermidor—and a lovely setting account for this spot's popularity. Closed Thursdays. Reservations advised. Across from *Posada de las Monjas* (a church), at 34 Calle Canal (phone: 20775).

Sierra Nevada The food served here is among the best in town. The menu includes pastries, escargots *à la Provençal,* and corn tortillas filled with mushrooms baked in a cilantro cream sauce. The food is international without being fussy, and there are surprises like homemade pasta. Coat and tie required for men for dinner; no shorts. Reservations necessary for dinner. In the *Casa de Sierra Nevada,* 35 Calle Hospicio (phone: 20415).

La Vendimia One of the most highly rated dining spots in town, where continental fare is served in a Southern California setting. Dishes range from warm scallop salad to charcoal-broiled tuna. Reservations advised, especially on weekends. 12 Calle Hidalgo (phone: 22645).

MODERATE

Bugambilia Mexican haute cuisine served in a lovely, century-old home. Among the specialties are *chicharrón guanajuatense* (fried pork rind, Guanajuato style), cold avocado soup, and *chiles en nogada* (stuffed peppers in a nut-based cream sauce, usually available only in September). Reservations advised. 42 Calle Hidalgo (phone: 20127).

La Fragua Like a country inn, with several dining rooms and terrace seating around an inner courtyard. The menu ranges from garlic soup to fried chicken. Thursdays through Sundays, there's live music for dancing. No reservations. Just west of the *zócalo,* at 3 Calle Cuna de Allende (phone: 20958).

Hacienda de las Flores Fine continental and local dishes, exquisitely served—and there's no extra charge for the magnificent view. Closed Mondays. Reservations unnecessary. 16 Calle Hospicio (phone: 21808 or 21859).

La Hacienda de Pepe A picture-book adobe patio with an international menu that includes delicious cream soups, homemade bread, and shredded beef. Closed Mondays. Reservations unnecessary. 101 Mesones (no phone).

Mama Mía This lively and popular beer hall has some cozy tables, where you can make a fine meal of the mouth-watering homemade pasta, or the cheesy pizza accompanied by light or dark beer on tap. There's good music, too. Reservations unnecessary. 8 Calle Umarán, just north of Plaza Allende (phone: 22063).

Villa Jacaranda Housed in the charming hotel of the same name, this pretty place offers delightful ambience as well as carefully prepared international and Mexican meals. The wine list is good, too. Reservations advised. 53 Calle Aldama (phone: 21015).

INEXPENSIVE

La Dolce Vita Pizza, pastries, coffee, and hand-cranked Italian ice cream are the highlights here. No reservations. No credit cards accepted. 74 Hernández Macías (no phone).

Posada Carmina This is a favorite for a quiet lunch in a courtyard under orange trees; breakfast and dinner are served as well. Try the paella *valenciana,* the Spanish-style tortilla (onion-and-potato omelette), or the cheese and vegetable salad. Reservations unnecessary. In the *Posada Carmina Hotel,* 7 Calle Cuna de Allende (phone: 20458).

Quinta Loreto The large portions here are perhaps the best bargain in town; stuffed pork chops are a tasty choice. Open for breakfast and lunch only. Reservations unnecessary. In the *Quinta Loreto Hotel,* 15 Calle Loreto (phone: 20042).

Taxco

(pronounced *Tahs*-co)

Nestled high in the folds of the Sierra Madre, halfway between Acapulco and Mexico City, sits an unusual treasure: a village of silversmiths that clings to the sides of the mountains and perches on the edge of the cliffs.

In Taxco, silver is undisputedly king. While there are also textile, clothing, tin, and curio stores, it seems that every other building in town houses a silver shop. The lure of lustrous jewelry and other silvery treasures, combined with the charm of the town itself, helped make Taxco—in the state of Guerrero, as is Acapulco—one of Mexico's first major travel destinations. In fact, there are those who grumble that Taxco has become too touristy, especially since the toll road linking Taxco with the Acapulco highway opened in 1989. Yet many visitors come back year after year to spend their entire vacations here. Taxco, filled with charming stucco houses, is Old Mexico as everyone expects it to be, and it is the rare traveler, Mexican or foreign, who regrets having made the trip.

Taxco's fortunes have always been closely tied to silver. The Spanish, who conquered Mexico in 1521, found rich sources of silver here and opened the first mine in 1529. By the end of the century, however, the mines were no longer commercially profitable, and the town's first "silver age" came to an end. Early in the 18th century, a Frenchman called Joseph de la Borde (who later changed his name to the more Mexican José de la Borda) struck a very rich vein of silver, thus inaugurating Taxco's second silver age. Unfortunately, this boom was just as short-lived as the first, and by the beginning of the 19th century the town was no longer of much interest to anyone.

Taxco pretty much slumbered away until 1928, when an enterprising American, William Spratling, opened the town's first silver shop (and modern mining techniques allowed more silver to be extracted from the old mines). Spratling's business prospered, and, as his apprentices went on to open their own shops, Taxco became a silver center yet again. Today, there are more than 250 silver stores in Taxco.

Happily, the modern world has not managed to encroach much on the traditional, almost fairy-tale quality of this town of 50,000 people. Narrow cobblestone streets still weave around the hills, over their tops, and along their gently curved sides. White and pink stucco houses, with Spanish tile roofs and wrought-iron balconies filled with flowering plants, line the thoroughfares. It is an artist's paradise, and if the Mexican government has its way, that's how the town will remain: Taxco itself has been declared a national monument. Indeed, few would dispute the idea that the town's charm is as precious a commodity as the metal that made it famous.

Taxco At-a-Glance

SEEING THE CITY

No visitor should miss the spectacular view of Taxco from the cable car that goes to the *MonteTaxco* hotel. The cable car may be boarded near the main highway, Route 95 (called Av. John F. Kennedy in town), by the arches near the northern entrance to town; the round-trip fare is 15 pesos (about $2). The views from the hotel itself are breathtaking, as are those from the *Posada de la Misión* hotel, overlooking the town (see *Checking In*); *Rancho Taxco* (14 Soto la Marina); *La Ventana de Taxco* restaurant; and the *Pagaduría del Rey* restaurant (see *Eating Out* for both). The Carretera Panorámica (Panoramic Highway) delivers what its name promises; take the *combi* (van) from *Iglesia de la Santísima Trinidad* (Holy Trinity Church), on Calles San Nicolás and San Miguel.

SPECIAL PLACES

Most of Taxco's places of interest are within walking distance of each other, and as you stroll around you'll invariably come across lush patios adorned with geraniums, cerise and orange bougainvillea, intricately carved doors, ornate ironwork, and cages of exotic songbirds. No serendipity is involved: Nearly every street in Taxco is special. Note that *Casa Figueroa,* a late 18th-century house that houses the studio and gallery of modern Mexican artist Fidel Figueroa, at press time was closed indefinitely for renovations; check with your hotel or at the tourist office (see *Tourist Information*) for current information.

IGLESIA SANTA PRISCA (ST. PRISCA CHURCH) Taxco's most important landmark was built in the mid-18th century by José de la Borda to express his gratitude to God for his success. The church's twin 130-foot Baroque towers and richly carved stone façade are impressive, but the blue tile dome and pink exterior walls are what account for the building's popularity with photographers. Inside, there are 12 altars, gold altarpieces, and paintings by 18th-century artist Miguel Cabrera in the sacristy. More than $3 million in gold and silver religious artifacts were stolen by burglars in 1988. Fortunately, the thieves overlooked *Santa Prisca*'s most valuable treasures: four 18th-century oil paintings by Spaniard Andrés Barragán. These works, and most of the remaining gold relics, still are on display. On the *zócalo,* or main plaza.

CASA BORDA José de la Borda constructed his Baroque, colonial-style home in 1759 on the *zócalo,* facing away from the *Iglesia Santa Prisca.* Because the house was built on the side of the mountain, the front section is two stories high, while the back descends five floors to the street below. The de la Borda family occupied only part of the home, using the other part to house priests from local churches. The building now houses both the *Palacio*

Municipal (City Hall) and a silver shop. Open daily. No admission charge. 2 Guadalupe (phone: 22278).

MUSEO GUILLERMO SPRATLING William Spratling, the American who sparked Taxco's modern reawakening, was a great collector of pre-Columbian artifacts, many of which are on display here. Downstairs exhibits are devoted to Spratling's life and the silver-mining industry. There are also fine exhibits on local history, photos of *Semana Santa* (Holy Week) festivities, and samples of silver ore. Closed Sundays and Mondays. Admission charge. Behind the *Iglesia Santa Prisca* (phone: 21660).

MUSEO DEL VIRREINATO (MUSEUM OF COLONIAL ART) Also known as *Casa Humboldt,* this Moorish-style house is notable for the fine details of the doors and windows, as well as its façade of bas-relief plaster. Originally built by Juan de Villanueva in the 18th century, it was renamed in honor of explorer and scientist Baron Alexander von Humboldt, who stayed here in 1803 during his extensive explorations in the Americas. Closed Mondays through Thursdays. Admission charge. 6 Calle Juan Ruiz de Alarcón, two blocks north of the *zócalo* (phone: 25501).

MUSEO DE LA PLATERÍA (SILVER MUSEUM) Prize-winning works by local artisans are displayed here. Open daily. No admission charge. Plazuela de los Artesanos (phone: 21645).

INSTITUTO DE ARTES PLÁSTICAS (MODERN ARTS INSTITUTE) These buildings, which house displays of contemporary art, are a fine example of modern architecture well integrated into a natural setting. It's possible to visit the workshops here. Open daily. No admission charge. On Route 95 next to the cable car stop for the *MonteTaxco* hotel, on the grounds of the former Hacienda del Chorrillo (phone: 23690).

ZOOFARI This wild-animal park is home to more than 100 species of birds and animals from all over the world. The part of the park where the animals roam freely must be visited by car (with windows closed). There is also a wide selection of pets for sale, rides on ponies and dwarf mules, a restaurant, and a handicrafts shop. Open daily. Admission charge. About 20 miles (33 km) east of Taxco on Rte. 95 (no phone).

EXTRA SPECIAL

Las Grutas de Cacahuamilpa (Caverns of Cacahuamilpa) are less than an hour's drive northeast from Taxco, near Route 33 and the Guerrero-Morelos state border. The astounding formations in this vast network of caves are aptly named: Sleeping Lady, the Hunchback, the Asparagus, the Snail, the Dawn, and the Champagne Bottle. They are well lit and have engineered walkways. Concerts occasionally are held in the caves—a real treat. Tours of the caverns are offered daily in English and Spanish. Admission charge (phone: 22279).

Sources and Resources

TOURIST INFORMATION

The *Subsecretaría de Fomento Turístico* (State Tourism Promotion Office; phone: 22279) is helpful; it's housed in Taxco's beautiful *Centro de Convenciones* (Convention Center), which was built on the site of a 450-year-old hacienda near the stone aqueduct at the northern entrance to the city. The office is closed Sundays. There are also information booths open daily at the northern and southern entrances to town, on Route 95 (no phone). Young boys wearing white shirts and brown ties in Plaza Borda lead tours under the auspices of the tourist office and expect a tip in return; $5 should suffice (US currency is preferred).

LOCAL COVERAGE *Casa Domínguez* (3 Calle del Arco) sells magazines from the US as well as *The News* and the *Mexico City Times,* both English-language dailies published in Mexico City.

TELEPHONE The city code for Taxco is 762. *Note:* Mexico's telephone company has embarked on a major expansion project that involves changing telephone numbers in many areas of the country. At press time, all numbers listed in this chapter were correct. However, if you have any difficulties reaching attractions listed here, contact the local tourist office.

CLIMATE AND CLOTHES The temperature hovers in the 60s and 70s F (16–26C) during the day virtually year-round, but dips at night, when a sweater or light coat is needed. Steep, cobblestone streets make comfortable, rubber-soled shoes a must. Dress is casual. Bring your umbrella if you visit during the rainy season, May through October.

GETTING AROUND

BUS Tiny, crowded *burritas,* as the small white buses are called, wend their way through the hilly streets along Avenida John F. Kennedy from the *zócalo* to Route 95. You can pick one up anywhere along the route. *Burritas* run from early in the morning until about 9 PM. The fare is 1 new peso (about 13¢).

CAR RENTAL The only agency in town is *Saturna Renta de Autos* (4 Calle Progreso; phone: 21130). It's also possible to hire a driver-guide; ask at your hotel or at the state tourism office.

TAXI Cabs—spiffy white Volkswagen Beetles with the front passenger seat removed—are readily available. They have meters; fares are reasonable.

SPECIAL EVENTS

Nowhere in the world is there anything quite like Taxco's *Semana Santa* (Holy Week). Beginning on *Domingo de Ramos* (Palm Sunday) with a procession, it builds in momentum; by *Jueves Santo* (Holy Thursday), the festivities involve the entire town. The forecourt of the *Iglesia Santa Prisca* is transformed into the Garden of Gethsemane (the olive grove where Jesus was betrayed), complete with guardian angels, Roman soldiers, and centurions. There is a reenactment of the Washing of the Feet, the Last Supper, the betrayal of Jesus by Judas, and Jesus' imprisonment in Nicholas Temple. At 11 PM, Pontius Pilate reads the sentence and washes his hands. While all this is going on, candlelit processions enter the town from surrounding villages. The crowd, including masked, black-gowned penitents bare to the waist, swells to as many as 3,000 people. Some of the participants carry heavy wooden crosses, others have their arms and backs laced with spiky branches of thorn, and you may see some carrying studded metal thongs with which they flagellate themselves.

On *Viernes Santo* (Good Friday), the Road to Calvary is re-created. A townsman portraying Jesus, bearing a cross, passes through the *zócalo* around noon. The Crucifixion takes place at the *Convent of San Bernardino,* on the Plazuela del Ex-Convento (about four blocks north of the *zócalo*). The man playing Jesus is tied to the cross and taken down later in the afternoon, usually between 3 and 5 PM, depending on the timing of the procession. The observance ends at midnight with a Procession of Silence in which hooded men dressed in black flowing robes parade in total silence. On Sunday morning, church bells ring out to mark the Ceremony of the Resurrection, and there is a final procession at 5 PM. You must make hotel reservations for *Semana Santa* months in advance.

The city's other major annual event is the *Feria Nacional de la Plata* (National Silver Fair), which takes place the last week in November. A cultural festival held in mid-May, *Jornadas Alarconas,* honors one of Mexico's greatest dramatists, Taxco native Juan Ruiz de Alarcón. Other holidays with parades and fireworks include pre-*Cuaresma* (Lent) *Carnaval* week; *Fiesta de la Candelaria* (Candlemas, February 2); *Fiesta del Santo Patrón de los Plateros, Felipe de Jesús* (Feast of St. Philip, the patron saint of silversmiths; February 5); *Fiesta de la Santa Prisca* (Feast of St. Prisca, January 18); *Fiesta de Vera Cruz* (Feast of the True Cross; in March, no fixed date); *Fiesta de la Santa Cruz* (Feast of the Holy Cross, May 3); *Jueves de Corpus Cristi* (Corpus Christi Day; the Thursday following the eighth Sunday after *Easter*); and the *Fiesta de la Virgen de las Mercedes* (Feast of Our Lady of Mercy, September 24). On the Monday following the *Día de los Muertos* (Day of the Dead, November 2), the entire town attends a picnic in Huixteco (northwest of Taxco), where everyone eats *jumiles* (small insects very much like termites, which are surprisingly delicious).

SHOPPING

Taxco is practically swimming in silver shops, but the heaviest concentration is around the *zócalo* and near the north entrance to town on Avenida John F. Kennedy, near the *Posada de la Misión.* Taxco also mines amethyst, tourmaline, nephrite, garnet, topaz, and various kinds of agates and opals.

At the public market, just off the *zócalo,* shawls, huaraches, straw products, leather goods, pottery, woodcarvings, bark paintings, and seed, bean, and nutshell jewelry are sold. Silver is also available in the market, but it is advisable to buy it in the shops. Shops are generally open from 10 AM until 9 PM Mondays through Saturdays; 11 AM until 7 PM Sundays.

Arnoldo's Fine ceremonial masks. The owner is a treasure trove of information about Mexican traditions. 1 Calle Palma (no phone).

Elena de Ballesteros A large, beautifully displayed selection of silver and gold jewelry. On the *zócalo* at 4 Calle Celso Muñoz (phone: 23767).

Galería de Arte Andrés A silver shop run by the eponymous Andrés Mejía Alvarez, a gentleman who produces some of the most innovative and impressive work in town. 28 Av. John F. Kennedy (phone: 23778).

Gracias a Dios Stunning Tachi Castillo jackets with appliqués of brightly colored ribbons. Also, a selection of regional crafts. 3 Bernal (phone: 20086).

Huarachería Los Angeles Carries a wide variety of sandals and other comfortable shoes. Near the *Platería Rancho Alegre,* on Av. John F. Kennedy (no phone).

El Mineral Joyeros Some outstanding work can be found here, including prize-winning pieces and silver and gold jewelry set with semi-precious stones. The shop itself is designed to look like a mine. 1 Plaza Borda (phone: 21878).

Pineda's Taxco Beautiful pieces in enameled silver are on display. 1 Plaza Borda (phone: 23233).

Spratling William Spratling's designs made in silver from traditional molds. Km 17 on Rte. 95 (phone: 20026).

SPORTS

BULLFIGHTS They're often held at a small bullring about 3 miles (5 km) from the city. Ask at the tourist office for specific details.

GOLF The *MonteTaxco* hotel (see *Checking In*) has a nine-hole golf course that's open to the public for a fee.

HORSEBACK RIDING Mounts are available at the *MonteTaxco* hotel (see *Checking In*).

SWIMMING The *Agua Escondida, MonteTaxco, Posada de la Misión, Hacienda del Solar, Posada San Javier,* and *Loma Linda* hotels (see *Checking In* for all) have pools that are open to guests only.

TENNIS The *MonteTaxco* and *Posada de la Misión* hotels (see *Checking In* for both) have tennis courts; all are open to non-guests for a fee.

NIGHTCLUBS AND NIGHTLIFE

Discotheques have sprung up all over Taxco, among them *Donde* (on the *zócalo;* no phone); *El Ascaparate* (1 Plaza Borda; no phone); and *Windows* disco-bar at the *MonteTaxco* hotel (see *Checking In*), which is the liveliest place in town. Mexican musicians often entertain at *Berta's* and the larger *Paco's Bar*. *Berta's* place is on the *zócalo,* next to the *Iglesia Santa Prisca,* and *Paco's* overlooks the lively street scene on the opposite side of the *zócalo.* For something a little out of the ordinary, buy a ticket for Tony Reyes's show at the *MonteTaxco.* Transportation, two drinks, a performance by the *Voladores de Papantla* (Flying Pole Dancers of Papantla), music, and dancing are included in the price. On Saturday nights, the *MonteTaxco* hosts a Mexican fiesta with a show and lavish buffet.

Best in Town

CHECKING IN

Taxco is one of the major destinations on the Mexican tourist trail, so it's a good idea to make reservations well in advance, especially if you intend to visit during festival time. Expect to pay about $100 per night for a double room in an expensive hotel; $50 to $70 in a moderate one; and $35 or less in an inexpensive place. Most Taxco hotel rooms don't have air conditioning (the climate makes it unnecessary), or telephones or TV sets in the rooms. All telephone numbers are in the 762 city code unless otherwise indicated.

We begin with our favorite haven, followed by recommended hotels, listed by price category.

A SPECIAL HAVEN

Hacienda del Solar Just outside town, this 22-unit property, which includes individual or twin cottages, sprawls across a hilltop for about 80 acres. Each of the bungalows (which are in the very expensive category) is named after a female friend or relative of the owner; "Isabel" is especially appealing for its tiled bathroom with plants and a skylight. The decor of all the units is natural brick and white stucco, with vaulted ceilings and arched doorways. All rooms are beautifully decorated with Mexican crafts, including the bathrooms, which are covered with hand-painted tiles. Breakfast is served on the terrace, which overlooks the surrounding mountains; huge open windows in the inn's restaurant, *La Ventana de Taxco,* provide spectacular views of the town (see *Eating Out*). A pool and tennis court are also on the grounds, though at press time the court was in need of renovation. Two miles (3 km) south of town on Rte. 95 (phone: 20323).

MonteTaxco Set on a steep mountainside overlooking Taxco, there are 156 air conditioned, TV-equipped rooms and suites, plus 32 villas (for four to six people) with kitchenettes. A cable car, a heated pool, Swedish massage, steambaths, tennis, golf, horseback riding, a disco, and three restaurants— *Toni's, Piccolo Mondo,* and *Taxqueño* (see *Eating Out* for all)—are available. North of town, off Rte. 95 to the right on a fearsomely steep road; it's possible to take the cable car up from Rte. 95 (phone: 21300; fax: 21428).

Posada de la Misión Decorated in colonial style, this 160-room inn offers comfortable rooms with TV sets, a heated pool, a Jacuzzi, shops, an inviting poolside restaurant and bar, and a tennis court. The Juan O'Gorman mural alongside the pool is an attraction on its own. Rooms and bathrooms are on the small side, except for Nos. 39 and 27, and the 39 exceptionally lovely— and more expensive—suites in the newer section. The rate includes breakfast. 32 Cerro de la Misión, off Av. John F. Kennedy, at the northern entrance to the city (phone: 20063; fax: 22198).

Agua Escondida It may lack the charm of many of the older establishments, but it's on the *zócalo* and rates high with young people. It has a pool, a Ping-Pong table, a restaurant, and parking. Ask for a room in back, away from the *zócalo* discos. 4 Guillermo Spratling (phone: 20726; fax: 21306).

Santa Prisca This old-fashioned downtown inn with two green courtyards and fountains has much charm and dignity. It has 40 comfortably furnished rooms, a bar, parking, and a lovely little restaurant, whose menu changes daily and includes homemade soups and other hearty fare for a low fixed price. Room rates include breakfast. 1 Cenas Obscuras (phone: 20080).

Los Arcos This small gem was a convent back in 1620; it has 25 rooms, including two two-level suites perfect for four people. There's no restaurant. A block from the *zócalo,* at 12 Calle Juan Ruiz de Alarcón (phone: 21836; fax: 23211).

Loma Linda A cheerful, small property with 55 rooms offering modest accommodations, plus a restaurant, a bar, a pool, and parking on the premises (but no trailers or RVs allowed). 52 Av. John F. Kennedy (phone: 20206; fax: 25125).

Posada de los Castillo With only 14 rooms, this hotel is run by a famous local silversmithing family. There's no restaurant. 3 Calle Juan Ruiz de Alarcón (phone: 21396; fax: 22935).

Posada San Javier This small hostelry has 14 rooms and four suites, as well as a nice garden, pool, and parking. There's no restaurant. No credit cards accepted. Just west of the *Palacio Municipal* (city hall). Two entrances: at 1 Estacas and at 4 Rastro (phone: 23177; fax: 22351).

EATING OUT

All the big hotels have restaurants that serve adequate to good food. Expect to pay $25 to $30 for a meal for two at a restaurant categorized as expensive; $20 to $25 at a place described as moderate; and under $20 at an inexpensive spot. Drinks, wine, tax, and tip are not included. Most restaurants below accept MasterCard and Visa, and a few also accept American Express and Diners Club; it's a good idea to call ahead and check. Unless otherwise noted, all restaurants are open daily for lunch and dinner. All telephone numbers are in the 762 city code unless otherwise indicated.

EXPENSIVE

Toni's Excellent prime ribs and lobster, along with a sensational view, make this a popular spot. Reservations advised on weekends. At the *MonteTaxco* hotel, north of town off Rte. 95 (see *Checking In*); it's possible to take the cable car up from Rte. 95 (phone: 21300).

La Ventana de Taxco There's a dramatic view of the city at night (the name means "window on Taxco") at this fine eatery, which features guitar music nightly except Mondays during high season (any festival time and December through *Semana Santa,* or Holy Week). The food, international but featuring Italian specialties, rates among the best in Mexico. Reservations advised on weekends. At *Hacienda del Solar,* Rte. 95, south of town (phone: 20587).

MODERATE

Carrusel A popular place, it has pleasant service, good steaks, and generous portions. Reservations unnecessary. 8 Calle Cuauhtémoc (phone: 21655).

Cielito Lindo Considerable Mexican charm accompanies carefully prepared Mexican dishes and such American favorites as breaded veal cutlet and fried chicken, followed by lemon meringue pie. Reservations unnecessary. On the *zócalo* at 14 Plaza Borda (phone: 20603).

La Pagaduría del Rey Steaks, seafood, and French, Italian, and Mexican fare are served in a colonial setting; the views are extraordinary. Closed Mondays. Reservations advised on weekends. 8 H. Colegio Militar, Cerro de Bermeja, east of the *zócalo* (phone: 23467).

Piccolo Mondo This pleasant spot at the *MonteTaxco* hotel specializes in *parrilladas* (meat grilled on a brazier at the table) and brick-oven pizza. Closed Mondays through Thursdays. Reservations unnecessary. Rte. 95 (phone: 21300).

Sr. Costilla's The name translates as "Mr. Ribs," appropriate for an eatery serving good steaks, ribs, and such. The mood at this branch of the popular

Carlos Anderson chain is lively and casual. Reservations unnecessary. Upstairs at 1 Plaza Borda (phone: 23215).

La Taberna Run by the same family that owns the *Bora Bora* (below), this eatery offers a more extensive menu, featuring shrimp shish kebab, beef Stroganoff, crêpes, salads, and pasta. There are table games, and the TV set airs major sports events from the US. Reservations advised. 8 Benito Juárez (phone: 25226).

Taxqueño Another popular dining spot at the *MonteTaxco,* this one specializes in Mexican dishes. On Fridays and Saturdays, lunch and dinner are accompanied by the lilting tropical sounds of a marimba. Reservations unnecessary. Rte. 95 (phone: 21300).

INEXPENSIVE

Bora Bora No South Seas rhythms and swaying palms here: this is the former site of William Spratling's workshop and store. The lure is good pizza and great people watching. Reservations unnecessary. 4 Callejón de las Delicias (phone: 21721).

La Hacienda This two-level eatery serves breakfast, lunch, and dinner. The Mexican platter reigns supreme here, enhanced by chilled mugs of beer. Reservations unnecessary. 4 Calle Guillermo Spratling and Plaza Borda (phone: 20663).

Tijuana
(pronounced Tee-*hwa*-nah)

Once the sin city of the Western Hemisphere, Tijuana has pretty much cleaned up its act. The wicked spots of old Tijuana—the *Chicago Bar* and the *Molino Rojo,* for instance—are still here, but pharmacies, dentists' offices, and medical centers are replacing the few stores whose shingles still advertise marriages and divorces (legally worthless on the US side of the border), and this most famous of Mexico's border towns now seeks to attract the family trade. Lots of people (especially college students) come here to shop, to bet on the jai alai games or the dog or horse races, to see a bullfight, to enjoy an authentic Mexican meal or alcoholic beverages (the legal drinking age here is 18), or just to send postcards. Some visitors come here simply because it's close, just 15 miles (24 km) south of San Diego. In any case, they come in droves—it's the foreign city most visited by American tourists.

Tijuana is a city of contrasts. Here the so-called Third World meets the so-called First, and the results make an indelible impression. Perhaps most striking is the border fence itself, 10 feet high, topped with barbed wire, and often cut or knocked down in places by would-be immigrants trying (often successfully) to enter the United States illegally. Recently the US border patrol has stemmed the high tide, and the illegals are turning to other areas of the 2,000-mile-long border to enter areas less patrolled.

Tijuana used to intimidate Americans who had heard too many horror stories—many of them apocryphal—about nights spent in jail, venal cops, and corrupt officials. To quell those fears, a state attorney's office for tourist assistance was established back in the 1970s, and sensitivity training is given to all public employees who come in contact with tourists. Interestingly enough, the vast majority of the complaints the office handles comes not from visitors who have run afoul of the law but from customers of dishonest jewelers who have misrepresented the worth of their merchandise. And although the city has figured prominently in recent headlines because of drug-related crime and the 1994 assassination of Luis Donaldo Colosio, the PRI party's presidential candidate, Tijuana is considered very safe for tourists.

To be sure, Tijuana earned the reputation it is now trying so hard to live down. It blossomed during Prohibition, since the city was the nearest place Californians could go to get a legal drink. During World War II, the crowds came for more than just drinks: The San Diego navy base swarmed with lonesome young men, and Tijuana was there waiting to satisfy every desire. It was literally "Sintown" until the sexual revolution more or less put it out of business.

In many respects, Tijuana spent much of its existence as a city without a country, ignored by the rest of Mexico because of its distance from the capital. (One Mexican president even tried to sell Tijuana to the US.) When the *maquilas* (factories that assemble products for foreign companies) started to crop up here in the 1970s, the huddled masses swept in, and Tijuana mushroomed into the fastest-growing city in Mexico. Only in recent years has the city tried to keep up with the demands of its population, launching urban-renewal projects to bring crucial services to the city's residents.

Today, outside investors are placing their bets on Tijuana's future, and progress is being made at breakneck speed. Modern Tijuana is not a *mañana* kind of place. With more than one million residents, it is a prosperous city with a sophisticated citizenry and a growing cultural life. It boasts one of the highest per capita incomes in Mexico, and many Mexicans are moving here from other parts of the country to take advantage of its employment opportunities and relatively high salaries. One of the areas near the border—formerly a bleak landscape of shacks and ramshackle buildings—is slowly being transformed into an impressive suburban neighborhood, known as Río Tijuana, linked by a maze of expressways. (Many dirt roads, wooden fences, and the feel of gritty Old Mexico still do exist uphill from town, however.)

It's easy for visitors to enter Tijuana from the US, since many of Mexico's immigration restrictions don't apply here. No tourist card or automobile permit is needed for a one-day visit to Tijuana; at the border checkpoint, visitors simply are waved through. But anyone planning to stay more than 72 hours, or heading into Mexico's interior, will need a tourist card and car permit, and customs laws and duties do apply in most cases when returning to the US. (See GETTING READY TO GO for details.)

Some people who come to Tijuana drive their own cars. Since US auto insurance policies are not valid in Mexico, it is advisable to get Mexican car insurance (again, see GETTING READY TO GO). Travelers renting automobiles also should be aware that many US car rental companies prohibit driving cars across the Mexican border. If you don't want to bring your car into Mexico, park just north of the international line, and either take a bus from the immigration building to Tijuana or walk across the border and then walk or take a taxi downtown. Doing so will prevent two problems: Parking spaces normally are in short supply in Tijuana, and, while driving into Mexico is easy enough, it often takes an hour or more to cross back into California because of long lines.

Despite these minor inconveniences, Tijuana—with its myriad shops, fine restaurants, and lively nightlife set against a backdrop of poverty and progress, seediness and sophistication—is worth exploring. Set right on the edge of the US but retaining its own distinctive identity, Tijuana is at once familiar and foreign, and always intriguing.

Tijuana At-a-Glance

SEEING THE CITY

From the hill leading to the *Casa de la Cultura* (House of Culture) in the Altamira district, Tijuana old and new can be seen crowding up to the border and extending to the sea—an unforgettable vista of Mexico meeting the US.

SPECIAL PLACES

SHOPPING DISTRICT The heart of the city is quite attractive, and the stores are tempting enough to lure thousands across the border every week. Once run-down and seedy, downtown Tijuana's main street, Avenida Revolución, is now a pleasant shopping boulevard. For more information, see *Shopping*.

BOULEVARD AGUA CALIENTE This southern extension of Avenida Revolución boasts some of the better hotels and good restaurants, as well as the racetrack and the country club.

PASEO DE LOS HÉROES One of Tijuana's major thoroughfares passes through the Río Tijuana section of the city, near the border. It's especially notable for its statuary: a larger-than-life replica of the beloved Aztec emperor Cuauhtémoc; Abraham Lincoln holding a broken chain (a gift from former US president Ronald Reagan to Mexico); and a modern sculpture in front of the *Centro Cultural* that commemorates the making of the canal from the Río Tijuana.

CENTRO CULTURAL (CULTURAL CENTER) This ultramodern complex houses a museum; a theater that stages dramatic presentations (in Spanish) by writers such as Genet, Albee, and even Aristophanes; a planetarium; a gigantic Omnimax theater; a restaurant; and some good shops. Combined, they have the wherewithal to keep visitors entertained for the better part of a day. Exhibits on the country's history and art are in English and Spanish; a few English-language volumes about Mexico and translations of books by Mexican authors are for sale. Open daily. There are separate admission charges for the complex and the Omnimax theater. Paseo de los Héroes and Av. Mina (phone: 841111).

PLAZA SANTA CECELIA The gateway to the honky-tonk part of town, at the opposite end of Avenida Revolución from the *Palacio Frontón* (Jai Alai Building), this little pocket features mariachis for hire in the evenings.

MEXITLÁN Covering one square block, this cultural park features precise scale-model replicas of such points of interest as Mexico City's Paseo de la Reforma, *Palacio de Bellas Artes* (Palace of Fine Arts), and the *Basílica de la Virgen de Guadalupe* (Shrine of the Virgin of Guadalupe); the archaeological sites of *Palenque, Teotihuacán,* and *Chichén Itzá;* and the Plaza Tapatía in Guadalajara. There's also a handicrafts shop. Closed Mondays. No admission charge for children under nine. Av. Ocampo between Calles 2 and 3 (phone: 384101).

"LA ZONA" Sometimes called the Zona Norte (North Zone), this is Tijuana's infamous red-light district. Many of the bars of yore are still here, sleazier than ever, but they don't do much tourist business these days; the crowd is local and rough. If you must visit, start at the *Molino Rojo* bar. Calle Coahuila near Av. de la Constitución.

RÍO TIJUANA (TIJUANA RIVER) Along the banks of the river, a new and attractive Tijuana is slowly developing into an exclusive residential and commercial district. Outstanding evidence of the renaissance includes the striking *Centro Cultural* (see above); the large, modern *Plaza Río Tijuana* shopping center next door; and the state government building.

PARQUE MORELOS (MORELOS PARK) Popular with locals as well as visitors, this is a delightful spot for a picnic or just to relax under the trees. There's a lake and a small archaeological site. On the road to Tecate, 20 minutes from downtown.

LAS PLAYAS DE TIJUANA (TIJUANA BEACH) This pleasant seaside community is the home of the locally famous bullring, two *charro* (rodeo) rings, a few handicraft shops, and seafood restaurants that are open only when there's a bullfight or *charreada* (traditional Mexican rodeo). About 5 miles (8 km) from the border.

EXTRA SPECIAL

The fast-growing resort of Playa Rosarito, 18 miles (29 km) south of Tijuana, is the top choice of the city's residents for a day's getaway. The area is also gaining a name for the high-quality home furnishings that are made and sold here. Several leading interior design shops are located here; exemplary is *Interiores del Río* (2500 Av. Juárez; phone: 661-21651), where custom furniture can be ordered. The wonderful little fish restaurants of Rosarito and Puerto Nuevo (known as "the Lobster Village") also deserve a visit. The modern *Quinta Terranova* resort (phone: 661-21648/9) and the landmark *Rosarito Beach* hotel (phone: 661-20144 or 661-21126; 800-343-8582) are good bets.

Another alternative is to continue 18 miles (29 km) south of Rosarito to the winsome cliffside *La Fonda* hotel (write to PO Box 430268, San Ysidro, CA 92073; phone: 66-287352/3), with its excellent Mexican terrace restaurant and fine beach below, or to the *New Port Baja* resort hotel (Km 45 of Rte. 1; phone: 661-41188; 800-582-1018; fax: 661-41174). Heading south from Tijuana, follow the toll road for fine beach views; the inland toll-free road for rural vistas.

Sources and Resources

TOURIST INFORMATION

The main tourist information offices are at two downtown locations (Av. Revolución, between Calles 3 and 4, and at the corner of Av. Revolución and Calle Primera; no phone for either). Small information booths are located at the border crossings at Puerta México (phone: 831405) and Mesa de Otai (no phone). The main branch of the *Secretaría de Turismo del Estado de Baja California* (Baja California State Tourism Secretariat), on the third floor of the *Plaza Patria Building* (Blvd. Díaz Ordaz and Las Américas; phone: 819492/3/4), provides general information on Tijuana and its environs. The secretariat also runs a tourist assistance office that handles complaints and helps visitors with a variety of problems (Calle 1 and Av. Revolución; phone: 880555). The *Cámara Nacional de Comercio Servicios y Turismo* (Chamber of Commerce; Avs. Revolución and México; phone: 858472) handles consumer complaints and offers a coupon booklet (also available at tourist information booths). The *Chamber of Commerce* and the tourist office in the *Plaza Patria Building* are closed weekends; all other offices and booths are open daily.

LOCAL COVERAGE Maps of the town and free brochures about Tijuana's attractions are available at the tourist office in the *Plaza Patria Building*.

TELEPHONE The city code for Tijuana is 66. *Note:* Mexico's telephone company has embarked on a major expansion project that involves changing telephone numbers in many areas of the country. At press time, all numbers listed in this chapter were correct. However, if you have any difficulties reaching attractions listed here, contact the local tourist office.

CLIMATE AND CLOTHES The weather in Tijuana is much like that in southern California, although sometimes more overcast and humid. It can be very hot in summer. Dress is casual yet conservative; going braless, shirtless, or shoeless, or even wearing short shorts, will invite unwelcome attention.

GETTING AROUND

US currency is accepted most places in Tijuana, including for bus, *colectivo* (jitney), or taxi fares. All fares quoted in this section are in US currency rather than pesos.

BUS Buses are inexpensive and convenient in Tijuana. To find out where to pick up the bus you need, ask at the tourist information booth downtown on the corner of Avenida Revolución and Calle Madero. The green and cream buses that go to the racetrack are marked "5 y 10," "Los Pinos," and "La Presa." The main terminal is on Avenida de la Constitución, between Calles 5 and 6. The cost of a ride is 25¢. *Mexicoach* buses (phone: 619-232-5040 in the US) make numerous trips daily from Avenida Revolución between Calles 6 and 7 direct to the border for $1 each way.

CAR RENTAL While handy if you plan to do any extensive exploring, a car is not essential if you are staying downtown. Most major international firms are represented downtown and at the airport.

COLECTIVO (JITNEY) Blue and white (or maroon and black, or yellow and black, depending on the route) *colectivos* pack in as many passengers as they can and run along the main boulevards. They charge 25¢ per head during the day, 40¢ at night. Yellow jitneys charge $2 per person to go from the Mexican side of the border to downtown Tijuana; a full load of five passengers is needed. Note: To the possible confusion of tourists, the locals often call these vehicles "taxis"—the same as the private-ride vehicles described below.

TAXI Rates are sometimes reasonable, sometimes not, and cabs are plentiful. You'll find them at the border, along Avenida Revolución, at stands by the *Palacio Frontón* (Jai Alai Building), and at the hotels. Ask the fare at the outset; try to bargain if it seems too high ($8 seems to be the going rate for in-town destinations).

TOURS *Baja California Tours* (phone: 619-454-7166 in the US) offers excursions to Tijuana that depart daily from San Diego every hour on the hour from 9 AM to 3 PM. The package includes shopping, sightseeing, and a packet of discount coupons.

SPECIAL EVENTS

The *Feria Tijuana* (Tijuana Fair), held for two weeks in late August or early September, is a food fair with many carnival touches added. *Día de la Independencia* (Independence Day; September 16) is celebrated with a big bash that gets started September 15 and attracts huge crowds.

SHOPPING

Reputable stores have replaced many of the tacky, honky-tonk joints that once lined Avenida Revolución, and European fashions, crystal, porcelain, perfumes, and Mexican handicrafts, as well as liquor, are now readily available.

So far (and for the foreseeable future), the passage of the North American Free Trade Agreement has not changed Tijuana's duty-free status. Savings on some items can be 40% or more, but serious buyers should arrive knowing what these items cost at home. Also beware of goods bearing phony designer labels such as Gucci. When it comes to purchasing imports, forget about bargaining: The law says price stickers must be on all goods, and a storekeeper offering a discount can be fined. Bargaining, on the other hand, is very much in order for anything made in Mexico, and the Generalized System of Preferences (GSP) waives duty on almost everything made in developing countries (see GETTING READY TO GO). On all other goods—such as imports from Switzerland and France—the duty-free limit is $400.

In Tijuana, the most pleasant shopping is often in the large ultramodern shopping centers. *Plaza Río Tijuana* is next door to the *Centro Cultural*. Across the street, *Plaza Fiesta* is filled with open-air cafés offering food from around the globe. Its other attraction is *Plaza del Zapato* (Shoe Square), with about 20 shoe stores. *Pueblo Amigo* (Av. Centenario), a colonial-style "village," is filled with shops, restaurants, and discos. Among the newest and largest of the shopping centers are *Viva Tijuana* (about 220 yards from the border, at 8800 Vía Juventud Ote.) and *Plaza Carousel* (1506 Blvd. Díaz Ordaz).

Note that dollars are used as often as pesos in Tijuana. Stores generally are open from 10 AM to 7 PM; some close on Sundays.

Noteworthy stores in Tijuana include the following:

Antón's A wide variety of children's *charrería* (Mexican riding gear), hats, and decorative items. Av. Revolución between Calles 3 and 4 (phone: 853585).

Avick Fifth Avenue This boot emporium has an inventory of 1,500 pairs, some made of exotic lizard, snake, or eel skin. 8207 Av. Revolución (phone: 852038). There's a branch with a different name but the same merchandise: *Exótica,* at 807 Av. Revolución (phone: 834208).

Azteca Pretty, but pricey, gold jewelry. 707 Av. Revolución (phone: 854318).

Castillo A saddle shop, it also carries some regional Mexican clothing. 2044 Av. Díaz Mirón (phone: 852895).

Galerías Vitrales Tiffany-style lamps and stained glass windows produced in their own factory, plus blown-glass items. At the *Arts and Crafts Market,* 8373 Calle Juárez (phone: 855333 or 881860).

Hand Art Table and bed linen, blouses, and handkerchiefs from Mexico, Europe, and Asia. 967 Av. Revolución (phone: 852642).

La Herradura de Oro A good place for *charrería* and western and English equestrian equipment. Paseo de los Héroes, in the *Plaza del Zapato* (phone: 842252).

Marco The specialties here are heavy Mexican doors and fireplaces. The carved wood doors, some with leaded or stained glass insets, are lovely. 1422 Av. Revolución (phone: 853551).

Maxim Imported clothing, porcelain, crystal, perfume, linen, and Mexican handicrafts. 605 Av. Revolución (phone: 880194).

Mosaicos Lomelí Lovely hand-painted Mexican and Spanish decorative tiles. 11330 Blvd. Agua Caliente (phone: 862248).

Ralph Lauren/Polo Lauren's designs are priced below the going rate in the States. Calles 7 and Madero, behind the *Palacio Frontón* (phone: 851389).

Sara's London Shop This landmark perfumery, which set up shop in 1929, has the finest French, Italian, Spanish, US, Israeli, and Swiss scents for less cents than you pay in the US. Av. Revolución and Calle 3 (phone: 850622).

SPORTS

BULLFIGHTS The regular season runs from May through September, with corridas scheduled most Sunday afternoons at one of Tijuana's two bullrings. The best matadors appear at the large *Plaza Monumental* (by the sea, at 100 Blvd. Agua Caliente; phone: 801808); the smaller *Toreo de Tijuana* (Las Playas de Tijuana; phone: 861510) hosts the lesser fights. Purchase tickets at the entrance to the *Sonia Arcade* beside *Caesar's* hotel (Av. Revolución and Calle 5) or at the bullring gates.

CHARREADAS (RODEOS) These popular events are held occasionally on Sundays at several rings, including *Misión del Sol* and *Cortijo San José,* both in Las Playas de Tijuana. The tourist information booths have details.

DOG RACES Greyhounds run for the money at *Hipódromo Agua Caliente* (Blvd. Agua Caliente; phone: 817747), with races nightly at 7:45 PM and 11:30 PM, plus Saturdays and Sundays from 2 PM until 5 PM. One of Tijuana's top attractions, the track has a restaurant and bar on the premises. There's no admission charge.

GOLF The challenging 18-hole course at the *Club Campestre* (Country Club; Blvd. Agua Caliente, near the racetrack; phone: 817855 or 817861) is a favorite with duffers and champions alike. Both the club and the restaurant are open to the public. Reserve at least a week ahead, and ask about special packages.

HORSE RACES The *Hipódromo Agua Caliente* (see *Dog Races*) features live races broadcast daily via satellite from the US. Admission (redeemable for betting vouchers) is charged only at the *Turf Club* in the track.

JAI ALAI The *Palacio Frontón* (Jai Alai Building; Av. Revolución between Calles 7 and 8; phone: 852524; 619-231-1910 in the US) is the best in Mexico. The game is exciting and fast (players propel balls at more than 160 miles per hour); dollar bets are welcome; and the language is English. The popular restaurant affords diners a view of the goings-on. The action starts Thursday nights at 8 PM. The admission charge, which usually is waived after 11 PM, is redeemable for betting vouchers.

TENNIS The *Gran Hotel Tijuana* hotel (see *Checking In*) has two lighted courts.

NIGHTCLUBS AND NIGHTLIFE

Tijuana is at its best after dark, especially when the dogs race and the jai alai matches are on. Most discos are open Thursday through Sunday nights, with *Baby Rock* (across from the *Lucerna* hotel—see *Checking In;* phone: 342404) the hands-down favorite, attracting hundreds of people a night on weekends (mostly Mexicans on Thursdays and Sundays, Americans on Fridays and Saturdays). Also popular are *Rodeo de Medianoche* (formerly *The News;* phone: 824967) and *Bananas Ranas* (phone: 824969), both at the *Pueblo Amigo* shopping center (Av. Centenario); and a recent addition, *Yuppies Sports Café* (Paseo de los Héroes and Av. Diego Rivera; phone: 342141 or 342324), in Río Tijuana. The *Lucerna* hotel (see *Checking In*) has a video bar and a small dance floor. Among several lively spots downtown on Avenida Revolución are *Club A* (corner of Calle 4) and *Tía Juana Tilly's* (see *Eating Out*). A branch of the *Hard Rock Café* operates on part of the site of the former *Bol Corona* bar (520 Av. Revolución; phone: 852513); also here is the small *Bol Corona* disco (no phone).

Best in Town

CHECKING IN

There are several very good hotels in Tijuana, with one of the latest additions a luxury 250-room *Camino Real,* scheduled to open as we went to press (for more information, call 800-7-CAMINO). Those listed as moderate charge about $50 to $80 per night for a double room; at an inexpensive hotel, expect to pay less than $45. All rooms have air conditioning, TV sets, and telephones unless otherwise noted. All telephone numbers are in the 66 city code unless otherwise indicated.

MODERATE

Gran Hotel Tijuana This property's 32-story tower dominates Tijuana's skyline. In addition to 422 comfortable rooms and suites, each with a king-size bed, it offers a sophisticated lobby bar, two restaurants (one open around the clock), 24-hour room service, two lighted tennis courts, a Jacuzzi, an outdoor pool, a gym, and a spa. Conveniently located near the racetrack and country club, at 4500 Blvd. Agua Caliente (phone: 817000; 800-472-6385; fax: 817016).

Lucerna This striking structure has 168 rooms, three suites, a fine restaurant (*Rivoli;* see *Eating Out*), a disco, a bar, and a smashing pool. Paseo de los Héroes at Rodríguez (phone: 342000; 800-LUCERNA; fax: 342400).

Plaza las Glorias Formerly the *Royal Inn,* the *Baja Inn,* the *Calinda, El Presidente,* and most recently the *Paraíso Radisson,* this pleasant chameleon has 197 rooms, three suites, a pool, a Jacuzzi, a restaurant, and a bar. Golf packages allow guests access to the facilities at the nearby country club. Near the racetrack, at 1 Blvd. Agua Caliente (phone: 817200; 800-342-AMIGO; fax: 863639).

INEXPENSIVE

Caesar's This spruced up 1930s landmark has 75 rooms and a collection of shops, but no restaurant. In the very heart of things, at Av. Revolución and Calle 5 (phone: 851666; fax: 853492).

Country Club Baja Inn A favorite with golfers and tennis enthusiasts because of its proximity to the local country club, this hotel (formerly the *Country Club*

Best Western) is casual and comfortable, with a pool and a restaurant. The 100 rooms are on the small side; the 20 suites and 11 master suites are considerably larger, and the best of the lot have a view of either the golf course or the racetrack. 1 Tapachula (phone: 817733; fax: 817066).

La Sierra Not elegant, but adequate, it has 60 rooms, a pool, a good restaurant (*La Fonda Roberto;* see *Eating Out*), and a sushi bar. 356 Av. 16 de Septiembre (phone: 861601; fax: 861577).

Motel Golf Rates at this clean, comfortable 40-room motel leave you plenty of money for betting on jai alai. There's a pool and the staff is most helpful, but there's no restaurant. 11420 Blvd. Agua Caliente, across from the *Plaza las Glorias* hotel (phone: 862018 or 862021; fax: 862876).

EATING OUT

Tijuana claims its great contribution to gastronomy is the Caesar salad, said to have been prepared first at the *Caesar's* hotel restaurant (an old standby that, alas, has closed, though the hotel remains open). While there is a fair spectrum of ethnic cooking in Tijuana, by far the best dishes are the Mexican specialties. People drive here from all over California to enjoy *carnitas* (cubes of roast pork) and Tecate beer. We consider a restaurant charging $50 or more for dinner for two expensive; $35 to $45, moderate; and $30 or less, inexpensive. Drinks, wine, tax, and tips are extra. Most restaurants below accept MasterCard and Visa, and a few also accept American Express and Diners Club; it's a good idea to call ahead and check. Unless otherwise noted, all restaurants are open daily for lunch and dinner. All telephone numbers are in the 66 city code unless otherwise indicated.

EXPENSIVE

Manhattan International haute cuisine has made its mark here, with lobster ravioli and smoked salmon just a few of the house favorites. Reservations advised. 19 Av. Hipódromo, behind the Hipódromo Agua Caliente; phone: 866061)

Boccaccio's Nueva Mariana A wide variety of international dishes fill the menu at this old favorite. When it's available, try the abalone prepared in a garlic or oyster sauce, or in black butter; another good bet is the grilled lobster. Reservations advised. 2500 Blvd. Agua Caliente, across from the *Gran Hotel Tijuana* (phone: 862266).

Rivoli The food and decor are strictly French; dishes include filet of sole prepared in white wine. Closed for lunch. Reservations advised. In the *Lucerna* hotel, at Paseo de los Héroes and Rodríguez (phone: 342000).

MODERATE

La Fonda Roberto Unusual regional specialties, such as beef tongue in *pipián* (a pumpkin seed–based sauce) and beef in *chipotle* chili sauce, are the dishes to try here. Reservations advised. In *La Sierra* hotel, 356 Av. 16 de Septiembre (phone: 864687).

Guadalajara Grill The Maya dish *cochinita pibil* (stuffed roasted pig with a special blend of spices) is the draw here, along with *ariero* (filet of beef prepared on a small hibachi with tomato, onions, and chilies) and strawberry margaritas. Reservations unnecessary. 19 Av. Diego Rivera and Paseo de los Héroes (phone: 343087).

La Leña The steaks and seafood are excellent at this attractive spot. Try *puños* ("fists"), made from marinated beef mixed with ham, pork, green onions, and cheese, or *gaonera* (meat pounded thin and stuffed with beans, guacamole, or cheese). Reservations unnecessary. 4560 Blvd. Agua Caliente (phone: 862920).

Tía Juana Tilly's Reason enough to cross the border, it has an international menu, a lively Mexican ambience, and good drinks. No reservations (expect to wait in line on weekends). 701 Av. Revolución, next to the *Palacio Frontón* (phone: 857833).

INEXPENSIVE

Birriería Guanajuato It's worth the trip up into the hills just for the house specialties—*cabrito* (roast kid), *gorditas* (melted cheese wrapped in cornmeal), and *birria* (a meat dish in a spicy sauce). Open from 8 AM to 8 PM. No reservations. No credit cards accepted. 102 Av. Abraham González (phone: 377070).

Chiki Jai Enjoy authentic Basque fare at this tiny, classic place (the name means "small party"). Closed Wednesdays. Reservations advised. No credit cards accepted. 1050 Av. Revolución and Calle 7, next to the *Palacio Frontón* (phone: 854955).

La Costa Seafood is the specialty at this down-home favorite; the *siete mares* (seven seas) soup is a meal in itself. Reservations unnecessary. Calle 7 between Avs. Revolución and Constitución (phone: 858494).

Giuseppi's Good pizza is served at this typical trattoria. No reservations. No credit cards accepted. Several locations, including 2600 Blvd. Agua Caliente (phone: 841018).

Margarita's Village The waiters here put on a show as patrons sample the Mexican food and 14 varieties of margaritas. Music for dancing completes the picture, making for a party atmosphere. Closed for dinner on Mondays and Tuesdays. No reservations. No credit cards accepted. At three locations: Av. Revolución and Calle 3 (phone: 857362); Av. Revolución between Calles 6 and 7 (phone: 854579); and the *Viva Tijuana* shopping center (phone: 828658).

Veracruz

(pronounced Ve-ra-*crooz*)

Fun-loving Veracruz, the first city founded by the Spanish in Mexico, is the country's largest international seaport. Few of its 800,000 residents depend on tourism for their livelihood, and while that means it lacks some of the more sophisticated tourist facilities of dyed-in-the-wool resorts, the atmosphere is comparatively free of the relentless consumerism associated with areas totally dependent on the tourist trade. Visiting Veracruz is a pleasant experience, but it isn't for those looking for posh hotels, unlimited fine restaurants, white beaches, and a never-ending nightlife.

Veracruz and its people are the product of a blend of the native Totonac, Spanish, Caribbean, and African cultures. About a quarter of a million African slaves were imported to and through this port between 1540 and 1640, and many were put to work in the surrounding sugarcane and rice fields. The vast majority of the slaves eventually married mestizos (people of Spanish and native blood) or Spaniards.

The Caribbean and African influence in Veracruz is most evident in the architecture and the music. The Spanish-style buildings, constructed of stucco or wood with long overhanging balconies and tile roofs, are painted in mellow Caribbean colors—pale pink, ocher, salmon, and sky blue. Instead of the mariachi bands characteristic of most of Mexico, local musicians play the marimba (an instrument similar to the xylophone), and strolling performers carry harps and stringed instruments. Their music can be languid or very lively, and is often filled with jokes and double entendres.

Veracruzanos call themselves *jarochos,* which means "shockingly rude." They are renowned throughout Mexico for their colorful and at times outrageously foul language: *Jarochos* have elevated profanity to an art form. They are equally famous for their refusal to take life too seriously and for their gracious hospitality. Indeed, their tolerance of outsiders is remarkable, considering the city's history of invasion by foreign powers. In 1519, Spanish conquistador Hernán Cortés landed about 20 miles north of Veracruz, planted a cross on shore, and christened the area *La Villa Rica de la Vera Cruz* (the Rich Village of the True Cross). From Veracruz, Cortés set out inland toward what is today Mexico City, conquering and plundering along the way. At the end of the Mexican War of Independence from Spain (1821), Spanish troops stationed in the *Castillo de San Juan de Ulúa* bombarded the town severely, practically reducing it to dust; 17 years later, the French attacked both the town and the fortress. During the Mexican-American War in 1847, American troops landed in Veracruz, subdued the resistance they encountered, and marched on to Mexico City. The French entered the city again in 1860, this time to prepare the way for Maximilian and Carlota. Finally, in 1914, the US Navy bombarded the port.

The town you see today was built by the Spanish and features the ubiquitous main plaza, or *zócalo,* lined with sidewalk cafés. Here, more than in any other city in Mexico, social life revolves around such cafés. Drinking *café con leche* (strong black coffee mixed with hot milk), talking, playing dominoes, and watching people go by are the favored pastimes. Street musicians stroll through the cafés in the evenings, and there are often band concerts in the plaza. The only slack hours are from 2 to 4 in the afternoon—lunch and siesta time. During these hours, visitors are well advised to join the rest of the population and eat or sleep. During the rest of the day, you can stroll, shop, swim and sun at nearby beaches, visit archaeological sites, and explore this bustling, Caribbean-influenced Mexican city.

Veracruz At-a-Glance

SEEING THE CITY

The best places from which to see Veracruz are from the glass-enclosed elevator at the *Emporio* hotel (four blocks east of the plaza on the *malecón,* or harborside walkway; phone: 316024); from the café at the *Howard Johnson Veracruz* hotel (also on the *malecón;* see *Checking In*); and from the terrace of the *Mocambo* hotel (see *Checking In*), 5 miles (8 km) south of town, overlooking Playa Mocambo, the area's best beach.

SPECIAL PLACES

PLAZA DE LA CONSTITUCIÓN Also known as the Plaza de Armas, this is the social center of the city. It was designed by the Spanish in the 16th century, and today it is attractively landscaped with tall palms, tropical flowers, and colored lights at night. During the day, people congregate here and at the surrounding sidewalk cafés while vendors hawk everything from chewing gum to gaudy crucifixes. Most nights strolling performers compete for attention, while on Tuesday and Thursday evenings outdoor band concerts hold sway. (In July and August and at *Christmas* and *Easter,* folkloric dance shows are staged daily.) The *Palacio Municipal* (City Hall) flanks the east side of the plaza, and hotels line the north and west sides. Also on the plaza is the 17th-century *La Parroquia* (The Parish Church), constructed on the site of an earlier church erected by the Spanish. Bordered by Avenidas Independencia and Zaragoza, and Calles Zamora and Lerdo.

MALECÓN This walkway along the harbor is a pleasant place for strolling and shopping. Three blocks northeast of the Plaza de la Constitución.

MUSEO HISTÓRICO DE LA REVOLUCIÓN VENUSTIANO CARRANZA Housed in a distinctive yellow and white building topped by a lighthouse, this museum pays homage to the life and times of Venustiano Carranza, who became President of Mexico in 1915. Closed Mondays. No admission charge. Calles Serdán and Xicoténcatl at the *malecón* (phone: 321864).

PLAYA MOCAMBO This is, hands down, the biggest, least crowded, and best beach in Veracruz. It's located 5 miles (8 km) south of town on the beach highway; take the bus marked *Costa Verde–Boca del Río* on Avenida Zaragoza at Calle Serdán downtown, or drive east along Boulevard Avila Camacho.

CASTILLO DE SAN JUAN DE ULÚA Now little more than a forbidding shell, this large island fortress is Veracruz's prime historical landmark. The Spanish built the fort in the late 16th century to defend the port from pirates; it was later used as a prison for criminals and political "undesirables," some of whom were thrust into dungeon holes that were half-flooded at high tide. Noted for its massive walls and ramparts, the *castillo* today houses a small historical and archaeological museum. Access is via the causeway that links the island to the city; take the bus marked *San Juan de Ulúa* at the *malecón* and Avenida Landero y Coss. Closed Mondays. Admission charge. In the harbor on Gallega Reef (phone: 385151). At press time, the fortress was closed for remodeling and due to reopen between March and September 1997; check with the tourist office for further information.

ENVIRONS

LA ANTIGUA This town is the spot where Cortés first planted a cross on the shore in 1519. The settlement was moved to "modern" Veracruz in 1600, but the remains of Cortés's house still stand on the main street, as does the *Capilla del Santo Culto del Buen Viaje* (Chapel of the Holy Rite for a Good Voyage) believed to be the first Christian chapel in the Western Hemisphere. Route 180, 35 miles (56 km) north of Veracruz.

MANDINGA Here you'll find a cluster of fishing shacks between two lagoons, one fished for shrimp, the other for oysters. Perch and bass are also good here. You can rent boats to fish, or feast in one of the several open-air restaurants that serve fresh seafood. Day and night, groups play traditional Veracruz music. Route 180, 11 miles (18 km) south of the village of Boca del Río (see *Fishing,* below), or a total of 18 miles (29 km) south of Veracruz.

CATEMACO This small fishing village, known for its native whitefish, has a 10-mile-long lake and three lovely waterfalls; rental boats and lodgings are available. Take a boat tour of the lake, which includes El Tegal grotto, where the Virgin of Catemaco is said to have appeared to a fisherman in 1710, and two islands, Isla de Agaltepec and Isla de los Changos, both of which are populated with monkeys (*chango* is a Mexican Spanish word for "monkey"). The state university carries out simian studies on the islands. Negotiate the details with any of the boat owners at the main dock. Located 75 miles (120 km) south of Veracruz on Rte. 180.

EXTRA SPECIAL

A visit to the archaeological zone of *El Tajín* is a must for anyone staying in Veracruz. While not as elaborate as ruins found in the Yucatán, the site of the ancient sacred city of the Totonac is still quite impressive. The *Pyramid of the Niches,* so named because its 365 niches mark the days of the year, is the highlight; the 150-acre area includes six restored temples, several pyramids, and ball courts as well. The site, about 135 miles (216 km) northwest of Veracruz on Route 180, is open daily; there's no admission charge on Sundays. *Autobuses de Oriente (ADO;* phone: 350783) offers a four-and-a-half-hour trip from Veracruz to *El Tajín.* Buses leave daily at 9 AM and 2:30 PM from the *ADO* station (1698 Díaz Mirón). For additional details on the site, see *Mexico's Magnificent Archaeological Heritage* in DIVERSIONS. For overnight trips, see the *Mexico City to Tampico and Veracruz* route in DIRECTIONS.

Cempoala (also spelled Zempoala), only about 30 miles (48 km) north of Veracruz on Route 180, along the coast, is the site of the well-preserved remains of the last capital of the Totonacan civilization. It was here that Cortés and Totonac leaders forged the alliance that eventually defeated the Aztec nation. The site is closed Mondays; admission charge. For additional information on *El Tajín* and *Cempoala,* contact the tourist office in Veracruz (see *Tourist Information*).

The discovery of another pre-Hispanic coastal city, thought to have been a flourishing political, commercial, and agricultural center more than 1,500 years ago, was announced in early 1994. Located about 60 miles (96 km) northwest of Veracruz and named for the nearby village of El Pital, the site comprises some 40 square miles and has more than 100 earth and stone structures, most of which currently are covered by dirt and dense vegetation. The area is not expected to be open to the public until at least 2015.

Sources and Resources

TOURIST INFORMATION

The *Dirección de Turismo Municipal* (City Tourist Office, in the *Palacio Municipal* on the Plaza de la Constitución; phone: 321999) is best for information, maps, and brochures. It's open daily.

TELEPHONE The city code for Veracruz is 29. *Note:* Mexico's telephone company has embarked on a major expansion project that involves changing telephone numbers in many areas of the country. At press time, all numbers listed in this chapter were correct. However, if you have any difficulties reaching attractions listed here, contact the local tourist office.

CLIMATE AND CLOTHES Veracruz is hot all year (the average high is 95F/35C) and humid in summer, the rainy season. August through December is the season of the *nortes,* storms from the north that bring high winds, more rain, and a dramatic drop in temperature (the average low is 65F/18C). The city enjoys its best weather from January through March. Dress is casual, although somewhat less so than at the Pacific Coast resorts; bathing suits are worn only at the beach.

GETTING AROUND

BUS The most scenic bus route is that designated *Mocambo–Boca del Río*. Two bus companies, *Autobuses del Oriente (ADO;* phone: 350783) and *Autobuses Unidos (AU;* phone: 322376), serve the city and the surrounding area. The fare within the city ranges from 1 to 2 pesos (approximately 13¢ to 26¢), depending on the destination.

CAR RENTAL *Avis* (phone: 326032), *Budget* (phone: 312139), *Dollar* (phone: 314535), *Hertz* (phone: 324021), and *National* (phone: 311756) have agencies in town and at the airport. Keep in mind that most agencies in Veracruz charge about 32¢ a mile on top of the basic rental fee.

TAXI You can pick up a cab on the *zócalo* or have your hotel call one for you. The fares are reasonable, and sightseeing by cab is less expensive than taking a city tour.

TOURS A great way to see the city is via the open-air, rubber-wheeled trolleys that leave from in front of the train station (on Av. Montesinos) every half hour between 9 AM and 10 PM daily (weather permitting). Tours last about an hour. Another excursionary option is a boat ride around the harbor on *La Orca*. It includes Isla Verde (a flora and fauna preserve) and Isla Sacrificios, where the main lighthouse stands. The half-hour trip is inexpensive; boats leave from the dock across the *malecón* from the *Emporio* hotel.

SPECIAL EVENTS

Carnaval is a full-scale blowout held just before *Cuaresma* (Lent). However, because of weather considerations—February in Veracruz is known for its cold, windy climate—local officials are discussing changing the date of the festivities; for current details, check with the tourist office. The festival features music, dancing in the streets, paraders in costume, fireworks, and all kinds of fervent and uninhibited frivolity. Make hotel reservations a few months in advance through a travel agent to ensure that your reservation has been accepted and will be honored.

SHOPPING

Follow Avenida 5 de Mayo east to Cortés, turn right, and go one block to reach the town's lively market, where you can buy anything from funeral wreaths to live iguanas. *Guayaberas Cab* (233 Av. Zaragoza, between Arista and Serdán; phone: 328427) carries a nice selection of *guayaberas,* the pleated and embroidered shirts that have become almost a uniform for men in the tropics and are considered suitable for formal occasions. *El Mayab* (Av. Zaragoza, just behind the *Palacio Municipal;* phone: 321435) and *El Campechano* (Mario Molina, between Independencia and Av.

Zaragoza; no phone) have good-quality Panama hats, straw baskets, and the like. *Silvett* (96 Av. Zaragoza; phone: 313060) has a fairly extensive selection of silver, handicrafts, and leather items. Hand-rolled cigars can be bought at *Puros La Prueba* cigar factory (500 Calle Miguel Lerdo; phone: 392061), where visitors are welcome to observe the cigar making process. If hunger strikes, go directly to *Panificadora París* (Av. 5 de Mayo and Calle Mario Molina; phone: 321213), whose shelves are lined with sweet rolls, cookies, and small whole wheat loaves. Grab a tray and tongs, and dig in with the rest. Weekday shopping hours are generally from 10 AM until 7 PM; Saturdays until 3 PM. Most stores are closed on Sundays.

SPORTS

FISHING For angling in the Gulf of Mexico, rent boats and gear through the *Hostal de Cortés* hotel (see *Checking In*). You can go after perch, bass, shrimp, and clams at Mandinga, rent a boat at Catemaco (see *Special Places* for information on both), or do some river fishing at Boca del Río, a small village 7 miles (11 km) south of Veracruz with several *palapa* (thatch-roofed) restaurants popular for fresh seafood.

The *Torneo Internacional Shad* (International Shad Fishing Tournament) is held annually in April or May at the *Club de Yates* (Yacht Club, on the north end of the *malecón;* phone: 325355).

GOLF The nine-hole course at the *Club de Golf La Villa Rica* (Km 1.5 on the road to Antón Lizardo; phone: 321202) is open only to guests of members.

JOGGING Join the locals for a run along the waterfront, from the *malecón* out to the beaches. Lots of folks do it, even at night.

SAILING The yearly *Regata Amigos* (Amigos Regatta) from Galveston, Texas, to Veracruz, takes place on selected dates between March and July. Contact the tourist office for schedule information.

SCUBA DIVING There are four large reefs just off the coast of Veracruz—La Blanquilla, Anegadita de Adentro, Isla Verde, and Pájaros—and an even larger area south of the city. La Blanquilla is Mexico's first national underwater park. *Tridente* (165A Blvd. Avila Camacho; phone: 327924) will arrange scuba lessons and diving trips; *Veraventuras* (see *Whitewater Rafting,* below) also arranges scuba lessons.

SWIMMING AND SUNNING Veracruz boasts several good gulf beaches, where chairs with umbrellas or canvas awnings can be rented for a small fee: Mocambo (see *Special Places),* Hornos, Costa Verde, and Villa del Mar are all within 3 miles (5 km) south of the city. There are lively musical performances at Villa del Mar on Sundays. Costa de Oro in Boca del Río (7 mi/11 km south of town) is also a good swimming spot.

TENNIS Most of the larger hotels have facilities; there are also 14 cement courts (six lighted) at *Las Palmas Racquet Club* in Mocambo (phone: 353484).

WHITEWATER RAFTING This is great fun for adventurous souls who enjoy a sense of danger under reasonably safe conditions. Three- to eight-day expeditions are arranged by *Veraventuras* in the town of Xalapa, about 80 miles (140 km) northwest (81-8 Santos Degollado, 91000 Xalapa, Veracruz; phone: 28-189579 or 189779; fax: 28-189680). Trips begin at the *Parque de Aguas Termales El Carrizal* (El Carrizal Hot Springs Park), 47 miles (75 km) northwest of Veracruz city, offering travelers the chance to explore three different rivers within a 100-mile radius of each other: the Antigua, the Bobos, and the Actopan, which also includes the striking El Descabezadero, or Guillotine Falls. Each trip is over Class III and IV rapids, winding through wide canyons, as well as jungles and mango groves. Food, transportation from the park to the rivers and other locations, and lodging—ranging from a first class hotel to tents—are included, though sleeping bags are not. Children must be at least 10. Reservations are advised. *Veraventuras* also offers hiking trips, horseback riding, and hot-air balloon tours in various locations throughout the state.

NIGHTCLUBS AND NIGHTLIFE

Veracruz is at its best after dark. Among the most appealing nighttime attractions are the musicians who entertain the crowds at the cafés surrounding the *zócalo*. Favorite discos include *La Capilla,* at the *Prendes* hotel (see *Checking In*); *Deus* (Blvd. Ruiz Cortines and Calle 22; phone: 372001); *Club Privado* (Blvd. Ruiz Cortines; no phone); and *Climax* (Blvd. Ruiz Cortines; phone: 383702). *Moruchos* disco, in the *Emporio* hotel (four blocks east of the plaza at the *malecón;* phone: 316024), is open Thursdays through Saturdays. Female impersonators perform at the *Hip Pop Potamus* in Costa Verde (Avila Camacho and Calle 1; phone: 313901), and there's music, dancing, and a midnight show in the *Gaviota* bar of the *Veracruz* hotel (see *Checking In*).

DANCING IN THE STREETS

Veracruz may be the only place in Mexico where dancing in the streets is a regularly scheduled event. Every Sunday evening, *jarochos* of all ages flock to the *Parque Ciriaco Vásquez* (six blocks southwest of the *zócalo*) to dance into the wee hours of the morning. The *danzón,* as the tradition is called, made its way to Veracruz from Spain and Africa by way of Cuba, and the *jarochos* have adapted it into a uniquely Veracruzan custom. There is also a *danzón* Friday evenings at the Plaza de la Constitución.

Best in Town

CHECKING IN

Expect to pay about $80 to $95 per night for a double room in an expensive hotel, about $50 to $70 in a moderate one, and $40 or less in an inexpensive one. A *Fiesta Inn* was due to open at press time; for more information, call 800-FIESTA-1. Unless otherwise noted, the hotels designated below have air conditioning, telephones, and TV sets in the rooms. Four of the hotels listed in the "expensive" category are on Boulevard Avila Camacho, across from Playa Mocambo (5 miles/8 km south of the city) in an area roughly 1 mile (1.6 km) long. All telephone numbers are in the 29 city code unless otherwise indicated.

EXPENSIVE

Fiesta Americana Opened in early 1996, this large hotel offers 208 rooms and 22 suites. There's also a gym, a weight room, aerobics and martial arts classes, massage and sauna facilities, four tennis courts, three restaurants, a coffee shop, three bars with live music, a swimming pool, a wading pool, free movies, and cable TV. Seven miles (11 km) south of town, in the Costa de Oro section of Boca del Río (phone: 898989; 800-FIESTA-1 in the US; 800-50450 in Mexico; fax: 898904.

Hostal de Cortés Very attractive, it has 103 rooms and five suites, each with a fully stocked mini-bar. There's also a pool and a restaurant. Blvd. Avila Camacho (phone: 320065; fax: 315744).

Howard Johnson Veracruz A modern and charming establishment, with 110 rooms and 60 suites. Amenities include a coffee shop, a restaurant, a nightclub, and a bar. Blvd. Avila Camacho (phone: 311121 or 310011; 800-446-4656 in the US; 800-50549 in Mexico; fax: 310867).

Mocambo The grande dame of local hotels has 120 spacious rooms, well-kept grounds, excellent room service, and a lovely terrace facing the ocean. There is also a good restaurant, a piano bar, a tennis court, one large outdoor and two indoor pools, a Jacuzzi, and a sauna. Blvd. Avila Camacho (phone: 371531; fax: 371660).

Playa Paraíso Small compared with the *Mocambo* next door, this hotel is its equal in comfort and exclusivity, with 41 villas and 34 suites in sparkling white three-story buildings, plus a restaurant, a pool, and a fine beach. Blvd. Avila Camacho (phone: 218600; fax: 378306).

Veracruz In this completely remodeled old favorite are 116 spacious rooms and suites, with pleasant, modern decor in pastel colors. A restaurant, a coffee shop, a nightclub, and a small pool are also on the premises. Downtown, Av. Independencia at the corner of Calle Miguel Lerdo (phone: 312233; fax: 315134).

MODERATE

Costa Sol This beachfront hotel has 108 rooms and 20 villas. There's a pool overlooking the beach, a pleasant dining room, and a lively bar. Rte. 180, corner of Ferrocarril, Boca del Río (phone: 860290; fax: 860364).

Imperial Here are 35 rooms, 26 suites, and an exceptionally attentive staff, all in a renovated 200-year-old colonial property that radiates Old World charm. There's a covered swimming pool, a restaurant, a piano bar, a heliport, and parking. On the *zócalo,* at 153 Miguel Lerdo (phone/fax: 328788).

Villa del Mar Among the draws here are 80 rooms and 23 fan-cooled bungalows (no air conditioning), as well as tennis, bar service, and a restaurant. Swing sets and a garden are in the back. On the beach, a mile (1.6 km) south of the *zócalo,* on Blvd. Avila Camacho (phone: 860056; fax: 860364).

INEXPENSIVE

Prendes Very popular and reasonably priced, with 34 rooms, a fine restaurant (see *Eating Out*), and a disco. On the Plaza de la Constitución, at 1064 Independencia, at the corner of Miguel Lerdo (phone: 310241; fax: 310491).

Real del Mar Offers 34 rooms, a pool, a restaurant, and a family atmosphere. 2707 Blvd. Avila Camacho (phone: 373634; fax: 377078).

EATING OUT

Veracruz is filled with restaurants that serve some of the world's best fish and seafood, rendered in such delectable local specialties as *caldo largo de camarones* (shrimp prepared in a rich, spicy broth) and *huachinango a la veracruzana* (red snapper in a tomato sauce). For a full dinner for two, excluding drinks, wine, tax, and tip, expect to pay $50 to $60 at expensive places; $35 to $45 at moderate ones; and $30 or less at inexpensive ones. Most restaurants below accept MasterCard and Visa, and a few also accept American Express and Diners Club; it's a good idea to call ahead and check. Unless otherwise noted, all restaurants are open daily for lunch and dinner. All telephone numbers are in the 29 city code unless otherwise indicated.

EXPENSIVE

La Bamba This is the best place in town for *huachinango a la veracruzana;* the house specialty is *cucaracha del mar* (shrimp). Closed Mondays. Reservations advised on weekends. Blvd. Avila Camacho and Zapata, next to the *Club de Yates* (phone: 325355).

Hostería Suiza Excellent Central European cooking, including meat and cheese fondues. Closed Mondays. Reservations unnecessary. Manuel Suárez between España and Estocolmo (phone: 210320).

MODERATE

El Gaucho This place specializes in Argentine food and has the best steaks in town. Those not feeling carnivorous should order the *tortilla de espinaca con camarón,* an enormous omelette filled with cheese, spinach, and shrimp.

Reservations unnecessary. Corner of Calle Colón and Bernal Díaz del Castillo (phone: 350411).

La Parroquia Stop in at this perpetually bustling spot for a meal, a nightcap, or just a breather. The *medianoches* ("midnights")—turkey, ham, and cheese sandwiches with tomato sauce—are very good, as is the strong coffee. When the diners tap their glasses, they aren't making a toast, but hailing the waiters, who bear kettles of hot milk to complete the *café con leche.* Reservations unnecessary. No credit cards accepted. On the Plaza de la Constitución (phone: 322584); another, less atmospheric branch is on the *malecón* (phone: 321855).

Prendes Fresh seafood dishes and regional music make it a local favorite, famous for its *filete relleno* (fish stuffed with seafood). Reservations unnecessary. In the *Prendes Hotel,* 1064 Independencia, at the corner of Miguel Lerdo (phone: 310241).

Submarino Amarillo Don't be fooled by the name, which translates as "Yellow Submarine"; this is actually one of the best steakhouses in Veracruz. Reservations unnecessary. On the *malecón,* at the corner of Rayón (phone: 327030).

Winner's This airy, plant-filled spot specializes in grilled steaks; fish and seafood are available, too. Open around the clock Tuesdays through Saturdays; closed from 11 PM Sundays to 7 AM Mondays. Reservations unnecessary. Midway to Mocambo at Bolívar and 23 de Noviembre (phone: 352517).

INEXPENSIVE

La Paella The name of this Spanish restaurant refers to the Iberian specialty—shellfish, chicken, and sausage served over rice—that reigns supreme here. Reservations unnecessary. No credit cards accepted. On the *zócalo,* at 138 Zamora (phone: 320322).

Pardiño's Centro The seafood here is exceptional, especially any dish served with *cangrejo* (crab). Portions are generous, and the service is friendly. The open terrace upstairs is great for watching the comings and goings on the *malecón.* Reservations unnecessary. No credit cards accepted. Two locations: 146 Landero y Coss (phone: 314881) and 40 Gutiérrez Zamora, Boca del Río (phone: 860135).

COOL COMESTIBLES

Make sure to save some room for *nieve* (ice cream), which for some reason tastes better in Veracruz than almost anywhere else. Try *mamey,* made from a sweet, native fruit; *sandía,* in which the flavor of watermelon is even more intense than in the fruit itself; *guanábana,* made from the tropical soursop fruit; or the peanutty *cacahuate.* There are vendors where Zamora dead-ends into Landero y Coss at the *malecón.*

Diversions

Unexpected Pleasures and Treasures

Quintessential Mexico

Among other things, traveling south of the border doubtless has taught you that the real spirit of Mexico lies somewhere between the Maya and *mañana*. If you've tried on the requisite number of sombreros, admired the blossoms at *Xochimilco,* and haggled over a colorful serape, you've certainly scratched the surface. You may even have ridden in a *calandria,* mixed it up with a marlin, tasted a *tamale,* and finally learned to pronounce Zihuatanejo. But, amigos, until you savor the places and pleasures listed below, you haven't experienced the true meaning of *"Viva México!"*

BALLET FOLKLÓRICO DE MÉXICO In every Mexican town and village, music and dance express the soul of the people. Pre-Hispanic Mexican music, simple and almost hypnotic, was dominated by percussion and wind instruments. The music was intended to accompany dances and religious rites; each of the many native cultures had its own dances and costumes. Despite very forceful efforts by the conquistadores to stamp out all traces of indigenous cultures, music and dance survived, mainly because the Spanish clergy realized that these arts could be used as tools for recruiting the "heathens" into the church. The "heathens," in turn, were clever enough to fuse their dances with European traditions in order to survive. Even today, a church festival isn't considered complete without the performance of brilliantly clad folk dancers.

Much of the credit for keeping the ancient dance tradition alive goes to Mexico's *Ballet Folklórico.* Though it has its imitators, *this* troupe is the real thing. For more details, see "Nightclubs and Nightlife" in *Mexico City,* THE CITIES.

WHALE WATCHING, Scammon's Lagoon, Guerrero Negro, Baja California Sur Every year the great gray whales journey 5,000 miles from the icy precincts of the Bering Sea to the warm, protected waters of Scammon's Lagoon, midway down the Baja Peninsula, where they spend the winter and mate or bear their young before returning north in the spring.

Wild creatures have always held a special fascination for humans, yet few of us have the opportunity to observe them at leisure in their natural habitat. Fortunately for us, expedition organizers and conservation groups convinced the Mexican government that it was good business to cater to this fascination (and, at the same time, protect the animals), and this gave rise to another migration to Baja—by whale watchers.

Today, Scammon's Lagoon and other protected areas stretching down to the southern tip of the Baja Peninsula are designated wildlife refuges that serve as havens for sea lions, porpoises, and a wide variety of migrating shore and sea birds as well as whales. With luck, it is possible to spot a humpback or gray whale from time to time. Calves swimming alongside their mothers are a common sight, and fortunate whale watchers may even catch a glimpse of one suckling the 50 gallons of milk each consumes every day.

Despite their tremendous size, whales seem genuinely friendly, hamming it up before an admiring public, as if they knew their lives depended on it. Agile, graceful swimmers, they are able to propel their massive bodies up out of the water in a movement called "breaching," sending up huge sprays as they make their dramatic re-entry. Before setting out to sea again, the grays often give a flick of their flukes, as if waving good-bye.

The thrilling spectacle of these amazing creatures cavorting in the water can be seen from the last week in December through mid-March (or sometimes early April) from several spots along the shore, or from whale watching vessels or small planes that can be boarded in Guerrero Negro—but note that boating in the lagoons during whale season is allowed only by special permission. Excursions are also available from Ensenada and San Diego. For information about naturalist-led tours to several whale watching sites, contact *Oceanic Society Expeditions* (Fort Mason Center, Building E, San Francisco, CA 94123-1394; phone: 415-441-1106; 800-326-7491); the *American Cetacean Society* (PO Box 2639, San Pedro, CA 90731; phone: 310-548-6279); or *Special Expeditions* (720 Fifth Ave., New York, NY 10019; phone: 800-762-0003).

POPOCATÉPETL and IZTACCÍHUATL VOLCANOES, State of México There was a time when the snow-covered peaks of these two volcanoes were a common, everyday sight in Mexico City. Now, on the few clear days of the year when they can be seen from the almost perpetually smog-blanketed capital, the awesome spectacle brings traffic to a halt on the busy *periférico* (beltway).

Popocatépetl ("Popo"), which rises to a height of 17,887 feet, last erupted in 1802; however, at press time the government had closed it to the public because of periodic signs of activity. (Scientists say there is no danger, but the government seems to be playing it safe.) Iztaccíhuatl ("Izta"), only 433 feet shorter than its neighbor, also has been inactive for almost two centuries. According to legend, the two volcanoes represent the love between an Aztec princess and a warrior. In exchange for the hand of his daughter, the king demanded that the warrior bring him the head of the most feared enemy of their people. But by the time the young swain returned with his prize, the princess had died of a broken heart. Grieving, he laid her body on a hill, knelt down, and remained in that position forever, watching over the eternal sleep of his beloved. The silhouette of Popo, whose full name means "smoking mountain," does resemble a kneeling man, and the outline of Izta, whose full name means "white lady," a sleeping woman.

From the town of Amecameca, a paved road leads to the Paso de Cortés, a scenic point on Popo that at press time was open to the public. It was at the Paso de Cortés that the conquistadores crossed into Tenochtitlán on their way from Veracruz in 1519 and where Cortés met with an envoy of Montezuma II, who tried to dissuade him from advancing on the Aztec capital. It was also from this place that the Spaniards first saw both the valley of Anáhuac spread out before them and Tenochtitlán, which Bernal Díaz del Castillo described as seeming to float on Lago de Texcoco (Lake Texcoco) like a silver ship.

To get to the Popo area from Mexico City, head east on Route 150 21 miles (33 km) toward Puebla, take the Chalco exit and continue 3½ miles (6 km) to the Amecameca-Chalco turnoff, and then follow Route 115 14 miles (22 km) to Amecameca. As an added treat, you can buy delicious nuts—especially pistachios—in Amecameca before heading on.

DÍA DE LOS MUERTOS (DAY OF THE DEAD) Although Mexicans fear and respect death as much as do other peoples, they face it, defy it, mock it, and even toy with it more than most cultures. Never is this more apparent than on the *Día de los Muertos*—an eminently Mexican holiday perpetuating a traditional belief in the cycle of death and rebirth.

The official date of *Día de los Muertos* (known elsewhere as All Soul's Day), is November 2, although the observances begin the day before (November 1 is for remembering dead children, November 2 for dead adults). By mid-October, in fact, bakeries and markets throughout Mexico are filled with death-themed sweets and toys. Bake shops are piled high with *pan de muerto,* a coffee cake decorated with meringues fashioned into the shape of bones. Children, friends, and relatives are given colorful sugar skulls with their names inscribed on them; death figures shaped from marzipan are on sale at most candy stores. *Calaveras* (literally "skulls," but in this case verses containing witty allusions or epitaphs) are written about living friends, relatives, and public figures, and by the end of October, shop windows take on a macabre air, with shrouded marionettes and other ghoulish-looking figurines heralding the holiday.

Families observe the holiday by gathering in graveyards to picnic and spend time with their departed, bringing along their loved ones' favorite foods and drink. Graves of adults are decorated with bright orange *zempasúchil* (a marigold-like flower), while graves of children are marked with dark red *mano de león* ("lion's paw," a velvety textured blossom); *copal,* an incense that dates to pre-Hispanic cultures, is burned. The celebration begins with prayers and chants for the dead, and usually ends with drinks to the departed's health. Homes are decorated similarly, with tables filled with *zempasúchil* and objects of which the deceased was especially fond.

One of the most moving observances of this tradition is held on Isla Janitzio in Lago de Pátzcuaro, in the state of Michoacán. On November 1, the descendants of the native Tarasco gather on the lake at dawn for a ceremonial duck hunt. Using ancient weapons, they paddle their canoes into a semicircle, trapping the ducks against the shore. At a signal from the leader of the hunt, the weapons are thrown. Shortly after midnight, the women make their way to the cemetery, laden with baskets of food (including traditional dishes of duck meat), incense, bouquets of *zempasúchil,* and thousands of candles, transforming the small graveyard behind the church of Isla Janitzio into a glittering outdoor cathedral. As the women and children meditate at the grave sites and the church bells toll, the men begin the slow, steady chants that they will continue through the night.

Similar cemetery observances are held November 1 and 2 in San Andrés Mixquic, in southern Mexico City near Xochimilco. Take Route 150 toward Puebla; at the Chalco exit (the first toll bridge), turn right and go 4 miles (7 km). Then follow the signs to Mixquic, another 6 miles (10 km).

SANTUARIO DE LAS MARIPOSAS MONARCA "EL ROSARIO" (EL ROSARIO MONARCH BUTTERFLY SANCTUARY), Angangueo, Michoacán Every year, hundreds of thousands of these dazzling winged creatures migrate from the cold climates of eastern Canada and the northern United States to a wildlife sanctuary that covers parts of the states of Michoacán and México. From late October through early March, monarchs blanket every inch of vegetation in a white-flecked, burnt-orange, and black batik—one of the most stunning sights imaginable.

The Tarasco, who lived in the area when the Spaniards conquered Mexico, considered the monarchs' nesting grounds sacred because they believed the butterflies carried the souls of the dead to their final resting place. Since the arrival of the monarchs traditionally occurs around the time of the *Día de los Muertos* (Day of the Dead), this myth has been incorporated into modern Mexican Christianity, and local tribes continue to intertwine the two events.

It's best to plan your visit for a weekday, when there are fewer crowds; try to get to the sanctuary after 10 AM, because the monarchs wait for the warming rays of the sun before putting on their spectacular show. Don't be discouraged by reports that millions of butterflies died following a snowfall last winter: although it's true that the snow killed some five million monarchs, a total of 65 million to 80 million winter here every year.

Reaching the butterflies is somewhat of a challenge. The sanctuary is located near the old mining town of Angangueo. We advise leaving your car in town and catching a ride on the back of one of the open-air trucks that make the dusty, hour-long trip up the eroded, unpaved road to the refuge. Dress warmly and wear comfortable shoes; once you reach the sanctuary, you face a grueling 40-minute walk up a steep pathway, but the experience is more than worth the hardship.

Overnight accommodations are available at the spa in San José Purúa, or in the town of Zitácuaro. *Turistoria* (Insurgentes Centro 114, 06470 México, DF, México; phone: 5-592-8137 or 5-703-1544; fax: 5-703-0391) offers several excursions to monarch sites each season. If you're planning an overnight stay, make reservations well in advance. There are also specialized tours available to scientists, study groups, or photographic expeditions through the nonprofit *Monarca AC* (Constituyentes 345, Eighth Floor, 11830 México, DF, México; phone: 5-515-9910 or 5-515-9646; fax: 5-271-3665). These tours (prices vary depending on the size of the group and the places visited) include visits to lesser-known sanctuaries.

CHARREADA Although there is evidence that horses once existed in the Americas, they disappeared centuries before the arrival of the conquistadores, who brought the first horses of Arabic origin to this continent. Though *charro* means "a man from the country" in Castilian Spanish, in Mexico it has come to denote a gentleman rider. Indeed, during the first decades of the colonial period, the use of horses was restricted to Europeans; criollos (Spaniards born in the colonies) and mestizos could be put to death if caught riding. But when more hands were needed to work the huge cattle ranches, the law was relaxed and the criollos and mestizos were allowed to ride. A true *charro* is said to love his horse at least as much as his wife.

Until *charrería* was formally organized in 1921 (it was declared a national sport in 1933), it was practiced spontaneously in cities and towns by groups of riders who wanted to improve and compare their skills. Today, most who participate in the events are professionals and businessmen who can afford to maintain their well-trained steeds and keep themselves outfitted in the costly costumes. The gala outfit, which has become a symbol of Mexico, is all black and consists of tight pants, a bolero jacket, and a wide-brimmed felt hat, all heavily adorned with silver. The saddle, bridle, and pistol are inlaid with silver, and sometimes gold.

Charreadas are especially popular in Guadalajara and Mexico City, where they are performed in *lienzos* (rings) on Sunday mornings. The activities usually begin with an enthusiastic mariachi rendition of the *Marcha de Zacatecas* ("Zacatecas March") and the presentation of the competing teams. Riders then charge at full speed into the arena, bringing their mounts to an abrupt halt in the center of the ring. Other riding feats—lassoing, and the wrestling of steers and calves—are followed by the *paso de la muerte,* in which the rider leaps from his galloping mount onto the back of a wild horse. On special occasions, the exhibition includes a display of equestrian ballet called *escaramuza,* performed by female riders executing elaborate crossing and intertwining patterns.

MARIACHI MUSIC The melodies pervade all of Mexico. Groups of musicians roam the streets of cities large and small, serenading under the windows of apartment buildings and in the doorways of restaurants and shops. Students, carrying guitars and flutes on subways and buses, often play for their fellow passengers in hope of earning some pocket money on the way to and from school. Although every region of Mexico has its own special music, none is more associated with the country as a whole than mariachi (said to have originated in Tecatitlán, with the word itself perhaps coming from the French for "marriage").

Mariachi groups—comprising at least one vocalist, a guitar player, a bass player, a violinist, and a trumpeter or two—are often hired to serenade girlfriends or to play at special events. Their vast repertoire includes such sentimental love songs as "Si estás dormida," "Las Mañanitas" (the Mexican equivalent of "Happy Birthday," but sung for almost any special occasion), "Guadalajara," and "Cucurrúcucu Paloma." The traditional Mexican fiestas frequently held at large resort hotels normally include at least one mariachi group, and any sizable town will have a few restaurants and bars where they provide the entertainment. Some of the best mariachis—dressed in close-fitting black pants, bolero-type jackets decorated with silver, and wide-brimmed hats—often congregate at the Plaza de los Mariachis in Guadalajara and at Plaza Garibaldi in Mexico City.

BARRANCA DEL COBRE (COPPER CANYON), Chihuahua The *Ferrocarril Chihuahua al Pacífico* (Chihuahua-Pacific Railway), an extraordinary feat of engineering that travels 420 miles through more than 80 tunnels and over 30 bridges, was begun in 1897, but wasn't officially inaugurated until 1961. A trip along this route combines awesome natural beauty with a fascinating ethnological experience: The giant canyons of the Tarahumara mountain range are home to some 60,000 Tarahumara, one of the most traditional indigenous groups still living in North America.

The 12- to 16-hour trip from Chihuahua (south of the Texas border) to Los Mochis (near the Pacific Ocean), or vice versa, can be made in a single day, with short stops along the way to enjoy the views. But it is best to leave enough time to spend a night or two in rustic comfort at one or more of the towns en route. The best time to go is late summer or early fall, after the rainy season, when the landscape is crowned with lush greenery. Starting from Chihuahua, the train winds its way west and then south to Creel, an almost abandoned mining town whose few remaining inhabitants eke out a living from timber from the Sierra Madre. From Creel, excursions go to Lago Arareco, the Cusárare Falls, and the abandoned Batopilas mine, situated in the depths of the canyon. Thirty-seven miles (59 km) beyond Creel, the train arrives in El Divisadero and then Posada Barrancas; it stops in both locations just long enough for passengers to capture the unforgettable views of the three canyons that make up the Barranca del Cobre (the Tararecua, the Urique, and the Cobre). After numerous other quick stops and before beginning the final descent to Los Mochis, the train stops in Bahuichivo, in the heart of some of Mexico's richest farming country. Overnight accommodations are available in Cerocahui (about a 40-minute bus ride away), at the very edge of the Urique Canyon. For more information on this trip, contact the *Ferrocarril Chihuahua al Pacífico* (Chihuahua-Pacific Railway; Apartado Postal 46, 31000 Chihuahua, Chihuahua, México; phone: 14-157756), or *Mexico by Rail* (PO Box 2782, Laredo, TX 78044; phone: 800-321-1699; fax: 210-571-3659).

Another option is to book a more leisurely five- or seven-day tour along a similar route on the luxurious *South Orient Express,* which features comfortable seating, fine food, and gracious hospitality in addition to splendid views. Hotel accommodations are arranged for passengers during the trip, as there are no sleeping cars on the train. For details, contact the *Mexican-American Railway Association* (16800 Greenspoint Park Dr., Suite 245 North, Houston, TX 77060; phone: 713-872-0190; 800-659-7602; fax: 713-872-7123). For more information on the *South Orient Express* and other Copper Canyon excursions, see *Ciudad Juárez to Mexico City,* DIRECTIONS.

MUSEO NACIONAL DE ANTROPOLOGÍA (NATIONAL MUSEUM OF ANTHROPOLOGY),

Mexico City Carved into a wall of this museum is the "Song of Huexotzingo," a lament composed by the Aztec after the Spanish conquest of Tenochtitlán:

> *Will I leave only this*
> *Like the flowers that wither?*
> *Will nothing last in my name*
> *Nothing of my fame here on earth?*
> *At least flowers! At least songs!*

The museum itself is a fitting answer to these poignant questions. Created by architect Pedro Ramírez Vázquez to house an unparalleled collection of archaeological treasures, these magnificent buildings combine metals and concrete with marble, wood, stone, and open spaces to capture the grandeur of an Aztec temple. If possible, allow a full day or, better, two half days to see the museum. For additional details, see "Special Places" in *Mexico City,* THE CITIES.

MOLE

To an uninformed gringo reading a Mexican menu, an entrée of turkey mole conjures up the unappetizing vision of a drumstick topped with hot fudge. Nothing could be further from reality. The word *mole* comes from the Nahuatl *mulli,* which means sauce—and this one is made of more than 30 ingredients, only *one* of which is unsweetened chocolate. Many Mexican housewives pride themselves on preparing the sauce from scratch, using a time-consuming recipe that calls for as many as a dozen types of chilies (which have to be seeded, deveined, and roasted), sesame seeds, almonds, peanuts, raisins, prunes, plantains, onions, garlic, coriander, anise, cinnamon, and an infinitesimal amount of the aforementioned chocolate. Traditionally, it is served with chicken or turkey, as a filling for tamales, or as a sauce for enchiladas. If you are served mole in a Mexican household, you know you're an honored guest.

SUNSETS ON THE PACIFIC Prime plaudits for the most spectacular sunset south of the border go to Playa del Amor (Lovers' Beach) at Land's End on the tip of the Baja Peninsula, where the Gulf of California (also called the Sea of Cortés) meets the Pacific and seems to divide the sky into a rosy gray on one side and a robin's-egg blue on the other. Sundown at Pie de la Cuesta and Barra Vieja in Acapulco, or at Playa Conchas Chinas in Puerto Vallarta, is also quite impressive. Just pick a spot, pull up a chair, sip your margarita, and watch the sun slip below the horizon—you may feel that you've just had a glimpse of heaven.

Mexico's Magnificent Archaeological Heritage

Astonishing ruins of ancient indigenous civilizations have been found and continue to be discovered in the central, southern, and far eastern reaches of Mexico. Excavation and restoration have opened up sites where early Mexican cultures flourished and have permitted visitors to take a close look at the country's extraordinary past. The following is a description of the architectural and cultural features of Mexico's most compelling archaeological zones. For an invaluable overview of the civilizations and their monumental sculpture, a visit to the awesome *Museo Nacional de Antropología* (National Museum of Anthropology) in Mexico City is strongly recommended. (For details, see *Quintessential Mexico,* above, and "Special Places" in *Mexico City,* THE CITIES.) In addition, most archaeological sites have a small museum on the grounds that will help visitors to understand the history of that particular area. The sites are listed alphabetically by location.

CENTRAL MEXICO

TULA, Hidalgo During the early Postclassic period (AD 900–1200), the Toltec culture dominated most of north and central Mexico from its capital at Tula.

Toltec legends recorded by the Aztec relate the story of Ce Acatl Mixcoatl and his people, who settled in the Valley of Mexico and conquered the surrounding peoples. Mixcoatl's son, Ce Acatl Topiltzin, moved the capital of the Toltec empire to Tula in AD 968. A priest of the religious sect of Quetzalcóatl, the peaceful ruler stimulated the expansion of the arts in Toltec culture. However, his opposition to the ritual of sacrifice and to slavery made him unpopular with the followers of Tezcatlipoca, the court magician, and in a power struggle between the opposing sects, Topiltzín was forced to flee Tula. According to one legend, he set himself ablaze adorned in his quetzal feathers and rose into the sky as a beautiful bird, to become the Morning Star; another, more widely circulated version has him journey out to sea eastward on a raft, vowing someday to return. He became associated with the god Quetzalcóatl himself, and his legend played a major role in the fall of the Aztec ruler Montezuma. (The Aztec believed that conquistador Hernán Cortés was the returning god.) Under the rule of the followers of Tezcatlipoca, Tula's militaristic expansion flourished until 1156, when a major drought drove out the Toltec, effectively precipitating Tula's fall.

The spacious central plaza of the *Tula* archaeological site is flanked by pyramids. *Building B,* east of the plaza, commemorates Quetzalcóatl as the Morning Star. To the west of *Building B,* the *Burnt Palace* has colonnades and decorated benches around the walls. Of the site's two ball courts, only one has been excavated and reconstructed.

The stone sculptures of reclining figures holding receptacles on their stomachs are probably rain gods; similar figures appear in the sculpture of the Tarasco and the Aztec. The site is closed Mondays. The admission charge includes parking and entrance to the museum; there's no admission charge on Sundays (no phone). *Tula* is 45 miles (72 km) north of Mexico City; follow Route 85 (the Pan-American Highway) to the western turnoff at Actopán. (For an alternate route, see *Nuevo Laredo to Mexico City* in DIRECTIONS.)

MEXICO CITY In 1978, electric-company workers discovered an eight-ton Aztec monolith under the streets of Mexico City. The massive structure depicted the legend of the god Huitzilopochtli, who avenged the death of his mother, Coatlicue, at the hands of his sister Coyolzauhqui. This amazing discovery led to excavations around the *zócalo,* the city's main square, which uncovered the foundations of the Aztec *Templo Mayor* (Great Temple), once the holiest shrine of that empire. Also unearthed were thousands of artifacts, including an enormous sculpture representing a decapitated and dismembered Coyolzauhqui, a Chac-Mool sacrificial stone, a sculptured seashell, the base of a temple ornamented with 240 stone skulls, and numerous weapons, masks, statues, and other artifacts which have since been exhibited in museums around the world. The treasures discovered at the site now can be seen in the city's *Museo del Templo Mayor,* whose design echoes that of the temple itself.

In 1988, the 12-ton Cuauhxicalli stone was unearthed from beneath the patio of the *Palacio del Arzobispo* (Archbishop's Palace), also near the *zócalo.* Human hearts were once sacrificed on this stone as "food" for the Aztec gods. The stone is now housed in Mexico City's *Museo Nacional de Antropología* (National Museum of Anthropology). For additional details on the *Museo del Templo Mayor* and the *Museo Nacional de Antropología,* see "Special Places" in *Mexico City,* THE CITIES.

TEOTIHUACÁN, México This archaeological zone of pyramids, temples, and ball courts, comprising more than 8 square miles, once made up what was probably the first true city in central Mexico, dating back to about AD 400. The city was abandoned long before the Aztec came to the valley; no one knows why Teotihuacán's inhabitants left, but it is surmised that they went south and eventually were incorporated into the Maya civilization.

The largest pyramid here (and the tallest in the New World) is the *Pyramid of the Sun*—216 feet high, with a base covering 750 square feet. In tunneling through the pyramid, archaeologists discovered a series of pyramids built on top of one another. The Teotihuacán people marked time in 52-year cycles, and it is believed that every 52 years a new pyramid was built over the older one.

The Avenue of the Dead, the main thoroughfare, runs on a north-south axis from the smaller *Pyramid of the Moon* past the *Pyramid of the Sun* to the spectacular *Temple of Quetzalcóatl* (the Plumed Serpent), which features carvings of feathered serpent bodies; heads of gods, including Tlaloc, the rain god; and marine shell motifs. For a distance of 1½ miles (2 km), the avenue is lined on both sides with smaller temples and shrines, all of them characterized by the *talud-tablero* architectural style (see *Cholula*, below).

Most of the inhabitants of Teotihuacán lived in apartment compounds—clusters of rooms organized around patios that contained small altar-shrines. *Tetitla, Zacuala, Xolalpán,* and *Tepantitla* are apartment compounds; the largest *(Tepantitla)* contains 176 rooms, 21 patios, and five spacious courts. Brightly colored mural paintings featuring the religious symbols of the early inhabitants are preserved in these areas. There's also an immense walled-in arena that presumably was used for games and religious spectacles.

To get to *Teotihuacán,* which is 33 miles (53 km) northeast of Mexico City, take Avenida Insurgentes Norte, which connects with the toll road to the site. There is also regular bus service from the Central de Autobuses del Norte (Av. 100 Metros) in Mexico City. The site and museum are closed on religious holidays; there's no admission charge on Sundays (phone: 595-60188).

CHALCATZINGO, Morelos Dating from the period between 1600 and 500 BC, the *Chalcatzingo* archaeological site is noted for its Olmec bas-relief carvings, altar, and stelae (upright stone slabs with inscriptions).

The site is on a hill, with some reliefs at the base. Ascending, visitors find the imposing relief known as *El Rey,* portraying a king seated inside a highly stylized jaguar earth-monster mouth. In Olmec culture, the jaguar cult was associated with fertility. This jaguar seems to signify agricultural fecundity: It's surrounded by rain clouds, and volutes symbolizing mist issue from its mouth.

On another slope, a variety of reliefs depict a procession, a scene with jaguars and humans, and a monster devouring a human. On the other side of the hill, the *Flying Olmec* relief portrays what is believed to be a ballplayer.

The altar at the site shows the design of an earth-monster face associated with human sacrifice, a celebrated event that served to appease the gods. In about 600 BC, when the altar was dedicated, several children and some 20 adults were sacrificed and buried in front of it.

One particularly interesting stela portrays a woman standing on a stylized earth-monster mouth. It is noteworthy because women in this society rarely reached a level of high political or religious power, and they were rarely represented in the monumental sculptures of this period.

To get to the village of Chalcatzingo from Cuautla (26 miles/42 km east of Cuernavaca), take Route 140 heading toward Azúcar de Morelos (in the state of Puebla) to the Amayuca turnoff (about 24 miles/40 km from Cuautla), then go south 1½ miles (2 km) and take the dirt road 8 miles (13 km) to Montefalco and Chalcatzingo. To reach the archaeological site, you must hike for about 30 minutes south from the village. The *Chalcatzingo* site is closed Mondays; there's no admission charge on Sundays (no phone).

XOCHICALCO, Morelos Constructed at the end of the Classic period (AD 1–900), *Xochicalco,* meaning "Place of the House of Flowers" in the Nahuatl language, is terraced from the top of the hill, the main ceremonial zone, down to the river. A series of walls and moats facilitated the 6-square-mile site's defense. The mountain is riddled with a honeycombed network of caves, which were used for ceremonies.

The *talud-tablero*–style (see *Cholula,* below) pyramid covered with bas-reliefs is the site's most interesting structure. Undulating feathered serpents and people with Mayaesque features are depicted, but the tribal identity of the builders is unknown. One of the pyramids houses a sunlit rooftop observatory once used to determine the date and time.

The *Temple of the Stelae* is south of the main pyramid. The palace where the rulers probably lived consists of many rooms, passages, courts, stairways, and baths. The ball court is similar to the one at *Tula,* though here the court has stone rings that served as goals.

The site is open daily; there's no admission charge on Sundays (no phone). To investigate the ruins more fully, you can take a guide with you from Cuernavaca, but for most people a good strong flashlight should do the job.

The site is 24 miles (38 km) east of Cuernavaca, reached via Route 95 to Alpuyeca, and then west for 5 miles (8 km) to the road marked "Xochicalco."

CHOLULA, Puebla Rising above the modern town of Cholula is the *Tepanapa Pyramid;* with a 40-acre span and a height of 230 feet, it's the largest ancient structure in the New World. Believed to have been constructed by the Toltec, the pyramid is almost twice the bulk of the great Cheops pyramid of Egypt. Still mostly buried under a hill, it has a few excavated tunnels that can be explored. On top of the pyramid towers is *Nuestra Señora de los Remedios* (Our Lady of Healing), a Catholic church built by the Spaniards in 1549. The church, which dominates the skyline and can be seen for miles around, serves as a stark symbol of the superimposition of Spanish culture over Mexico's native culture.

The town of Cholula is situated on a complex built between 1600 and 500 BC, an era that witnessed the first of the four constructions of the *Tepanapa Pyramid,* as well as the construction of a smaller pyramid painted with polychrome murals that can be seen by entering one of the excavated tunnels. According to early Spanish accounts, the walls of the site once were covered with the blood of sacrificial victims. Much of the area has not been excavated because it would involve tearing down a large part of the modern town—now virtually a suburb of Puebla—at a prohibitive cost and great inconvenience.

Cholula survived the disruption following the fall of Teotihuacán, central Mexico's first true city. It shows influences of the Teotihuacán culture in the prevalence of the *talud-tablero* architectural form (rectangular spaces used for painting and sculpture, supported with sloping walls decorated with frescoes) and mural painting; some of the murals depict life-size figures engaged in a drinking ritual.

Cholula was conquered in AD 800 by an invading tribe and was liberated by the Toltec-Chichimec in AD 1292. During this period it was famous for crafts, including goldwork, turquoise mosaics, and lacquered, polychrome pottery so fine that the Aztec ruler Montezuma had some made to decorate his table.

Five miles (8 km) northwest of Puebla on Route 190, the *Cholula* archaeological site is open daily; there's no admission charge on Sundays (no phone).

EL TAJÍN, Veracruz This site was contemporaneous with and influenced by Teotihuacán. The ruins here are believed to date from around AD 800— the height of the Totonac culture—although some archaeologists speculate that the Olmec built the site during the 5th or 6th century. El Tajín survived the upheaval that occurred with the fall of Teotihuacán and the ensuing militarism. The site was destroyed by fire during the 13th century.

The older section of the city is the site of the famous six-stepped *Pyramid of the Niches,* with its 365 niches (one for each day of the year) in the *talud-tablero* architectural style (see *Cholula,* above). The typical El Tajín style of architecture employs numerous scrolls and volutes. Two of the area's seven ball courts have been reconstructed; one bears a bas-relief depicting the sacrifice of a player. The preponderance of yokes, *hachas,* and *palmas*— stone sculptures associated with the native ball game—has given rise to theories that the ball game was invented in lowland Veracruz. The game was played with a hard rubber ball, and such theories are supported by the abundance of rubber trees in the area.

Excavations are ongoing, and still-uncovered sites extend for several hundred acres beyond the older section. The encroaching jungle only adds to the charm and mystery of the site. It is 8 miles (13 km) southwest of the town of Papantla; take the road toward Espinal, turn right at El Chote, and drive one-half mile (1 km) past El Tajín to the ruins. The site is open daily; there's no admission charge on Sundays (no phone).

SOUTHERN MEXICO

PALENQUE, Chiapas *Palenque* is unique in that it is the only Maya ruin site buried in a rain forest and yet accessible by car. It remains lost from sight until a final hairpin turn reveals it, standing against the jungle's deep green—probably the most spectacular Maya site in all of Mexico. Set on a high plateau surrounded by lush mountain jungles where monkeys and wild birds still manage to survive, the pyramids here evoke a precision and order that stand in sharp contrast to their primordial surroundings. From the top of any of these elaborate structures is a sweeping view of the lowlands of Tabasco, a seemingly limitless stretch of forest and savanna. These ruins are believed to be the remains of a great holy city that once spread over as many as 25 square miles; in the small museum near the entrance to the ruins is a model that offers some idea of how the place once might have looked. The museum also displays a vast assortment of Maya work and artifacts, including intricate reliefs, jade masks, necklaces, beads, rings, and pottery vessels, all of which were found in the temples.

The largest of the site's pyramids is the *Temple of the Inscriptions,* which was found to contain the funerary crypt of Lord Pacal, the greatest ruler of Palenque. The remains of the body were tightly sealed in a stone sarcophagus in about AD 620. He was buried with a jade cube in his left hand, a jade ball in his right hand, and jade rings on his fingers; his body was covered with red dust. Artifacts from the tomb can be seen in the *Museo Nacional de Antropología* (National Museum of Anthropology) in Mexico City. The walls of the chamber are decorated with stuccoed figures. Guarding the chamber were the skeletal remains of his servants, who had been killed and then entombed with their master to accompany him on his journey to the next world. Discovered in 1950, this was the first tomb found in a Maya pyramid. Since then, archaeologists have found that many Maya pyramids contain royal crypts. Interestingly, the process of entombment here is similar to that practiced by the Egyptians, though it seems unlikely that there was any contact between the Maya and that ancient Middle Eastern civilization.

Note also the *Temple of the Sun,* which houses a tablet carved with a mask of the Jaguar Sun before crossed spears, and the *Temple of the Cross,* where the tablet is inscribed with branching trees topped by quetzal birds. The palace is a complex gallery of rooms organized around patios where exquisite reliefs portray prisoners in submission. The four-story square tower probably served as an astronomical observatory or strategic lookout post. Underneath the palace runs the stream that crosscuts the site, enclosed in a corbel-vaulted aqueduct.

Palenque is 87 miles (139 km) southeast of Villahermosa, Tabasco. Take Route 186 for 71 miles (114 km) to the turnoff at Catazaja, then go south for 16 miles (26 km) on Route 199 to the ruins. The site is open daily; no admission charge on Sundays (no phone). The museum is closed Mondays and has a separate admission charge (no phone).

Note: At press time, *Palenque* and the surrounding area were back to normal after being somewhat affected by the rebel uprisings elsewhere in the state of Chiapas. Previously, however, the government was setting up roadblocks on Route 199, and hotels and restaurants in the area sometimes closed without notice. Before you leave home, check the situation with the *US State Department*'s 24-hour travel advisory hotline (phone: 202-647-5225). For updates on tourist facilities in the area, contact the *Palenque* tourist office (phone: 934-50356); however, it's closed weekends.

MITLA, Oaxaca This site, whose name means "Place of the Dead," was an important religious center during the early Postclassic period (around AD 1000). Beneath the buildings lie the catacombs that gave Mitla its name. Its five groups of buildings once housed the high priest and secondary priests of the Zapotec, as well as the Zapotec king and his advisers.

The complex was started by the Zapotec but taken over and heavily influenced by the Mixtec, an enemy tribe, and the architecture here is totally different from that of any other ruins in the area. The layout features rectangular patios surrounded by long, narrow rooms. The doorways and façade are covered with mosaics, some of which show the Mixtec influence in the form of step-and-fret motifs. Unlike other ancient buildings in North America, there are no human figures or mythological events represented here—only designs. A colonial church was constructed on one of the precincts of the site—another graphic illustration of the superimposition of the Spanish culture on that of the original inhabitants.

The site is 27 miles (46 km) southeast of Oaxaca on Route 190. The ruins and museum are open daily, though they close earlier during the rainy season (roughly mid-May through mid-October); there's no admission charge on Sundays (no phone).

MONTE ALBÁN, Oaxaca This imposing place occupies a mountaintop overlooking the city of Oaxaca. The site was first occupied by the Zapotec from 300 BC to AD 300. Sometime around 1,000 years ago, the Zapotec were conquered by the Mixtec. These new inhabitants converted Monte Albán into a massive cemetery of lavish tombs, more than 160 of which have been discovered.

The Zapotec constructed Monte Albán around a large plaza. The buildings are carefully arranged on a perfect north-south axis, with the exception of one structure, thought to have been an observatory, which is more closely aligned with the stars than with the poles. The hilltop bore a sophisticated network of dams and 2,000 terraces used by the Zapotec as foundations for dwellings. The *talud-tablero* architecture, similar to that at Teotihuacán, predominates here; at one time, the buildings were stuccoed and painted.

An I-shaped ball court lies in one corner of the main plaza. The ball game was a religious ceremony in which two teams competed to knock a hard rubber ball through the stone rings on either side of the court. When a team put the ball through a ring, it had the right to claim anything worn by the spectators—at which point the spectators usually fled. Atypical of most Oaxacan ball courts, however, the one at the *Monte Albán* site is devoid of stone rings. The two niches in the diagonal corners of the court probably served as shrines for the patron deities of the ball game.

The *Templo de los Danzantes* (Temple of the Dancers) has interesting bas-reliefs, including carved, numbered slabs on the façade that suggest the use of the Calendar Round, the calendric system based on a 52-year cycle. Originally thought to be figures of dancers, the Danzantes are now believed to represent patients in a hospital or a school of medicine or, more likely, dead captives: The rubbery postures of the figures are interpreted as death poses, and the depiction of sexual organs in Mesoamerican art designates prisoners, because nudity was considered degrading. Some instances of sexual mutilation are represented in the reliefs.

Building J is an interesting arrowhead-shaped structure harboring a series of internal chambers. Its exterior is set with carved slabs that relate a story of conquest; the inverted heads inscribed above the town names represent the defeat of the rulers.

The subterranean Mixtec tombs, consisting of clusters of chambers decorated with frescoes, can be found throughout the site. Inside *Tomb 104*, at the northern end of the site, pottery—including a magnificent gray urn representing Cocijo, the Oaxacan rain god—was discovered, along with a skeleton. *Tomb 105* has a fresco similar to those discovered at Teotihuacán depicting a procession of nine male and nine female deities. In 1932, *Tomb 7* yielded dazzling treasures, including gold breastplates; jewelry made of jade, pearls, ivory, and gold; and fans, masks, and belt buckles of precious stones and metals. Most of these finds can be seen in Oaxaca's *Museo Regional* (see "Special Places" in *Oaxaca*, THE CITIES).

The site is 6 miles (10 km) southwest of the city of Oaxaca. From Oaxaca, take Calle García Vigil, cross the *zócalo,* and continue on Miguel Cabrera to the *periférico;* then cross the bridge and take the right fork. The site is open daily, but closes earlier during the rainy season (mid-May through mid-October); there's no admission charge on Sundays (no phone).

THE YUCATÁN PENINSULA

CHICHÉN ITZÁ, Yucatán Spanning two great eras of the Maya civilization, this site offers fine examples of the Classic and Postclassic architectural styles, with a powerful Toltec influence. By the time of the coming of the Toltec, the Maya were in decline, and the commingling of the two groups produced a new race, the Maya-Toltec. The Toltec brought to the "marriage" their ideas and gods, but they incorporated the Maya culture and knowledge of the skies. The Maya-Toltec rebuilt Chichén Itzá from a tiny village to a major center for the entire region. The site was abandoned in AD 1224.

The more interesting part of the *Chichén Itzá* site, the "new" city, lies on one side of the highway, surrounding the *Temple of Kukulcán* (also known as *El Castillo,* or The Castle). The *Temple of Kukulcán* features a mixture of architectural elements, from Maya corbeled vaults to Toltec warrior reliefs. At the base of the balustrade are giant carved heads of the feathered snake god Quetzalcóatl (called Kukulcán in Maya; thus the name of the structure), and at the top of the pyramid is a temple to that god. The pyramid rises in a series of terraces that cast shadows on the balustrade. On the first day of spring and the first day of autumn (the vernal and autumnal equinoxes), the undulating shadows form a serpent's body leading from the temple on top to the bottom. Even in this age of pocket calculators, the mathematics required to get those shadows to strike the right way on the right day boggle the mind. The phenomenon draws more than 100,000 sightseers and Maya pilgrims each year.

The math that went into building the rest of the *Temple of Kukulcán* is also impressive. The entire structure is scaled by four stairways of 91 steps on each of its four sides; add to that figure the top platform, and you get a total of 365: the number of days in the Maya calendar. The structure has 52 panels on its sides, which correspond to the number of years in a Maya century. There is a total of 18 terrace sections, representing the 18 months of the Maya year. Those who manage to climb to the very top of the pyramid and then descend a long, slippery stairway into its secret depths are rewarded with a glimpse of a stone throne in the shape of a jaguar with jade eyes, vestiges of red paint, and still-intact white flint fangs. The pyramid's giant 16-foot statues of warriors and the huge serpent columns are typically Toltec.

Sculptures of Toltec warriors can also be seen carved on the columns of the *Temple of the Warriors,* whose murals recount battles between the Toltec and surrounding groups. The temple is topped by a sculpture of a reclining Toltec Chac-Mool figure. Chac-Mools were the centerpiece on sacrificial altars, and they held large bowls in which were placed the still-beating human hearts torn from living victims. Scattered throughout the area are more Chac-Mool figures that, despite their name, bear no relation to Chac, the rain god.

The acoustics of the immense ball court, the largest in Mesoamerica, are so fine that a voice scarcely louder than a whisper can be heard 500 feet away. The games played here lasted 10 to 15 days; a bas-relief on the walls depicts one team's captain getting killed, though scholars are still not sure whether it was the captain of the losing team or the winning team. In any case, sacrificial death was considered a great honor by the Toltec.

The sacred cenote (sinkhole, or natural well) for which Chichén Itzá was named is believed to have been used by priest-kings seeking mystical visions. They first purified themselves in the sweat baths on the cenote's brink, then dived into its murky depths. In 1901–04, a US treasure hunter dredged the cenote and found thousands of figurines and artifacts that had been thrown in as offerings to the rain god. He also found skeletons of about 50 people, mostly children, which gave rise to fantasies of "sacrificial virgins." However, most experts today doubt that human sacrifice was practiced in the cenote, believing instead that the skeletons were those of people who drowned by accident over the centuries.

The *Group of a Thousand Columns* was probably the complex's marketplace. Several acres in size, the area is completely surrounded by colonnades resembling plumed serpents; it is surmised that at one time they supported a huge thatch roof.

Across the road, the ruins of "Old" Chichén are somewhat less impressive. There is a much smaller cenote, as well as a circular astronomical observatory. A spiral stairway leads to a small tower, whose windows align with certain stars at the equinox and solstice in such a way as to record the longest and shortest days of the year. Its circular structure makes the observatory a rarity among Maya buildings.

Also in this group of ruins is the ossuary, or bone house, a 30-foot-high pyramid with stairways on each side and a miniature temple on top. The temple is in the same form as the *Temple of Kukulcán;* the building was used by the Toltec as a burial place. Nearby are the *Temple of the Sculptured Tablets,* the *Nunnery* (it wasn't really a nunnery, but the Spanish thought it looked like one because of all the tiny rooms), the *Abbey* and the *Church* (two more Spanish-bestowed misnomers), and the *Akad-Dzib,* a building adorned with obscure writings and red handprints.

A smaller group of buildings in "Old" Chichén is still overgrown with jungle vegetation, and you have to walk along some rough trails to get to them. The structures in this part of *Chichén Itzá* include the *Temple of Old Chichén,* the *Temple of the Jaguar,* the *Temple of the Turtle,* the *Temple of the Sculptured Jambs,* the *Temples of the Lintels,* and the *Temple of the Hieroglyphic Jambs.* The paths leading among the different temples are known as *sacbes* (holy paths).

Chichén Itzá is about 100 miles (160 km) east of Mérida, Yucatán, on Route 180. There's a sound-and-light show with English narration nightly at 9 PM (in Spanish at 7 PM). The site is open daily; no admission charge on Sundays (no phone).

UXMAL, Yucatán Built around AD 825, this site was the major center of the Maya late Classic period. Its name means "three times built," referring to the multiple levels of the *Temple of the Magician,* which vividly demonstrate the Maya practice of burying older temples within pyramids that have new temples on top. Why Uxmal was abandoned is not as hard to fathom as why it was built in the first place, since it has no water. The Maya had to carve their own giant reservoirs, but clearly there were years when the rains failed to come. Chac, the elephant-nosed rain god, was the most important god in the hill country, and sculptures of him remain throughout the *Uxmal* site.

Uxmal was occupied well into the Postclassic period. In the 12th century, it was part of a triumvirate known as the League of Mayapán, which also included Chichén Itzá and Mayapán. (The latter city was overthrown and destroyed so completely that little remains to be seen at its site near the present-day village of Telchquillo.) *Uxmal* and other sites in the Puuc hill country show no Toltec influence. *Uxmal*'s beautifully proportioned and lavishly decorated temples and other buildings are generally considered the best example of unadulterated Classic Maya architecture.

The largest pyramid—the *Temple of the Magician* (also called the *Temple of the Dwarf*)—contains intricate masks, panels, and mosaics. (Be aware that the steps of the *Temple of the Magician* make for a very steep climb.) The *Governor's Palace,* a majestic structure 320 feet long and 40 feet wide, is considered the most beautiful of all Maya structures in North and Central America. Built on multiple levels with vaulted passages and lateral wings, the place contains some 20,000 hand-cut stones set into acres of geometric friezes. Northeast of the *Governor's Palace* is the *House of Turtles,* a well-proportioned, simply adorned structure.

The breathtaking *Nunnery Quadrangle,* whose façade contains many carved rain god masks, intertwined rattlesnakes (symbolizing transition), and figures of astronomers, is said to have served as a kind of learning center where Maya nobility from throughout the Yucatán shared knowledge of arts, sciences, and religion. Like many places in native ruins, the *Nunnery* was named by early Spanish explorers, who had little idea of the real purpose of the various buildings; in this case, the Spanish thought the small rooms in the group of buildings resembled nuns' cells. The *House of the Doves,* so named for the dovecote design in the roof comb, is also well worth a look.

Many of the ruins at *Uxmal* remain almost unexplored, and there is plenty to see. Archaeologists move slowly among the remote sections of the ruins, sifting through every spoonful of earth as it is removed. The *House of the Old Woman* and the *Temple of the Phalli* (named for a group of giant phallic monuments that were removed in the early 20th century after tourists complained that they were obscene) still await further exploration. Freelance guides usually gather at the ruins awaiting tourists; guided tours through the ruins usually take about two hours. Many visitors like to return after a tour and wander among the monuments on their own.

A sound-and-light show with a recorded English narrative of the history of *Uxmal* is presented nightly except Mondays at 9 PM (in Spanish at 7 PM). *Uxmal* is 50 miles (80 km) south of Mérida along Route 180. The site is open daily; no admission charge on Sundays (no phone).

Devotees of Maya culture usually continue on to the ruins at *Kabah,* 14 miles (23 km) from *Uxmal.* Formerly a disappointing pile of rubble, *Kabah* is now undergoing extensive restoration. Even more beautiful are the ruins of *Labná,* with its huge palace and beautiful city gate, a few miles farther down the road. Both sites are open daily; there's no admission charge on Sundays (no phone).

THE CARIBBEAN COAST

COBÁ, Quintana Roo This 81-square-mile Maya city, not far from the *Tulum* archaeological site (see below) and Cancún, is slowly being reclaimed from the jungle. Discovered in 1897, the site was only opened to the public in 1973, with major excavations beginning a year later. Cobá was one of the largest cities in the Yucatán and boasted a population of 50,000. Much older than Tulum, it is thought to have been a major trading and religious center. It was connected by a network of highways with such major Maya cities as Chichén Itzá and Uxmal. Already uncovered are a 150-foot-high pyramid surrounded by smaller ones; a nine-tiered castle; and remnants of a ball court. Along the coast, north of *Tulum,* are hundreds of smaller sites. A NASA satellite survey using special infrared photography revealed a massive network of irrigation canals between raised terraces that scientists believe allowed the Maya to raise crops in this swampy region.

Cobá is on Route 307, 26 miles (42 km) from *Tulum. A Club Med Villa Arqueológica* (no local phone; 5-203-3086 or 5-203-3833 in Mexico City; 800-CLUB-MED; fax: 5-203-0681 in Mexico City) is at the site. The ruins are open daily; there's no admission charge on Sundays (no phone).

TULUM, Quintana Roo Tulum was the only Maya city known to have been encircled by a wall fortification. Built around AD 1280 by seafaring Maya traders, it is also one of the few Maya sites on the seacoast. This late Postclassic city is often referred to as "decadent"; that is, it dates from the time of the waning of the Maya civilization. Although it was built by the Maya, the site lacks their refinement of style; the squarish structures are crudely designed and constructed.

The structures found at *Tulum* (about 60 in all) are comparatively small in scale. *El Castillo* is the zone's most prominent—and curious—structure; it does resemble a castle, and for all we know it may actually have been one. Walk carefully to the side facing the sea for a stunning view of white, sandy beaches at the bottom of 80-foot limestone cliffs. About 400 yards offshore is a "blue hole," the ocean equivalent of a cenote. The *Temple of the Frescoes* contains rare Maya paintings, vivid murals, and sculptured decorations. *Tulum*'s most intriguing building is the *Temple of the Descending God,* whose entrance is dominated by a large sculpture of a winged deity descending headfirst from the heavens. The conventional theory is that this may represent the rain god; an alternative theory is that it represents a descending spaceman. Yet another theory suggests that it is actually a rather obscure bee god who helped the city's residents to produce honey. (Then again, it may have represented a special god of divers, as undersea diving was an important occupation here.) Other buildings of note are the *Temple of the Initial Series* and the *Great Palace.*

This area offers some natural, as well as manmade (however old), amenities. The beach just below the site is beautiful, and the local waters can be fished year-round. *Tulum* is 81 miles (129 km) south of Cancún via Route 180 east to Puerto Juárez, then south along Route 307. The site is open daily; there's no admission charge on Sundays (no phone).

Bullfights: The Kings of the Rings

Ernest Hemingway once said there are two kinds of spectators at a bullfight: those who identify with the bull and those who identify with the matador. The first group cannot hope to enjoy a bullfight and never will. While bullfighting is certainly a part of the culture of Mexico, some people will be much happier if they leave this Mexican experience to the aficionados.

A spectacle rather than a sport, the bullfight dates from before the Christian era; modern bullfighting originated on the Iberian Peninsula during the 12th century. The Spanish brought bullfighting to Mexico just eight years after the conquest, and the first official bullfight in the New World took place in 1529.

Little has changed over the centuries. The elaborate bullfighting ceremony opens with the *desfile* (starting parade). First, the *alguacil* (horseback rider) rides across the ring, salutes the authorities, and asks permission to begin the spectacle. Dressed in black, the *alguacil* then returns to the portal from which he came, signaling the beginning of the *desfile.* The *alguacil* leads off, followed closely by the three matadors, costumed in tight-fitting, beautifully embroidered *trajes de luces* ("suits of lights"). Their *banderilleros* (assistants) walk behind them in similar but less costly uniforms; by comparison, the *picadores* (mounted lancers) appear most businesslike, attired in yellow breeches, velvet jackets, and frilled shirts. The *picadores* are followed by lesser ring attendants and, finally, the team of mules that eventually will drag away the dead bull. After the parade, the ring is cleared, the crowd hushed, the *presidente,* who is in charge of the bullfight, waves a handkerchief, and a trumpet announces the first bull. As the bull rushes into the ring, a barb is thrust into the animal's hide.

Every bullfight has three *tercios* (thirds). Like an act in a play, each *tercio* has its own particular character and action; tension builds from *tercio* to *tercio,* culminating in the end of the third "act." During the first *tercio,* the *banderilleros* test the behavior of the bull, who is least dangerous at this time, charging quickly but wildly. The matador stands behind a wooden *burladero* (barrier) and observes the bull before he handles the animal himself. During this phase of the drama the matador uses a heavy gold silk cape. The pass he almost always uses at the very beginning, when he is first facing the bull, is the *verónica:* The matador profiles himself to the bull holding one end of the cape in front of himself and extending the other end with either his right or left arm. A good pass is smooth and flowing, with the bull passing by and the matador moving nothing but his arms. If the matador is jumpy, or the pass jerky, the pass is considered poor work. After these preliminaries, the horses come in, and the *picador* pokes the bull with a long pointed pole. The matador then lures the bull away from the horse and does more *quite* (capework).

The second *tercio* begins with the clearing of the ring, leaving the bull alone with a *banderillero,* who must thrust into the bull's hump *banderillas* (26-inch wooden poles that end in vicious, harpoon-like barbs). The purpose: to weaken the huge tangle of muscles that controls the bull's head, forcing the animal to keep its head lowered, which facilitates the kill in the third *tercio.*

The final "act" features the matador's bravest and most artistic work. The matador exchanges the large cape of the previous two *tercios* for a small *muleta* (piece of red flannel). By now familiar with the bull and its charges, he will have decided exactly what kinds of passes to use in the last flourish. If he feels the bull has been weakened too much by the lance and barbs, he will fight it *por arriba* (from above), passing the *muleta* over the bull's horns to keep its head up. If the bull is still strong, he will fight it *por abajo* (from below), dragging the cape along the ground to lower the animal's head. It is not unusual for an artistic fighter confronted with a good bull to lead the animal in a complete circle with one fluid, graceful movement. The matador will execute a series of passes—from three to a dozen—that end with a concluding *pase de pecho* (chest pass), when the bull's horns seem almost to scrape the chest of the matador. When the matador decides the bull is slowing down, he goes in for the killing pass—a special way of stabbing the animal so that it dies instantly.

Don't be disappointed if you don't see a great variety of showy passes—this is not the sign of a bad matador (sometimes a poor matador uses fancy passes to hide his lack of skill). If the matador stands close to the bull, doesn't jump back when the horns almost graze his body, passes the bull smoothly, and dominates it while staying out of trouble, you are seeing a good fight.

At the end of a creditable fight, the matador will be called to the center of the ring to take a bow. If he has done a very good job, the audience will wave white handkerchiefs, petitioning the judge to award an ear to the matador. Depending on the quality of the fight, the judge will award one or two ears. If the fight has been truly extraordinary, the matador will be given both ears and the tail. When the triumphant matador takes his tour of the ring, it is customary to throw hats, jackets, flowers, and wine flasks to him. (Never throw a seat cushion, which is an insult and is also against the law.)

The top matadors in Mexico today are Miguel Espinoza ("Armillita Chico"), Manuel Mejía, Eloy Cabazos, Jorge Gutiérrez, Mariano Ramos, Francisco Daddoli, and Alejandro and David Silveti. Although bullfighting is still mainly practiced by men, Conchita Cintrón, Raquel Martínez, and Spain's Cristina Sánchez have emerged as leading female matadors; their skills in the bullring have gained them a degree of respect and fame in this macho sport.

There are two seasons in bullfighting: *temporada grande* (the big season), with veteran matadors; and the corridas *novilladas* (the little season), when the novices fight. In the border towns, the *temporada grande* is in the autumn, but in the rest of the country, it is in the winter. During the big season, there are usually some Spanish matadors in Mexico, as there are no bullfights in Spain between October and *Easter*.

In Mexico City, Guadalajara, and Tijuana, corridas are regularly scheduled events (for additional details, consult the individual reports in THE CITIES). Many smaller towns hold bullfights (or at least matches with aspiring bullfighters practicing on whatever taurine opponent is at hand), and local tourist offices can provide information. You can also visit haciendas where the bulls for Mexico City and Guadalajara rings are bred. Las Peñuelas, near Aguascalientes in north-central Mexico, is one of the best; visits there can be arranged through local hotels.

Shopping at the Source

Almost any regional Mexican craft, from handwoven serapes to native pottery and fine silver jewelry, can be found in the shops of Mexico City's Zona Rosa. But it's far more fun to buy them in the marketplace of their original provincial town, perhaps even from the artisan who made them. In many places, shoppers are expected to bargain; to do this, a buyer really should know some basic Spanish, even if it's just a few numbers (see *Useful Words and Phrases* in the GLOSSARY). When absolutely necessary, however, body language will suffice. There are several approaches to bargaining, depending on the place, the item you are after, and your personality. One way to shop is simply to look carefully, decide upon a fair price, and make a firm offer. Or you can offer half to two-thirds of the requested price and argue firmly from there.

Although bargaining is fun, very often the amount in question is so small that it is easier for most tourists to be generous. Also be aware that haggling over prices is not always appropriate or allowed. Don't bargain in shops that have the sign *"Precios Fijos"* (fixed prices), in government shops (often called *Artes Populares*), or in the shops of hotels.

Native crafts are usually less expensive in local markets than in shops, but it is better to buy more valuable items—jewelry or gems—in reputable shops. If someone offers to sell an archaeological relic from a Mexican ruin, turn him or her down flat. In most cases these "relics" are manufactured by the truckload, and if by some wild chance you are being offered a genuine artifact, the sale is illegal, and the item cannot be exported from Mexico.

Check carefully the quality of any merchandise you are considering buying. Often, goods presented as hand-crafted are patently machine-made—although if the price is right and the item attracts you, this is certainly no reason to refrain from buying it. Just try to make sure you are paying what the item is worth.

Besides native crafts, Mexico does have occasional bargains on items produced outside the country. Many tourists flock to the Mexican border towns to buy duty-free items ranging from French perfume and Japanese and Chinese silks and laces to Irish linen tablecloths. (*Warning:* Some expensive items carrying the name of Gucci and other top European designers, and sold in shops of the same name, are *not* the real thing, no matter what you're told—they are imitations made in Mexico and sold through a quirk in Mexican laws that will gradually disappear as the North American Free Trade Agreement takes effect.) Tijuana is the largest duty-free shopping zone in Mexico, though many exemptions will fade away in time under NAFTA.

You are allowed to bring most Mexican crafts into the US duty-free under the Generalized System of Preferences (GSP) program. For additional information about US customs regulations, see GETTING READY TO GO. Certain items are produced or crafted especially well in Mexico. Below, we offer a description of some uniquely Mexican materials, products, and arts. (For a list of the best shops in Mexico's major cities and resorts, see the *Shopping* entries in THE CITIES.)

COPPER AND TIN GOODS Copper was the favorite metal of the Mixtec and the Aztec, and items made from copper and tin can be found all over Mexico. Kettles, pots, pans, and pitchers are sold in markets, as well as in the more expensive shops. Always check for quality—some articles are actually made of iron sprayed with copper-toned paint.

Many towns in the state of Michoacán are famous for their copper crafts, especially the village of Santa Clara del Cobre, about 20 minutes southwest of Pátzcuaro. The town hosts a colorful *Fiesta del Cobre* (Copper Festival) each August. To appreciate the importance of copper to the area, visit the *Museo del Cobre* (on the main street in Santa Clara), which has a broad selection of pieces on exhibit and for sale. Interestingly, all copper items here are made from recovered electrical wire, not metal from mines.

FINE ARTS AND CRAFTS Mexico is the home of many working artists and artisans, some of whom combine new materials and design with the art of the past to produce original painting, sculpture, weaving, jewelry, and much more. In many ways, Mexico is the perfect place for an artist to live: Life moves slowly and has been relatively inexpensive; also, the country's great natural beauty is inspiring.

You can see the work of resident artists in galleries and shops in towns and cities throughout the country. San Miguel de Allende and Puerto Vallarta have some of the best work.

MUSICAL INSTRUMENTS Should you plan to serenade someone back home, visit Paracho in the state of Michoacán. The town is the largest producer of handmade guitars in Mexico. Here, you'll also find excellent hand-crafted violins and mandolins. This is also the site of Mexico's annual *Feria de la Guitarra* (Guitar Fair), held in late July or early August.

POTTERY AND LACQUERWARE One of the major crafts of Mexico, there's a lot of it—some of high artistic value—and it's usually inexpensive. To play it safe, don't buy Mexican pottery to cook in, and *never* store acidic foods in it, since lead compounds are often used in glazing. (If you can ascertain that the pottery is fired at high temperatures, it's safe; lead is dangerous only in pottery fired at low temperatures.) Each area of the country has its special designs and materials. Oaxaca pottery is satiny black or glazed with an unusual green. You can choose as well from delicately painted Tlaquepaque pottery, Puebla earthenware, or Mexico City's modern designs.

Lacquerwork and ceramics also are often of high quality. The lacquer is made from *chía* oil (a combination of wild sage and *aje,* the remains of plant lice). Dolomite and other minerals are added to produce a lacquer as fine as that made from the sap of the Asian sumac. Lacquer trays usually have polished black backgrounds painted with flowers or designs in gold lacquer. The state of Michoacán is famous for its exquisite lacquerware; some fine examples are available in the market and the handicrafts shops in Morelia and Pátzcuaro. Uruapan, a Tarasco town near Pátzcuaro, boasts some of the finest lacquerwork in the region, as well as a Sunday market and an excellent regional crafts museum—the *Museo de Artes Populares*—whose annual competitions attract the finest work in the state. In Chiapa de Corzo, a village located 8 miles (14 km) east of Tuxtla Gutiérrez, Chiapas, you will find colorful, elaborately painted lacquered gourds of varying sizes, called *jícaras.*

PRECIOUS AND SEMI-PRECIOUS STONES Be wary of gems that are sold as bargains. Jade has not been found in Mexico since the Spanish conquest; turquoise, like all other stones, should only be bought in reputable stores.

Mexico does, however, have high-quality amethysts and opals and some lovely onyx and black obsidian. Mexico's coral jewelry also is beautiful. But beware: Some species of coral—especially black coral, sold in Cozumel and nearby areas—are protected and cannot be imported into the US.

Querétaro is mainly known for its fine gems, especially amethysts, opals, and topaz. Onyx is of high quality here, also. One reliable store is *El Rubí* (3 Av. Madero Pte., just off Plaza Principal, between Juárez and Allende; phone: 42-120984), which carries a wide assortment of fiery opals, as well as amethyst, topaz, agate, and alexandrite, sold set or loose. Other small towns in the area, including San Juan del Río and Tequisquiapan, boast fine stonecutting, polishing, and jewelry-making industries.

RESORTWEAR Resort areas specialize in locally designed sportswear that is machine-made but of high quality and style.

SILVER This precious metal has been plentiful in Mexico since before the Spanish conquest. Silver items should be marked *sterling* or *.925,* which indicates that there are not less than 925 grams of pure silver for every 1,000 grams of weight. If you are told that the silver in the jewelry came from local mines, be skeptical: Nowadays, all silver from Mexican mines goes to the central Bank of Mexico, where it is melted into bars and then resold around the country to craftspeople.

Taxco, in the state of Guerrero and a major silver-mining area since the arrival of Cortés, remains famous throughout Mexico for its silver crafts. Saltillo, southwest of Monterrey, also has some fine silver shops, including *Platería Taxco* (428 Victoria; phone: 84-112854). Nearby is the *Moeller Platería Saltillo* (Moeller Silversmiths of Saltillo; 212 Victoria; phone: 84-142726), which offers tours and sells silver items.

WOVEN GOODS Serapes, rebozos (shawls), blankets, and other woven articles are usually great bargains. They should be handloomed from wool; examine the weave to make sure that other yarns weren't used. Jocotepec, a village on the shores of Lago de Chapala southwest of Guadalajara, is famed for its white wool serapes. Pátzcuaro, in the state of Michoacán, is also well known for high-quality serapes and for embroidery and rugs, plus it has a native market that shouldn't be missed: Every Friday, residents of the nearby hill and lake villages stream into town with their wares. Also in Pátzcuaro is the *Casa de los Once Patios* (House of the Eleven Patios), a colonial-era convent building in which local crafts are displayed and sold. Other towns around Lago de Pátzcuaro are noted for their fine crafts. Erongaríquaro is a small Tarasco village that has some of the best cambric handloomed fabrics and native embroidery; Tzintzuntzan also has fine fabrics. (For more information on all these locations, see *The West Coast: Nogales to Mexico City,* in DIRECTIONS.

Izúcar de Matamoros, a village near Puebla, produces exceptional rebozos. Hand-embroidered blouses and ponchos are also made in the Puebla area.

Other top spots for handmade garments include the Mezquital region, east of Querétaro, where the natives produce hand-embroidered clothing. In the state of Guanajuato, the twin villages of Uriangato and Moroleón specialize in well-crafted rebozos and blankets.

Saltillo, southwest of Monterrey, is famous for its fine wool serapes. Here, you can watch the process—spinning the wool, dyeing it in bright colors, and weaving it the old-fashioned way on a handloom—at the family-run *El Sarape de Saltillo* (305 Hidalgo Sur; phone: 84-120187). Saltillo's central market also has stalls that sell other woven articles and rugs.

East of Mexico City, in central Mexico, is the state of Tlaxcala, one of the country's most famous wool-weaving centers. Santa Ana, less than 2 miles (3 km) south of the capital city, also called Tlaxcala, has shops with bolt textiles and serapes. Toluca, 33 miles (53 km) southwest of Mexico City, has long been famous for its Friday market; woolens, especially sweaters, are a good buy here. *CASART,* a handicrafts center featuring indigenous crafts, has a branch in Toluca's zoo (700 Paseo Tollocán Ote.; phone: 72-147830).

Spa-Hopping Special

Montezuma, the 16th-century Aztec emperor, was one of Mexico's earliest *balneario* (spa) enthusiasts. In fact, three of the mineral baths that Montezuma visited—in Tehuacán, Ixtapán de la Sal, and Oaxtepec—are still in use today. A number of Mexican *balnearios* are true resorts, with swimming, tennis, horseback riding, and hiking available; spas with these facilities are the most expensive. Others are mainly places to "take the waters," either outside in natural mineral springs or inside in spring-fed pools.

As more Americans discover the pleasures and benefits of mineral baths, the number of spas continues to grow. And Mexico's spa potential is formidable—there are more than 570 known warmwater mineral springs in the country. But beware: Many spas still have rustic facilities that may not be that clean.

Most mineral waters contain a mixture of sulfate of soda, sulfate of lime, carbonate of lime, sodium chloride, magnesium, and some sulfuric acid. This may not sound appetizing, and it certainly doesn't look appetizing (the mineral waters are usually a murky brown color), but for most people the waters are amazingly soothing.

Most of Mexico's spas are in the states of Aguascalientes (literally "hot waters"), Guanajuato, Michoacán, Morelos, Puebla, Querétaro, San Luis Potosí, Jalisco, Sinaloa, and México. These are our favorites; the entries are listed alphabetically by location.

BAJA CALIFORNIA NORTE

RANCHO LA PUERTA, Tecate Some 52 miles (83 km) southeast of San Diego, this 83-unit health and fitness resort has been operating for more than 50 years. The spa, on a 150-acre mountain site, has pools, tennis courts, gyms, a jogging track, hiking trails, and about 30 different exercise classes daily. However, it does not have mineral or thermal waters. Reservations should be made at least six months in advance, particularly for the popular spring, fall, and holiday periods. Information: *Rancho La Puerta,* PO Box 463057, Escondido, CA 92046 (phone: 665-41155; 800-443-7565; collect calls from Canada accepted at 619-744-4222; fax: 665-41108).

GUANAJUATO

SPA LA CALDERA, Abasolo This resort on the Guanajuato–Mexico City route, 19 miles (30 km) southwest of Irapuato on the Carretera Abasolo, has 117 rooms, a restaurant, a bar, gardens, outdoor thermal pools, four tennis courts, a Jacuzzi, and a variety of sports facilities. Information: *Spa La*

Caldera, 201 Guerrero Ote., 36970 Abasolo, Guanajuato, México (phone: 469-30020; phone/fax: 469-30021).

BALNEARIO COMANJILLA, Comanjilla About 18 miles (29 km) southeast of León (235 miles/376 km northwest of Mexico City) on Route 45, this restful, pleasant spa offers three outdoor pools, 124 rooms (each with its own thermal bath), horseback riding, a restaurant, a bar, movies, steamrooms, and even a playground. The León airport is an hour's flight from Mexico City, and transportation from the airport to the spa (15 minutes away) is available for an extra charge. Information: *Balneario Comanjilla,* Apdo. Postal 111, 37000 León, Guanajuato, México (phone/fax: 47-146522; 47-120091 phone/fax in León).

HACIENDA TABOADA, San Miguel de Allende This lovely, family-oriented resort has 64 pleasant rooms, two pools, a restaurant, a bar, a disco, horseback riding, tennis, and badminton. The bathtub taps offer hot and cold thermal water for soothing soaks. Rate includes three meals a day. It's 6 miles (10 km) north of San Miguel on Km 8 of Route 51, with complimentary bus service into town. Information: *Hacienda Taboada,* Apdo. Postal 100, 37700 San Miguel de Allende, Guanajuato, México (phone: 415-20850 or 415-20888; 212-750-0375 in New York City; 800-447-7462 elsewhere in the US; fax: 415-21798).

JALISCO

RANCHO RÍO CALIENTE, La Primavera Here is a vegetarian resort that combines thermal mineral springs, a spa, and a diet center. This 50-room property, an hour northwest of Guadalajara on Route 15, has three pools fed by hot mineral springs and a cold-water pool as well. It offers massages, facials, mud baths, scalp reflexology, yoga instruction, good food (much of it home-grown), and fireplaces in every room. Information: *Spa Vacations Ltd.,* PO Box 897, Millbrae, CA 94030 (no local phone; 415-615-9543 in California; fax: 415-615-0601 in California).

MÉXICO

IXTAPÁN, Ixtapán de la Sal This sprawling facility offers thermal and freshwater pools, Roman baths, tennis, private pools, Swedish massage, a large beauty clinic and spa, movies, a playground, horseback riding, a nine-hole golf course, and 250 suites and chalets. *Balneario Nuevo Ixtapán,* the public baths, offers thermal pools and a scenic train ride through beautiful gardens. Avoid weekends, when it is very crowded. The hotel does not accept personal checks. Information: *Hotel Ixtapán,* Tonalá 177, Ixtapán de la Sal, 06700 México, DF, México (phone: 714-30125 or 714-30021; 5-264-2613 in Mexico City; 800-90472 elsewhere in Mexico; 800-223-9832 in the US); or *International Spa Promotions,* 9311 San Pedro, Ste. 1110, San Antonio, TX 78216 (phone: 800-638-7950; fax: 210-342-9789).

Best Beaches off the Beaten Path

Unless it were to become an island floating freely between the US and Guatemala, it is hard to imagine how Mexico could be any better endowed with coastlines and beaches. Except for the borders with neighboring countries, it is entirely surrounded by warm, tropical waters: 5,500 miles of shoreline on the Pacific Ocean and the Gulf of California (also called the Sea of Cortés) in the west, the Gulf of Mexico and the Caribbean Sea in the east. And by virtue of the spiny finger of the Baja Peninsula shooting 800 miles south into the Pacific, it actually has *two* coasts on both the Pacific Ocean and the Gulf of California. Mexico is a particularly favored haven for beach lovers, with as varied and vital a beach life as any place east of Maui.

The west coast, the traditional sunning spot, boasts some of North America's most celebrated beach resorts, including Mazatlán, Ixtapa, Puerto Vallarta, Acapulco, and farther south, the rapidly growing resort of Huatulco. Wide, powder-white beaches, a tropical climate, warm waters, and spectacular sunsets (on this coast, the sun usually plunges into the sea with great drama, since most vistas look directly westward) attract thousands of tourists from Mexico and around the world, year-round, year after year. But the Gulf of California–Pacific Ocean coast extends thousands of miles above and below the famous strip of resorts, and there are pristine beaches and lagoons, tiny fishing villages, and unexplored coves, from the start of the Gulf of California to Puerto Madero (near the Guatemalan border).

On the eastern coast, the beaches on the Gulf of Mexico tend to be darker and less developed than those in the west, although Mexico's Caribbean coast has white, soft beaches and fine resorts at Cancún, Cozumel, and Isla Mujeres. The 1,400 miles of eastern shore are, however, susceptible to tropical storms and strong currents. The beach season peaks from December through *Semana Santa* (Holy Week), after which the rains and winds tend to increase. Though there is certainly a winter "season" on the west coast, it is social, not seasonal; the beaches of the Pacific, from Mazatlán to all points south, can be enjoyed all year.

All beaches in Mexico are open to the public, meaning that visitors can swim and use all the facilities, even those near luxurious hotels (although the only way to get to some beaches is to walk through a hotel lobby). Beaches designated "public recreational areas" are maintained by the government and are much used by resident Mexicans. For details on the beaches that grace the larger resort areas—Acapulco, Los Cabos, the Cancún-Cozumel–Isla Mujeres area, Ensenada, Huatulco, Ixtapa-Zihuatanejo, Manzanillo, Mazatlán, Puerto Escondido, Puerto Vallarta, and Veracruz—consult the individual reports in THE CITIES. For those who prefer privacy and seclusion, there are hundreds of miles of undeveloped, largely untouched beaches along all of Mexico's coasts.

The following is a list of the best of those off-the-beaten-track strands, listed in geographical order, north to south, along each coast.

BAJA—THE PACIFIC AND GULF OF CALIFORNIA COASTS

PUNTA BANDA This peninsula on Bahía Todos Santos, near Ensenada, has 8 miles of beaches and coves. Cabins and campgrounds are open to the public.

VALLE DE SAN QUINTÍN An agricultural town 120 miles (192 km) south of Ensenada, San Quintín has beautiful beaches; the pismo clams that flourish here attract as many visitors as does the sea. The beach in front of *La Pinta San Quintín* (phone: 616-52878; 800-336-5454) is a lovely stretch of sand where clam diggers and horseback riders can be seen from dawn till dusk.

MALARRIMO Off the dirt road from Bahía Tortugas, this west coast beach attracts people looking for seashells and driftwood—it has an abundant supply of both.

SANTA ROSALÍA On the east coast of the Baja Peninsula, facing Guaymas across the Gulf of California, Santa Rosalía's beautiful beaches start south of town and get better all the way past Mulegé and into Bahía Concepción. Overnight accommodations are available at *El Morro* (Km 1.5 on the Carretera al Sur; phone/fax: 115-22390). *La Terraza* (Carretera Norte; phone: 115-20578) has decent food.

MULEGÉ This charming town in Baja California Sur has several outstanding stretches of white sand. Playa El Coyote is shaded by trees (a rarity at the beach), and Punta Arena provides a good setting for windsurfing. A couple of other beaches here have unique touches: Playa Santispaquis, the biggest (and most crowded), has a hidden hot spring, and Playa El Requesón leads to its own private island. There are several good choices for lodging. The *Serenidad* is the oldest and most comfortable hotel in the area (2 miles/3 km south of Mulegé on Rte. 1; phone: 115-30111); *Las Casitas* (right in town on Calle Madero; phone: 115-30019) is also recommended.

LORETO On the Gulf of California, north of La Paz, Loreto's beaches are shaded with date palms. Delicious seafood can be found at nearby restaurants. Loreto and its environs are slowly being developed into a major resort area. Renovated in 1995, the *Loreto Diamond* (Blvd. Misión de Nopoló, south of town; phone: 113-30700; 800-858-2258; fax: 113-30377) overlooks some of the area's finest beaches.

PUERTO BALANDRO, Isla Carmen In the Gulf of California, across from Loreto, this island port city is surrounded by wide, nearly empty, white-powder beaches and clear waters. It's accessible by boat from Loreto.

LA PAZ The charm and tropical weather of this capital on the Gulf of California coast lend themselves to a pleasant, easygoing beach life. Playa Coromuel, 3 miles (5 km) north of town, and Playa Pichilingue are both excellent for swimming.

GUAYMAS The beaches here are known more for shell collecting, clamming, sport fishing, and skin diving than for sunbathing, but the swimming conditions are usually adequate. Twelve miles (19 km) north on Bahía San Carlos are the area's best beaches, which rival the shorelines of Acapulco and Puerto Vallarta. Both Playa San Francisco and Playa Algodones, a white sand beach with a *Club Med* resort (you must buy the all-inclusive package to stay here; phone: 622-60166; 800-CLUB-MED; fax: 622-60070), have good swimming, snorkeling, windsurfing, fishing, and boating. The *Club Med* is open from early March through mid-October.

SAN BLAS Not far down the coast from Mazatlán, in the state of Nayarit, is this unspoiled port city. Easy to reach, free from the tourist deluge, and surrounded by lagoons and coconut, papaya, banana, and mango trees, San Blas's beautiful white beaches begin 1 mile (1.6 km) south of town. San Blas may lack the charged, day-and-night-party atmosphere of Mazatlán's resort beaches, but it has all the requisite facilities—bathhouses, food stands—as well as a peaceful, relaxing atmosphere. Playa del Rey, on a peninsula opposite the port of San Blas, is a beautiful virgin beach reached by boat from the *San Blas Pier*, near the *Aduana* (customs) building. Remote beaches such as Matanchén, south of San Blas, are good for camping and surfing.

RINCÓN DE GUAYABITOS This tiny village about 40 miles (65 km) north of Puerto Vallarta has the local reputation of being the poor man's Vallarta because of such fine beaches as Playa Chacala, Playa Chacalilla, Playa los Ayala, and Playa Rincón de Guayabitos. Other good choices are Playa Latracadero, a dreamy expanse of sand fringed with palm trees; and Playa San Francisco, an excellent sun-and-siesta beach (swimming in the churning surf here is risky, however). Farther south, surrounding Huanacaxtle, are Punta de Mita, Playa Anclote, and Playa Destiladeras—great spots for swimming, surfing, and snorkeling. A good hotel in Rincón de Guayabitos is the 145-room *Los Cocos* (Retorno las Palmas; phone/fax: 327-40190); for ritzier lodgings, there's the *Club de Playa Costa Azul* in nearby San Francisco (off Rte. 200; no phone).

YELAPA Except for the few hours when the *Sarape* (phone: 322-44777, 322-10262, or 322-10415) and other tour boats unload their passengers, Yelapa, from the native word meaning "Place of Reunions," is an ideal refuge from civilization. A one-hour boat ride from Mismaloya, which is 7 miles (11 km) south of Puerto Vallarta, this small fishing village with lovely beaches and tropical rustic surroundings has no telephones or TV sets. (You can also get here by motor launch from Boca de Tomatlán; see *Puerto Vallarta* in THE CITIES for more information.) A fairly sizable number of US, Canadian, and European expatriates have taken up residence here. The *Lagunita* hotel has comfortable accommodations, including a few cabins for rent, but because there are no phones, you must take your chances on finding a vacancy. The *Yacht Club* has disco dancing in the evenings.

In Yelapa you can ride horseback along the beach, or take the mountain trails to where townsfolk make huaraches (leather sandals), pottery, and woodcarvings. About a mile south of the village is a beautiful waterfall with a dramatic 150-foot drop. After a seafood lunch at one of the many thatch-roofed beachfront eateries, enjoy a relaxing stroll along the beach.

BARRA DE NAVIDAD This small, isolated vacation village, about 37 miles (59 km) north of Manzanillo, is mainly frequented by Mexicans, but that may change once word gets out about the great beaches here. Playa Barra de Navidad and Playa Melaque, nestled along the Bahía de Melaque, are the more popular choices, but don't overlook the quieter Boca de Iguanas and Playa Manzanilla, which merge to form a nearly 6-mile (10-km) length of coastline south of the village. Playa Tenacatita, set in a banana grove, is another wonderful beach; it's a good place for snorkeling. Beachfront accommodations can be found at the *Sands* hotel (24 Calle Morelos; phone: 333-70018) or at the more posh *Cabo Blanco* (Pueblo Nuevo; phone/fax: 335-55136 or 335-55103). The beaches are also home to such low-rise, inexpensive accommodations as the *Delfín* (23 Av. Morelos, Barra de Navidad; phone: 335-70068) and *De Legazpi* (Av. las Palmas, San Patricio; phone: 335-70397).

LA VENTOSA Seven miles (11 km) south of the port town of Salina Cruz, near the border between the states of Oaxaca and Chiapas, is this beachcomber's paradise; principal accommodations are hammocks stretched out beneath thatch-roofed canopies. Not for the Acapulco-loving crowd, but a beautiful beach on the Pacific's Gulf of Tehuantepec.

ISTMO DE TEHUANTEPEC (ISTHMUS OF TEHUANTEPEC) Where Route 200 follows the Pacific Coast to the Guatemala border, there are numerous side roads to almost unexplored, certainly uncrowded Pacific beaches. The sand is hot, the climate humid, and the accommodations rustic—but it's heaven for the sauna-and-steambath school of beach lovers.

THE GULF OF MEXICO COAST

CHACHALACAS Some 52 miles (83 km) north of Veracruz off Route 80, this resort area offers a never-ending expanse of gulf beach and huge sand dunes that can be explored in rented dune buggies. Although the waters can be rough, swimming is safe near the shore, and surfing and fishing are good. Boats are for rent near the Río Jalcomulco. Restaurants, baths, and showers are available, and there are a number of small, inexpensive hotels.

TECOLUTLA This enticing, palm-fringed beach in Papantla country, about 120 miles (192 km) north of Veracruz, is one of the few good gulf coast beaches. The *Balneario Tecolutla* (phone: 784-60071; fax: 784-60183) and *Marsol* (phone/fax: 784-60151) hotels offer simple but adequate rooms and meals. Although it shows signs of deterioration from its palmier 1980s resort days, it remains a quiet spot to enjoy warm water and a relaxed atmosphere.

PLAYA DEL CARMEN The white, powdery sand and crystal-clear blue waves of the shoreline of this fishing village 41 miles (66 km) south of Cancún draw swimmers, snorkelers, and divers galore. *Las Molcas* hotel (phone: 987-24609; fax: 987-30138), the posher *Continental Plaza Playacar* (phone: 987-30100; 800-88-CONTI; fax: 987-30348), and the *Diamond Playacar* (phone: 987-30341; 800-642-1600 outside New York State; 800-858-2258 outside Florida; fax: 987-30105) are good places to stay. Not only is Playa del Carmen a fine beach destination in its own right, but it also is a great jumping-off point for exploring some of the stunning beaches farther south toward and beyond *Tulum,* such as Playa Paamul, Playa Akumal, and Playa Chemuyil, as well as the little-known wilderness of the *Reserva de la Biósfera Sian Ka'an* (Sian Ka'an Biosphere Reserve) and the Boca Paila Peninsula. Playa del Carmen is also where you catch the ferry to the island of Cozumel, 11 miles offshore.

Scuba and Skin Diving: Best Depths

Some of the world's most noted diving spots lie off Mexico's long coasts. On the Caribbean, the clear, warm lagoons of Cozumel, Cancún, and Isla Mujeres teem with tropical fish and incredible coral deposits of intricate formation and colorful hues. All the major resort areas off the mainland Pacific Coast and on Baja California also offer ideal diving conditions. Every major Mexican beach resort rents equipment and offers instruction and organized diving tours. For details on diving opportunities in the larger coastal resort areas—Acapulco, Los Cabos, the Cancún-Cozumel–Isla Mujeres area, Ixtapa-Zihuatanejo, Manzanillo, and Puerto Vallarta—consult the individual reports in THE CITIES. Besides those well-known locales, the following out-of-the-way spots are sensational for underwater exploration.

BAJA—THE PACIFIC COAST

There are innumerable beaches and lagoons that offer great scuba diving along the Baja's Pacific Coast; most of these areas, however, have no formal access trails. In addition, there are few convenient places to get tanks filled along the Pacific Coast; they're especially scarce on Baja Sur. Divers on the good beaches around Ensenada find the water very cold in winter, and most wear wet suits.

BAJA—THE GULF OF CALIFORNIA COAST

This side of the peninsula offers better scuba facilities than the Pacific Coast side. Tanks, regulators, fins, snorkels, and masks can be rented in La Paz, where deep-sea diving is one of the biggest attractions. (Fishing is still the number-one draw.) Boats are available for daily rental, and *Baja Diving and Service* (*Plaza Cerraldo* shopping center, on the *malecón,* or boardwalk, La Paz; phone: 112-21826) offers a diesel-propelled houseboat (it sleeps six) that can be rented for a four-day cruise to the islands in the Gulf of California. *Baja Expeditions* (2625 Garnet Ave., San Diego, CA 92109; phone: 800-843-6967) operates week-long scuba trips from La Paz from early May through mid-November. Hotel-based trips are available during the entire period, while live-aboard trips are offered beginning in early June.

In Los Cabos, there are two superb dive operations: *Cabo Acuadeportes* (on Playa Chileno, by the *Cabo San Lucas* hotel; phone: 114-30117; 713-680-2090) and *Amigos del Mar* (at the entrance to the *Solmar* hotel on Blvd. Marina; phone: 114-30505; 800-344-3349). *Cabo Acuadeportes* offers one-, two-, and three-dive packages. *Amigos del Mar,* a *PADI* dive center, offers one- and two-dive packages and also takes reservations for the *Solmar V* diving and fishing boat, which has live-aboard accommodations. *Sea Safaris* in Manhattan Beach, California (phone: 800-821-6670) handles reservations for diving tours.

MAINLAND—THE PACIFIC COAST

The unspoiled waters, rocky coves, and resort facilities of Guaymas, a coastal town on the eastern side of the Gulf of California, make it an ideal diving spot. Bahía San Carlos, 13 miles (21 km) northwest of town, is a particularly popular diving area, with a yacht club, marina, numerous rocky coves, and nearby islands. Small craft and a complete line of diving equipment are available for rent at the *Marina San Carlos* (phone: 622-60230 or 622-60565) and *Gary's Place* (on Calle San Carlos, next to the *San Carlos* hotel; phone: 622-60049). Bahía Bocachibampo, 2 miles (3 km) west of Guaymas, is another popular diving spot; the Playa de Cortés has shops with all kinds of diving equipment for sale and rent.

Sensational Surfing on Mexico's Pacific Coasts

Although surfing is not an inherently Mexican sport, American surfers claim that Mexico's Pacific coastline—with its abundance of reef breaks, point breaks, and river-mouth breaks—offers some of the best waves in the world. Despite the dangerous undertow in many areas, as well as a distinct lack of appreciation of surfing on the part of most Mexicans, dedicated American surfers readily travel up and down the Pacific coasts (on Baja and on the mainland) to try waves at beaches big and little. Windsurfing also has become a popular sport at most major resorts. There is some surfing on the Gulf of Mexico and Caribbean coasts, but waves along Mexico's east shore are erratic.

A word of warning: There are few surfboards—and almost no rental facilities—in Mexico. Of the rental shops that do exist, many are stocked mostly with boards that US surfers in the area swear were stolen. Surfers familiar with the Mexican scene report that US-made boards are prime targets for theft, and advise visitors to take particular care of their equipment.

For details on fine surfing opportunities available at Ensenada, Ixtapa-Zihuatanejo, Los Cabos, Manzanillo, Mazatlán, Puerto Escondido (said to have the best surfing in the country), and Puerto Vallarta, consult the individual reports in THE CITIES. Many excellent surfing beaches now visited by US surfers are off the tourist track, however. Below, we offer a survey of Mexico's superlative out-of-the-way surfing spots, listed in geographical order (north to south), first on the Baja Peninsula and then along the long Pacific Coast.

BAJA—THE PACIFIC AND GULF OF CALIFORNIA COASTS

The entire Baja Peninsula is covered with hundreds of ideal surfing areas. Because many of them are near rugged terrain accessible only to four-wheel-drive vehicles, however, we include below only those that can be reached with relative ease.

HALFWAY HOUSE Halfway between Tijuana and Ensenada, where the Baja's Route 1 skids along the Pacific Coast, this spot, at the bottom of a 100-foot cliff, is a Baja favorite. Most surfers camp out or stay in Ensenada, spending the days on the waves or on the sand. Idyllic, anarchistic, hard-core, laid-back California surfer style reigns here.

EL ROSARIO DE ARRIBA Also known as Punta Baja, this area about 150 miles (240 km) south of Ensenada has excellent, long, right-point waves in the summer only. Take Route 1 to El Rosario, then take the exit (in town) for Bahía Rosario. Finally, look for the sign pointing to Punta Baja.

SANTA ROSALÍA This friendly fishing village, with excellent waves for all surfers, is about 9 miles (14 km) off a dirt road from the Punta Prieta turnoff on Route 1. In all, it's 330 miles (528 km) south of Ensenada. The amiable, relaxed atmosphere of the village adds to the pleasure of good surfing. Accommodations are available at *El Morro* (Km 1.5 on the Carretera al Sur; phone/fax: 115-22390), but many surfers prefer to camp out on the beach and enjoy the local supplies of fish.

THE PACIFIC COAST

SAN BLAS Just south of San Blas, on the harbor of Bahía Matanchén, there is a mile-long stretch with excellent right-point waves for beginners. Playa Las Islitas, on the bay, is the overall best place for surfing in the area. Just north of the bay, about a half mile on foot, there is a well-known area for advanced surfers called Stoners Point. South of San Blas, in a small fishing village called Santa Cruz, thrives a small community of American surfers—most of whom came to enjoy the surf and never left. Here the left-point waves are ideal. Playa del Rey, on a peninsula opposite the port of San Blas, is best place around for windsurfing; it can be reached by boat from the pier near the *Aduana* (Customs) building.

PLAYA AZUL TO BAHÍA PETALCALCO Mexico's most dangerous waves, comparable to the largest ones in Hawaii, are found along this stretch of warm coastal water about 60 miles (98 km) up the coast from Ixtapa, off Route 57. Although Bahía Petalcalco offers a spectacular vista point for ocean surfing, the area is also noted for robberies and unpleasant relations between natives and strangers. There are no accommodations, but the waves are definitely worth a day's journey for advanced surfers.

Great Golfing

Maintenance of golf greens is generally excellent throughout Mexico. Although many of the best Mexican courses are part of private country clubs or resort hotel complexes, it is possible for visitors to play at some of them. In the larger cities, as well as at most other inland points, it is extremely difficult for an outsider to gain access to private courses unless invited by a member who accompanies the guest (although several places do allow non-members to play on weekdays). In resort areas such as Acapulco, Cancún, and Manzanillo, and certain inland points—Avándaro, Cuernavaca, and Querétaro, for example—access is generally easier. And at any hotel that is connected with a golf course, or openly offers to secure greens privileges for its guests, few obstacles to entry are found. For more information on private clubs and tournaments, write to the *Confederación Mexicana de Golf* (Mexican National Golfing Association, Cincinnati 40-104, Colonia Nápoles, 03710 México, DF, México; phone: 5-563-9194). *Best Golf Tours* (332 Forest Ave., Suite 27, Laguna Beach, CA 92651; phone: 800-227-0212) offers golf packages to Acapulco, Cocoyoc, Guadalajara, Ixtapa, Los Cabos, Manzanillo, Mazatlán, and Puerto Vallarta that include several rounds of golf on some of Mexico's best courses.

For details on the prime golf courses located in major cities and resorts, see *Golf* in the individual reports in THE CITIES. The following is a selective list of top tee-off spots that lie away from the tourist track. They are listed alphabetically by location.

PUERTO AVENTURAS GOLF CLUB, Puerto Aventuras Part of the expanding Puerto Aventuras development on Mexico's Caribbean coast, this extraordinary 18-hole course was designed by Tommy Lehman to incorporate natural cenotes (sinkholes) and ancient Maya ruins into the playing field. With so many spectacular sights from one hole to the next, it is almost impossible to keep your eye on the ball. It's a tough par 72 for men and 74 for women. Almost every green is surrounded by sand traps; the long, winding course also has an exceptionally high share of doglegs, and the roughs are literally jungles. Take a lot of extra balls. Electric carts and clubs can be rented from the pro shop, and the 19th hole is a favorite watering hole for golfers and yachting enthusiasts alike. The manager is Edgar H. Giffenig; the pro,

Desiderio Coot. About 13 miles (21 km) south of Playa del Carmen on the Yucatán Peninsula's Rte. 307 (phone: 987-2221l or 987-22233).

HACIENDA JURICA, Querétaro This 18-hole, par 72 golf course often hosts tournaments, and lessons are offered. Carts are available for rent, and there's a pro shop. The facility also has tennis courts, a pool, squash courts, and horseback riding. (See *Mexico on Horseback,* below.) The manager is Francisco Gómez and the pro is Olaf Ferreira. Six miles (10 km) north of Querétaro on Rte. 45, then 2 miles (3 km) west on Rte. 57 (phone: 42-180622).

QUERÉTARO, Querétaro The 18-hole course here was designed by Percy Clifford; the par is 72. To play, a visitor must be a member's guest or must be a member of a golf club in the US (bring a letter from your club secretary). On the premises are a pool, tennis courts, and horseback riding. Golf lessons are available, and there's a pro shop on the premises. However, there are no golf carts. The manager is Manuel Contreras; the pro is Mario Moreno. Km 223 of the Pan-American Hwy. (phone: 42-162011).

SAN GIL, San Juan del Río In the heart of the Bajío region, this 18-hole course, next to *La Mansión de Andrea* hotel, is rated among the five best in the country by the *Confederación Mexicana de Golf.* It is also a favorite training course for Mexico's golf pros. In the middle of the grounds is a 54-acre lake that is visible from more than half of the holes. The par is 72, and electric carts are available for rent. Guests of *La Estancia* and of the *Antigua Hacienda Galindo,* which is 3 miles (5 km) away, may play here. The manager is Carlos Díaz; the pro, Enrique Serna. On Rte. 57 (phone: 467-20050).

AVÁNDARO, Valle de Bravo/Lago de Avándaro Percy Clifford designed this 18-hole, par 72 course, which is considered one of the finest in Mexico. A river flows through, and most of the holes have sand traps. At 6,000 feet, the course offers lovely views. Accommodations are available nearby at the *Avándaro* hotel (phone: 726-60366; fax: 726-60122), *Loto Azul* hotel (phone: 726-22747), and *Los Arcos* hotel (phone: 726-20042). Alejandra Simon is the manager; Ricardo Plata is the pro. About 80 miles (128 km) west of Mexico City. Mailing address: Vega del Río, Fracc. Avándaro, 51200 Valle de Bravo, Estado de México, México (phone: 726-60370).

Mexico on Horseback

Along with Catholicism, a lust for gold, and a host of Spanish traditions, Hernán Cortés introduced one thing to Mexico that proved to be an outright blessing: the horse. Actually, it's more accurate to say that Cortés *reintroduced* the horse to Mexico—although there were none in the country when he arrived, cave paintings discovered in northern Mexico indicate that a smaller species once existed here, but apparently became extinct. Mexicans are enthusiastic and skilled riders, and the tradition of horsemanship here is a perfect marriage between the equestrian heritage of Spain and the workaday requirements of ranches and farms throughout Mexico's northwestern mountains and plains country.

Anyone driving from the US border to central Mexico will cross arid ranch and cattle country, where opportunities to ride are plentiful; most towns of any size have independent stables or hotels with riding facilities. But opportunities are just as rife along the eastern and western seacoasts. Beach riding is a favorite pastime, and horses can be rented in such resorts as Acapulco, Cancún, Mazatlán, and Puerto Vallarta, as well as up and down the Baja Peninsula. Horseback riding is offered at the *Club Med* resorts at Guaymas (phone: 622-60166; 800-CLUB-MED; fax: 622-60070) and Playa Blanca (on the Costa Careyes, in the state of Jalisco; phone: 335-10001/2/3 and 335-10005; 800-CLUB-MED; fax: 335-10004), which also has an intensive English riding program for an additional cost.

The vicarious equestrian has the option of experiencing a *charreada,* a fantastic display of traditional riding skill and bravado. (For details, see *Quintessential Mexico.*) For the active horseback rider, two kinds of equestrian experiences can be enjoyed in Mexico: short rides on horses rented by the hour, and longer horseback expeditions.

RIDING BY THE HOUR

It is possible throughout Mexico simply to rent a horse by the hour for a leisurely ride around the countryside or for practice in the ring of the renting stable. Several places noted for good riding (you don't have to be an overnight guest) are listed below; there are scores more. Entries are listed alphabetically by location.

EL MOLINO DE LA ALBORADA, Chiapas The state of Chiapas in southern Mexico offers beautiful, unspoiled lakes and forests. *El Molino,* a lovely 10-room (all with fireplaces) hotel, is located on the mountain slope above picturesque San Cristóbal de las Casas (in the Valle de Hueyzacatlán, or Hueyzacatlán Valley). It offers fine horseback riding, plus a good restaurant and a panoramic view of San Cristóbal. (*Note:* At press time, Chiapas seemed peaceful following the anti-government uprising in 1994; still, you may want to check with tourism authorities before traveling there.) Two miles (3 km) southeast of San Cristóbal on Rte. 190. Mailing address: Apdo. Postal 50, 29200 San Cristóbal de las Casas, Chiapas, México (phone: 967-80935).

RANCHO LA ESTANCIA, Chihuahua This ranch is situated in the midst of a Mennonite colony at the entrance to the Sierra Madre. Horseback excursions to nearby Barranca del Cobre (Copper Canyon), as well as hunting and fishing, are offered. There are 40 rooms with TV sets, a bar, a restaurant, a pool, a sauna, and a disco. 85 miles (136 km) southwest of the city of Chihuahua at Km 32 of Rte. 16. Mailing address: Apdo. 986, Venustiano Carranza 507B, 31000 Chihuahua, Chihuahua, México (no local phone; phone in Chihuahua: 14-161657; fax: 14-104688).

HACIENDA JURICA, Querétaro Horseback riding, along with golf (10 minutes away), tennis, squash, and volleyball, are featured at this hotel, a restored hacienda whose 180 rooms are beautifully decorated in Mexican colonial style. Km 229 of Rte. 57. Mailing address: Apdo. Postal 338, 76100 Querétaro, Querétaro, México (phone: 42-180022; 5-207-0562 in Mexico City; fax: 42-180136).

EXPEDITIONS ON HORSEBACK

It's also possible to join treks on horseback into the Sierra Madre Oriental outside Chihuahua, or into the jungles of the Yucatán Peninsula, or even through the forests of the state of Chiapas. In fact, some of the most beautiful sights in Mexico are reserved for those who get out of their cars and venture up mountains or into jungle valleys on horseback. Mexico is not a country tamed by highways; it has mountains, valleys, and beaches yet to be discovered by even the most enterprising visitor.

BARRANCA DEL COBRE (COPPER CANYON), Chihuahua If your idea of a riding vacation is to rough it, explore the magnificent Barranca del Cobre (actually a series of three canyons) and environs west of Chihuahua via horse or burro. Three lodges at the canyons rent horses: *Cabañas Divisadero-Barrancas* (phone: 14-123362 in Chihuahua; fax: 14-156575 in Chihuahua), *La Mansión Tarahumara* (phone: 14-162672 in Chihuahua), and *Posada Barrancas* (reserve through the *Santa Anita* hotel in Los Mochis; phone: 681-87046; 14-165950 in Chihuahua; fax: 681-20046). Less expensive accommodations and horse rentals are available at the *Copper Canyon Sierra Lodge* (phone: 14-560179 in Chihuahua; phone: 800-776-3942; fax: 14-560036) in Creel, a small railroad town a bit removed from the canyons. For additional details on the area, see *Quintessential Mexico* in this section and *Ciudad Juárez to Mexico City* in DIRECTIONS.

RANCHO OJO DE AGUA, Jalisco Based in Puerto Vallarta, this ranch offers five-day horseback tours that include a stop at an archaeological site and treks through jungles and pine forests, as well as custom-designed tours. They also operate twice-daily tours through back roads and villages. 227 Cerrada de Cárdenas (phone: 322-40607).

Fishing Mexico's Rich Waters

Mexico's ocean coasts offer some of the best deep-sea fishing in the world, and American anglers travel thousands of miles up and down the Baja, the Pacific Coast, the eastern Gulf, and the Caribbean coasts for snook, bass, dorado (also known as mahimahi), striped marlin, sailfish, red snapper, billfish, and shark. Many experienced anglers come to Mexico just for the numerous fishing competitions held in the major seaports each year. There is no problem bringing any kind of fishing gear into the country, and every major port has charter boats and fishing gear for hire (figure an average of

$275 a day, gear and bait included). Even the smallest fishing village is likely to have at least one fishing boat that can be hired for a half day or a day. (Note, however, that many areas are establishing catch-and-release policies so as not to deplete the waters.)

Visiting anglers are required to obtain fishing permits; they are readily available from the *Secretaría de Medio Ambiente, Recursos Naturales y Pesca* (Secretariat of the Environment, Natural Resources and Fisheries; Periférico Sur 4209, Colonia Jardines de la Montaña, Tlalpan, 14210 México, DF, México; phone: 5-628-0600) or from any one of its more than 140 offices throughout the country. Permits are free for fishing from the shore. There is a charge for permits to fish from a small vessel; daily, weekly, and monthly rates are available. Tour packagers and fishing boat outfits often include the permit in the package. Temporary permits are issued for boats and trailers entering Mexico; try to get one at a *Mexican Consulate* in the US, if you can, to avoid possible hassles with border personnel. (For information on consulates, see GETTING READY TO GO.) Anglers who bring a boat will be asked at the border to pay a small fee based on the weight of the vehicle. They will also be required to register the boat with the port captain, and they must obtain a license (for a small fee), which is good for one year. More information on fishing in Mexico, including guides, regulations, fishing seasons, and tournaments, is available from the *Secretaría de Medio Ambiente, Recursos Naturales y Pesca.*

Besides the prime angling spots in Acapulco, the Cancún-Cozumel–Isla Mujeres area, Ensenada, Huatulco, Ixtapa-Zihuatanejo, Los Cabos, Manzanillo, Mazatlán, Puerto Vallarta, and Veracruz (see *Fishing* in the individual reports in THE CITIES for details), the fishing areas below, listed by region from north to south, are considered tops in Mexico.

THE BAJA PENINSULA

SAN FELIPE This sandy fishing village 125 miles (200 km) south of Mexicali is best known for its sweet-tasting *totoaba;* however, in 1994 the Mexican government outlawed *totoaba* fishing altogether. Anglers interested in other kinds of fish, such as marlin and sailfish, can rent a boat from *Pesca Deportiva* (phone: 657-71052), located on the waterfront, or launch their own at the village pier.

BAHÍA DE LOS ANGELES Set on a magnificent bay 600 miles (960 km) north of La Paz, this harbor and famed fishing camp has spectacular sport fishing, particularly during the spring, when fish nearly clog the channel waters. Charter boats can be rented.

MULEGÉ About 313 miles (500 km) northwest of La Paz, on the brackish estuary of the Río Santa Rosalía, this village is the winter home of the black snook, a prized game fish that measures up to six feet and weighs up to 80 pounds.

Clam digging and lobster diving are favorite sports at nearby Bahía Concepción. The *Serenidad* hotel, 2 miles (3 km) south of town, on Rte. 1 (phone: 115-30111; fax: 115-30311) has charter boats; fishing packages include gear, crew, and refreshments.

LORETO Marlin and sailfish, which run from June through July and September through November, are the main attraction of this fishing village 230 miles (370 km) northwest of La Paz on Baja's Gulf of California coast. Mahimahi, roosterfish, and other fighting fish, as well as Loreto clams, are found here year-round. The beachfront *La Pinta Loreto* hotel (phone: 113-50025; 800-336-5454; fax: 113-50026) arranges for fishing boats and equipment.

LA PAZ The springtime run of marlin and the autumn run of sailfish are La Paz's biggest fishing attractions, with mahimahi, roosterfish, swordfish, yellowtail, tuna, sierras, and black sea bass available all year in the southern waters of the Gulf of California. The rates for motorboats and deep-sea charter cruisers with equipment are set by the captain of the port. Boats with equipment are available at leading hotels, including *Los Arcos* (498 Alvaro Obregón; phone: 112-22744).

LOS CABOS For fishing enthusiasts, Los Cabos is still "Marlin Alley," taking the moniker from its record years for blue and black marlin in the 1940s and 1950s. The waters teem with sport fish during the same seasons as its northern neighbor, La Paz (see above). Most hotels have their own fishing fleets, and charters can easily be arranged. Two good bets are *Cabo Acuadeportes* (on Playa Chileno, by the *Cabo San Lucas* hotel; phone: 114-30117; 713-580-2090) and *Solmar Fleet* (phone: 114-33535). *Solmar Fleet* also has the Solmar V diving and fishing boat, which has live-aboard facilities. *Cabo Resort Reservations* in Pacific Palisades, California, can assist with reservations for *Solmar*'s fishing excursions (phone: 800-344-3349; fax: 310-454-1686).

THE PACIFIC COAST

GUAYMAS Near two bays 250 miles (400 km) south of Nogales, Guaymas is a genuine anglers' paradise. Sport fishing enthusiasts favor Guaymas for its abundant supply of marlin, sailfish, and other game fish. Marlin, sailfish, and mahimahi season begins in early June and ends in mid-October; yellowtail fishing lasts through February.

Although there are no longer any fishing boats for hire in Guaymas, hotels can easily arrange to have a vessel sent down from nearby San Carlos.

LOS MOCHIS/TOPOLOBAMPO In the state of Sinaloa, about halfway between Guaymas and Mazatlán, Topolobampo is the port for nearby Los Mochis and is well loved by aficionados of big-game fishing. From June through October, the Gulf of California at Topolobampo runs with marlin and sailfish. Pompano are available from November through April, and ladyfish, roosterfish, and yellowtail live in the waters year-round. Boats for up to 12 people can be rented through the *Santa Anita* hotel (corner of Calle Gabriel

Leyva and Hidalgo; phone: 681-87046; 14-165950 in Chihuahua; fax: 681-20046). There is good bass and perch fishing at nearby Lago Domínguez.

THE GULF OF MEXICO COAST

TAMPICO This river port city is known to sports enthusiasts around the world. Although the tarpon population was nearly eliminated by commercial fishing companies in the past, the *Torneo Internacional de Shad* (International Tarpon Tournament) now takes place in Tampico every year in August, and there are other tournaments in February, April, May, and June. Snook and yellowtail thrive in the area's rivers and lagoons, while sailfish, marlin, snook, mackerel, red snapper, bonito, pompano, and yellowtail fill the Gulf of Mexico seas. The *Club de Regatas Corona* (Laguna de Chairel, at the far west end of town; phone: 12-125902) will arrange boat rentals for the duration of the tournaments.

INLAND

Mexico's many lakes, rivers, lagoons, streams, and reservoirs offer an enormous variety of fish, including black bass, catfish, trout, snook, and carp. Valle de Bravo, beyond Toluca, has excellent black bass and trout. The Brockman Dam, in the state of México at El Oro, has rainbow trout. There is good bass fishing 90 miles (144 km) east of Hermosillo, Sonora, at Novillo Dam. In Lago de Chapala, 32 miles (51 km) southeast of Guadalajara, a native species of catfish called *bagre,* a species of sunfish called *mojarra,* and a native whitefish called *blanco* can be found. (However, pollution tends to make Chapala catches unsafe to eat.) Lago de Pátzcuaro, near Morelia, is famous for its whitefish.

In the southern part of the state of Veracruz, Laguna Catemaco also is renowned for whitefish. Ask at your hotel desk for assistance in arranging a fishing excursion, or speak to a member of one of the local fishing cooperatives; they often congregate at the town dock.

Hunting

Once a hunter's paradise, Mexico is no longer an easy place to hunt, as the country is becoming more ecologically conscious. Yet game is still plentiful from the hills of the Sierra Madre to the jungles of the Yucatán, and Mexico remains relatively popular with hunters. Wild turkey, most kinds of duck, geese, quail, wild boars, deer, grouse, doves, agoutis, peccaries, and armadillos are still fair game, provided the hunter is armed with the proper papers. A special (and very expensive) permit is required to hunt white-tailed Texas deer and bura deer, whether or not you bag your catch.

Venados (deer) are most heavily concentrated in the northern border states—Sonora, Chihuahua, and Coahuila. The state of Tabasco also has deer, especially mule deer. The northern border states are the best hunting grounds for *codornices* (quail) and *palomas* (doves). *Patos* (ducks)—especially teal, pintail, and mallard—*gansos* (geese), and wild turkeys are found mostly along the west coast and in central Mexico. Wild boar is found in Nayarit and Guerrero. *Important:* Check an updated list of endangered species before you decide what game to go after. Right now, bighorn sheep, lynx, Canadian gray geese, jaguar, puma, black bear, crocodiles, and ocelots are on the endangered list. Your local zoo will be able to help.

There is quite a bit of red tape involved in obtaining Mexican hunting permits and licenses, bringing guns into the country, and taking game out. Plan a hunting trip well in advance, in order to obtain all the necessary papers. We strongly recommend that you engage an outfitter to take care of all the paperwork, especially since you must have all your papers in order before you enter Mexico. Two good outfitters are *Mexhunt Booking* (3302 Josie Ave., Long Beach, CA 90808; phone/fax: 310-421-6215), which primarily arranges hunting trips in western Mexico, and *Sunbelt Hunting and Travel* (PO Box 3009, Brownsville, TX 78523-3009; phone: 800-876-4868; fax: 210-544-4731), which concentrates on the state of Tamaulipas. The *Mexican Hunting Association* (6840 El Salvador St., Long Beach, CA 90815; phone: 310-430-3256) provides information on current requirements for hunters and assists with processing licenses and permits.

Hunting seasons and bag limits vary according to the region and the abundance of game each year. For general information on permits and hunting regulations, for answers to specific hunting-related questions in English or Spanish, or to request the *Calendario Cinegético* (official hunting season calendar), write to the *Dirección de Fauna Silvestre* (Wildlife Bureau; Nuevo León 210, 20th Floor, Colonia Roma, 06700 México, DF, México; phone: 5-574-5489). It will supply an application for a hunting license and special permits for any game that require them (see below). What follows is a description of the process of obtaining the required license and permits to hunt in Mexico; once again, we strongly suggest that you have an experienced outfitter make the arrangements for you.

HUNTING LICENSES AND PERMITS

Each hunter in Mexico *must* have a hunting license. Hunting licenses are good only in the state for which they are issued. To obtain a license for hunting birds or small mammals, you must fill out an application, pay the fee, and, most important, prove that you have obtained a permit to transport arms temporarily into Mexico (see below). You must also show proof that you have hired a local hunting organizer (names and addresses are listed in the hunting calendar); every hunter in Mexico must be accompanied by a registered Mexican hunting guide. The cost per state for a license to hunt birds and small mammals is about $50; costs of licenses for other species vary. A medical certificate of the hunter's good health is also required to hunt certain species. Finally, a special permit is required for hunting some species. It's realistic to begin making plans at least three months before arriving in Mexico.

GUN PERMITS

Hunters also must obtain a permit to transport arms temporarily into Mexico. To get a gun permit, you must bring the following documents to the *Mexican Consulate* nearest your US address: a valid passport or birth certificate, a notarized letter from your sheriff or police department stating that you have no criminal record, five passport photos, and a letter asking to take firearms temporarily into Mexico. The letter must state the brand name, caliber, and serial numbers of the arms you intend to take into the country. Hunters are allowed only one high-powered rifle of any caliber, or two shotguns of any gauge. Automatic weapons are prohibited. The *Mexican Consulate* will issue a permit for firearms and a certificate of identity with a description of your weapons. The fee for this service is about $50. To facilitate re-entry into the US, you should register your firearms with *US Customs* before departure. No more than three nonautomatic firearms will be registered for one person. Once in Mexico, you will also be asked to register your weapons with the office of the commander of the local military garrison. Ammunition may not be imported, but you can buy it at any sporting goods store. You will need to present your hunting license and gun permit, and you can buy up to two boxes per gun registered. Note that ammunition in Mexico costs roughly three times what it costs in the US.

RETURNING TO THE US

Once you've obtained your licenses and permits, made it into the country, tramped through the jungles, and bagged your game, your final task is to get your game out of Mexico and back into the US. First, check bag limits, both with the *Dirección de Fauna Silvestre* and with *US Customs*—they're different, and they change. Taking game mammals and migratory game birds out of Mexico requires a Mexican export permit or the permission of a Mexican game official. In addition, US law requires that a permit be issued from the *Fisheries and Wildlife Service* before wild game birds, wild fowl, or wild game animals may be brought into the country. Animals may be protected by international law, by US law, or by both, and the regulations covering them change periodically, so before going to Mexico, consult the *Division of Law Enforcement* (PO Box 3247, Arlington, VA 22203-3247; phone: 703-358-1949) and the *Office of Management Authority* (4401 N. Fairfax Dr., Room 430, Arlington, VA 22203; phone: 800-358-2104 or 703-358-2095)—both part of the *Fisheries and Wildlife Service* of the *US Department of the Interior*—about the specific laws and regulations involved in bringing game back into the US.

WHERE TO HUNT

In addition to the hunting opportunities found near major cities (consult the individual reports in THE CITIES), we offer below a survey of Mexico's best hunting grounds, in alphabetical order by state.

BAJA CALIFORNIA NORTE and SUR Mexico's 800-mile peninsula of coast, desert, and mountains has good hunting near the available freshwater supplies, such as its inland oases and mountain streams. Californians regularly flock across the border for the annual autumn dove season. Mexicali Valley, just below the US border, has ducks, doves, quail, pheasant, and partridges. The *Meling Ranch,* just outside San Telmo de Arriba, organizes pack trips. Reservations for the ranch can be made by calling Duane Barré Meling in San Diego, California (phone: 619-758-2719; be sure to leave an evening-contact phone number). Baja California Sur is known for good hunting, especially near La Paz, Mulegé (for quail and ducks—especially during the winter), and El Mejor (for rabbit, doves, quail, and duck). Buena Vista is a good spot for deer, though the season runs only from mid-December through late January.

CHIHUAHUA Near the Chihuahua state border with Sonora, Nuevo Casas Grandes is a little-known but rich hunting area especially good for deer, turkey, quail, and doves. The Sierra Madre Occidental range is breathtaking, but the high altitude may not be comfortable for everyone. Hunting season runs from late September through February for birds; from August through March for small mammals. Nuevo Casas Grandes can be reached either by road (123 miles/197 km off Rte. 10); by train; by bus; or by chartering a plane. The area is known not only for its hunting and camping, but also for the ruins of *Paquimé,* probably an outpost of a North American Southwest Indian culture. It was later colonized by Mexican tribes who were influenced by the Toltec. For more information on *Paquimé,* see *Ciudad Juárez to Mexico City* in DIRECTIONS.

GUERRERO Duck hunting is excellent in the lagoons around Acapulco; farther inland are deer, wild pigs, and small game. *But be alert:* The wilder parts of the state of Guerrero are reputed to have bandits lurking in the hills.

SINALOA Many different duck species can be found in the Pacific coastal state of Sinaloa, especially in the area between Los Mochis and Mazatlán. Pintail, teal, mallard, redhead, and bluebill are a few; there are also speckled geese and quail. Hunting season for birds is from late October through mid-February; for small mammals, from mid-August through late March. Nearby duck ponds and lagoons (with blinds) are just 25 to 40 minutes from Los Mochis. The surrounding mountains also hold wild pigs and deer. Isla Palmito de la Virgen, between Laguna Caimanaro and the ocean, has great duck shooting opportunities, as do the surrounding marshes and fields.

SONORA About 175 miles (280 km) south of Nogales, Hermosillo, Sonora's capital, offers good duck, deer, coyote, and rabbit hunting in the immediate area. Bahía Kino, some 65 miles (104 km) west of Hermosillo (on Rte. 15 between Nogales and Guaymas), is a favorite with campers who like to hunt quail, duck, and deer. The Guaymas countryside offers some of the best white-winged-dove hunting in the country.

TAMAULIPAS Some 375 miles (600 km) south of Brownsville, Texas, Tampico is a leading port and refining center. It's also on the flyway of eastern migratory birds, and a good place to hunt deer, quail, turkey, and duck.

Mountains and Mountain Climbing

For a country as well endowed with mountains as Mexico, there is surprisingly little general interest in mountain climbing among Mexicans. There are, however, an increasing number of organized climbs in the Sierra Madre Occidental and the Sierra Madre Oriental, the two gigantic arms that sweep parallel to Mexico's eastern and western coasts. There are good climbing opportunities on two volcanoes relatively close to Mexico City: Iztaccíhuatl (visible from Mexico City, though the climb is strenuous and not recommended for beginners), and Orizaba, in the state of Veracruz. (At press time, the Popocatépetl volcano near Mexico City was closed to the public due to periodic activity.) Organized climbing parties with guides and equipment are offered at both Iztaccíhuatl and Orizaba.

Depending upon snow conditions, ropes may not be needed, though it is advisable to carry at least one rope on any climbing expedition. Tents, ropes, and other major equipment are available in Mexico City and from guides at the mountains, but plan to bring your own personal equipment, such as a sleeping bag, boots, and a backpack. Never climb during the rainy season, March through September, when the weather greatly increases the hazard. Bring along crampons, despite their weight.

It's possible to arrange for guides through the *Club de Exploraciones de México* (Exploration Club of Mexico; Juan A. Mateos 146, Colonia Obrera, 06800 México, DF, México; phone: 5-740-8032). *Club Citlaltépetl de México* (Dr. Mora 9, Suite 25C, Colonia Doctores, 06720 México, DF, México; phone: 5-512-2534) runs mountain climbing expeditions for both experts (high mountain) and beginners. *Grey Line Tours* (Calle Londres 166, Colonia Juárez, 06600 México, DF, México; phone: 5-208-1163) offers daily departures with professional mountain-climbing guides to Orizaba. The company also rents all the necessary equipment. *Trek México* (Havre 67, Suite 305, Colonia Juárez, 06600 México, DF, México; phone: 5-525-5113 or 5-525-5213) also offers adventure trips to Iztaccíhuatl and Orizaba.

IZTACCÍHUATL (IZTA) This challenging volcanic peak, about an hour east of Mexico City, has two marked routes, but should be scaled only by experienced climbers. Guides and some equipment are available in Amecameca, the Aztec town near the foot of Iztaccíhuatl, as well as through the groups listed above.

ORIZABA Mexico's highest mountain (the third highest in North America), near the town of Orizaba in the state of Veracruz, Pico de Orizaba (also known as Citlaltépetl) reaches an elevation of 18,700 feet. Covered with snow year-round, it is considered sacred by the natives, who believe it contains the spirit of the god Quetzalcóatl. To begin the climb at Piedra Grande, take the road from Tlachichuca (in the state of Puebla) to La Blatchichieca. From there, a four-wheel-drive truck is needed to travel the rough road to Piedra Grande. Some of the Orizaba trails are marked, but many of the markers are stripped away by storms as quickly as they are put up. Climbing experience is recommended, since some sections may require the use of ropes and crampons. It's best to avoid this mountain during the rainy season.

Camping and Hiking in Mexico's National Parks

In striking contrast to the US, organized camping and backpacking are not generally popular forms of recreation among Mexicans. Yet despite the relative lack of interest, trailer parks and national parks are an increasing concern of the government—due in no small part to the burgeoning tourist trade and greater mobility of Mexico's growing urban middle class.

Most camping in Mexico, however, is still done outside national parks. The many free beaches and absence of laws prohibiting camping on public land open thousands of miles of secluded grounds to the adventurous camper. *But beware:* There are *bandidos* who prey on unwary campers in remote sites.

Of all the regions of Mexico, the west coast of the mainland and the Baja Peninsula are by far the most popular for informal and trailer camping. Mexico's western Pacific Coast offers beach after beach open to the public; because of its popularity, the region has excellent trailer hookups. The Baja Peninsula is a far more informal affair, and camping here requires more knowledge and competence. There are thousands of miles of four-wheel-drive-only trails in the Baja, but only experienced campers should take off into the isolation of the Baja wilds.

The national parks listed below are the only areas in Mexico specifically set aside for camping and hiking. No permits or fees are required for camping, which is allowed anywhere within all park areas. Campers can obtain maps and trail information at the headquarters of each park or through *Parques Nacionales* (National Parks Headquarters; Insurgentes Sur 1478, Eighth Floor, Colonia Roma, 06700 México, DF, México; phone: 5-584-6944). Several parks have protected campsites with services. Some, such as Lagunas de Chacahua on the coast of Oaxaca, have fully equipped cabins.

THE BAJA PENINSULA

PARQUE NACIONAL CONSTITUCIÓN DE 1857, La Rumorosa Cradled in the Sierra de Juárez, 90 miles (144 km) southwest of Mexicali, this lovely forested area with striking granite formations, towering ponderosa pines, and a large warmwater lagoon is a secluded haven for hikers and campers. The park can be reached by taking the La Rumorosa turnoff off Route 2, 45 miles (72 km) west of Mexicali and traveling for 45 more miles (72 km) to the park.

PARQUE NACIONAL SAN PEDRO MÁRTIR, San Telmo de Arriba About 135 miles (216 km) south of Ensenada, at an altitude of 9,000 feet, the breathtaking granite rock formations and majestic ponderosa pines of this park—surrounded by contrasting rolling valleys and prairies—make it a sensational spot for camping and hiking. The *Observatorio Nacional de México* (National Observatory of Mexico) is at the top of the park area, across from the north face of the Picacho del Diablo (Devil's Peak). Although camping near the observatory is not permitted, it is possible to enjoy the magnificent view of steep, forested cliffs dropping into eastern desert highlands. There are streams, forests, and trails throughout the park. To get here, take Route 1 through the town of Colnett. Then, 6 miles (10 km) south of town on Route 1, take the turnoff to the town of Misión de San Telmo. Follow the road to the park.

CENTRAL MEXICO

DESIERTO DE LOS LEONES, Mexico City "Desert of the Lions" is a rather deceptive name for this park, 15 miles (24 km) west of downtown Mexico City, for neither lions nor cacti live here. There are, however, tall pine trees, the remains of a 17th-century Carmelite monastery, and many good hiking trails. The spot is popular with the Mexico City weekend crowd, so visit during the week if you want peace and quiet. Take Avenida Revolución or the Periférico (beltway) to Calle Desierto de los Leones, which leads though delightful hill country into the park. Another route is to take Paseo de la Reforma west until it becomes Route 15 to Toluca (make sure you take the old road, *not* the newer toll road, or *cuota*). Watch for the sign marking the turnoff to the park, on the left. Because both routes go through heavy traffic, the trip is likely to about an hour and 10 minutes.

LA MARQUESA (PARQUE NACIONAL MIGUEL HIDALGO Y COSTILLA), México Besides a government trout hatchery and an artificial lake, this 4,500-acre valley, surrounded by mountains, has many picnic sites near the highway, horseback riding, and good hiking. It is on the road to Toluca (Rte. 15) from Mexico City. Take the road marked "Chalma" near the entrance of the park to reach the Valle de Silencio (Valley of Silence), where there are lovely, quiet meadows and woodland areas for picnicking and relaxing. The park is less crowded on weekdays, but avoid getting too far off the beaten path: robberies and assaults have been reported in the remote areas.

SOUTHERN MEXICO

PARQUE NACIONAL LAGUNAS DE MONTEBELLO, Chiapas Almost all the colors of the rainbow can be found in the dozen or so accessible lakes of this 13,000-square-mile area on the Mexico-Guatemala border. (Numerous other lakes in the park are hidden in the woods and cannot be reached.) Besides the exquisite lakes and lush woodland areas, there is a cave, the Río Comitán, and the nearby *Chinkultic* archaeological zone, an ancient ceremonial site that has not been fully explored. Although there are no tourist facilities in the park, there are many lovely hiking trails. (*Note:* Though at press time conditions were peaceful following the anti-government uprising in Chiapas in 1994, you should check on the present situation with tourism authorities before traveling there.) For more information, see *Mexico City to the Guatemala Border* in DIRECTIONS.

Directions

Introduction

Approaches to travel through Mexico have undergone a dramatic change in recent years, as more and more visitors to the lands south of the border have discovered that there's much more to Mexico than that which lies along the familiar Mexico City–Taxco–Acapulco Highway. Exploring a land so rich in archaeological treasures, dramatic history, spectacular scenery, and evocative accommodations can be pure pleasure for those folks willing to do a bit of roaming on their own.

Our favorite parts of Mexico are those that attract the fewest typical tourists—our idea of wonderful traveling experiences doesn't include hand-to-hand combat for a chaise longue beside a crowded pool, or fending off vendors determined to wear visitors down by their constant hawking. With this in mind, we've created touring itineraries that offer the best and most authentic Mexican experiences—and a minimum of anonymous high-rise hotels.

What follows are what we consider the choice driving routes through Mexico, including the Baja's Transpeninsular Highway, the best routes to and from Mexico City, itineraries across the Yucatán Peninsula, and roads through the jungles of Oaxaca and Chiapas to the Guatemalan border. Each of the chapters that follows discusses the highlights of the route, including suggestions for shopping and dining; the *Best en Route* sections list the best available hotels and inns along the way. A map outlines each itinerary and notes major landmarks and reference points.

Some words of advice about driving in Mexico: Although many of the roads included in our driving routes are four-lane divided highways, it's still a good idea to give yourself plenty of travel time to reach your destination before dark. In Mexico, many drivers do not turn on their headlights, and in the countryside, especially in the north-central states, animals roam freely on the roads. In addition, many highways do not have center lines, and if they do, the markers are often worn and difficult to see in the dark. Many roads have no shoulder, and stalled vehicles often block traffic.

When entering a town, however small, you will frequently encounter a row of speed bumps set in the road to slow traffic. These obstacles are often, but not always, marked by the signs *Topes* or *Bordos* (Bumps). Be alert and slow down or you could easily ruin the front suspension system of your vehicle. Also keep in mind that on Mexico's highways the left-turn signal is often used to notify drivers that it's safe to pass, rather than to indicate a left turn. A sign reading *Puente Angosto* (Narrow Bridge) or *Un Solo Carril* (One Lane Only) indicates that there's room for only one vehicle to cross at a time. The rule: The first driver to flash his or her car lights on and off has the right of way. See *Useful Words and Phrases* in the GLOSSARY for other Spanish traffic signs and terms. For additional details on renting a car and driving in Mexico, see GETTING READY TO GO.

Finally, as anywhere in the world, picking up strangers, camping on a lonely beach, or sleeping in a car in some isolated area can invite serious trouble. It takes only a little common sense, and some very basic planning, to make a driving tour of the Mexican countryside both a safe and a memorable travel adventure.

The Baja Peninsula

The Baja Peninsula drops from Mexico's border with southern California like a strong, slim root seeking anchorage in the Pacific Ocean—800 miles of desert and semidesert separating the Pacific to the west from the Sea of Cortés (or Gulf of California) in the east, and facing the rest of Mexico across the gulf like a thumb. Until the mid 1970s, its secrets were safe with the very few four-wheel-drive, off-the-road adventurers willing to risk the severity of the terrain—single-track sand lanes that shifted with the wind and often disappeared entirely with the coming of winter—for the exquisite pleasures of hunting, fishing, rock hunting, fossil collecting, bird watching, and surfing in one of the Western Hemisphere's purest natural environments.

Originally inhabited by the native Cochimi, the peninsula wasn't settled by Europeans until the 18th century, when Jesuits arrived to minister to and convert the indigenous people. They built the first missions, taught the natives to farm, planted vineyards, olive trees, and date palms, and spread The Word. For years, the only means of access from one settlement to another was by foot along the shore or by boat. When the first primitive road—the Camino Real—was built down the peninsula, it was used primarily by traffickers in smuggled goods and carriers of news from one isolated village to the next.

That all changed when the Mexican government inaugurated the 1,050-mile Route 1 (Transpeninsular Highway) in the mid 1970s, effectively opening the full length of the Baja to mainstream tourism. The giant, sleeping peninsula slowly awakened: Hotels and resorts began to dot the landscape, travelers from the US began to wander down, and Mexicans from the mainland began to cross the Sea of Cortés by ferry to visit, and settle in, this part of their country. In an effort to speed up the region's economic and tourist development, the federal government exempted the entire peninsula from import taxes, attracting bargain hunters. As the population grew, several villages developed into fairly large towns. Los Cabos, for example, on the peninsula's southern tip, has become a popular mega-resort and is becoming a golf destination.

To be sure, Baja still reserves its finest moments for the strong and brave who trek off the main road, but many of its pleasures are accessible even to the less intrepid traveler. With coasts along both the Pacific Ocean and the Sea of Cortés, Baja is a paradise for anglers, swimmers, and surfers. Its beaches are laden with huge clams and oysters, and both the emerald-green gulf waters and the deep blue Pacific support an incredible variety of big fish. As the highway traverses Baja, crossing into the south, the dry landscape breaks into sudden, always surprising oases. The coasts are dotted with innumerable fishing villages and several excellent resort lodges devoted to fishing and all types of water sports.

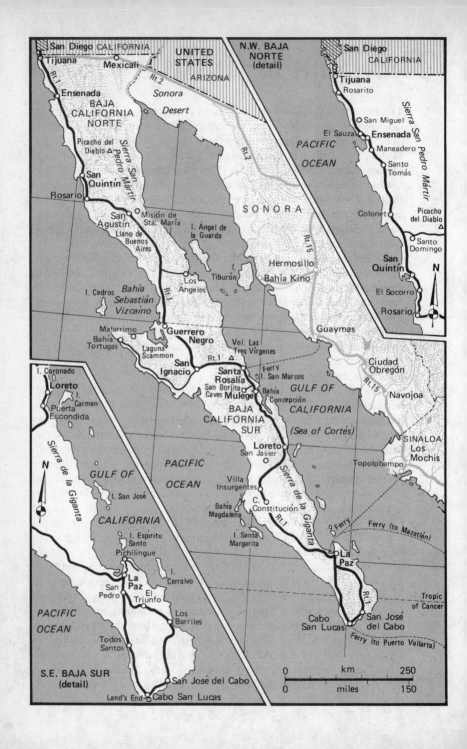

Baja California is divided into two states: Baja California Norte (the northern part) and Baja California Sur (the southern part). The state of Baja California Norte comprises the area from the US border south to the 28th parallel (just about midway down the length of the peninsula); Baja California Sur stretches down to Cabo San Lucas, at the tip of the peninsula. The northern state has a population of more than 2.6 million; Baja Sur, only 350,000. Mexicali (pop. 800,000) is the capital of Baja California Norte; La Paz (pop. 200,000), on the Sea of Cortés, is the capital of Baja California Sur. The climate of the northern state is mild, dry, and sometimes quite hot during the day in the summer, cool to cold (especially at night) with a little rain during the winter. Southern Baja is warm and humid in summer, tepid and dry in winter. Although rain is usually rare in the region, a week of heavy downpours and flooding in the northern state in 1993 killed at least 43 people and left thousands homeless.

At Baja's widest point (the "elbow" just below the 28th parallel), the peninsula measures about 105 miles; at its narrowest point, near La Paz, the distance is only 28 miles from the Sea of Cortés to the Pacific Ocean. Along the length of the peninsula run two major mountain chains, the Sierra San Pedro Mártir in the northern state and the Sierra de la Giganta in the southern. The highest crest of the chains rises to more than 6,000 feet, but, as in the lowlands surrounding them, the terrain is essentially semidesert.

Route 1 passes through all the major Baja towns. From Tijuana to Ensenada, the highway is a divided toll road, but beyond Ensenada it narrows to a two-lane, two-way route that, although in good condition, is not recommended for night driving. (Roaming cattle, as well as other large quadrupeds, have caused many an accident; cattle seem especially prevalent on the road between La Paz and Los Cabos.) Good accommodations and some elaborate resorts can be found in and between cities all along the way. Just remember to drive carefully, in full daylight, and to fill up at every gas station along the way.

En Route to Tijuana For regulations regarding entry into Mexico, see GETTING READY TO GO.

TIJUANA For a detailed report on the city, its hotels, and its restaurants, see *Tijuana* in THE CITIES.

En Route from Tijuana The journey into Baja begins on the scenic toll road that follows the Pacific Coast (or the pastoral toll-free road just east of it) for 70 miles (112 km) to Ensenada. Small resorts, other tourist facilities, and beaches mark the way. The ocean water is cold here, and surfers normally wear wet suits. Playa Rosarito (Rosarito Beach) is a popular resort where many families, fleeing the intense city heat of Mexicali and southern California, spend the summer months. The seafood eateries here are particularly good. Thirty miles (48 km) south is the Cantiles exit, which leads to Puerto Nuevo, a small fishing village well worth a small detour for its several restaurants that serve fresh lobster *a la Puerto Nuevo* (with refried beans, rice, flour tortillas, and hot sauce). The town, which calls itself "the Lobster Village," is particularly busy on Sundays; most of its restaurants are closed Mondays.

Beyond Puerto Nuevo, Route 1 closely follows the coastline, with Pacific breakers lapping its rocky base. When there is no fog, the view is magnificent, with the ocean's deep blue framed by snatches of brown cliffs and green landscape as the road twists and turns along the coast. There's an excellent restaurant in *La Fonda* hotel (phone: 66-287352/3), on a cliff above the ocean, 19 miles (30 km) north of Ensenada.

Here the highway crosses Río San Miguel, one of the largest streams in Baja. Nearby San Miguel village has a popular resort with a restaurant and camping areas, tennis courts, horses, and a beautiful beach with good surfing. Shortly after El Sauzal, Ensenada comes into view, a vista that inspired the late Mexican journalist Fernando Jordán to write: "Ensenada is the only city on the Pacific Coast of Baja California that did not fear the ocean, for it deliberately turned its back to the land and spends its life facing its ocean window and running down the mountain to the beach."

ENSENADA For a detailed report on the city, its hotels, and its restaurants, see *Ensenada* in THE CITIES.

En Route from Ensenada The road continues through Maneadero, a large agricultural valley where chilies, melons, beans, and corn are grown. The highway narrows and turns down into the broad valley of Santo Tomás, an old agricultural community. In the town of Santo Tomás are the adobe ruins of an 18th-century Dominican mission and the *Viñedos de Santo Tomás* (St. Thomas Vineyards), which produce Mexico's best wine.

Five miles (8 km) past Colonet, a tiny farming town with an excellent bakery, the highway crosses Meling Road, which leads to the *Meling Ranch,* a cattle ranch and comfortable lodge with a swimming pool. From here you can rent horses and guides and ride to the Sierra San Pedro Mártir, the highest mountains in Baja, and 10,100-foot Picacho del Diablo (Devil's Peak). Make reservations for the ranch by calling Duane Barré Meling in San Diego (phone: 619-758-2719; be sure to leave an evening-contact phone number). La Grulla, about 35 miles (56 km) from the ranch, is a lovely spot in the fir-pine forest, a valley strewn with ponds and streams where trout abound. The town of Valle de San Quintín is about 36 miles (60 km) farther down the main road.

VALLE DE SAN QUINTÍN Valle de San Quintín was part of a concession granted to an American agricultural firm in 1885. The Americans soon discovered there was too little water for profitable farming; seeking to get rid of the property, they sold it to an English firm whose interest was aroused after an unusually heavy rainy season had garlanded the valley in green. It became evident soon after the purchase, however, that the English had been snookered. Deciding to unload the property themselves, they devised an elaborate hoax, digging water wells and irrigation channels, and spreading the word about the fine prospects of their project. The deceit never bore fruit, however, because before any buyers could be found, the Mexican government annulled the concession that had been granted the company, and the English departed, leaving behind only an English cemetery and the remains of a railroad and loading wharf—all still there, on the southern shore of the bay.

In 1931, the government sent 500 families here to settle and farm the lands, which had long since returned to their normal, desolate state. The hapless settlers soon found themselves stranded in the desert without food, water, or the means to obtain necessities, and all but 11 of the original families left. But 11 was a lucky number, because one of this group discovered water running nearly 100 feet below ground; soon after, the valley became even more fertile than the English had ever dreamed it could be.

Today, San Quintín is remarkably fecund, with potatoes, tomatoes, carrots, chilies, and grain growing profusely. Many of the 20,000 residents are settlers from the north and south. Most of the people here live in nearby ranches, but there is a strip with stores that cater to the people who come here to enjoy the beaches, to fish, and to dig for pismo clams. If you want to stop for a meal, *Gaston's Cannery* restaurant at the *Old Mill* motel on the estuary serves outstanding seafood (Km 196 of Rte. 1; no phone). It's open daily.

En Route from San Quintín The highway parallels the ocean, with many side roads leading to the beach. But beware of sand traps that have snagged hundreds of innocent vacationers who drove too close to the beach and had to be pulled out by tractors. Playa El Socorro has excellent clamming and good camping.

In Rosario, a small farming village, the café run by Señora Espinosa serves good meals, and she provides information about the history of the area. Rosario is also the site of the Dominicans' first mission (1774), whose remains can still be seen. South of Rosario grows vegetation unique to the Baja desert, including the cardon cactus, a giant that can grow 60 feet high. Prickly pear cacti grow profusely here, though they are not unique to Baja; their edible fruit (*tunas,* or prickly pears) ripens in the summer.

Past San Agustín, the highway enters the Llano de Buenos Aires, a sandy desert with a landscape of gigantic boulders and cardon and cirio plants. *La Pinta San Quintín* hotel is a good choice for lodging (see *Best en Route*).

Eleven miles (17 km) away, via a small road, lie the ruins of *Misión de Santa María,* the last Jesuit mission founded in Baja (1767). Legend holds that the Jesuits established another mission in the area named Santa Isabel, where they hid a huge treasure of gold, silver, and pearls after discovering that they were about to be expelled from the peninsula. For years, adventurers have been searching for the "lost mission" without success, so keep your eyes open.

Some 64 miles (102 km) farther south, a branch of the highway shoots off to the left, crossing to the Sea of Cortés coast. The offshoot leads to Bahía de los Angeles, a harbor right across from the Isla Angel de la Guarda in the Sea of Cortés. The bay offers shelter to vessels of all sizes, and the small fishing village of Los Angeles graces its shore. Cabin lodgings and fine meals are provided at *Casa Díaz* (no phone); if you take this detour, try the special stew said to contain coyote meat. The fishing season in the area lasts from April until September. Caguama turtles abound here as well. *Note:* The turtles should only be viewed; hunting them is prohibited.

From the Bahía de los Angeles turnoff, the main highway continues south along the Pacific side of the peninsula, across a plain thick with desert plants. You are now about an hour away from the 28th parallel, which forms the boundary between Baja Norte and Baja Sur. The boundary is marked by a stylized eagle monument located in the town of Guerrero Negro.

GUERRERO NEGRO This important town has a promising industrial future, for it claims the world's largest salt flats, as well as oil and natural gas deposits. But Guerrero Negro is also the site of the annual migration of gray whales and humpbacks, and staunch environmentalists want to keep the area pristine. For example, when a French company proposed installing offshore oil-drilling platforms in the mid 1980s, conservationists objected that the installations would interfere with the mating habits of migrating whales, and the local government voted down the company's proposal. More recently, leading environmentalists strenuously protested proposals in late 1994 to expand the salt industry into nearby Laguna San Ignacio. To date, the government has not cancelled the project.

Meanwhile, increasingly large numbers of whale watchers come to Guerrero Negro to view the annual migration. Scammon's Lagoon, also known as Laguna Ojo de Liebre, is a shelter for many migrating gray whales and one of the most interesting spots in Baja. It's in Bahía Sebastián Vizcaíno, which is part of a 6-million-acre desert and ocean biosphere reserve; access is via a fairly well marked 17-mile (27-km) dirt road 8 miles (12 km) south of the eagle monument. The whales usually can be seen from the last week of December through mid-March (or sometimes early April). The whales also take refuge in Laguna San Ignacio. Though whales are not violent, they are huge and naturally protective during calving season; you can observe them from the shore or hire a small plane in Guerrero Negro to fly overhead, but boating in the lagoons during whale season is not recommended and requires special permission. For additional details, see *Quintessential Mexico* in DIVERSIONS.

En Route from Guerrero Negro Here Route 1 turns inland and southeastward, crossing the desert mainland to the Sea of Cortés coast, some 130 miles (208 km) away. About midway along the hot, tedious route is San Ignacio.

SAN IGNACIO After the drive from Guerrero Negro through some 80 miles (128 km) of sunbaked desert, this oasis town (pop. 3,500), shaded by date palms, provides a welcome respite. Like many other towns in Baja Sur, San Ignacio started out as a Jesuit mission, established in 1728 by Dominican priest Juan B. de Luyando. Located at the heart of town, the well-preserved mission faces a little plaza shaded by a lush canopy of Indian laurels. Don't be surprised to find that food and lodging prices are higher here than in surrounding towns.

The region's main crop is dates, which are harvested in October and then set out to dry all around the town. Many of the men from San Ignacio are anglers. During fishing season, they set up camps on the Pacific Coast to catch cabrillas and other types of sea bass, lobsters, and abalones. A dirt road at the southern end of town leads to Bahía Tortugas (Turtle Bay), the largest fishing establishment on the west coast of Baja. Sport fishing is good here from May through August, and rustic accommodations are available. Farther along this road lies Playa Malarrimo, where shells and driftwood wash ashore from as far away as Alaska, Japan, and the China Sea; swimmers should beware of the strong undertow.

The area's mysterious painted prehistoric caves are almost impossible to find on one's own, but consummate explorers can track one down by driving 22 miles (35 km) north to the tiny goat-raising community of San Francisco (pop. 300), asking directions of someone there, and backtracking slightly. Oscar Fischer, who runs *La Posada* hotel in San Ignacio (see *Best en Route*), offers tours to the caves.

En Route from San Ignacio The highway passes the volcano of Las Tres Vírgenes (The Three Virgins), believed to be the most recently active volcano in the area and, according to local lore, used in colonial times as a natural lighthouse. The ground surrounding the volcano is covered with hardened lava. The Sea of Cortés comes into view just before you reach Santa Rosalía.

SEA OF CORTÉS Also known as the Gulf of California and the Vermilion Sea, it is bounded by the Mexican mainland on the east, the Baja Peninsula on the west, and Baja and the state of Sonora to the north. The sea originates at the mouth of the Colorado River, 50 miles south of the US-Mexico border, and ends at the peninsula's tip, where it merges with the Pacific Ocean. Its formation was a result of the San Andreas Fault, which separated a large chunk of the west side of Mexico from the mainland, in the process creating a peninsula linked to the mainland on the north and open to the Pacific Ocean on the south. When the volcanic peaks of the mountainous Baja Peninsula split off and slid into the crevasse, their tops projected above the water's surface, creating the many islands that stand off the eastern coast.

The Sea of Cortés reaches great depths and, because its warm, calm waters provide an abundant supply of food and ideal conditions for spawning, harbors more than 650 species of fish. It is a paradise for fishing enthusiasts, but it also attracts many others who come to swim in its clear waters, collect shells on its beaches, water-ski on its mirror-smooth surface, or go scuba diving. Many resorts have sprung up in the area for the ever-increasing numbers of travelers who make their way here.

SANTA ROSALÍA The tiny church in this town of 14,000 was designed by Gustave Eiffel, of Eiffel Tower fame. The apparent geographic incongruity does have an explanation: Santa Rosalía was founded in 1855 by a rancher who discovered rich copper deposits in the area. Two years later, El Boleo, a French mining company, obtained the concession for extracting the metal. At a world exposition in Brussels, one of the directors of El Boleo purchased a church designed by Gustave Eiffel and transported the galvanized structure section by section from Europe to Santa Rosalía. This charming church, the *Iglesia de Santa Bárbara,* stands in the center of town, quite beloved by the local populace. Catholic services are still held here.

No longer a mining center, Santa Rosalía today bases its economy mainly on boat building, for which the coastal fishing industry creates a constant demand. Santa Rosalía is also the Baja terminus of the Guaymas ferry, which runs fairly often.

Stroll along Calle Obregón, Santa Rosalía's main street, past the bakery and shops, to get the feel of this friendly place. *La Terraza* (1 mile/1.6 km north of town; phone: 115-20578) is a good choice for breakfast or a seafood meal. The beaches to the north and south of town are beautiful. For a stunning view of the surrounding area, drive or take a taxi up the hill capped with the dish antenna; from here you can see the Tres Vírgenes and Reforma peaks and Isla Tortuga (Turtle Island), better known for snakes than turtles.

En Route from Santa Rosalía Several miles south of town, a side road leads to San Borjita, site of the oldest cave paintings found in Baja. Although the road to the entrance is only about 1 mile (1.6 km) long, it is in very poor condition and takes more than three hours (honest!) to negotiate by pickup truck; undertaking the drive with a car is not recommended. (The road is deliberately left in a run-down state to discourage a mass influx of tourists.) The entrance to the caves faces west, so it is best to visit in the afternoon, when plenty of sunlight pours in. The main themes of the paintings are war and hunting; life-size works depict humans, lions, deer, fish, and rabbits. Reds, blacks, whites, and yellows—all still very bright—predominate.

From the caves, return to the main road and continue 19 miles (30 km) south to Mulegé.

MULEGÉ (pronounced Moo-lay-*hay*) This lush green town (pop. 4,570) lies at the mouth of Río Santa Rosalía, better known as the Río Mulegé. An oasis springing up in the midst of barren country, it is a place where groves of date palms and semitropical fruit trees grow densely. The environs look like John Wayne territory, and, indeed, the "Duke" was fond of visiting here.

The *Misión de Santa Rosalía,* founded by Jesuit Juan Basaldúa in 1705, lies across the river. Below the mission is a stone dam, a small lake, and roads running the 2 miles (3 km) to the Sea of Cortés. Above town stands an interesting old prison; the view is worth the climb. Cemetery buffs will enjoy the one here.

Good bathing beaches are found at Playa el Cacheno near the *Serenidad* hotel (see *Best en Route*) and in front of El Sombrerito, the tall hill on the north side of the river mouth; it gets its name from the lighthouse on top, which resembles a little hat. Mulegé is gaining a reputation for scuba diving and kayaking; if you're interested, stop in at *Mulegé Divers* (on Calle Madero, the town's main street; no phone). Off Punta Chivato, a point of land 12½ miles (20 km) north of Mulegé, there's excellent swimming, snorkeling, and diving. Boats for nearby Isla San Marcos leave from the dock.

Don Johnson, a former US consul who owns the *Serenidad* hotel, can offer advice on everything from where to buy shells to how to find a boat that's strayed from its moorings. He also takes reservations for kayak trips organized by local Americans.

Eat in town at the *Candil* (phone: 115-30185) or *Maranatha* (no phone), both on the main square, or, if it's Saturday afternoon, go out to the *Serenidad* for a barbecue.

En Route from Mulegé The highway plays hide-and-seek with immense Bahía Concepción for some 20 miles (32 km) on the way to Loreto, passing Santispaquis, a beautiful cove, and El Coyote, so named because of a rock painting found in the area that shows a coyote in an attacking position. The most beautiful beach on the bay is El Requesón, where a small island is connected to the mainland by a strip of stark white sand. This is a great place to get clams, when the fishermen come in around 5 PM. Camping sites are available in the bay area.

LORETO In 1697, Jesuit Juan María de Salvatierra initiated the work of missionaries in the Californias by building the *Misión de Nuestra Señora de Loreto* (Mission of Our Lady of Loreto) here. Loreto was the mission center and the headquarters of the civil government of Baja Sur until 1829, when a devastating hurricane leveled Loreto and the capital was moved to La Paz (where it remains today). The town, with some 20,000 people, is garlanded in the green of its vineyards, date palms, and fig and olive trees, all introduced by the missionaries. A car is absolutely essential for getting around. More than 43,000 visitors come to the area every year, primarily to fish. (Hotels will pack and freeze the fish, and there is no problem flying back to the US with it.)

For the last 20-odd years, *FONATUR,* the government tourism development fund, has been trying to design a full-blown resort here, so far with no success. The resort would encompass three separate areas: the existing village of Loreto; Bahía Nopoló, a few miles south of town, which eventually will be the site of luxury hotels (at present, the *Loreto Diamond* stands alone; see *Best en Route*), two 18-hole golf courses (one of which has been built), and a marina; and the harbor at Puerto Loreto, 16 miles (26 km) south of Loreto in the shadow of Gorilla Mountain. Across the street from the *Loreto Diamond,* the *Loreto Tennis Center* (phone: 113-30408) offers year-round clinics.

Loreto's original mission, in the heart of town, has been almost completely rebuilt. One of its bells dates from 1743, but the tower is newer, and its clock is modern. The *Museo de las Misiones Californias,* next door to the mission church, was organized by personnel from Mexico City's *Museo Nacional de Antropología e Historia;* it offers exhibits of artifacts and manuscripts related to the old mission days. It's closed Mondays; there is an admission charge (phone: 113-50441).

Northeast of Loreto, Isla Coronado is home to a large colony of sea lions. Make arrangements for boat excursions to Isla Coronado at *Alfredo's Viajes* travel agency (Blvd. López Mateos and Calle Hidalgo; phone: 113-50165) or at the *Loreto Diamond* and *La Pinta Loreto* hotels (see *Best en Route* for both). Next to Isla Coronado, at Isla Carmen, more than 100,000 tons of salt are extracted annually from a salt mine. It's possible to go snorkeling or scuba diving off the islands, as well as at Puerto Loreto, and there's wonderful swimming at Bahía Nopoló.

En Route from Loreto South of the Loreto junction, a dirt road painstakingly crosses the mountains toward San Javier, site of the best-preserved of the many Jesuit missions in Baja; unfortunately, the 20-mile (32-km) trip takes two and a half hours. Founded in 1699 by Padre Juan de Ugarte, the mission was originally named *Rancho Viejo.* The architectural style is Moorish, and you'll see remarkable stonework, a gilded high altar brought from Mexico City, and a statue of St. Francis. The first wheat fields and the vineyards in the peninsula were planted in the mission garden, where two stone reservoirs built by the Jesuits are still in use.

Farther southwest, the highway climbs dramatically across the Sierra de la Giganta and swings toward the Pacific side of the peninsula. You'll go through Villa Insurgentes, a rich agricultural, industrial, and cattle raising center, and Ciudad Constitución, which lies in the fertile Santo Domingo Valley and, with a population of 43,500, is the second-largest city in Baja California Sur. The nearby Bahía Magdalena, the largest bay in Baja, attracts lots of gray whales—so many, in fact, that the Mexican government recently declared it a gray whale sanctuary. Plans are in the works for the development of federal whale watching facilities here. Isla Santa Margarita, one of the three islands in the bay, is a major shelter for sea lions—up to 3,000 may gather here at one time. At this point, the highway turns southeastward again, to La Paz, about 235 miles (376 km) away.

LA PAZ The capital of Baja California Sur (pop. 200,000) is on a deep inlet in Bahía La Paz on the Sea of Cortés. Overlooking the bay, the city is protected from the open waters of the sea by a long sandbar called El Mogote.

Only 51 miles north of the Tropic of Cancer, La Paz enjoys a sunny and mild climate nearly all year.

Hernán Cortés landed in La Paz in 1535, naming it Bahía de la Santa Cruz (Bay of the Holy Cross). The land was inhabited by the Guaicuru, who were friendly to the European invaders; it was their amiability that prompted another explorer, Sebastián Vizcaíno, to change the name to La Paz ("Peace") when he came here in 1596. Other Spanish expeditions soon arrived, as well as pearl hunters in search of the area's renowned black and pink pearls, some of which adorn various crowns in Europe. (The pearls are nearly nonexistent now.) It wasn't until the Jesuits arrived in 1720 and founded the mission of *Nuestra Señora de la Paz,* however, that the town really began to develop.

In 1830, La Paz became the capital of Baja Sur, at that time a Mexican territory (it did not become a state until 1974). Though new hotels and shopping areas have been built (today there are more than 1,600 hotel rooms), the city retains a provincial and tranquil atmosphere and maintains its old colonial structures. The Sea of Cortés can be seen from every point in town, and at sunset, a blazing spectacle of red and yellow, its waters appear red—thus the moniker Vermilion Sea.

La Paz received almost 130,000 visitors in 1994 (about 40% of the state's total), many attracted by the area's deep-sea fishing, which is reputedly among the finest in the world. Anglers catch marlin, sailfish, swordfish, roosterfish, yellowtail, mahimahi, cabrilla, tuna, and sierras in the bay. The best season for deep-sea fishing is March through August. Marlin are caught March through July; sailfish, June through September. Rental of fishing gear and boat charters can be arranged through any of La Paz's leading hotels (see *Best en Route*). Larger (and more expensive) boats with sleeping facilities can be rented for overnight excursions; a 38-foot boat that sleeps four people comfortably is available from *Baja Diving and Service* (*Plaza Cerraldo* shopping center, on the *malecón,* or boardwalk; phone: 112-21826).

La Paz is ideal for other water sports, especially scuba diving, jet skiing, and water skiing. The area around El Mogote is good for scuba; rent gear at *Los Arcos* hotel (see *Best en Route*). The kiosk across from *Los Arcos,* on Avenida Alvaro Obregón, has information about equipment rental, yacht cruises, fishing, and bike rentals. Joggers will find company along the promenade beginning at the arched Mill Bridge just north of town, but golfers will be disappointed to learn that there still is no golf course nearby (though there has been talk of building one next to *La Concha* hotel).

Coromuel, 3 miles (5 km) south of downtown and the beach closest to the city, has a sandy swimming area, a little dock for diving, a water slide, and a refreshment stand. Only half a mile (1 km) south of the *Gran Baja* hotel, it's accessible via the beach by maneuvering over some rocks along the way. Perhaps the most popular family beach is Pichilingue, which has a couple of open-air restaurants and fishing docks; to get there, drive north on Calle Abasolo, one block west of the *Gran Baja.* This road also leads to

Balandra, Coyote, and Tecolote beaches, all of which have bathhouses and rustic restaurants. Balandra is excellent for snorkeling, while Coyote and Tecolote are a little more remote and face the open sea. Readily available, taxis can be hired for the day for jaunts to local beaches, or you can drive yourself—the road used to be rather rough on a car's shock absorbers, but it recently was repaired.

The *malecón,* or boardwalk, is a great place for strolling in La Paz. The *paceños* (as the locals are known) go there to meet friends, enjoy the sunset, and exchange news as the *coromuel* (evening breeze) cools the town. Above the *malecón* on a hill is the main plaza, along one side of which stands an old Catholic church (1861) that's now the cathedral. The strikingly contemporary *Palacio de Gobierno* (Statehouse) is nearby (on Av. Isabel la Católica; no phone). La Paz's very helpful tourist office (Km 5 of Route 1; phone: 112-40100) is closed weekends.

One of the city's greatest attractions is shopping, and the best hunting grounds are along Calle 16 de Septiembre and just off it, on Calles 5 de Mayo, Madero, and Revolución. Among the fine stores in town are *La Perla de la Paz* (the largest and oldest department store on the peninsula; Calles Mutualismo and Arreola; phone: 112-51701); *El Trébol* (Independencia between Calles Revolución and Madero; phone: 112-59885); and *Importaciones Mary* (Revolución and Independencia; phone: 112-21480). *La Paloma* (on the *malecón,* between Obregón and Calle 16 de Septiembre; no phone) carries all types of hand-crafted items. High-quality wool blankets, clothing, and other items are available at *México Lindo* (on Av. Alvaro Obregón, just off Lerdo de Tejada; no phone). The *Mercado Francisco Madero* (at Revolución and Santos Degollado) is a colorful produce market. Most stores accept credit cards and are open daily, but close from 2 to 4 PM.

The *Museo de la Antropología de Baja California Sur* (Museum of Anthropology of Southern Baja California; Calle 5 de Mayo and Av. Altamirano; phone: 112-20162) has an extensive exhibition on Baja's cave paintings. These mysterious primitive representations of humans and animals, painted in red and black as high as 40 feet above the floor of some 160 caves, have never been fully explained. The museum is closed weekends; there's no admission charge. The *Palacio Municipal* (City Hall; Calle 16 de Septiembre; no phone) has a lovely inner courtyard decorated with handsome historical murals. It's open daily, and there's no admission charge.

Several restaurants in town serve fresh seafood and meat. The top choice for lobster is *Bismark II* (Santos Degollado and Av. Altamirano; phone: 112-24854); *El Moro* (Km 2 on the road to Pichilingue; phone: 112-24084) also is worthwhile. *Sunset Mike's* (on the *malecón,* a block west of *Los Arcos;* no phone), with Mexican, American, and German fare, is a fun addition to La Paz's restaurant scene. "In" nightspots include *La Paz Lapa* restaurant/disco (Calle 16 de Septiembre and Av. Alvaro Obregón; phone: 112-29290) and *Quinto Patio* (Av. Alvaro Obregón; phone: 112-59717). If you're in town during February or March (just before *Cuaresma,* or *Lent*), La Paz has a lively *Carnaval,* complete with cockfights and other festivities.

Visitors can cruise the bay, as well as visit the islands and beaches in the immediate vicinity. Several excursions—among them a sunset cruise and a trip to Isla Espíritu Santo, with its emerald coves and brick-red rocks— are available from *Baja Diving and Service* (see above). From La Paz it's also possible to explore the Sea of Cortés on adventurous kayaking trips offered by San Diego–based *Baja Expeditions* (phone: 619-581-3311 in San Diego; 800-843-6967 elsewhere in the US; fax: 619-581-6542 in the US). And there's erratic ferry service from La Paz to Mazatlán (for a detailed report on the city, see *Mazatlán* in THE CITIES); for schedule information, call 112-53833 or 112-54666.

En Route from La Paz Here, as the peninsula narrows to its southern tip, resorts on both the Pacific and the Sea of Cortés coasts are equally accessible. South of town, you'll come to a junction; at this point, you can drive to San José del Cabo alongside the Pacific or travel via an inland route, 20 minutes longer but more scenic.

The Pacific route leads to Todos Santos (64 miles/106 km from La Paz), a colonial village 1 mile (1.6 km) from the ocean that is popular with surf bathers and artists. (For more information on Todos Santos, see "Extra Special" in *Los Cabos,* THE CITIES.) Should you opt to follow the inland route, you'll pass through El Triunfo, once an important mining town but practically a ghost town today. Its few inhabitants eke out a living by selling handmade palm-fiber crafts.

San Bartolo offers the hot and weary traveler a freshwater spring shaded by banana and palm trees. The townspeople prepare jams and jellies from homegrown bananas and dates and sell them at roadside stands. Los Barriles is a small fishing village with several nice resorts, each with its own fishing fleet and airstrip. The resorts are *Playa del Sol* and *Palmas de Cortez* (no local phone; 818-222-7144 in California; 800-368-4334 elsewhere in the US) and *Punta Pescadero* (no local phone; 800-426-BAJA, also receives faxes), which is the most deluxe and has a private beach.

Just south of Los Barriles on the highway, *Rancho Buena Vista* (no local phone; 805-928-1719 in California; 800-258-8200 elsewhere in the US; fax: 114-10055; 805-925-2990 in the US) is a fine resort with its own fishing fleet, tennis courts, a beach and a pool, and a lighted airstrip, plus opportunities for horseback riding, diving, and hunting for doves, quail, and rabbits.

A few miles farther south is *Punta Colorada* (no local phone; 818-222-5066 in California; 800-368-4334 elsewhere in the US), which has a private beach and a fishing fleet.

The 20-mile stretch between San José del Cabo and Cabo San Lucas, 23 miles (37 km) south of *Punta Colorada,* is known as Los Cabos (The Capes).

LOS CABOS For a detailed report on San José del Cabo and Cabo San Lucas, their hotels, and their restaurants, see *Los Cabos* in THE CITIES.

BEST EN ROUTE

For a double room for one night, expect to pay $90 to $110 at an expensive hotel; $40 to $85 at a moderate place; and $35 or less at an inexpensive one. All hotels listed below have air conditioning, TV sets, and telephones in the rooms unless otherwise indicated. For each location, hotels are listed alphabetically by price category.

PLAYA ROSARITO

Rosarito Beach A 1920s-vintage, hacienda-style property overlooking the ocean, it's Baja's oldest hotel and a longtime celebrity favorite. It features 280 rooms (150 with air conditioning), two pools, two Jacuzzis, a spa, tennis, golf, two restaurants, three bars, and a Mexican fiesta on Friday and Saturday nights. It's received many refurbishings over the years, but it's still as charming as it was when it first opened. Km 27 of Rte. 1 (phone: 661-20144 or 661-21126; 800-343-8582; fax: 661-21176). Expensive.

Quinta Terranova Formerly the *Quinta del Mar,* this sprawling resort underwent a complete renovation of its guestrooms and public areas in 1993. The 83 rooms and two suites are attractively decorated in contemporary style (but are not air conditioned); one suite has a Jacuzzi. Other facilities include a restaurant serving good Mexican fare (but open only June through August), a bar, and a pool. A block from the beach, at 25500 Blvd. Benito Juárez (phone: 661-21648/9; fax: 661-21642). Moderate.

PUERTO NUEVO

New Port Baja In town, overlooking the beach, it has 147 rooms, a restaurant, a sports bar, pool, Jacuzzi, two tennis courts, and a volleyball court. Km 45 of Rte. 1 (phone: 661-41188; 800-582-1018; fax: 661-41174). Moderate.

VALLE DE SAN QUINTÍN

La Pinta San Quintín In this attractive Mexican colonial structure are 56 rooms and one suite with ocean views (but no phones), a restaurant, a bar, tennis courts, and fishing. The long beach here is perfect for clamming. Km 189 of Rte. 1 (phone: 616-52878; 800-336-5454). Moderate.

GUERRERO NEGRO

La Pinta Guerrero Negro With 28 rooms (no air conditioning or phones), a restaurant, and a bar, this place arranges whale watching excursions and trips to the salt mines. On Rte. 1 at the 28th parallel, facing the eagle monument (phone: 115-71305; 800-336-5454; fax: 115-71306). Moderate.

SAN IGNACIO

La Pinta San Ignacio A lovely patio, 28 comfortable rooms (no air conditioning or phones), a restaurant, a bar, a small pool, and volleyball are highlights here. Just south of town (phone: 115-140300; 800-336-5454). Moderate.

La Posada Clean and basic, this motel has six rooms with TV sets, but no phones or air conditioning. Check here for information about whale watching and visiting the area's painted caves. No credit cards accepted. 22 Av. Carranza (phone: 115-40313). Inexpensive.

SANTA ROSALÍA

El Morro This motel has 30 rooms (no phones), a restaurant, a bar, and a pool in a tropical setting. Nearly 1 mile (1.5 km) south of town, on the Carretera al Sur (phone/fax: 115-22390). Inexpensive.

MULEGÉ

Serenidad A dining room, a pool, a bar, scuba gear rental, fishing, kayaking, and even an airstrip are available at this beachfront place. There also are 45 rooms, five two-bedroom casitas, and nine trailer hookups (none of the units has phones or TV sets). Owner Don Johnson, a former US consul, is a good source of tourist information. There's a pork barbecue every Saturday night and a Mexican fiesta every Wednesday. Two miles (3 km) south of town on Playa el Cacheno (phone: 115-30111; fax: 115-30311). Moderate.

Las Casitas An eight-room family-run hotel (no TV sets or phones in rooms), it offers fishing and scuba diving expeditions, plus visits to the nearby cave paintings. On the premises is a restaurant and bar. There's a 10% surcharge if you pay with a credit card. On Plaza Hidalgo, at 50 Francisco Madero (phone: 115-30019; fax: 115-30340). Inexpensive.

LORETO

Oasis The perennial favorite of fishing diehards, it has 35 rooms (no phones or TV sets), a restaurant, a bar with satellite TV, a pool, and a tennis court. Rooms can be booked with or without three meals daily. Two blocks north of downtown, on Calle Baja California (phone: 113-50112 or 113-50211; fax: 113-50795). Moderate to expensive.

Loreto Diamond The erstwhile *Stouffer Presidente Loreto* is now an all-inclusive Diamond Resorts hotel, and a 1995 renovation may put it in the top ranks again. Its attractive 224 rooms are equipped with plenty of amenities, and its spectacular setting on the Bahía Nopoló—surrounded by a meticulously manicured landscape—makes a stay here especially worthwhile. Water sports are available on the premises; there's also a disco open nightly, as well as nightly live shows (very risqué—no minors allowed) at a new theater on the premises. Across the street is a tennis center; the hotel staff can arrange fishing and diving excursions, as well as tours to Isla Coronado. Because the hotel is about 30 minutes south of downtown, you'll need a car to get around (there's a car rental desk at the hotel); otherwise, plan to pay a lot of taxi fares. Blvd. Misión de Nopoló (phone: 113-30700; 800-858-2258; fax: 113-30377). Expensive.

La Pinta Loreto A modern, comfortable hotel with 48 large rooms (no phones), a bar, a small pool, a gameroom, and shuffleboard, it boasts the best beach in town. The restaurant is known for its Mexican food. On the beach, six blocks north of the plaza (phone: 113-50025; 800-336-5454; fax: 113-50026). Moderate.

Tripuí Trailer Park Outstanding among its genre, it offers 31 traditional hookups, a restaurant, a large pool, and laundry facilities. Perfect for fishing enthusiasts. Puerto Loreto (phone: 113-30818; fax: 113-30828). Inexpensive.

LA PAZ

Los Arcos In this attractive colonial-style structure are 145 balconied rooms and suites (there are 52 thatch-roofed cabañas next door at *Cabañas de los Arcos*), a restaurant, a coffee shop, two pools, a car rental desk, a gift shop, and fishing facilities. The wonderful bar here was a favorite hangout of John Wayne and Humphrey Bogart. Rooms in back are quietest. Right on the bay, at 498 Av. Alvaro Obregón (phone: 112-22744; 800-347-2252; 714-476-5555 in California; fax: 112-54313; 714-476-5560). Expensive to moderate.

La Concha This three-story hotel has 103 rooms, four suites, a large pool, an outstanding restaurant, a bar, an excellent beach, and diving, boating, and fishing excursions. Playa Caimancito, at Km 5 on the road to Pichilingue (phone: 112-26544; 619-260-0991 in California; 800-999-BAJA elsewhere in the US; fax: 112-26218; 619-294-7366). Expensive to moderate.

Mar y Sol American expatriate Carol Palenzona runs this cozy inn with six rooms, three suites and a two-bedroom penthouse, all decorated in Mexican style with kitchens and dining areas (but no phones). On the grounds are a pool and a large, pretty garden. There is no restaurant. Insurgentes and Margaritas, a block north of *La Posada de Engelbert* (phone: 112-52467; 415-346-6337; fax: 112-20180; 415-346-6337). Expensive to moderate.

La Posada de Engelbert Owned by pop singer Engelbert Humperdinck, this colonial-style hostelry is cool and peaceful. There are lovely tiled baths, a small pool, 21 rooms, four casitas, a restaurant, and a bar. Nueva Reforma and Playa Sur (phone: 112-24011; fax: 112-20663). Expensive to moderate.

Aquario's This 60-room property has a pool, a restaurant, a piano bar, and a staff that's eager to please. Three blocks south of the center of town, at 1665 Ramírez (phone: 112-29266; fax: 112-55713). Inexpensive.

The West Coast:
Nogales to Mexico City

The 1,450-mile (2,320-km) drive from Nogales (Nogales, Arizona, on the US side of the border; Nogales, Sonora, on the Mexican) to Mexico City provides one of the most fascinating journeys in Mexico. If the objective is to reach Mexico City as quickly as possible, the trip can be made in just under four days of hard driving; to do so, however, would mean passing up an unparalleled opportunity to explore the endless beaches along the Golfo de Cortés (Sea of Cortés, also known as the Gulf of California) and the Pacific Coast, which are only accessible by car, and to unheedingly speed by an astounding diversity of landscape, climate, and culture.

This western route leads from Nogales 225 miles (360 km) southwest to Guaymas, where the long coastal stretch of the trip begins. Eventually, at Tepic, the route leads inland again for the 400-mile-plus (640-km) final lap to Mexico City. During the course of this epic journey travelers will traverse the dry, naked desert hills of the state of Sonora, drop south through the subtropics of Sinaloa into the very real tropics of Nayarit (passing along the way the very best—and many of the least known—resorts and fishing spots on the western coast), and at last turn east to cross the Sierra Madre Occidental through the lake districts of Jalisco and Michoacán into the state of Mexico, and finally to reach Mexico City. It could well be called the "route of contrasts," for the traveler driving this road can find in the same day the adobe huts of Mexico's northwestern rural dwellers and the beautiful mansions of the rich. The trip offers the chic discos of Mazatlán and the undeveloped simplicity of Bahía Kino, where it's tough to find a postcard for friends; in addition, you'll encounter incredibly plush resorts on the Golfo de Cortés, as well as the best sport fishing and hunting in the country (see *Fishing Mexico's Rich Waters* and *Hunting* in DIVERSIONS).

From Nogales to Guaymas and from Ciudad Obregón to Navojoa, the route follows a divided four-lane highway. Farther south, from Los Mochis, a toll road leads to Culiacán, and more stretches of divided highway lead to Guadalajara. From here, the road is a narrow, two-lane highway along which you might see as many cows, horses, burros, goats, dogs, old men, and children as you will fellow drivers. From Toluca you'll reach the toll road leading to Mexico City. We strongly discourage you from driving at night, especially on the undivided, two-lane roads, most of which do not have shoulders.

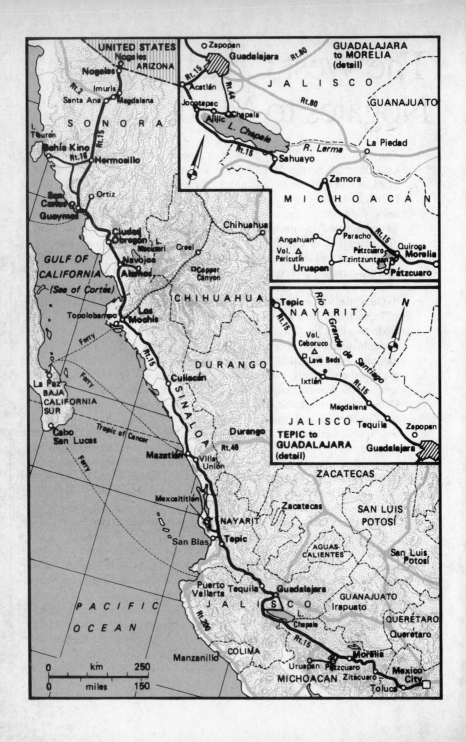

En Route to Nogales, Mexico A fence along the international boundary separates the cities of Nogales, Arizona, and Nogales, Sonora. The United States and Mexican governments each maintain 24-hour customs facilities for tourists crossing the border. In the Mexican immigration office just beyond the border, officials will issue tourist cards or validate the one you already have. For regulations regarding entry into Mexico, see GETTING READY TO GO. There is little of interest to keep you dallying in Nogales, a commercial center for farmers, ranchers, and the dairy industry.

En Route from Nogales, Mexico Hermosillo, the first major town along the way, is 175 miles (280 km) from the border via Route 15, about a four-hour trip. Head out of Nogales on the one-way street onto Route 15. After some 15 miles (24 km), you will reach a customs check, where your baggage may be examined. The highway then passes through a series of narrow valleys before emerging on the rim of a cultivated plain watered by the Río de los Alisos and Río Magdalena.

Forty-five miles (72 km) south of Nogales, in the small town of Magdalena, the remains of renowned priest Padre Eusebio Kino were discovered in 1966. This amazing Italian-born Jesuit came to Mexico in 1687, at the age of 32. During the next 24 years he established 25 missions and converted seven native tribes (the Apache, Yuma, Seri, Maricopa, Papago, Pima, and Cocopa). In his spare time the priest proved that Baja California was not an island and introduced fig, pear, peach, apricot, and citrus trees and wheat and grapes to these fertile river valleys. Padre Kino died in Magdalena in 1711, and his remains are on display in a mausoleum (on the Plaza Monumental, or *zócalo*). Magdalena's tourist office is in the *Presidencia Municipal* (City Hall; phone: 632-21085); it is closed weekends.

HERMOSILLO The capital of the state of Sonora is not really a tourist town. Most American visitors stop for lunch and move on, but the town, tucked between sea and mountains, does have a few interesting sights. Its mild, dry winters have made it a popular winter resort.

The town was named in honor of José María González Hermosillo, a revolutionary leader during Mexico's War of Independence. The city's few early colonial buildings, all in the center of town, offer an excellent introduction to Spanish colonial architecture. For exhibits of pre-Columbian artifacts, visit the *Museo de la Universidad de Sonora* (University of Sonora Museum; Rosales and Luis Encinas; no phone). It's closed Mondays; admission charge.

Other points of interest in Hermosillo include the Plaza Zaragoza in the center of town and the fine cathedral there, and *Parque Madero* (Madero Park), a favorite promenade and sports center in the southeast section of the city, with areas for baseball, tennis, and handball. Also of interest is the *Museo Costumbrista* (History Museum; off the Plaza Zaragoza; phone: 62-131234), converted from an old prison. It's closed Mondays; admission charge. The scenic Cerro de la Campana (Hill of the Bell) is also worth seeing. Hermosillo's tourism office is in the Edificio Pitic (100 Eusebio Kino; phone: 62-146304 or 800-62555 toll-free in Mexico). It's open daily.

Good choices for a meal here are *Merendero la Huerta* (136 Calle 11 Ote.; phone: 62-148288), which has a no-frills atmosphere and serves some of the best seafood in town at reasonable prices, and *Miyako* (Km 4 of the Carretera Bahía Kino; phone: 62-131697), a fairly expensive, but authentic, Japanese restaurant, with chefs from Japan and seating on the floor. For tasty steaks and ribs—this cattle state's specialty—head for *Jardines de Xochimilco* (51 Calle Obregón, off Blvd. Rosales in Colonia Villa de Seris; phone: 62-133489); while you eat, strolling musicians will serenade you with regional *ranchero* songs.

Lago Rodríguez, Rodríguez Dam, and Boulevard Rodríguez, which leads into town, are all named for former Mexican President Abelardo Rodríguez, a native of Sonora who served from 1932 to 1934 and promoted industry in this area. The large earthfill dam, which checks the flow of the Río Sonora, has played a major role in converting this desert region into a substantial agricultural producer.

Deer, coyote, rabbit, dove, pigeon, and duck hunting are good in the immediate area.

En Route from Hermosillo At this point, you have the option of going directly south to Guaymas and San Carlos or detouring 65 miles (104 km) west to Bahía Kino, a worthwhile stop for those who enjoy comfortable seclusion and the absence of push-button anything.

To head directly for Guaymas, continue on Route 15 south over dry range country for 84 miles (134 km).

To reach Bahía Kino from Hermosillo, leave Route 15 at Transversal just before the university and continue on Route 16 west, a good two-lane road that leads you right to the Golfo de Cortés.

BAHÍA KINO With its immaculate beaches and excellent fishing, Bahía Kino is giving Guaymas a run for its money as Sonora's most popular resort. There are beach houses and accommodations on this short stretch of sand. Offshore are a number of islands, the largest of which is Isla Tiburón (Shark Island). Now a wildlife refuge, the island can be visited only by special permission; contact the tourist office in Hermosillo (see above) for additional details. Until 1956, the 40-mile-long island was the home of the Seri Indians, who were forcibly removed by government troops to make way for the wildlife refuge. The proud Seri now live in two settlements near Old Bahía Kino, Punta Chueca and El Desemboque. For an illuminating look at Seri culture, visit the *Museo de los Seris* (Seris Museum), which offers excellent exhibits of traditional clothing, reed kayaks, and other artifacts (Calle Progreso and Av. Mar de Cortés). It's open daily; no admission charge (no phone).

The paved road leads directly into town, with the beach on the west side. The main road ends in a dirt road that wanders away from the beach to a

Seri camp about a quarter of a mile down the road. Seri women often can be seen weaving heart-shaped baskets, while men fish or carve ironwood animals, some fine enough to be considered collectors' items. Be forewarned that people have been stoned for taking photographs of the Seri without permission.

Beyond the Seri settlement, the road winds along the jagged coastline, where groups of fishermen venture out in boats to net mackerel, which they sell locally and in Mexico City. Beyond the tiny fishing villages, the beach is great for secluded sunbathing.

Sport fishing is not commercialized here as it is in Mazatlán or Acapulco; many people bring their own boats to Bahía Kino, rent space at one of the local trailer camps, and launch their own excursions.

En Route from Bahía Kino Take Route 16 east, back toward Hermosillo. About 35 miles (56 km) out of Bahía Kino, take the right fork (marked "Guaymas"); this shortcut takes you 56 miles (90 km) to Route 15 south, right into Guaymas.

GUAYMAS Backed by high mountains, Guaymas is one of Mexico's finest seaports. Spanish explorers landed here as early as 1535, but the area was not settled until the 18th century, after it had become a mission base under Fathers Salvatierra and Kino. The settlement was opened as a general trading post in 1841 and served as a Spanish-Mexican free port, a prized outlet for Sonora's rich mineral resources.

Guaymas was attacked by US naval forces in 1847 during the Mexican War and was occupied until 1848. It was the scene of battle once again in 1854, when the French buccaneer Count Gastón Raouset de Bourbon and some 400 pirates attempted to seize the city. Bourbon was captured and executed by General Yáñez, defender of the port. Eleven years later, the French under Maximilian took the port. During the US Civil War, supplies destined for troops in Arizona were shipped in through Guaymas from San Francisco, California, and then transported overland.

Guaymas today is actually two communities. The city section, with its 18th-century *Catedral de San Fernando,* shrimp docks, and freighters in the harbor, is divided by a mountainous peninsula from the resort areas along Bahías Bocachibampo and San Carlos. Most of the city's inhabitants are active in the all-important shrimp and oyster trade with the United States.

For the tourist, Guaymas's chief draw is sport fishing. The Golfo de Cortés teems with fish all year: Sailfish, marlin, and dolphin run heavily June through September; yellowtail, red snapper, bass, whitefish, and sea perch run October through April. There also is fine shore fishing, with plentiful corbina, sierra mackerel, and roosterfish. Arrangements for fishing trips can easily be made through the *Marina San Carlos* (see *San Carlos*). The *Fiesta de la Pesca* (Fishing Festival) and *Torneo Internacional de Pez Deportivo* (International Game Fish Tournament) are held here every July.

In the surrounding area, duck and dove hunting are excellent. Farms in the area produce wheat, safflower, and corn, and products from them are sold locally. Sesame seeds, chick-peas, and cotton are grown and exported.

Guaymas is also noted for its abundance and variety of seashells. Each year, during the period of lowest tide (November through March), conchologists visit the area to gather specimens. *La Casona* (3 Calle 24; no phone), a shop with a large collection of shells and shell jewelry, delights gatherers of a different ilk.

If you aren't interested in bagging your own dinner, *El Paradise* (20 A. L. Rodríguez; phone: 622-21181) is a small, clean place offering sand lobster, shrimp (the house specialty), and frogs' legs; there's also a branch in San Carlos. For steaks and lobster served in colonial decor, try *Del Mar* (Calle 17 and Av. Serdán; phone: 622-20226).

Besides the cathedral, Guaymas's attractions include the Plaza de los Tres Presidentes (Plaza of the Three Presidents, one block west of the dock), a monument to fishermen (on Plaza del Pescador, one block southwest of the dock), the *Palacio Municipal* (City Hall; on the Plaza de los Tres Presidentes), and the decorative façade of the late 19th-century municipal jail (Av. XII and Calle 13). All are within walking distance of each other. Guaymas's tourist office is at 437 Avenida Serdán (phone: 622-22932); it is closed Sundays.

En Route from Guaymas San Carlos is about 13 miles (21 km) northwest.

SAN CARLOS This town offers more tourist facilities than Guaymas in a more resort-like atmosphere, with plush motor inns, condominiums, and sleek sport fishing boats. San Carlos is famous for its accessibility to deep-sea fishing.

The *Marina San Carlos* (phone: 622-60230 or 622-60565) is the best base of operations for fishing. *Lanchas Deportivas de Sonora* (phone: 622-60011 or 622-60565) has about a dozen boats, from 30 to 42 feet long. Eight-hour fishing trips are available, which include a guide and boat hand, bait, ice, and tackle. If you'd rather just sightsee, a large glass-bottom boat leaves from the marina daily for two-hour daylight and sunset cruises of the bay area (phone: 622-20026).

Gary's Place (Calle San Carlos, next to the *San Carlos* hotel; phone: 622-60049) outfits scuba divers with everything from wet suits to weights. They also rent small fishing boats to individuals and groups. (For more information, see *Best Beaches off the Beaten Path* in DIVERSIONS.) There are also several stables in San Carlos that rent horses by the hour for rides through the country.

The best place to eat in San Carlos is the dining room of the *Posada San Carlos* (see *Best en Route*), which serves seafood. *La Terraza* (Km 9.5 of the Carretera San Carlos; phone: 622-60039), 1 mile (1.6 km) from the *Teta Kawi* trailer park (see *Best en Route*) and overlooking Bahía San Carlos, serves international food and seafood at moderate prices. *La Roca* (phone: 622-60160), across the highway from *Teta Kawi,* also serves good seafood.

En Route from San Carlos Route 15 passes through several agricultural and industrial towns before reaching Mazatlán, almost 500 miles (800 km) down the road. The highway is the same two-lane blacktop along the entire route, with the exception of short four- and six-lane stretches that bypass Ciudad Obregón and Los Mochis, respectively.

At the village of Cruz de Piedra (Cross of Stone), 16 miles (26 km) out of Guaymas, begins a Yaqui reservation that extends southeast to Río Yaqui. The Mexican government set aside this tract for the indigenous Yaqui after an uprising in 1928. The fierce group is known for its *danza de venado* (deer dance) and the *matachines* (masquerade and coyote dance) performed during the festivities of *Semana Santa* (Holy Week) and in late June.

The next stop of major interest is Ciudad Obregón, about 78 miles (125 km) south of Guaymas. Along the way, notice how the brown cacti and scrub brush blossom into lush vegetation—the result of huge irrigation projects for the cultivation of cotton, corn, and sugarcane.

CIUDAD OBREGÓN Founded in 1928, Ciudad Obregón is a flat, open city with wide streets, contemporary buildings, and an absolute lack of colonial atmosphere. The concentric rings of storage elevators and granaries that circle the city spread out across the surrounding Mexican countryside.

Ciudad Obregón is a popular base for hunters after deer and wild turkeys in the Sierra Madre foothills 50 miles (80 km) to the east. From November through February, there's some of the best duck hunting in Mexico. The *Museo Yaqui* (Calles Allende and 5 de Febrero; no phone) covers the entire history of the Yaqui people in exhibits of their clothing, jewelry, dances, weaponry, music, and even a re-creation of a Yaqui home. It's closed Mondays; admission charge.

Mr. Steak (near the *Norotel Cajeme Valle Grande* hotel; phone: 641-33570) has a western atmosphere and serves lunch and dinner for modest prices. *El Cortijo* (Calle 5 de Febrero, two blocks west of Rte. 15; phone: 641-52343) specializes in *cabrito* (kid) and paella.

En Route from Ciudad Obregón About 44 miles (70 km) south of Ciudad Obregón, in the middle of a vast agricultural area devoted to cotton, is Navojoa, a large center for the Mayo (a native regional group, not to be confused with the Maya). From here, the route leaves Route 15 long enough to visit the beautifully maintained antique city of Alamos, 33 miles (53 km) to the east on Route 19. The way to Alamos is peppered with *ejidos,* or collective farming settlements.

ALAMOS A once-prosperous mining town and capital of the area, Alamos is now a national monument that testifies to its past grandeur. One of the few Spanish settlements in this part of Mexico to have escaped modernization, it is equipped with electricity, telephones, good hotels, and an airstrip, but the newest building is more than 100 years old. Federal decree prohibits construction of new buildings or alteration of the town's colonial atmosphere.

Exploitation of the area's gold and silver deposits had attracted a population of 30,000 to Alamos by 1781. The wealthy governors and mine owners built large, lavish Moorish-style homes, and the town became one of Mexico's colonial jewels. By the beginning of this century, however, Alamos was a fading star. A combination of exhausted mineral resources, successive attacks by indigenous groups, drought, famine, and the 1910 revolution left Alamos a ghost town. After World War II, a group of American artists and retirees, drawn by the invigorating climate and warm winters, reclaimed and restored the ancient manor houses. The influx from the US has not ended, and many of the renovated buildings are among the town's biggest attractions.

The most famous restored house in Alamos is the *Casa de los Tesoros,* now a hotel (see *Best en Route*) and located on the Plaza de Armas (main plaza). The plaza is surrounded on three sides by arched *portales* and fine buildings, and, on the fourth side, by the *Iglesia de la Señora de la Concepción* (Church of Our Lady of the Immaculate Conception), built in 1784 on the site of the old mission, which had been burned by Indians. The worthwhile *Museo Costumbrista de Alamos* (Alamos History Museum; Calles Victoria and Cárdenas; no phone) is closed Mondays and Tuesdays; no admission charge.

The colonial cemetery, located about four blocks south of the Plaza de Armas, is interesting for its aboveground vaults and wrought-iron crosses. Alamos also has *La Uvulama,* an outdoor market where female potters buy and sell clay bowls; it's located about two blocks southwest of the Plaza de Armas.

La Aduana, 6 miles (10 km) outside Alamos on the only road leading north, is a ghost town built around the great smelter works where Alamos silver was once cast into ingots. Every November 20, the Mayo have a festival in honor of the Virgen Balvanera, which includes fireworks and pilgrimages.

Another big, if bizarre, attraction of Alamos is that it is the home of the so-called Mexican jumping bean. Powered by a hyperactive larva, the beans are picked from wild plants that grow in the hills nearby. Some Alamos natives earn fairly comfortable livings by catering to the largely American market for these frisky little "creatures," known in Alamos as *brincadores.*

The hills around Alamos are a treat for duck, blue pigeon, white-wing dove, and quail hunters. Halfway between Navojoa and Alamos is a road heading 10 miles (16 km) north to Lago de Macuzari and a dam where the bass fishing is excellent.

Any of the self-styled guides at the Plaza de Armas will give you a two-hour tour of the town in English for a small fee. On Saturdays, the *Amigos de la Biblioteca* (Friends of the Library) offer an inexpensive tour (in English) that includes the interiors of some of the faithfully reconstructed homes; just show up at the library at 10 AM. From November through March, the desk clerk at *La Mansión de la Condesa Magdalena* (see *Best en Route*) will arrange one-day raft trips, which include fishing and bird watching.

Both *La Mansión de la Condesa Magdalena* and *Casa de los Tesoros* have excellent restaurants, and *Polo's,* on the plaza, serves charcoal-broiled steaks and chicken in a no-frills atmosphere.

En Route from Alamos Route 15 travels inland in the shadows of the Sierra Madre for 98 miles (157 km) to Los Mochis.

LOS MOCHIS This town was just a small group of huts in 1893, when entrepreneur Benjamin Johnston arrived from the United States and started to grow sugarcane. He later built a sugar mill, which became one of the biggest in Mexico. Johnston laid out streets, constructed a huge mansion, and watched Los Mochis mature.

Today, Los Mochis is an agricultural boomtown, and the 250,000 farmers in the region produce more sugarcane than any other area on Mexico's west coast. The city is literally wrapped in marigolds, which are a cash crop here (they produce a dye used in chicken feed).

Los Mochis is the major coastal terminal of the *Ferrocarril Chihuahua al Pacífico* (Chihuahua-Pacific Railway), though technically the line ends in Topolobampo, 10 miles (16 km) to the southwest. The railroad leaves Los Mochis daily for points east via the Barranca del Cobre (Copper Canyon), a series of huge, deep gorges that surpass the Grand Canyon in both size and beauty. If you decide to take a train excursion from here, you may safely leave your car in the train station parking lot until you return. For additional details, see the *Ciudad Juárez to Mexico City* route in this section and *Quintessential Mexico* in DIVERSIONS.

If train rides don't beckon, you can take the southwest branch of Route 32 to Topolobampo, a small fishing village known for its shrimp fleet and abundant sport fish—including skipjacks, yellowtail, sierra mackerel, and roosterfish. Sailfish and marlin run heavily from July through October. The town has good beaches and duck hunting as well. Nearby Islas Las Animas, a breeding place for sea lions, are great for offshore sunbathing and spearfishing. The ferry that links Topolobampo with La Paz, Baja California, makes the journey twice a week. You also can charter a fishing boat for up to 12 people at the *Santa Anita* hotel in Los Mochis (see *Best en Route*).

The best food in Los Mochis is available at the hotels, particularly at *El Dorado* and *Santa Anita* (see *Best en Route* for both). For seafood, try *El Farallón* (495 Obregón, around the corner from the *Santa Anita* hotel; phone: 68-121428 or 68-121273). Los Mochis's tourism office is at Calles Allende and Cuauhtémoc; it's closed Sundays (phone: 68-150405).

En Route from Los Mochis Route 15 takes you through 127 miles (197 km) of flat, fertile farmland en route to Culiacán.

CULIACÁN The capital of the state of Sinaloa derives its name from the Nahuatl word *colhuacán,* meaning "place where two rivers meet." The city, which was founded by the cruel and despised conquistador Pedro Beltrán Nuño de Guzmán, in 1533, is now a busy mining, agricultural, and fish-processing center. The surrounding region, between the foothills of the Sierra Madre and the Pacific, abounds in cotton, peanuts, and some of the world's finest tomatoes.

Culiacán is a progressive city whose modern buildings have almost eclipsed traces of its colonial past. On the *zócalo* (Plaza Obregón), for instance, a lovely old cathedral faces the park near some of the most avant-garde architecture in the country.

On the outskirts of Culiacán there are two thermal swimming spots: the hot springs of Carrizalejo, 9 miles (14 km) southeast of the city on Route 30, and those at Ymala (12 miles/19 km beyond Carrizalejo on the right bank of the Río Ramazula). Two beaches popular with Culiacán residents are Playa Altata (42 miles/67 km west, at Boca del Río) for surfing and fishing, and El Dorado (43 miles/69 km south). Culiacán's tourism office is in the *Palacio de Gobierno* (Statehouse; phone: 67-140610); it's closed weekends.

En Route from Culiacán Just a few miles north of Mazatlán, which is 135 miles (216 km) from Culiacán, the road crosses the Tropic of Cancer; a sign marks the exact spot.

MAZATLÁN For a detailed report on this city, one of the most popular resorts in Mexico, see *Mazatlán* in THE CITIES.

En Route from Mazatlán Beyond the resort town, the highway crosses rolling country, and the vegetation changes from semi-arid to tropical. To the east rises the Sierra Madre Occidental. At this point you can take an interesting side trip to the city of Durango. Route 40 cuts inland across the mountains from a junction 1 mile (1.6 km) south of Villa Unión (15 miles/24 km south of Mazatlán) to Durango. (For a detailed description of Durango, see the *Ciudad Juárez to Mexico City* route.)

The 183-mile (293-km) stretch between Mazatlán and Tepic affords travelers the chance to make a worthwhile side trip to the island of Mexcaltitlán or the village of San Blas, or to both.

MEXCALTITLÁN Four miles (6 km) beyond the crossing at the village of Río Chilapa (136 miles/218 km south of Mazatlán), a bumpy, winding, and unmarked gravel road leads from the highway to this island village, in a large, peaceful lagoon and connected to the mainland by a causeway. Turn right down the road, which is paved after about 12 miles (20 km). After about 7 miles (11 km) more, take a right at the second water tower; then take the first left to the causeway that leads to the village, for a total of 30 miles (49 km), or more than an hour's drive from the highway. (Make sure you turn right at the water tower; if you don't, you'll come to a dead end in about 3 mi/5 km and have to turn around and come back.) The road passes through tobacco and cornfields, and farther along swamps seep up on both sides. You may see one or two villagers from Mexcaltitlán fishing while standing in hip-deep water.

When the causeway ends, you'll see the tiny island of Mexcaltitlán, which resembles a *National Geographic* foldout in three dimensions, complete with children playing on the shore and dugout canoes.

The small island village is laid out in a circle, divided into four sections representing the four cardinal points (some say it's a template for the Aztec calendar). Legend has it that this is actually Aztlán ("the place of herons"), whence the Aztec left in 1111 to wander for 200 years in search of their promised land.

Though few tourists come through Mexcaltitlán, there's always someone to take visitors for a canoe ride around the island. The fewer than 3,000 residents fish and farm tobacco and corn. On shore you can stroll to a stately church with a cracked bell tower.

En Route from Mexcaltitlán Return to Route 15 and travel 24 miles (38 km) south to the San Blas turnoff, where you pick up Route 54 and drive for another 24 miles (38 km) west to San Blas. The drive takes three to four hours.

SAN BLAS This tropical seaside village (pop. 8,400) could have been taken right out of a Hemingway novel or a Bogart movie. In fact, San Blas is better known as the place about which Longfellow wrote his last poem, "The Bells of San Blas."

Part of the fun of visiting San Blas is getting there. The paved road drops rapidly from an altitude of 1,000 feet to sea level, passing vibrant vegetation and large coquito palms that form a living green canyon. As you near the sea, there are estuaries and dark mangrove swamps, the exposed roots of the trees crusted with oysters. Coconuts, papayas, bananas, and mangoes grow everywhere.

Adobe and thatch houses line San Blas's sandy streets. High on a rise of ground behind the village is Old San Blas, the stark, stone ruins of a fortress and ancient mission church built by the Spanish. This is the best vantage point from which to get a perspective of the entire area; most hotels will arrange for guides. There was once a waterfront here from which Coronado launched many of his colonizing expeditions. Across from the port on a spit of land stands the San Blas lighthouse, built on Cerro de Vigía (Lookout Hill) in the 18th century. San Blas used to be a major Spanish shipbuilding center, and many of the ships that sailed the Philippine trade route were constructed here.

Fishing is one of the major pastimes here. You can go deep-sea fishing for sailfish, marlin, and dorado (mahimahi), or fish closer to shore for mackerel, yellowtail, and bonitos. Antonio Aguayo, a member of the *Unión de Lancheros Pesca Deportiva* (Sport Fishermen's Union), operates fishing trips for tourists. You can reach him through the desk clerks at the *Garza Canela* hotel (see *Best en Route*). Aguayo's boat can accommodate four passengers, although only two can fish at one time; trips last from 7 AM until 2 PM and bait, tackle, and ice are included. Abraham Murillo has a larger boat on which five can fish (phone: 328-50362).

Jungle boat trips also are popular with San Blas visitors. A three- to four-hour trip departs from Estero San Cristóbal (St. Christopher Estuary), at the bridge at the mouth of Río la Tovara on Route 15 toward Tepic; it goes down the river for a short way, and then up the La Tovara tributary to *Los Manantiales de la Tovara* (La Tovara Springs), where the water is crystal clear. A shorter, hour-and-a-half trip departs farther up Río la Tovara at El Embarcadero on the road to the village of Matanchén, southeast of town. You can swim and get refreshments at the springs. The *Unión de Lancheros Pesca Deportiva,* in front of the *Presidencia Municipal* (City Hall) in San Blas rents boats for these trips. Any hotel in town will help with arrangements, or visit the San Blas tourist office in the *Presidencia Municipal* (no phone).

Good meals are served at the *Garza Canela* hotel (see *Best en Route*) and the *Misión* hotel (on Cuauhtémoc; no phone). *La Familia* (18 Batellón; phone: 328-50258) is another good restaurant, set in a colonial home. *Tony's,* also known as *La Isla* (Calle Paredes Sur; no phone), serves excellent steaks and seafood.

Along with San Blas's undeniably positive assets—mystique, history, great deep-sea fishing, and a casual pace—come two equally undeniable liabilities: grade B accommodations and *jejenes* (pronounced hay-*hay*-nays), tiny gnats that proliferate during the summer months. Bring lots of insect repellent.

En Route from San Blas Return to Route 15 and continue south to Tepic; the total trip from San Blas is about 42 miles (67 km).

TEPIC At the foot of the extinct Sangangüey Volcano, this town is the capital of Nayarit, one of the smaller and lesser-known states in Mexico. It presents an interesting mixture of Mexico's past and present.

The town's historical claim to fame is that in 1524, Francisco Cortés de San Buenaventura, a relative of Hernán Cortés, occupied the indigenous village that stood on the site. Tepic didn't really get moving, however, until 1912, when the first locomotive whistled through.

Points of interest include the old cathedral, which was completed around 1750 and is noted for its two fine Gothic towers, and the *Iglesia de la Santa Cruz* (Church of the Holy Cross), founded in 1744 and once part of a Franciscan convent of the same name. The *Museo Regional de Nayarit* (91 Av. México Nte.; phone: 32-121900) has exhibits of Mesoamerican pottery and jewelry; admission charge.

At the stores bordering the main plaza, you can buy items embedded with thousands of tiny beads worked into colorful designs by the Huichol and Cora Indians, who sell their handiwork in town on Sundays. If you're lucky, you may see the beautiful and mysterious ceremony during which they make offerings to the sea. The ritual takes place several times a year along the Nayarit coastline, most frequently near Santa Cruz, a coastal town 12 miles (19 km) of Tepic; it has no set date or time.

From Tepic, you can take an excursion to El Salto, a breathtaking water-fall, and to Playa Miramar on the Pacific, both west of the city. Other attractive spots are El Salto de Ingenio de Jala (Jala Falls), which flow only during the rainy season, and Laguna Santa María, a volcanic crater lake 20 miles (32 km) southeast of Tepic.

There are several decent places to eat in the area. *Roberto's,* also called *Internacional* (at Militar and Insurgentes; 32-133005), serves good food at modest prices. The *Beachcomber* (at Insurgentes and Durango, east of the *Corita* hotel, near *Parque Loma;* phone: 32-120636) serves seafood specialties, as does *Maryskos* in *El Farallón* hotel (Rte. 15, across from *Parque Loma;* phone: 32-124887). Tepic's tourism office is at 253A Avenida México Sur; it's closed Sundays (phone: 32-130993).

En Route from Tepic Here Route 15 turns inland, first to Guadalajara and then on to Mexico City. If you are loath to leave the Pacific Coast, however, you can follow Route 200 southwest to the pretty resort town of Puerto Vallarta (for a detailed report on the city, its restaurants, and its hotels, see *Puerto Vallarta* in THE CITIES) and then travel even farther south to Manzanillo. The total trip is about 275 miles (440 km).

Route 15 leaves Tepic in the opposite direction—inland over the Sierra Madre to Guadalajara, 140 miles (224 km) east on a road that whips from side to side for most of the journey. Forty miles (64 km) down this roller coaster, the famous lava beds of Ceboruco are stacked along both sides of the road—a gray moonscape of volcanic formations that is impossible to miss. Seventeen miles (27 km) beyond the lava beds, the road passes the *Ixtlán* archaeological site, most of which is yet to be uncovered. About 36 miles (58 km) beyond the *Ixtlán* ruins is the small village of Magdalena, tucked away in the Sierra Madre and famous for the quality of its opals. Two small shops side by side on the west side of the plaza sell these gems as well as beautiful carved black obsidian objects. The next major town is Tequila.

TEQUILA The word *tequila* means "the rock that cuts" in Nahuatl, an appropriate name for this town surrounded by hills of sharp obsidian rock. To most people, however, the word tequila is the name of the world-famous liquor that's produced here. Tequila is made from the juice of the heart of the spiny *agave azul* plant, which grows in profusion in this part of the country; you've seen them constantly along the last 50 miles of road. The heart of the plant is cooked, and the juice that's drawn from the pulp is fermented, distilled, and bottled.

Tequila, the town, was founded in 1530 by a Spanish captain, Cristóbal de Oñate; tequila, the liquor, was first distilled here in 1600. The town now claims about 25 tequila distilleries. Since 1875 the Sauza family has been operating La Perseverancia, the oldest and largest tequila distillery in Mexico. The Cuervo family has been operating La Rojena since 1888, which makes it the second-oldest firm. For a tour of Sauza's La Perseverancia, free drinks, and tequila at discount prices, call Aurora at the distillery (phone: 374-20243). Visitors are also welcome at La Rojena distillery (no phone).

If you'd like a guide to escort you through either distillery and around town, stop in at *Mario's* restaurant (on Rte. 15, close to Calle Morelos just before the bridge over Arroyo de Atizocoa on the way to Tepic; phone: 374-20088). Mario Sánchez, who is well regarded at both distilleries, is often available for half-hour or hour-long tours. Alternatively, you can walk around the town on your own, or hire as a guide one of the dozens of nervy little kids who will swamp your car when you drive into town.

Tequila is a nice place to visit, but don't plan to stay overnight—the hotels are strictly for an emergency situation.

En Route from Tequila About 20 miles (32 km) from Tequila is Zapopan, a municipality on the edge of Guadalajara and site of a shrine (inside the *Basílica de Zapopan,* on the *Plaza de las Américas,* the area's main square) to the Virgin of Zapopan. In the shrine is a six-inch figurine of the Virgin, which is said to have special powers. The shrine is considered the second-holiest place in Mexico (after the shrine to the Virgin of Guadalupe in the capital); Pope John Paul II made a pilgrimage here during his visit to Mexico in 1979. Ten miles (16 km) beyond Zapopan is the junction of Route 15 and the bypass route around Guadalajara. Route 15 leads straight into town; travelers pushing on to Morelia and Mexico City should take the bypass. (For detailed information on Guadalajara, see THE CITIES.)

The journey from Guadalajara and Morelia, the next-to-last leg on the road to Mexico City, is one of the most beautiful and interesting sections of the entire route. Continue on Route 15 (which bypasses downtown Guadalajara) 5 miles (8 km) past the Minerva traffic circle to the junction of Route 44. Then take Route 44 south some 32 miles (51 km) to the town of Chapala, on the northwest side of Lago de Chapala, Mexico's largest lake, and within a stone's throw of several other lakeside villages. These villages have become popular summer resorts for Mexicans and retirement spots for Americans.

CHAPALA Mountain-ringed Lago de Chapala, on which the town is located, offers pleasant vistas and a pretty shoreline park. The lake traditionally offers fairly good fishing, but be aware that pollution problems often render the native Chapala whitefish unsafe to eat.

Chapala itself (pop. 25,700) is primarily a resort town, dotted with restaurants, cafes, and small shops. Souvenir sellers set up stalls every day in the lakeside park, and there's a small crafts market at the park's eastern end. A few miles west of town is the Chula Vista subdivision, where many American and Canadian residents have built homes.

For steaks or a drink and snack, try *Cazadores Chapala* (phone: 376-52162) across from the lake, next to the church at the corner of Avenida Madero, the main street. On the other side of Avenida Madero, also overlooking the lake, is the *Beer Garden* (376-52257), a terraced establishment that serves seafood, chicken, and meat dishes.

AJIJIC About 4 miles (6 km) west of Chapala, down Route 94 along the lake, is Ajijic (pronounced A-hee-*heek*). A haven for bohemians, would-be writers, and aspiring artists since the early 20th century, the town has acquired some real talent over the years, with a number of Mexican and American writers, artists, and photographers in residence. Shops, galleries, and restaurants spring up here constantly.

One good place to start is *Mi México,* where there's a colorful selection of pottery, blown glass, and local and imported textiles (8 Morelos; phone: 376-60133). At *La Nueva Posada,* near the lake at 9 Donato Guerra, the restaurant overlooks luxuriant gardens and offers tasty variations on Mexican and American specialties (see *Best en Route*). On the highway toward Jocotepec, *Trattoría di Giovanni* has a wide-ranging selection of Italian dishes, as well as steaks and chicken (phone: 376-61733).

The *Chapala Society Information and Library Center,* in the middle of town, is run by the Americans and Canadians who live in the area; it's a handy place for information on everything from fishing to home rentals (16A Av. 16 de Septiembre; no phone). It's closed Sundays.

SAN JUAN COSALÁ This village on Lago de Chapala, about 3 miles (5 km) west of Ajijic (heading toward Jocotepec), has thermal waters and is a popular weekend spot.

JOCOTEPEC Some 10 miles (16 km) west of Ajijic is this unspoiled fishing village and refuge for writers and artists. The village is noted for its fine serapes. In January, the locals hold a lovely fiesta, featuring bullfights and cockfights, and regional dances performed on the shores of the lake.

En Route from Jocotepec The road passes through increasingly beautiful mountain terrain and scores of small villages that suggest turn-of-the-century Colorado mining towns. One village, Pátzcuaro, near Morelia, is definitely worth a stop. From Jocotepec, take Route 44 to the junction of Route 15. Follow Route 15 to Quiroga; Pátzcuaro is about 40 miles (64 km) south.

PÁTZCUARO Hidden high in the mountains of the state of Michoacán, Pátzcuaro is veiled from the outside world by a curtain of tall pine trees. About 1½ miles (2 km) to the north, via Calzada de las Américas, is Lago de Pátzcuaro, notable for both its location (Mexico's highest lake) and for its fishermen, who traditionally used delicate "butterfly" nets on poles to snare whitefish and then pull them in. These fishermen have become Pátzcuaro's trademark, though they have actually given up the butterfly nets in favor of more modern fishing techniques. However, in return for a tip they often will give demonstrations, which make excellent subjects for photographs.

The town is an eclectic combination of Mexico's past and present, its good and bad, its mysterious and mundane. Pátzcuaro has always been of interest to Mexican history buffs because it was central to the careers of two diametrically opposed characters in Mexico's colonial past. The first was Pedro Beltrán Nuño de Guzmán, the vicious conquistador who plundered the area for gold. He burned alive the local Tarasco chief, who couldn't or wouldn't tell him where gold was hidden. Eventually his crimes against the Indians became so extreme that the Spanish were forced to arrest him. In his place they sent Don Vasco de Quiroga, a priest. As bishop of the state of Michoacán, "Tata" ("Daddy") Vasco, as his followers affectionately called him, helped the Tarasco by introducing new crops and establishing schools, churches, and hospitals. He also taught the inhabitants of each of the surrounding towns a trade (today, Quiroga still is known for its colorful masks; Santa Clara for its fine copperwork; Uruapan for its lacquerware; and Paracho for its guitars and masks). He died at the age of 95, and in these parts he is considered a saint for his good works.

The stoical Tarasco still live in the region, though many of them exist in dire poverty. The people usually have little to say, but the town itself and the surrounding area speak of the valiant efforts by Vasco de Quiroga, who lent his name to Quiroga, a small town on Route 15 north of Pátzcuaro. The *Posada de Don Vasco,* named for the bishop, is the finest hotel in the immediate area (see *Best en Route*).

Plaza Vasco de Quiroga, Pátzcuaro's central square, is a private little world surrounded by high buildings and treetops that lend it an air of isolation. A statue of Quiroga stands in the center of the grass-covered plaza. The town, which consists largely of one-story adobe or plaster-over-brick buildings with red tile roofs, retains its colonial atmosphere. Horses and autos alike travel its steep cobblestone streets (bring comfortable shoes). There's a tourism office at 2 Calle Ibarra, Room 4, on the plaza (closed weekends; phone: 434-21214).

Also in Pátzcuaro is the *Centro Regional de Educación de Adultos y Alfabetización Funcional para América Latina* (CREFAL; Regional Center for the Education of Adults and Functional Literacy for Latin America), a *UN* training school for Latin American teachers and one of *UNESCO*'s earliest and largest projects. The school's main building was once the mansion of former President Lázaro Cárdenas (1934–40), who donated it to the *UN.*

Friday is the big market day in Pátzcuaro, when residents of surrounding villages come to sell their wares in the market square. Town shops carry henequen rugs, serapes, masks, wooden boxes, and lacquered trays. Pátzcuaro's lacquered trays are quite famous; the lacquer is made from the crushed bodies of purple insects, which provides the deep, rich finish and durability. The masks sold here are especially interesting because each design has a special significance and role in Indian dances. Mask collecting is a growing hobby among Mexicans and foreigners alike, but the quality, originality, and variety has declined significantly over the years.

On the east side of downtown, two blocks northwest of the Plaza Vasco de Quiroga, is the 16th-century *Basílica de Nuestra Señora de la Salud* (Basilica of Our Lady of Salvation), the city's patron saint. Don Vasco de Quiroga directed the construction of the corn pith and orchid honey statue. From November 25 through December 16, fiestas honor *Nuestra Señora de la Salud* with folk dances and crafts exhibitions.

The *Colegio de San Nicolás,* south of the basilica on Calle Arciga, was a school founded by Don Vasco in 1540. It now houses the *Museo de Artes Populares y de la Arqueología* (Museum of Archaeology and Folk Arts; no phone), which exhibits carvings, pottery, weaving, and archaeological artifacts. The museum is closed Mondays; admission charge.

Near the museum, at the corner of Cuesta de Portugal and Lenín, is the moss-covered *Templo de la Compañía de Jesús* (Church of the Jesuits). Built by Don Vasco and opened in 1547, it was Michoacán's first cathedral, but lost its status when the state capital was later moved to Morelia. However, it is still Pátzcuaro's main church.

A block south of the cathedral, the *Casa de los Once Patios* (House of Eleven Patios; half a block from the main plaza on Larín) is the best place in town to purchase handicrafts. In the artisans' workshops housed in the building, 24-karat gold leaf is applied to finely painted plates; you'll also see Indian women weaving on the porches. Merchandise includes hammered copper from Villa Escalante, black clay pottery from Tzintzuntzan, woodcarvings from various nearby towns, straw work, textiles, fine lacquerwork, and sets of furniture and woodwork.

Located in the 16th-century *Templo de San Agustín* (Church of Saint Augustine), the public library houses a mural by Juan O'Gorman depicting the history of the region and the struggles of the Tarasco for land. The library faces the Plaza de San Agustín, with its neatly kept gardens and quiet atmosphere. A statue of Gertrudis Bocanegra, born in 1765 of a Spanish father and a Tarasco mother, stands in the center. Known as the Heroine of Pátzcuaro, Bocanegra was a genuinely liberated woman who, with her husband and their 10-year-old son, joined the independence cause in 1810. In 1811, they helped in the attack on Morelia (then called Valladolid). When her husband and son were killed in combat, Gertrudis continued sending messages from Pátzcuaro to the rebel forces; eventually she tried to join the battle herself. Commanders sent her back to Pátzcuaro to study the possibility of an attack and to seduce various royalists to get more information. When the Spanish discovered her purpose, she was tried and sentenced to death; she was executed by a firing squad in 1817 in this plaza.

The *Danza de los Viejitos* (Dance of the Old Men), one of the best and most widely known native dances of Mexico, is presented at the *Posada de Don Vasco* (see *Best en Route*) on Wednesday and Saturday nights at 9 PM. The dancers wear wooden masks that depict smiling old men to show that old age is not a time of listless despair, but rather a season to enjoy the fruits of life.

The area surrounding Pátzcuaro has several interesting attractions. The lake is dotted with seven islands, and Janitzio should be the first one on your list. You can drive to the dock (also called the *Embarcadero* or the *Muelle General;* just off Rte. 120) and arrange for the 30-minute boat ride out to the island (sightseeing boat rides on the lake are also offered). Proceeds from the nominal dockside parking fee pay for the clearing of water lilies and other plant growth from the lake. Less expensive than hiring a boat is a launch that holds up to 80 people; it makes six trips daily and round-trip tickets may be bought at the dock (no phone). Along the boat route to Janitzio, elderly fishermen will demonstrate (for a small tip) how the traditional butterfly nets are made and how they are manipulated on the lake.

The fishing village of Janitzio is huddled near the shoreline, and above it on the island's crest towers the statue of José María Morelos y Pavón, a famous revolutionary-era general and hero. Morelos was a native of this state (the city of Morelia was named in his honor), a country priest, a school-teacher, and a leader for Mexican independence. Those in good physical shape can tackle the taxing 135-foot climb to the top of the hollow statue, past more than 50 murals depicting Morelos's life. The top affords a magnificent view of the lake and exhibits the death mask of Morelos.

To celebrate the *Día de los Muertos* (Day of the Dead, November 2), Janitzio families hold all-night candlelight vigils the night before at the island's cemeteries by the graves of their loved ones. For more information, see *Quintessential Mexico* in DIVERSIONS.

Back at the *Embarcadero* in Pátzcuaro, stop at one of the restaurants that serve tiny whitefish that are deep-fried, wrapped in a tortilla, and sprinkled with lime juice and hot sauce. Inevitably, you'll be serenaded by mariachi groups. You can easily spend a couple of hours here, eating fish and drinking cold beer while you watch the boats on their way to Janitzio. Outside restaurants on the dock, you'll be hounded by numerous little boys offering to be guides around the town. It's a good idea to hire one, for it saves time. Rather than shop at the profusion of handicrafts stands here, however, make your major purchases in downtown Pátzcuaro.

Several of the hotels in the area have good restaurants, including the *Posada de Don Vasco, Mesón del Cortijo, Posada de la Basílica,* and *Posada San Rafael* (see *Best en Route* for all). Also good are *El Patio* (Plaza Vasco de Quiroga; no phone), which serves whitefish, and *Fonda del Sol* (Calzada de las Américas; no phone), which specializes in regional dishes. The café at the *Mansión Iturbe,* on lamplit Plaza Vasco de Quiroga (see *Best en Route*), is a wonderful spot to sip cappuccino.

Several other nearby towns are interesting to visit; though they have overnight facilities, they are close enough to Pátzcuaro to allow for a comfortable all-day excursion and an early return to Pátzcuaro's better accommodations. The largest of these is Uruapan, 40 miles (64 km) west of Pátzcuaro. Uruapan is known primarily for its proximity to the famous Paricutín Volcano, which first erupted in 1943 and for the next 10 years spewed boulders and lava across surrounding terrain. Drive to the village of Angahuán, about an hour northwest of Uruapan, and hire a donkey to take you on the 15-minute ride to one of the most startling sites in Mexico. Paracutín's lava flow buried a small village under 40 feet of molten rock. The only building that withstood the wave of red-hot rocks was the church, whose steeples can still be seen jutting some 70 feet above the lava. In the northeastern part of the city is the *Parque Eduardo Ruiz Barranca* (no phone), a national park on Barranca del Cupatitzio featuring aqua-blue terraced waterfalls and a beautiful tropical garden. It is open daily; there's an admission charge.

Uruapan is famous for its lacquered goods. The *Mercado de Artesanías,* near the entrance to the national park, carries reasonably priced hand-painted lacquered items. Good buys can also be had on embroidered clothing, pottery, and copper. On the high side of the main plaza are an ancient hospital and chapel, which have been converted into the *Museo de Artes Populares* (Regional Folk Art Museum; Calles Alcantarrilla and Lenín; phone: 434-21019), whose annual competitions attract the finest work in the state. The museum is closed Sundays and Mondays; there's an admission charge. Museum employees will either sell the items on display or provide the names and addresses of the artisans so you can buy directly from them. Also worth seeing is the *Mercado de Antojitos Típicos,* a market filled with typical regional foods, at Constitución and Corregidora. In July, folk dances and parades are held to honor St. Mary Magdalene. Uruapan is also the avocado capital of the world, and each year, in late May or early June, the city holds a festival in honor of this fruit. If you're lucky enough to be in town at the time, make sure to try the avocado ice cream or, even more exotic, hot avocado punch.

Just north of Uruapan along Route 37 is Paracho, the city of guitars. Look around and then bargain with dealers, because prices are negotiable (for additional details, see *Shopping at the Source* in DIVERSIONS).

At Tzintzuntzan, 8 miles (13 km) north of Pátzcuaro on Route 120, there's an interesting market specializing in pottery and other Tarasco arts and crafts. The remains of some small pyramids are within walking distance.

Quiroga, on Route 15 at the junction of Route 120, has a fine selection of lacquerware. And at Erongaríquaro, a pretty town of 2,500 on the west side of Lago de Pátzcuaro, the villagers weave cambric fabrics on handlooms and barter at market. The rocky road leading there makes the journey from Pátzcuaro difficult but satisfying.

En Route from Pátzcuaro The next major stop is Morelia, about 34 miles (54 km) east via Route 15 or 120.

MORELIA For a detailed report on the city, its hotels, and its restaurants, see *Morelia* in THE CITIES.

En Route from Morelia Between Morelia and Mexico City lie *Parque Nacional Morelos, Mirador de Mil Cumbres* (View of a Thousand Peaks), and *Parque Nacional Bonsecheve,* plus 154 miles (246 km) of hairpin turns along steep mountains that take about four hours to negotiate.

If you travel between late October and early March, your next stop after Morelia should be Zitácuaro, where you can experience the spectacle of the monarch butterflies (during the rest of the year, drive on to Toluca). Beginning in late October, hundreds of thousands of them migrate from Canada and the northern US to certain areas in the states of México and Michoacán. The beautiful creatures literally cover every inch of rock and weigh down all the tree branches in the areas the Mexican government has set aside as refuges. To see the butterflies at their best, it is wise to stay overnight in one of the hotels in the area (see *Best en Route*). Weekdays, when the crowds are smaller, are the best times for a visit; it's next to impossible to get hotel reservations on weekends when the monarchs are in town. The next morning, put on comfortable shoes and warm clothes and, after breakfast, drive to the nearby town of Angangueo, where you can leave your car and board an open truck (negotiate the fare with the truck driver—a group of four or more will get a better deal) for the rough, 45-minute drive up to the fields where the butterflies are found. After that, you'll have to negotiate a long, tough walk up a steep pathway, but take heart: it's an unforgettable spectacle and well worth the trek. For additional details, see *Quintessential Mexico* in DIVERSIONS.

TOLUCA The capital of the state of México, Toluca is a busy commercial center, producing sausage, liqueurs, dried meat, wines, dairy products, native needlecraft, pottery, and baskets. It's well worth a visit, especially on Fridays, when the native open-air market—one of the country's largest—is held on the outskirts of town, on the *periférico* (beltway). The market has a wide selection of regional handicrafts, including woolen blankets, *jorongos* (ponchos), thick woven sweaters, pottery from Metepec, colorfully painted furniture from Tenancingo, baskets, lathe-turned kitchen utensils, and more straw hats than you've ever seen before.

Don't miss the government showrooms called *CASART* (Center for Mexican Handicrafts; 700 Paseo Tollocán Ote.; phone: 72-147830), which specialize in regional handicrafts. The selection includes stoneware, furniture, copper, metalwork, jewelry, silver, woolens, and clay pottery. In the center of town, a covered colonnade area called Portal 20 de Noviembre has rows of turn-of-the-century iron, brass, and tin candy stands where all kinds of typical candies and local glacé fruits can be bought for pennies.

The *Jardín Botánico* (Botanical Garden) is just off the main square in an Art Nouveau structure that was once the main market. Inside, 48 spectacular stained glass windows depict man's relationship to the universe. The garden is closed Mondays; there's no admission charge (phone: 72-147830). Toluca's tourism office (101 Lerdo Ponte; phone: 72-141099 or 72-133014) is closed weekends.

The Nevado de Toluca, an extinct volcano, towers above the city. Its 15,036-foot peak is snow-capped most of the year and frequently is obscured by clouds. In the crater are Lago del Sol and Lago de la Luna (Sun Lake and Moon Lake), where rainbow trout fishing is especially good.

For Mexican food, Toluca's best restaurant by far is the *Real de Oro,* in the *Del Rey Inn* (see *Best en Route*). *Hostería las Ramblas* (107D Portal 20 de Noviembre; phone: 72-142308) serves good, inexpensive Mexican dishes. Another popular, if pricey, spot is *La Cabaña Suiza,* offering fondue and other international specialties in a lovely Swiss chalet–like building. St. Bernard dogs and ponies (children may ride the latter) stroll and graze in the surrounding gardens. Reservations suggested weekends and holidays (Km 63 of Paseo Tollocán Pte.; phone: 72-161885).

En Route from Toluca You actually descend through the mountains that surround the Valley of Mexico to enter Mexico City. If you approach after sunset, Mexico City looks like a gigantic bowl filled with sparkling lights, floating in a dark sea. If you make the descent while there is still light, the bowl will be filled with what looks like mushroom soup "steaming" with the smog retained by the surrounding mountains.

MEXICO CITY For a complete description of the city and its hotels and restaurants, see *Mexico City* in THE CITIES.

BEST EN ROUTE

At hotels along this route categorized as expensive, expect to pay $75 or more per night for a double room; at moderate places, $45 to $70; at inexpensive hotels, $40 or less. Unless otherwise indicated, all hotels feature private baths, TV sets, and phones in rooms. For each location, hotels are listed alphabetically by price category.

HERMOSILLO

Bugambilia This motel has 109 units, 82 in a newer section. The older section consists of bungalows in neatly landscaped grounds. The rooms have cable TV showing US programs. There also is a pool and a restaurant. 712 Blvd. Padre Eusebio Kino (phone: 62-145050; fax: 62-145252). Expensive.

Calinda A high-rise with 115 rooms, plus a pool, a restaurant, a bar, and a cafeteria. Downtown, at Rosales and Morelia (phone: 62-172396; 800-228-5151 in the US; 800-90000 in Mexico; fax: 62-172424). Expensive.

Fiesta Americana All 218 units have wet bars and satellite TV. There's also a pool, a restaurant, a nightclub, a coffee shop, and a tennis court. 369 Blvd. Padre Eusebio Kino (phone: 62-596000; 800-FIESTA-1 in the US; 800-50450 in Mexico; fax: 62-596060). Expensive.

Gándara You can stay in a newer, hotel-type section or in a completely remodeled older section that has bungalows and larger rooms (two double beds) at slightly higher rates. There are a total of 154 units, all with cable TV. On the premises are a coffee shop, a cocktail lounge, a restaurant, and a lobby bar. 1000 Blvd. Padre Eusebio Kino (phone: 62-144414 or 62-144241; fax: 62-149926). Moderate.

Kino Here are 114 rooms, a restaurant, a heated pool, a hot tub, and a sauna. Downtown, at 151 Pino Suárez Sur (phone: 62-133131 or 62-133138; 800-62624 in Mexico; fax: 62-133852). Moderate.

Kino Bay Trailer Park This place has modern facilities and good connections to the highway. Just outside town on Rte. 15 (phone/fax: 62-153197). Inexpensive.

BAHÍA KINO

Bahía Kino This clean, comfortable, 18-unit motor hotel has a small restaurant noted for good shrimp. Also on the premises are a trailer park and two furnished bungalows, with boat launching facilities nearby. On the north side of Playas Kino Nuevo, a 3-mile (5-km) stretch of beach where the new resorts are located (phone: 62-420216; fax: 62-200283). Moderate.

Posada del Mar All 48 units here have ocean views; there's also a colonial-style restaurant. Across from the beach in Kino Nuevo (phone: 62-420155; 62-181237 in Hermosillo). Moderate.

Posada Santa Gemma In addition to 14 bungalow units with bedrooms, kitchenettes, and satellite TV, there's a trailer court with hookups, but no restaurant. Kino Nuevo (phone: 62-420026 or 62-420001; fax: 62-145579 in Hermosillo). Moderate.

Islandia Marina Here are 100 trailer hookups and eight rustic cabins (each has a kitchen) on the beach. There's no restaurant. A boat ramp is available. Bahía Kino (phone: 62-420081). Moderate to inexpensive.

GUAYMAS

Club Med Sonora An outstanding property that resembles an adobe village, it has 375 rooms, two beaches (one on a lagoon), 30 tennis courts (15 lighted), two saunas, a gym, two restaurants, a pool, and all water sports. Deep-sea fishing, rafting trips down the Río Yaqui, and overnight horseback riding excursions are available for an extra charge. Guests here must buy the Club Med package. Closed November through March. On the rugged road past the marina, 17 miles (27 km) north of Guaymas in Los Algodones (phone: 622-60166; 800-CLUB-MED; fax: 622-60070). Expensive.

Plaza Hotel and Resort San Carlos This Howard Johnson property has 172 rooms and suites, all with ocean views; a spectacular lobby atrium with a waterfall, bridges, and streams; convention facilities; a pool; a spa; two tennis courts; a restaurant; a cafeteria; and a lobby bar. All rooms have ocean views, satellite TV, and mini-bars. One mile (1.6 km) from *Club Med,* in Los Algodones (phone: 622-60777 through 622-60796; 800-446-4656 in the US; 800-50549 in Mexico; fax: 622-60777, ext. 503). Expensive.

Armida With 164 rooms, this property also has a pool, a lobby bar, a disco, a French restaurant, a steakhouse, and a coffee shop. Arrangements can be made for tennis, skin diving, fishing, and water skiing. In town, on Rte. 15 (phone: 622-43035; 800-64705 in Mexico; fax: 622-20448). Moderate.

Playa de Cortés Gándara This old hotel features an excellent dining room and bar, a pool, two tennis courts, fishing, and a nightclub with dancing; there are 122 guestrooms. Four miles (6 km) north of town on Bahía Bocachibampo (phone: 622-40131 or 622-40142/3/4; 800-782-7602; fax: 622-20135). Moderate.

Flamingos A 65-unit motel with a restaurant, a bar, and a pool. Some of the rooms have kitchenettes. Two miles (3 km) north of town on Rte. 15 (phone: 622-12061; fax: 622-10961). Inexpensive.

Las Playitas This trailer park with 120 spaces and all connections also has 30 rooms and seven bungalows with kitchenettes. On the grounds are an excellent restaurant, a bar, a pool, a dock, and a boat ramp. On the bay at Km 6 of the road to the *Varadero Nacional* (National Shipyard; phone: 622-22727 or 622-22753). Inexpensive.

SAN CARLOS

Posada San Carlos The hotel offers 136 modern, well-furnished units with good facilities—two pools, access to an 18-hole golf course, a boat ramp, fishing, and skin diving. On the premises is a western-style saloon with live music and dining rooms specializing in seafood with live entertainment. 10 Privada del Delfín, in town (phone: 622-60015 or 622-60122; fax: 622-60451)). Expensive.

Solimar Here are 135 rooms, 83 condominiums, three pools, two Jacuzzis, a restaurant, a bar, satellite TV, and access to the 18-hole golf course and 13 tennis courts at the *San Carlos Country Club* next door (phone: 622-60007 or 622-60231). Moderate.

Fiesta The 33 modern motel units here have balconies overlooking the bay. There's a pool and a dining room. Km 8.5 of Carretera San Carlos, across from the beach, 5 miles (8 km) west of Rte. 15 (phone/fax: 622-60229). Inexpensive.

Teta Kawi Here are spaces—with all connections—for 132 trailers, plus a restaurant, a Jacuzzi, and some cable TV hookups. Km 8 of Carretera San Carlos, across from the beach, 5½ miles (9 km) west of Rte. 15 (phone: 622-60220; fax: 622-60248). Inexpensive.

Totonaca There are 140 full trailer hookups here, along with a laundry, a restaurant and bar, a coffee shop, gardens, and showers. Some rooms and apartments also are available. Km 8 of Carretera San Carlos (next to the *Teta Kawi*), across from the beach, 5½ miles (9 km) west of Rte. 15 (phone: 622-60481 or 622-60323; fax: 622-60523). Inexpensive.

CIUDAD OBREGÓN

Costa de Oro This motel has 122 units, a restaurant, a bar, a disco, and a pool. Miguel Alemán and Allende (phone/fax: 641-41775). Moderate.

Norotel Nainari Obregón An inn with 135 rooms, a restaurant, a pool, and satellite TV. Miguel Alemán and Tetabiate (phone: 641-41775; fax: 641-33475). Moderate.

NAVOJOA

El Rancho An excellent choice, with 61 units, satellite TV, a disco, a restaurant, a bar, and a coffee shop. Fishing and hunting trips can be arranged. Km 1788 of Rte. 15 (phone/fax: 642-20310 or 642-20004). Moderate.

Del Río A 65-unit motel with a pool and a restaurant. Off Alameda (phone/fax: 642-25601 or 642-25402). Moderate.

ALAMOS

Casa de los Tesoros The "Treasure House" is a fine 14-unit colonial-era inn with period furnishings, excellent food, a pool, and nightly music. Breakfast, lunch, and dinner are included in the room rate. Reservations are necessary. In town, a block and a half from the plaza at 10 Calle Obregón (phone: 642-80010; fax: 642-80400). Expensive.

La Mansión de la Condesa Magdalena This well-run gem has hosted several Mexican presidents, among other dignitaries. There are 12 charming rooms with fireplaces, a Jacuzzi, an exercise room, and a cozy restaurant. 2 Calle Obregón (phone/fax: 642-80221). Moderate.

Acosta Ranch Here are six hotel rooms and 25 trailer spaces; camping and guides for hunting, fishing, and bird watching are available. Meals are served in the owner's home (with 24-hour notice). A half mile (1 km) beyond Alamos (phone: 642-80246). Inexpensive.

El Caracol Spaces for 40 trailers are available. There's also an excellent restaurant, and horses to rent. Ten miles (16 km) west of Alamos (no phone). Inexpensive.

LOS MOCHIS

Las Colinas This hotel offers 120 comfortable rooms, two tennis courts, basketball, volleyball, a water slide, heated pools and wading pools, a coffee shop, two discotheques, and a restaurant. Just south of the Rte. 15 interchange (phone: 68-118111; fax: 68-118181). Expensive.

Plaza Inn Besides 125 well-appointed rooms and six suites, two international restaurants, a video bar, a pool, and conference and convention center, this downtown establishment houses the most popular disco in town. Calz. Mateos, between Blvd. Jiqílpan and Calle Rendón (phone: 68-181043; fax: 68-181042). Moderate.

Posada Real Here are 35 motel units and a pool, but no restaurant. Calles Gabriel Leyva and Buelna (phone: 68-122179 or 68-122363). Moderate.

Santa Anita A total of 133 rooms, with a bar and dining room specializing in fish dishes. Fishing, hunting, and Copper Canyon trips can be arranged. Downtown, at Calle Gabriel Leyva and Hidalgo (phone: 68-187046; fax: 68-120046). Moderate.

El Dorado A good-size property with 93 rooms with cable TV, a restaurant, a bar, a pool, and parking. Calle Gabriel Leyva and H. Valdéz (phone: 68-181111 or 68-181546). Inexpensive.

Los Mochis Copper Canyon Offers 100 RV spaces with complete hookups, 12 complete bathrooms, laundry facilities, and fishing, but no restaurant or cafeteria. Half a mile (1 km) past the Rte. 15 overpass toward Navojoa (phone: 68-126817). Inexpensive.

CULIACÁN

Hotel Ejecutivo It has 229 units with satellite TV, a restaurant, a bar, a nightclub, a pool, tennis, and a solarium. Madero and Obregón (phone: 67-139300; fax: 67-139310). Expensive.

San Luis Linda Vista This 91-room hostelry lives up to its name, offering guests a lovely view of the city. Surrounded by beautiful gardens, it has a restaurant with good international fare, a bar, a nightclub, a pool, and meeting facilities. Av. las Palmas between Blvd. Hermanas and Av. Bravo (phone: 67-168490 and 67-168490; fax: 67-151819). Moderate.

Los Tres Ríos One of the most popular places in town is a combination motel with 70 bungalow-type units and a 100-space trailer park with all connections. It offers a good international restaurant, a pool, two bars, and a nightclub. Km 1423 of Rte. 15 and República de Brasil (phone: 67-505262 or 67-505279/80; fax: 67-525283). Moderate.

Del Valle Pleasant modern decor and 42 units are offered here; there's also a restaurant. 180 Blvd. Solano Ote. (phone: 67-139020, 67-139080, 67-139120, or 67-139170). Inexpensive.

SAN BLAS

Garza Canela One of the better establishments in town, offering 42 units (some air conditioned), a restaurant, a bar, and a pool. Paredes (phone: 328-50112 or 328-50480; fax: 328-50308). Moderate.

Playa Amor A 40-unit RV facility on the beach. Hookups, showers, toilets, hot water, a security wall, and a guard are available. Take the San Blas turnoff to the Santa Cruz–Aticama exit on the outskirts of San Blas; then 13 miles (21 km) to Santa Cruz (no phone). Inexpensive.

Suites San Blas It has 23 suites with kitchenettes, plus a pool, a playground, and parking, though no restaurant. Aticama and Palmas (phone: 328-50505). Inexpensive.

Tresora de San Blas This tiny property offers three bungalows and one guestroom, though no restaurant. Each cottage offers a kitchenette and a beautiful view. On Estuario el Pazo (El Pazo Estuary), near the fishing dock (phone/fax: 328-50537). Inexpensive.

TEPIC

Ejecutivo Inn Features 34 units, a pool, a restaurant, a disco, and a bar. 310 Av. Insurgentes Pte. (phone/fax: 32-120477). Moderate.

Fray Junípero Serra An 85-unit hotel with a restaurant and a bar. Across from the main plaza at 23 Lerdo Pte. (phone: 32-122525, 32-122290, or 32-122175; fax: 32-122051). Moderate.

La Loma This motel has 52 rooms, a restaurant, a bar, and a pool facing a lovely park. 301 Paseo de la Loma (phone: 32-132222, 32-132057, or 32-132947; fax: 32-134001). Inexpensive.

Sierra de Alica A colonial-style hotel, it has 60 units—some with air conditioning—a restaurant, and parking. Near the main plaza (phone: 32-120322, 32-120324, or 32-120325; fax: 32-121309). Inexpensive.

AJIJIC

La Nueva Posada Seventeen colonial-style suites (some with terraces), a pool, gardens, an excellent restaurant, and bar are featured here. 9 Calle Donato Guerra (phone: 376-61444; fax: 376-61344). Moderate.

Real de Chapala A colonial-style inn with 79 spacious suites, some offering a view of the lake. There's a restaurant, tennis, access to golf at the *Chapala Country Club,* a barbecue on Saturdays, and a Mexican fiesta on Sundays. 20 Paseo del Prado, in La Floresta (phone: 376-60028; fax: 376-60025). Moderate.

Posada de las Calandrias In a two-story brick building are 29 suites and apartments. There's a lovely garden, but no restaurant. Carretera Pte. 8, two blocks north of the *zócalo,* or main square (phone: 376-61052). Moderate to inexpensive.

SAN JUAN COSALÁ

Balneario San Juan Cosalá A 32-unit motor hotel on the lake, with a restaurant and thermal water pools. On the road into town, about 5 miles (8 km) before Jocotepec (phone: 376-30302). Inexpensive.

Villas Buenaventura Cosalá Seven apartments at this great bargain spot have Jacuzzis, while the other 9 have tubs with thermal water. All but two have kitchenettes. There's no restaurant. 423 Av. de la Paz (phone: 376-10303 and 376-10202). Inexpensive.

JOCOTEPEC

Posada del Pescador Features 21 units, a cafeteria, and a pool. Just outside town on Rte. 94 (no phone). Inexpensive.

PÁTZCUARO

Posada de Don Vasco The best place in town, this colonial-style hotel with 104 rooms and a 56-site trailer park has excellent food, a good bar, a tennis court, a playground, a heated outdoor swimming pool, a movie theater, a billiards room, and a bowling alley. 450 Av. de las Américas (phone: 434-20227; 5-207-2369 in Mexico City; 800-528-1234; fax: 434-20262). Expensive.

Posada San Rafael A colonial setting with 104 units and a decent restaurant. On Plaza Vasco de Quiroga (phone: 434-20770 and 434-20779; fax: 434-21097). Moderate.

Mansión Iturbe This charming 14-room hostelry is housed in a restored 17th-century mansion. There's a restaurant and a souvenir shop on the premises. 59 Portal Morelos, on the south side of Plaza Vasco de Quiroga (phone: 434-20368). Inexpensive.

Mesón del Cortijo A former hacienda with 14 units in Tarasco decor, complete with fireplaces; the dining room serves decent food. Beyond the Tanganzhuan traffic circle on Av. Alvaro Obregón (phone: 434-21295 or 434-21037). Inexpensive.

Mesón del Gallo An extremely well maintained colonial-style inn offering 25 small but comfortable rooms, a restaurant, and a pool. 20 Dr. Coss (phone: 434-21474; fax: 434-21511). Inexpensive.

Misión de San Manuel Near the *zócalo,* or main plaza, this is an old townhouse converted into a plain but cozy 42-unit hotel and restaurant-bar. 12 Portal Aldama (phone: 434-21313). Inexpensive.

Posada de la Basílica An 11-room colonial inn with modest prices and a good restaurant. At the south end of town at 6 Calle Arciga (phone: 434-20659). Inexpensive.

El Pozo Twenty lakefront trailer spaces with all connections—one of the nicest in the country. There's no restaurant. On the shores of Lago de Pátzcuaro, 2 miles (3 km) north of town on Rte. 120 (phone: 434-20937). Inexpensive.

URUAPAN

Mansión de Cupatitzio A lovely, colonial-style hotel with 56 units with satellite TV, a restaurant, a bar, and a handicrafts shop. About 2 miles (3 km) from town next to the national park at the source of the Río Cupatitzio (phone: 452-32100, 452-32090, or 452-32070; fax: 452-46772). Moderate.

Paraíso Uruapan Another attractive colonial-style hostelry, this one with 56 rooms and a lovely garden setting. There's a dining room, a bar, a pool, and parking. At the east end of town on the road to Pátzcuaro (phone: 452-38478, 452-38511; fax: 452-43681). Moderate.

Pie de la Sierra Fine motel accommodations in Spanish colonial decor with fireplaces in each of the 72 rooms, a playground, a heated pool, a restaurant, and a bar. Km 4 of Rte. 37 (phone: 452-21510; fax: 452-42511). Moderate.

Plaza Uruapan Here is a hotel with 124 rooms, a bar, a restaurant, a coffee shop, and a disco. 64 Ocampo (phone: 452-33700, 452-33866, or 452-30333; fax: 452-33980). Inexpensive.

El Tarasco This 55-unit hotel has a pool, a restaurant, and a bar. Two blocks from the main plaza, at 2 Calle Independencia (phone/fax: 452-41500). Inexpensive.

ZITÁCUARO

Villa Monarca Inn de Zitácuaro All 56 rooms and seven suites here feature Jacuzzis; other amenities include a good restaurant serving international fare, a video bar, a bar/disco with live music, a swimming pool, a wading pool, a children's playground, and meeting rooms. Guided tours of the monarch butterfly sanctuary can be arranged here. Km 103.5 of Rte. 15 (phone: 715-35365 or 715-35371; fax: 715-35350). Expensive.

Rancho San Cayetano The accommodations—eight rooms and two suites—are as fine as the food. Reservations necessary on weekends, especially from late December to early April. No credit cards. Km 2.5 on the road to Tuzantla (phone: 715-30285). Moderate.

TOLUCA

Castel Plaza las Fuentes This hotel has 150 rooms, a restaurant, a bar, a tennis court, a basketball court, and a gameroom. About 6 miles (10 km) from downtown, at Km 57.5 of Paseo Tollocán (phone: 72-164666; fax: 72-164798). Expensive.

Del Rey Inn An excellent hotel, featuring 257 rooms, a heated indoor pool, a playground, an outstanding restaurant, a video bar, and a coffee shop. Km 63.5 of the Carretera México-Toluca (phone: 72-122122; fax: 72-122567). Expensive.

Ciudad Juárez
to Mexico City

The 1,200-mile (1,920-km) route from Ciudad Juárez (in the state of Chihuahua, across the border from El Paso, Texas) to Mexico City is not the most popular entry route into Mexico. The cities along the way, especially in the northwest, are not as large or exciting as those farther east, and the distances to be covered are mammoth. But the route burrows straight through the center of the country, a landscape offering magnificent mountain and desert sunsets, long-abandoned archaeological ruins, and, in the Bajío region near Mexico City, the country's most beautiful colonial cities.

The harsh landscape of north-central Mexico has never supported an agricultural economy, perhaps one of the reasons that native cultures did not prosper here as they did in the south. Most of the indigenous civilizations that developed here were largely destroyed by the Spanish, who were attracted to—and exploited—the area's fabulous mineral wealth. Today, only two major indigenous groups live in the region: the Yaqui and the Tarahumara. The cultural ties of Mexico's northern border region are closer to Texas—whose cultural traditions also come from the Spanish settlers—than to the rest of Mexico, which helps to explain the relative lack of native tradition encountered here.

North-central Mexico has had a tumultuous past, filled with bandits, Apache and Comanche raids, revolutionary battles and assassinations, Spanish conquests, and ruthless struggles for gold and silver. It was here that Padre Miguel Hidalgo y Costilla, the father of Mexican independence, was killed in 1811. As Hidalgo—defeated in central Mexico—returned with his ragged army from a fruitless effort to reach the US for help, he was betrayed and turned over to the Bishop of Monterrey. Captured and then tried by the Inquisition, Hidalgo recanted, but he was nonetheless defrocked, executed, and finally beheaded in the city of Chihuahua.

The region was the center of government later in the 19th century, when President Benito Juárez moved his armies north to continue the battle against the invading French, led by Emperor Maximilian. Maximilian was finally captured by Juárez in Querétaro and executed in 1867.

Some of Mexico's most dramatic sights are found here: the Sierra Tarahumara canyon country (best experienced on the breathtaking train ride across the mountains from Chihuahua to Los Mochis); the Cascada de Basaséachic (Basaséachic Falls) in the Sierra Madre; the compelling ruins of Casas Grandes, south of Ciudad Juárez; and La Quemada, near Zacatecas, believed to have been linked to the Teotihuac culture from the 4th through the 6th centuries. Farther south, near the fertile Bajío region,

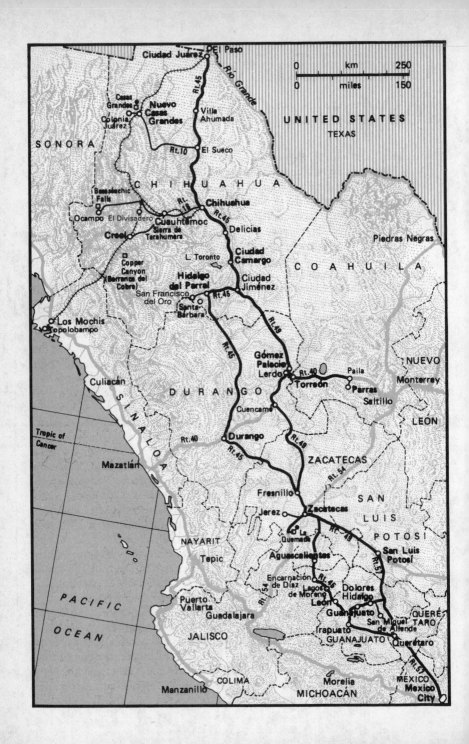

are Guanajuato, San Miguel de Allende, and Querétaro—some of the most attractive colonial cities in Mexico.

En Route to Ciudad Juárez Take one of four bridges from El Paso, Texas: the Good Neighbor Bridge (Stanton St.) or the Del Norte Bridge (Av. Juárez), both of which enter downtown Juárez; the Bridge of the Americas, which enters the suburb of San Lorenzo, east of the city; or the eight-lane Zaragoza Bridge, off Loop 375, which passes through the south side of town. All bridges charge a toll. *US Customs* is open 24 hours, as are Mexican customs and immigration offices. For regulations regarding entry into Mexico, see GETTING READY TO GO.

CIUDAD JUÁREZ The fifth-largest city in Mexico (pop. 900,000) was originally known as Paso del Norte (Pass to the North), because it was the only passage across the Río Bravo (called the Rio Grande in the US) and through the mountains within hundreds of miles. Once a stop on the old Santa Fe Trail, it is still reminiscent of the Old West. In 1888 it was renamed in honor of Benito Juárez, who overthrew Maximilian while headquartered in the city.

Juárez has the requisite racy nightlife typical of a border town, though it has never been quite as honky-tonk as some of the other border cities. Bizarrely, among the most popular stops for one-day visitors are the numerous dental clinics in town, where US citizens find bargain rates; some folks combine a root canal with a vacation in the sun.

If you have come to Mexico for its sights, however, Juárez is filled with places to visit. From the colonial era, for example, there's the *Misión de Nuestra Señora de Guadalupe* (Mission of Our Lady of Guadalupe; Calles Venustiano Carranza and Guerrero), built in 1659 by Friar García de San Francisco to honor the patron saint of the Americas.

When the French army occupied Mexico City from 1864 to 1867, President Juárez established his government here; the building that served as his headquarters, now known as the *Museo Xalana,* is at Calle 16 de Septiembre, between Calles Mariscal and Venustiano Carranza (phone: 16-124707). Exhibits cover the the pre-Hispanic to revolutionary eras with a regional emphasis. The museum is closed Mondays; there's no admission charge.

Bullfights are held at the *Plaza Monumental de Toros* (Av. 16 de Septiembre; phone: 16-131182) about six Sundays a year, spring through fall, usually coinciding with long US holiday weekends. At the *Galgodromo* (Prolongación Vicente Guerrero; phone: 16-255138), greyhounds race at 8:30 PM; closed Mondays and Tuesdays.

The picturesque shops in the *Plaza de las Américas* shopping center (off Lincoln and Calle 16 de Septiembre) carry a variety of Mexican wares. The *Museo de Arte e Historia* (Museum of Art and History; phone: 16-167414), which has archaeology and art exhibitions, is also in the complex. It's closed Mondays; there's an admission charge.

There are a number of excellent restaurants in Juárez. *Casa del Sol* in the *Plaza de las Américas* (phone: 16-130509 or 16-160088) serves international fare at reasonable prices; black bass is a specialty. The *O. K. Corral* (735 Av. de las Américas Nte.; phone: 16-135200 or 16-163511) has good Mexican and international dishes, and *Sanborns* (Paseo Triunfo de la República and López Mateos; phone: 16-169105) is always a safe choice. *Café Corona* (Calle 16 de Septiembre; phone: 16-133397) tones down *picante* (spicy) Mexican dishes for tourist palates.

En Route from Ciudad Juárez Don't forget to fill up your gas tank at one of the Pemex gas stations; it is 100 miles (160 km) to the next one at Villa Ahumada, on Route 45. You will pass an immigration and customs checkpoint just south of the city. Route 45 leads directly into Chihuahua, the state capital, in three to four hours. To take a highly recommended side trip to the ruins of *Paquimé,* near Nuevo Casas Grandes and Casas Grandes, turn right off Route 45 at El Sueco (some 150 miles/240 km south of Juárez). Follow Route 10 to Nuevo Casas Grandes, about 123 miles (196 km) farther.

PAQUIMÉ About 4 miles (7 km) northwest of Nuevo Casas Grandes along the local road to Colonia Juárez, the ruins of *Paquimé,* on a ridge overlooking the village of Casas Grandes, are similar to those of the pueblo dwellers of Arizona and New Mexico. Excavations have unearthed a ball court and a strange foundation in the form of the Latin cross. Some of the adobe dwellings are four stories tall. Little is known of the people who lived here or even when they lived here, but there are traces of influences from the Anasazi culture.

Beyond Colonia Juárez—a Mormon settlement established in 1885— are streams offering excellent fishing; the best stocked are San Juan de Dios, Tres Ríos, Gavilán, Paraíso, Largo, and Cañada del Oro. The fishing season is May through mid-October. However, the roads get rough here, and you'll need a guide to take you over the trails leading to the streams (contact the *Piñón* hotel; see *Best en Route*). When you're ready to go on to Chihuahua, backtrack to Route 45.

CHIHUAHUA The broad boulevards and congenial squares of this city are a welcome contrast after the long journey through the desolate plateau from Ciudad Juárez. For a detailed report on the city, its hotels, and its restaurants, see *Chihuahua* in THE CITIES.

BARRANCA DEL COBRE (COPPER CANYON) EXCURSION Chihuahua is an excellent jumping-off point from which to explore some of Mexico's most spectacular scenery. Just west of the city are the massive canyons and trenches in the Sierra Madre known as the Barranca del Cobre (Copper Canyon). This area is the site of the 980-foot-high Cascada de Basaséachic (Basaséachic

Falls) and some of the best hiking in all of Mexico. You can reach the canyon country in three ways: by rail on the *Ferrocarril Chihuahua al Pacífico* (Chihuahua-Pacific Railway) or the more luxurious *South Orient Express;* by road via Cuauhtémoc and Creel; or by air from Chihuahua to Creel. Package tours, which make many of the arrangements easier, also are available.

The *Ferrocarril Chihuahua al Pacífico,* quite rightly called the "world's most scenic railroad," is one of the best ways to see the Barranca del Cobre. Completed by the Mexican government in 1961, it is an exceptional engineering feat. The railroad includes a difficult 161-mile (258-km) section crossing Tarahumara territory to the Barranca del Cobre and through the mountains: In order to construct this stretch, 86 tunnels (one a full mile long) and 37 bridges had to be built.

The *Chihuahua al Pacífico* train leaves from the station in Chihuahua (Méndez and Calle 24) at 7 AM, arriving in Los Mochis (in the state of Sinaloa) between 7 and 11 PM. The trip includes stops at Creel, El Divisadero, Posada Barrancas, Bahuichivo-Cerocahui, El Fuerte, and Los Mochis. The return trip leaves the Los Mochis train station at 7 AM and arrives in Chihuahua between 7 and 11 PM. Passengers are served a box lunch. You can buy a round-trip ticket to and from Los Mochis or to and from any point between. If you want to stop along the route, you must specify your destination and stopovers, as well as the length of each stay, at the time you buy your ticket. The trip has become very popular, so it is advisable to make reservations well in advance with *Mexico by Train* (PO Box 2782, Laredo, TX 78044; phone: 800-321-1699; fax: 210-571-3659); many US travel agents, or travel desks in Chihuahua hotels, will reserve a seat for you as well. (See *Getting Ready To Go* for additional information on Copper Canyon train trips.) Note that this 400-mile (640-km) trip is more scenic on the way back (that is, from Los Mochis to Chihuahua), when you can experience the most spectacular scenery by daylight.

Another option is to book a more leisurely (and much more expensive) five- or seven-day trip from Chihuahua to Los Mochis on the luxurious *South Orient Express.* This train, made up of carefully restored cars from the 1940s and 1950s, offers comfortable seating, fine food, and gracious hospitality, plus some stupendous scenery: In addition to the glorious Copper Canyon, the famous Sierra Madre mountain range can be seen. There are no sleeping compartments, so hotel accommodations are arranged for the passengers. The all-inclusive trips are available in spring, fall, and early winter; a less luxurious (and less expensive) train runs year-round. Return trips from Los Mochis to Chihuahua run regularly. For details, contact the *Mexican-American Railway Association* (16800 Greenspoint Park Dr., Suite 245 North, Houston, TX 77060; phone: 713-872-0190; 800-659-7602; fax: 713-872-7123).

The journey to the canyon by car can take as long as a day, since the mountain roads are rough. Take Route 16 west for 67 miles (108 km) to

Cuauhtémoc, a city near the Cascada de Basaséachic. The city's population of about 145,000 people includes a Mennonite community of 55,000. The Mennonites, who fled from Prussia, the Ukraine, and other parts of Europe, have maintained their religious customs and native languages in Mexico; they are known for their excellent cheese. From Cuauhtémoc, take the mountain road to Creel, a small town on the *Ferrocarril Chihuahua al Pacífico* line about 20 miles (32 km) from the canyons along a twisting mountain road. From Creel, you can explore more distant points by train or through package tours (see below). It is safe to leave your car in one of the attended parking lots here while you are away. If you want to continue exploring by car, you also can drive on to the tiny village of Batopilas at the end of the mountain road. Once a major silver mining center, this now-sleepy town at the bottom of the canyon makes a pleasant base for exploring the area, with one of the area's best hotels, the *Copper Canyon Riverside Lodge* (see *Best en Route*).

Finally, small, noncommercial aircraft fly to the canyon country from Chihuahua. For information, contact the state tourism office in Chihuahua (*Palacio de Gobierno,* 1300 Calle Libertad and Calle 13; phone: 14-159124 and 14-162436); it's open daily.

The trip through the Barranca de Cobre takes you deep into Tarahumara territory. Closely related to the Pima Indians of southern Arizona, the Tarahumara are the largest and least-known native group of northern Mexico. People who keep to themselves, they have managed to avoid both extermination and modernization. More than 60,000 Tarahumara live in this region in small settlements scattered throughout the mountains; they can be identified by their long jet-black hair tied with a headband. The men often wear little more than a loincloth. Traditionally, the Tarahumara are excellent runners who hunt deer by chasing them for days, until the animals drop from exhaustion.

Many of the Tarahumara use the small town of Creel (near the start of the canyon and also the first stop on the *Ferrocarril Chihuahua al Pacífico* route) as a trading post; the men come in on weekends to buy supplies. Dressed in their best clothes—a long, loose-fitting white shirt over a loincloth and a tall hat with eagle feathers—they usually congregate in the main square. Creel is an excellent jumping-off point for half-day or longer excursions into the canyons.

Another interesting point along the way into the canyon is El Divisadero, where you will find a native market and two hotels, as well as the best vantage point for seeing the canyons. You can also see the loincloth-garbed Tarahumara men here and watch the Tarahumara women at work on their exceptional baskets. Bahuichivo, near the mission village of Cerocahui, is a good base from which to explore the beautiful Cañón de Urique (Urique Canyon). At each location, hotel management can arrange your trips—by van, horseback, or foot—into the canyons. Those who enjoy camping should certainly do so. The climate at the bases of the canyons is almost tropical, with bamboo, oranges, and orchids in abundance. In fact, many of Tarahumara "go south" for the winter simply by walking from the top of the canyons to the base.

On your way back to Chihuahua, explore the Cascada de Basaséachic, a sight well worth the journey. The falls can be reached by car by heading northeast from Creel to Cuauhtémoc (also a stop on the railway line). Follow Route 16 west from Cuauhtémoc directly to Basaséachic. The walk down to the falls takes about 15 minutes. Tours can be arranged through travel desks at the larger Chihuahua hotels. (For more information on the falls, see the section on the Cascada de Basaséachic in *Chihuahua,* THE CITIES.)

Sanborn Viva Tours (2015 S. 10th St., McAllen, TX 78503; phone: 210-682-9872 in Texas; 800-395-8482 elsewhere in the US) and its sister agency at the same location, *Sanborn Tours* (phone: 800-531-5440), offer a variety of excursions to the Barranca del Cobre and other destinations in Mexico. *Copper Canyon Lodges* (2741 Paldan St., Auburn Hills, MI 48326; phone: 800-776-3942) offers nine- and 12-day trip packages that take in the bottom of the canyon and rustic Batopilas, as well as shorter excursions.

En Route from Chihuahua Route 45 south from Chihuahua is quite good for the next 150 miles (240 km) to Ciudad Camargo.

CIUDAD CAMARGO This lively town of 45,000 people was founded in 1740 and almost destroyed by Apache attacks in 1797. A new settlement grew quickly, however, and today the city is a busy industrial center, with meat-packing plants, textile mills, and other industries. The *Fiesta de Santa Rosalía* is celebrated here from September 4 through 12. Within 7 miles (11 km) of town are a number of hot springs—Ojo de Jabalí, Ojo Caliente, and Ojo Salado—all known for their curative powers. Ojo Caliente is generally considered the best of the lot.

About 18 miles (29 km) southwest of Ciudad Camargo is La Boquilla dam and adjoining Lago de Toronto (Lake Toronto), so named because it was first stocked with black bass from the Toronto, Canada, area. Spring is the best time for fishing here (no fishing is allowed on the lake in July and August), and you'll find bluegills, perch, and catfish, in addition to black bass. The nearby *Club de Esquís* rents small boats and launches (no phone).

En Route from Ciudad Camargo About 45 miles (72 km) south of Ciudad Camargo on Route 45 is Ciudad Jiménez, an agricultural center and a nice rest stop. At Jiménez, the route divides, and you may take either Route 49, which passes through the town of Gómez Palacio en route to Torreón, or Route 45, which passes through Hidalgo del Parral and Durango. Route 49 rejoins Route 45 at Fresnillo (see below), about 490 miles (784 km) south of Ciudad Jiménez on Route 45 and 390 miles (624 km) south of Jiménez on Route 49.

Along Route 49, Gómez Palacio is one of the government's three "La Laguna" land reclamation projects, and it's of interest mainly for the irrigation projects that surround it. Northwest of town, at Ojuelo, is a 990-foot-high pedestrian bridge that is suspended across a vast canyon. (Take Route 49 for 26 miles/42 km to Bermejillo; turn left on Route 30 and proceed 12½ miles/20 km; turn left again on a dirt road and proceed 4½ miles/7 km to the bridge.) Nearby is Mapimí (from Ojuelo, return to Route 30 and continue 2½ miles/4 km), bejeweled with quartz, geodes, and other glistening minerals. Further information can be obtained from Gómez Palacio's tourist office (250 Blvd. Miguel Alemán Ote.; phone: 17-144434). It's open daily.

TORREÓN Founded in 1887, Torreón is another "La Laguna" city. After 1907, when the railroad came to town, Torreón became a major thoroughfare and commercial center, serving as a strategic point during the 1910 revolution. Residents say that Pancho Villa's roughriders were so delighted when they saw telephones in Torreón—the first they'd ever seen—that they went from house to house making phone calls.

The *Teatro Isauro Martínez* (Isauro Martínez Theater; at Matamoros and Galeano; phone: 17-127199) is considered one of the most beautiful in Mexico. Pre-Hispanic artifacts are on display at the *Museo Regional de la Laguna* (Laguna Regional Museum; at Juárez and Carranza; phone: 17-139545). It's open daily; there's an admission charge.

Torreón offers the traveler some good, inexpensive places to eat. For seafood, try the *Apolo Palacio* (259 Valdéz Carillo Sur, on the main plaza; phone: 17-120774). *La Majada* (Blvd. Independencia and Donato Guerra; phone: 17-134715) has good meat, especially roast kid, as does *Rodeos* (Colón and Ocampo; no phone). The *Atenas* (239 Acuña Sur; phone: 17-120368) offers Greek and Arab fare.

Some spectacular sites are within easy driving distance of Torreón. The Bilbao dunes (take Rte. 40 east 25 miles/40 km and turn right at the *Ejido Hermosa*) and the *Biósfera de la Zona del Silencio* (Zone of Silence Biosphere Reserve; about 87 miles/139 km northeast on Rte. 49) are abundant with giant turtles, fossils, and aerolites, as well as brilliantly colored cacti. Be especially careful around the *Zona del Silencio,* whose name comes from its interesting, but puzzling, environment: Nothing that depends on electricity, radio, or television waves works within it. Airplanes are routed around the zone, electrical systems on cars stop functioning, and no broadcast signals can be sent or received within the region. The government has established a research station here to investigate the phenomenon.

The lovely, uncommercialized town of Parras de la Fuente is also worth a detour. In the state of Coahuila, Parras is midway between Torreón and Saltillo, off Route 40. Founded in 1598, the town is the birthplace of Francisco I. Madero, father of the Revolution of 1910. Nowadays Parras is best known for its wine industry, specifically the winery of *San Lorenzo*

(2 miles north of Parras off Rte. 35; no phone), which has been in operation since 1626. At the *Casa Madero* winery (6 miles north of Parras off Rte. 35; no phone), you can tour the premises and taste samples of the local crop in a lovely vineyard setting. Inquire at your hotel for additional details. Notice the still-functioning ancient aqueduct adjacent to one of the winery buildings. A *Feria de la Uva* (Grape Fair) is held in the town in August.

En Route from Torreón Route 49 rejoins Route 45 at Fresnillo (see below), 247 miles (412 km) south.

HIDALGO DEL PARRAL If you chose to travel via Route 45, this old mining town (pop. 250,000) will be your first stop. The mining boom hit Parral in 1629, when what is now La Prieta mine was discovered. Early on, more than 7,000 Indian slaves were literally worked to death by the Spaniards in area mines. In 1862, when Napoleon's troops occupied much of Mexico to prop up Emperor Maximilian, Parral served as the capital from which Benito Juárez and his cabinet led the nation.

Pancho Villa was assassinated here in 1923; the house where he was killed, now the *Biblioteca Francisco Villa* (Francisco Villa Library; corner of Calle Juárez and Calle M. Herrera; no phone) is a major attraction. It's closed Sundays; there's no admission charge.

The *Palacio Municipal* (City Hall), on the central plaza, has pleasant gardens; it's closed weekends. The *Iglesia de la Virgen del Rayo* (Church of the Virgin of the Thunderbolt) is definitely worth a visit. Completed in 1728, it is a source of special pride to the indigenous inhabitants of the area. A Tarahumara miner financed much of the construction, arriving each week with a gold ingot to pay the workmen. When the church was completed, the Spanish governor demanded to know where the miner had found his gold. Refusing to answer, he was tortured to death; the location of his mine remains a mystery.

A more modern church, the *Iglesia de Nuestra Señora de Fátima* (Church of Our Lady of Fatima, the patron saint of miners), right off the central plaza, was built entirely of raw rock taken from the mines and from unfinished oak. Gold, silver, manganese, zinc, copper, and antimony are embedded in the structure.

The *Casa Alvarado* (12 Calle Riva Palacio) is an amazingly ornate building constructed in the beginning of this century by a miner who struck it rich in a local silver mine. He became famous when he offered to pay Mexico's national debt (the government declined his offer). Admire the outside only; the house is not open to the public.

En Route from Hidalgo del Parral Continue south on Route 45 for about 250 miles (400 km) to Durango.

DURANGO This place has a special claim on modern travelers: To date, more than 100 American, British, and Mexican films have been made in the surrounding area, including *A Man Called Horse, Five Card Stud, The Sons of Katie Elder,* and *Fat Man and Little Boy.* John Wayne hunted bandits in the desolate hills outside the city more than once, and many of the sets are still standing. *Chupaderos,* the most popular of the western movie sets—with a saloon, a hotel, a bank, a livery stable, a mine, and even a public execution site— can be reached by taking Route 45 north for 9 miles (14 km) before turning onto a dirt road for a quarter of a mile (0.4 km). *Calle Howard,* another movie set, is also on Route 45, about 5 miles (8 km) north of Durango. One of the newer movie sets is at *Alamos,* at Km 35 on the road to La Flor. Free one-day passes to visit a movie set can be obtained from the *Turismo y Cinematografía* office (408 Calle Hidalgo Sur; phone: 181-11107 or 181-12139); it's closed weekends. *Viajes Anamar* (1204 Negrete Pte.; phone: 181-25080) operates tours of the city and its environs.

More important than movie sets, however, is Durango's wealth of natural resources—as the Spanish discovered in 1563, when they arrived in search of precious metals. Gold, silver, lead, copper, and iron line the inside of Durango's hills. In fact, one of the largest iron deposits in the world— El Cerro del Mercado (Market Hill)—is just north of town.

Plain evidence of the wealth of the mines can be found in the massive, Baroque *Catedral de Durango* (Cathedral of Durango), which faces the Plaza de Armas, or main square. Built between 1695 and 1750, it contains oil paintings from the 18th and 19th centuries. Legend has it that the cathedral is haunted by a lovesick Spanish maiden named Beatrice, who died of a broken heart during the War of Independence (1810). Her ghost is said to appear in the tower on nights of the full moon; Avenida Constitución is reputed to be a prime ghost viewing spot.

You can hear *serenatas* (concerts) performed by the *Banda del Estado de Durango* (Durango State Band) on Sunday and Thursday evenings at the Plaza de Armas.

The *Palacio de Gobierno* (Statehouse; 143 Calle Bruno Martínez; phone: 181-15562) houses two contemporary murals, one by Ernesto Flores Esquivel and the other by Francisco Montoya; they're considered to be among Durango's finest artistic displays. It's closed weekends; no admission charge. In the *Santuario de Guadalupe* (Sanctuary of Guadalupe; off Esplanada Insurgentes in the northern, Guadalupe section of town) lie the remains of the priests who were executed near Durango in 1812 for participating in the fight for independence.

Durango's *Parque Guardiana* (Guardiana Park, at the entrance to Rte. 40 east, toward Mazatlán; phone: 181-14575) houses the *Escuela de Artesanías* (Arts and Crafts School), where hand-blown glass objects, ceramics, sculptures, and woven products can been seen. It's closed weekends. For purchases, go to *Los Tlacuilos,* a market on the Plaza de Armas (no phone). Other handicrafts, including a wealth of scorpion (Durango's trademark) souvenirs, are sold in the *Mercado Francisco Gómez Palacio,* the central marketplace, near the Plaza de Armas.

Although none of the restaurants in Durango rates a rave review, there are several adequate spots. *La Majada* (2000 Calle 20 de Noviembre; phone: 181-84377) serves Mexican beef and goat dishes at moderate prices. *La Bohemia* (Calles 20 de Noviembre and Hidalgo; phone: 181-15422) offers typical Mexican and German fare. *Far West* (1106 Calle Florida; no phone) is highly recommended for meat dishes. For an afternoon or evening coffee accompanied by live music, try *Café y Arte Plaza los Condes* (201 5 de Febrero Pte.; phone: 181-26263).

Two reservoirs near Durango offer opportunities for fishing, swimming, and water skiing: Peña del Aguila, about 20 miles (32 km) north of town on Route 39, an asphalt road that branches off from Route 45; and Guadalupe Victoria, 15 miles (24 km) south of Durango on an unnumbered asphalt road. The tourist office (480 Calle Hidalgo Sur; phone: 181-12139) can provide detailed information and maps to the reservoirs; it's closed Sundays.

En Route from Durango About 22 miles (35 km) south of Durango, on Route 45, the Cascadas de El Saltito (El Saltito Waterfall) has amazing rock formations that western movie buffs might recognize.

FRESNILLO Route 45 rejoins Route 49 near Fresnillo (pop. 35,500), a colonial town 108 miles (180 km) south of Durango, where you might want to stop for a rest on your way to Zacatecas, about 40 miles (64 km) farther south.

ZACATECAS Named from the Nahuatl words *zacatl* (grass or hay) and *tecatl* (people), the city was originally the home of the indigenous Zacateco. You enter the city along a winding road that passes picturesque houses sprawled across a mountain called Cerro de la Bufa. Its steep cobblestone streets give the city a medieval look.

In 1546 the Spanish declared Zacatecas property of the Crown; the area's first mining expedition was launched soon after, and the town, like most in the region, became a profitable silver mining center. Between the 16th and 18th centuries the mines yielded more than a billion dollars worth of silver, and some of those mines are still being worked. Guided tours through the tunnels of the *Socavón el Edén* (Edén Mine), which stretch out below the city, are available in English daily except Mondays. Make arrangements for tours through your hotel.

Zacatecas has some stunning colonial architecture made of pink quarry stone called *cantera rosa*. In fact, this "pink city" is among the best preserved in the region. The *Catedral de Nuestra Señora de Zacatecas,* completed in 1752, is on the south side of the main plaza. The *Iglesia de Santo Domingo* (a block west of the plaza) is a good representative of Spanish Baroque style. The *Palacio de Gobierno* (Statehouse, on the Plaza de Armas) and the *Teatro Calderón* (Calderón Theater, on Av. Hidalgo, across the Plaza de Armas from the *Palacio de Gobierno*) are both fine examples of colonial Spanish buildings. Not to be missed is the *Museo Pedro Coronel* (near the Plaza de Armas on Plaza Santo Domingo; phone: 492-28021), which houses the extensive private collection of the renowned artist, a native Zacatecan. In it are pieces from Mexico's pre-Columbian period; Greco-Roman, Oriental, and contemporary art; works from Mexico's colonial era, including two magnificent Christ figures by Zacatecans; and two rooms devoted to Goya and Piranesi. Coronel's mausoleum is also on the premises. The museum is closed Mondays; admission charge.

One of Zacatecas's major attractions is the *Museo Rafael Coronel* (in the 16th-century Convento de San Francisco, on Calle Abasolo; phone: 492-28116). Named for the aforementioned Pedro's brother, this museum boasts a collection of 6,000 Mexican masks—the most extensive in the country. It's closed Mondays; admission charge. Another museum not to be missed is the *Museo Francisco Goytia (Parque General Enrique Estrada;* no phone), which houses works of Goytia, among other artists. It's closed Mondays; no admission charge.

For a good view of the city, visit *La Capilla de los Remedios* (Chapel of Healing) on the summit of El Cerro de la Bufa, on the northeast edge of town. A cable car makes the trip between Cerro del Grillo and Cerro de la Bufa when it's not too windy. The chapel, also known as *El Patrocinio,* contains an image of the Virgin that, according to the Indians, has magical powers.

Among the recommended restaurants in the city are *La Cuija* (downtown, in the *Mercado González Ortega;* phone: 492-28275), which serves steaks and international fare, and *Hostería de la Moneda* (501 Dr. Hierro; phone: 492-23888), a good place to sample local specialties.

The tourist office (Av. Hidalgo and Callejón de Santero; phone: 492-24170, 492-20170, or 492-25137) is very helpful. It's closed weekends.

Just south of Zacatecas, in Guadalupe, is the *Museo Regional de Guadalupe,* located in the former *Convento de Nuestra Señora de Guadalupe* (Convent of Our Lady of Guadalupe) and considered one of Mexico's most important monuments. Worth seeing are the valuable colonial-era paintings, a rare-book library, and lovely chapels, especially the *Capilla de Nápoles* (Naples Chapel), with its gilded stucco walls and extraordinary cupola. The convent is closed Mondays; there's an admission charge (phone: 492-32089).

You can visit the *Ruinas de Chicomoztoc,* ruins of the pre-Hispanic city of *La Quemada,* which are 30 miles (48 km) southwest of Zacatecas. Follow Route 54 toward Guadalajara for about 28 miles (45 km); take the turnoff on the left and drive another 2 miles (3 km). *La Quemada* is fairly well preserved, probably because of the dry air of the region. Divided into three sections—the temple, the palace, and the citadel—the ruins are spread over a large area. They are Postclassic Toltec, dating from the 13th century.

Back on Route 54, about 100 miles (160 km) southwest of the *La Quemada* ruins, are the ruins of *El Teul* and *Las Ventanas,* at Highway 70 West. Because the road is bad and the ruins are in a very primitive state, it is a good idea to hire a guide. You would also do better with a guide at the ruins of the fortress-like city *Chalchihuites.* Located northwest of *La Quemada,* near the Zacatecas-Durango state line and south of the railway town Súchil, these ruins have characteristics similar to those of *La Quemada.*

Finally, about 30 miles (48 km) west of Zacatecas, in the midst of the best cattle raising country in Mexico, is Jerez de García Salinas. This colonial town of about 100,000 is best known for its 10-day *Festival de Primavera* (Spring Flower Fair), which begins on *Sábado de Gloria* (Holy Saturday), and for the old and very romantic *Teatro Hinojosa*, on Calle Aquiles Serdán (phone: 494-52212).

En Route from Zacatecas From Zacatecas you can take Route 49 to Querétaro via San Luis Potosí, or you can take Route 45 toward Querétaro through Aguascalientes and León, perhaps with a side trip to Guanajuato, Dolores Hidalgo, and San Miguel de Allende.

SAN LUIS POTOSÍ Named after Louis, "the saintly monarch" of France, and *potosí,* the Quechua word for "extremely wealthy" (originating from the rich Potosí mines of Bolivia), this town was founded by Fray Magdalena and Captain Miguel Caldera in 1583. Its history, however, began much earlier; the Chichimec, a seminomadic tribe, inhabited this site (which they called Tangamanga) for three centuries before the Spanish arrived. Although the bulk of the region's gold and silver, which brought the Spanish flocking to the area, was in a town called San Pedro, 25 miles (40 km) south of San Luis Potosí, the mineral springs of the latter made it a better place to settle. Much of the spectacular colonial architecture still remaining in San Luis Potosí is the result of the zealousness of missionaries who expended their energies protecting the city and the Indians from the speculators who rushed here during boom mining days, only to leave when the mines played out.

From 1863, when Benito Juárez led the fight against further French colonization, until 1867, when—from the *Palacio de Gobierno,* on the main plaza—he pronounced the death sentence on Maximilian and his two generals, San Luis Potosí functioned as the de facto capital of northeast Mexico.

It also was here that Francisco I. Madero, while being held prisoner by dictator Porfirio Díaz, drafted the famous *Plan de San Luis Potosí,* which called for a revolt against the dictatorship. Madero designated November 20, 1910, as the day for all Mexicans to rise up against Díaz; that date marks the official start of the Mexican Revolution. (Though the insurrection would last until 1917, Díaz was overthrown in 1911.)

San Luis Potosí is today a picturesque and prosperous city of about one million people. Its main plaza, the Plaza de Armas (or Jardín Hidalgo; between Calle Francisco I. Madero and Avenida Venustiano Carranza), provides a central point for exploring the town. Overlooking the plaza are two of the city's landmarks, the *Palacio de Gobierno* (Statehouse), dating from 1770, and the *Catedral de la Virgen.* Both of these structures have undergone change and restoration since their construction, but both retain some aspects of their original structure and decor. The statehouse's lower floors and façade remain from the original building; inside are the ornate *Salón de los Espejos* (Hall of Mirrors) and the *Galería de Héroes* (Heroes Gallery). Both rooms are open daily; there's no admission charge. The prominent structure on the north side of the cathedral, facing the Plaza de Armas, was built by the Count of Monterrey, and was once a lavish palace. Since 1921, however, it has functioned as San Luis Potosí's *Palacio Municipal* (City Hall).

The beautifully proportioned *Catedral de la Virgen* was built between 1670 and 1740 on the site of two earlier churches. Inside, it is a potpourri of architectural styles, including Byzantine, Doric, and Gothic.

On the Plazuela del Carmen, three blocks east of the Plaza de Armas, is the unusual *Iglesia de Nuestra Señora del Carmen* (Church of Our Lady of Mt. Carmel), which was built in Churrigueresque style in 1764. The unique façade of this church is adorned with shells, columns, and a dome of blue, yellow, green, and white tiles. The interior, designed by the noted architect Francisco Eduardo Tresguerras, contains an intricately carved pulpit and paintings by Francisco Antonio Vallejo. One block past this church is the *Teatro de la Paz* (Plazuela del Carmen; no phone), where folkloric ballets, concerts, and operas are performed. Across the street from the theater is one of Mexico's most fascinating museums, the *Museo Nacional de la Máscara* (2 Vilerías; phone: 48-123025), which contains about 1,500 masks from pre-Hispanic to modern times. They show the effects of the conquest of Mexico; the subsequent marriage of native and Spanish cultures; and the influence of the Catholic religion. The museum is closed Mondays; no admission charge. Just east of Plazuela del Carmen is *Alameda Juan Sarabia*, the city's largest park. Well shaded with trees and far enough from the busy center of town to provide a peaceful retreat, this is a fine place to picnic, stroll, and relax. Just past the southwest corner of Alameda, along Avenida Universidad, is the *Plaza de Toros Fermín Rivera* (phone: 48-220236). If you don't catch a bullfight, you might settle for a visit to the photographic exhibit in the *Centro Taurino* (Bullfighting Museum; phone: 48-221501) next door to the Plaza España, where a variety of bullfighting exhibits are open to the public. The *Centro Taurino* is closed Sundays and Mondays; there's no admission charge. Across from the northwest corner of the Alameda, where Othón and Azteca intersect, stands the city's railroad station, where Fernando Leal's magnificent frescoes depicting the history of transportation in Mexico cover the walls.

Three blocks south and one block west of the Plaza de Armas, along Calle Aldama, is the Plaza de San Francisco, once a vast Franciscan monastery. On the south side of the plaza is the *Iglesia de San Francisco,* with a lovely blue-and-white tile dome on the exterior and a substantial display of 18th-century paintings within. On the west side of the plaza, in striking contrast to the 18th-century cathedral, stands the *Museo Regional de Arte Popular* (Regional Museum of Folk Art; 1 Parque Tangamanga; phone:

48-276217). Set in a completely renovated turn-of-the-century mansion, the collections cover the full spectrum of local crafts from ceramics, inlaid wood, and papier-mâché sculpture to rebozos (shawls), pottery, and other artifacts. The museum is open daily; no admission charge. Many of these crafts are sold at the government-operated *Tienda de Arte Popular* (6 Jardín Guerrero; phone: 48-127521). The shop is closed Sundays.

Shopping is particularly pleasant in San Luis Potosí along Calle Hidalgo. If you follow the tiled street north from the Plaza de Armas, you will pass many of the smaller, fine shops of the city that sell the famous silk rebozos made in the nearby village of Santa María de Oro. You will also pass the flower market, housed in the renovated structure of the city's old marketplace. Eventually, you will reach the central marketplace, an enormous building containing a vast array of local crafts, foods, and other delights of all kinds. Among the special attractions are the local culinary treat called *queso de tuna* (a sweet paste made from the prickly pear cactus fruit), baskets, straw furniture, pottery, leather goods, and a variety of produce.

Eating is a special pleasure in San Luis Potosí. *La Virreina* (830 Venustiano Carranza; phone: 48-123750), one of Mexico's best restaurants, is set in an elegantly converted mansion and has excellent regional and international dishes. Another good spot for local and international fare is *La Lonja* restaurant and bar (Madero and Aldama; phone: 48-128119). *La Gran Vía* (620 Venustiano Carranza; phone: 48-122899) serves first-rate international food in a formal setting.

For tourist information, city maps, and general information, call or visit the tourist office (325 Venustiano Carranza; phone: 48-129939 or 48-129943). It's closed Sundays.

En Route from San Luis Potosí Take Route 57 south for 121 miles (202 km) to Querétaro (see below).

AGUASCALIENTES If you took the alternate route from Zacatecas (Rte. 45), your first stop is the city of Aguascalientes, about 77 miles (123 km) to the south. Named for the thermal springs found in the area, Aguascalientes is also known for the extensive system of tunnels beneath it. The tunnels are clearly made by human beings, but no one knows by whom; native histories shed no light.

In 1522, the conquistador Hernán Cortés ordered Pedro de Alvarado into the western territories near Aguascalientes. His troops were badly mauled by the native Chichimec, and for a number of years the city was deserted except for a small group of Chichimec. The discovery of rich silver mines at Tepezala infused life into the area. First the mines, then the Jesuits, then rapid growth: the same pattern of development followed in almost all of the silver cities of north-central Mexico.

One of the most famous festivals in all of Mexico is Aguascalientes's *Feria de San Marcos* (San Marcos Fair), which is held from about April 20 to May 5. Bullfights, cockfights (usually illegal, but allowed during the fair), fireworks, rodeos, and crafts exhibits make the city come alive, and there's much merriment and consumption of tequila. Most of the activities take place in the *Jardín de San Marcos,* one of the city's many pleasant parks.

A stroll in the parks is the best way to begin a tour of this city; fine weather is almost guaranteed. Also of interest, in the center of town on the Plaza Principal, is the *Palacio de Gobierno* (Statehouse; open daily; no admission charge), known for its fine historical mural by the Chilean painter Oswaldo Barra. Other sites worth visiting are the *Palacio Municipal* (City Hall; on Plaza Patria), the *Iglesia de San Diego* (Calle Rivera y Gutiérrez), the *Iglesia de San Antonio* (Calles Pedro Parga and Zaragoza), and the *Teatro Morelos* (Plaza República). The *Palacio Municipal* and the churches are open daily, while the theater is open for performances only. (Call the state tourism office for information about upcoming events; see below for details.) *El Museo de la Ciudad* (City Museum; 505 Calle Zaragoza; phone: 49-159043) concentrates on exhibits of Mexican art. It's closed Sundays; there's an admission charge. More information on local sites is available from the state tourism office (*Palacio de Gobierno,* ground floor; phone: 49-151155), which is closed weekends.

Aguascalientes is also known for fine hand-embroidered and crocheted articles, which can be purchased in local shops. Local hotels can arrange visits to *Las Peñuelas,* a bull-breeding hacienda near the city, and to local wineries.

Travelers can also visit the nearby hot springs. Within a short ride are *San Nicolás de la Cantera, Ojo Caliente,* and *Valladolid,* where you can submerge yourself in a mixture of sulfate of soda, sulfate of lime, carbonate of lime, chloride of sodium, magnesia, and sulfuric acid. It's supposed to make you feel like a new person.

For a good binge before you get healthy, try the restaurant at the *Francia* hotel (see *Best en Route*); the *Rincón Gaucho* (110 Arturo Pani; phone: 49-163191); *El Caballo Loco* (310 Venustiano Carranza; 49-157869); *Aguas 'n' Charlie's* (902 José María Chávez; phone: 49-171775); or *La Vendimia* (102 Arturo Pani; no phone).

En Route from Aguascalientes You may want to stop off at the town of Encarnación de Díaz, 16 miles (26 km) south of Aguascalientes on Route 45. Replicas of Christopher Columbus's *Niña, Pinta,* and *Santa María*—all sculpted from the trees—grace the *zócalo* (main plaza). Otherwise, your next stop will be the city of León, 77 miles (123 km) from Aguascalientes.

LEÓN In 1888, a huge wall of water from the Río Gómez crushed León, in the state of Guanajuato, destroying 2,230 houses, killing more than 200 people, and leaving 20,000 homeless. El Puente del Coecillo, a huge dike nearly a mile long and 10 feet thick, was constructed to prevent another disaster.

Today León is an important commercial center with a number of parks, colonial buildings, and a busy market. León is also one of the three leading shoe manufacturing cities in Mexico and a major production center for leather goods, which means that boots, shoes, and saddles are good buys here.

If you don't really care for shoe shopping, you might want to visit the *Templo Expiatorio* (Church of Atonement; Calle Pedro Moreno). Construction workers are still attempting to finish the church, which was begun 53 years ago. Make sure to see the catacombs beneath the church, which house a series of chapels, statues, altars, and paintings.

Also worth a visit are the *Palacio Municipal* (City Hall), with its richly carved stone façade, and the *Catedral de la Madre Santísima de la Luz* (Holy Mother of Light Cathedral), both on the main plaza and both open daily. The beautifully proportioned cathedral was built by the Jesuits in 1746.

On *La Fiesta de San Sebastián Mártir* (St. Sebastian Martyr Day), January 20, a fair and folk dancing are held in town.

Good restaurants include *El Molinito* (111 Hidalgo; phone: 47-146915); *Los Venados* (511 Blvd. López Mateos; phone: 47-161770); and *La Casa Grande* (in the *Centro de Exposiciones;* phone: 47-162018).

En Route from León While the Mexico City toll road can be picked up in León, we highly recommend a side trip to Guanajuato, about 30 miles (48 km) southeast. Take Route 45 as far as Silao (about 19 miles/30 km), then turn onto the stretch of Route 110 that heads to Guanajuato. From here it's a twisting, 16-mile (26-km) drive through the hills to the city.

GUANAJUATO For a detailed description of the city, its hotels, and its restaurants, see *Guanajuato* in THE CITIES.

About 10 miles (16 km) west of Guanajuato, via Route 110, is the Cerro del Cubilete, considered the geographic center of Mexico. An enormous bronze statue of *Cristo Rey* (Christ the King)—82 feet high and weighing 200 tons—stands atop the 9,442-foot peak. Pilgrims from all over Mexico flock to the monument and climb the interior stairway to a chapel near the figure's heart.

En Route from Guanajuato Head northeast on Route 110 toward Dolores Hidalgo, about 32 miles (54 km) away. About 3 miles (5 km) out of town is Valenciana, a worthwhile stop because of its beautiful church and incredibly rich working silver mine. For details on Valenciana, see "Special Places" in *Guanajuato,* THE CITIES.

DOLORES HIDALGO Padre Miguel Hidalgo y Costilla made this town famous on September 16, 1810, when he proclaimed Mexico's independence from Spain. That morning at dawn, Hidalgo rang the bell of the parish church to gather his flock, and then delivered his battle cry—known as *el grito de Dolores* (the shout of Dolores): *"Mexicanos, viva México!"* Afterwards, a makeshift army, armed mainly with sticks and farm tools, set out for San Miguel. This, the first phase of the independence movement that finally came to fruition in 1821, is why Dolores Hidalgo is known as the *Cuna de la Independencia* (Cradle of Independence). The bell that Hidalgo rang is said to be the one that's now above the *Palacio Nacional* (National Palace) in Mexico City. Historians argue that it's only a replica and that the original bell was melted down for munitions during the 11-year war. In 1821, after independence was won, the town of Dolores was renamed Dolores Hidalgo, to honor Hidalgo's heroism.

Tradition today holds that each Mexican president send a representative to Dolores Hidalgo during the annual reenactment of the *grito de Dolores.* The president himself also must visit the town and proclaim the *grito* at least once during his six-year term.

Stores around the plaza and connecting side streets are jammed with locally made ceramic goods, generally of unimaginative design. The town is, however, well known for its colorful tiles.

Casa de Don Miguel Hidalgo (1 Morelos, at the corner of Hidalgo; no phone) is a museum containing many of Padre Hidalgo's personal effects, including his eyeglasses, clothing, furniture, books, and papers. Patriotic paintings and independence-era memorabilia fill the rooms and the surrounding two patios. It's closed Mondays; admission charge.

About 8 miles (13 km) south of town on Route 51 is the Presa las Peñuelitas (Peñuelitas Dam). *La Gruta,* with thermal baths, is about 12½ miles (20 km) from town.

En Route from Dolores Hidalgo Take Route 51 to San Miguel de Allende, 20 miles (32 km) away.

SAN MIGUEL DE ALLENDE For a detailed description of the city, its hotels, and its restaurants, see *San Miguel de Allende* in THE CITIES.

En Route from San Miguel de Allende Take Route 111 east 21 miles (35 km) to Route 57; then take Route 57 south 17 miles (28 km) to Querétaro.

QUERÉTARO Querétaro (pop. 900,000) is one of the most historic cities in Mexico. The most famous of Querétaro's residents was Doña Josefa Ortiz de Domínguez, known as "La Corregidora." In 1810, she warned the rebels that the Spanish planned to capture them. These fighters, including Ignacio Allende and Padre Miguel Hidalgo, escaped and started the campaign that would eventually bring freedom to Mexico. Her home is now the site of the *Palacio de Gobierno* (Statehouse; Calles 5 de Mayo and Pasteur; no phone). Open to the public (no admission charge), it sits downtown at Plaza de Armas, a charming restored colonial square.

Querétaro was founded by the Spanish in 1531, when they conquered the native Chichimec and Otomí who lived in the area. Agriculture expanded, mining began, and the city eventually became a colonial center. In 1848, Querétaro was the site of the signing of the Treaty of Guadalupe Hidalgo, in which Mexico lost more than half its national territory to the US after the Mexican War. Querétaro was also the place to which Emperor Maximilian fled in 1867 after Napoleon III pulled out France's troops (which had been propping Maximilian up); Maximilian eventually was court-martialed and executed here. In 1916, after the overthrow of dictator Porfirio Díaz, Mexico's new constitution was written in Querétaro. Thirteen years later, Mexico's dominant political party, now called the *Partido Revolucionario Institucional* (PRI, or Institutional Revolutionary Party), was founded here as the *Partido Nacional de la Revolución* (PNR, or National Revolutionary Party).

Today the city has several thriving industries. Tractors, sewing machines, fork lifts, oil drilling rigs, and food products are manufactured here. Automobiles produced in the US by Ford and Chrysler are equipped with standard transmission gearboxes manufactured in Querétaro by one of Mexico's largest exporters of manufactured products.

The Jardín Obregón is the city's main square. (In this region, squares are sometimes called *jardines,* or gardens.) A large wrought-iron bandstand in the middle of the square is the site of concerts on Sunday evenings. There is also an ornate 19th-century fountain and water tank of cast iron produced by a foundry in Philadelphia. The Jardín Obregón is a hangout for many vendors of opals and amethysts of generally low quality; buyers beware.

The *Iglesia de San Francisco* dominates Jardín Obregón. Frequently mistaken for the city's cathedral because of its high tower, the church was completed in 1545 and has undergone subsequent architectural modifications. The structure served as a hospital and surgery ward during the siege of 1867, in which Maximilian was defeated, and soldiers were quartered here during the 1810–17 War of Independence. The church steeple affords a great view of *Nochebuena* (Christmas Eve) celebrations in which *fantoches*— huge papier-mâché dolls—are carried playfully around the square, accompanied by music and fireworks.

In the convent section of the *Iglesia de San Francisco* is the *Museo Regional de Querétaro* (Regional Museum of Querétaro; 3 Corregidora; no phone). Its exhibits cover numerous stages of Mexican history, as well as archaeology, natural history, and Indian artifacts. The most interesting items include the keyhole and door latch of a household prison where "La Corregidora" whispered instructions to a servant to warn the Allende brothers and Padre Hidalgo that their plot had been discovered. As a result of this information, the date of the revolt was pushed ahead by three months. In the same exhibit is the table on which the Treaty of Guadalupe Hidalgo was signed by interim Mexican President Manuel de la Peña. According to the terms of the treaty, Mexico turned over to the US the territory of Texas, the territory between the Nueces and Bravo (Grande) rivers belonging to the state of Tamaulipas, the territory of New Mexico, and the territory of Alta (Upper) California. Mexico lost more than half of its total area at the time, for which the US paid 15 million pesos (worth 15 million dollars at the time). In an adjoining room stands the desk at which sat the council of war that heard the case of Emperor Maximilian and signed his death sentence in 1867. Also on display is the flatbed press that printed the first copies of the *Constitución Política de 1917,* the Mexican

Constitution, which is still in effect today. The museum is closed Mondays; there is an admission charge.

The Plaza de la Constitución is covered with the rose-colored *cantera* rock for which Querétaro is famous; in it is a large statue of the controversial Venustiano Carranza, who headed the triumphant Constitutionalists during the 1910 revolution and later became President of Mexico. Bordering the plaza are posts bearing the names of Mexico's states and territories and the names of individual delegates to the constitutional convention.

The Jardín de Santa Clara's *Fuente de Neptuno* (Neptune Fountain) is an imaginative, neoclassical work designed by Francisco Eduardo Tresguerras, one of Mexico's best-known architects.

The Jardín de la Corregidora, at 16 de Septiembre and Corregidora, is the site of the *Arbol de la Amistad* (Friendship Tree)—actually two conifers growing together, with a plaque between them stating: "Querétaro is the crossroads of all roads of the country and center of gravity of national history." Also in the square is a monument to "La Corregidora." Dedicated in 1910, it features a symbolic reproduction of the keyhole through which she whispered her messages. The base of the statue is surrounded by large bronze eagles; the slave breaking out of chains represents freedom from Spanish domination.

The *Iglesia de Santa Rosa de Viterbo* (Calle General Arteaga and Calle Ezequiel Montes) is one of the most exotic, if not downright bizarre, examples of ecclesiastical architecture in Mexico. Completed in 1752, the church has two enormous flying buttresses that help shore up the central structure, upon which an octagonal cupola is set. The lower half of the cupola is sculpted in stone, and the dome has patches of painted, blue and white Talavera tile. The intricate bell tower is topped with what appears to be an Oriental pagoda; it contains the first multiple-face clock built in the Americas. The outermost extremities of the flying buttresses, which extend from the tower to the street, are flanked by ornately carved dragon faces. Inside the church are huge gold leaf *retablos* (altarpieces) and murals, some by colonial-era artist and muralist Miguel Cabrera, and a pulpit with a giant crown of Oriental origin finished with silver and ivory inlay. A pipe organ and choir section are in the back section of the nave. Across the street, in the Plaza Ignacio Mariano de las Casas, named for the church's architect, stands a group of municipal government buildings.

In contrast, the *Iglesia de San Felipe Neri* (Av. Madero at Ocampo) is a refreshing change from the gold and silver resplendence of most Mexican churches. Although the façade is ornate, inside there is no gold leaf, and the large dome allows plenty of light to filter in. The small pipe organ in the choir loft is one of the best in the city. Construction on the church began in 1755, and mass was first said here in 1763. It was completed in 1804 and was later restored.

Yet another Querétaro church, the *Iglesia de la Congregación de Guadalupe* (16 de Septiembre and Pasteur), is well worth a visit for its huge pipe organ, which reverberates magnificently throughout the building. The twin towers of the church are topped with wrought-iron crosses, and the upper portions of the towers are decorated with mosaic tiles in Mexico's national colors of red, white, and green.

Also noteworthy is the *Iglesia y Convento de la Cruz* (Church and Convent of the Cross; Av. Venustiano Carranza and Calle Acuña), which was built in the late 17th century. It became the center of operations for a Franciscan order, which established its *Colegio de Propaganda Fide* (Academy for Propagation of the Faith), the first such institution in the Americas. Father Junípero Serra and other friars left the school to establish missions in other parts of Mexico and California. The monastery was an important scientific and artistic center; its library had more than 7,000 volumes, a record for that period of history. The building also served as the prison of Emperor Maximilian in 1867; his cell is still furnished with his desk, sleeping cot, and chair.

Querétaro's *acueducto* (aqueduct), which still carries water into the city, was completed in 1735. Nearly 6 miles (10 km) long and almost 100 feet high in some spots, it is composed of 74 arches, which are lit dramatically at night. Drive on Calzada de los Arcos for a good view. Alternately, you can take the cutoff to San Luis Potosí under the arches.

West of the city, the Cerro de las Campanas (Hill of the Bells) has a statue of Benito Juárez at the top and, farther down the slope, a chapel marking the site where Maximilian was executed. The emperor surrendered here in 1867 and was killed later that year by a firing squad. An expiatory chapel financed by the last Emperor of Austria, Franz Josef, was built here in 1901. In front of the altar are the three truncated columns below which Maximilian and his two generals stood facing their executioners. The walls of the chapel are lined with photographs and paintings from the Maximilian period.

The *Plaza de Toros Santa María* (Av. Libre a Celaya; phone: 42-161617), with a seating capacity of about 18,000, is one of the best bullrings in Mexico, second only to those of Mexico City and Tijuana. Querétaro's corridas often feature top matadors from Mexico and Spain, especially during the main season in November and December.

Querétaro is known for its opals, but the region's famed opal mines are becoming exhausted, and the better stones are scarce and expensive. For the best buy, consult the shopkeepers for prices and quality. Buy gems only from reputable sources; the goods offered by the street vendors may or may not be the real thing. And don't be afraid to bargain. Perhaps the most common stone and the best buy now is the brown fire agate. Examine gems under low light—only opals or agates of high quality will show "fire" under those conditions. A reliable store is *El Rubí* (3 Av. Madero Pte., just off Plaza Principal, between Juárez and Allende; phone: 42-120984), which carries a wide assortment of fiery opals, as well as amethyst, topaz, agate, and alexandrite (sold set or loose).

The tourist office (5 de Mayo and Pasteur; phone: 42-138483, 42-138443, 42-139802, or 42-138512) offers free two-hour tours of historic Querétaro sites; they leave from the office at 10:30 AM, except on Sundays, when the office is closed.

For a good meal, try *La Fonda del Refugio* (26 Corregidora; phone: 42-120755), which offers an international menu, including such expensive dishes as pepper steak and chateaubriand. On warm days, tables are set on the plaza. You can also eat in the covered porch facing the plaza where the monument to "La Corregidora" stands.

En Route from Querétaro The toll road (Rte. 57) to Mexico City is good, but be careful—mist and clouds reduce visibility, and the moisture makes the road surface dangerously slick. There is also heavy traffic, with trucks carrying goods to and from the border.

BEST EN ROUTE

Along this route, expect to pay more than $100 per night for a double room at an expensive hotel; $50 to $95 at a moderate one; and $45 or less at an inexpensive one. Most hotels deep in the Barranca del Cobre (Copper Canyon) area have no air conditioning, TV sets, radios, or phones; most of the expensive and moderate hotels throughout the rest of the route do. For each location, hotels are listed alphabetically by price category.

CIUDAD JUÁREZ

Plaza Misión Juárez Park Inn This motel has 175 rooms, a swimming pool, a coffee shop, a nightclub, and a dining room. In the *Plaza de las Américas* shopping center (phone: 16-131310 or 16-131414; fax: 16-130084). Expensive.

Colonial las Fuentes Its 250 colonial-style motel rooms are arranged around a beautiful garden and courtyard. There are three pools, a 24-hour *Denny's* restaurant, and even a stockbroker on the premises. 1355 Av. de las Américas (phone: 16-135050; fax: 16-134081). Moderate.

Sylvia's This hotel offers 100 refurbished rooms, a pool, gardens, bar service, a barbershop, a dining room, and free parking. 16 de Septiembre and Venezuela (phone: 16-150442). Moderate.

Plaza Continental In addition to 64 rooms, this property offers bar service, a restaurant, parking, and a barbershop. 112 Lerdo Sur (phone: 16-150084; fax: 16-140531). Inexpensive.

NUEVO CASAS GRANDES

La Hacienda A highly recommended motel with 126 rooms, a pool, a tennis court, a restaurant, and a bar. 2603 Av. Benito Juárez (phone: 169-41048; fax: 169-44818). Moderate.

Piñon This 40-unit motel has a pool, a fair dining room, and a museum with a collection of Casas Grandes artifacts. 605 Av. Benito Juárez (phone: 169-40655, 169-40847, or 169-40166). Inexpensive.

BARRANCA DEL COBRE (COPPER CANYON)

Cabañas Divisadero-Barrancas All 54 rustic but comfortably furnished rooms have spectacular views; there's a wing with balconies overlooking the canyons. Rate includes meals. Excursions to the Tarahumara caves and settlements on foot and horseback can be arranged. At the edge of the three canyons that make up the Barranca del Cobre, two hours from Creel. Divisadero stop on the railway (phone: 14-123362 in Chihuahua; fax: 14-156575). Expensive.

Copper Canyon Riverside Lodge A rustic, interesting 19th-century hacienda with 14 rooms; meals are served in the gardens. Excursions can be arranged. In Batopilas, at the bottom of a 6,000-foot canyon, 80 miles (128 km) from the Creel train station (phone: 14-560179; 800-776-3942; fax: 14-560036). Expensive.

Copper Canyon Sierra Lodge A lodge with 29 primitive log and adobe rooms, this place is pricey, although there is no heat, only occasional hot water, and no electricity (only kerosene lamps and wood-burning stoves). However, good family-style meals are served. Hiking excursions can be arranged. In Creel (phone: 14-560179; 800-776-3942; fax: 14-560036). Expensive.

Misión In the midst of paradise, this comfortable hostelry offers 30 rooms, a restaurant, and trips to nearby waterfalls, the startling Cañón de Urique (Urique Canyon), the *Iglesia de San Francisco,* and the defunct *Mina Urique* (Urique Mine). Get off at Bahuichivo on the *Ferrocarril Chihuahua al Pacífico;* a bus will take you to the hotel, 75 minutes away in Cerocahui. Reservations necessary; make them through the *Santa Anita* hotel in Los Mochis (phone: 681-57046; 14-165950 in Chihuahua; fax: 681-20046). Expensive.

Posada Barrancas Offers 45 rooms, a restaurant, tours of the canyons and Tarahumara caves, and horseback trips. Posada Barrancas station on the *Ferrocarril Chihuahua al Pacífico,* or a few minutes' walk from Divisadero. Make reservations through the *Santa Anita* hotel in Los Mochis (phone: 681-57046; 14-165950 in Chihuahua; fax: 681-20046). Expensive.

Parador de la Montaña A colonial-style motel with 49 rooms and a small restaurant with ho-hum service, it offers several delightful tours into the canyons. Room maintenance could be better, but the location in Creel is more practical than the *Copper Canyon Sierra Lodge.* 41 López Mateos (phone: 145-60075; 14-122062 or 14-155408 in Chihuahua; fax in Chihuahua: 14-153468). Moderate.

CIUDAD CAMARGO

Florido A comfortable motel with 42 rooms, a pool, bar service, and a decent café. Av. Juárez and 20 de Noviembre, in nearby Jiménez (phone: 154-20186). Inexpensive.

Los Nogales One of the better establishments in town, with 31 rooms, a restaurant, parking, and a pool. 402 Av. Juárez (phone: 146-21247; fax: 146-24442). Inexpensive.

TORREÓN

Del Prado Torreón A modern building with 146 units, a pool, a sauna, a restaurant, a coffee shop, and a bar. Paseo de la Rosita and Diagonal de las Fuentes (phone: 17-212424; fax: 17-212958). Expensive.

Palacio Real A remodeled older hotel with 140 rooms and suites, cable TV with US programming, a restaurant, a bar, and access to the golf and tennis facilities at *La Rosita Country Club*. On the main square, at 1280 Av. Morelos Pte. (phone: 17-160000; fax: 17-168608). Moderate.

Paraíso del Camino Pleasant and clean, with 81 rooms, cable TV, a pool, a bar, a restaurant, and seven trailer spaces with full hookups. Juárez and Reforma (phone: 17-200333). Moderate.

Paraíso del Desierto This hotel offers 164 rooms, a restaurant, a cafeteria, a pool, a garage, and cable TV with US programs. Blvd. Independencia and Jiménez (phone: 17-161122). Moderate.

El Paso A newer motel that has 45 rooms and a bar, but no restaurant. 400 Saltillo at Carranza (phone: 17-137364 or 17-137079). Inexpensive.

Posada del Rey A downtown spot with 38 rooms and a restaurant. 333 Valdez Carrillo Sur (phone: 17-168004 or 17-160015). Inexpensive.

PARRAS DE LA FUENTE

Rincón del Motero The 85 rooms, suites, and bungalows here have fans and showers; some also have heat and air conditioning. Pluses include a nine-hole golf course, a pool, a tennis court, horseback riding, extensive gardens, and an excellent restaurant. At the north end of town (phone: 842-20540; fax: 842-20872). Moderate to inexpensive.

HIDALGO DEL PARRAL

Adriana Features 62 clean, comfortable motel rooms and a restaurant. 2 Colegio (phone: 152-22570; fax: 152-24770). Expensive.

San José The 51 rooms are decent; there's a restaurant, too. 5 Santiago Méndez (phone: 152-22453; fax: 152-22712). Inexpensive.

DURANGO

El Gobernador Set in lovely gardens, this hotel has 100 comfortable rooms, an excellent restaurant, a bar, a cafeteria, and a pool. 257 Av. 20 de Noviembre Ote. (phone: 181-31919 through 181-11422; fax: 181-11422). Expensive.

Los Arcos Here are 68 motel units, a restaurant, a bar, and gardens. 2204 H. Colegio Militar Ote. (phone: 181-81239; fax: 181-87777). Moderate.

Campo México This property features 80 pleasant rooms with satellite TV. There's also a bar and a dining room, plus a trailer park on the grounds. Far east on Av. 20 de Noviembre Ote. (phone: 181-87744; fax: 181-83115). Moderate.

Casablanca Some of the 46 units here are suites. Every indoor area is air conditioned, and there's a restaurant and bar on the premises. 811 Av. 20 de Noviembre Pte. (phone: 181-13599; fax: 181-14704). Inexpensive.

Plaza Catedral In a colonial building, with 40 large units (four suites have refrigerators) and a restaurant-bar. Beside the *Catedral de Durango,* at 103 Av. Constitución Sur (phone: 181-32480; fax: 181-32660). Inexpensive.

ZACATECAS

Aristos Zacatecas A highly recommended hotel with 102 rooms, a restaurant, a coffee shop with an impressive view of the city, a nightclub, a pool, and even secretarial services. Loma de la Soledad (phone: 492-21788; 800-527-4786; fax: 492-26908). Expensive.

Continental Plaza Zacatecas The 18th-century façade of this building has been declared a colonial monument. Formerly the *Paraíso Radisson,* its 115 spacious rooms are decorated with colonial furniture; some have charming balconies overlooking the main square. There is a restaurant as well. 730 Av. Hidalgo, down the street from the cathedral (phone: 492-26183/4/5/6/7; 800-882-6684; fax: 492-26245). Expensive.

Quinta Real Beautifully designed to blend in with the aqueduct and the old bullring next door, this hotel has 49 rooms, a fine restaurant, a bar, and lovely gardens in the courtyard. 434 Av. Rayón and González Ortega (phone: 492-29104/5/6/7; 800-445-4565; fax: 492-28440). Expensive.

Del Fresno An extremely clean, sun-filled hotel with 55 rooms; there's also a restaurant and parking. 411 Av. Hidalgo, in Fresnillo, about 40 miles (64 km) north on Rte. 45 (phone: 493-21126 or 493-21120; fax: 493-20731). Moderate.

Del Bosque This 60-room motel with a restaurant offers guests a great view of the city. Only Visa is accepted. A 10-minute drive from downtown, on Paseo Díaz Ordaz (phone: 492-20745 or 492-21034). Inexpensive.

Posada de los Condes Here are 58 colonial-style rooms, plus a restaurant and bar. Downtown, corner of Rayón and Juárez (phone: 492-21412 or 492-21093; fax: 492-24254). Inexpensive.

Hostal del Quijote This hotel offers 211 comfortable rooms, a restaurant, a nightclub, two pools, and tennis. Km 420 on Rte. 57 (phone: 48-181312 or 48-181411; fax: 48-186105). Expensive.

María Dolores A newer hotel, with 213 rooms, two pools, a garden, a restaurant, a coffee shop, a disco, a lobby bar, and a playground. Km 1 on Rte. 57 (phone: 48-221882; fax: 48-220602). Expensive.

Cactus This spacious Howard Johnson property has 110 rooms, some with refrigerators and mini-bars. There is a steambath, a dining room, a cocktail lounge with entertainment, a nightclub, convention facilities, a pool, satellite TV, a playground, and a 30-space trailer park with full services. Just south of Juárez Circle, next to the *María Dolores* on Rte. 57 (phone: 48-221995; 800-456-4656 in the US; 800-50549 in Mexico; fax: 48-144259). Moderate.

Real de Minas A colonial-style hostelry with 200 rooms, a heated pool, a coffee shop, and a shopping center on the premises. Km 426.6 of Rte. 57, about 500 yards from Juárez Circle (phone: 48-182616; fax: 48-186915). Moderate.

Real Plaza Modern and centrally located, with 138 units, a restaurant, a bar, a pool, and a coffee shop. 890 Carranza (phone: 48-146969; fax: 48-146639). Moderate.

María Cristina Its 71 units are equipped with fans, and there's a restaurant. 110 Juan Sarabia (phone: 48-129408; fax: 48-128823). Inexpensive.

Sands A motel with colonial decor, pleasant grounds with gardens and a pool, 50 spacious rooms, and a nice restaurant. Km 422 on Rte. 57, across from the *Cactus* (phone: 48-182533; fax: 48-182533). Inexpensive.

Tuna Another well-kept motel, it has 50 units, cable TV, a pool, a playground, and a restaurant-bar. 200 Dr. Manuel Nava (phone: 48-131207; fax: 48-111415). Inexpensive.

AGUASCALIENTES

De Andrea Alameda Here is a lovely colonial-style hotel with 40 rooms and two suites, a restaurant, a bar, and meeting rooms. Av. Madero, on the *zócalo* (phone: 49-184417; fax: 49-183759. Expensive.

Fiesta Americana This property has 200 rooms with satellite TV and mini-bars, three restaurants, a coffee shop, a piano bar, a pool, tennis courts, and a gym. Paseo de los Laureles (phone: 49-185059; 800-FIESTA-1 in the US; 800-50450 in Mexico; fax: 49-185362). Expensive.

Quinta Real The most luxurious hotel in town, with 81 suites, a fine restaurant, a bar, and meeting and banquet rooms. 601 Av. Aguascalientes Sur (phone: 49-181842; 800-445-4565; fax: 49-181859). Expensive.

Las Trojes One of the nicest places in Aguascalientes, it has 160 rooms, restaurants, bars, a disco, tennis courts, and a pool. Blvds. Zacatecas and Campestre (phone: 49-630006 or 49-630007; fax: 49-730434). Expensive.

La Cascada Here are 78 rooms, a restaurant, a bar, and a pool. 501 Blvd. José María Chávez (phone: 49-711010; fax: 49-711108). Moderate.

Francia This imposing hotel has 87 rooms and a good restaurant and bar. In the lobby is a huge print of Aguascalientes as it looked a century ago. Av. Madero and Plaza Patria (phone: 49-156080; fax: 49-160140). Moderate.

Medrano A motel with 85 rooms, a restaurant, a bar, a nightclub, and a pool. 904 Blvd. José María Chávez (phone: 49-155500; fax: 49-168066). Moderate.

La Vid Modern, with 68 rooms, a restaurant, a bar, a disco, and a pool. 1305 Blvd. José María Chávez (phone: 49-139150). Inexpensive.

LEÓN

La Estancia A classy motel with 162 rooms, restaurants, a bar, a pool, and a Jacuzzi. 1311 Blvd. López Mateos Ote. (phone: 47-163939; fax: 47-163940). Expensive.

Fiesta Americana This upscale hostelry has 211 rooms with cable TV, bars, restaurants, and a pool. 1102 Blvd. López Mateos (phone: 47-136040; 800-FIESTA-1 in the US; 800-50450 in Mexico; fax: 47-135380). Expensive.

Balneario Comanjilla In this 124-room spa, guests can spend the day playing tennis or horseback riding, with a reward of thermal waters and steambaths to soothe the tired muscles. For additional details, see *Spa-Hopping Special* in DIVERSIONS. In Comanjilla, Km 387 of Rte. 45, about 18½ miles (30 km) from León (phone/fax: 47-146522; 47-120091 phone in León). Moderate.

Real de Minas A colonial-style inn with 175 comfortable rooms, a restaurant, a heated pool, and a lobby bar featuring live music at night. 2211 Blvd. López Mateos Ote. (phone: 47-710660; fax: 47-712400). Moderate.

DOLORES HIDALGO

Caudillo This 32-room establishment has a restaurant and bar. 8 Querétaro (phone/fax: 418-20198). Inexpensive.

Posada Cocomacán In the middle of town, the 40 units here are rustic and clean. The inn has a restaurant. 4 Plaza del Grande Hidalgo (phone: 418-20018). Inexpensive.

QUERÉTARO

Casablanca A favorite getaway for Mexico City's elite, this 65-room resort has direct-dial long-distance telephone service, a restaurant, a bar with live entertainment, a pool, tennis, and lovely gardens. The service is exceptional. 69 Av. Constituyentes Pte. (phone/fax: 42-160100 or 42-160102/3). Expensive to moderate.

Hacienda Jurica The most elegant accommodations in the area feature 180 rooms (24 with computers), a heated pool, a discotheque, restaurants, two lighted tennis and squash courts, horseback riding, and access to the *Club de Golf Jurica,* 10 minutes away. Km 229 of Rte. 57, northwest of Querétaro (phone: 42-180022, 5-207-0562 in Mexico City; fax: 42-180136). Expensive to moderate.

Mesón de Santa Rosa This, one of the best of Mexico's small, intimate properties, was originally built as a hostel for visitors from the countryside. Eventually, the structure was converted to an all-suite hotel, a masterpiece of elegance and colonial restoration work. There are 20 suites, an excellent restaurant, three patios, and a swimming pool. All rooms have satellite TV, and most have VCRs. Plaza de Armas, 17 Pasteur Sur (phone: 42-145781 or 42-145993; fax: 42-125522). Expensive to moderate.

Real de Minas There are 200 rooms with TV sets, six tennis courts, a pool, billiards, a piano bar, and private dining rooms. Guests have access to an 18-hole golf course. 124 Constituyentes Pte., next to the *Plaza de Toros Santa María* (phone: 42-160444; fax: 42-160662). Expensive to moderate.

Azteca A hotel with 51 immaculately clean rooms and suites. Facilities include a 24-hour cafeteria, a restaurant, a handicrafts shop, a pool, two tennis courts, and a gasoline station. There are also 30 spaces for trailers, many with full hookups. Nine miles (14 km) north of the city on the old road (phone/fax: 42-180076). Moderate.

Impala One of the nicer downtown hotels, featuring 102 units with TV sets, and a restaurant. 1 Zaragoza at Colón (phone: 42-122570; fax: 42-124515). Inexpensive.

Nuevo Laredo
to Mexico City

The border crossing from Laredo, Texas, to Nuevo Laredo, Mexico, is one of the entry points into Mexico most used by US drivers. The Constitutional Highway, the 693-mile (1,109-km) road from Nuevo Laredo to Mexico City, comprises three major sections: Route 85 from the border to Monterrey, Route 40 from Monterrey to Saltillo, and Route 57 from Saltillo to Mexico City. This route traverses some of Mexico's major mining, industrial, and agricultural regions, and passes through the most interesting towns in Mexico's northeast—Monterrey, Saltillo, and San Luis Potosí.

The geography of the journey is rather starkly divided between the arid deserts of the north and the rich farmlands of the central highland area. The change occurs as the road leaves the plains below Texas and enters the Sierra Madre Oriental, the mountain range whose spiny cliffs, canyons, winding roads, peaks, and valleys you actually travel twice in the course of the journey. After crossing a 250-mile (400-km) stretch of nearly empty desert plateau, the road continues past the hills of Mexico's richest mining regions to the Bajío and the fertile farmlands of the central highlands district, where trees, mineral springs, rivers, farms, and maguey fields dominate the landscape.

Besides large, interesting cities, this route offers opportunities for adventure and off-the-road exploration. By burro, jeep, turn-of-the-century railroad coach, or car, travelers can journey to a ghost town, hidden caves, an abandoned mining tunnel, natural health spas, and the major archaeological zone of *Tula*.

In the high altitudes of the Sierra Madre, the weather is mild and dry all year. It can become chilly at night, but seldom cold. The desert and northernmost regions along this route tend to be very hot and dry, with few breezes. In the areas covered on this drive, March through October are the warmest months, while November through February are the coolest; in cooler months, you might need a sweater at lower altitudes and a light coat at higher ones.

En Route to Nuevo Laredo The twin cities of Laredo, Texas, and Nuevo Laredo, in the state of Tamaulipas, Mexico, are connected by two bridges; if you plan to continue beyond Nuevo Laredo, you must use the old bridge, the only entry that handles immigration papers. After paying a $2 per car toll, you will go through customs and immigration. For regulations regarding entry into Mexico, see GETTING READY TO GO.

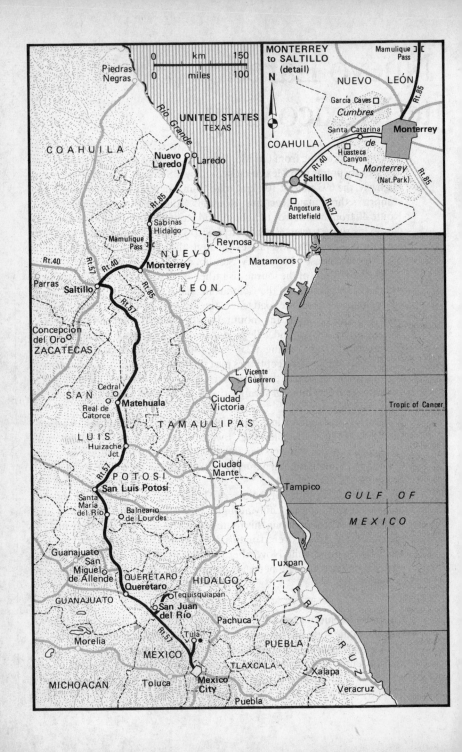

NUEVO LAREDO Besides the thousands of tourists who visit Nuevo Laredo each year, a stable population of 220,000 inhabits this 400-year-old city. Like most border towns, Nuevo Laredo offers a wealth of accommodations, restaurants, shopping areas, and nightlife. The town is renowned for its picturesque greyhound dog races, held every Sunday afternoon at the *Galgodromo,* 6 miles (10 km) south of town on Route 85. Emotions run high at this heated event, and betting can get very fierce. A note of warning, though: This place is infamous for its light-fingered pickpockets, so watch your wallet or purse.

The one-square-block *Mercado de Artesanías Maclovio Herrera* (Maclovio Herrera Handicrafts Market) at Guerrero and Belden features products from all over the country. Lunch or snacks may be had at the pleasant umbrella-shaded restaurant-bar in the patio. Before undertaking the long journey south, you might want to eat at *México Típico* (on Guerrero; no phone), which offers dining inside or out with wandering Mexican musicians, or *Victoria 3020* (3020 Victoria; no phone), where fine Mexican food is accompanied by house beer.

En Route from Nuevo Laredo Follow Avenida Guerrero out of town to Route 85 toward Monterrey, about a one-and-a-half-hour drive away on the toll road that starts after the customs checkpoint. (Look for the signs that say "Monterrey Vía Rápida" or "Monterrey Cuota." The tolls are high—they'll total 62 pesos, or about $8.25—but they are worth it. Taking the freeway—"Monterrey Libre"—will add another two hours to your trip.) Seventeen miles (27 km) out of town is the only customs and immigration checkpoint on this entire route, though there are sometimes additional spot customs checks, particularly in December. At the 17-mile checkpoint, officials generally look at your tourist card, and the driver of each vehicle is usually asked to push a button on a machine at the checkpoint. If a red light goes on, the customs officials will examine the car's trunk and any packages. During slow seasons the button system is not used and the officials inspect cars on a random basis.

Sabinas Hidalgo, a small town 81 miles (130 km) from Nuevo Laredo, has become an important textile center over the past two decades. It is a good place to purchase local fabrics, which incorporate traditional designs with modern techniques. Since it is the only town on the route between Laredo and Monterrey (63 miles/101 km south of here), you might want to take advantage of its filling stations, stores, and restaurants. The *Ancira* (no phone), right on Route 85, has adequate food.

Mamulique Pass, a vista point in the Sierra Madre, is a good place to rest and catch a glimpse of surrounding cliffs and distant valleys before the descent to Monterrey, Mexico's main industrial center and third-largest city. The pass is marked on the road.

MONTERREY For a detailed report on the city, its hotels, and its restaurants, see *Monterrey* in THE CITIES.

En Route from Monterrey Take Avenida de la Constitución out of the city to Route 40. (Follow the signs to Saltillo—53 miles/85 km away.) Turn left at the sign to Santa Catarina on Monterrey's outskirts and follow a paved road for 2 miles (3 km) to reach the breathtaking Cañón de la Huasteca (Huasteca Canyon), site of a 1,000-foot gorge with towering walls and unusual rock formations caused by the erosion of the area's soft stone. The paved road ends at a tidy fenced-in picnic area and playground (admission charge); a stony, unpaved road leads into the canyon. This is a desolate place, but a police car usually is stationed at the entrance for security. Backtrack to Route 40 from here.

About 16 miles (26 km) beyond Monterrey on Route 40 is the turnoff for the village of Villa de García and the nearby *Grutas de García* (García Caverns)—the most spectacular caverns in North America and a sight not to be missed. Discovered a century ago, the *Grutas de García* have 16 different chambers and natural pools, magnificent stalactite and stalagmite formations, and spectacular natural stairways (open daily, except December 12; admission charge). The caves are dangerous to explore alone; instead, sign up for one of the many guided tours (in English upon request) offered through *Infotur* in Monterrey (Calles Matamoros and Zaragoza; phone: 8-345-0870; closed Mondays). Be sure to wear sensible shoes—climbing around requires some agility. Just outside Villa de García, a cable car travels up 2,460 feet, providing terrific panoramic views; you can also rent a burro to make the trip.

SALTILLO The capital of the state of Coahuila, at an altitude of 4,125 feet in the Sierra Madre Oriental, has a population of about 445,000. The modern city is a major industrial center that manufactures pottery, silverware, engine parts, and textiles. The city's two universities attract students from around the world. Because of its mild, sunny, dry climate, Saltillo has become a regional recreational center of the northeast. Its golf courses and tennis courts are open all year, while swimming facilities remain full from March through October.

Saltillo was founded in 1575, when Captain Francisco de Urdiñola selected the site as a teaching center for the native peoples of Mexico's north. By importing the Tlaxcala, who were more faithful to the Spanish, from the central highlands, Urdiñola hoped to influence the more rebellious northern plains peoples. Under his leadership the northeast underwent an initial stage of colonial development. Soon, Saltillo became a staging area for northern expansion, as well as the capital of an enormous area extending across Texas to Colorado.

Although modernization has destroyed much of Saltillo's original architecture and flavor, several remnants of its early colonial life remain, particularly in the southwest section of town, on Avenida Allende, by the central square, Plaza de Armas (also known as the Jardín Hidalgo). The 18th-century *Catedral de Santiago,* which overlooks the Plaza de Armas, is considered one of the finest examples of Churrigueresque architecture in North America. Its main tower offers a panoramic view of Saltillo. Across from the cathedral, also overlooking the plaza, is the *Palacio de Gobierno* (Statehouse), of more historical than visual interest: It was here that Governor Venustiano Carranza recruited an army to avenge the assassination of Mexico's first revolutionary president, Francisco I. Madero, in 1913.

Other points of interest in Saltillo are the *Alameda* and the *Fortín* (Fortress) *de Carlota.* The *Alameda,* west of Plaza de Armas (off Victoria and Ramos Arizpe), is a quiet, pleasant spot containing the *Fuente de la República* (Pond of the Republic), which is built in the shape of Mexico, and an equestrian statue of General Ignacio Zaragoza. The fortress, not far from the Plaza de Armas, was dedicated to Maximilian's wife, Carlota, who fled to France in an unsuccessful attempt to seek Napoleon III's aid against the Mexican independence forces.

In the center of town between Aldama and Carranza, Plaza Acuña is the city's busiest square and the place to go to get a sense of Saltillo's daily life. This is where vendors hawk their wares, senior citizens gather, and late lunch crowds tarry over coffee.

Saltillo is a center for a wide variety of reasonably priced, well-made handicrafts and decorative pieces. Colorful serapes, silver goods, pottery, grotesque tin masks, furniture, and leather goods are all good buys here. At the *Mercado Juárez,* the central marketplace (between Padre Flores and Allende), Mexican curios and embroidered blouses are sold at reasonable prices; the selection of other local handicrafts is not so great here, though. Calle Victoria, the main street, and nearby side streets have the largest concentration of interesting local products. For silver goods, such as tea sets and jewelry, *Platería Taxco* (428 Victoria; phone: 84-112854) and *Moeller Platería Saltillo* (212 Victoria; phone: 84-142726) offer a good variety; *Moeller* also offers tours. For leather, *La Azteca* (159 Acuña Nte.; no phone) has a wide selection of purses, billfolds, saddles, and belts, while *Zapatería Victoria* (642 Allende Nte.; no phone) has good boots. For hand-crafted colonial-style furniture, *Muebles Coloniales el Arte* (1036 Zarco Ote.; no phone) has a reasonably priced, varied, high-quality stock. *Artesanías del DIF* (Blvd. Francisco Coss and Acuña; no phone) carries a range of handicrafts, from paper flowers and wrought-iron chandeliers to sculptured candles and copper, brass, alabaster, and glass items. You can watch the entire process of serape and rug making, from the carding of the wool to the final weaving (done on handlooms), at the family-run *El Sarape de Saltillo* (305 Hidalgo Sur; phone: 84-120187).

Saltillo is the site of the *Universidad Autónoma del Noroeste* (Blvd. E. Reyna and Américas Unidas), a liberal arts university, and the *Instituto Tecnológico de Saltillo* (2400 Blvd. Venustiano Carranza), as well as three schools where foreigners come to learn Spanish.

Most of Saltillo's festivals take place in late summer and early fall. *Festival del Cristo de la Capilla* (August 6) is the major event. According to the legend that inspired the festival, an unattended donkey wandered into town on August 6, 1608, carrying a box so heavy that it finally collapsed under the load. Curious townspeople pried open the box to find inside an image of Christ. As soon as the box had been breached, the donkey disappeared. A chapel, or *capilla*, was built on the site of the miracle, and the festival commemorates the event with fireworks, bullfights, and *La Malinche*, the Huastec dance in which participants wear carved wooden masks signifying betrayal between blood brothers. (La Malinche was a native princess who fell in love with Hernán Cortés and betrayed her own people by helping him conquer the Aztec empire. To this day, *malinchista* is a derogatory term for someone who prefers foreign goods and culture over his or her own.)

The *Festival del Agua* (Water Festival) is held during the first week of September, and the *Festival de Queso y Vino* (Wine and Cheese Festival) takes place on October 4 in nearby Parras, east of Saltillo.

Two side trips from Saltillo warrant special mention. The *Ferrocarril Coahuila-Zacatecas* (Zacatecas and Coahuila Railroad) leaves Saltillo daily for the mining town of Concepción del Oro. The journey follows narrow mountain ridges in turn-of-the-century coaches; for railroad buffs it could be a high point of the entire route. The 164-mile (262-km) round trip constitutes a day's excursion; consult the tourist offices (see below) or any local hotel for schedules and ticket information.

Just outside Saltillo is *La Angostura*, also known as *Buena Vista*, the site of a major battle between US and Mexican forces during the Mexican-American War. In 1847, US general Zachary Taylor and his army confronted Mexican general Antonio López de Santa Anna and his (far more numerous) forces here. After capturing most of Taylor's strongholds in two days, Santa Anna inexplicably withdrew, leaving the field to the US forces. Historians say the battle left 694 Mexicans dead; the US lost 267 troops.

In Saltillo, make sure to try *dulces de leche*, a boiled milk candy; *pan de pulque*, a sweet bread made with pulque, a fermented drink made from the maguey cactus; mescal, a drink distilled from maguey; and—in season, from July through October—concoctions made from *huitlacoche*, a corn fungus with a delicate mushroom-like flavor. *La Reina Panadería* (at Allende and Alvarez; no phone) is the best bakery to sample pastries and sweet rolls. *El Tapanco* (225 Allende Sur; phone: 84-144339) is the best, and loveliest, restaurant in the area. Located in a converted 17th-century home, it serves Mexican and international food. Other decent eateries are *La Canasta* (2485 Venustiano Carranza and Michoacán; no phone) and *El Principal* (702 Allende Nte. and Rte. 40; no phone).

Saltillo has two helpful tourist offices, both with an English-speaking officer on hand. One is at the *Centro de Convenciones* (Convention Center; Blvd. Fundadores; phone: 84-154902; fax: 84-158390) and the other is downtown (Blvd. Francisco Coss and Manuel Acuña; phone: 84-154050). Both offices are open daily.

En Route from Saltillo East of town, Route 57 ascends for 9 miles (14 km) through rugged mountain terrain before reaching the rim of a broad semi-arid plateau that continues until you make the descent into real desert. The desert road, which you will follow before and after Matehuala, has its own particular blend of native charm and high risk. Although it looks unpopulated, occasional desert dwellers do unexpectedly stray into the road. Those with two legs (usually young boys carrying boxes) are likely to wave you down and try to sell you a rattlesnake, an eagle, a falcon, or *tuna,* the fruit of the prickly pear cactus tree. It is best to keep an eye out for these unexpected visitors along these long, flat stretches of desert road.

MATEHUALA The only town along the 282-mile (451-km) stretch between Saltillo and San Luis Potosí, Matehuala is a welcome sight to most travelers. It has a pleasant *zócalo,* or main plaza, and some good eateries. *Las Palmas* restaurant (on Rte. 57; no phone) serves a superb version of the regional dish *enchiladas potosinas,* a cheese-filled soft tortilla topped with peas, carrots, and chorizo (a type of sausage). *San Angel* (301 Altamirano; phone: 488-20536) and *Santa Fe* (709 Morelos; no phone) have international menus, and *Fontella* (618 Morelos; no phone) is good for steaks. All are downtown.

Matehuala is a convenient departure point for two interesting side trips. Some 31 miles (50 km) west of town, across difficult mountain terrain, is the ghost town of Real de Catorce (some maps refer to it as El Catorce). The name, which literally means "Royal 14," commemorates 14 royal guards who were shot here during a colonial-era battle. In 1773, the first silver and gold mines were opened here; by the beginning of the 19th century, Real de Catorce's veins had become Mexico's third most productive mines, and the town claimed a population of 40,000. No longer a boomtown, Catorce, whose residents today number fewer than 400, still offers adventure to the desert traveler. Some of the hazards of past mining days remain: The entrance to Catorce, for instance, is a 2-mile-long abandoned mining tunnel. Park your car and take a taxi from the entrance to the city. Once you pass through the tunnel and enter the town of Catorce, the *Iglesia de la Purísima Concepción* (Church of the Immaculate Conception) and the abandoned government mint are among the most interesting of the many empty colonial structures on streets that once teemed with fortune seekers and speculators.

Fifteen miles (24 km) northwest of Matehuala is the *Mina de Mármol el Cedral* (Cedral Marble Quarry), where visitors can watch marble being cut and sculpted or shop among the slabs and beautifully carved statues of marble for sale.

En Route from Matehuala Back on the main highway, you are likely to see native women and children selling the fauna of the surrounding desert—

roadrunners, desert rats, snakes, and sometimes even baby coyotes. Fourteen miles (22 km) south of town, a monument marks the spot where the road crosses the Tropic of Cancer.

The *Mina la Paz* (La Paz Silver and Gold Mine), just 10 miles (16 km) southwest of Matehuala off Route 57, has been in operation since 1864; it's well worth a visit.

The plateau road from Matehuala to San Luis Potosí (a total of 115 miles/191 km) along Route 57 remains curveless and deserted until the Huizache junction, where the terrain begins to roll and rise.

SAN LUIS POTOSÍ This bustling city is the capital of the state of the same name, as well as one of Mexico's most picturesque mining towns. For additional details, see the *Ciudad Juárez to Mexico City* route.

En Route from San Luis Potosí About 45 miles (72 km) south of San Luis Potosí on Route 57, just before a tiny chapel and cemetery on the left-hand side, is the *Santo Domingo Ranch,* where the Labastida family breeds fighting bulls. The family will usually allow anyone interested in bullfighting to wander around the old hacienda. The bulls are kept far away and out of sight, however, in the belief they will not perform well in the arena if they become too accustomed to humans.

Back on Route 57, you'll pass through fertile farmlands and see stone fences, red tile roofs, and church towers in the small towns dotting the valley landscape. Thirty miles (48 km) south of San Luis Potosí is Santa María del Río, a small village where most of the rebozos (shawls) found in San Luis Potosí are produced. It is a charming, peaceful spot to visit and watch the women at their work.

A few miles south of Santa María del Río on Route 57 is the *Balneario de Lourdes* turnoff; follow the dirt road for 7 miles (11 km) to reach the *Balneario y Manantiales de Lourdes* (no local phone; 48-171404 in San Luis Potosí). In this thermal spa and hotel, you can enjoy the cold river water of the Río Santa María and the warm, relaxing mineral water of the village's natural springs. The spare, impeccably clean, and inexpensive hotel offers guests unheated pools, a dining room, tennis courts, horses, a game-room, a cordial staff, and free parking.

Some 72 miles (115 km) south of San Luis Potosí is a junction where Route 57 meets Route 110. Here you enter the Bajío country, rich in ancient, colonial, and revolutionary history. At this junction you can take roads west leading to Dolores Hidalgo and Guanajuato or, farther down Route 57, you can take the turnoff for San Miguel de Allende. Just before Querétaro, 121 miles (202 km) from San Luis Potosí, Route 57 meets Route 45, a junction called Cruce a Querétaro (Querétaro Crossing). Stay on Route 57, which from here all the way to Mexico City is a four-lane toll road.

QUERÉTARO The capital of the state of Querétaro, with a population of 1.3 million, is an ancient and fascinating city of tree-filled plazas, splendid mansions, busy marketplaces, and colonial architecture. For additional information, see the *Ciudad Juárez to Mexico City* route.

En Route from Querétaro Returning to Route 57, you will begin winding up through a stretch of maguey fields known as La Cuesta China (the Chinese Slope). Beyond it lies San Juan del Río, 30 miles (48 km) from Querétaro, a small town of special interest for its crafts, wine, and cheese.

SAN JUAN DEL RÍO This town (pop. 130,000) is one of the weaving centers of Mexico. Most of San Juan's better handicrafts shops are in the colonnades along the main street. The nearby Trinidad opal mines supply the stone-cutting, polishing, and jewelry making industries here, in nearby Tequisquiapan, and in Querétaro. Although this is the center of the Mexican gem industry, not all the stones sold are domestic. Many come from Brazil, Colombia, and the US, and are cut and polished locally. Purchase expensive items only in well-established shops; items sold by street peddlers and small stands often turn out to be bogus. *Lapidaria Gabriel Guerrero M.* (4 Calle Juárez Pte.; no phone) is one of the largest lapidary shops, specializing in opals, turquoise, amethyst, and topaz. Items range from finely set rings, bracelets, necklaces, and earrings to loose cut and polished stones and geodes.

Wicker and *carrizo* (reed-grass) basketry competes with semi-precious stones for the title of leading merchandise in San Juan del Río, although the basketry and weaving are finer in Tequisquiapan (see below).

Wines are another important regional product. The vineyards of San Juan del Río produce some quite passable red and white table wines. A Querétaro state law forbids wine tasting in the wineries, but sometimes this ban is overlooked during the wine and cheese festivals held in Tequisquiapan during the last 10 days of May. Wine can be bought by the case, half case, or bottle in San Juan del Río at attractive savings over supermarket prices. The largest winery is *Cavas de San Juan* (phone: 427-20102), less than a mile out of town on the road to Tequisquiapan, on the left. Of Spanish descent, the owners blend local grapes and grapes from the state of Aguascalientes to produce their Hidalgo-brand wines. You can tour their cellars, where thousands of bottles age for three or four years each. Their cabernet sauvignon and pinot noir are especially good, and their blanc de blanc is considered the best in the country. The winery is closed Sundays; there's no admission charge.

Also in San Juan del Río is *La Madrileña* (no phone), another large winery that specializes in port, vermouth, muscatel, sherry, brandy, rum, and liqueurs. You can pick up a bottle at the winery's showroom at Carretera Tequisquiapan; it's open daily.

En Route from San Juan del Río Head for Tequisquiapan, about 12 miles (19 km) northeast on Route 120.

TEQUISQUIAPAN This peaceful village of cobblestone streets and adobe houses is populated by indigenous Otomí. One of Mexico's most noted natural health spas, it appeals to harried city dwellers, tired travelers, and health seekers. At one time, all the hotels in town had water piped in from the area's hot springs; now only *Las Delicias* and *Balneario el Relox* do (see *Best en Route* for both). Besides the mineral springs, Tequisquiapan offers horseback riding, fishing, and hunting. The stores right on the *zócalo* are good spots to purchase the baskets for which the town is noted.

En Route from Tequisquiapan *Tula,* one of Mexico's major archaeological zones, is 14 miles (22 km) off Route 57 at the Tepeji del Río interchange.

TULA This was once the capital city of the Toltec. The site is closed Mondays; admission charge includes parking and entrance to the museum (but admission is free on Sundays). For additional details, see *Mexico's Magnificent Archaeological Heritage* in DIVERSIONS.

En Route from Tula Return to Route 57 and head south for the final 45 miles (72 km) to Mexico City.

MEXICO CITY For a detailed report on the city, its hotels, and its restaurants, see *Mexico City* in THE CITIES.

BEST EN ROUTE

Along this route, expect to pay $70 to $90 for a double room in an expensive hotel; $40 to $65 in a moderate place; and less than $40 in an inexpensive one. All hotels have air conditioning, telephones, and TV sets in the rooms unless otherwise indicated. For each location, hotels are listed alphabetically by price category.

NUEVO LAREDO

Hacienda A motel with 74 units, two tennis courts, a pool, and a restaurant-bar. Four miles (6 km) south of the old bridge on Rte. 85, at 5530 Reforma (phone: 87-170000; fax: 87-140420). Moderate.

El Río This motel has spacious grounds, 132 large units, two pools, a bar, an excellent dining room, a business center, and great service. Three miles (5 km) south of the old bridge on Rte. 85, at 4402 Reforma (phone: 87-143666; fax: 87-151232). Moderate.

Tres Caminos With a good restaurant, a bar, a pool, and 82 rooms, this modest, family-run motel is a pleasant choice. Off the main drag, it's quieter than most of its competitors—a godsend for light sleepers. Three miles (5 km) south of the old bridge, at 2450 Calle Chihuahua (phone: 87-149300; fax: 87-149349). Moderate.

Reforma In this established motel are 36 rooms and three junior suites, all with showers, cable TV, phones, and bar service. Avoid the mediocre dining room, though. In the center of town, at 822 Av. Guerrero (phone: 87-126250; fax: 87-120714). Inexpensive.

SALTILLO

Camino Real Saltillo This member of the chain is one of the finest hotels in northern Mexico, with acres of landscaped gardens, a heated pool, two tennis courts, a putting green, a playground, a restaurant, a coffee shop, a cocktail lounge with live music, a disco, cable TV with US programs, and 116 rooms. Located 3½ miles (6 km) southeast of Saltillo on Rte. 57, at 2000 Blvd. Los Fundadores (phone: 84-300000; 800-7-CAMINO in the US; 800-90123 in Mexico; fax: 84-301030). Expensive.

Hotel del Norte A colonial-style motel with 72 rooms (23 at inexpensive rates), a pool, a restaurant and bar, cable TV, ample parking, and a 20-vehicle-capacity trailer park with all hookups. Located 1 mile (1.6 km) north of town, at 3800 Venustiano Carranza (phone: 84-150011; fax: 84-167543). Expensive to inexpensive.

San Jorge This modern, 120-room hotel has a restaurant, a bar, an indoor pool, cable TV, and parking. Downtown, at 24 Manuel Acuña Nte. (phone: 84-122222; fax: 84-129400). Expensive to moderate.

Eurotel Plaza Best Western One of Saltillo's newer hostelries, it offers 182 rooms with cable TV, a heated pool, a restaurant, a bar, a cafeteria, a gym, and pleasant service. 4100 Venustiano Carranza (phone/fax: 84-151000; 800-528-1234). Moderate.

Rancho los Magueyes Hotel la Torre Also known by locals as "La Torre," this establishment has 86 units distributed between an older colonial-style section and a modern 12-story structure. There are two tennis courts, a restaurant-bar, a coffee shop, a pool, a disco, and cable TV. Km 869 on Rte. 57 (phone: 84-153333; fax: 84-160512). Moderate.

Plaza Urdiñola A 46-room hostelry with definite charm. There's a good restaurant, too. Downtown, at 211 Calle Victoria (phone: 84-140940). Inexpensive.

Rancho El Morillo A small establishment offering 14 units, a restaurant, a bar, a pool, tennis, basketball, volleyball, and horseback riding at a neighboring ranch. Two miles (3 km) east of Saltillo, on Periférico Luis Echeverría, Prolongación Alvaro Obregón (phone: 84-174078; fax: 84-141376). Inexpensive.

MATEHUALA

Misión del Real Repainted in gaudy colors, this 66-unit complex is still pleasant and well maintained, with a good restaurant and a bar. There is plenty of parking. Km 608 on Rte. 57 (phone: 488-20641; fax: 488-23198). Moderate.

Las Palmas Not elegant, but clean and tastefully decorated, with good service. There are 89 rooms, a restaurant, a big pool, nice grounds, a miniature golf course, a couple of bowling alleys, and an excellent restaurant. There are also 28 trailer spaces with all connections, a bathhouse, and the use of hotel facilities. Km 617 on Rte. 57 (phone: 488-20002; fax: 488-21396). Moderate.

El Dorado Here is a 42-room motel with spacious gardens, a restaurant, a pool, and a small playground. Km 615 on Rte. 57 (phone: 488-20174). Inexpensive.

SAN JUAN DEL RÍO

Antigua Hacienda Galindo The region's most luxurious hotel, built on a remodeled 17th-century hacienda, has 163 units (18 with Jacuzzi and private terrace), six tennis courts, horseback riding, a pool, and an 18-hole golf course nearby at San Gil. On the highway going into town off Rte. 57 (phone: 427-50250; 5-533-3550/1/2/3 in Mexico City; 800-90138 elsewhere in Mexico; fax: 427-50300; 5-208-7799 in Mexico City). Expensive to moderate.

La Mansión de Andrea Formerly *La Estancia de San Juan,* this fine, 108-room hotel is housed in a 16th-century hacienda. Its amenities include four tennis courts, a large pool, and the nearby *San Gil* golf course. There is ample covered parking. About 5 miles (8 km) north of San Juan del Río at Km 172 of Rte. 57 (phone: 467-10061 or 467-10096; 5-533-3188 in Mexico City; 800-90138 in the rest of Mexico; fax: 467-10030). Moderate.

TEQUISQUIAPAN

Balneario el Relox This 110-room resort has a restaurant with bar service and 14 pools fed by hot mineral springs. Meals are included in the rate. 8 Morelos (phone: 427-30006 or 427-30066). Expensive to moderate.

Del Parque In this 21-suite property are an excellent restaurant, a bar, a pool, and ample parking. Some of the rooms have Jacuzzis. 1 Privada Camelinas (phone/fax: 427-30938). Expensive to moderate.

Suites Paraíso Tequis Very exclusive, this colonial-style hostelry has 18 suites (some with kitchenettes), a restaurant, cable TV, and pleasant gardens. 12 Privada Camelinas (phone: 427-31035; fax: 427-31085). Expensive to moderate.

Las Cavas Tequisquiapan Another colonial-style structure, it has 88 rooms, a huge pool, lush gardens, two tennis courts, a gameroom, movies, a putting green, volleyball, a restaurant, and a bar. About 1½ miles (2 km) north of town at 8 Paseo de la Media Luna (phone: 427-30704 or 427-30764; fax: 427-30671). Moderate.

Las Delicias A well-kept hotel with 23 units, three spring-fed pools and a wading pool, a TV lounge (but no TV sets in rooms), lovely gardens, and a fair restaurant. All meals are included in the room rate. 1 Calle 5 de Mayo (phone: 427-33259 or 427-30017; fax: 427-30240). Moderate.

The Bajío

About 150 miles (240 km) northwest of Mexico City, the Bajío country begins. This part of Mexico was an agricultural center as early as 3,500 years ago; because of its rich soil, the region's first settlers were able to grow corn, beans, chili peppers, and squash here. The earth also yielded clay, which the early inhabitants molded into pottery and shelters. In the 11th century, the Chichimec invaded the Bajío country from the north, conquering the earlier civilization; the Aztec arrived about a century later.

But the Bajío really came into its own after the 16th-century Spanish conquest. It was here that the first colonial cities were built, and as a result the Bajío contains an abundance of colonial and other historic monuments. The main battles of Mexico's War of Independence were fought in Querétaro and Guanajuato, the two states that make up most of this rugged area. It also was in this area, in 1810, that revolutionary leader Captain Ignacio Allende allied himself with Padre Miguel Hidalgo y Costilla in the movement against Spain. They were captured and decapitated in 1811 by the Spanish, who hung their heads on public display in Guanajuato for the next 10 years. After independence was won in 1821, two cities in the area—San Miguel and Dolores—were renamed San Miguel de Allende and Dolores Hidalgo in honor of the two heroes. Decades later, in 1867, Mexico's Austrian ruler Maximilian was executed on Bajío soil, in Querétaro.

The Bajío remains one of Mexico's richest agricultural regions. Farmers regularly harvest two or three crops of strawberries, asparagus, tomatoes, sorghum, corn, wheat, and other important produce in the course of a year. The Bajío also is rich in minerals, especially silver, which made it a center of Spanish colonial activity. Today, it also is a center of heavy manufacturing, petrochemical processing, and petroleum refining plants.

Though by no means as popular with American tourists as Mexico City or the better-known coastal resorts, the Bajío region is well equipped to handle visitors. Besides its splendid colonial towns, it has outdoor sports facilities, comfortable accommodations, and numerous vineyards and crafts pavilions. The weather is cool, dry, and moderate year-round, with days tending to be sunny. Temperatures drop at night (usually to between 45 and 50F, or 7 to 10C), so bring warm sweaters. Otherwise you needn't worry about what to wear in this informal part of the world.

We suggest you tour this part of the country via a circular route from Mexico City, beginning with Route 57, stopping at San Juan del Río, Tequisquiapan, and Querétaro (the junction of several major highways), then taking Routes 111 and 51, respectively, to San Miguel de Allende and Dolores Hidalgo, Route 110 to Guanajuato and Route 45 to Celaya, then traveling west (still on Route 45) to Salamanca, then south on Route 43 to Valle de Santiago, Yuríria, and Morelia. From there, Route 15 takes you

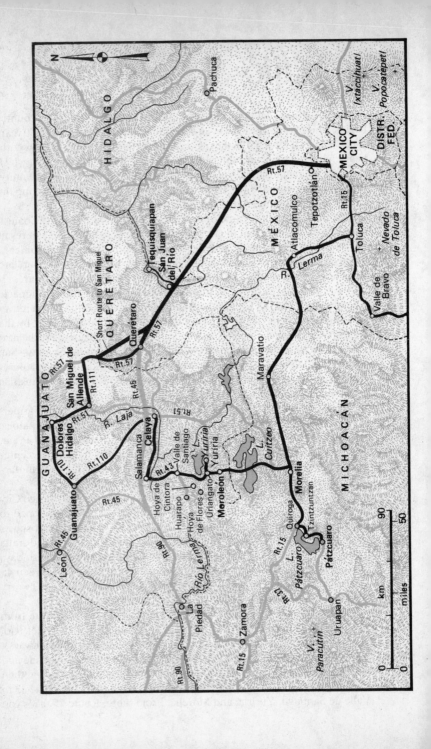

to Pátzcuaro by way of Quiroga. From there, return to Morelia; Route 55 will take you to Toluca, from where you can take a worthwhile side trip to Valle de Bravo. Finally, you can return to Mexico City from Toluca via Route 15.

Because each of the larger cities takes more than one day to cover, this circuit requires a bit more than five days, if you want to do it justice. And we suggest that you do take the time, as this is one part of Mexico that is still relatively undiscovered. You can enjoy yourself, absorb the country's history and tradition, and get a sense of what Mexico was like before 20th-century North American architecture planted itself on the horizon.

En Route from Mexico City From the *Fuente de Petróleos* monument at Plaza Comermex, where the Paseo de la Reforma crosses the *periférico* (beltway), it is 23½ miles (38 km) on Route 57 to the turnoff for Tepotzotlán. Make sure that you do not go through the tollgate to Tepotzotlán. The turnoff comes before the tollbooths and takes you on an overpass. About a half mile (1 km) west of the overpass going toward Tepotzotlán, the road becomes Avenida Insurgentes.

Before you reach Tepotzotlán, you might want to stop at the *Balneario San Pedro Tepotzotlán,* a recreational park that offers natural springwater baths and traditional swimming pools. Parking is available for campers and trailers, but there are no full hookups. Other facilities include handball, volleyball, and tetherball courts. It's open daily; there's an admission charge (no phone).

From the park, continue west on Avenida Insurgentes; Tepotzotlán is actually only about 1 mile (1.6 km) from Route 57.

TEPOTZOTLÁN This town (pop. 30,000) is at a comfortable altitude of 7,500 feet. Its most notable attraction is the *Museo Nacional del Virreinato* (National Museum of the Vice-Regency; Av. Insurgentes; phone: 5-876-0245), one of the most important historic museums in the country, located in a former Jesuit seminary built partly in the late 17th century and completed in 1762. It's closed Mondays; there's an admission charge.

The *Instituto Nacional de Antropología e Historia* (*INAH,* or the National Institute of Anthropology and History), which runs the museum, has edited an excellent English-language guidebook explaining the collection; it's available at the museum. The astounding collection includes artifacts, paintings, statuary, silver and gold objects, and vestments owned and used by the Catholic church in colonial Mexico. Among the items are bone fragments allegedly from St. Peter and St. Paul, an Italian silver chalice with coral inlays, and some of the most opulent gold leaf *retablos* (altarpieces) in Mexico. There's also a major collection of religious paintings. Possibly the museum's most interesting feature is the circular *Camarín de la Virgen* (Chamber of the Virgin), dating from the early 1700s. In the center of the room is a statue of the Virgin Mary, behind a low partition; above, a dome decorated with a frieze depicts a scene from the Pentecost. The frieze can be viewed by means of a large, tilted mirror mounted on the floor below. The museum is closed Mondays; there's an admission charge.

Tepotzotlán may well be the capital of Mexico's elaborate adaptation of the already ornate Spanish Churrigueresque style of architecture, with almost every inch of several buildings gilded, flourished, curlicued, and topped with statues of beaming cherubs.

The *Hostería del Convento de Tepotzotlán* (1 Plaza Virreinal; phone: 5-876-0243) is a lovely restaurant that serves food with lots of mole sauce, to the accompaniment of a group of lively musicians. Sit at a small table inside or outside the portals, sip a mug of beer, and sample some *huerepos* (small dried, salted fish) or *huitlacoche* (delicately flavored corn fungus) crêpes. A *Christmas* pageant—the *pastorela,* or comic retelling of the shepherds' journey to Bethlehem—is held nightly in the restaurant's patio from December 16 through 23. The event comes complete with mariachis, spiked punch, food, piñatas, and fireworks, and is well worth sitting outside in the nippy weather.

En Route from Tepotzotlán It is 76 miles (121 km) from Tepotzotlán to the turnoff for San Juan del Río on Route 57.

SAN JUAN DEL RÍO This town is a good place to purchase a wide range of handicrafts and choose from extensive selections of semi-precious stones. For additional details, see the *Nuevo Laredo to Mexico City* route.

En Route from San Juan del Río Drive northeast about 12 miles (19 km) on Route 120 to Tequisquiapan.

TEQUISQUIAPAN The mineral hot springs and resorts of this village attract travelers seeking rest and relaxation. For additional details, see the *Nuevo Laredo to Mexico City* route.

En Route from Tequisquiapan Return to San Juan del Río. From here to Querétaro, a distance of 43 miles (72 km) northwest on Route 57, numerous roadside stands offer cheese, butter, cream, candied fruit, sausages, and *cajeta,* a sweet, thick syrup made of caramel and goat's milk. Thanks to mass production, *cajeta* is now available in jars in supermarkets all over Mexico. It comes in wine, vanilla, and other flavors. Known for their sweet tooth, Mexicans spread *cajeta* on bread or dinner rolls or eat it by the spoonful; however, the best way to savor *cajeta* is in crêpes—most good restaurants serve them, and the waiters will usually flambée them in tequila at your table if you ask.

Another delicacy often sold with *cajeta* is *rompope,* a yellow liqueur that tastes similar to eggnog. (The *rompope* made in Mexico generally has a low alcoholic content compared with that of rum.) Like eggnog, *rompope* is often served during the *Christmas* season.

This part of the route is a wine-and-cheese circuit well traveled by Mexico City residents on one-day outings. The best cheeses are produced by the El Sauz company, which has stands on both sides of the road. Their *patagrás,* originally a Cuban cheese, is excellent. Other good choices are *manchego,* gouda, *holandés,* and *asadero* or *tipo Oaxaca,* used for baked dishes. Productos Walter, whose original owners came from Switzerland, also makes very good cheeses. The company has a selection of approximately the same kinds of cheeses as El Sauz, as well as butter and cream. There is hardly a more Mexican activity than sampling the wine and cheese along this leg of the Bajío route; not to do so would be to miss one of its chief pleasures.

If you prefer to bypass Querétaro and go directly to San Miguel de Allende (see below), take the turnoff marked "San Miguel Vía Corta" (Short Route to San Miguel) about 5 miles (8 km) before Querétaro.

QUERÉTARO A city of 1.3 million people, Querétaro is one of the principal centers of Spanish colonial architecture in the Bajío region, and both literally and figuratively an important crossroads in Mexican history. For additional details, see the *Ciudad Juárez to Mexico City* route.

En Route from Querétaro To continue counterclockwise through the Bajío, head north on Route 57 toward San Luis Potosí. On the right, you will pass the Cerro de las Campanas (Hill of the Bells), where Emperor Maximilian was executed, and then several multinational manufacturing plants and the burgeoning Querétaro industrial park. About 17 miles (28 km) from Querétaro is a junction with Route 111, at which you turn left to San Miguel de Allende. The road passes a lake formed by a dam, goes through extensive cornfields, winds up into the hills, and crosses the state line into Guanajuato. Then you suddenly drop down a winding, hillside, cobblestone street into San Miguel de Allende. Make sure your car's brakes are in good order.

SAN MIGUEL DE ALLENDE For a complete description of the city, its restaurants, and its hotels, see *San Miguel de Allende* in THE CITIES.

En Route from San Miguel de Allende The 18th-century *Santuario de Atotonilco* is about 8 miles (13 km) from San Miguel de Allende on Route 51, on the way to Dolores Hidalgo (12 miles/19 km northwest of San Miguel). The sanctuary was the first stop of the disheveled Army of Independence, under the leadership of Padre Hidalgo and Ignacio Allende, on its march to San Miguel. At the sanctuary, Hidalgo seized the banner of the Virgin of Guadalupe, which his army carried into battle against the Spanish. The mystic quality of the Virgin helped attract indigenous followers to the cause. The sanctuary is actually a complex of six connected chapels and a lofty assembly hall decorated with a great deal of gold leaf, silver, and flamboyant frescoes. The sanctuary also contains a large collection of early pagan-Christian native art.

DOLORES HIDALGO This town (pop. 112,000) is best known for its parish church, whose bells Padre Hidalgo rang in 1810 to convene an army and declare independence from Spain. For additional details, see the *Ciudad Juárez to Mexico City* route.

En Route from Dolores Hidalgo Route 110 is a well-paved but tricky, twisting mountain road that can easily overheat a car's brakes. Don't try to break any speed records here. Guanajuato, the next stop, is 32 miles (54 km) west.

GUANAJUATO For a complete description of the city, its hotels, and its restaurants, see *Guanajuato* in THE CITIES.

En Route from Guanajuato Take Route 110 southeast for 15 miles (24 km) to the Route 45 toll road, from which it's another 59 miles (94 km) to Celaya.

CELAYA One of the Bajío's most important urban areas, this city (pop. 345,000) is known for its colorful street vendors, who offer fresh strawberries, *cajeta,* and *jícama,* a tasty white root similar to turnips that can be eaten raw. Mexicans eat *jícama* in slices, often sprinkled with powdered (and fiery!) *chile piquín,* and lime juice.

Celaya also is renowned for its antiques. There are, however, many modern pieces being passed off as antiques—would-be buyers beware.

The *Templo del Carmen* (Temple—or Church—of the Virgin of Mt. Carmel; Calle Madero and Obregón; no phone) is considered to be the masterpiece of Celaya's illustrious architect, sculptor, painter, poet, and engraver, Francisco Eduardo Tresguerras (1759–1833). Set on a slim rectangular lot, it has a single central tower, behind which a long nave ends in a dome. Viewed from the corner, the church is symmetrical, with a clean, neoclassical elegance unusual in Mexico. The present building was rebuilt in 1807 after a fire destroyed the original church in 1802.

The *Iglesia y Convento de San Francisco* (Church and Convent of St. Francis; Calles Madero and Guadalupe) was originally built in the 17th century, then substantially rebuilt by Tresguerras. The master architect is buried here in a chapel he designed. The façade of the church has four Ionic columns and an entablature topped by a curved frontispiece, also rare in this part of the world. A three-tiered bell tower stands to the left of the entrance, while the end of the nave is topped by an egg-shaped cupola.

Celaya's Jardín Principal (Main Plaza) has manicured trees that have grown together to form a large overhead hedge; in the center of the square, the trees form a circle. In the early evening, hundreds of chattering birds come to roost here.

En Route from Celaya Return to the Route 45 toll road headed west. (Don't take the old road, which is invariably filled with slow trucks wending their way through cornfields and cow pastures.) At Salamanca, 28 miles (45 km) farther, the fields turn into petrochemical plants serving the Pemex oil refinery, one of the largest in Latin America.

SALAMANCA Besides the oil refinery, the *Convento y Iglesia de San Agustín* (Convent and Church of St. Augustine; Revolución and Andrés Delgado), also called *San Juan,* is Salamanca's chief attraction. The convent was founded in 1615; the church wasn't completed until 1750. The balustrade of the presbytery and communion altar is similar to that of the *Catedral Metropolitana* in Mexico City and is said to have been brought from Macao. The style is Chinese, and it contains gold, silver, and bronze. The pulpit, filigreed with wood and ivory, was also reportedly transported from Macao. The front is lined from top to bottom with paintings depicting the devil, paradise, the four races, and the four elements.

En Route from Salamanca Take Route 43 south for 13 miles (22 km) to Valle de Santiago.

VALLE DE SANTIAGO Known as the "country of the seven fires" because of its once-active volcanoes, the area around Valle de Santiago has green farmlands that provide a striking contrast to adjacent stark areas of rough volcanic rock. Some of the dormant craters here have filled with water, forming lakes that are used for swimming, rowing, canoeing, or fishing. One such lake, La Alberca, is in a dormant volcano that rises more than 8,000 feet from the valley floor. It is some 2,400 feet in diameter, and its deep inner pool changes colors according to the seasons of the year. The crater's sides have fissures of basalt rock, and its slopes are covered with different kinds of cactus. Craters that have not filled with water can be explored on foot; hire a guide in Valle de Santiago.

Every year thousands of waterfowl visit the Hoya de Rincón de Parangueo during their annual migration south, making the site a favorite place for duck hunters; it's 6 miles (10 km) west of Valle de Santiago on a dirt road, then almost 2 miles (3 km) farther on a turnoff. The forest area on the crater's slopes is home to badgers, coyotes, and foxes, all of which can be hunted in their respective seasons (for information on hunting seasons, regulations, and restrictions, see *Hunting* in DIVERSIONS). Also nearby are the Hoya de Cintora, a saltwater crater lake, and Hoya de Flores, with ruins of a pre-Hispanic ceremonial center on the edge. To get to the craters, take the road from Valle de Santiago to Huarapo, then turn left at Km 5.5, about 3½ miles (6 km) from town. On the way back, you can stop off at Yuríria; backtrack to Route 43; go south 30 miles (48 km) to Uriangato (see below) and then east on the local road about 10 miles (16 km).

YURÍRIA Alongside the lake of the same name, this town is the site of the fortress-like former Augustinian *Convento de San Pablo* (Convent of St. Paul), built by Fray Diego de Chávez y Alvarado in 1556 and today a national monument. The structure's façade is said to be the most richly ornamented in the country and is often compared to the *Convento de Acolman,* on the road to Teotihuacán, near Mexico City. Yuríria's lake, with a dam constructed under Fray Chávez's supervision in 1548, supports swimming, fishing, rowing, and regattas.

En Route from Yuríria Returning to Route 43 and continuing south, you pass through two small villages, Uriangato and Moroleón. Uriangato is famous for its rebozos (shawls), bedspreads, and woolen sweaters. Nearby Moroleón also has excellent woven goods. A 2-mile causeway crosses mirrorlike Lago Cuitzeo, where fishermen can be seen in dugout canoes. Continue to Morelia, 35 miles (56 km) from Moroleón.

MORELIA For a complete description of the city, its hotels, and its restaurants, see *Morelia* in THE CITIES.

En Route from Morelia Drive west on Route 15 about 9 miles (15 km) to Quiroga. At Quiroga, head south 15 miles (24 km) to Pátzcuaro.

PÁTZCUARO A town that shouldn't be missed. The Tarasco, who founded Pátzcuaro in 1324, developed a rich artisan tradition that continues today, and you'll find beautifully made handicrafts here. For additional details, see *The West Coast: Nogales to Mexico City*.

En Route from Pátzcuaro Return to Morelia the way you came and pick up the road to Maravatio, which leads to the road to Atlacomulco (these roads are unnumbered, but signposts point the way). At the town of Atlacomulco—112 miles (69 km) east of Morelia—head south on Route 55 for 40 miles (64 km) to Toluca. The journey will take about four hours.

TOLUCA This city (pop. 500,000) has many clean, quaint 1890s buildings, as well as some from the colonial period. For additional details, see *The West Coast: Nogales to Mexico City*.

En Route from Toluca Take Carretera Valle de Bravo west for 50 miles (80 km) to Valle de Bravo.

VALLE DE BRAVO This is a charming village of cobblestone streets and thatch-roofed houses set into the pine-covered hills surrounding Lago Avándaro, the large, artificial lake that forms part of the vast hydroelectrical system that furnishes electricity to the valley of Mexico.

"Valle," as it is known, is something of an artists' colony, and has become a favorite weekend retreat for well-to-do Mexican families. Market day is Sunday, when the streets around the plaza become crowded with vendors from surrounding villages who come into town to sell produce and handicrafts, including a distinctive brown pottery, stoneware, and colorfully embroidered textiles. Hang gliding is also popular, and sailing and windsurfing are practiced on the lake. (Sailboats and windsurfing equipment are available for rent at some of the clubs around the lake.)

Two excellent places to eat in the vicinity are the restaurant in the *Avándaro* hotel (see *Best en Route*) and the very popular *Patio de Valle*

(Calle Francisco González Bocanegra; phone: 726-20954 or 726-21574), in the patio of a lovely old home, a half-block from the plaza.

En Route from Valle de Bravo Retrace the route to Toluca, then travel east on Route 15 for 40 miles (64 km) back to Mexico City.

BEST EN ROUTE

At the hotels along this route described as expensive, expect to pay $65 or more per night for a double room; moderate, $30 to $60; and inexpensive, $30 or less. All hotels have air conditioning, telephones, and TV sets in the rooms unless otherwise indicated. For each location, hotels are listed alphabetically by price category.

CELAYA

Celaya Plaza Here are 150 rooms, a coffee shop, a restaurant, a bar, a disco, a tennis court, a health spa, and a pool. Blvd. Adolfo López Mateos Pte. and Carretera Panamericana, also called Rte. 45 (phone: 461-46149; fax: 461-46869). Moderate.

Isabel This 80-room hotel, remodeled in 1995, is closer to the center of town than the *Mary* (below). A lovely pink marble fountain bubbles in the center of the lobby. There's a restaurant but no air conditioning; a small fee is charged for use of the garage. 207C Calle Hidalgo (phone: 461-22095). Inexpensive.

Mary A good place for drivers, since the covered parking area is locked at night. There are 125 rooms with window fans (but no air conditioning) and a good restaurant. It's popular with families traveling the Mexico City–to–Guadalajara route. Blvd. Adolfo López Mateos and Zaragoza (phone: 461-20450 or 461-20497; fax: 461-30250). Inexpensive.

MOROLEÓN

Moroleón Plaza This modern 54-room complex has a restaurant-bar and a good-size pool. López Bermúdez and 12 de Octubre (phone: 466-74400 or 466-74450). Moderate.

Posada Carreta A pool, a restaurant, tennis and basketball courts, and a bar are the facilities at this 24-room hotel. Km 1 of Rte. 43 to Morelia (phone: 466-71090). Moderate.

VALLE DE BRAVO

Avándaro Popular with weekend visitors, this charming hostelry has 108 elegantly rustic cabins with window fans (but no air conditioning), plus a pool, a restaurant, a bar, horseback riding, an excellent 18-hole golf course, a spa, and two tennis courts. Vega del Río, in Avándaro, a suburb 7½ miles (12 km) west of Valle de Bravo (phone: 726-60366; fax: 726-60122). Expensive.

Loto Azul Forty-two bungalows are set in a lovely garden; some are equipped with saunas, Japanese tubs, and herbal steambaths. Also on the premises are a pool, a restaurant-bar, and two tennis courts. Av. Toluca (phone: 726-20796; fax: 726-20157). Expensive.

Los Arcos About three blocks up the hill from the plaza, its 25 rooms (10 with TV sets) are built around an interior patio. There's a restaurant and pool, as well as a TV room with a fireplace. 310 Calle Francisco González Bocanegra (phone: 726-20042; 5-510-2563 in Mexico City; fax: 726-21878). Inexpensive.

Mexico City to Tampico and Veracruz

One of the most interesting routes in Central Mexico, although one not frequently traveled by tourists, is a circuit from Mexico City through the cities of Pachuca, Tampico, Tuxpan, Papantla, and Veracruz. This route, which winds through a variety of terrains, has something for everyone—from mountainous pine forests to lush orchid jungles to fine beaches.

From Mexico City the drive takes you to Pachuca, the capital of the state of Hidalgo, high in pine country in the heart of the silver-mining area. The route continues across the eastern finger of the Sierra Madre, immortalized by B. Traven in *The Treasure of the Sierra Madre,* to Tampico, a colorful port city on the Gulf of Mexico. This turn-of-the-century oil boomtown is no longer booming, but its old flavor still lingers; for hunting and fishing enthusiasts, the city and its environs offer game and both salt- and freshwater varieties of fish. (See *Fishing Mexico's Rich Waters* and *Hunting* in DIVERSIONS.)

Leaving Tampico and traveling south, you'll come to Tuxpan, a fishing town at the mouth of the Río Tuxpan, another good place for angling, swimming, camping, or just relaxing on the fine, hard-sand beaches that stretch along the gulf.

The route next goes inland a bit to Papantla, the center of Mexico's vanilla industry. Papantla is nestled in a rich valley surrounded by lush vanilla orchid jungles. Nearby is *El Tajín,* the sacred city of the Totonac civilization, and its famous *Pyramid of the Niches.* Papantla is also the home of the *voladores,* or flying pole dancers, who perform their ancient ceremonial dance every weekend (weather permitting) in the town square and at other times at *El Tajín.* From Papantla, the route takes you back to the Gulf of Mexico and down to Veracruz along a beautiful stretch of coast road that wanders through picturesque villages and passes the nearby *Cempoala* (also known as *Zempoala*) ruins, part of another great Totonac city dating from the 14th and 15th centuries.

En Route from Mexico City Head northeast on Avenida Insurgentes Norte to Route 85 past the Indios Verdes (two bronze statues of Aztec warriors, now green with age), which face away from the city, ready to defend it against intruders. It is 14½ miles (23 km) from downtown Mexico City to the tollbooth where Route 85 to Pachuca begins. The road continues north over a high desert plateau; on either side are Joshua trees, smaller than those of southern California's Mojave Desert but something of a surprise

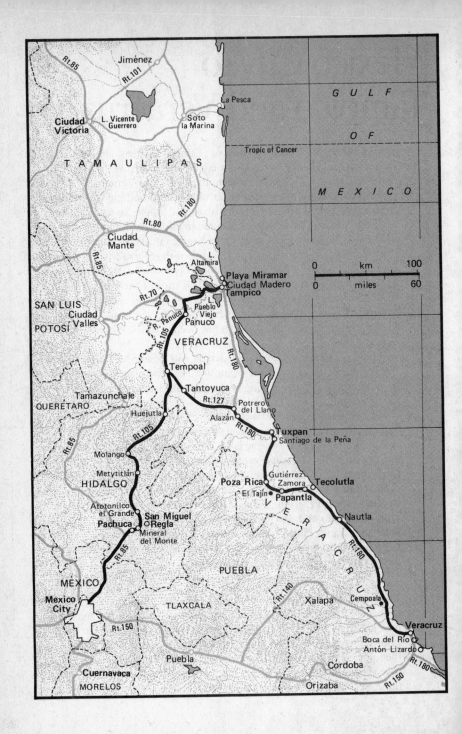

here, so close to Mexico City. From here to Pachuca, the trip is 60 miles (96 km).

PACHUCA The capital of the state of Hidalgo, Pachuca (pop. 200,000) lies at an altitude of 8,000 feet. The road into town is lined with massive contemporary bronze statuary that depicts the silver-mining activity that first attracted the Spanish to this area. Also on the road into town is a gigantic statue of revolutionary leader Emiliano Zapata, as well as a Victorian gingerbread house, constructed for a British mine administrator. It is one of the few wooden houses you will see in the high valleys of Mexico, where lumber is at a premium and bricks are less expensive.

Pachuca was founded in 1534, on the site of an Otomí village that was under the domination of the great Aztec center of Tenochtitlán at the time of the Spanish Conquest.

In 1739, a silver vein that would eventually lead to the development of the Real del Monte mine was discovered by a muleteer, Pedro Romero de Terreros, who detected silver in the soil when he lit a fire to camp overnight. "La Vizcaína," as his discovery was called, became such a bonanza that Romero de Terreros was soon lending money to the King of Spain. After making the Crown a gift of a fully equipped warship, he was granted the title "Conde de Regla" (Count of Regla) in 1769. His generosity was felt closer to home as well, for he established schools, missions, and churches in Mexico. In 1775 the count founded the *Monte de Piedad* (National Pawnshop, literally "Mountain of Pity") in Mexico City.

The privately owned Compañía Real del Monte y Pachuca now controls the Real del Monte silver mine, which has honeycombed the mountains with 1,240 miles of tunnels. Some of these tunnels emerge from vertical shafts at the town of Mineral del Monte, on a mountainside above Pachuca. The town still supplies approximately 10% to 15% of the world's silver; area mines have been successfully operated by Spanish, English, Mexican, and US firms since the 16th century.

In 1826, a wave of British immigration began: 250 families were imported from Cornwall, England, to work Pachuca's mines and, during the next 100 years, thousands more British miners arrived. Vestiges of their influence can be seen in the high peaked roofs of many of the structures in the town of Mineral del Monte; in the many Cornish names found in the area; in a Cornish cemetery; and in the meat pies, known as pasties, that are a local specialty. Pachuca's Cornish miners also introduced soccer to the New World.

In town, the two most obvious symbols of British influence are the *Torre del Reloj* and the *Iglesia Metodista* (Methodist church). The 130-foot clock tower, inaugurated in 1910 and built as a tribute to the British settlers, is a replica of London's Big Ben. It's located in the Plaza Independencia, in the northeastern part of the city; the church is on Calle Matamoros, facing the plaza.

Inside Pachuca's contemporary *Palacio de Gobierno* (Statehouse) is a replica of the three-paneled fresco presented to the *United Nations General Assembly* in 1974 by Luis Echeverría, President of Mexico at the time. The slightly surrealistic mural, by Pachuca artist Jesús Becerril, depicts the liberation of mankind to be realized by the signing of the Charter of Economic Rights and Duties of Nations. The artist gave some of the delegates the faces of people who actually attended the signing; others are drawn from history. Among the famous faces in the fresco are those of Archbishop Makarios, Pope Paul VI, Fidel Castro, Gerald Ford, Queen Elizabeth II, and Indira Gandhi. The mural brings together such diverse historical figures as Columbus, Emperor Cuauhtémoc (the last Aztec ruler), 17th-century Mexican nun and poet Sor Juana Inés de la Cruz, the heroes of Mexican independence, and Benito Juárez, restorer of the republic after the final defeat of the French in 1867. The building is on the Plaza Cívica, at the intersection of Avenida Juárez and Fernando Soto.

History buffs will enjoy the collection of photographs chronicling Mexico's history from the late 19th to the early 20th century displayed in the *Archivo Fotográfico Exclaustro, Colección Casasola* (Casasola Archives) in the 16th-century former *Convento de San Francisco* on Calle Hidalgo, along Plaza Bartolomé de Medina. The archive, which includes a large collection of 20th-century photographer Tina Modotti's work, is closed Mondays; no admission charge (no phone). The *Museo de la Historia Regional,* also in the former *Convento de San Francisco,* has several halls displaying Hidalgo folk arts and photographs (no phone).

In the large square between the *Palacio de Gobierno* and the small, neo-classical replica of the old *Teatro Bartolomé de Medina* (now the *Teatro de la Ciudad*) stands a large bronze statue of Benito Juárez sculpted by Juan Leonardo Cordero and dedicated in 1957.

About 10 miles (16 km) north of Pachuca is *Parque Nacional El Chico,* a camping spot of unequaled beauty. *El Chico* may well be the only forest in Mexico where the grass is mowed every week. Horses can be rented here, and there is a government-run hostel in the park. Check with the Pachuca tourist office (Centro Minero, Km 93.5 of the Carretera México-Pachuca, on the southern edge of town; phone: 771-13806 and 771-14237); it's closed weekends.

Food in Pachuca is acceptable. Try *Noriega* (305 Matamoros; phone: 771-51591), which offers a wide range of dishes and serves a particularly good breakfast.

En Route from Pachuca Head north from the Plaza Independencia on Route 105 to Mineral del Monte, where you can see the elevator towers and one of the main entrances to the Real del Monte mine. About 13 miles (22 km) farther along the winding mountain road is the picturesque town of Huasca, and 4 miles (6 km) farther is San Miguel Regla, where Route 105 becomes a well-paved mountain road. Crossing the Sierra, it passes through such small towns as Atotonilco el Grande, Metytitlán, and Molango, a mining town at the site of one of the largest manganese ore deposits in the Western Hemisphere.

At the town of Huejutla, take a left on Route 105 to Pánuco and Tampico; it joins Route 127 after about 32 miles (52 km). Here, take a left to Tempoal and then proceed downhill toward Tampico. Along the way you'll see oil wells operating in what were Mexico's very first oil fields, vividly described in the opening chapters of *The Treasure of the Sierra Madre. A caveat:* Don't drive the Pachuca-Tampico stretch of Route 105 at night, when there are often heavy fogs or rain. Stay over in Pachuca or San Miguel Regla instead.

TAMPICO The largest city in the state of Tamaulipas, Tampico (pop. 500,000) is a busy port and petroleum-refining center. The town enjoyed a boom at the turn of the century, when oil was discovered in the region, but the international flavor of those days is largely gone. However, Tampico still offers a variety of things to do and see to those willing to dig a bit beneath the somewhat commercial surface.

Tampico was founded in 1533 on the site of a Huastec settlement that was destroyed by the forces of Cortés in 1523. In 1560 a Franciscan monastery was completed, and the town became known as San Luis de Tampico. The oldest buildings in modern Tampico, however, date from only the late 19th century; earlier structures fell victim to the periodic hurricanes and flooding of Río Pánuco, which at times rises 15 feet above its normal level. Weather conditions in Tampico are erratic at best. Strong afternoon winds often blow off the river. The hot, humid season begins in April and reaches its height in July and August, with rains bringing some relief in September. Beginning in November, and sometimes extending through January and occasionally into February, is the hurricane season, when strong, cold winds blow through the area, lasting anywhere from a day to a week.

Most of the nighttime action and port atmosphere for which Tampico is famous occurs around the Plaza de la Libertad, a block from the waterfront. The plaza is bordered by Calles Madero, Rivera (sometimes Ribera on street signs), Juárez, and Aduana.

Facing the plaza, the *Palacio* (401 Rivera Ote.; no phone) is the kind of place Tennessee Williams and Ernest Hemingway would have frequented (not, one hopes, on the same evening). Founded in 1897, until the mid 1980s it had the reputation of a wild seaman's saloon; it also served as the rowdy movie set for *The Treasure of the Sierra Madre.* Women (as long as they're tourists) are occasionally allowed in the saloon, but there are tables and chairs on the wide porch facing Calle Rivera, where a mixed group can get courteous service. (Groups of women are likely to be targets of persistent pick-up attempts.)

Tampico bars are the venue for an extraordinary parade of itinerant vendors; in a typical night you're likely to encounter a man selling pens and lighters, a fellow from Veracruz displaying kerchiefs embroidered by Totonac women, a lad selling lottery tickets, a newsboy hawking local papers, a shoeshine boy, and a young man in the white dress of the Totonac selling scorpion-shaped figures fashioned from vanilla-bean stalks. Habitués are often serenaded by a vocalist accompanied by wandering musicians.

Walk south from the plaza on Fray Andrés de Olmos past the *Inglaterra* hotel (see *Best en Route*) to Calle Rivera, where the street dips down toward the riverbank. As steep as any in San Francisco, California, this section of Rivera is lined with stands selling a wide range of shiny merchandise, including flashlights, pocket mirrors, knives, cosmetics, and portable radios, many of them made in Hong Kong and Japan.

At Calle Pedro Méndez is the beginning of the public market, which sprawls across a full city block and spills into the adjacent streets. This is the place to choose from all manner of fresh produce, including the huge, beautiful avocados grown in Tamaulipas and northern Veracruz. The market area still retains some of the flavor of older and better days. Venerable buildings with fake balconies and cast-iron grillwork line Calle Pedro Méndez; this area, along with the closed hotels along the Plaza de la Libertad, gives Tampico some of the flavor of old New Orleans.

North of the market, beneath the portals of Calle Rivera, you will come upon the desks of *evangelistas* (public scribes), who, for a fee, help the illiterate and the poor (and anyone else who pays them) write letters, fill out tax forms, or complete documents. East of the market past the long, Victorian customs house is the railroad station, an ersatz mission-style monstrosity with hand-painted Talavera tiles set in the lower inside walls. Here, an iron bell is still rung by hand to announce train departures. The telegraph office in the station (for railroad use only) still relies on ancient equipment; it's worth a look for antique buffs. The great flood of 1955 left its mark on the walls of the waiting room and in the telegraph office, where the water rose eight feet high.

Near the train station are Tampico's wharves, where ships from Eastern Europe and South America, as well as Mexican freighters, can be seen.

Tampico's main square and daytime social center is the Plaza de Armas, bordered by Calles Emiliano Carranza, Díaz Mirón, Colón, and Fray Andrés de Olmos. The plaza is a peaceful park shaded by slim palms, Oriental elms, and other trees and enlivened by squirrels, ravens, and pigeons. The bandstand in the center of the plaza is called the *Kiosco Monumental Tampico.* A pink concrete curiosity of Moorish provenance (twisted candy-cane columns on the inside and blue and yellow mosaic on the dome, which is supported by eight enormous, incongruous flying buttresses), it was dedicated in 1945. The bandstand is the focal point of Mardi Gras *Carnaval* celebrations, usually held during the first two weeks of February.

On the north side of the plaza is Tampico's *Catedral,* which was constructed in 1931 with funds donated by Edward L. Doheny and his wife. Doheny, the California oil tycoon who was linked with the Teapot Dome scandal of 1923–24, had extensive oil interests in the Tampico region until the expropriation of foreign holdings in 1938. *El Globito* (no phone), on the plaza, offers root beer and the juice of fresh oranges, carrots, strawberries, or anything else that happens to be in season and can fit in a blender.

The modest restaurants in the downtown area have some of the best and freshest seafood in Mexico. *Jaiba* (crab) is king; indeed, *tampiqueños* are known throughout Mexico as *jaibas,* a reflection on their food and not their temperaments. The people of Tampico are especially friendly to foreigners, particularly visitors from the United States, who have been coming to Tampico since oil was discovered at the turn of the century. Incongruously, most longtime Tampico residents conclude deals by announcing, "All right!"

One of Tampico's best seafood houses is the inexpensive *Mariscos Diligencia* (415 Rivera Ote., on the corner of Calle César López de Lara, two blocks from Plaza de la Libertad; phone: 83-137642). If the weather is really hot, sit in the air conditioned rear section. Start with oysters on the half shell or raw crab and go on to a shellfish plate called *fuente de mariscos frescos,* or *carne a la tampiqueña,* Tampico's famous beef cooked in a spicy sauce. Other offerings are clams, marinated trout, hot bell peppers stuffed with crabmeat, and octopus in brine with rice. With your meal, try a can of Tecate beer. After sprinkling salt on the top of the can and squeezing lime juice over the salt, drink it straight from the can the way the locals do. The owners have a second restaurant, *Diligencias Norte* (Av. Ayuntamiento; no phone). Another downtown restaurant, *Café y Nevería Elite* (211 Díaz Mirón Ote.; 83-120364), offers inexpensive specialties, including a *comida corrida* (fixed-price full meal) at lunchtime. It's a good place for breakfast or dinner, too; the menu, in English and Spanish, includes hotcakes with bacon, hamburgers with onion rings, steaks, and, naturally, a variety of fish and seafood. Locals consider *Jardín Corona* (1915 Av. Miguel Hidalgo; no phone) the city's finest restaurant; it has seafood, steaks, and its own rendition of *carne a la tampiqueña.*

Downtown Tampico is the place for antiques collectors to browse. Stop in at *El Porvenir* (1401 Hidalgo; no phone) for a drink and a look at the owner's collection of antique bottles. *Bazar Numismático y Filatélico* (201 Fray Andrés de Olmos Nte.; no phone) carries a rather limited selection of old clocks, telephones, ceramics, stamps, and currency. If you're interested in chinoiserie, the *Chung King* (507 Emiliano Carranza Ote., in the *Tampico* hotel; no phone) has a good assortment of Chinese porcelain.

The *Museo de la Cultura Huasteca,* in Tampico's twin city, Ciudad Madero, about 4 miles (6 km) away (in the *Instituto Tecnológico de Madero,* or Madero Technological Institute building; no phone), is a must-see. In pre-Hispanic times, the influence of the Huastec extended south from the Ohio and Mississippi valleys all the way into Guatemala. Often at war with their neighbors, they were involved in dynastic disputes in Tula that eventually led to the fall of the Toltec metropolis. The Huastec were finally made to pay tribute to the Aztec, whom they loathed so much that they allied themselves with the Spanish against Tenochtitlán. They then spent the next two decades resisting Spanish attempts at genocide. Now only about 50,000 strong, the Huastec are found primarily in parts of the states of San Luis Potosí, Veracruz, and Tamaulipas. The museum houses ancient ceramic pots; delicate terra cotta figurines; and articles made of shells, semi-precious stones, gold, silver, and copper. It's closed weekends; admission charge.

If the weather is hot, cool off at Playa Miramar, a beach only 10 minutes by car from Tampico. Drive east on Avenida Alvaro Obregón through Ciudad Madero past the Petróleos Mexicanos oil refinery, one of the country's largest. The left fork of the road approaching the beach leads north through a pine grove to a place called Pinar del Mar, where you can stay at the *Centro Recreativo* (see *Best en Route*). Take the right fork to reach Playa Miramar, several miles of sandy beach lapped by the placid gulf surf. Miraculously unpolluted by the nearby refinery, the shallow water is fine for swimming. Unfortunately, waste from the refinery has tainted the last section of Río Pánuco, which is separated from the beach by a long jetty. If you have a recreational vehicle, this is an ideal spot for camping. Separate toilet and shower facilities are available at intervals across the paved access road.

For fishing enthusiasts, the Río Pánuco and surrounding freshwater lagoons offer plentiful shad, porgies, catfish, and trout; Laguna del Chairel and Laguna del Carpintero are particularly good. There is deep-sea fishing in the Gulf of Mexico for tarpon, white sea bass, sailfish, and mackerel, among others. Fishing from the shore along the gulf is not recommended, however, since the waters are choppy and not so clean. The larger hotels will arrange fishing trips for you. Information about sport fishing (no license is required, except for a fishing vessel) can be obtained at the local fisheries offices (407 Carranza; phone: 12-122751; and 310 López Rayón and Avila Camacho; phone: 12-135737 or 12-133873). Boat rentals are available from the *Club de Regatas Corona* (at Laguna de Chairel; phone: 12-125902 or 12-137410).

Bass and tarpon tournaments are held annually, but the foremost fishing event is the *Torneo Internacional de Shad* (International Shad Fishing Tournament) in February or March. North of Tampico, at the mouth of the Río Soto la Marina, Italian investors are developing a resort area where saltwater, river, and lagoon fishing yield white sea bass, trout, saurels (yellow jack), corbinas, and porgies.

There's hunting in the Tampico area for white-tailed deer from early December through late January (special permit required); duck and quail from late October through mid-February; coyotes from early December through January; white-wing doves from mid-August through mid-November; geese from late October through February; and rabbits from mid-August through March. Quail and deer can be hunted in the Laguna Altamira; ducks in the Escondida, Jancal, and Pueblo Viejo lagoons; and duck, coyotes, and deer at the Laguna Chila. For more information, see *Hunting* in DIVERSIONS.

Information on hunting and other tourist activities is also available from Tampico's tourist office, located downtown (218 Calle 20 de Noviembre Nte.; phone: 12-122668 or 12-120007). It's closed Sundays.

En Route from Tampico The next stop is Tuxpan, 110 miles (177 km) south, and there are two possible ways to get there from Tampico. One is Route 180, which runs close to the coast but doesn't provide much in the way of scenery. It's more interesting to take Route 105 and then 127 to Route 180. The stretch from Tempoal (where you pick up Rte. 127) is paved, but it is constantly being beaten out of shape by the hundreds of oil trucks that drive on it. However, the scenery is well worth the bumps; you will pass through the rich farm country of northern Veracruz state, past Tantoyuca, with its hillside houses, and on to the towns of Potrero del Llano and Alazán, where Route 127 joins Route 180. If you are driving on a winter day, you will see farm girls at roadside stands selling grapefruit and tangerines on strings as well as pineapples, honey, and oranges at unbelievably low prices (at press time, six pounds of oranges were going for about 15 pesos, or $1.95).

TUXPAN Sometimes spelled Tuxpam by traditionalists, this clean, pretty town (pop. 120,000) is a good place to fish, swim, or just soak up the lazy, romantic atmosphere. The *embarcadero,* or dock, is on the main street as you enter town, on the north bank of the Río Tuxpan.

On the other side of the river is Santiago de la Peña, a working class residential area. The locals pay a small fee to cross the river in small boats rather than make the long walk downriver to the bridge. The boats, some with outboard motors, will take up to eight people across the river; they can also be hired for excursions.

About 7 miles (11 km) east of town is a long stretch of beautiful, hard-sand beach, with showers and dressing rooms.

The inexpensive *Reforma* restaurant (in the *Reforma* hotel; 25 Benito Juárez; phone: 783-40210) makes a delicious salad containing both large saltwater shrimp and the smaller lagoon shrimp. For a delectable—if salty—treat, try *hueva de lisa* (striped mullet roe), which is served in thick bars, sliced, fried in butter, and sprinkled with hot sauce. *Villa Tamiahua* (134 Independencia; no phone), *Las Palmas* (Independencia, next to the bridge; phone: 783-40799), and *Los Coquitos* (on the road to the beach; no phone) are also good choices for seafood. *Trendy Fisher's* (Calle Hernández on the *malecón,* or seaside promenade; phone: 783-40392) serves rich seafood casseroles and meat and chicken dishes in an air conditioned dining room and on an outdoor patio.

During February or early March, *Carnaval* (before *Lent*) is a big event here. At the end of June, Mexicans and foreigners alike pour into town for the *Pesca Internacional del Sábalo* (Annual Tarpon Tournament). August brings the annual *Feria y Exposición Regional,* an agricultural and livestock fair.

En Route from Tuxpan Head south on Route 180 for about 50 miles (80 km) to Papantla.

PAPANTLA Nestled in a rich mountain valley, the city (pop. 130,000) is surrounded by lush jungles fragrant with the aroma of the vanilla orchid. Papantla is one of the world's largest vanilla producers. As you enter the city from the north you will see a gingerbread Gothic church perched on the side of the hill on your left. This twin-spired edifice, with its vaulted ceiling, is the *Santuario del Cristo Rey* (Sanctuary of Christ the King); it boasts more than two dozen brilliant stained glass windows, as well as tropical hardwood doors carved in high relief.

The Totonac, descendants of the great pre-Hispanic civilization, have become relatively wealthy here, thanks to the vanilla industry. Their cultural heritage has been maintained in a beautiful ceremony featuring *voladores* (flying pole dancers). One of the most spectacular ritual displays in Mexico, the dance is also one of the few ancient religious ceremonies that survived efforts to eradicate the indigenous culture by the Spanish, who were duped into believing the ceremony was a sporting event. In the dance, the five participants, dressed in red velvet pants, embroidered white shirts, and cone-shaped headdresses made of eagle or macaw feathers, dance their way to the pole as the group's "captain" plays a haunting melody on a flute, a drum, or both. The dancers climb 100 feet to take their places on the frame balanced atop the pole. They are followed by the captain, who performs a dance and then sits on a tiny platform in the center. The dancers let their bodies fall backward into space, and the ropes tied around them begin to unwind, leaving them free to "fly" around the pole, arms extended. They slowly circle the pole 13 times, to represent the four periods of 13 years that made up the ancient Totonac life cycle of 52 years.

The dance is now performed every weekend (weather permitting) at the ruins of *El Tajín* (no phone), the sacred city built by the ancestors of the present-day Totonac. Located 8 miles (13 km) southwest of Papantla on a mostly paved road, the site is open daily; admission charge. For additional details, see *Mexico's Magnificent Archaeological Heritage* in DIVERSIONS.

The Totonac are also known for their beautiful clothing, particularly the men's long, full white pants that tie at the ankle. These "pantaloons" are both picturesque and practical, for the jungle abounds in chiggers. When you visit *El Tajín,* you should take care to wear long pants with narrow cuffs or tie the bottoms, Totonac-style. If you stick to roads, paths, and fully cleared areas, you ought to be able to avoid these maddening little insects.

The Totonac are Mexico's only polygamous people. The wealthier men keep up to five wives, and in some cases a young boy, to sate their sexual appetites. In addition, the Totonac produce some of the most realistic ceremonial masks in the country. The beautiful masks are covered with a thin coating of plaster and painted in lifelike tones.

On either side of Route 180 in Papantla there are stores selling animal figures, baskets, and other aromatic and decorative items woven from the long pods of the vanilla bean. They are often used as sachets in closets and bureau drawers.

En Route from Papantla Route 180 now leads back to the coast through prosperous-looking citrus groves and banana and coconut plantations visible from the road. From here to journey's end in Veracruz, 135 miles (217 km) south, the highway runs right along the gulf, where sandbars create lagoons of shallow water and small, placid waves. Even in the winter (except when the *nortes*—cold winds from the north—are blowing), the warm breeze that blows shoreward off the water often tempts people to roll up their trousers and wade, or even to go for a moonlight swim. This beautiful stretch of coast is dotted with small hotels and motor courts that do their best business during *Semana Santa* (Holy Week); May, July, August, and December; and the mid-September *Día de la Independencia* (Independence Day) holiday. Most of these places are open all year.

Tecolutla, an enticing, palm-fringed beach about 19 miles (30 km) south of Papantla, is one of the few good east coast beaches. Although it shows signs of deterioration from its palmier resort days, it remains a quiet spot to enjoy warm water and a relaxed atmosphere. For more information, see *Best Beaches off the Beaten Path* in DIVERSIONS.

About 29 miles (40 km) south of Palma Sola, on a turnoff to the right, are the *Cempoala* (also known as *Zempoala*) ruins. *Cempoala* (no phone) was the last capital of the great Totonac civilization, built much later than *El Tajín,* in the 14th and 15th centuries. There are pyramids and several temples, among them one that resembles the *Pyramid of the Sun* in Teotihuacán. The site is closed Mondays; admission charge.

About 52 miles (84 km) south of Nautla is the controversial Laguna Verde nuclear power plant, the object of sporadic protests ever since its construction began in the early 1980s. It is now complete and partially on-line.

VERACRUZ For a detailed report on the city, its hotels, and its restaurants, see *Veracruz* in THE CITIES.

BEST EN ROUTE

For a double room at an expensive hotel, expect to pay $95 to $160 per night; at a moderate one, $65 to $90; at an inexpensive one, $35 to $60; and at a very inexpensive one, less than $30. Unless otherwise noted, all hotels listed below have air conditioning, TV sets, and telephones in the rooms. For each location, hotels are listed alphabetically by price category.

PACHUCA

Calinda Pachuca Set in a beautiful garden, this modern hotel-country club is (so far) undiscovered by foreign tourists. It has 112 rooms, two junior suites, and three presidential suites with Jacuzzis, along with a restaurant, a bar, a thermal pool, a tennis court, and a nine-hole golf course. Km 8.5 of Rte. 85 (phone: 771-39911; 800-228-5151 in the US; 800-90000 in Mexico; fax: 771-39896). Expensive.

Emily A bright hostelry with 30 large rooms and a dining room. There's no air conditioning, but the climate is brisk and breezy. Calle Hidalgo, facing Plaza Independencia (phone: 771-50816 or 771-50849; fax: 771-51964). Moderate.

De los Baños An older, well-kept hotel with 60 rooms and a restaurant. Again, no air conditioning, but a cool climate. 205 Matamoros (phone: 771-30700 or 771-30701; fax: 771-51441). Very inexpensive.

SAN MIGUEL REGLA

Hacienda San Miguel Regla Picturesquely situated in a pine grove next to the ruins of Pedro Romero de Terreros's famous silver smelter, this rather exclusive hotel has 53 rooms and cottages, plus a restaurant. There is hiking, horseback riding, and trout fishing right outside the entrance, and nearby are pools from the old refinery and a waterfall. Just north of town (phone: 5-651-6369 in Mexico City; fax: 5-550-4706 in Mexico City). Expensive.

Hacienda Santa María Regla The second of the former haciendas of the Conde de Regla, dating from the 1840s, is now a hotel with all the amenities of the other ex-hacienda (above), plus a much better restaurant. This is the smaller of the two, with 24 cabins and rooms. Two miles (3 km) farther north of town than *Hacienda San Miguel Regla,* on the same road (phone: 771-54400 or 771-54447; 5-550-0254 in Mexico City; fax: 5-550-4706 in Mexico City). Expensive.

TAMPICO

Camino Real Tampico This luxury hotel has 101 units surrounding a courtyard with a large pool. *El Flamboyán* restaurant is Tampico's fanciest, and there's a bar and a cafeteria. Meeting rooms, free parking, and the golf facilities of the *Club Campestre Laguna del Chairel* are available. Downtown, at 2000 Av. Hidalgo (phone: 12-138811; 800-7-CAMINO in the US; 800-90123 in Mexico; fax: 12-139226). Expensive.

Posada de Tampico Here are 130 rooms, each with two double beds, plus four suites. On the premises are a tennis court, a pool with a bar, a nightclub featuring dance music and international entertainment, the *Laguna del Chairel* restaurant, and a bar. Convention facilities also are available. The hotel will arrange hunting, fishing, golf, and tennis. On Rte. 80 (an extension of Av. Hidalgo) to Ciudad Mante, 6½ miles (10 km) northwest of downtown and 1 mile (1.6 km) southeast of the airport (phone: 12-280515; 5-533-4454 in Mexico City; fax: 12-280855). Expensive.

Centro Recreativo This small (five-bungalow) seaside hotel, little known to foreign tourists (although they're most welcome), is owned and operated by a section of the Petroleum Workers' Union. It caters primarily to Mexicans of modest means. There's a restaurant and a freshwater pool with showers; basketball courts and baseball diamonds are nearby. Also on the premises is a vegetarian spa offering weight-reduction programs and the like, with homeopathic physicians in residence. The hotel's summer season runs March through November; the winter season lasts December through February. The rooms have no air conditioning, TV sets, or telephones. About 10 minutes southeast of Tampico by car, at Pinar del Mar (no local phone; 12-150301 in Tampico). Moderate.

Inglaterra It has 130 rooms and suites, a good restaurant, and a lobby bar. Other features are parking, a rooftop heliport, and a large ballroom that offers a great view of the city. Downtown, at 116 Salvador Díaz Mirón Ote., corner of Fray Andrés de Olmos (phone: 12-125678; 800-57123 toll-free in Mexico; fax: 12-140556). Moderate.

Impala Here is a modern, 83-unit hotel with a restaurant-bar and parking. 220 Salvador Díaz Mirón Pte. (phone: 12-120990/1/2; fax: 12-120684). Inexpensive.

TUXPAN

El Tajín A hostelry with 167 rooms, suites, and villas. It also has a restaurant and bar, a discotheque, a tennis court, and a pool. Near Tuxpan, on the shores of the Río Pánuco, Km 4 of the Carretera a Cobos, a local road (phone: 783-42260; fax: 783-45429). Expensive.

Plaza This downtown 57-unit hotel also has a small restaurant. 39 Av. Benito Juárez (phone: 783-40738 or 783-40838; fax: 783-40738). Inexpensive.

PAPANTLA

El Tajín In this colorful hilltop hostelry are 60 rooms, plus a restaurant and a bar. 104 Calle Dr. José de Jesús Nuñez y Domínguez (phone/fax: 784-21062). Inexpensive.

TECOLUTLA

Flamingo A 62-unit hotel on the beach with a restaurant and a bar. Some rooms are air conditioned, and all have ceiling fans, but no telephones. 17 Aldama (phone/fax: 784-60368). Moderate.

Balneario Tecolutla A beach hotel with 72 rooms, a restaurant, a bar, a billiards room, and a freshwater pool. At the end of the road turning off Rte. 180 to Tecolutla (phone: 784-60071; fax: 784-60183). Inexpensive.

Marsol On the beachfront, this property has 52 spacious rooms, all with ceiling fans and some with air conditioning and sea views; no in-room telephones, though. There are also two swimming pools and a restaurant. Calle Aumas (phone/fax: 784-60151). Very inexpensive.

The Yucatán Peninsula

The Yucatán Peninsula encompasses the three Mexican states—Yucatán, Campeche, and Quintana Roo—that jut into the Gulf of Mexico where it joins the Caribbean Sea. Best known for the magnificent Maya-Toltec ruins at *Chichén Itzá,* the Yucatán also has a walled city that could have come right out of a late show pirate movie, outposts of an empire that novelist Graham Greene might have invented, and some of the most enchanting resorts in the entire Caribbean.

In many ways, the Yucatán is a country within a country. While Mexico's mainland is made up of hills, forests, and deserts originally settled by the Toltec and related groups, the peninsula consists of the flat jungles of the Maya. About the size of Arizona, the peninsula was isolated from the rest of Mexico for centuries; several times in the course of its history the Yucatán has in fact almost become a separate country.

Historically, the Yucatán Peninsula has been the domain of the Maya, who for countless centuries have lived not only in the Yucatán and what is now the nearby state of Chiapas, but also the countries of Guatemala, Belize, El Salvador, and Honduras. The Yucatec Maya began to emerge as a separate culture and linguistic group around 2000 BC. Archaeologists divide the Maya civilization into three periods: the Preclassic (2000 BC until AD 250), the Classic (AD 250 until AD 900), and the Postclassic (AD 900 until AD 1520). The great Maya pyramids, sculptures, and hieroglyphic inscriptions are from the Classic period, which coincided with the early Middle Ages in Europe.

The Maya were the only indigenous civilization to develop a true writing system before the arrival of the Europeans. However, except for dates and astronomical events, experts were unable to decipher the Maya hieroglyphs until quite recently; in fact, breakthroughs did not come until the late 1970s and early 1980s. (The biggest discovery was that the hieroglyphs spelled out words in the Maya language still spoken today—which earlier generations of archaeologists never realized, because they never learned spoken Maya.) Now, for the first time, scientists are able to reconstruct much of the ancient history of the Yucatán, and practically everything scholars believed to be true a generation ago has turned out to be wrong. So much outdated misinformation is still circulated by tour guides and New Age cultists that travelers who are serious about exploring the peninsula's fascinating ruins should be sure to read up on the subject first. (Two good sources are Michael Coe's *The Maya* and *Breaking the Maya Code,* both published by Thames Hudson. Prices are $24.95 for hardback, $14.95 for paperback.) In particular, tales of sacrificial virgins and a time-worshiping priest class are now considered pure nonsense.

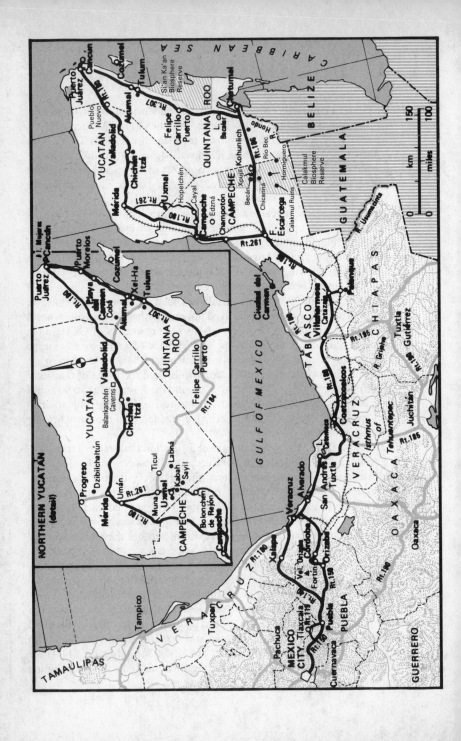

The reasons for the decline of the Classic Maya civilization and the abandonment of its great cities remain perhaps the greatest mystery to tantalize modern visitors. Architecture degenerated during the Postclassic period, and much writing was done in books rather than on stelae (large stone monuments), as in previous centuries. Tragically, almost all Maya books were destroyed by Spanish priests during the conquest; only four of the books (known as codexes) are known to exist today.

While the Yucatec Maya built some of the earliest Maya cities, including the huge Preclassic zone at Dzibilchaltún, north of present-day Mérida (see *Mérida* in THE CITIES), they are best known for cities built at the very end of the Classic period. It was then that the formerly minor city of Chichén Itzá was conquered by the Toltecs, the predominant culture of Central Mexico at the time. Under Toltec influence, the city's unique architecture developed, and Chichén Itzá became the capital of the peninsula for about two centuries. When the first Spanish conquistadores arrived in the early 16th century, however, most of the large ancient cities in the Yucatán were already abandoned. The common people lived much the same as they had during ancient times (and still do today), but no trace remained of the leadership that had built the great civilization.

Although the Maya lands were eventually occupied by the Spaniards, the Maya could claim with some justification that they were never really conquered. The first Europeans to arrive were immediately chased away. The Yucatán was finally breached by Europeans in 1517, when Francisco Hernández de Córdoba was shipwrecked on the peninsula's coast. Some 20 years after the Aztec capital of Tenochtitlán (the location of modern-day Mexico City) fell to Hernán Cortés and his army in 1521, Francisco de Montejo founded Mérida in the western Yucatán. But the surrounding area never completely fell under Spanish domination, and Mexico's independence in 1821 did little to change things. The Caste War, in which the remaining Maya people battled foreign domination, dragged on from mid-19th century through 1901.

Finally, economics did what force of arms could not. The US and European nations needed rope for their ships, and the Yucatán had an abundant supply of *henequén,* or sisal, of which rope was made. Great *henequén* plantations began to thrive, and a feudal system of land ownership developed. The Yucatán natives became peons on great Spanish haciendas. The hacienda owners were able to ignore the rest of Mexico partly because, before the age of air travel and modern highways, it was difficult to reach and partly because, as far as the aristocracy was concerned, it was not worth the effort.

Only since the 1950s has a paved highway linked the Yucatán with the rest of the country. Today, a highway system completely circles the peninsula, and driving is the best way to get a feeling for the entirety of this magnificent area—from the Gulf Coast to Mérida, from the resort area of

Cancún on the Caribbean to the inland routes passing *Chichén Itzá* and other major archaeological areas.

The Yucatán today is still vastly different from the rest of Mexico. The Yucatán accent is as distinct as a Southern drawl in the US. *Henequén,* still the area's major crop (although it's now primarily used to make rugs and is not a major revenue producer in the Yucatán economy), can be seen growing in expansive fields along the highways. In the villages, people still speak Maya, live in white thatch huts called *chozas,* and wear white garments—embroidered *huipiles* for the women, tailored *guayaberas* for the men. Almost nowhere else in Mexico are native costumes seen with such frequency as in the Yucatán. You'll see a good many Panama hats as well; they are made of straw from the *jipijapa* palm, which grows in the region.

Besides maintaining their unique costumes, the inhabitants of the Yucatán have their own distinctive fare. Pork *pibil,* baked in banana leaves, is a favorite dish, while venison and pheasant are still basic staples. Yucatán beer and ale, particularly the Montejo brand of stout, rare outside the immediate region, are prized throughout Mexico, as is *Xtabentún* (pronounced Shta-ben-*toon*), a potent honey-and-anise liqueur. Teetotalers will want to sample *soldado* (soldier), a local chocolate-flavored soft drink available across the peninsula.

Plan your journey carefully. Places to eat are scarce, as are places to spend the night. You can't count on pulling into a roadside hotel when you get weary of driving. You should know where you expect to arrive at the end of each day and about how long it will take to get there. As donkeys and cows are fond of turning highways into after-hours barnyards, night driving should be avoided.

Travelers have a choice of two routes at the start of this tour of the Yucatán. One starts in Mérida, the other in Mexico City. From Mérida, you'll head southwest via Uxmal and Campeche, while the route from Mexico City takes you along the Gulf of Mexico, a jungle route through coffee country, banana plantations, fishing villages, coastal boomtowns, and a river port out of a novel. The two routes converge in the town of Francisco Escárcega (see *Francisco Escárcega to Chichén Itzá,* below). From there, you'll head northeast to the town of Chetumal, then north along the Caribbean coast, and then west across the peninsula to Mérida.

MÉRIDA ROUTE

MÉRIDA It's possible to fly directly into Mérida and then rent a car in town. For a detailed report on the city, its hotels, and its restaurants, see *Mérida* in THE CITIES.

En Route from Mérida The drive directly to Francisco Escárcega, 220 miles (352 km) southwest, takes about six hours. That leaves time to poke around the Maya ruins at *Uxmal* (pronounced Oosh-*mal*), about 50 miles (80 km) south of Mérida, and still get to Campeche by dusk. If you have time to spend the night in *Uxmal,* you should also plan to see the ruins of *Edzná,* which will add at least 25 miles (40 km) to your trip.

To get to *Uxmal,* head southwest on Route 180. Just beyond Mérida, take the left-hand fork at a town called Umán and keep going for about 30 miles (48 km) to Muna, where the road divides again. Bear right. These instructions may seem overly explicit, but Mexico is not a country in which to depend on road signs. Whenever there is any doubt, ask and ask again. Language is no barrier. If the response to "Uxmal?" is a shaking head or wagging finger, turn around.

UXMAL Although you can make it to Campeche the same day, you will probably want to spend the night at *Uxmal* if you have the time. Apart from the exotic appeal of staying at an inn adjacent to an abandoned Maya city, you'll have a chance to see the nightly (except Mondays) sound-and-light show, presented in Spanish at 7 PM and in English at 9 PM. The script offers a fascinating explanation of Maya artistic symbolism in an entertaining blend of history, myth, and legend, and the lighting is spectacular. For additional details, see *Mexico's Magnificent Archaeological Heritage* in DIVERSIONS. The *Uxmal* ruins are open daily; no admission charge on Sundays (no phone).

From *Uxmal,* you can also visit the archaeological sites at *Kabah* (undergoing major restorations—likely to continue for years—at press time), *Sayil,* and *Labná,* along the border separating the states of Yucatán and Campeche. Take the paved road from *Uxmal* to these remote ruins; all are open daily; no admission charge on Sundays (no phone). Styles intermingle at these sites. The Maya of Campeche built in what is called the *Puuc,* or Hill, style; the Maya of Yucatán proper created the *Chen,* or Well, forms. Both architectural styles are pure Maya, with no Toltec influence. In the 1840s, explorer John Lloyd Stephens clambered around these ruins and wrote of his experiences in his fascinating *Incidents of Travel in Yucatán.* The suffering endured by Stephens during his visit to the *Uxmal* area seems incredible, but if you get to *Sayil* and *Labná,* you might well come away convinced that little has changed. Since there are no accommodations here, you will have to head back to *Uxmal,* where there are extremely comfortable hotels in jungle settings (see *Best en Route*).

For more information on the sites mentioned above, call or visit Mérida's tourist office, which is open daily (*Teatro Peón Contreras,* 59 Calle 60; phone: 99-249290).

En Route from Uxmal Route 261 runs south 150 miles (241 km) to Campeche. You may want to stop at the *Bolonchén de Rejón,* a series of caverns about 34 miles (55 km) south of *Uxmal* near the Campeche state line, as well as *Edzná,* which has one of the tallest Maya pyramids in the Yucatán.

BOLONCHÉN DE REJÓN This is a must for spelunkers; even for amateurs, these stalactite-studded caverns 200 feet below the earth are worth a look. For a small fee, guides will escort you through the subterranean passages; it is too dangerous to explore them on your own. The caverns are open daily; there's an admission charge.

En Route from Bolonchén de Rejón Continue south on Route 261 for 21 miles (34 km) to the town of Hopelchén. Then, head east (still on Route 261) 26 miles (42 km) to the village of Cayal, where you will find the turnoff to Route 188 leading to *Edzná,* 12 miles (19 km) southwest.

EDZNÁ *Edzná* is believed to have been inhabited since 600 BC, making it one of the oldest groups of ruins in the Yucatán. The main pyramid here is huge—about 50 percent taller than the famous *El Castillo* pyramid at *Chichén Itzá,* although the others are not particularly impressive. The site also has the most advanced hydraulic system in the Maya world. Because the area receives little or no rain except in the summer, resourceful engineers designed a complex network of dammed reservoirs and irrigation canals. There is also a ball court and an elongated annex that probably served as living quarters for *Edzná*'s chieftains and shamans. The site is open daily; no admission charge on Sundays (no phone).

En Route from Edzná To get back to Route 261, backtrack on Route 188 to Cayal. Then head east 27 miles (43 km) on Route 261 to Campeche.

CAMPECHE One of Mexico's least visited and most picturesque port towns, Campeche has been walled and fortressed from the early days of the Spanish conquest.

Founded by the Spanish in 1540, Campeche's importance began to increase after the conquistadores discovered logwood, a rare and costly source of dye, growing in the nearby forests. By the mid-1550s, they were getting rich by exporting the precious commodity to Europe. Campeche rapidly grew into one of New Spain's most thriving cities, duly attracting the attention of a series of pirates who proceeded to sack it throughout the next century. In 1686, construction began on a fortress and a wall. Parts of the wall have since been removed, but the two main gates and seven of the original eight fortresses remain.

The former *Fuerte de San Pedro* is now an arts exhibition gallery and houses a branch of the local tourist office (Calle 18, corner of Calle 51; no phone). There is another branch of the tourist office in the former *Fuerte de Santa Rosa* (Circuíto Baluartes, near Calle 65; phone: 981-67364, 981-66068, or 981-66767), where you can find a guide to show you around town; both tourist offices are closed weekends. *San Pedro*'s rooftop has changed little since its days as a fort, its fighting deck heavy with quaint cannon. With a bit of persuasion and a few pesos, your guide will take you to the secret passageways beneath the fort. Mostly sealed off with bricks, these tunnels once linked many houses in the city and sheltered women and children when pirate ships came into view. Some of the passages were built in the Maya period and were simply expanded by the Spanish.

The *Fuerte de San Miguel,* the handsomest of all Campeche's fortresses, is now the *Museo Regional de Campeche,* displaying pirate arms, portraits of the most infamous scoundrels to plague the city, and a model of 17th-century Campeche. Also displayed is an interesting collection of Maya objects, including a jade mask and jewelry discovered in the *Calakmul* tomb, which contained the richest finds of jade jewelry in Campeche (see *Calakmul Biosphere Reserve,* below, for details). The guides seem to delight in telling horror stories about how San Miguel's moat was stocked with crocodiles; they tend to equivocate when asked whether any malefactor actually tumbled into it. The museum is open daily; admission charge (Av. Escénica, at the top of the hill; no phone).

Church lovers will be culturally and spiritually rewarded in Campeche. The *Catedral,* on the main plaza, was completed in 1546; nearly as old is the *Monasterio de San Francisco* (St. Francis Monastery), just off the *malecón* (seafront esplanade, three blocks west of the main plaza).

The city has its modern side, too. The brightly colored *Palacio de Gobierno* (Statehouse) has been dubbed "the jukebox" by irreverent local citizens, and the modern *Palacio Legislativo* (State Legislature building) is known as "the flying saucer." The two buildings are next to each other on Avenida 16 de Septiembre at Calle 61. Also among Campeche's modern elements are the city's growing network of wide, handsome boulevards and the futuristic *Ciudad Universitaria* (University City), home of a local state university and rivaled only by the *Universidad Nacional Autónoma de México* campus in Mexico City.

Campeche is noted for its seafood, especially shrimp. It's famous for such intriguing seafood combinations as the *campechano,* a cocktail of shrimp and oysters. (Light beer and dark beer also are served half-and-half on request.) *Cangrejo moro* (stone crab), pompano, and *esmedregal* (black snapper) are favorites, too. The restaurant in the *Baluartes* hotel (see *Best en Route*) serves good seafood. The *Miramar* restaurant (phone: 981-62883), in a run-down colonial building across the street from the *Palacio de Gobierno,* is less expensive and more crowded, but serves food that's at least as good. Also across from the government buildings are three eateries— *Restaurant 303* (no phone), *Cafeteria Bamboo* (no phone), and *Bar la Escala* (no phone)—all good for a relaxing meal.

En Route from Campeche From Campeche, Route 180 heads 41 miles (66 km) south to Champotón, the last stop on the Gulf of Mexico coast. It was here that the first Spanish blood was shed in Mexico, in 1517, when Francisco Hernández de Córdoba was mortally wounded by the Maya leader Moch-Cohuó while exploring the area. Route 261 leaves Route 180 at Champotón, continuing south to Francisco Escárcega (see below). There, the Mérida route converges with the route from Mexico City.

MEXICO CITY ROUTE

En Route from Mexico City The total distance from Mexico City to Chetumal is 892 miles (1,427 km), at least a three-day drive. We recommend a minimum of two overnight stops—including one at Veracruz, 264 miles (422 km) from Mexico City, and another at Villahermosa, 297 miles (475 km) from Veracruz. This trip can be completed in four easy days of driving, seldom with more than six hours spent on the road in any one given day. But there's so much to see that for an in-depth look, even a week is not enough.

Leave Mexico City via Route 150, heading south toward Puebla, about 78 miles (126 km) away. The town of Tlaxcala, about 42 miles (67 km) from Mexico City, makes an interesting side trip along the way.

TLAXCALA Until the mid 1980s, when some important pre-Hispanic murals were restored and the town was spruced up, the city of Tlaxcala was almost unknown to tourists. Today it is very much worth a slight detour on the way to Puebla. Take the Tlaxcala turnoff from Route 150; just before the town of Nativitas, about 12 miles (19 km) before Tlaxcala, you'll see an open-sided, stadium-like structure protecting the *Cacaxtla* archaeological zone. You will have to leave your car in the parking lot and walk about a quarter of a mile to the site. The small visitors' center on the right describes the history of the area, which was settled by a group known as the Olmec-Xicalancas. The zone itself contains the finest examples of Toltec-era murals in Mexico. The archaeological zone is open daily; no admission charge on Sundays (no phone).

Continue on the road to Tlaxcala; once in town, follow Route 119 toward Puebla. After about 1½ miles (2 km), take a left and you will see the *Basílica de Ocotlán* rising from the top of a hill. The basilica was built in the 17th and 18th centuries at the site of a miracle said to have occurred during a drought in the 16th century, when the *Virgen de Ocotlán* answered the prayers of an Indian by causing water to flow from the ground. The sanctuary is noteworthy for its eight-sided *Camarín de la Virgen* (Chamber of the Virgin), with its white plaster façade, two red-tiled towers, and a profusion of Baroque decorations covering the walls and cupola. The *Fiesta de la Virgen de Ocotlán* (Feast of the Virgin of Ocotlán) is usually celebrated at her basilica on May 15 with fireworks, music, and much food and drink.

Have lunch at one of the restaurants near Tlaxcala's main square or at the *Misíon Tlaxcala* hotel (see *Best en Route*). Return to Route 119 to connect with Route 150 to Puebla.

PUEBLA For a detailed report on the city, its hotels, and its restaurants, see *Puebla* in THE CITIES.

En Route from Puebla Between Puebla and Veracruz, there is a choice of roads. Route 150 is a four-lane toll road that shoots east for 111 miles (178 km) from Puebla through Orizaba and Fortín de las Flores to Córdoba, where it becomes an ordinary highway running the 81 miles (130 km) to Veracruz (see Orizaba, below).

The alternative, Route 140, goes through Xalapa. The Xalapa route makes sense if you plan to drive straight to Veracruz.

XALAPA (pronounced Ha-*la*-pa) About 180 miles (288 km) northeast of Puebla on Route 140, Xalapa is famous for its flowers. The capital of the state of Veracruz, the city has come into its own as a provincial cultural center, with frequent concerts and ballet and modern dance recitals. Drizzle is frequent, too. There are moments when the sun shines, but usually Xalapa is a lovely, misty greenhouse.

Xalapa is a necessary stop for archaeology buffs, because the town has one of Mexico's most beautiful archaeology museums, the *Museo de Antropología de Xalapa* (Av. Xalapa and 1 de Mayo; phone: 28-150920 or 28-154952), whose exhibits are from the Olmec, Huastec, and Totonac civilizations. Designed by the New York firm of Edward Durell Stone, the museum displays more than 25,000 items. Among the most compelling exhibits are replicas of the famous colossal Olmec heads dating from 1100 to 900 BC discovered at the *San Lorenzo de Tenochtitlán* archaeological site; charming sculptures of *caras sonrientes* (smiling faces) from the Central Gulf region; and a sculpture of the *Sacerdote de las Limas,* the figure of a priest holding the body of the Sun Child in his arms. The museum is filled with bright interior patios. It is closed Mondays; there's an admission charge.

The *Xalapa* hotel (see *Best en Route*) or *La Pérgola* (Loma del Estadio; no phone) are good choices for lunch. For more tourist information, consult the city tourist office (*Palacio Municipal,* third floor; phone: 28-182775 or 28-184829) or the state tourist office, located on the southeastern outskirts of town (5 Blvd. Cristóbal Colón, ground floor: phone: 28-127345 or 28-128500). Both offices are closed Sundays.

En Route from Xalapa *El Lencero,* in the town of Coatepec, 5 miles (8 km) southwest of Xalapa, is a beautifully restored hacienda that was once home to General Antonio López de Santa Anna, who led troops in both the War of Independence and the later Mexican-American War. The hacienda is closed Mondays; there's no admission charge (no phone). On the way to Coatepec, don't miss the *Jardín Botánico Francisco Javier Clavijero,* botanical gardens located 2 miles (3 km) southwest on the old highway to Coatepec. The gardens are closed Mondays; there's an admission charge (phone: 28-186009, ext. 3110/1/2). From here, continue on to Veracruz (see below), 80 miles (134 km) away.

ORIZABA If you have chosen Route 150 from Puebla, this will be your first stop. The town, 39 miles (62 km) past Tehuacán, is where much Mexican beer is made. The *Cervecería Cuauhtémoc Moctezuma* (Cuauhtémoc Moctezuma Brewery; Calles 10 Sur and 9 Poniente, behind the Cinema Orizaba; phone: 272-61222, ext. 1681 and 1693) offers tours in English daily (except Sundays) so you can see how superior *cerveza* is made and taste free samples of the brew. A manufacturing town, Orizaba has a pleasant climate. Overlooking the town to the west, the 18,700-foot Orizaba Volcano, also known as Citlaltépetl, is the highest mountain in Mexico.

A huge monolith in the local cemetery depicts a fish, a man, a rabbit, and two human feet that look as if they had been set in cement outside *Mann's Chinese Theatre* in Hollywood. In a canyon near the brewery, the *Estanque de la Reina,* an area surrounding a pond, is filled with sensational vegetation, including orchid-covered trees. Both places are well worth a visit.

En Route from Orizaba Some 4 miles (6 km) up Route 150 as it curves toward Córdoba is perhaps the most enchanting stop along the route.

FORTÍN DE LAS FLORES With the majestic Orizaba volcano towering in the distance, Fortín, whose full name is Spanish for "Fortress of the Flowers," is a tropical village of gardenias, orchids, camellias, and azaleas. Nearby are sugar, coffee, and citrus plantations.

En Route from Fortín de las Flores About 4 miles (6 km) east on Route 150 is Córdoba, the Mexican equivalent of Yorktown.

CÓRDOBA Independence from Spain was finally won here in 1821. Córdoba is a lovely town of pink and blue buildings with red tile roofs, mango-shaded streets, and an occasional squawking parrot or a peacock. We recommend spending the night in Fortín, then driving to Córdoba in the morning for breakfast at the *Palacio* (see *Best en Route*) before continuing on to Veracruz.

En Route from Córdoba Veracruz is another 66 miles (106 km) on Route 150.

VERACRUZ Whether you take Route 140 or Route 150, plan to spend at least one night in the port city of Veracruz. For a detailed report on the city, its hotels, and its restaurants, see *Veracruz* in THE CITIES.

En Route from Veracruz If you leave around noon, you will arrive in Alvarado—45 miles (72 km) southeast down Route 180—in time for a late lunch.

ALVARADO This town is famed throughout Mexico for its foul-mouthed citizens, who will neither offend nor delight you if you don't speak the language. More to the point, Alvarado is a leading fishing port. A good lunch stop is *El Bosque* (1 Av. Carranza; phone: 297-30576).

En Route from Alvarado Route 180 leads about 60 miles (96 km) to picturesque San Andrés Tuxtla, one of the prettiest towns on the gulf. Next door, Laguna Catemaco is largely unvisited.

LAGUNA CATEMACO The 50-square-mile lagoon was formed centuries ago by the eruption of seven volcanoes. Trout, perch, and a small species called *pepesca* inhabit the lake, from which the town of Catemaco derives a thriving fishing industry. There is also a launch area on the lake, where you can arrange for boat rides and water skiing.

Dine lakeside at *La Ola* (Paseo del Malecón; no phone), an open-air restaurant and bar set under a woven roof, where *mojarra* (sunfish) is caught fresh from the lake.

En Route from Laguna Catemaco Follow Route 180 for 91 miles (146 km) to Coatzacoalcos.

COATZACOALCOS This vibrant, booming port, fed by Mexico's national Pemex petroleum monopoly, affords a glimpse of the lusty, tackier side of life in Mexico. The *zona de tolerancia* (red-light district) on the outskirts of the city features a slew of bars and discos where women of ill repute hustle for a share of the nation's oil money. If you're looking for a *Casablanca*-esque atmosphere and an inexpensive meal, eat at the *Valgrande* (Hidalgo and Morelos; phone: 921-21624).

En Route from Coatzacoalcos Continuing on Route 180, cross the river into the fabled state of Tabasco. Tabasco pretty much lives up to its reputation as a remote region of jungles and swamps, where just yesterday the only highways were rivers. Today an excellent road cuts through about 107 miles (171 km) of the densest jungle between Coatzacoalcos and Villahermosa, the state capital. It's an adventure just to pass through. Banana trees and vanilla orchids are everywhere, and roadside stands sell fresh unsweetened chocolate and even cacao fruit (similar to a giant lychee in texture and flavor). The ambience is hot and steamy, and if there's not too much traffic, you may even glimpse a spider monkey swinging from tree to tree.

VILLAHERMOSA Famous for its beauty and charm, Villahermosa ("beautiful town") is a favorite honeymoon destination, and it's one of the prettiest cities in Mexico. It boasts a river walk, a historic downtown section, and tons of museums. The tourist office (1504 Paseo Tabasco; phone: 93-163633) is closed Sundays.

One of the city's most distinctive attractions is the spectacular *Tabasco 2000* complex, which includes a shopping center with a department store, art galleries, boutiques, and a *Woolworth's;* a planetarium; the 18-hole *Club de Golf;* and the *Holiday Inn Tabasco Plaza* (see *Best en Route*).

Also worth visiting is the *Museo la Venta* (Blvd. Grijalva and Paseo Tabasco, 2 miles/3 km northwest of the center of town; phone: 931-52228), an outdoor archaeology museum with artifacts placed in the same type of jungle setting in which they were found in the oil fields of *La Venta* (100 miles northwest), a former Olmec ceremonial site dating back more than 3,000 years. The park also has monkeys swinging in the trees, some animals roaming loose, and others caged. A path winds among the palms and vines, and around the various artifacts, including altars, stelae, and three ancient, giant sculptures of heads approximately six feet tall and weighing 20 to 30 tons. English-speaking guides are available. Be sure to bring insect repellent. The museum is open daily; admission charge.

The Olmec, thought by many experts to have established the earliest known civilization in Mexico, settled in the rain forest along the gulf coast around 1200 BC. They constructed plazas, ceremonial centers, and giant sculpted heads without bodies—the head was perceived as the most important part of the body. The ritual of cutting off someone's head evolved from the belief that this was the most effective way of stealing an enemy's power, and heads were considered good sacrifices to the gods. The Olmec were also fond of carving figures of jaguars and babies with jaguars' heads. Although it is impossible at this time to determine the precise significance of this symbol, it is probably an image of esteem, as jaguars were the biggest felines on the continent.

The *Museo Regional de Antropología Carlos Pellicer Cámara* (203 Calle Sáenz, one block west of the Río Grijalva, downtown; phone: 931-23202) is one of the best-regarded museums in all of Mexico. Carlos Pellicer was one of Mexico's greatest poets and a native of the state of Tabasco. He directed this archaeology museum for 26 years, and is credited with amassing the outstanding collection of Olmec and Maya artifacts currently on display. Exceptional exhibits include a drinking vessel, one of the finest examples of Maya art, which depicts a governor and his subjects; carved bricks used in the construction of *Comalcalco,* a Maya ceremonial center about 34 miles (54 km) northeast of Villahermosa; stelae; and colossal heads. The full-scale reproductions of the murals at the jungle ruins of Bonampak depict a young warrior being presented to the Maya lords, as well as war dances, prayers for victory, and a battle. The paintings at this museum in Villahermosa are the next best thing to being in Bonampak, which is remote and difficult to visit. The museum is closed Mondays; there's an admission charge.

En Route from Villahermosa Continue east on Route 180 and then turn right (south) at the town of Catazaja, 71 miles (114 km) from Villahermosa, onto Route 199. Then, continue 16 miles (26 km) to the *Palenque* archaeological site, a total of 87 miles (139 km) from Villahermosa.

Note: At press time, *Palenque* and the surrounding area were back to normal after being somewhat affected by the rebel uprisings elsewhere in the state of Chiapas. Earlier, however, the government was setting up roadblocks on Route 199, and hotels and restaurants sometimes closed without notice. Before you leave home, check the situation with the *US State Department*'s 24-hour travel advisory hotline (phone: 202-647-5225). For updates on tourist facilities in the area, contact the *Palenque* tourist office (Calle Jiménez at Calle 5 de Mayo; phone: 934-50356), which is closed weekends; there's also a tourist information booth at Avenida Juárez and

Calle Abasolo that's open daily (no phone). In addition, it's a good idea to reconfirm your hotel reservations.

PALENQUE Of all the surviving Maya archaeological zones, none is more majestic than *Palenque,* in the state of Chiapas. The site is open daily; no admission charge on Sundays (no phone). For additional details, see *Mexico's Magnificent Archaeological Heritage* in DIVERSIONS.

En Route from Palenque Return to the main highway (Rte. 186), turn right, and head for Francisco Escárcega, 115 miles (184 km) northeast.

FRANCISCO ESCÁRCEGA TO CHICHÉN ITZÁ

FRANCISCO ESCÁRCEGA Little more than a collection of unsightly concrete-block buildings and noisy streets, Escárcega is where the Mérida and Mexico City routes converge. At this point, our route heads east on Route 186 to Chetumal. From here on, the jungle closes in. Although the roadside vegetation is typical low shrub, the deep rain forest of the *Calakmul Reserva de la Biósfera* (Calakmul Biosphere Reserve) is never far from the highway.

The 171-mile (274-km) drive to Chetumal from Escárcega will probably take more than four hours, and may run as long as six, if you stop to see the ruins at *Kohunlich,* and even longer if you decide to explore any of the sites in the accessible regions of the *Calakmul Biosphere Reserve.* (You may also elect to stay overnight at the Calakmul reserve and explore some of the sites within; see below.) This section of the route is a long, tedious odyssey, punctuated every few miles with industrial-strength *topes* (speed bumps) and potholes that can wreak havoc on your timetable and your shock absorbers. This is wild jungle country; amenities are few and far between. Take along a box lunch and make sure to fill up your gas tank at Escárcega (there's only one gas station between here and Chetumal, and it doesn't always have unleaded gasoline).

Underscoring the remoteness of the region is the customs shed at the Quintana Roo (pronounced Keen-*tah*-na *Row*) state line. No one entering has to stop, but vehicles leaving Quintana Roo are sometimes required to submit to a customs inspection. Quintana Roo is exempt from Mexico's protective tariffs. For many years, there was no way for Mexican goods to get into the area (and no place for them to go once they were here), so the government eliminated import taxes to stimulate the state's almost nonexistent economy. To some extent, this made the region a legal base for smugglers, and contraband became big business. However, the situation is gradually changing as the North American Free Trade Agreement takes effect.

From Francisco Escárcega, it is 83 miles (133 km) to the western edge of the *Calakmul Biosphere Reserve.* However, there are no signs or entrance gates.

CALAKMUL BIOSPHERE RESERVE Just over the Quintana Roo state line in the southeastern section of Campeche, this vast expanse of tropical rain forest extends to the Guatemala border, where it adjoins the *Maya Biosphere Reserve.* Together, the two reserves make up the largest surviving area of rain forest in North America. The jungle conceals the ruins of many Maya ceremonial centers. Most of the sites are small compared to *Chichén Itzá, Uxmal,* and *Tulum* (though larger than *Kohunlich,* below), but their architecture is just as fascinating—temples with elaborate sculptures and carved doorways, huge stone jaguar and eagle masks, and towers that look like pyramids. The most accessible places are *Chicanná, Xpujil,* and *Becán,* set within a few miles of each other just off Route 186. Although all three have been cleared and excavated, they were formerly difficult to visit because of the lack of accommodations in the area; however, the nearby village of Xpujil has been greatly developed over the past few years, emerging as a center of ecotourism in the biosphere reserve. The *Ramada Ecovillage* (see *Best en Route*) can arrange expeditions for guests to the less accessible sites of *Calakmul, Hormiguero,* and *Río Bec;* four-wheel-drive vehicles and guides (both essential) can be hired at the hotel. Attempt travel within the reserve only during dry season, as there are no paved roads.

The reserve's namesake, *Calakmul,* one of the largest Classic-era Maya cities, is still being excavated. The site lies 33 miles (53 km) south of Route 186, but travel through the jungle is very slow; the trip from *Xpujil* to *Calakmul* takes a full day each way. Built in a similar architectural style as *Xpujil* and other sites in the area, *Calakmul* is estimated to have had a population of more than 50,000 at its peak (around AD 800). Most of the restoration efforts have focused on the massive pyramids that flank the central plaza, one of which was found to contain the richest royal tomb yet discovered on the Yucatán Peninsula. There are no hotels near *Calakmul,* but the *Ramada Ecovillage* (see *Best en Route*) offers trips to the ruins, including camping gear and meals. All the archaeological sites in the reserve are open daily (no admission charge on Sundays; no phones).

About 156 miles (260 km) east of Francisco Escárcega (and 35 miles/56 km from the eastern edge of the Calakmul reserve), along a poorly maintained stretch of Route 186, are the ruins of *Kohunlich.*

KOHUNLICH A Maya city whose name means "Place of the Palm Trees," *Kohunlich* dates from about AD 100. The site was discovered in 1967, when construction workers were cutting a *trocha,* or path, for Route 186. Highlights are several pyramid-shaped temples and an acropolis built around large ceremonial plazas, plus a number of large stone monuments and a ball court.

The hard, dense clay once used to stucco the pyramids and other structures here has eroded away over the centuries, so the ornamentation that originally decorated the temples has been lost. While excavating one of the temples, however, archaeologists found buried on both sides of the stairway a series of eight intact stucco masks, each about six feet tall, thought to represent the Maya sun god. The pyramid is now called the *Temple of the Masks*. Continuing excavation has also turned up several royal burial chambers at the foot of the *Temple of the Masks* and of other temples. (Archaeologists once believed that Maya pyramids were not used as burial places; recent discoveries have proven them wrong, disclosing royal tombs within many, and perhaps most, of them.) These revelations merely hint at discoveries that may await future explorers; analysis of satellite photographs reveals some 200 pyramids throughout the remote jungles of southern Quintana Roo.

Kohunlich is by no means as well ordered as such sites as *Uxmal* and *Tulum*. You can get a sense of ongoing exploration and feel you are actually in the midst of potentially important discoveries. The palm-studded grounds are extremely beautiful, and the lush carpet of green grass and thick jungle that frames the site gives it a mystical quality. If you go, be sure to take insect repellent, because the local mosquitoes can be vicious. The site is open daily; no admission charge on Sundays (no phone).

En Route from Kohunlich Chetumal is 43 miles (69 km) farther west on Route 186.

CHETUMAL It's hard to imagine a more exotic introduction to Mexico's Caribbean coast. By no means as glamorous as the resorts farther north, Chetumal is more like the setting of a grade B Hollywood thriller of the 1940s. It's balanced delicately on Mexico's border with Belize and on the deep Bahía de Chetumal. Because Quintana Roo is a free-trade zone, this odd little town is aglitter with shops selling Japanese electronic devices, Dutch cheese, Italian silk, and French perfume. Mexicans usually have to pay 20% to 40% duty on goods from abroad, so for people from nearby Mérida or Villahermosa, Chetumal is the next best thing to Hong Kong. (Under the North American Free Trade Agreement, however, the city's duty-free status is gradually changing; furthermore, increasing numbers of shoppers are coming from neighboring Belize, which is not a member of NAFTA.) In addition to attracting shoppers, Chetumal is a staging point for fishing expeditions.

If you're ready for a tasty meal, *La Cascada* at the *Continental Caribe* hotel (see *Best en Route*) has a good selection of seafood and international dishes. If you prefer Italian food or grilled steaks, try *Sergio's Pizza* (182 Av. Obregón, just off the Av. Héroes, the main boulevard; no phone). Late-night snackers will appreciate *24-Horas* (no phone), open around the clock, also on the main drag.

You can spend the afternoon in Quintana Roo just lying around or swimming at Laguna Bacalar, about 29 miles (46 km) north of downtown Chetumal via Route 307, or at the nearby Cenote Azul, just 3 miles (5 km) south of Bacalar on Route 307.

LAGUNA BACALAR AND CENOTE AZUL According to Maya legend, the Laguna Bacalar is the birthplace of the rainbow. The lagoon's turquoise waters, which reflect many colors, are as clear as the air above it, ideal for snorkeling. Cenote Azul is an azure sinkhole, the perfect place for a dip in the water, Maya-style. The limestone pool of fresh water, 600 feet wide and almost 280 feet deep, is surrounded by eucalyptus and other shade trees. The small, open-air *Cenote Azul* restaurant, on the banks, serves fresh seafood; try the giant shrimp stuffed with cheese, wrapped in bacon, and deep-fried. It's open daily (no phone).

Although the main reason for stopping off in Bacalar is the lagoon, the town has a bonus attraction that is often overlooked: *Fuerte San Felipe Bacalar,* a stately stone fort constructed by colonists during the first half of the 18th century to protect the city from pirates. Today, the fort is a museum housing old weapons and other local artifacts; it's open daily, and there's an admission charge (no phone).

En Route from Chetumal From Chetumal, Route 307 goes north to the resorts that spot Mexico's fabulous Caribbean coast. The first stop is Felipe Carrillo Puerto, 99 miles (158 km) north of Chetumal.

FELIPE CARRILLO PUERTO This town gets its name from a populist Yucatán governor of the 1920s who loved an American woman named Alma Reed. The story of the two lovers could easily have been invented by a novelist. A reporter from San Francisco, Reed took up the cause of a young Mexican convicted of murder. Her article persuaded the authorities that the jury had made a mistake, and the governor signed a pardon. The Mexican government, pleased to have found a friend, invited Reed to tour the country as its guest.

In the course of her journey, Reed visited Mérida, where she interviewed Carrillo Puerto, governor of the state of Yucatán. Apparently, he was taken with Reed, because later he had a mariachi band drop by her hotel to serenade her. He even had a tune, "Peregrina" (Pilgrim), written especially for her; it's still considered a classic among Mexican love songs. Reed booked passage on a steamer for New York, where she planned to buy her wedding dress. While she was there, however, political fortunes turned in Mérida, and Carrillo Puerto was executed. Reed became a great promoter of Mexican culture and archaeology. She died in 1966 and is buried in Mérida, very close to Carrillo Puerto.

The extraordinary restaurant on the highway called *El Faisán y el Venado* (no phone) serves pheasant and other wild game perfectly prepared at extremely reasonable prices. You won't find venison on the menu, despite the restaurant's name (*venado* is "venison," as well as "deer"; *faisán* is "pheasant"), because commercial deer hunting is *verboten* in Quintana Roo.

En Route from Felipe Carrillo Puerto To continue to the Caribbean coast, bear right at the highway junction and continue north 96 miles (154 km) on Route 307 to the Maya ruins of *Tulum*. (Do not take the local road that leads from Felipe Carrillo Puerto to the *Reserva de la Biósfera Sian Ka'an;* the trip is much easier from *Tulum,* because the road is considerably better.)

TULUM This small archaeological zone has some fine Maya buildings. In fact, it was one of the few Maya cities still inhabited when the Spanish arrived. Juan de Grijalva described it from his ship in 1518 as a city "so large that Seville would not have seemed more considerable." He was mistaken; even in its heyday, only 500 to 600 people lived in this walled city overlooking the fine white beaches and crystalline blue Caribbean waters. For additional details, see *Mexico's Magnificent Archaeological Heritage* in DIVERSIONS.

From *Tulum,* travelers have a choice of two interesting side trips. Nature lovers may want to backtrack south to the *Reserva de la Biósfera Sian Ka'an* (Sian Ka'an Biosphere Reserve), while archaeology buffs may opt for an excursion to the Maya city of *Cobá*.

SIAN KA'AN (pronounced *See-*an *Kahn*) If you have decided to head south to *Sian Ka'an,* fill your gas tank before you leave—this route is quite isolated. Also, do not attempt to visit *Sian Ka'an* during the rainy season (roughly mid-May through mid-October), when the route is often impassable. From the Route 307 turnoff for the *Tulum* ruins, take the local, unnumbered coastal road south. After 5 miles (8 km), the pavement ends, and you will be heading into the reserve on a dirt road, though there is no designated entrance gate (or admission charge). Boca Paila, a small community that caters to fly fishing enthusiasts (see below), is about 6 miles (10 km) farther down the road. The village of Punta Allen, which is the southernmost part of the reserve reachable by car, is some 24 miles (38 km) south of Boca Paila. For a meal, stop at Candy Guzmán's *Restaurant Candy,* an open-air, flower-filled *palapa*-style eatery on the road from the boat dock to the beach (no phone).

Jungles, salt marshes, mangrove swamps, palm beaches, and coral reefs make up this 1.3-million-acre biosphere reserve. It's a paradise for bird lovers and for biologists, who have established crocodile and butterfly farms here. The pricey hotels on the reserve, *Club de Pesca Boca Paila* and *Pez Maya* (see *Best en Route*) are frequented by millionaire yachting enthusiasts, who come to fish and sun. Unfortunately, the more rustic *palapa* (thatch-roof) establishments (including our favorite, *Posada Cuzán*), were destroyed by Hurricane Roxanne in 1995; at press time, none had plans to rebuild. For information on guided visits, contact the *Association of Friends of Sian Ka'an* (Plaza Américas, Suite 50, 5 Av. Cobá, Cancún, QR 77500, México; phone: 98-849583; fax: 98-873080).

COBÁ This archaeological site is about 26 miles (42 km) inland from *Tulum*; take the inland turnoff from Route 307. Discovered in 1897 and first opened to the public in 1973, *Cobá* contains more than 6,500 Maya structures, most of them uncharted. For additional details, see *Mexico's Magnificent Archaeological Heritage* in DIVERSIONS. To get back to the main road (Route 307) and *Tulum,* backtrack on the local road from the site.

En Route from Tulum From here to Cancún, this part of Quintana Roo—known as the Cancún-Tulum Corridor—is peppered with some delightful seaside hotels and restaurants. It's hard to predict how many more years of peace and tranquillity remain here, since more and more resorts are springing up. For example, about 32 miles (51 km) north of *Tulum* is Puerto Aventuras, a huge development of villas, condominiums, hotels, restaurants, tennis courts, a golf course, and a marina. There's also a maritime museum. For more details, see *Cancún, Cozumel, and Isla Mujeres* in THE CITIES and *Great Golfing* in DIVERSIONS.

Our first stop along the Cancún-Tulum Corridor is Xel-Ha, 12 miles (19 km) from *Tulum.*

XEL-HA (pronounced Shel-*Ha*) This series of lagoons, operated as a national park, forms a natural aquarium filled with colorful tropical fish and turtles. Recently restored to near-pristine condition by a massive conservation effort, it is a great place for novice snorkelers to test their fins. It's best to visit on weekdays, when the area is less crowded. Across the road is the *Xel-Ha* archaeological zone, which is run independently of the national park. The ruins here are interesting, if uninspiring. The main structure, a 10-minute hike over jagged limestone terrain, is the *Temple of the Birds,* where a faint image of Chac, the rain god, and several plumed flamingos can be discerned in the western wall. The park and the ruins are open daily; each has a separate admission charge (no phone).

En Route from Xel-Ha Continue north 8 miles (13 km) on Route 307 to Akumal.

AKUMAL This was once a private Mexican undersea explorers' club; members would fly down in private aircraft to don wet suits and scuba tanks for expeditions to the sunken wrecks of Spanish galleons in the seas nearby. They also came upon submerged Maya ruins where the sea had swallowed up the land. Today Akumal is open to the public, with three delightful luxury hotels, plus a beachfront campground cum bar (see *Best en Route*).

En Route from Akumal Playa del Carmen is another 24 miles (38 km) north. This popular beach and resort community (see *Best Beaches off the Beaten Path* in DIVERSIONS) is also where ferries depart for the island of Cozumel. Ferries leave every half hour from the town dock, from 5:30 AM to 7:30 PM, but they do not take cars. Ferries to Cozumel from Puerto Morelos, another 20 miles (32 km) north along Route 307, do take cars, but the wait can be quite long.

COZUMEL Cozumel is Mexico's original international Caribbean resort. For a detailed report on the island, its hotels, and its restaurants, see *Cancún, Cozumel, and Isla Mujeres* in THE CITIES.

En Route from Cozumel Return to the mainland and continue north on Route 307. Cancún is 50 miles (80 km) from Playa del Carmen and 30 miles (48 km) from Puerto Morelos.

CANCÚN AND ISLA MUJERES Cancún is Mexico's great resort success story of the 1970s and 1980s. Isla Mujeres, Quintana Roo's other island resort, is 6 miles (10 km) north of Cancún, and almost everybody staying on Cancún takes a boat over from Puerto Juárez for lunch and a swim. For a detailed report on both islands, their hotels, and their restaurants, see *Cancún, Cozumel, and Isla Mujeres* in THE CITIES.

En Route from Isla Mujeres From Puerto Juárez, it is about 55 miles (88 km) west on Route 180 to Pueblo Nuevo, the border town on the Quintana Roo–Yucatán state line. The next city—Valladolid—is about 41 miles (66 km) west of Pueblo Nuevo.

Note: The stretch of Route 180 between the east coast and Mérida has been declared a nature preserve in which it is forbidden to hunt animals or cut down flora.

VALLADOLID This city made the history books as the site of a bloody massacre during the mid-19th-century Maya uprising known as the Caste War, when the Maya rebelled against the wealthy landowners. The two sides slaughtered each other from 1848 until 1901, when the Mexican army claimed victory.

The outdoor *Cenote Zaci* restaurant (Calle 36, between Calles 35 and 37, three blocks east of the *zócalo;* no phone), beside a cenote, serves delicious *poc chuc* (barbecued pork) and *pavo escabeche* (turkey stewed in a spicy onion sauce), and the restaurant at the *Mesón del Marqués* hotel (see *Best en Route*) offers both regional and international dishes.

En Route from Valladolid It's a total of 29 miles (46 km) to *Chichén Itzá.*

CHICHÉN ITZÁ When people say you haven't seen Mexico until you've been to the Yucatán, this is what they are talking about. The most famous and complete of the ancient Maya cities, this site is a testament to their engineering genius. For additional details, see *Mexico's Magnificent Archaeological Heritage* in DIVERSIONS.

En Route from Chichén Itzá Five miles (8 km) past *Chichén Itzá* on Route 180 are the *Grutas de Balankanchén* (Balankanchén Caverns). Discovered only in 1959, they were apparently abandoned 1,000 years ago and completely forgotten. The caverns served as a secret Maya temple, the *House of the Sacred Jaguar.* Formed by a stalactite joined to a stalagmite, the throne resembles a ceiba, the tree revered by the Maya, with the little stalactites on the cavern ceiling serving as the "leaves." The copal incense burners and hundreds of pots, bowls, and other artifacts in the chamber are believed to be exactly where the priests left them centuries ago. By a pool so still it scarcely seems to contain any water stands an altar to the rain god, although there is some question as to whether it is the Toltec rain god, Tlaloc, or the Maya deity, Chac. It is also possible that the caverns were the secret temple of a persecuted religious group, whose members had to abandon the caves when they were discovered. There are guides to lead you through the interior, but exploring the place is rough going. The caverns are closed Mondays; there's an admission charge (no phone).

Continue 94 miles (150 km) west on Route 180 to Mérida. From Mérida, you can take Route 180 and Route 161 south to Francisco Escárcega and, from there, Route 186 toward Villahermosa and Coatzacoalcos. From Coatzacoalcos, it is possible to detour south on Route 185 and cross the Isthmus of Tehuantepec in four hours. The 574-mile (918-km) trip heads back to Mexico City via Oaxaca.

BEST EN ROUTE

Expect to pay $60 to $100 for a double room at an expensive place; $30 to $55 at a moderate place; and $25 or less at an inexpensive place. Hotels in the expensive category have air conditioning unless otherwise noted. Most expensive and moderate hotels have TV sets and telephones in the rooms, except at archaeological sites, where there are no in-room phones, and at remote beach locations, where in-room phones usually cannot be used to make outside calls. For each location, hotels are listed alphabetically by price category.

UXMAL

Misión Park Inn Uxmal A well-managed establishment with 50 rooms, a pool, a dining room, and a bar. A half mile (1 km) from the ruins (phone: 99-247308 in Mérida; 800-437-PARK; fax: 99-247308 in Mérida). Expensive to moderate.

Hacienda Uxmal Here you'll find old-fashioned tropical luxury amid ample gardens, 80 large, cool rooms (some with air conditioning), two pools, a fine dining room, shops, and a good bar. About a five-minute walk from the ruins (phone: 99-247142 in Mérida; 800-235-4079; fax: 99-252397 in Mérida). Moderate.

Villa Arqueológica Run by Club Med (but not all-inclusive), this place has 49 spartan (but air conditioned) rooms, a dining room serving simple French cuisine, a bar, tennis courts, and a nice pool. On the main road, in front of the site (phone: 99-247053 in Mérida; 5-203-3086 or 5-203-3833 in Mexico City; 800-CLUB-MED; fax: 5-203-0681 in Mexico City). Moderate.

CAMPECHE

Ramada Inn This fine hotel offers 119 rooms, a pool, a bar, a disco, and a restaurant. 51 Av. Ruiz Cortines (phone: 981-62233; 800-854-7854; fax: 981-11618). Expensive.

Alhambra Its 100 rooms have satellite TV, and there is a restaurant, a coffee shop, a disco, and a pool. 85 Av. Resurgimiento (phone: 981-66988; fax: 981-66132). Moderate.

Si-Ho Playa If you want to stay for more than one night, this 78-unit resort is perfect. With a tennis court, boat rental (about 3 miles/5 km from the hotel), a pool, and a restaurant, the ambience is very relaxing. Km 35 of the Carretera Campeche-Champotón (phone: 981-64044; fax: 981-66154). Moderate.

Baluartes Here is a handsome 102-unit (most with air conditioning) hotel that is close to everything, with a pool and a restaurant. Near the sea, at 61 Av. Ruiz Cortines (phone: 981-63911; fax: 981-65765). Moderate to inexpensive.

TLAXCALA

Misión Tlaxcala This pleasant, comfortable hostelry sits next to a rushing waterfall. In addition to 120 units, it has a heated pool, three tennis courts, satellite TV, a restaurant, and a bar. Ten minutes from downtown, on the Carretera Tlaxcala-Apizaco, in Atlihuetzía (phone: 246-24000; fax: 246-20178). Moderate.

XALAPA

Xalapa Xalapa's best hotel boasts 200 rooms equipped with satellite TV, plus a restaurant, a coffee shop, and a pool. Victoria and Bustamante (phone: 281-82222; fax: 281-89424). Expensive.

ORIZABA

Trueba Clean, comfortable, and somewhat generic, this place has 60 rooms with TV sets, a restaurant, and a bar. Arrangements can be made for golf at the nearby club. 6 Oriente and 11 Sur (phone: 272-42930; fax: 272-52773). Inexpensive.

FORTÍN DE LAS FLORES

Fortín de las Flores A fine, old-fashioned resort and inn, it is noted for its extensive gardens. It also offers 75 units (one with a fireplace), a pool, access to a tennis club, a video bar, a restaurant, a gameroom, and movies. Av. 2, between Calles 5 and 7 (phone: 271-30055; fax: 271-31031). Inexpensive.

Posada Loma Like the *Fortín,* this great favorite is known for its tropical gardens. The 20 or so nicely furnished rooms and bungalows have fireplaces. There's a pool on the grounds, and the service is friendly and competent. Km 333 of Rte. 150 (phone: 271-30753; fax: 271-31454). Inexpensive.

CÓRDOBA

Real Villa Florida A modern hotel with 81 pleasant rooms, gardens, a restaurant-bar, and cable TV. 3002 Av. Primero (phone: 271-43333; fax: 271-43336). Moderate.

Palacio This pleasant hostelry has 75 air conditioned rooms, a restaurant, a cafeteria, color TV sets, and a garage. Just a block from the main plaza, at Av. 3 and Calle 2 (phone: 271-22188). Inexpensive.

LAGUNA CATEMACO

La Finca All 36 rooms have balconies and a view of the lake. There's a pool and a restaurant. Km 147 of Rte. 180 (phone/fax: 294-30322). Moderate.

Berthangel Each of the 23 rooms here has a balcony and lovely views overlooking the plaza and the lake. There's also a small cafeteria. Madero and Boettiger (phone: 294-30089). Inexpensive.

Playa Azul This hotel arranges boating, fishing, and water skiing. There are 80 units, a pool, and a disco. Its restaurant serves local fish. On the shores of the lagoon (phone: 294-30001). Inexpensive.

COATZACOALCOS

Terranova An outstanding modern hotel with 200 rooms, satellite TV, a bar, a pool, tennis courts, a disco, and even a heliport. The dining room serves exceptionally good food. Carretera Transístmica (phone: 921-45100 or 921-45600; fax: 921-45482). Expensive.

Valgrande A typical commercial hotel one would expect to find in a thriving seaport, this place is good, but unexceptional. There are 60 units (including two suites), with TV sets, a restaurant, and a bar. Hidalgo and Morelos (phone: 921-21443, 921-21624, or 921-21387; fax: 921-23139). Moderate.

VILLAHERMOSA

Calinda Viva Villahermosa This urban resort-like property has 264 units, shops, a restaurant, a disco, a nightclub, and a pool. A bit out of the way, at Av. Ruiz Cortines and 1201 Paseo Tabasco (phone: 931-50000; 800-228-5151 in the US; 800-90000 in Mexico; fax: 931-53073). Expensive.

Hyatt Villahermosa Here are 214 units, two tennis courts, a pool, a restaurant, a disco, and a bar. 106 Av. Juárez (phone: 931-34444 or 931-51234; 800-233-1234 in the US; 800-00500 in Mexico; fax: 931-51235). Expensive.

Holiday Inn Tabasco Plaza A hostelry with 156 guestrooms, a restaurant, a bar, a pool, satellite TV, and access to the adjoining country club's 18-hole golf course and tennis courts. 1407 Paseo Tabasco (phone: 931-64400; 800-HOLIDAY in the US; 800-00999 in Mexico; fax: 931-64540). Expensive to moderate.

Cencali This hotel has 116 units with color TV sets, a pool, and a restaurant. Next to the *Parque la Venta* museum, at Av. Juárez and Paseo Tabasco (phone: 931-51999, 931-51997, or 931-51996; fax: 931-56600). Moderate.

Maya Tabasco In addition to the 153 units and a pool, there is a fine dining room, satellite TV, a disco, a coffee shop, and a *Hertz* rental car agency. 907 Av. Ruiz Cortines (phone: 931-21599; 800-334-7234; fax: 931-21097). Moderate.

PALENQUE

Chan Kan Ruinas Village This place has 30 cottages, a restaurant, and a pool. On the road leading to the ruins (phone/fax: 934-51100). Moderate.

Misión Park Inn Palenque A 160-unit hotel with a restaurant, a lobby bar, a tennis court, a pool, and minibus service to the ruins. About 5 miles (8 km) from the archaeological site (phone: 934-50066, 934-50455, or 934-50241; 800-437-PARK; 934-50300). Moderate.

Nututun Viva Here are 42 suites and bungalows with satellite TV, a restaurant, a bar, extensive gardens, and river swimming. About 5 miles (9 km) from the ruins (phone: 934-50161; fax: 934-50100). Moderate.

XPUJIL

Ramada Ecovillage The first of several planned hotels in the area, this 20-unit establishment opened in 1995. Set in thatch-roofed duplexes surrounded by lush tropical forest, some of the guestrooms have king-size beds and balconies overlooking the *Xpujil* ruins (but none has air conditioning, TV sets, or phones). The lodge also has a restaurant, a pool, and a Jacuzzi. Rte. 186, west of *Xpujil* (no local phone; 981-62233 in Campeche; fax: 981-11618 in Campeche). Expensive.

CHETUMAL

Azteca A pleasant hotel, with 22 air conditioned units, parking, a restaurant, and a bar. 186 Belice (phone: 983-20666). Moderate.

Los Cocos Run by one of Mexico's largest hotel chains, with 76 rooms, a pool, a restaurant, and a bar, this is by far the best in town. 134 Av. Héroes, at Chapultepec (phone: 983-20544; fax: 983-20920). Moderate.

Continental Caribe This first class hotel offers 64 rooms and 11 suites, plus a pool, a bar, a garage, movies, and a restaurant. 171 Av. Héroes (phone: 983-21100; fax: 983-21676]). Moderate.

Jacaranda Clean and comfortable, this unforgettable bargain with an on-premises restaurant glows with an outpost-of-empire atmosphere. 201 Alvaro Obregón (phone: 983-21455). Moderate.

LAGUNA BACALAR

Rancho Encantado The gardens are wonderful for leisurely strolls at this cozy, lakeside, five-cottage resort; all have ceiling fans, but no air conditioning. Its restaurant offers a continental menu. The place itself is worth an extra day's layover. The rate includes breakfast and dinner. Reservations essential. Rte. 307, just north of Bacalar City (phone/fax: 983-80427; 800-505-MAYA; 505-776-5878 in New Mexico; fax: 505-776-2102). Expensive.

La Laguna A clean, family-run, 34-unit air conditioned establishment with a pool, a restaurant, and very slow service. The view of the lagoon is spectacular, and there is a small boat dock. 316 Bugambilias (phone/fax: 983-23517). Moderate.

BOCA PAILA

Club de Pesca Boca Paila This rustic little lodge has six cabins with no air conditioning, no TV sets, and no other amenities to speak of. What it does offer is superb saltwater fly fishing. The place is booked months in advance, and there is a house policy not to receive drop-ins. For reservations, contact Frontiers, PO Box 959, Wexford, PA 15090-0959 (no local phone; 987-21176 on Cozumel; 800-245-1950). Expensive.

Pez Maya From the same folks who brought you the *Club de Pesca Boca Paila* comes this set of seven cabins, stripped bare (and we do mean bare!) of the usual necessities and with little else to offer but fly fishing (no local phone; 800-327-2880; 305-664-4615 in Florida). Expensive.

COBÁ

Villa Arqueológica The only hotel at the ruins is set in an isolated jungle environment close to many unexplored sites. Run by Club Med (but not all-inclusive), it has 40 units, tennis courts, a pool, and a library on Mesoamerican archaeology. You actually can get out of bed and hack your way through the jungle; the ruins are a five-minute walk away. Visitors may choose the American plan, with all meals included, or the European plan, with no meals included (phone: 5-203-3086 or 5-203-3833 in Mexico City; 800-CLUB-MED; fax: 5-203-0681 in Mexico City). Expensive to moderate.

AKUMAL

Akumal Cancún Right on the beach, it has 81 rooms with terraces, 11 two-bedroom suites with kitchenettes, a pool, two lighted tennis courts, all water sports, a dive shop, a disco, two restaurants, a video bar, and miniature golf.

Right on the beach (phone: 987-22453 on Cozumel; 98-842272 or 98-842641 on Cancún). Expensive.

Club Akumal Caribe This lovely 61-room place is also a fine spot for lunch. Room rates include all meals. Near *Tulum* (phone: 987-22532 on Cozumel; 800-351-1622 in the US; 95-800-351-1622 in Mexico). Expensive.

El Dorado This all-suite property sits on 280 acres on the Bays of Kantenah, between Akumal and *Xel-Ha.* The hotel offers 51 one-bedroom units (with another 84 currently being built) in several brightly painted villas surrounded by jungle. On the grounds are two pools, a private beach, two tennis courts, and extensive gardens. Other amenities: two restaurants, a supper/dance club, and two bars. All meals, drinks, and on-site activities are included in the rate. Located 1 mile off Rte. 307 (phone: 98-843705 or 98-843242 on Cancún; 800-544-3005; fax: 98-846722 or 98-846952 on Cancún). Expensive to moderate.

Chemuyil On this quiet beach, the Román family has 12 tents for campers and additional camping space, plus a bar that also serves local catch seafood. (At press time, 10 cabañas here that were destroyed in 1995 by Hurricane Roxanne were scheduled to be rebuilt). Relax on a hammock and have a drink served in a fresh coconut. Km 123, Carretera Tulum, about 4 miles (6.5 km) north of Xel-Ha (no phone). Make reservations well in advance by writing to *Don Lalo Román Chemoir Fideicomiso,* Xel-Ha, Tulum, QR 77500, México (no phone). Inexpensive.

PLAYA DEL CARMEN

Continental Plaza Playacar This elegant Mediterranean-style complex has 200 units, two restaurants, two pools, a tennis court, a shopping arcade, and a nine-hole golf course. All rooms have a scenic ocean view, a private balcony, kitchenettes, and satellite TV. Next to the ferry dock (phone: 987-30100; 800-88-CONTI; fax: 987-30105). Expensive.

Diamond Playacar This "ecological" luxury resort has 300 rooms and suites in a cluster of four-plexes styled after jungle lodges, all with thatch roofs and ceiling fans. Amenities include two pools, two restaurants, three bars, tennis courts, and one of the finest stretches of beach on the Caribbean coast. Just south of the ferry dock (phone: 987-30341; 800-642-1600 in all states but New York; 800-858-2258 in all states but Florida; fax: 987-30348). Expensive.

Costa del Mar This 34-room mom-and-pop establishment has a pool, homey touches, and a terrific restaurant. At the northern edge of town along the beach (phone/fax: 987-30058). Moderate.

Las Palapas These 30 or so thatch-roofed cottages are a favorite destination for Germans and other Europeans seeking a taste of the tropics with very few of the comforts of home. There is a pool, a restaurant, and a gameroom, but no telephones or TV sets in the rooms. Each cottage has its own porch with a hammock. A very peaceful setting with a beautiful beach, just north of town (no local phone: phone/fax: 5-379-8641 in Mexico City). Moderate.

Las Molcas Here are 65 air conditioned rooms, a pool, a restaurant, a boutique, and three bars. At the ferry landing (phone: 987-24609; fax: 987-30138). Moderate to inexpensive.

VALLADOLID

María de la Luz Pleasantly modern, it's a provincial 33-room hotel with a pool, a restaurant, and a bar with live entertainment. The rooms have air conditioning, ceiling fans, and cable TV. 195 Calle 42 (phone: 985-62071; fax: 985-91985). Moderate.

Mesón del Marqués Heavy on atmosphere, this old-fashioned colonial inn is one of a dying breed, with 26 units, a restaurant-bar, and gardens. 203 Calle 39 (phone: 985-62073; fax: 985-62280). Moderate.

CHICHÉN ITZÁ

Dolores Alba A nice change of pace from hotel stays, this lovely country house has six air conditioned rooms and 14 with ceiling fans; all have private terraces. There's also a cozy dining room, a pool, and tropical grounds. Km 122 on Route 180, between *Chichén Itzá* and the *Grutas de Balankanchén* (no local phone; 99-213745 in Mérida; fax: 99-283163 in Mérida). Expensive.

Mayaland In this luxury resort are 34 large air conditioned rooms in the main building, plus 31 more (with ceiling fans, but no air conditioning) in villas and thatch-roofed huts, a restaurant, a cocktail terrace, a pool, and evening entertainment. Overlooking the ruins, on Rte. 180 (phone: 985-62777; 99-252133 or 99-252122 in Mérida; 800-235-4079; fax: 99-250727 in Mérida). Expensive.

Misión Park Inn Chichén Itzá A modern hotel with 50 air conditioned rooms, a bar, a restaurant, a pool, and lovely grounds. Pisté, about a mile (1.6 km) from *Chichén Itzá* (phone: 985-62671; 800-437-PARK in the US; 800-90038 in Mexico; fax: 985-62671). Moderate.

Villas Arqueológicas Club Med runs this "inn," which features 44 rooms, a pool, tennis, and a good French restaurant. Only five minutes from the ruins (phone: 985-10034; 5-203-3086 or 5-203-3833 in Mexico City; 800-CLUB-MED; fax: 985-10018; 5-203-0681 in Mexico City). Moderate.

Pirámide Inn The plethora of facilities here—which include a pool, tennis courts, lush gardens, a restaurant, a bar, and even a book exchange—make it hard to leave the premises to explore the ruins. The 47 air conditioned rooms are adequate. Pisté (phone: 99-252122, ext. 151 in Mérida; 800-262-9296). Moderate to inexpensive.

Mexico City to the Guatemala Border

If you want to lounge in the sun and be pampered in luxurious surroundings, go to Acapulco, Cancún, or Puerto Vallarta. If you want cosmopolitan culture and sophisticated nightlife, Mexico City has facilities unmatched elsewhere in the country. And if it's colonial charm and quiet living that you're seeking, Taxco, Guanajuato, and San Miguel de Allende are perfect. But for Indian Mexico—hot and tropical, cold and mountainous, ancient, colorful, and costumed Mexico—you must go south and east to the states of Puebla, Oaxaca, and Chiapas. And to get there, you must take the famous Carretera Panamericana (Pan-American Highway) southeast.

From Mexico City to Guatemala, the Pan-American Highway traverses some of Mexico's most fascinating and rarely visited regions. The route offers the traveler an opportunity to explore 850 miles of almost every conceivable terrain and climate, as well as to sample a vast range of cultures and languages.

From Mexico City through the western part of the state of Puebla, you will witness the splendor of the Sierra Madre ranges, including the Iztaccíhuatl and Popocatépetl volcanoes and the lower slopes of the giant Orizaba peak.

Along this leg of the route are small indigenous villages with colonial-era churches and native markets where various dialects are spoken and regional handicrafts are sold. The town of Texmelucán is known for its weaving, Acatlán and Izúcar de Matamoros for pottery, and Puebla, the state capital, for pottery and polychrome tiles.

Crossing through to the state of Oaxaca, you will find a wonderland of contrasts, from cool, forest-covered mountains and lush tropical valleys to a hot, humid coastline of beaches pounded by the Pacific surf. The contrasts are cultural as well as topographical, with ancient ruins lying within sight of old Spanish colonial towns. Oaxaca boasts more ethnic groups than any other state except for Chiapas. Most have maintained their original languages, customs, and dress, making Oaxaca's villages and markets seem like tiny individual countries to the visitor. Even nature contributes to the exotic atmosphere of the state: The rivers of Oaxaca often overflow their banks during the spring and summer rainy season, minor earthquakes occur frequently, and the state plays host to a diversified wildlife population. Tapir, pumas, jaguars, ocelots, and ocelot-like margays, though tragically reduced in numbers by the lumber, oil, and mining industries, can still be found in some of the forests. Crocodiles, alligators, and boa constrictors thrive in the more humid southern areas.

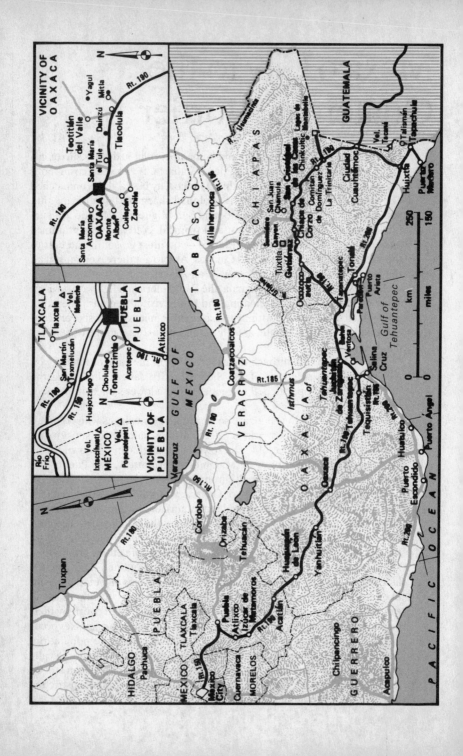

Two proud cultures dominate Oaxaca's many ethnic groups—the Mixtec and the Zapotec. These civilizations reached great heights long before the Europeans made their way to Mexico, as attested to by the impressive sacred cities of Monte Albán, Yagul, Dainzú, and Mitla.

The state of Oaxaca encompasses three major geographical regions: the Valle de Oaxaca (Valley of Oaxaca), the Istmo de Tehuantepec (Isthmus of Tehuantepec), and the Pacific Coast. The Pan-American Highway crosses the first two. The valley, the part closest to Mexico City, is the cultural, historical, and economic center of the state. The isthmus is where the west coast veers northeast to form Mexico's narrow belt. The winds of this area are treacherous and the climate hot and humid, but a handful of interesting towns and beaches make it a fascinating part of the trip.

Just below the isthmus, the Pan-American Highway crosses over into Chiapas, Mexico's southernmost state. This incredibly scenic land stretches from the hot, humid Pacific coastal area to fertile highlands, where the temperature varies from cool to downright cold. Chiapas has the most fascinating folklore of any of Mexico's states, thanks to the rich variety of peoples whose dress, customs, and language differ from one village to the next. As recently as 1950, this region was inaccessible except by horseback. To this day, huge tracts of jungle and forest teeming with exotic flora and fauna remain unexplored. Also found in these unexplored and roadless jungles are hundreds—perhaps thousands—of Maya ruins, most of which can only be reached by helicopter or on horseback.

BE CAREFUL

In January 1994, an armed uprising was staged in Chiapas by guerrillas protesting the government's treatment of indigenous peoples. At press time, negotiations were proceeding and the situation had calmed, but travelers are advised to check with the *US State Department* (phone: 202-647-5225) or the *US Embassy* in Mexico City (305 Paseo de la Reforma; phone: 5-211-0042) before planning a trip. If you decide to travel here, don't stray into isolated areas. It is also inadvisable to go on hunting trips in Chiapas or to bring weapons here, although the state is considered to be the finest hunting region in all of Mexico.

Finally, if you are driving a rental car and want to enter Guatemala, be sure to check with the rental company first. Many firms will not allow renters to drive their cars out of Mexico; those that do require renters to buy special insurance to drive in Guatemala.

En Route from Mexico City Try to leave early—about an hour before sunrise—to avoid the early-morning traffic jams for which Mexico City is infamous. If the weather is good, an early start will also reward you with the spectacular sight of the sunrise reflecting off Popocatépetl and Iztaccíhuatl, two of the four snow-capped volcanoes in this region. It is a vision that will set a charmed, almost magical tone for your whole trip.

Shortly after leaving the city via Calzada Ignacio Zaragoza or Ixtapalapa, you will have to choose between the toll road, Route 150, which goes only as far as Puebla (81 miles/130 km away), and the old free road, Route 190. Of the two, the toll road is faster and less tiring, if less interesting. Either route will take you through picturesque, pine-covered mountains and will get you to Puebla in two hours, more or less.

Forty miles (64 km) out of Mexico City, the Río Frío (Cold River) marks the border between the states of Mexico and Puebla; it is also the halfway point between Mexico City and the city of Puebla. This aptly named spot is always cold, but there are facilities for picnicking, nature trails for hiking, icy water for hardy swimmers, and a restaurant for snacking.

Eight miles (13 km) beyond Río Frío is the Continental Divide—10,480 feet above sea level. No marker indicates the crossing, but it may be of interest to those who enjoy following the map and acting as navigator.

Fifty-seven miles (91 km) east of Mexico City is San Martín Texmelucán, an important weaving center.

SAN MARTÍN TEXMELUCÁN At Tuesday's native market, the town's chief attraction, you'll find serapes and other woolen products of fine quality. During the rest of the week, there is not much to entice you out of your car.

If you pass through on November 11, when the town celebrates the *Fiesta de San Martín* (Feast of St. Martin, the town's patron saint), however, it is worth a stop. Regional dancing, fireworks, music, and even a bullfight mark the festivities.

En Route from San Martín Texmelucán Continue to Huejotzingo, another 8 miles (13 km) southeast on Route 190.

HUEJOTZINGO (pronounced Way-hote-*seen*-go) An infamous bandit town, Huejotzingo was the headquarters of guerrilla-turned-bandit Agustín Lorenzo, and on *Martes de Carnaval* (Shrove Tuesday), Huejotzingo celebrates Lorenzo's capture during the war with the French in 1862 with a colorful, fireworks-filled fiesta. *Carnaval* is celebrated during the five days before *Miércoles de Ceniza* (Ash Wednesday). Saturday is market day, and while it offers a fascinating assortment of people, animals, colors, and sounds, some goods may be inferior and should be checked closely. Across the highway from the market are two of Mexico's oldest colonial monuments, the *Iglesia* and *Monasterio de San Francisco de Huejotzingo.* Begun in 1525, the church and monastery are among the finest Gothic buildings in the country and well worth a visit.

En Route from Huejotzingo Ten miles (16 km) farther is the *Cholula* archaeological site.

CHOLULA This was once the holy city of the Aztec Confederation. The site is open daily; admission charge. For additional details, see *Mexico's Magnificent Archaeological Heritage* in DIVERSIONS.

En Route from Cholula On the descent into Puebla, 5 miles (8 km) away, a first glimpse can be caught of Orizaba (Citlaltépetl) and Malinche, the other two large volcanic mountains of this region.

PUEBLA Puebla is a good city in which to think "car," because if there is the slightest hint that yours is not functioning at its best, this is the time to have it checked. The rest of the trip covers rugged, often isolated mountain terrain, where the nearest repair facilities may be 20 miles away and necessary parts are unlikely to be in stock. (However, the *Angeles Verdes,* or "Green Angels," do patrol the highway; see GETTING READY TO GO for more information.) For a detailed report on Puebla, its hotels, and its restaurants, see *Puebla* in THE CITIES.

Before leaving Puebla, stock up on lunch and snacks for the next segment of the journey to Oaxaca; satisfactory restaurants are few and far between on this leg of the trip.

En Route from Puebla It takes approximately eight hours to drive along the Pan-American Highway (Route 190) to Oaxaca, and all of the trip should be done in daylight. Much of the 264-mile (422-km) journey is on winding roads through arid, semidesert land and an occasional fertile valley. At some points the drop-off at the side of the road is a good half mile to the bottom. Beware of animals and people walking, standing, or sitting beside or actually in the road. And heed the speed limits; many curves should not be taken at even 2 miles per hour faster than indicated.

Along the way, the small village of Tonantzintla is well worth a 20-minute detour. Take the Acatepec turnoff 8 miles (13 km) beyond Puebla, and continue 1 mile (1.6 km) northeast.

TONANTZINTLA (pronounced To-nan-*tseent*-la) The center of this village is dominated by the 16th-century *Iglesia de Santa María Tonantzintla,* whose dull façade belies its exuberant interior. Inside, town residents have created one of the most breathtaking examples of popular art in Mexico, featuring intricately carved, vividly painted reliefs, embellished with gold leaf, flying cherubim, and dancing angels.

The village also boasts an ultramodern *Observatorio Nacional* (National Observatory) equipped with a Schmidt camera that, with a 20-minute exposure, can record an image 300 million light-years away. There are only two other cameras like it in the world: in Hamburg, Germany, and in Mount Palomar, California.

En Route from Tonantzintla Back on Route 190 and 20 miles (32 km) from Puebla, a banner across the highway proclaims that drivers have just entered "the best climate in Mexico"—you've arrived in the town of Atlixco.

ATLIXCO (pronounced At-*leeks*-co) A thriving textile center, Atlixco is surrounded by maize and wheat fields. The ancient *aguacate* (avocado) trees here provided the original stock for California's avocado industry. The colorful *zócalo,* or central plaza, features a beautiful domed bandstand and bright tile benches. Fortunately, you can see everything of interest without a pause in your journey, since Route 190 runs through the center of town. Atlixco is a Nahuatl word meaning "on the surface of the water," and indeed the town's major points of interest are the *Balneario Agua Verde* (Agua Verde Spa, on the local road to Metepec, several miles west of town; no phone) and the *Salto de Axocopán* (Axocopán Spring, on the same road; no phone). The Metepec turnoff will be on your left as you head south through town. If you pass through during the last weekend in September, stop to check out the big dance festival held in town. Performers come from miles around, and regional dancers fill the *zócalo* all weekend.

En Route from Atlixco Twenty-two miles (35 km) beyond Atlixco, the town of Izúcar de Matamoros is hidden a mile off the highway. If you have an extra 40 minutes or so, especially in October or on a Monday, which is market day, it is worth a quick look-see.

IZÚCAR DE MATAMOROS Izúcar is the source of the colorful ceremonial ceramics—brightly glazed tree-of-life candelabra decorated with angels, skulls, and fruit—traditionally used for the *Día de los Muertos* (Day of the Dead) fiesta on November 2. On *Corpus Cristi* (the Thursday following the eighth Sunday after *Easter*), don't miss the presentations of the dance of the Moors and Christians. There is also a year-round resort, the *Salto de Amatitlán* (Amatitlán Spa), 1 mile (1.6 km) east of town, which boasts a mineral spring and dry air, said to be good for the liver and kidneys (no phone).

En Route from Izúcar de Matamoros About 54 miles (86 km) farther, still on Route 190, is Acatlán, an important pottery-making town.

ACATLÁN Some of the most attractive pottery in Mexico originates here. White clay, sculpted with curiously shaped animals, birds, and human figures, is built up into a pyramid or tree of life and decorated with bright colors. The figures are not entirely covered with paint; color is only used as a highlight on the white background. The final product is unglazed, an example of folk art that has remained unchanged for centuries. Other potters in this town specialize in the black Coyotepec kitchenware typical of Oaxaca.

A number of artists have shops at the north edge of town, and although the dominant language here is Mixtecan, you should have no problem. All the merchants speak Spanish and enough English to make bargaining a stimulating but conquerable challenge, and well worth the effort.

En Route from Acatlán Roughly 21 miles (34 km) beyond the village, the road enters the state of Oaxaca. It's 39 miles (62 km) to Huajuapán de León, a town that marks the halfway point in the journey between Puebla and Oaxaca. Route 190 cuts through the town, most of which lies south of the highway, in the Valle del Río Mixteco (Mixteco River Valley).

HUAJUAPÁN DE LEÓN (pronounced Wa-hwa-*pahn*) Huajuapán (pop. 50,000) was the birthplace of General Antonio de León, a hero of the Battle of Molino del Rey during the 1847 US invasion of Mexico. (Mexico won this battle, though the US ended up winning the war.) The town was completely rebuilt after 1980, when a strong earthquake, whose epicenter was nearby, wiped out about 60% of its buildings.

This is the mescal-producing region of Mexico. Mescal, a fermented alcoholic drink made from hearts of the maguey plant (a type of agave) and bottled with each plant's own maguey worm, is similar to tequila and highly potent. The Mexicans have an expression, *"Para todo mal mezcal y para todo bien también,"* which translated freely means, "Mescal makes the bad times good and the good times better." That may be, but don't drink too much of it if you're going to continue driving.

Huajuapán de León is also known for its textiles, woven from palm leaves and sold at the Sunday market. The town holds annual fairs on May 19 and July 23, and if you are in the area, the dancing is well worth seeing.

En Route from Huajuapán Yanhuitlán is 48 miles (77 km) away.

YANHUITLÁN (pronounced Yahn-weet-*lahn*) The only point of interest in this tiny hamlet looms up at you from miles away and grows to gigantic proportions as you get nearer. It's Yanhuitlán's 16th-century *Convento Dominicano* (Dominican Convent), whose carved and painted 100-foot ceilings shelter dozens of chirping birds. There is a bas-relief behind one of the altars and several interesting carved wooden ornaments. Many of the church's decorations have been restored to their original splendor.

The convent is infamous for an incident that took place here in 1642. The Inquisition prohibited a native rite involving the use of hallucinogenic mushrooms, but the Indians ignored the edict. The Inquisitors seized a number of Indian chiefs, tortured them until they confessed to being in league with the devil, and promptly burned them in the churchyard.

En Route from Yanhuitlán From here the route to the city of Oaxaca, 48 miles (77 km) away, involves difficult mountain driving and should not be attempted at night. Tiring even in daylight, the road becomes especially dangerous after dark.

About 7 miles (11 km) before the city of Oaxaca, there is a turnoff from Route 190. If you are traveling with a list of all the people to whom you must bring gifts, a short side trip at this point might do much to ease your mind. At the end of the road is the little town of Santa María Atzompa, where you will find an amusing type of pottery. The object is a small horned animal with an unglazed, striated body and a glazed green head. The animal is filled with water, chia seeds are planted in the surface grooves, and soon it becomes covered with a green, mosslike coat. A generic version of this pottery is now sold in the US, but this is the genuine article. It is particularly popular with children.

OAXACA This lovely, easygoing city closes early, and if you are planning to spend the night, try to find a hotel immediately upon arrival. For a detailed report on the city, its restaurants, and its hotels, see *Oaxaca* in THE CITIES.

There are several worthwhile side trips from Oaxaca.

MONTE ALBÁN Only 6 miles (10 km) southwest of Oaxaca, this is one of Mexico's most spectacular archaeological sites. For additional details, see *Mexico's Magnificent Archaeological Heritage* in DIVERSIONS and Oaxaca in THE CITIES.

CUILAPÁN (pronounced Cwee-la-*pahn*) This tiny Mixtec village, 9 miles (14 km) southwest of Oaxaca on a local paved road, is the site of another and very different kind of ruin. Here, in 1555, a group of Dominican friars began work on a massive basilica next to their monastery, but the project was never completed nor given a name. Today it has deteriorated into an odd combination of functioning parts (still used for worship) and crumbling ruins. The walls of the basilica hold the tombs of perhaps the last of the Zapotec and Mixtec royalty, the Mixtec Prince of Tilantongo and his wife Cosijopi, daughter of the King of Tehuantepec; they reigned during the late 14th or early 15th century.

In its heyday, Cuilapán was the hub of the cochineal (red dye) industry, so important in the development of Mexico's traditional textiles. Long before the Spanish invasion, the Zapotec used this enduring scarlet dye, derived from the dried female cochineal mite. During the colonial period, the Spanish crown had a monopoly on cochineal, and vast haciendas were built around the industry. The Spanish took their monopoly so seriously that anyone caught removing from Spanish territory the cactus on which the mites laid their eggs was sentenced to death. Only the Spanish were allowed to export the dye, and scarlet soon became the rage in Europe. Even the resplendent red coats of the British army were dyed with cochineal.

ZAACHILA Three miles (5 km) farther down the same road that Cuilapán is on is this lovely pastoral village, the last capital of the Zapotec nation. The archaeological site on the edge of town has been only partially excavated. What has been unearthed so far in the way of clay figurines, gold plate, carved reliefs, and royal remains is quite fascinating, and much more is yet to be revealed. However, the site is not yet open to the public.

En Route from Oaxaca Go back to Route 190 and continue 4 miles (6 km) southeast to Santa María el Tule.

SANTA MARÍA EL TULE This little town has two claims to fame: Its mangoes are said to be among the most delicious in the world, and it is the home of Mexico's oldest living tree, the *Arbol Tule* (Tule Tree). Towering above the churchyard in which it stands, this huge ahuehuete cypress (which is still growing today) reaches 140 feet into the air, measures 136 feet around, and has a trunk 55 feet thick. Naturalists estimate that this grand cypress is between 2,500 and 3,200 years old. Close by stands another tree that would otherwise be impressively large. In a few hundred years, *El Hijo,* "the son," may take over as the successor of a mighty arboreal tradition and serve as guardian of Santa María el Tule. Lively festivities are held in town on *Día de la Candelaria* (Candlemas; February 2), which features colorful dances, horse racing, water sports, and fireworks.

En Route from Santa María el Tule Two miles (3 km) farther on Route 190 are the famous ruins of one of the finest of the Zapotec centers—*Dainzú,* which has a symmetrical ground plan and a magnificent view of the surrounding valleys. Two miles (3 km) past *Dainzú* on Route 190 is the turnoff to Teotitlán del Valle, another 4 miles (6 km) down the paved side road.

TEOTITLÁN DEL VALLE A pleasant village at the foot of the Sierra Madre, Teotitlán is the center of Oaxaca's serape industry, and almost every home in town has a loom. The typical Teotitlán serape is all wool, usually of two panels, of light to medium weight, loosely woven, and decorated with stylized animal figures.

En Route from Teotitlán del Valle Return to Route 190; about 10 miles (16 km) farther is Tlacolula, a town that dates from 1250. The native village has a wonderful Sunday market, and in town there is also a beautiful 16th-century church with a fine chapel.

From Tlacolula head south to the turnoff to the ruins of *Mitla,* at the end of a marked side road off Route 190, about 27 miles (46 km) southeast of Oaxaca.

MITLA Originally the home of the Zapotec and later the Mixtec, *Mitla* has puzzled archaeologists, who have found no recorded representations of people, animals, or mythological symbols here. The designs in the large *Sala de Monolitos* (Hall of Monoliths) are reminiscent of Greek fretwork. About 4½ miles (7 km) north of the ruins is the town of Mitla, where you can see the fine collection of Mixtec and Zapotec artifacts in the small *Museo de Arte Zapotec Frissell,* located in the center of town (no phone). The museum is open daily; there's no admission charge on Sundays. For additional details, see *Mexico's Magnificent Archaeological Heritage* in DIVERSIONS.

En Route from Mitla Head back to Route 190, which now begins its sinuous progress through rugged mountains with an occasional vista over the lush countryside. Curving, twisting, and winding back on itself, the two-lane road soars from peak to sweeping valley in rapid succession, rising, dipping, turning right and left, with every diabolical twist a road can make. It is no route for an inexperienced or timid driver, or for a passenger who suffers from motion sickness, and there are few places to pause for a breather. The driver's undivided attention is required at all times. Although the driving surface is excellent, be on the lookout for the occasional surprise boulders offered up by the surrounding mountains. Again, heed the maximum speeds posted: The road is narrow, and it's a long drop.

After about 72 miles (115 km) the road descends from 4,900 feet to 800 feet in a 39-mile (62-km) series of long, winding curves through magnificent scenery. The road eventually levels out at the riverside town of Tequisistlán, which will, from this time on, occupy a warm place in your memory as the place the road stood still. From here you enter the tropical lowlands of the Istmo de Tehuantepec (Isthmus of Tehuantepec), with the town of the same name only 30 miles (48 km) down the road. Numerous unexplored beaches line the coast here; for more information, see *Best Beaches* in DIVERSIONS.

TEHUANTEPEC One of two major cities on the isthmus, Tehuantepec is the subject of great controversy in the rest of Mexico. Here, in a country dominated by machismo, a society exists in which women have social and cultural dominance (though history is cloudy on why the society developed this way). Women handle the commerce and trade, hold the purse strings, and run the banks, while the men plant and harvest the fields.

The elaborate daily attire of the *Tehuana* (women of Tehuantepec), characterized by gold embroidery on red cloth, is modest compared with their dress for special occasions. Fiestas call for satin or velvet skirts, sleeveless blouses, and starched ruffled petticoats of finely pleated white lace. On their heads the women sport magnificent bonnets of white lace fashioned after a baby's baptismal dress, with two tiny sleeves uselessly hanging down over the ears. This particular form of headdress is said to have originated when a hapless sailor returned home from a long voyage without a gift for his wife, who promptly put him out of the house, telling him not to return empty-handed. He roamed all the way to Oaxaca, where in desperation he grabbed a package from a Spanish *doña* who was just leaving a local shop with a baptismal gown for her new baby. When the sailor returned home and his wife opened his offering, she didn't know what to make of it. The quick-thinking sailor, wishing to enjoy the comforts of home once again, told her the baptismal gown was a hat and the latest rage in Oaxaca. When she wore it outside, it was so successful that all the women of the town followed suit, and soon its popularity moved it from style to tradition. Much like the Gypsy women of Europe, the women of Tehuantepec wear the family wealth in the form of heavy chains, necklaces, and bracelets made of gold coins. The most valuable of the coins are worth $2,000 apiece; some women wear as much as $30,000 in gold.

Unfortunately, the town has little to recommend it other than its exceptional social structure and traditional attire. Sweltering under the tropical sun, with only one paved road, it is one of the least attractive towns along the route. But the sight of the local women filling the *zócalo* at night, sitting around in the drowsy tropical air, swapping salty stories, and whistling at any attractive man passing by, is truly a pleasure. A final word about the *Tehuana:* These women are known for their fiery tempers and are provoked by having their pictures taken or being approached by foreign men.

The town name, Tehuantepec, is Nahuatl for "Jaguar Hill." According to legend, fierce jaguars once roamed this country, forcing the natives to appeal to a sorcerer for aid. He, in turn, called upon a giant turtle to rise from the sea and drive the jaguars away. When the last jaguar was gone, the sorcerer transformed the turtle into a hill and ordered it to keep guard and see that none of the jaguars returned. If you climb the brush-covered path to the top of this mound, you, like the turtle, will get a spectacular view stretching from from Juchitán in the east to the great lagoon of Tehuantepec along the Pacific in the west. If you visit during June, you can go to the *Fiesta de las Calendas,* an annual regional arts and crafts fair held in town.

En Route from Tehuantepec If you are ready for a little ocean and beach life before continuing west, a side trip should more than satisfy you. Eleven miles (18 km) south of Tehuantepec on Route 185 (take the turnoff from Rte. 190) is the once booming port town of Salina Cruz, whence an unpaved but good road leads east for 20 minutes to Bahía Ventosa.

BAHÍA VENTOSA (VENTOSA BAY) This beautiful 4-mile stretch of beach curves to form a small bay bordered by lush tropical vegetation. There are a number of thatch-roofed beach restaurants offering the local catch of seafood and generously providing hammocks for weary travelers. If you decide to stay overnight, there are a few rooming houses (ask for the *Casa de Huéspedes* when you arrive); campers have taken over a coconut grove near the beach, although the facilities are primitive. *Ventosa* means "windy," and the bay is very aptly named. Make sure to do all your sunbathing before about 3 PM, when the wind begins to blow. All that soft, fine sand becomes airborne at a speed of about 30 mph, in effect sandblasting the tan off any uncovered skin. For more information, see *Best Beaches* in DIVERSIONS.

En Route from Bahía Ventosa The only road out of Bahía Ventosa is the one leading into it. From Tehuantepec, take Route 190 east 16 miles (26 km) to Juchitán de Zaragoza, on the way to Chiapas.

JUCHITÁN DE ZARAGOZA (pronounced Hoo-chee-*tahn* day Sah-rah-*go*-sah) At times in their history, Juchitán de Zaragoza and its neighbor Tehuantepec have been known to struggle over everything from political allegiances to the length of hemlines and depth of necklines. Eternally vying with Tehuantepec for eminence in weaving, pottery, gold jewelry, and poetry, this busy isthmus town has succeeded in becoming the more important cultural and economic center for the area. For instance, the market and fiestas of Juchitán are cleaner and more elaborate than those of its rival. Juchitán is also the straw hat, basket, and weaving center of the isthmus, and handloomed and finely embroidered textiles can be found in shops near the *zócalo,* or main square. The women of Juchitán, known as *Juchitecas,* take pride in adorning themselves with colorful clothing and gold jewelry. A festival featuring native dancing is usually held in the spring.

En Route from Juchitán de Zaragoza Before embarking on the 57-mile (91-km) journey to Tapanatepec, just west of the Oaxaca-Chiapas border, consider resting or eating in the Juchitán area. Just over the Río los Perros is the clean, air conditioned *Colón* restaurant (no phone). As you continue toward Tapanatepec, you'll come across a strip of road, near the junction of Routes 190 and 185, that warrants a word of caution. The wind is so fierce along this stretch that it has been known to blow strips of chrome off the sides of cars. It sometimes requires a herculean effort to stay on the right side of the highway, so slow down to avoid problems with oncoming vehicles.

At Tapanatepec the road to Guatemala divides. Route 200, the newer road, glides quickly along the level Pacific Coast. For anyone eager to reach Central America quickly, or, conversely, for those with enough time to dally along some of the country's most beautiful beaches (with a guarantee of privacy more secure than anywhere else on Mexico's sweeping Pacific Coast), it can be delightful.

The longer trip, northward and inland along Route 190, offers a far better picture of exotic Chiapas. We recommend, however, that you avoid driving this stretch of Route 190 during the rainy season (November and December); just after Tapanatepec the road can become muddy and dangerous, especially in the mountains. In addition, though the political situation in Chiapas appeared to be stable at press time, remember to exercise general caution and avoid straying into isolated areas in this region. Also, under no circumstances should you ever take photographs—this includes videos—of native peoples without getting their permission first. Many indigenous people in this region believe that photographs can capture their souls, and they have sometimes attacked shutter-happy tourists.

Both routes are described below. Note that no matter which road you take, the highways in Chiapas are in far worse repair than those in Oaxaca. Chiapas is a poor state, a situation made patently obvious when the middle-of-the-road white lines disappear from the highway and the pavement becomes rougher and harder.

CHIAPAS'S PACIFIC COAST—ROUTE 200

En Route from Tapanatepec Route 200 crosses the Chiapas border and then rolls along the Pacific Coast for 198 miles (317 km) before entering Guatemala. While it parallels the coastline, it is several miles from the sea; to find the best beaches and fishing villages you must leave the highway occasionally and drive south. The first really interesting stop is Tonalá, 42 miles (67 km) from Tepanatepec. Tonalá also has roads to several marvelous sea spots.

TONALÁ and PAREDÓN A seafood-shipping center, Tonalá is the turnoff point for Paredón and Puerto Arista, two of Chiapas's seaside resorts. Fifteen miles (24 km) southwest of Tonalá via a local paved road, Paredón is on a bay known deceptively as the *Mar Muerto* (Dead Sea), an angler's paradise. Besides magnificent catches, the waters here promise perfect swimming year-round. A popular activity is a *cayuco* (dugout canoe) excursion along the 40-mile coastline of the bay; the trip can also be made by motorboat. (Bargain with local boat owners at the town dock for either type of excursion.) There are facilities for camping and trailers, and there are also a couple of small hotels. The *Grajandra* (204 Av. Hidalgo in Paredón; phone: 966-30144) has a restaurant, bar, pool, and disco.

Another road, leading 7 miles (11 km) southeast from Tonalá, goes to the pristine beaches of Puerto Arista. The only sign of human encroachment here is a few thatch-roofed restaurants, for which you will be grateful.

En Route from Tonalá To reconnect with Route 200 you must return to Tonalá, from which it is a fast, fairly flat stretch all the way to Tapachula, 11 miles (18 km) from the Guatemala border. Along this undeveloped section of the route, you'll see dense forests of rare woods and exotic orchids, fields of sugarcane, and stock farms.

TAPACHULA This city is the center for local coffee, cotton, cocoa, and banana plantations. Set at the foot of the extinct Tacaná volcano, Tapachula has a charming *zócalo* with neatly trimmed tropical trees, lively sidewalk cafés, and a choice of pleasant accommodations. The small tourism office (phone: 961-39396/7/8/9), in the *Palacio Municipal* (City Hall) on the south side of the *zócalo,* will provide maps and advice on the Guatemala border crossing. The office is closed Sundays. A day in Puerto Madero is a recommended side trip.

PUERTO MADERO At the end of a 15-mile (24-km) paved road south of Tapachula is the beautiful Pacific resort of Puerto Madero, where there are facilities for all sorts of water sports, plus the usual thatch-roofed restaurants serving freshly caught fish. You are likely to find yourself the only non-Mexican on this idyllic, unspoiled, and totally relaxing beach.

En Route from Tapachula You are now at the edge of Mexico, ready to enter Guatemala. By backtracking to Huixtla (pronounced *Weesh*-la), 26 miles (42 km) west of Tapachula along Route 200, you can pick up a mostly dirt road north and drive 82½ miles (132 km) roughly parallel to Mexico's border with Guatemala to connect with Route 190 just before it crosses the border at Ciudad Cuauhtémoc. Or you can continue on Route 200 for 20 minutes more and cross into Guatemala from Talismán. (For details regarding entry into Guatemala, see *En Route from Lagunas de Montebello,* below.)

INLAND CHIAPAS—ROUTE 190

OCOZOCOAUTLA (pronounced O-ko-so-*kwout*-la) This town populated by almost pure-blooded Zoque is 74 miles (123 km) from Tapanatepec, along Route 190. Of Maya descent, the Zoque are a tall, stout people who farm and work as laborers. The men of the village wear shirts and pants of a rough woven fabric called *manta,* and the women wear dresses cinched at the waist with blue fabric rolled into a belt. Above Ocozocoautla, a half-hour walk up the side of the mountain, is the tiny village of Ocuilpa, where artisans make beautifully decorated pots that have wavy black-and-white-lined designs around the rims.

En Route from Ocozocoautla Forty miles (64 km) east along Route 190 is Tuxtla Gutiérrez.

TUXTLA GUTIÉRREZ The capital city of Chiapas, Tuxtla Gutiérrez replaced San Cristóbal de las Casas as the seat of state government in 1892 and is now a prosperous commercial distribution center for the surrounding coffee and tobacco plantations. The town's 45 or so hostelries are booked to 95% capacity year-round, so it is advisable to make reservations in advance through a travel agent in Oaxaca. Although the city is not particularly picturesque, it is filled with tropical flowers and interesting sites, and it offers a good opportunity to rest up before continuing along the route. The *Palacio de Gobierno* (Statehouse), on the Plaza Principal (central plaza) is a handsome building of Mexican and Spanish design with a monument to the state's benefactor, Friar Bartolomé de las Casas, a Dominican missionary and later bishop of Chiapas, who ended the Spaniards' oppressive treatment of the native people in the region. In the town market and in shops near the central plaza is a large selection of inlaid wooden boxes, lacquered gourds, carved deer antlers, leather goods, native amber, and gold jewelry. The Zoque women of the area wear rosary-like necklaces of amber beads and small gold coins with gold filigree crosses, heirlooms much sought after by collectors.

On the southeastern side of the city is Tuxtla's fabulous zoo and ecological park, the *Parque Zoológico Miguel Alvarez del Toro* (phone: 961-29943 or 961-23754), where more than 100 species of animals native to the state—such as monkeys, jaguars, anteaters, ocelots, boars, snakes, and birds—roam free in lush vegetation. (Visitors observe from protected areas.) This impressive collection has been written up in renowned scientific publications throughout the world. The zoo is closed Mondays; no admission charge, though donations are welcome.

Another place worth visiting is the *Museo Regional de Chiapas* (Regional Museum of Chiapas, on the Calzada de los Hombres Ilustres; phone: 961-34479), designed by Pedro Ramírez Vázquez—architect of the *Museo Nacional de Antropología* in Mexico City—and devoted to pre-Hispanic treasures. It is closed Mondays; admission charge. Be sure to stop at the tourist office (950 Blvd. Dr. Belisario Domínguez; phone: 961-34499 or 961-24535). The staff speaks English and has done a remarkable job compiling tourist information for the entire state. The office is closed Sundays. Several long blocks east is the *Casa de las Artesanías,* which sells fine examples of handicrafts made throughout the state. Also inside is an excellent ethnographic museum of the state's indigenous groups (1030 Blvd. Dr. Belisario Domínguez; phone: 961-21612). Both the shop and the museum are closed Sundays; no admission charge.

Excursions from Tuxtla include tours of coffee and tobacco plantations, which can be arranged through any hotel or the tourist office. For an amazing side trip from Tuxtla, drive 15 miles (24 km) north of town to Cerro de Tierra Colorada (Tierra Colorada Hill). From a lookout point here, one can see the spectacular formations of the Cañón del Sumidero.

CAÑÓN DEL SUMIDERO (SUMIDERO CANYON) This 26-mile-long, 4,875-foot-deep canyon was cut by the churning waters and treacherous rapids of the Río Grijalva at the bottom. The river was tamed somewhat after the completion of the *Presa Manuel Moreno* (Manuel Moreno Dam, popularly called the *Presa Chicoasén*) in 1980.

It was here that the fiercely independent natives of Chiapas made their final stand against the invading Spaniards in the middle of the 16th century. Spanish troops pushed into Chiapas to subdue the united tribes that had thus far managed to resist them. Over a period of years, the tribes were driven to the edge of the canyon. In the last prolonged battle, they held off the Spaniards for days with arrows and spears, until their food ran out. Their numbers dwindling, the Indians fought on with their few remaining weapons, then with rocks, and finally with their bare hands. When they could no longer hold off the enemy, they threw themselves into the ravine; all told, some 1,000 Indians committed suicide rather than submit to Spanish rule. The awed invaders, not wanting to be a party to further genocide, withdrew their troops to Oaxaca, and the natives of Chiapas were left to rule their own land.

En Route from Tuxtla Gutiérrez Continue on Route 190 for 8 miles (14 km) to Chiapa de Corzo.

CHIAPA DE CORZO This picturesque colonial village, built on a bluff overlooking the Río Chiapa, was founded in 1528 by conquistador Diego de Mazariegos on the site of a native settlement. The *zócalo* is dominated by a strange and beautiful 16th-century fountain shaped like the crown of the King of Spain. This imposing octagonal structure is considered the finest example of Mozarabic (Spanish-Arabic) architecture in Mexico. Another 16th-century legacy is the Gothic *Iglesia* and *Convento de Santo Domingo* (Church and Convent of St. Dominic; one block south of the *zócalo,* at the corner of Calles Mexicanidad and Chiapas). Hanging in the tower is a huge bell made of silver, gold, and copper.

Also in the convent building is the small but colorful *Museo Regional de la Laca* (Regional Lacquer Museum; phone: 961-60055), devoted to exhibits of regional handicrafts. It is closed Mondays; no admission charge. The specialty of the region is colorful lacquered gourds called *jícaras,* and local potters specialize in green and black glazed ware.

Local festivals include *Día de San Sebastián* (St. Sebastian Day, January 20), celebrated with a fair, folk dancing, and a reenactment of a naval battle on the Río Grijalva. The next day is the famed dance of the Parachicos, put on by hundreds of performers in brightly colored native dress and masks. In the spring, there's an annual *Easter* carnival.

On the eastern edge of town is an interesting Maya ruin with pyramidal platforms. In addition, Chiapa de Corzo is the point of departure for river trips that go some distance into the Cañón del Sumidero (Sumidero Canyon). You can also bargain with local boat owners at the town dock for a ride downriver to Alcalá, 17½ miles (28 km) away, and from there take a bus another 10 miles (16 km) to the native village of San Bartolomé de los Llanos, whose inhabitants dress in some of the most unusual and attractive native costumes in all of Mexico. The women wear colorfully embroidered dark blue skirts and lovely white lace blouses. The men wear white cotton jodhpur-like trousers, flared from the hip to the knee and narrow from there to the ankle. These pants are covered with tiny red embroidered figures, which also appear on the men's lacelike shirts. Both men and women leave their midriffs uncovered.

En Route from Chiapa de Corzo The 44-mile (71-km) drive east on Route 190 to San Cristóbal, the next major stop, is an amazing 5,000-foot climb through magnificent mountain scenery, with spectacular vistas at every turn. Watch out for local people careening down the hillsides in tiny homemade wooden carts stuffed with the day's shopping or goods destined for the market: The carts have no brakes.

SAN CRISTÓBAL DE LAS CASAS Set in the lovely valley of Hueyzacatlán, this town exudes a colonial ambience. The buildings are mostly one-story stucco houses painted in pastel tones and topped with red tile roofs. Peering down from the two hills east and west of town are two churches, carefully and somewhat threateningly placed—one atop each hill—by the Spanish conquistadores. Members of the nearly 30 tribes from the surrounding mountains fill the town and marketplace, each group wearing its own particular clothing and speaking its own language. The pace is slow; the weather is warm under a morning sun, but cold (lows in the high 40s F, or around 9C) at night. At press time, San Cristóbal was calm in the wake of the armed uprising that occurred here in January 1994; the Zapatistas, as the rebels call themselves, are negotiating with the government and are in the process of becoming a legitimate political party. (But they still wear black ski masks to hide their identities, giving rise to a new item in the local markets—dolls with ski masks.) Although peace seems to have been declared, exercise normal precautions and don't stray into isolated areas.

Captain Luis Marín and the famous soldier-historian Bernal Díaz del Castillo led their troops into this valley in 1524. The native Chamula fought bravely against the Spanish until their losses became too heavy. Four years later, when the Spaniards had consolidated control, the Spanish governor,

Juan Enrique de Guzmán, instituted repressive tactics. In 1545, when Bishop Bartolomé de las Casas arrived in this former capital of Chiapas, conditions were at their worst. The bishop fought vigorously on behalf of the Chamula, speaking out against the political practices of the governor and writing a detailed report to Madrid about the deplorable situation. He earned himself the hatred of the conquistadores, and his report was widely circulated by the enemies of Spain in the rest of Europe. But it was not until 20 years later, when the king issued "New Ordinances Governing Treatment of Indians in the New World," that the bishop's report had any effect. The new ruling, which in effect recognized the natives as humans, went largely ignored. Nevertheless, Bishop de las Casas won a place in the hearts of the Chamula, and the town is named in his honor.

Among the many places of interest in San Cristóbal is the *Catedral* (on the *zócalo,* also known as Plaza 31 de Marzo), notable for its Baroque *retablos* (altarpieces) and magnificent gold-encrusted pulpit. Across from the southeast side of the Plaza 31 de Marzo, at the corner of Calles de Diego de Mazariegos and Insurgentes, is the palatial, elaborate *Casa de Mazariegos,* once the mansion of the city's founder and now the *Santa Clara* hotel (see *Best en Route*). The *Iglesia de Santo Domingo,* begun in 1547, stands six blocks north of the plaza, on Avenida 20 de Noviembre. The carvings on its Baroque façade have weathered to a dusty pink; its interior is covered with elaborate gilt *retablos.* Visitors are also drawn to the town's 16th-century *Iglesia del Carmen* and its Moorish-style tower. The church is three blocks south of the *zócalo* on Calle Hidalgo; the base of the building is an arch through which a street runs.

It is impossible to visit San Cristóbal and not see *Na Bolom Centro de Estudios Científicos* (Na Bolom Center of Scientific Studies; 33 Av. Vicente Guerrero; phone: 967-81418), a home-library-museum founded by the late Gertrude Duby Blom, a Swiss writer, photographer, and linguist, and her husband, Franz "Pancho" Blom, a Danish archaeologist who had lived in Mexico since 1919. (Franz died in 1963, and Gertrude—then in her nineties—died in 1994.) The Bloms, who married in the early 1940s, devoted themselves to the study of the customs, language, and history of the area's inhabitants. They are credited with having saved the once-dwindling Lacandón Maya civilization from extinction. In recognition of their work, the Mexican government bestowed on them the rare honor of Mexican citizenship. The entire center is dedicated to the ecology of Chiapas and the preservation of the Lacandón region. The center's museum is closed Mondays; the library is closed Sundays and Mondays; admission charge. There's also a guesthouse on the premises (see *Best en Route*).

Anfitriones Turísticos de Chiapas (15 Avenida 5 de Febrero; phone: 967-82550 or 967-82557) arranges charter flights from San Cristóbal to the ruins of *Bonampak* and *Palenque,* and to the Lacandón region. The company also arranges river trips, horseback rides, and bird watching expeditions. For general tourist information, visit the state tourist office at 2 Av. Miguel

Hidalgo (open daily; phone: 967-86570) or the municipal office, on the ground floor of the *Palacio Municipal,* or town hall (closed Sundays; phone: 967-80660).

For a fascinating overview of the area's attractions and regional clothing, visit the *Museo de Traje Regional* (Museum of Regional Dress; 32 Av. 16 de Septiembre; phone: 967-84289), run by Sergio Castro, an agricultural engineer who has worked with the local Indians for most of his life. The museum offers a slide show and is open evenings only; no admission charge, but donations are welcome.

About 2 miles (3 km) northeast of the *zócalo* is the *Muxviquil* archaeological zone, which contains some barely explored Maya ruins that make a fascinating afternoon outing. And about 4 miles (7 km) south of town, just off Route 190 via a rough trail, are the partially explored *Grutas de Rancho Nuevo* (Rancho Nuevo Caverns), an enticing series of caves for the experienced spelunker. They can be entered only during the dry season (generally from January through June). Group tours of the caves are offered by *Na Bolom Centro de Estudios Científicos* (see above).

While a main attraction in San Cristóbal is people watching, bear in mind that the Indians strongly dislike being stared at and—once again—definitely do not want to be photographed without permission. Be discreet and considerate in observing them. The variations in clothing can give you clues as to which indigenous group an individual belongs. For example, the Chamula women wear *huipiles* (shapeless blouses) tucked into wraparound skirts of heavy black wool streaked with red and gray stripes. The only adornments on the *huipil* are two tassels of red wool or silk hanging down the front. The *huipil* is belted by a red woolen sash with a large pleat in front; women cover their heads with a folded piece of the same material. The men wear white calf-length pants and shirts covered by black or white woolen tunics. The men of San Juan Chamula have white sleeves on their tunics; those from San Andrés Chamula, red; those from Santiago, brown; and those from Santa Marta and Magdalenas, blue. They all wear flat, handwoven straw hats tied under the chin by bands. The Chamula seldom wear ribbons on their hats, except in combination with black tunics that indicate the wearer is or was an official of the village. Around their waists, the Chamula wear goat horns, in which salt is kept to use as a condiment and for barter.

Zinacantec women wear *huipiles* of white homespun wool, often beautifully embroidered, that reach to their calves. The upper part is completely covered by diamond-shaped patterns; the lower part and sleeves follow the same pattern but are embroidered in a smaller, more delicate stitch. The men wear short white or pale pink cotton tunics with very short pants designed to show off their well-formed, muscular legs—Zinacantec males are said to have the most beautiful legs in the world. They also sport handsome flat hats bedecked with gaily colored ribbons, which have an important meaning: Married men wear their ribbons tied, while bachelors let their ribbons blow freely in the wind. A word of warning is in order regarding these hats. While they are an attractive purchase in the local markets, wait until you leave the area before wearing them. The Zinacantec resent strangers, especially women, wearing their finery.

The Huisteco women wear short cotton *huipiles* embroidered lengthwise in very fine red lines. Across these lines are diamond-shaped decorations embroidered in orange, green, and magenta yarn. The *huipil* is worn with a dark blue wraparound skirt held up by a red-and-black-striped woolen waistband. The costume of the Huisteco men is one of the region's most interesting, consisting of a wide piece of cotton material placed waist-level in the back and then crossed between the legs in numerous folds, diaper-fashion. The ends are brought up and fastened with a braided sash whose ends hang to either side. The shirt, a sleeved *huipil* split up the sides, is worn tucked inside the pants. It is made from heavy cotton embroidered on the back of the shoulders with one line of simple geometric figures in red or blue.

The Huisteco headdress is also unique. The hat has a small, flat, straw crown with an upturned brim reminiscent of a dinner plate. It is worn at a rakish angle, slanted over the forehead and attached at the nape of the neck by a red ribbon. Under the hat, hanging from a strap and dangling down the back all the way to the waist, is a small, colorfully embroidered flat bag used to carry small items. It is interesting to note that women usually go barefoot, even on the most festive occasions, while the men are shod in huaraches, often with built-up heel guards—a relic of Maya days.

An interesting side trip from San Cristóbal is San Juan Chamula, 8 miles (13 km) northwest.

SAN JUAN CHAMULA This is one of the more accessible of the many fascinating indigenous villages in the mountains north of San Cristóbal. While it can be reached by car, a guided horseback trip will make more adventurous, out-of-the-way detours possible. Horses can be rented and guides hired in San Cristóbal through most hotels. Whether you drive to San Juan Chamula or go on horseback, take the local road toward Zinacantán for a little over 4 miles (about 6 km), and then turn right down the unpaved road, where it's another 3½ miles (5½ km) to San Juan.

Try to attend Sunday mass in San Juan Chamula's church, where the services are conducted in Tzotzil, the native tongue. A permit must be obtained in advance at the *Palacio Municipal* (City Hall, in a one-room building in the center of town, on the *zócalo*) for a small fee. Absolutely no photographs may be taken inside the church.

En Route from San Cristóbal de las Casas Continue on Route 190 to Comitán de Domínguez, which marks the halfway point in the 110-mile (176-km) drive from San Cristóbal to the Guatemalan border.

COMITÁN DE DOMÍNGUEZ Long before the Spanish settled here in the early 16th century, Comitán de Domínguez was the most populated Maya-Quiché kingdom in southeast Chiapas. It was then called Bulumcanán, Maya for "new star." Today, this small colonial community, built on the side of a mountain, is the chief entry port for Guatemalan products as well as the main marketing center for the native Tzeltal. Here you will find colonial houses perched atop huge rocks and connected by tortuous uphill-downhill streets, each with its own amazing view. The climate is superb, and the whole area is teeming with some 500 varieties of orchids. A Moorish-style kiosk, in the form of a six-pointed star, stands in the center of the plaza surrounded by these tropical blossoms. The area also makes a sugarcane brandy called *comitecho* or *chicha,* a fiery spirit not to be taken lightly. The *Lagos de Montebello* hotel (14 Blvd. Dr. Belisario Domínguez Nte.; phone/fax: 963-21092, 963-21198, or 963-20657) is a pleasant place to stay in town.

En Route from Comitán de Domínguez Between Comitán and the border town of Ciudad Cuauhtémoc, 55 miles (88 km) away, is the last stretch of Route 190 in Chiapas, and in Mexico. This leg offers a side trip to the Lagunas de Montebello (Montebello Lakes, also called Lagos de Montebello). To get there, drive south from Comitán on Route 190 for 11 miles (18 km). Just before La Trinitaria, turn east on the paved road that leads 27 miles (43 km) to Laguna de Colores, one of three more accessible lakes in the area. (Esmeralda and Tziscao are two others.)

Near the end of the road is the tiny village of San Rafael de Arco, where you can hire a guide to accompany you through the forest to the natural bridge over the Río Comitán and just beyond to a cave into which the river seems to disappear.

LAGUNAS DE MONTEBELLO This chain of more than 50 magnificent lakes, set in forest and mountain country, is one of the most beautiful and isolated places in Mexico. The waters of the lakes glow in spectacular shades of amethyst, turquoise, emerald, azure, and steely gray. In 1960, the Mexican government made the Lagunas de Montebello and the surrounding Selva Lacandona (Lacandón Rain Forest) into the *Parque Nacional Lagunas de Montebello.* The fishing here is reputed to be among the finest in Mexico. However, the only sleeping facility nearby is very run-down, so it's better to return to Comitán for the night. The park is open daily; there's an admission charge.

The forest and the vast unexplored lands to the east are the home of the Lacandón Maya. Totally isolated from the rest of the world, these people were near extinction when they were aided in the early 1920s by Franz "Pancho" Blom (see *San Cristóbal de las Casas,* above). The Lacandón continue to live in isolation, following their own ancient lifestyle and religion and speaking a rarely heard dialect of Maya. Some of them do speak Spanish, and they are aware of, if not totally familiar with, the presence of other people beyond the forest. There is no possibility of confusing a Lacandón with a member of any other native group. All members of the community wear their hair long, and the women, once they have reached puberty, tie brightly colored bird feathers to the back of their hair. Men and women dress alike, in loosely fitting white robes. The Lacandón are a reticent people who have opted to continue their life of seclusion. They do not feel comfortable around strangers, nor do they like having their pictures taken. Any contact with them must be carried out in a spirit sensitive to their lifestyle.

En Route from Lagunas de Montebello When you return to Route 190, you will be about 44 miles (70 km) from the border crossing at Ciudad Cuauhtémoc. Do not, under any circumstances, attempt this section of road at night. The consideration is not only one of safety, but also one of pure pleasure, for if you do drive at night you will deprive yourself of some of the most spectacular scenery in Mexico. The area overflows with a profusion of exotic flora and fauna; lush tropical plants and trees host more than 60 species of orchids. The bright plumage of this area's incredibly beautiful birds and butterflies sometimes eclipses the gorgeous scenery. If you are lucky, you might see a jaguar streaking across the road.

If you are planning to continue your trip into Guatemala, be prepared for the usual hassle at the border (and remember that if you're driving a rental car, you have to have already made arrangements for insurance to cover you in Guatemala). US citizens will need a visa or tourist card to enter the country; to obtain either, you must show your passport. Free three-year visas that allow multiple 30-day entries can be obtained at *Guatemalan Consulate General* offices in New York, New Orleans, Houston, Chicago, Los Angeles, San Francisco, or Miami; or at the consular sections of the *Guatemalan Embassies* in Washington, DC (2220 R St. NW, Washington, DC 20008; phone: 202-745-4952) or Mexico City (1025 Av. Explanada, Lomas de Chapultepec; phone: 5-520-2794). Tourist cards, good for one entry (and one 30-day stay) only, can be purchased at the Guatemalan border. However, obtaining a tourist card at the border can often be time-consuming, confusing, and more expensive than the actual $5 fee, so we advise you to get the paperwork done before leaving the US. Also note that at press time, the *US State Department* was advising travelers to be cautious in Guatemala due to threats against US citizens following rumors of US involvement in abductions of Guatemalan children. Check with the *US State Department* (phone: 202-647-5225) or the *US Embassy* in Mexico City (305 Paseo de la Reforma; phone: 5-211-0042) before setting off on your trip.

If you are not continuing into Guatemala, there is a highway that intersects with Route 190 at El Jocote, 3 miles (5 km) northwest of the border city of Ciudad Cuauhtémoc. From here it is a pleasant 130 miles (208 km) to Route 200 at Huixtla, and another five hours (155 miles/248 km) over the flat coastal road back up to Tapanatepec and the Pan-American Highway north.

BEST EN ROUTE

Along this route, expect to pay more than $100 per night for a double room in an expensive hotel; $50 to $100 in a moderate place; and less than $50 at an inexpensive one. The hotels in this region tend not to have air conditioning, TV sets, or telephones in rooms (exceptions are noted). In fact, fireplaces are a more attractive feature in San Cristóbal de las Casas, where it gets cold at night. For each location, hotels are listed alphabetically by price category.

HUAJUAPÁN DE LEÓN

Casablanca This hotel has 20 rooms with TV sets and ceiling fans, a pool, a restaurant, parking, and even a disco. 1 Amatista (phone: 953-20779; fax: 953-20979). Moderate.

García Peral Here are 32 rooms equipped with TV sets and telephones, a restaurant, and parking. Calle Colegio Militar (phone: 953-20777 or 953-20742; fax: 953-22000). Inexpensive.

TEHUANTEPEC

Calli The best lodging place between Oaxaca and Tuxtla Gutiérrez includes 100 modest, air conditioned rooms, plus a pool and a dining room. About a mile (1.6 km) past the turnoff to Tehuantepec, at Km 790 on Rte. 190 (phone: 971-50085/6/7/8/9; phone/fax: 971-50113). Moderate.

JUCHITÁN DE ZARAGOZA

La Mansión Here are 43 units with ceiling fans, plus a restaurant, a bar, and parking. 11 Prolongación Av. 16 de Septiembre (phone: 971-21055). Expensive to moderate.

TONALÁ

Granjandra The 24 comfortable rooms all have ceiling fans. There's a coffee shop and parking. 304 Av. Hidalgo (phone: 966-30144). Moderate.

TAPACHULA

Kamico In this two-story motor inn are 92 air conditioned units, a restaurant, and a pool. Rte. 200, on the east edge of town (phone: 962-62640; fax: 962-61878). Expensive.

Loma Real This property has 86 units with ceiling fans, a coffee shop, a restaurant, a bar, a pool, and a boutique. On a hilltop on Rte. 200 north of town (phone: 962-61440; 800-28006 elsewhere in Mexico; fax: 962-64816). Expensive to moderate.

Camino Real Perched on a hill overlooking the city, this establishment opened in 1995 and offers 200 rooms and 10 suites, all with air conditioning and cable TV. There are three swimming pools, a gym, two lighted artificial-lawn tennis courts, three restaurants, three bars, and convention and meeting facilities. 1195 Blvd. Dr. Belisario Domínguez (phone: 961-77777; 800-7-CAMINO in the US; 800-90123 in Mexico; fax: 961-77771). Expensive.

Balún Canán All 38 units have bathtubs and ceiling fans, and there is a restaurant. 944 Av. Central Ote. (phone/fax: 961-23050, 961-23102, or 961-23048). Moderate.

Bonampak This modern hotel has 88 air conditioned units with cable TV (including 15 bungalows). There is a pool, a handball and tennis court, a coffee shop, a cocktail bar, a video bar, and a dining room. 180 Blvd. Dr. Belisario Domínguez (phone: 961-32050; fax: 961-27737). Moderate.

Flamboyán A circular building houses 118 air conditioned rooms overlooking a central garden. There's a swimming pool, a wading pool, a tennis court, a restaurant, a coffee shop, and free movies. 2900 Blvd. Dr. Belisario Domínguez (phone: 961-50888; fax: 961-50087). Moderate.

La Hacienda Here are 42 units with ceiling fans, complemented by a restaurant, parking, and a pool, plus nine full hookups for trailers. 1197 Blvd. Belisario Domínguez (phone/fax: 961-27986 or 961-27832). Moderate.

Humberto A 112-room hotel with a dining room, a cafeteria, and a garage. Rooms are equipped with TV sets. 180 Av. Central Pte. (phone: 961-22081/2/3; fax: 961-29771). Moderate.

Posada del Rey Comfortable but modest, with 42 rooms and three suites (all with air conditioning and TV sets), and a rooftop restaurant. On the plaza at 310 Calle Primera (phone: 961-22871, 961-22924, or 961-22755; fax: 961-22210). Inexpensive.

SAN CRISTÓBAL DE LAS CASAS

Bonampak Offers 49 air conditioned units with cable TV, a restaurant-bar, a tennis court, a pool, and miniature golf. There are also 21 spaces with complete trailer hookups. At the entrance to town on 5 Av. México (phone: 967-81621; fax: 967-81622). Moderate.

El Molino de la Alborada Ten comfortable rooms with fireplaces (nice for the chilly nights); good food and horseback riding are available. Two miles (3 km) southeast of town on Rte. 190 (phone: 967-80935). Moderate.

Na Bolom This memorable place is on the grounds of the *Na Bolom Centro de Estudios Científicos*. The 12 rooms—each named for and decorated in the style of a particular regional pueblo—are comfortable. Meals feature food from the late Gertrude Blom's organic garden and orchard. 33 Av. Vicente Guerrero (phone: 967-81418; fax: 967-85586). Moderate.

Palacio de Moctezuma A 38-room hostelry with three lovely gardens, a restaurant, and a bar. 16 Av. Juárez (phone: 967-80352 or 967-81142; fax: 967-81536). Moderate.

Posada Diego de Mazariegos A colonial-style, 71-unit hotel with fireplaces and TV sets in every room, a restaurant, a bar, and a video bar. 2 María Adelina Flores (phone: 967-81825, 967-80621, or 967-80513; fax: 967-80817). Moderate.

Santa Clara Here is a delightful inn with 22 original rooms and another 40 in a newer addition, all with bathtubs. There's also a pool, a dining room, a bar, a cafeteria, and a handicrafts shop. On the Plaza 31 de Marzo, at Av. Insurgentes and 1 Plaza Central (phone: 967-81140; fax: 967-81041). Moderate.

Maya-Quetzal This 50-room hotel has a restaurant and a disco. Km 1171 on Rte. 190 (phone: 967-81181; fax: 967-80984). Moderate to inexpensive.

Español Flamboyán This tranquil hotel has 60 rooms, all with fireplaces. There's also a restaurant-bar. Avs. 16 de Septiembre and 1 de Marzo (phone: 967-80045 or 967-80623; fax: 967-80514). Inexpensive.

Villa Real A colonial building with 38 clean, comfortable rooms and a restaurant. No frills, but it's efficient and economical, and the service is friendly. 8 Av. Benito Juárez (phone: 967-82930). Inexpensive.

Reynosa to Mazatlán

The 720-mile (1,152-km) drive along Route 40 from Reynosa to Mazatlán is the shortest route to the Pacific from the southern and eastern US. It offers a variety of interesting stops and spectacular terrain in a region filled with mines, major industries, large-scale agriculture, and cattle ranches.

Beginning at the northeastern border of Mexico, along the Río Grande (called the Río Bravo in Mexico), this route rolls along flat plains before ascending, descending, and winding through the valleys, deep canyons, desert highlands, towering peaks, and rugged rolling hills of Mexico's Sierra Madre Oriental and Sierra Madre Occidental to the Pacific Ocean. In addition to passing through the states of Tamaulipas, Nuevo León, Coahuila, Durango, and Sinaloa, this route takes you to the major cities of Monterrey, Saltillo, Torreón, Durango, and Mazatlán, as well as to subterranean caverns, picturesque villages, mountain hideaways, locations used in movies, and dramatic mountains. The last 40-mile (64-km) stretch, climbing 9,000 feet into the Sierra Madre Occidental, is renowned for its beautiful scenery.

The climate along the route varies according to altitude and season. You can expect mild, dry weather with pleasant breezes at higher altitudes, and warm, dry weather at lower altitudes. Although the warm season is March through October, the colder season is never too cold; however, at night temperatures drop, and you will need a jacket.

The history of the regions along this route is one of conquest and violence. During the 1800s the Comanche and Apache raided throughout the state of Coahuila, and the northeastern territories were the site of numerous battles during the Mexican-American War. At the turn of the century, Durango-born Francisco "Pancho" Villa and Coahuila-born Francisco I. Madero both fought to overthrow Mexico's dictator, Porfirio Díaz.

The people of northern Mexico are considered to be more "North American" in their style of living and attitudes than are their compatriots farther south. The ancient cultures and traditions so prevalent in the southern and central regions are scarcely evident here.

En Route from McAllen, Texas Cross the international toll bridge over the Río Bravo into Reynosa. If you are planning to venture farther into the country, you must go through customs and immigration (open 24 hours) before continuing your journey. For regulations regarding entry into Mexico, SEE GETTING READY TO GO.

REYNOSA This town (pop. about 300,000) is a junction for roads to Matamoros, Nuevo Laredo, and Monterrey. Founded by the Spanish in 1749, Reynosa was little more than a village until oil was discovered in 1940. After that it quickly blossomed into one of the main urban centers in the state of

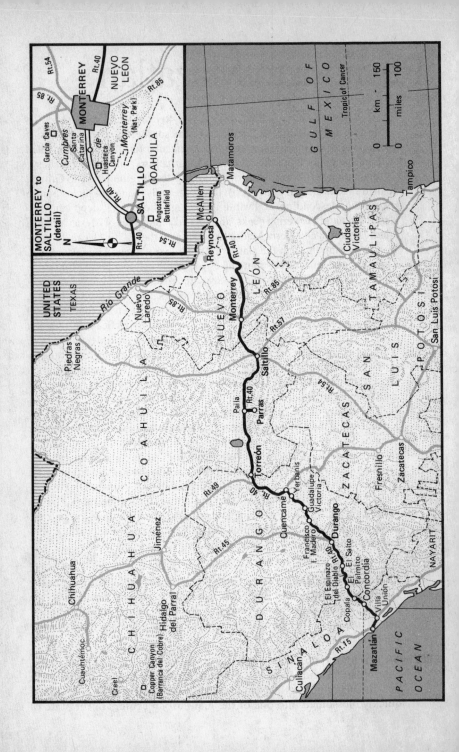

Rt.54

Rt.85

Rt.40

NUEVO
LEÓN

García Caves

MONTERREY

Santa
Catarina

Cumbres
de
Monterrey

Huasteca
Canyon

Monterrey
(Nat. Park)

Rt.85

SALTILLO

COAHUILA

Rt.40

Angostura
Battlefield

Rt.54

N

UNITED
STATES

TEXAS

Rio Grande

Piedras
Negras

Nuevo
Laredo

Rt.85

C O A H U I L A

Jiménez

Rt.45

Rt.49

Chihuahua

C H I H U A H U A

Hidalgo
del Parral

Copper Canyon
(Barranca del Cobre)

Creel

Cuauhtémoc

D U R A N G O

Cuencamé

Francisco
I. Madero

El Espinazo
del Diablo

Copala

El Salto
Palmito

Durango

Rt.40

Rt.40

Verbanis

Guadalupe
Victoria

Concordia

Villa
Unión

Mazatlán

S I N A L O A

Culiacán

Rt.15

P A C I F I C

O C E A N

McAllen

Reynosa

Rt.40

Matamoros

N U E V O

L E Ó N

Monterrey

Rt.85

Saltillo

Rt.57

Paila

Rt.40

Parras

Torreón

Rt.40

Z A C A T E C A S

Rt.54

Fresnillo

Zacatecas

S A N

L U I S

P O T O S Í

San Luis Potosí

Ciudad
Victoria

T A M A U L I P A S

Tampico

G U L F   O F
M E X I C O

Tropic of Cancer

km - 150

miles 100

NAYARIT

Tamaulipas. Today, Reynosa has thriving cattle ranching, agricultural, textile manufacturing, and commercial industries. It has all the trappings of a typical border town—plenty of hotels, commerce, and nightlife—but few uniquely Mexican features. The colonial-era *Catedral de Reynosa* on the Plaza Principal (main square), however, is worth seeing.

A large commercial area called the Zona Rosa is the location of one noteworthy restaurant—*Sam's Place* (Allende and Ocampo; phone: 89-220034)—as well as some curio shops and several discos, including *Alaskan Club Disco* (1020 Ocampo Nte.; phone: 89-220481) and *Treviños Bar* (Calzada Los Virreyes; phone: 89-221444). Heading toward downtown, you will come to the main pedestrian mall, Calle Hidalgo, and the Plaza Principal. Swarming with shoppers and vendors, Hidalgo stretches from the Plaza Principal to an open-air produce market. Reynosa also has a bullring, the *Plaza de Toros Reynosa* (Calle Guerrero, in the center of town; phone: 89-225493); bullfights are usually held on Sundays August through November, but there is no regular schedule.

If you want to try Mexican-style *cabrito* (kid), stop in *El Pastor* (710 Juárez Ote.; phone: 89-224191) or *La Mansión* (Calles Emilio Portes Gil and Pedro J. Méndez; phone: 89-229914). The tourist office is located at the International Bridge (phone: 89-221189); closed weekends.

En Route from Reynosa Head out of downtown Reynosa on Zaragoza, turn left onto Chapa, then right onto Calle Hidalgo to Route 40, a four-lane toll road. Along the 140-mile (224-km) drive to Monterrey on Route 40 (which will take about three hours), you will encounter a customs and immigration checkpoint (16 miles/26 km from Reynosa), several small towns, and some of the largest steel mills in North America. In Monterrey, Route 40 becomes Avenida Benito Juárez, which then merges with Calzada Francisco Madero (heading west) and Avenida Colón (heading east). Take Calzada Francisco Madero into the downtown area.

MONTERREY For a detailed description of the city, its hotels, and its restaurants, see *Monterrey* in THE CITIES.

En Route from Monterrey Avenida de la Constitución (also known as Avenida General Pablo González Garza) will lead you back to Route 40, heading for Saltillo (52 miles/83 km), and Mazatlán (580 miles/928 km). About 8 miles (13 km) from Monterrey on Route 40 (now also called Avenida Gonzalitos) is the turnoff to Chipinque Mesa. For a magnificent view of Monterrey and the surrounding valley, drive 14 miles (22 km) up the road, which climbs 4,920 feet (1,500 meters) to the mesa.

Another interesting site off Route 40 is Cañón de la Huasteca (Huasteca Canyon), a breathtaking 1,000-foot gorge with distinctive rock formations about 10 miles (16 km) west of Monterrey. Take a left at the Santa Catarina turnoff from Route 40 and follow the signs. The pavement ends at a tidy, fenced-in picnic area and playground (admission charge). A stony, unpaved road leads into the canyon, which was once used by Spanish settlers as a haven from Apache raiding parties. The area is rather isolated, but a police car is usually parked at the canyon's entrance for security.

A third side trip, to the *Grutas de García* (García Caverns), 28 miles (45 km) west of Monterrey off Route 40, is highly recommended. Discovered in 1834, these lighted caverns, with 16 different chambers, many natural pools, and magnificent stalactite and stalagmite formations, are among the most dramatic in North America. A cable car takes vistors from the parking area to the entrance of the caves, which are more than 1 mile (1.6 km) away and 3,700 feet (1,100 meters) up the mountainside. Wear flat shoes (so you can climb around easily) and long pants (to protect your legs from the jagged rocks). The caves are open daily; the admission charge includes the cable car journey, a 90-minute tour, and use of the playground and swimming pool next to the parking lot.

SALTILLO In addition to being the capital of the state of Coahuila, the site of two universities, the center of the area's ranching and farming industries, and the headquarters of the Chrysler and General Motors factories, Saltillo is also the main source of the famous Mexican serape. Traces of its eventful 400-year history can be seen in its colonial architecture and narrow streets, making Saltillo a fascinating place to explore. For additional details, see the *Nuevo Laredo to Mexico City* route.

En Route from Saltillo Travel west on Calzada Venustiano Carranza, pick up Route 40, and continue to Paila, 81 miles (130 km) from Saltillo. The highway winds through arid mountains before straightening out and passing through semidesert highland terrain. Take the road to the left at the junction at Paila and continue 18 miles (29 km) past vineyards, groves of pecan trees, and a rustic mill to the town of Parras de la Fuente.

PARRAS DE LA FUENTE The lush country road leading to Parras provides an appropriately pleasant introduction to the town itself, which was founded in 1598 as Santa María de las Parras. Parras is most famous as the cradle of the North American wine industry. *San Lorenzo,* the oldest winery on the continent, was started here in 1626 and continues to operate to this day. For additional details, see the *Ciudad Juárez to Mexico City* route.

En Route from Parras de la Fuente Backtrack to Paila and Route 40, then head west through the desert highlands to Torreón, 91 miles (146 km) away. The trip takes approximately three hours.

TORREÓN At 6,400 feet, with a population of about 439,400, Torreón was founded in 1887 and flourished with the advent of the railroad 20 years later. For additional details, see the *Ciudad Juárez to Mexico City* route.

En Route from Torreón Return to Route 40 via Torreón's Calle Ramos Arizpe and head southwest for Durango, about four hours away (158 miles/253 km). The first 18 miles (29 km) of this stretch, along the Río

Namas Valley highway, are tricky and require cautious driving; in addition to stray cattle who like this path, there are sharp curves and bits of worn, uneven pavement. After leaving the valley, the road climbs through high desert country where cactus and *topes* (small, tire-jarring bumps built into the road to slow down traffic) abound. Since many of the *topes* are unmarked, it is best to exercise caution, particularly around the towns of Cuencamé, Yerbanis, Guadalupe Victoria, and Francisco I. Madero.

DURANGO Capital of the eponymous state and featuring a population of 348,000, Durango is a colonial city that for many years rated second only to Hollywood as the major movie making location of the world. For additional details, see the *Ciudad Juárez to Mexico City* route.

En Route from Durango Leave Durango (no later than 10 AM to avoid late afternoon fog on the road ahead) via Avenida 20 de Noviembre around *Parque Guardiana* (Guardiana Park), which will bring you back to Route 40 and the final and most spectacular stretch of your journey to the Pacific. After climbing gradually and steadily through 40 miles (64 km) of semi-desert terrain covered with cactus and shrubs, you will begin your ascent into the Sierra Madre Occidental.

The last lap through the mountains is the most impressive part of the route to Mazatlán because of its extraordinary terrain and views. Although the highway is in good condition, the turns and curves around canyons and steep cliffs require maximum concentration and a speed of no more than 45 mph. Since the road sustains a heavy flow of traffic, you are likely to encounter many trucks along the way. Rather than becoming impatient and inviting disaster, wait for the truck driver ahead of you to blink his left taillight as a signal for you to pass. This is the acknowledged etiquette on Mexican roads and seems to work to everyone's benefit.

El Salto, a lumber camp 63 miles (101 km) from Durango, is noted for good freshwater fishing (catfish and carp) and hunting (red deer, mule deer, mountain quail, and wild turkeys); see *Hunting* in DIVERSIONS for more information about regulations and restrictions. Fine stands of pine and oak grow abundantly throughout the camp area, which lies at the end of a steep, sharply curved 2-mile (3-km) road. There are also two small hotels. Just before El Salto you'll see the *El Bosque* restaurant, railroad tracks, and signs reading *Curva Peligrosa* (Dangerous Curve). The high ridge above you marks the Continental Divide.

About 45 miles (72 km) farther down the highway, at 7,000 feet, El Espinazo del Diablo (the Devil's Backbone) overlooks a steep 1,000-foot drop into deep canyons—the breathtaking view will immediately let you know where you are. After coming down the Backbone, you enter El Palmito, 125 miles (200 km) from Durango, the spot where central time changes to mountain time and watches should be set back one hour. Ten miles (16 km) beyond El Palmito, *La Sombra del Paraíso* (no phone) is a charming mountain restaurant beside a waterfall. Since there are few places along the road where it's possible to pull over and snap photos, you might want to take the opportunity here. The descending highway to Mazatlán winds through scenic hills covered with wildflowers and traverses a *vado* (place where the riverbed crosses the road) to Copala.

COPALA This quiet town of narrow cobblestone streets and picturesque colonial buildings is inhabited by only about 600 people. More than 400 years old, Copala was once a thriving mining town. Today the village has become popular as a day-trip destination for tourists from surrounding cities. The main attraction is the 18th-century *Iglesia de San José* (Church of St. Joseph), which overlooks the surrounding countryside.

Daniel's, one of the village's few eateries, is owned by American expatriate Daniel Garrison, who came to visit decades ago and decided to stay. The restaurant, part of a small hotel also owned by Garrison (see *Best en Route*), serves good Mexican fare, followed by banana-coconut cream pie.

En Route from Copala Continue on Route 40 for 20 miles (32 km). Just beyond a restaurant and a furniture factory on the left side of the road, turn right onto a paved road, which leads to Concordia's *zócalo* (main square).

CONCORDIA Founded in 1565, this small village (pop. 25,000) features Baroque architecture, colonial furniture, and fine ceramics. The 17th-century *Iglesia de San Sebastián* (Church of St. Sebastian), the oldest church in the state, with its pink stone portal and richly carved columns, stands on the tree-lined, sleepy *zócalo*. In the center of the plaza stands a giant rocking chair, which symbolizes the town's fame in furniture making.

En Route from Concordia Continue on Route 40. At Villa Unión, Route 40 merges with Route 15, which becomes Avenida Gabriel Leyva when you enter Mazatlán (about 15 miles/24 km from Concordia).

MAZATLÁN For a detailed description of the city, its hotels, and its restaurants, see *Mazatlán* in THE CITIES.

BEST EN ROUTE

For a double room, expect to pay $70 to $80 per night at hotels in the expensive category; $30 to $65 at places in the moderate category; and less than $30 at hotels in the inexpensive category. All hotels have air conditioning, telephones, and TV sets in the rooms unless otherwise indicated. For each location, hotels are listed alphabetically by price category.

REYNOSA

Engrei A 110-unit hotel with a restaurant, a bar, and a pool. On Route 40 (phone: 89-231730; fax: 89-245587). Moderate.

San Carlos Here are 83 clean, simple rooms. There is also bar service, an excellent restaurant serving international and Mexican dishes, and parking. 970 Calle Hidalgo Nte. (phone: 89-221280; fax: 89-222620). Moderate.

Virrey Modern and popular with tourists, this hotel offers 162 rooms, spacious grounds with gardens, a pool, a parking lot, and a good restaurant. On Hidalgo and Praxedis Balboa Pte. (phone: 89-231050; fax: 89-238869). Moderate.

COPALA

Daniel's Buoyed by the success of his restaurant, Daniel Garrison decided to open an 11-room hostelry that also has flourished. Facilities include a Jacuzzi, a pool, and a small gym. On the road heading into Copala off Route 40 (no phone). Inexpensive.

Posada San José Once the headquarters of a mining company, this 400-year-old building has cozy guestrooms, a billiards room, and the *Copala Butter Company* restaurant downstairs, which serves standard Mexican fare prepared to please Yankee tastes. Located on the square (no phone). Inexpensive.

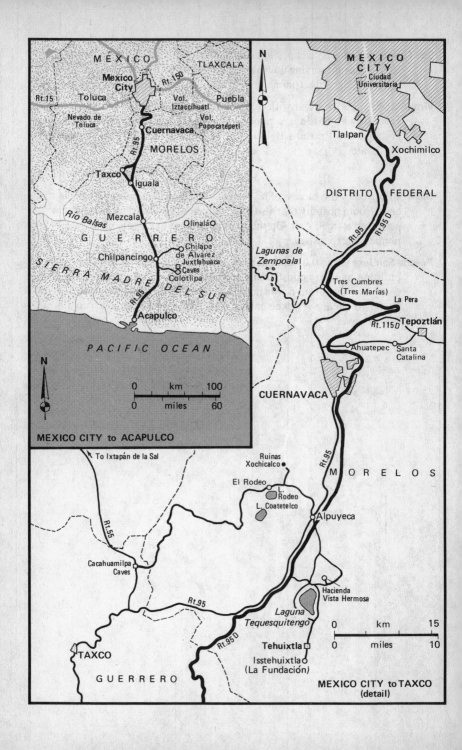

MEXICO CITY to ACAPULCO

N

MEXICO

TLAXCALA

Mexico
City

Rt. 150

Toluca

Puebla

Rt. 15

Vol.
Iztaccíhuatl

Nevado de
Toluca

Vol.
Popocatépetl

Cuernavaca

MORELOS

Taxco

Iguala

Mezcala

Olinaláo

Río Balsas

G U E R R E R O

Chilapa
de Álvarez
Juxtlahuaca

Chilpancingo

Caves
Colotlipa

S I E R R A   M A D R E   D E L   S U R

Rt. 95

Acapulco

P A C I F I C   O C E A N

N

0   km   100

0   miles   60

MEXICO
CITY

Ciudad
Universitaria

Tlalpan

Xochimilco

DISTRITO   FEDERAL

Rt. 95

Rt. 95 D

Lagunas de
Zempoala

Tres Cumbres
(Tres Marías)

La Pera

Rt. 115 D

Tepoztlán

Ahuatepec

Santa
Catalina

CUERNAVACA

To Ixtapán de la Sal

Ruinas
Xochicalco

El Rodeo

L.
Rodeo

L. Coatetelco

Rt. 95

M O R E L O S

Alpuyeca

Rt. 55

Cacahuamilpa
Caves

Rt. 95

Hacienda
Vista Hermosa

Laguna
Tequesquitengo

TAXCO

Rt. 95 D

Tehuixtla

Isstehuixtla
(La Fundación)

G U E R R E R O

0   km   15

0   miles   10

**MEXICO CITY to TAXCO
(detail)**

Mexico City to Acapulco

One of the most traveled routes in all of Mexico is the road that leads south from Mexico City to the Pacific Ocean, linking the capital with Acapulco. The route passes through the beautiful city of Cuernavaca and can be extended to include Taxco, the colonial showpiece of the state of Guerrero. There are also suggested stopovers at lakes, caves, archaeological ruins, and resort spas before you arrive in the most popular and populated of Mexico's seaside playgrounds. The several hours of mountain driving take you through dramatic scenery and highly varied topography. Although the 224-mile (358-km) trip can be made in five hours or less (traveling on a new four-lane superhighway), if time allows, we suggest more scenic alternatives. The first leg of the journey, from Mexico City to Cuernavaca, can be either a leisurely hour on the four-lane toll road, Route 95D, or an almost equal amount of time spent driving the older but more dramatic mountain highway, Route 95. Taxco is 90 minutes from Cuernavaca on Route 95; the longest part of the journey, from Taxco to Acapulco, takes approximately three hours, along rising and falling mountain roads with sweeping views and a spectacular descent into palm trees and coastline luxury.

Much of this region is Aztec in history and culture, with many residents still speaking their original language, Nahuatl, rather than Spanish. While several of the resorts and hotels mentioned here cater mostly to Mexican tourists, they are more than happy to extend their hospitality to visitors from the US and other foreign countries. If your time is short and you want a rich mixture of cities, villages, recreation areas, mountains, and beaches, this driving route offers it all.

En Route from Mexico City Traveling south along Avenida Insurgentes, you will pass the *Ciudad Universitaria,* or campus of the *Universidad Nacional Autónoma de México* (National Autonomous University of Mexico) and then the *Villa Olímpica* (Olympic Village) housing complex, constructed for athletes participating in the *1968 Olympics* and later turned into condominiums. Along this street, too, are various sculptures presented to Mexico by the participating nations. About 2 miles (3 km) farther is the Tlalpan interchange, a fork where Route 95 (the old mountain road) and Route 95D (the newer four-lane toll road) separate. Both roads go to Cuernavaca, which is 35 miles (56 km) away.

There are two other routes to the Tlalpan fork: the Tlalpan freeway, just south of the *zócalo* (main square) downtown; and west on Paseo de la Reforma, through *Parque Chapultepec,* to the sign for Periférico Sur, the expressway entrance.

While both Route 95 and Route 95D will take you to Cuernavaca, very different side trips are possible from each. From Route 95D, the village of Tepoztlán is accessible. Also, about 32 miles (51 km) south of the tollbooth, there is a lookout with an amazingly clear view of Popocatépetl and Iztaccíhuatl, the snow-topped volcanoes that dominate the surrounding countryside. The more scenic Route 95, narrow but well-maintained, will take you to the Lagunas de Zempoala, a group of mountain lakes.

TEPOZTLÁN (pronounced Te-pos-*tlan*) After La Pera, a pear-shaped curve on Route 95D, take the Cuautla turnoff, Route 115D, to Tepoztlán. Less than half an hour northeast of Cuernavaca, Tepoztlán is a beautiful village set at the foot of a mountain in a lush, green valley. The predominant language is Nahuatl, and the customs are ancient, but the town is prepared to deal with tourists quite happily.

Tepoztlán's most interesting sites are the temples and pyramids constructed on the mountain peak 1,200 feet above town. The most famous, the *Santuario del Cerro de Tepozteco* (Shrine of Tepozteco), was dedicated to Tepoztecatl, god of pulque—a popular alcoholic beverage fermented from the sap of the maguey plant, a member of the cactus family. A steep climb through the thin mountain air leads to the pyramid-shaped base of this shrine. A narrow stairway on the western side leads up to the inner shrine, whose walls are covered with bold-relief hieroglyphs. The hike up is very strenuous and should only be attempted if you are in good shape, but the awe-inspiring view from the heights is worth it. The shrine is open daily; there's no admission charge (no phone). Plans are afoot to build a golf course in Tepoztlán, but local farmers and environmentalists nationwide have raised opposition.

The *Museo del Convento de Tepoztlán,* an archaeological museum in the town's 16th-century Dominican convent, has an interesting collection of pre-Hispanic art and of objects that will give you a full sense of the lives of the people who worshiped at the *Santuario del Cerro de Tepozteco.* A Spanish-language guided tour of the huge convent covers the building's past, from the 16th-century destruction of native idols to an early 20th-century incarnation as revolutionary army barracks. *"El convento"* is closed Mondays; there's an admission charge (no phone).

During the *Natividad de la Virgen María* (Nativity of the Virgin Mary) fiesta on September 8, the whole town honors Tepoztecatl's connection with pulque by getting drunk. One other unusual festival is held annually during the week before *Miércoles de Ceniza* (Ash Wednesday), when the men of the area perform the *brincos,* or jumps, an ancient Aztec dance performed in conquistador costumes, beards, wigs, and masks.

En Route from Tepoztlán To continue to Cuernavaca (see below), about 18 miles (29 km) away, take the paved road that leads through the towns of Santa Catalina and Ahuatepec.

LAGUNAS DE ZEMPOALA If you chose to follow the old mountain road (Rte. 95) from Mexico City, you will pass through Tres Cumbres (also referred to as Tres Marías), a small lumber town. From there, veer west and drive 8 miles (13 km) on a winding paved road to Lagunas de Zempoala.

Known to the Indians as "Lakes of the Windy Place," these seven small bodies of water are more than 9,000 feet above sea level. Each is very beautiful and well stocked with trout, but don't get any ideas about casting a line: Fishing is strictly forbidden. Part of the *Parque Natural de Zempoala* (Zempoala Wildlife Reserve), the lakes are set amidst pine woods and offer lovely picnic areas. Note that camping is prohibited because of the danger presented by *bandidos*. Take along a jacket or heavy sweater; it gets quite cool here, particularly after sunset. Weekends draw crowds, but weekdays are quieter, offering an idyllic contrast to the modern bustle of Mexico City. The local artisans are famous for their varnished wood furniture and lamps made from tree trunks.

En Route from Lagunas de Zempoala Unfortunately, there is no way to drive from the lakes to Cuernavaca other than returning to Route 95 and continuing south to the city, 34 miles (54 km) away.

CUERNAVACA For a detailed report on the city, its hotels, and its restaurants, see *Cuernavaca* in THE CITIES.

En Route from Cuernavaca South of Cuernavaca, you can choose from several routes. You can take Route 95D straight through to Iguala, bypassing Taxco. If you choose to include Taxco in your route, however, three options are available to you from the Alpuyeca interchange.

ALPUYECA From here, you can take Route 95 directly to Taxco (below), a 45-mile (72 km) drive; you can take an eastern route that includes a visit to a lake and an exotic bathing resort; or you can follow a western route that takes in mysterious ruins, vast caverns, and a mineral spa town.

EASTERN ROUTE TO TAXCO

If you opt for the eastern route, about 5 miles (8 km) southeast of the Alpuyeca interchange, on a well-paved road in the village Jojutla de Juárez, is the *Hacienda Vista Hermosa,* a resort spa created by incorporating the ruins of a 400-year-old colonial sugar mill. Even if you don't plan to stay overnight, it is a good place to spend an afternoon (see *Best en Route*).

LAGUNA TEQUESQUITENGO (pronounced Tay-kays-kee-*ten*-go) About a mile (1.6 km) south of the *Hacienda Vista Hermosa,* on the same paved road, this natural lake is popular with Mexico City's water enthusiasts. There are motorboats and water skis for rent, as well as swimming, fishing, tennis courts, restaurants, hotels, guesthouses, and snack bars. Weekends tend to get a little hectic, but weekdays are simply lively. In the middle of the lake, whose water level rises and falls drastically, are the submerged remains of an indigenous village that once stood above water.

En Route from Laguna Tequesquitengo Either branch of the road surrounding the lake will take you 8 miles (13 km) south to Tehuixtla.

TEHUIXTLA Less than a mile (1.6 km) south of the town of Tehuixtla (Tay-*weeks*-tla) is a bathing resort named *La Fundación* but better known simply as *Issstehuixtla* (Ees-tay-*weeks*-tla; phone: 5-592-7744 or 5-592-7755 in Mexico City). Run by the *Instituto de Seguro Social y Servicios de Trabajadores del Estado* (*ISSSTE,* the social security institute for federal employees), the resort is open to the public. There is an admission fee and a charge for locker rentals, but you can enjoy the sulfur baths and five pools to your heart's content. The main pool is very deep, filled with waters rising from the depths of the earth. A fast-flowing river runs through the property, and a suspension bridge connects the two banks. Swaying wildly as you walk across it, and surrounded by tropical growth, the bridge calls to mind a Tarzan movie. This exotic atmosphere is only enhanced by the poolside waiters who serve you whole coconuts, chopping off the top to form a natural cup of cooling coconut milk. There are snack stands and the very pleasant *La Fundación* restaurant, with such specialties as *chiles rellenos* (peppers stuffed with cheese or ground meat) and *gorditas* (small tortillas lavished with sausage and green sauce).

A short walk across the bridge takes you to another restaurant, pool, and bar, part of *La Rivera* hotel (see *Best en Route*). It's not associated with *La Fundación,* but a friendly exchange back and forth is taken for granted. No English is spoken in either place, but almost anything you might want can be pretty easily indicated with smiles, shrugs, and pointing. The people of Tehuixtla are friendly and helpful.

En Route from La Fundación To get back to Route 95, return to Laguna Tequesquitengo; whichever side of the lake you drove down, you can now drive up the other. Almost at the top, before reaching Vista Hermosa, you'll come to a road that will take you back to Route 95; continue to Taxco.

WESTERN ROUTE TO TAXCO

If you opt for the western route to Taxco, the *Xochicalco* ruins will be your first stop.

RUINAS XOCHICALCO (pronounced So-chee-*cahl*-co) About 5½ miles (9 km) northwest of the Alpuyeca interchange, you'll see a sign to the right for the mysterious ruins for which this area is famous. For additional details, see *Mexico's Magnificent Archaeological Heritage* in DIVERSIONS. The ruins are closed Mondays; there's an admission charge. To investigate the ruins more fully you can take a guide with you from Cuernavaca, but for most people a good strong flashlight should do the job.

En Route from Xochicalco About 21 miles (34 km) farther along this road, near the Morelos-Guerrero state border, are the largest caverns in central Mexico.

GRUTAS DE CACAHUAMILPA (CACAHUAMILPA—pronounced Ca-ca-wa-*meel*-pa— CAVERNS) Discovered in 1835, these caves still have not been fully explored. At present they rival their northern neighbors at Carlsbad in size and in variety of formations; once fully explored, they may prove to be even larger and more extensive. Stalactites, stalagmites, arches, and boulders are lighted in the more central caves for easier exploration, and guided tours for groups or private parties are available daily; call a day in advance to request a tour in English. In addition to the tours, there is a sound-and-light show. For details, check with the tourist office in Taxco (in the *Centro de Convenciones,* at the northern entrance to the city; phone: 762-22279; closed Sundays).

En Route from Grutas de Cacahuamilpa Before heading south to Taxco, travelers seeking a little pampering can opt to head 23 miles (37 km) north-west of the caverns on Route 55 to the spa town of Ixtapán de la Sal in the state of México. Long before the Spanish conquistadores set foot on Mexican soil, the Aztec traveled over this mountainous terrain to soak themselves in the mineral waters here. Aztec shamans claimed the waters of Ixtapán— which in Nahuatl means "on the salt"—were endowed with magical qual-ities that could heal the sick and relieve the aches and pains of the aged. Modern-day pilgrims will find this a welcome and relaxing respite along the route. In addition to the public baths, there are two excellent hotels, a public park, golf, tennis, and a complete range of water sports. If time allows, a full day—or more—will refresh even the most weary spirit. (For addi-tional details, see *Spa-Hopping Special* in DIVERSIONS.)

To get to Taxco, take Route 55 south from the caverns, pick up Route 95, and continue southwest to the city, another 20 miles (32 km).

TAXCO For a detailed description of the city, its hotels, and its restaurants, see *Taxco* in THE CITIES.

En Route from Taxco Twenty-two miles (35 km) southeast of Taxco on Route 95 and halfway between Mexico City and Acapulco on Route 95D is Iguala.

IGUALA (pronounced Ee-*gwa*-la) This is the area's most important agricultural cen-ter. Market day is Friday, when farmers from the surrounding countryside pour into Iguala to sell their produce. Pineapples, cantaloupes, watermel-ons, delicious peanuts, and mangoes (for which this city is famous) fill the marketplace with luscious colors and smells. Baskets and pottery are also on sale, and, occasionally, the amethysts for which the state of Guerrero is renowned.

Iguala has a special place in Mexican history, for it was here that the flag of Mexico was created. In 1821, Agustín de Iturbide combined his troops with those of rebel leader Vicente Guerrero, for whom the state is named; in celebration, Guerrero ordered Magdaleno Ocampo, a local tai-lor, to design and deliver a flag within 24 hours. Ocampo returned with the red, white, and green flag that is still in use today. Iguala's main plaza, known as Plaza de la Bandera (Plaza of the Flag), commemorates this event with a vast monument. On it are inscribed the following words in Spanish: "Here the consummation of Mexico's independence from Spain was proclaimed on February 24, 1821." The peace plan was known as the Plan of Iguala, which Iturbide wrote in Taxco. The monument is surrounded by 32 tamarind trees (one for each Mexican state)—a gift from the Chinese government. Near the *zócalo,* the lovely town church is also worth a visit.

If you happen to pass through Iguala during the first week in December, stop by the *Feria del Caballo* (Horse Fair), which attracts traders from all over the country. Iguala is also the center of northern Guerrero's mask-making region. The selection ranges from inexpensive carved wooden masks to costly antique masks, a rare few made of silver.

En Route from Iguala Just 9 miles (15 km) past Iguala on the right side of Route 95 is *Sendi Stop,* which offers spotlessly clean restrooms, safe food, a playground, and a well-equipped pharmacy. There also is an enclosed parking area and well-landscaped grounds for stretching your legs.

Five miles (8 km) farther south on Route 95, where the highway crosses the Río Balsas, is Mezcala.

MEZCALA This town offers an interesting diversion. Flat-bottom wooden rafts can be rented at the riverside dock for exhilarating trips down the river. The trip can be extended as far as Ciudad Altamirano, where a second class bus will take you back to Iguala (and from there, you can catch a first class bus back to Mezcala). Be sure to check out information about the return trip carefully at the dock in Mezcala before you board the raft. We advise you to seek two corroborating reports, since Mexicans are likely to answer you whether they know the correct information or not, just to be polite.

En Route from Mezcala Chilpancingo is another 30 miles (48 km) down Route 95.

CHILPANCINGO The capital of the state of Guerrero, Chilpancingo is primarily an agricultural center; home to a large university, it has a significant place in Mexico's history. In colonial times, Chilpancingo reached its economic zenith as a major stopover for caravans of silver, gold, ivory, silk, spices, and other luxury items that were traded between Mexico City and Manila from the port of Acapulco. The town was also the site of the first Mexican Congress, convened in 1813. Three heroes of the War of Independence, brothers Nicolás, Leonardo, and Victor Bravo, were born here. Moreover, Chilpancingo has the distinction of being the first sovereign capital in all of Latin America, having been declared independent from Spain by José María Morelos y Pavón in 1813. During the revolution the city was a hotbed of political unrest; it was taken by Emiliano Zapata in 1911.

The city's glorious past goes much farther back than colonial times. Chilpancingo was inhabited as long ago as 100 BC by the Olmec, the probable creators of the cave paintings in the *Grutas de Juxtlahuaca* (Juxtlahuaca

Caverns; see below) and the crude rock pyramids along the banks of the nearby Río Azul. Later, the region was occupied by the Yope and Mexica civilizations; both left vestiges of their heritages behind. The cave paintings and simple pyramidal mounds are visible on the south edge of town.

Closed to vehicular traffic, the city center is concentrated around the *Palacio de Gobierno* (Statehouse), *Palacio Municipal* (City Hall), and the *Catedral.* All three buildings are on the large *zócalo,* or main plaza, which comes alive with music and dancing every weekend. The entire *zócalo* is shaded by giant jacaranda and elm trees, interrupted only by a modern sculpture-mural celebrating the nation's struggle for independence. Across Avenida Miguel Alemán from the *Palacio de Gobierno* is the *Museo de la Antropología,* which features a wall-to-wall mural around the patio that depicts the history of the area. Inside are pre-Columbian artifacts and mementos from the War of Independence. The museum is closed Mondays; there's an admission charge.

Off to the right of the *Palacio de Gobierno* stands the *Cámara de Diputados* (Chamber of Deputies, where the state legislature meets), which is well worth a visit if you can persuade the guard to let you sneak a peek inside. The building is crowned by a beautiful overhead stained glass mosaic featuring the portraits of four of the city's greatest heroes: the three Bravo brothers and José María Morelos.

Also of interest in Chilpancingo is the *Zoológico del Estado de Guerrero* (State Zoo), with more than 270 species of birds and mammals indigenous to the region, many of them rarely found in captivity. To get there, drive south through town on Route 95 and take the turnoff for the zoo; it's located four blocks east of the highway. The zoo is closed Mondays, and there's an admission charge (no phone). More information is available from the tourist office (*Palacio de Gobierno,* second floor); it's closed Sundays (no phone).

En Route from Chilpancingo Follow the paved road stretching east for about 19 miles (30 km), then take a left a few miles beyond Ojitos de Agua; in about 3 miles (5 km) you will come to Chilapa de Alvarez.

CHILAPA DE ALVAREZ A tiny, fascinating town, Chilapa de Alvarez is noted for the beautiful handloomed rebozos (shawls) made here and for its Sunday market, one of the largest in the nation. You'll find bargain prices on all sorts of native handicrafts, from ceramics to woodcarvings. Be sure to check out the 16th-century *Convento de San Agustín* (Convent of St. Augustine) on the *zócalo,* in the center of town. Shaped in the form of a cross, the Baroque-style convent's façade is adorned with figures of Juan Diego, the second Mexican ever beatified (St. Felipe de Jesús was the first), and images of the Virgin of Guadalupe, who appeared to him. In late June, the town takes on a particularly festive mood, as locals dress in Renaissance costumes and reenact the 13th-century war in Spain between the Moors and Christians in a fascinating dance ritual. Chilapa is one of the last places in

Mexico where the dance is still performed in its original form; people flock here annually to observe this extraordinary event.

Chilapa is a takeoff point for a much more adventurous trek by horse to the mountain village of Olinalá, home of some of the most elaborate lacquerware made in Mexico. For additional details on equestrian excursions to Olinalá, consult the *Ayuntamiento* (City Council) in the *Palacio Municipal,* located on the *zócalo,* where some employees speak English (phone: 747-50015).

En Route from Chilapa de Alvarez To continue south to Acapulco, return to Chilpancingo and reconnect with Route 95. Acapulco is 85 miles (136 km) away.

But before heading for the sun, sand, and surf, adventurous travelers may want to take a side trip to the *Grutas de Juxtlahuaca* (Juxtlahuaca Caverns). Four miles (6 km) south of Chilpancingo is the small town of Petaquillas. From here, there is a dirt road going east, rough but passable in the dry season (November through April), and a big adventure after a long drive any time of year. If you're considering a trip to the caverns, ask in Chilpancingo and Petaquillas about the condition of this road; you can also hire a guide at the tourist office in Chilpancingo (see above). With advice and an escort, you can now continue the 30-mile (48-km) drive east to the village of Colotlipa, where you must hire another local guide. The magnificent caverns are a comfortable hike from the village.

GRUTAS DE JUXTLAHUACA (JUXTLAHUACA—pronounced Hooks-tla-*wa*-ka—CAVERNS) Among the largest in Mexico, these caverns contain Olmec paintings estimated to date from the first millennium before Christ—some of the oldest yet discovered in North America. Remarkably, the bright yellow, red, and black paintings of humans and snakes have not faded over the centuries. There are also several caves that are home to thousands of vampire bats and a rare species of giant spider (these creatures are not harmless, so the caves they inhabit are off-limits to explorers; visitors can peek in from the outside). Another cave houses an underground lake. Footpaths connect the principal chambers of the caverns, but the going is treacherous, with little illumination. Old clothes, practical footwear, and anything waterproof will be appropriate because of the spray from subterranean waterfalls. These caverns are very beautiful and exciting, but lest we have not yet made the point clear, let it be stressed again: Don't explore them on your own. The caverns are closed Mondays; there's an admission charge (no phone).

En Route from Grutas de Juxtlahuaca To reconnect with Route 95, retrace your route exactly. Now you're back on the road for the last 59 mountainous miles (94 km) to Acapulco, rising and dipping until the first thrilling glimpse of the sea appears. Suddenly you're in a world of coconut palms, high-rise hotels, sighing surf, and smooth golden beaches.

ACAPULCO For a detailed description of the city, its hotels, and its restaurants, see *Acapulco* in THE CITIES.

BEST EN ROUTE

In this region, expect to pay about $100 per night for a double room in an expensive hotel; $50 to $70 in a moderate one; and less than $35 in an inexpensive one. The hostelries listed are the nicest en route; however, in this area they generally do not have TV sets or telephones in the rooms (exceptions are noted). Because of the altitude, air conditioning is rarely necessary until you reach sea-level Acapulco, though all the establishments below have ceiling fans. For each location, hotels are listed alphabetically by price category.

TEPOZTLÁN

Posada del Tepozteco On a hill overlooking Tepoztlán, this colonial-style inn has 20 units. Facilities include two pools, extensive gardens, a fine dining room (request a window seat for an outstanding view of the surrounding valley and mountain peaks), a bar, and a specially equipped room for table tennis. 3 Calle del Paraíso (phone: 739-50010 or 739-50323). Moderate.

Tepoztlán Short on character, but comfortable nonetheless, this place offers 36 rooms, two suites with Jacuzzis, a restaurant-bar, and a heated pool. On weekends the hotel fills up with families and gets quite noisy. At the entrance to town, at 6 Calle de Industrias (phone: 739-50522; fax: 739-50503). Moderate.

JOJUTLA DE JUÁREZ

Hacienda Vista Hermosa Built more than 400 years ago, this former sugar mill is now a fine resort offering swimming, tennis, bowling, and horseback riding. There's also a bar and alfresco dining, and all rooms have telephones and TV sets. Meals are good all week, but Sundays and holidays are particularly special, with a generous buffet drawing visitors from as far as Cuernavaca. Colonial-style furnishings fill the 105 air conditioned units. About 30 miles (48 km) southeast of Cuernavaca, off the Alpuyeca interchange (phone: 734-70492; 5-566-7700 in Mexico City; 800-421-0767; fax: 734-70492). Expensive to moderate.

TEHUIXTLA

La Rivera Adjacent to the famous bathing resort of *Issstehuixtla,* the rooms and cottages of this 36-unit hotel are scattered over spacious riverfront grounds. There is a restaurant, a bar, and a pool; foreign visitors are made to feel more than welcome. Off Route 95 and 95D, southeast of the Alpuyeca interchange or the Vista Hermosa–Tequesquitengo cutoff, about 3 miles

(5 km) south of Laguna Tequesquitengo (phone: dial national directory assistance, then request Operator No. 23 in Tehuixtla). Moderate.

IXTAPÁN DE LA SAL

Villa Vergel Formerly *Kiss,* this informal, family oriented establishment across the street from the *Ixtapán* is run by a distant relative of the Hungarian-born Kiss family that previously ran the business. There are 64 rooms and six suites, a bar, and a pool. Its restaurant offers continental dishes, as well as some down-home Yiddish specialties—such as matzoh ball soup and fresh apple strudel—the Kisses used to offer. Blvd. Las Jacarandas and Diana Circle (phone: 714-30901; fax: 714-30842). Expensive to moderate.

Ixtapán This longtime favorite has 250 air conditioned junior suites and chalets, plus a full complement of resort-type amenities. All units have telephones and TV sets. Avoid weekends, when it is very crowded. Major credit cards accepted, but the hotel does not accept personal checks. For additional details, see *Spa-Hopping Special* in DIVERSIONS. Blvd. Las Jacarandas and Diana Circle (phone: 714-30304; 800-223-9832; fax: 714-30856). Moderate.

CHILPANCINGO

Jacarandas This modern, government-run complex set in a spacious jacaranda garden boasts a splendid view and an oversize pool. The service is a bit slow, but the 70 large, comfortable rooms are extremely clean. In the far south end of town, on Av. Circunvalación (phone: 747-24444; fax: 747-24506). Moderate.

Parador del Marqués More centrally located than the *Jacarandas,* this colonial-style establishment is almost as old as the city itself. It has 40 rooms, a restaurant that offers good, simple fare, and a small disco off the lobby. Km 276.5 on Rte. 95 (phone: 747-29532 or 747-10644; fax: 747-10641). Moderate.

Glossary

Useful Words and Phrases

Unlike the French, who tend to be a bit brusque if you don't speak their language perfectly, the Mexicans do not expect you to speak Spanish, but appreciate your efforts when you try. In many circumstances, you won't have to, because the staffs at most hotels, museums, and tourist attractions, as well as at a fair number of restaurants, speak serviceable English, which they are eager to use. Off the beaten path, however, you will find at least a rudimentary knowledge of Spanish very helpful. Don't be afraid of misplaced accents or misconjugated verbs. Mexicans will do their best to understand you and will make every effort to be understood.

Mexican Spanish has a number of regional dialects, but the dialect of educated people in Mexico City is regarded as standard, is used on national television, and is understood by almost everybody. The spelling of standard Mexican Spanish is a very reliable guide to pronunciation.

The list below of commonly used words and phrases can help you get started.

Greetings and Everyday Expressions

Good morning (also, Good day).	*Buenos días*
Good afternoon	*Buenas tardes*
Good evening	*Buenas noches*
Hello	Use *"Buenos días," "Buenas tardes,"* or *"Buenas noches,"* as appropriate for the time of day.
How are you?	*Cómo está usted?*
Pleased to meet you.	*Mucho gusto en conocerle.*
Good-bye!	*Adiós!*
So long!	*Hasta luego!*
Yes	*Sí*
No	*No*
Please	*Por favor*
Thank you	*Gracias*
You're welcome	*De nada*
I beg your pardon (Excuse me)	*Perdón*
I'm sorry	*Lo siento*
It doesn't matter	*No importa*
I don't speak Spanish.	*No hablo español.*
Do you speak English?	*Habla usted inglés?*
I don't understand.	*No comprendo/entiendo.*
Do you understand?	*Comprende?/Entiende?*
My name is . . .	*Me llamo . . .*

What is your name?	*Cómo se llama?*
miss	*señorita*
madame	*señora*
mister	*señor*
open	*abierto/a*
closed	*cerrado/a*
entrance	*entrada*
exit	*salida*
push	*empujar*
pull	*jalar*
today	*hoy*
tomorrow	*mañana*
yesterday	*ayer*

Checking In

I have a reservation.	*Tengo una reservación.*
I would like . . .	*Quisiera . . .*
a single room	*una habitación sencilla*
a double room	*una habitación doble*
a quiet room	*una habitación tranquila*
with bath	*con baño*
with shower	*con ducha*
with a sea view	*con vista al mar*
with air conditioning	*con aire acondicionado*
with balcony	*con balcón*
overnight only	*sólo una noche*
a few days	*unos cuantos días*
a week (at least)	*una semana (por lo menos)*
with full board	*con pensión completa*
with half board	*con media pensión*
Does that price include . . .	*Está incluído en el precio . . .*
breakfast?	*el desayuno?*
taxes?	*los impuestos?*
Do you accept traveler's checks?	*Acepta usted cheques de viajero?*
Do you accept credit cards?	*Acepta tarjetas de crédito?*
It doesn't work.	*No funciona.*

Eating Out

ashtray	*un cenicero*
(extra) chair	*una silla (adicional)*
table	*una mesa*
bottle	*una botella*

cup	*una taza*
plate	*un plato*
fork	*un tenedor*
knife	*un cuchillo*
spoon	*una cuchara*
napkin	*una servilleta*
hot chocolate (cocoa)	*un chocolate caliente*
black coffee	*un café negro*
"American-style" coffee	*café americano*
coffee with hot milk	*café con leche*
cream	*crema*
milk	*leche*
tea	*un té*
fruit juice	*un jugo de fruta*
lemonade	*una limonada*
orange juice	*jugo de naranja*
orangeade	*una naranjada*
water	*agua*
mineral water	*agua mineral*
carbonated	*con gas*
noncarbonated	*sin gas*
beer	*una cerveza*
port	*oporto*
sherry	*jerez*
red wine	*vino tinto*
white wine	*vino blanco*
cold	*frío/a*
hot	*caliente*
sweet	*dulce*
(very) dry	*(muy) seco/a*
bread	*pan*
butter	*mantequilla*
bacon	*tocino*
eggs	*huevos*
hard-boiled	*un huevo cocido*
fried	*huevos fritos*
omelette	*un omelette*
soft-boiled	*un huevo pasado por agua*
scrambled	*huevos revueltos*

honey	*miel*
jam, marmalade	*mermelada*
pepper	*pimienta*
salt	*sal*
sugar	*azúcar*

Waiter!	*Camarero!/Mesero!*
I would like ...	*Quisiera ...*
a glass of	*un vaso de*
a bottle of	*una botella de*
a half bottle of	*una media botella de*
a carafe of	*una jarra de*
a liter of	*un litro de*
The check, please.	*La cuenta, por favor.*
Is a service charge included?	*Está el servicio incluído?*
I think there is a mistake in the bill.	*Creo que hay un error en la cuenta.*

Shopping

bakery	*la panadería*
bookstore	*la librería*
butcher shop	*la carnicería*
camera shop	*la tienda de fotografía*
department store	*el almacén*
grocery	*la tienda de comestibles*
jewelry store	*la joyería*
newsstand	*el puesto de periódicos*
pastry shop	*la pastelería*
perfume (and cosmetics) store	*la perfumería*
pharmacy/drugstore	*la farmacia*
shoe store	*la zapatería*
supermarket	*el supermercado*
tobacconist	*la tabaquería*

inexpensive	*barato/a*
expensive	*caro/a*
large	*grande*
larger	*más grande*
too large	*demasiado grande*
small	*pequeño/a*
smaller	*más pequeño/a*
too small	*demasiado pequeño/a*
long	*largo/a*
short	*corto/a*
old	*viejo/a*

new	*nuevo/a*
used	*usado/a*
handmade	*hecho a mano*

Is it machine washable?	*Es lavable en lavadora?*
How much does it cost?	*Cuánto cuesta ésto?*
What is it made of?	*De qué está hecho?*
camel's hair	*pelo de camello*
cotton	*algodón*
corduroy	*pana*
filigree	*filigrana*
lace	*encaje*
leather	*cuero*
linen	*lino*
suede	*ante*
synthetic	*sintético/a*
wool	*lana*

brass	*latón*
copper	*cobre*
gold	*oro*
gold plated	*dorado*
silver	*plata*
silver plated	*plateado*
stainless steel	*acero inoxidable*
tile	*azulejo* or *baldosa*
wood	*madera*

Colors

beige	*beige*
black	*negro/a*
blue	*azul*
brown	*marrón*
green	*verde*
gray	*gris*
orange	*anaranjado/a*
pink	*rosa*
purple	*morado/a*
red	*rojo/a*
white	*blanco/a*
yellow	*amarillo/a*
dark	*oscuro/a*
light	*claro/a*

Getting Around

north	*norte*
south	*sur*
east	*este*; also (in street addresses), *Oriente (Ote.)*
west	*oeste*; also (in street addresses), *Poniente (Pte.)*
right	*derecho/a*
left	*izquierdo/a*
Go straight ahead.	*Siga todo derecho.*
far	*lejos*
near	*cerca*
airport	*el aeropuerto*
bus stop	*la parada de autobuses*
subway station	*la estación de metro*
train station	*la estación de ferrocarril*
map	*el mapa*
tourist information	*información turística*
one-way ticket	*un boleto de ida*
round-trip ticket	*un boleto de ida y vuelta*
first class	*primera clase*
second class	*segunda clase*
smoking	*fumar*
no smoking	*no fumar*
track	*el andén*
gas station	*la gasolinera*
gasoline	*gasolina*
leaded	*Nova*
unleaded	*Magna sin*
diesel	*diesel*
Fill it up, please.	*Llénelo, por favor.*
oil	*el aceite*
tires	*las llantas*
Where is . . . ?	*Dónde está . . . ?*
Where are . . . ?	*Dónde están . . . ?*
How far is it from here to . . . ?	*Qué distancia hay desde aquí hasta . . . ?*
Does this train go to . . . ?	*Va este tren a . . . ?*

| Does this bus go to . . . ? | *Va este autobús a . . . ?* |
| What time does it leave? | *A qué hora sale?* |

Danger	*Peligro*
Caution	*Precaución*
Detour	*Desviación*
Do Not Enter	*Paso Prohibido*
No Parking	*Estacionamiento Prohibido*
Tow-away Zone	*Se Usará Grúa*
No Passing	*Prohibido Pasar*
One Way	*Dirección Unica*
Pay Toll	*Peaje*
Pedestrian Zone	*Zona Peatonal*
Reduce Speed	*Despacio*
Steep Incline	*Fuerte Declive*
Stop	*Alto*
Use Headlights	*Encender los Faros*
Yield	*Ceda el Paso*

Personal Items and Services

aspirin	*aspirina*
Band-Aids	*curitas*
condom	*condón*
laundry	*la lavandería*
sanitary napkins	*toallas femininas*
shampoo	*champú*
shaving cream	*espuma/crema de afeitar*
soap	*el jabón*
tampons	*unos tampones*
tissues	*Kleenex*
toilet paper	*papel higiénico*
toothpaste	*pasta de dientes*

barbershop	*la peluquería*
beauty shop	*el salón de belleza*
dry cleaner	*la tintorería*
hairdresser's	*la peluquería*
laundromat	*la lavandería*

| post office | *el correo* |
| postage stamps | *estampillas* or *timbres* |

| Where is the bathroom? | *Dónde está el baño?* |
| toilet | *el sanitario/inodoro* |

| MEN | *Caballeros* |
| WOMEN | *Señoras* |

Days of the Week

Monday	*lunes*
Tuesday	*martes*
Wednesday	*miércoles*
Thursday	*jueves*
Friday	*viernes*
Saturday	*sábado*
Sunday	*domingo*

Months

January	*enero*
February	*febrero*
March	*marzo*
April	*abril*
May	*mayo*
June	*junio*
July	*julio*
August	*agosto*
September	*septiembre*
October	*octubre*
November	*noviembre*
December	*diciembre*

Numbers

zero	*cero*
one	*uno*
two	*dos*
three	*tres*
four	*cuatro*
five	*cinco*
six	*seis*
seven	*siete*
eight	*ocho*
nine	*nueve*
ten	*diez*
eleven	*once*
twelve	*doce*
thirteen	*trece*
fourteen	*catorce*
fifteen	*quince*
sixteen	*dieciséis*
seventeen	*diecisiete*
eighteen	*dieciocho*

nineteen	*diecinueve*
twenty	*veinte*
thirty	*treinta*
forty	*cuarenta*
fifty	*cincuenta*
sixty	*sesenta*
seventy	*setenta*
eighty	*ochenta*
ninety	*noventa*
one hundred	*cien* or *ciento*
one thousand	*mil*
1997	*mil novecientos noventa y siete*

WRITING RESERVATIONS LETTERS

Restaurant/Hotel Name
Street Address
Postal Code, City
México

Dear Sir:

I would like to reserve a table for (number of) persons for lunch/dinner on (day and month), 1997, at (hour) o'clock.

or

I would like to reserve a room for (number of) people for (number of) nights from (day and month) to (day and month), 1997.

and

Would you be so kind as to confirm the reservation as soon as possible?

Thanking you in advance,

(Signature)

Estimado Señor:

Me gustaría reservar una mesa para (number of) personas para comer/cenar el día (day) de (month), 1997, a las (time) horas.

or

Me gustaría reservar una habitación para (number of) personas por (number of) noches desde el (day) de (month) al (day) de (month), 1997.

and

Sería tan amable de confirmar la reservación lo más pronto posible?

Agradeciendo de antemano sus atenciones,

(Signature)

(Print or type your name and address below your signature.)

Climate Chart

Average Temperatures (in °F)

	January	April	July	October
Acapulco	72–88	73–88	77–91	77–90
Cancún and Cozumel	68–82	72–90	74–91	72–90
Chihuahua	36–65	54–82	66–99	52–81
Cuernavaca	54–75	63–86	61–79	57–77
Ensenada	45–64	52–68	61–75	55–73
Guadalajara	45–73	52–86	59–79	54–77
Guanajuato	46–70	55–81	57–77	54–75
Huatulco	71–88	73–88	77–91	77–90
Ixtapa and Zihuatanejo	48–68	62–84	71–90	64–80
Los Cabos	55–77	61–84	73–91	68–90
Manzanillo	68–80	68–81	77–91	75–88
Mazatlán	63–73	66–77	79–91	75–86
Mérida	64–82	70–91	72–90	70–90
Mexico City	37–72	48–82	50–76	46–75
Monterrey	48–68	64–86	72–93	63–81
Morelia	45–70	54–81	57–73	54–73
Oaxaca	46–72	57–81	59–82	55–77
Puebla	45–70	54–79	54–73	50–73
Puerto Escondido	72–88	73–88	77–91	77–90
Puerto Vallarta	61–86	64–88	73–93	73–93
San Miguel de Allende	48–79	59–90	61–84	57–82
Taxco	57–79	64–88	63–79	57–70
Tijuana	43–68	50–72	61–82	55–79
Veracruz	64–75	73–82	75–88	73–86

Weights and Measures

APPROXIMATE EQUIVALENTS

	Metric Unit	Abbreviation	US Equivalent
Length	1 millimeter	mm	.04 inch
	1 meter	m	39.37 inches
	1 kilometer	km	.62 mile
Capacity	1 liter	l	1.057 quarts
Weight	1 gram	g	.035 ounce
	1 kilogram	kg	2.2 pounds
	1 metric ton	MT	1.1 tons
Temperature	0° Celsius	C	32° Fahrenheit

CONVERSION TABLES

METRIC TO US MEASUREMENTS

	Multiply:	by:	to convert to:
Length	millimeters	.04	inches
	meters	3.3	feet
	meters	1.1	yards
	kilometers	.6	miles
Capacity (liquid)	liters	2.11	pints
	liters	1.06	quarts
	liters	.26	gallons
Weight	grams	.04	ounces
	kilograms	2.2	pounds

US TO METRIC MEASUREMENTS

	Multiply:	by:	to convert to:
Length	inches	25.0	millimeters
	feet	.3	meters
	yards	.9	meters
	miles	1.6	kilometers
Capacity	pints	.47	liters
	quarts	.95	liters
	gallons	3.8	liters
Weight	ounces	28.0	grams
	pounds	.45	kilograms

TEMPERATURE

Celsius to Fahrenheit $(°C \times 9/5) + 32 = °F$

Fahrenheit to Celsius $(°F - 32) \times 5/9 = °C$

Index